Nutritional Anthropology

Biocultural Perspectives on Food and Nutrition

Alan H. Goodman

Hampshire College

Darna L. Dufour

University of Colorado

Gretel H. Pelto

Cornell University

Mayfield Publishing Company

Mountain View, California

London • Toronto

The editors dedicate their collective efforts to members of their immediate families, who are among their most important sources of support:

To DEBRA MARTIN, life partner, fellow anthropological traveler, and inspiration, from Alan

To PAUL PATMORE, life partner, for his encouragement on this and other anthropological endeavors, from Darna

To my children, JONATHAN, ARI, and DUNJA, for their wonderful support, understanding and encouragement, from Gretel

Library of Congress Cataloging-in-Publication Data

Nutritional anthropology : biocultural perspectives on food and
    nutrition / [edited by] Alan H. Goodman, Darna L. Dufour, Gretel H.
    Pelto.
        p.   cm.
    Includes bibliographical references (p.   ) and index.
    ISBN 0-7674-1197-8
    1. Nutritional anthropology.   I. Goodman, Alan H.   II. Dufour,
Darna L.   III. Pelto, Gretel H.
    GN407.N878   1999
    306.4—dc21   99-16016

Manufactured in the United States of America
10 9 8 7 6 5 4 3 2 1

Mayfield Publishing Company
1280 Villa Street
Mountain View, California 94041

Sponsoring editor, Janet M. Beatty; production, Penmarin Books; manuscript editor, Adrienne Armstrong; design manager, Susan Breitbard; text designer, Cynthia Bassett; cover designer, Diana Coe; illustrations, Lineworks, Inc., and Carto-Graphics; print buyer, Danielle Javier. The text was set in 10/12 New Baskerville by TBH Typecast, Inc., and printed on 45# Chromatone Matte by The Banta Book Group.

 This book was printed on recycled, acid-free paper.

Preface

Whether you are a professor or a student, we hope that this book will contribute to your enthusiasm for nutritional anthropology. The anthropological study of food and nutrition is both rewarding and important for understanding ourselves and others. Such studies bridge diverse parts of anthropology—past and present, theoretical and applied, biological and cultural—and between anthropology and other disciplines concerned with nutrition, such as nutritional science, nursing, and public health. An anthropological perspective on nutrition offers great potential for understanding the multifaceted nature of human relationships to food. Food is "good to think" and "good to eat." Food is richly symbolic; nutrition is essential.

If you have previously taught a course in nutritional anthropology, then you might also share some of our frustrations in conveying the excitement and knowledge of this diverse field to students within the limitations of a semester. What topics can reasonably be included? How can one present diverse theoretical perspectives? Finding the right mix of reading materials for our courses has been difficult. Our collective disappointment over the lack of an appropriate collection of articles to introduce students to nutritional anthropology is one of the chief motivations behind this book. Beyond filling a need, we also hope that this reader will help to solidify and define the field.

Nutritional anthropology came into being as a distinct area of inquiry in the 1970s. Before that time, anthropologists, including such notables as Margaret Mead and Audry Richards, had studied food and nutrition, but in the 1970s interests in the evolution of diets and contemporary nutrition problems coalesced. Since that time, the field of nutritional anthropology has continually expanded. Courses in nutritional anthropology are now regularly taught on many college campuses. Although the name of the course might vary from campus to campus (for example, "Nutritional Anthropology," "The Anthropology of Food and Nutrition," "Food and Culture," and so on), most such courses are taught to advanced undergraduates. We sense that the students who take these courses come from diverse backgrounds and have diverse aspirations. Where once nutritional anthropology seemed to be an anthropological child, it is now frequently a means to introduce nutritionists to culture and anthropological perspectives, and it is even making inroads into public health, nursing, and medical school curricula.

The greatest challenge we faced in designing this reader stemmed from the great variability of topics and approaches found across the spectrum of nutritional anthropology courses taught. Our challenge was to define a core set of readings that would provide a foundation for the field and, at the same time, be appropriate for students of different backgrounds and for instructors with various needs and foci. Here is how we went about doing it.

THEORETICAL PERSPECTIVE

The dominant perspective of the book is a biocultural one. As foods transform to nutrients, culture blends into biology. How food tastes is a matter of both culture and biology. What is defined as food and what is eaten may have reverberations in domains as diverse as ethnic identity and health. Nutritional anthropology from the start has been an arena in which ecology, biology, and culture come together. Our chief aim was to ensure that *Nutritional Anthropology: Biocultural Perspectives on Food and Nutrition* reflected the biocultural richness of food and nutrition. Some articles are very biological or very nutrient-focused, and others are very food-focused, symbolic, and social. But almost all of them speak to an integration of perspectives and expertise.

In addition to the boundary between biology and culture, there are other borders that we aimed to bridge, including those between the present, the historic, and the prehistoric. *Nutritional Anthropology: Biocultural Perspectives on Food and Nutrition* not only is concerned with foodways today but also includes articles on how foodways have come together, mixed, and evolved. It is about the state of nutrition today, and also about what our ancestors ate, what problems they encountered, and what their nutrition might mean for us.

Finally, learning comes from reading and from doing. Thus, another border we wished to span was the one that tends to separate theory and learning from doing and implementing. Many of the articles have been selected because they show "nutritional anthropology in action," and this perspective is further supplemented by our "suggestions for doing nutritional anthropology." This focus on linking theory to action reflects the emerging situation in which an anthropological perspective is an increasingly valued component of public health and international nutrition programs. From these readings and the optional activities, students may gain a better sense of how nutritional anthropologists work, and hence a deeper appreciation of issues in this evolving field of inquiry.

TOPICAL COVERAGE AND ORGANIZATION

After the first part, which contains materials that introduce the field and provide a "taste of nutritional anthropology," we divided the reader into eleven sections of two to four readings each. In a semester-long course, the topic of each section may be used as a weekly focus. The section introductions are intended to provide a sense of the area of inquiry, how questions have evolved, and what some of the current key questions are. In the introductions we briefly note the purpose and salient points of each article, explain some of the more difficult parts, and provide questions to guide students in reading the articles that follow. These questions may also provide the basis for class discussions. We end each introduction with suggestions for further reading and for "thinking and doing nutritional anthropology."

In addition to the twelve sections, the articles in the book are grouped into four main parts:

+ Part I provides an introduction and a "taste" of the topics to follow.

+ Part II covers the evolution of human food procurement and an overview of contemporary human food systems. It includes primate and fossil studies, the importance of the development of agriculture, and examples of the food systems found in some contemporary populations.

+ Part III covers diverse theoretical perspectives on the analysis of food systems. Included are sections on materialist perspectives, symbolism and the power of symbols, food as medicine, adapting to foods, and cultural modifications of food.

+ Part IV takes on the issues of under- and overnutrition in the contemporary world. The specific areas addressed include the significance of mild undernutrition, the "small but healthy" hypothesis, the increasing "delocalization" of diets, infant feeding

as a critical nexus, and nutritional issues in rich nations.

THE SELECTION OF ARTICLES

The process of selecting articles to include in *Nutritional Anthropology: Biocultural Perspectives on Food and Nutrition* was both our most difficult and most rewarding task. We relied on the experience and wisdom of many colleagues, as well as our own experiences. Selecting articles involved a great deal of give-and-take because tastes in reading, like tastes in food, are individualistic. One of the rewards of the selection process was discovering little-known "gems." Our selections were guided by the following criteria.

+ Clarity and readability. Even if the material is detailed or technically difficult, it must be clearly presented.

+ Current issues. A few of the articles were originally published in the 1960s and 1970s. We include these as historical pieces and because the issues they addressed, and their means of addressing them, are still timely. The majority of the articles are more recent, and they address issues of relevance today.

+ Representation of diverse perspectives. Although the dominant perspective is biocultural, we wish to show that there is much variety in how one might approach various nutrition and food issues.

+ Ethnographic and geographic spread. We have selected articles to maximize geographic diversity and at the same time have endeavored to provide a focus on the nutritional anthropology of the United States.

+ A spectrum of types of articles. We have intentionally selected articles that were written for different audiences and with different purposes. Some of the articles are written for general audiences, others are reviews for specialists, and others are primary research articles written for professional anthropologists, nutritionists, medical doctors, or epidemiologists. The variety provides a sense of the goals and purpose of different types of writings.

USING THIS READER

Our aim is for this reader to be flexibly included in a variety of courses on food and nutrition. For example, in an anthropology course we expect that it might be supplemented with a monograph that provides more ethnographic detail. Conversely, in a more nutritionally oriented course it may be supplemented with a nutrition text.

Many of the articles we selected were included to provoke discussion. Did the Aztecs really perform human sacrifice because they needed the protein? Should we focus on mild malnutrition or more severe forms of undernutrition? Who is responsible for persistent undernutrition, and how can we combat this problem? We hope that these controversial areas will provide students with a sense of the currency of important debates.

The introductions and appendices include reference materials that we have found useful. For example, the inclusion of National Center for Health Statistics (NCHS) growth charts allows students to estimate their and their classmates' percentiles of weight and height, one of the central methodologies of nutritional anthropology. "Some Principles: Nutrition ABCs, Measurement, and Classification" provides a capsule summary of key issues in nutrition for those who have not taken a course in nutrition and in classes that are not supplemented with a nutrition text.

Finally, we apologize for possibly leaving out any of your favorite topics or articles. We have not, for example, focused on eating disorders, because this topic is covered well in other edited books and monographs. We have not included fictional writing that focuses on food, although there are many excellent examples. These may be assigned alongside the reader.

We hope this volume will mark a stage in the development of nutritional anthropology. We also hope readers will provide feedback on articles that did not meet their expectations and offer suggestions of new ones to consider. Good reading!

ACKNOWLEDGMENTS

A wide network of colleagues provided support and advice. Individuals who read part or all of this book and who helped us to select among articles include Barry Bogin, Peter Brown, Lynne E. Christenson, Carole Counihan, Debra Crooks, Elliot Fratkin, Nina Etkin, Jean Pierre Habicht, Thomas Leatherman, Jonathan Marks, Debra Martin, Ellen Messer, Geraldine Moreno-Black, David Pellitier, R. Brooke Thomas, Wenda Trevathan, and Warren Wilson. Students, particularly those at Hampshire College, "pretested" many of the articles, and we thank them, particularly Kelly Keenan and Kimberly McKenty, for their good advice. Thanks to Bonnie Connor for handling requests for permissions and Deborah Houy for help with copy editing. Pertti Pelto is owed a special debt of thanks, as it is he, more than any other single colleague, who nurtured this project.

We owe a great debt of gratitude to individuals associated with Mayfield Publishing Company who have so amicably helped a vague idea to become a book. April Wells-Hayes has been the most pleasant of production managers. We also wish to thank Marty Granahan and Star MacKenzie at Mayfield and Hal Lockwood of Penmarin Books. Finally, Jan Beatty first encouraged this project an embarrassing number of moons ago. We particularly want to thank her for not playing too heavily on our collective guilt, for her constant good humor, and for her many bright ideas.

Contents

1

The Biocultural Perspective in Nutritional Anthropology

Gretel H. Pelto, Alan H. Goodman, and Darna L. Dufour

INTRODUCTION

Scenario 1. Jane and Frank are discussing the house renovations their neighbors, Jeff and Carol, are doing. Jane reports to Frank the sum of money that is being spent on the kitchen, an amount that vastly exceeds the amount that they themselves would be willing to spend. Frank reacts, "That's nuts—just for the kitchen? Think what else they could do with that money; they could even put in a tennis court." Jane replies, "Well, dear, you have to remember that Jeff lives to eat."

Scenario 2. Bill and Joe have finished lunch and are lingering over coffee and a fruit tart before they return to their offices to continue work. Peter, another colleague, walks into the café and orders a "sandwich to go." While it is being prepared, he comes over to the table to greet Bill and Joe, and they chat amiably for a few minutes. "Number 10, peanut butter and jelly," the clerk announces. "That's me," says Peter, who proceeds to pay for the sandwich and then turns to wave as he leaves. "Does that guy ever sit down to lunch?" Bill asks. "Not likely," Joe replies. "Peter eats to live, you know."

"He lives to eat."
"He eats to live."

These two variations of an aphorism that describes the relationship between some individuals and their food have become commonplace in popular American discourse. The first is often intended as a thinly veiled accusation of gluttony. It good-naturedly caricatures an individual whose interest in food exceeds a level that is "seemly" (that is, culturally appropriate). The second is also often used with a mildly pejorative intent. It carries the implication that the individual being described is insufficiently interested in the "finer" (that is, culturally valued) aspects of food. It conjures up an image of someone who "wolfs down" food and is oblivious to the sensory and social pleasures of eating. Together, these two variations of the aphorism capture the extremes of an implicit cultural dimension about how people should relate to food, and in so doing they reveal the varied significance of food in American culture.

As is true of many aphorisms, the characterizations in the "eat-to-live" and "live-to-eat" observations derive their punch from the fact that they rest on an underlying truism. In this case, the truism is that humans, like all living organisms, must eat food to obtain the nutrients that are essential to life, and, at the same time, we humans invest food with a host of symbolic and social qualities that enhance its meaning beyond that of sustaining physical functioning. A tacit recognition of the interplay of these two elements is invoked in the popular aphorism.

This interplay between food as a biological necessity and the social and cultural factors that condition its availability and consumption is the focus of a number of fields of research. Nutrition and/or food are the subjects of study in many disciplines, from biochemistry and molecular biology to philosophy, folklore, and history. Contemporary scholarship on food and nutrition covers the full range from questions that are exclusively biological to ones that are exclusively about social issues. Some disciplines, including nutritional epidemiology, public health nutrition, community nutrition, and nutritional anthropology, focus on the middle ground in the spectrum from biological to social aspects of food and nutrition. Each of these "middle-of-the-spectrum" disciplines has its own identity and orientation, which are determined to a large extent by the types of questions with which it is concerned.

As a field of study, *nutritional anthropology is fundamentally concerned with understanding the interrelationships of biological and social forces in shaping human food use and the nutritional status of individuals and populations.* Food, or what is bioculturally defined as edible, contains nutrients and other substances. Once food is consumed, the human digestive tract begins to convert food to its chemical constituents. One result of variation in the amount and quality of foods consumed is variation in nutritional status, or the state of balance resulting from the supply and expenditure of nutrients. Nutritional status is important because it is linked to a host of health and functional consequences. A simplified flow of the process linking food to function is presented below.

Culture/Environment → Food → Nutrients → Nutritional Status → Functional Outcomes

In pursuing knowledge of this important process, nutritional anthropologists utilize theory from both biological and social sciences and employ research

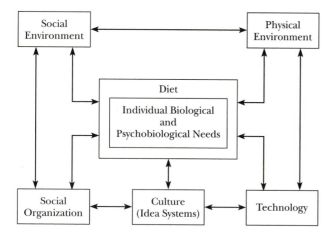

Figure 1.   An ecological model of food and nutrition *(Source: Redrawn from Jerome, Kandel, and Pelto, 1980.)*

methods from biological sciences, from cultural anthropology, and from other social sciences. In addition, they also draw on humanistic scholarship as a source of insights into the cultural and historical aspects of food. In this essay, we will outline key elements of the concepts and approaches that characterize the field of nutritional anthropology.

AN ECOLOGICAL MODEL OF FOOD AND NUTRITION

A number of years ago Jerome, Kandel, and Pelto (1980) published an essay on nutritional anthropology in which they presented an ecological model of food and nutrition (see Figure 1). This model identifies the main social and environmental sectors in a truly holistic analysis of the factors that affect the nutrition of a population. In any particular study, investigators may focus their attention primarily on one of these sectors, but *the hallmark of a biocultural approach is the examination of interactions* among them. Augmented with a chronological perspective and attention to interactions of genetics, disease, and the biological characteristics of foods, the ecological model provides a framework for a biocultural approach to the understanding of food and nutrition.

Jerome and colleagues (1980:15) define the sectors in the model as follows. The *physical environment* includes climate, water resources, soil characteristics, naturally occurring flora and fauna, and other features that establish the conditions for food procurement and production. The *social environment* refers to the larger, external environment (other societies, regions, and communities) whose food production and distribution behavior can have profound effects on the soci-

ety or social group in question. *Social organization* encompasses a large set of social institutions and arrangements, from the structure and organization of the household to the political and economic structures that relate to the production, distribution, and consumption of food. *Technology* includes the entire range of tools and techniques that are utilized for production, distribution, acquisition, storage, and preparation of food. *Culture* (idea systems) refers to ideas and concepts related to food, such as food preferences and restrictions, the use of food in social interactions, religious beliefs involving food, and ideas about food and health. In our own society, the knowledge that we refer to under the rubric of "nutritional science" would be part of the *culture,* or *idea systems,* component of the ecological model.

The arrows in the diagram are intended to indicate the dynamic, interactive nature of the model. Only some of the interrelationships are shown because the diagram would be difficult to decipher if all the sectors were connected to each other with two-way arrows. In theory, however, there are multiple ways in which these sectors are linked, and changes and developments in each affect all of the others. To illustrate, consider the effects of global warming—an aspect of the physical environment. This phenomenon can be examined in terms of not only its immediate effects on the food supply in specific locations but also changes in idea systems (culture) as new language, new concepts, and even new fears enter the vocabulary of daily life. The effects of global warming are identifiable in the invention of new technologies and in alterations in economic exchanges and in the policies and organizational structures that facilitate these exchanges. No sector in the ecological model is unaffected by a major change in the physical environment, and each of these changes influences dietary intakes to some degree. The same principle of "interconnectedness" holds for changes that begin in other sectors of the model. In other words, the ecological model on which research in nutritional anthropology is based is fundamentally a *systems model.*

THE PROCESS OF ADAPTATION

The adaptive process—how humans cope and adjust to meet material needs—is a distinguishing focus of nutritional anthropology. It informs and guides the development of hypotheses about the interactions of biology and culture. With respect to food and nutrition, we distinguish three types or levels of adaptation: (1) genetic adaptation, (2) physiological adaptation, and (3) sociocultural adaptation.

A genetic adaptation is a change that is passed from one generation to the next through biological inheritance of a gene (or set of genes) that improves the survival (hence the reproductive potential) of individuals who have the advantageous gene. The concept of genetic adaptation is illustrated by the studies of population differences in the ability of older children and adults to consume milk without experiencing serious gastric distress. Kretchmer examines the historical process that may have led to this adaptation in his article, "Genetic Variability and Lactose Tolerance," in this book (article 23).

Genetic adaptations are relatively rare, whereas physiological and sociocultural adaptations are common and rapid. They provide a means of responding to environmental change. One form of physiological adaptation is a reduction in basal metabolic rate in the face of chronic caloric deficits. The significance of a physiological adaptation to inadequate food in early childhood—growth stunting—is examined by Martorell in his article in this book titled "Body Size, Adaptation and Function" (article 30). One important point made by Martorell is that this adjustment is not a cost-free one. Adaptation is a compromising process.

Sociocultural adaptations involve behavioral and technological innovations rather than biological adjustments. The development of maize-processing techniques that prevent pellagra (see Katz and colleagues, article 22) and manioc-processing techniques that make it possible to utilize bitter manioc (see Dufour, article 21) is an example of cultural adaptations that improve people's ability to successfully exploit food resources that would otherwise be closed to them. Agriculture is certainly an innovation that improves the yield of energy, but it may come with other costs (articles 8–10).

When one finds food patterns of long standing, it seems reasonable to suggest that they represent positive cultural adaptations that optimize nutritional well-being. Although this is sometimes the case, it is not always so. Both biological and sociocultural adaptations can have negative consequences for the individuals who experience them. One of the most pervasive negative or maladaptive food practices is the denial of some kinds of foods to certain classes of people within a society—notably women and children. In some cases, discriminatory food patterns are maintained through informal custom and may not even be readily verbalized by the people who practice them. However, food prohibitions can also be highly structured by traditional health beliefs or ritual food restrictions. For example, many years ago D. A. McKay (1971) documented the role of food prohibitions as a factor in xerophthalmia (eye disease due to

vitamin A deficiency) in Malaysian children. Unfortunately, it was commonly believed that the early signs of vitamin A deficiency, which was thought to be caused by a kind of worm, were made worse by feeding children green or yellow vegetables. This belief is related to the traditional hot/cold medical belief system (see Anderson, article 25). The practice of withholding the vegetables further reduced vitamin A in the children's diet and increased the likelihood of blindness.

Many other instances of food prohibitions, especially related to pregnancy and lactation, have been described by anthropologists and nutritionists. However, it is wise to be very cautious in interpreting these reports. Often people's reports about their food "rules" and "taboos" turn out, in practice, to be widely ignored or reinterpreted in ways that do not lead to negative food restrictions.

Jelliffe and Bennett (1961) suggested that traditional food practices can be classified into four categories from the perspective of their impact on health: practices that are beneficial, practices that are harmful, neutral practices, and practices whose health impact is unknown. Human cultures are not infallible, although it is obvious that seriously maladaptive practices are likely to be eliminated if they threaten the overall survival of the population. Table 1 (page 4) outlines various types of beliefs and practices in relation to their positive or negative nutritional consequences.

FOOD SYSTEMS IN NUTRITIONAL ANTHROPOLOGY

The concept of food systems is fundamental to the development of theory in nutritional anthropology. Anthropologists use this concept in at least two distinctly different ways. The phrase "food system" can be used to refer to the totality of activities, social institutions, material inputs and outputs, and cultural beliefs *within* a social group that are involved in the production, distribution, and consumption of food. This holistic definition is clearly related to the ecological model described previously. The different components of physical and social actions that are concerned with food are seen as constituting an interactive and interdependent system. Many of the articles in this book examine the internal workings of specific food systems (see, for examples, articles 2, 14–20).

A second definition of "food systems" is based on the means of food acquisition. The food quest is so central to the functioning of societies that anthropologists have made extensive studies of subsistence systems. The differences in the ways that human groups

Table 1.   Examples of cultural beliefs and practices that may have either positive or negative effects on nutritional status.

Positive	Negative
1. Sacred and/or secular beliefs that prevent consumption of contaminated food	1. Beliefs that lead to withholding of food in times of stress
2. Food preparation techniques that improve nutrient availability	2. Beliefs that restrict consumption of nutritionally important foods to infants, young children, and pregnant and lactating women
3. Sacred and/or secular beliefs and rituals that result in increased food in times of stress (for example, warfare, pregnancy, lactation)	3. Food preparation techniques that reduce nutrient bio-availability (for example, boiling)
4. Food storage practices that improve nutritional quality (for example, fermentation)	4. Food storage practices that introduce contaminants or reduce nutritional quality

obtain and utilize food resources have powerful effects on social organization, kinship structure, religious practices, child rearing practices, and many other aspects of life. In the most simplified form, the categorization distinguishes among (1) hunting-gathering subsistence systems; (2) pastoralist systems; (3) agricultural systems, which are subdivided into horticultural (or gardening) systems and advanced (or plow) agriculture systems; and (4) industrialized agricultural systems (articles 6, 11–13). Before we turn to an overview of these different types of food systems, we should review the fundamental similarities that have characterized human food use throughout our evolution as a species, regardless of the type of systems we create.

Universals in Human Food Use

The wide variation that one finds in contemporary and historical food systems is a function of interactions among ecological/cultural determinants in relation to the plasticity and flexibility of the human biological template. Compared with those of other animals, human food systems are distinctive in a number of ways, and despite their great diversity, it is possible to identify core characteristics of basic human biocultural food patterns:

✦ *Homo sapiens* have an extremely omnivorous diet compared to most other animals.

✦ All human groups prepare at least some of their food by cooking, which includes boiling, roasting, frying, and steaming, usually with the addition of various flavoring elements, including salt, sweeteners, or other substances that modify the taste of the prepared foods.

✦ The use of fire and other food preparation techniques means that humans spend more time in the

preparation and alteration of foods than do other animals.

✦ Compared to other animals, humans have elaborate systems of food distribution, sharing, and exchange. These systems of food sharing have resulted in complex ideologies of meaning.

✦ From the process of selecting foods to eat from the larger pool of potentially edible plants and animals, all human groups have created food prohibitions as well as food preferences. Together with the symbolic structures that have developed through the regulation of social exchanges around food, these ideological elements of preference and prohibition have powerful influences on dietary intakes.

Hunting-Gathering Subsistence Systems

For most of our history, humans lived as hunter-gatherers, collecting food from land and water, but not cultivating plant foods or raising animals. In most environments, the distribution of food resources was such that human groups were small, seminomadic bands, utilizing fairly large land areas. Population density was low, and population growth was slow. Only in unusually rich environments, especially riverine and coastal areas, were food resources sufficiently concentrated to allow for permanent settlement and the development of more complex social organizations.

A review of hunting-gathering systems reveals a wide range in the types of food consumed, and in the ratio of animal to vegetable foods. Two of the articles in this book examine the evidence concerning diet and nutritional status in hunting-gathering adaptations to food acquisition (see articles 8–9). Data from archaeological research, as well as studies of foraging peoples who maintained this form of subsistence into the twentieth century, suggest that in general nutritional status was good to excellent. Seasonal food shortage was a problem in many environments, but chronic malnutrition and deficiency diseases were extremely rare.

Pastoralism

Pastoralism refers to a form of subsistence that is based on herd animals. Two types of pastoralist food systems have evolved—nomadic and seminomadic. Nomads do not build permanent housing and do not practice agriculture, whereas seminomadic pastoralists live in settlements, and some members of the group (usually women and children) cultivate crops. Goldschmidt has described pastoral subsistence as "a cultural adjustment to semiarid open country in which native vegetation will support large ruminants but in which hoe agriculture without advanced technologies cannot be satisfied or sustained" (1968:240).

The diets of pastoralists are highly dependent on the animals they herd, with milk products playing a central role. The article in this book by Galvin and colleagues (article 12) examines the characteristics and nutritional implications of "the pastoralist strategy." Today, fewer and fewer peoples are able to pursue this subsistence strategy as economic and political forces push them into permanent villages and other forms of obtaining food. However, for more than 3,000 years, pastoralists inhabited areas from the Atlantic shore of the Sahara to the steppes of Mongolia, as well as parts of North and South America.

Agricultural Food Systems

Beginning approximately 12,000 to 15,000 years ago in several different parts of the world, human groups developed ways of cultivating, and hence domesticating, a variety of food sources. All over the world the transition from hunting and gathering to cultivation and animal keeping appears to have developed through a process of interactions between increased population pressures and technological-environmental factors. The "idea" of plant and animal domestication spread widely, and by 2,000 years ago a very large proportion of the world's peoples were fully dependent on agricultural production to supply most of their food. These inventions came about rather gradually, over many centuries, but their impact on human lifeways was profound. The effects of the "agricultural revolution" not only radically altered diet, nutrition, and health but also brought about social and technological changes that altered the nature of human societies in very fundamental ways.

From a cultural perspective, agriculture led to new patterns of social organization. Social interactions in hunting-gathering groups were heavily influenced by fluctuations in food availability, whereas in agricultural systems, the demands of plant and animal production shaped the nature of social institutions. New technologies for food production were accompanied by technological innovations in food preservation and preparation. The distribution of food within and across populations was also dramatically altered with the advance of agricultural production.

Physical environments experience very major changes as a consequence of human agricultural activities. New species are introduced into the ecosystem, and old ones are forced out. Often, agriculture results in overcultivation and overgrazing, with land erosion following as a consequence. On the other hand, the extent to which agricultural production results in environmental degradation depends on multiple environmental and social factors, and some agricultural systems have been relatively nondestructive. For example, the shifting cultivation practiced by many rain forest cultivators appears to represent an effective use of land that is well adapted to the conditions of the tropics (see Dufour's discussion in article 11).

The earliest forms of agricultural food systems, which have continued to the present day, are referred to as "horticultural" or "gardening" systems. These systems, which rely on the hoe (as contrasted with a plow) and do not utilize irrigation, produce foods for household consumption rather than for commercial sale. Typically, the production unit is a household, which functions as a self-provisioning entity (Wolf, 1966). There is relatively little interdependence with external groups, and expanded market networks are generally not present. Instead, the social relations around food are played out through ceremonial and ritual interactions.

Agriculture that involves only some members of a society in food production (albeit a substantial proportion) arose with the development of plow agriculture, irrigation, and the emergence of a class of producers who are commonly referred to as peasants. Wolf (1966) has described *peasants* as rural cultivators who raise crops and livestock in the countryside for household consumption, while the surplus production of their more efficient methods is transferred to a dominant group of rulers in the city who use it to underwrite other activities, including a higher standard of living for themselves.

Although food systems based on horticultural production use surplus production for social (often ritual) exchanges, peasants lack control over their production and often are not able to keep adequate amounts to meet their own nutritional needs. The malnutrition that plagues rural food producers in many developing countries today is not new but came about with the development of state societies that were built on intensive agriculture. In Mesoamerica, for example, there is substantial evidence from archaeological data to suggest that the average stature of Mayan males decreased from the Early Classic Period (A.D. 250–550) to the Late Classic Period, as intensive cultivation proceeded and rural producers experienced increasing nutritional stress. The decrease in dietary adequacy was due to a number of factors, including increasing environmental degradation under the pressure of overproduction. The reasons for overproduction are also complex, but there is little doubt that the demand of the ruling class for food to support their own non–food production activities played a significant role. Thus, the class differences in diet that are found in Mexico and Guatemala today represent the continuation of long-standing patterns of dietary inequality (see discussion by Pelto in article 13).

Cash Cropping and the Rise of Industrialized Agriculture

In modern times, the production of nonfood crops (such as tobacco and sisal) and nonnutritive foods (such as coffee and tea) came to play an increasingly important role as household food production shifted away from subsistence to a cash economy. Changes in household production patterns are just one aspect of the vast social, cultural, and environmental changes that are associated with the "delocalization" of food production and the globalization of economies. During the second half of the twentieth century, the industrialization of food production and food preparation has brought further transformations. Understanding the short-term and long-term consequences of this new stage in the evolution of human food systems claims the attention of researchers across a range of social science disciplines, as well as scholars in the humanities. In nutritional anthropology, the dietary and nutritional consequences of cash cropping at the community, household, and individual level have been a particular focus of research. However, along with scholars in other disciplines, anthropologists are also studying other aspects of the social and biological changes that these transformations are bringing about. (Articles 31–34 provide some examples of anthropologically informed work on these contemporary processes.)

Research Approaches in Nutritional Anthropology

We suggested previously that one of the features that distinguishes among the different disciplines concerned with food and nutrition research is the type of questions that the members of a discipline address in their work. Together with the theoretical approaches that they draw on in forming their hypotheses about "how the world works," and the methods they use to investigate these hypotheses, the types of questions that investigators ask tend to have a different cast, depending on their disciplinary orientation. Thus, sociologists, psychologists, anthropologists, political scientists, economists, epidemiologists, humanists, and individuals whose basic training is in the biological or medical sciences frame their questions in different ways. In an article on nutritional anthropology prepared for the *Encyclopedia of Cultural Anthropology*, Pelto (1996) outlined the main orientations of work in nutritional anthropology. We have drawn on this discussion in the sections that follow.

Sociocultural Processes and Nutrition

The evolution of human lifeways can be described in terms of both long-term and short-term "sociocultural processes." In nutritional anthropology, the most significant long-term evolutionary change is the transition from hunting-gathering subsistence to settled, agriculturally based societies. The large-scale sociocultural processes that are currently ongoing, which are also the subject of study by nutritional anthropologists, are often subsumed under the labels of "globalization," "modernization" (including the growth of cities), delocalization of energy resources, and industrialization. The explosive increase of contact with mass media and the expansion of women's participation in the paid labor force are also among the significant sociocultural processes of concern to nutritional anthropologists.

The basic structure of the questions that nutritional anthropologists ask about the relationship of sociocultural processes to nutrition is: "What is the impact of X on nutrition?" The X in this question is a particular process or set of events, such as the transformation of a subsistence system from one form to another, the introduction of a new technology, or migration from rural to urban areas. Some anthropological scholars are concerned with synthesizing knowledge from many specific historical or geographic conditions in order to derive broad generalizations about sociocultural processes. For example, biological anthropologists and archaeologists have proposed generalizations about the consequences for human nutrition and health of the shift from hunting-gathering to agriculture (Cohen and Armelagos, 1984). Similarly, cultural anthropologists have examined the effects on nutrition of recent large-scale social processes, such as neocolonialism (Franke, 1987) and cash cropping (article 33).

A common mode of research in nutritional anthropology is to focus on a specific factor or related set of factors in a particular place in order to understand how it is affecting food intake and nutrition. The types of factors that have been selected for study cover a broad range from technological and social characteristics found only in traditional hunting and herding societies to factors that have become important to human experience only in recent times. For example, the well-known studies of the !Kung San (represented in this book by Lee's articles 2 and 6) describe the linkages between the social organization of the group, the environment, and dietary intake in hunting-gathering food systems. Studies of dietary changes associated with cross-national migration caused by warfare and political upheaval are another example of this mode of questions. A number of anthropologists have been concerned with the effects on nutrition of maternal work, child care, and seasonal food availability. In this book, the article by Levine (article 37) on this subject is an excellent example of research that follows the basic format of investigating the effects of sociocultural processes on nutrition.

The Social Epidemiology of Nutrition

This research orientation has many similarities with studies of social processes and nutrition. However, there is a different emphasis in that the initial focus is on a nutritional condition, and the researcher seeks to identify the role of social factors in the etiology of those conditions. The general structure of the research question is: "What are the determinants of (or the factors associated with) outcome Y?" The Y in this question is a nutritional condition, such as deficient levels of intake of a single nutrient (for example, vitamin A or iron); a macro dietary feature (for example, total energy intake, saturated fat intake); measures of growth (such as attained height, arm circumference); or a nutritional pathology (such as the protein-energy deficiency diseases of marasmus and kwashiorkor, or obesity) (see articles 38–40).

The following are examples of the types of questions studied by nutritional anthropologists who are concerned with the social epidemiology of nutrition:

(1) What are the factors that account for the adequacy of weaning practices *in a given population?* (2) What are the determinants of duration of breastfeeding or the selection of breastfeeding versus bottle-feeding *in a particular population?* (3) What are the sociodemographic correlates of vitamin A intake? (4) What are the factors that determine inadequate nutrient intake of women in conditions of food scarcity as contrasted with environments where the food supply is adequate? (5) What are the social factors that contribute to high saturated fat intake *in a particular cultural group?*

Idea Systems and Nutrition

The study of cultural systems of belief as they relate to nutritional outcomes is another focus of research for nutritional anthropology. The structure of questions takes the form: "What is the relationship of X [beliefs] to Y [nutritional outcome]?" In this statement, the word "beliefs" is used broadly to cover the range from specific elements of knowledge, such as the concept of "vitamins" or "iron-rich foods," to more general cultural constructs. An example of the latter is the humoral medical system of "hot/cold" beliefs, which imputes qualities of "hot" or "cold" to individual food items as well as to illnesses. In this book, Anderson (article 25) explores this widespread cultural theory in traditional Chinese food systems, and Dubisch (article 26) applies this perspective to the health foods movement.

Anthropological studies linking beliefs to dietary intake and nutritional status cover a range of topics, from the analysis of traditional beliefs to contemporary nutrition ideas. Illustrative topics are studies of the impact on maternal nutrition of pregnancy and lactation food proscriptions and prescriptions; the nutritional consequences of religious systems with frequent fasting cycles; the effect of maternal nutrition knowledge on infant and young child feeding practices; and the study of how concepts of food qualities and health influence dietary intake.

Physiological Adaptation, Population Genetics, and Nutrition

Nutritional anthropologists who pursue studies in which they apply principles of human adaptation to understanding the relationship of nutrition to certain biological experiences of populations often study how the nutritional history of a population has shaped or influenced its physiological or genetic characteristics.

The general form of the research question is: "What is the role of X [biochemical feature of a food or a pattern of food use] in explaining the distribution of Y [physiological or genetic trait or condition] in this *population?*"

The previously noted study of lactose tolerance (article 23) is an example of this type of research interest. Other research interests that can be classified under the heading of "adaptation and nutrition" are studies in human reproduction and body composition, including obesity (see articles 39–40). Together with other types of investigators, nutritional anthropologists have undertaken studies of pregnancy outcome, low birth weight, growth stunting, and obesity, all of which involve complex interactions of diet, environment, disease, and social organization.

COMMONALITIES IN METHOD AND THEORY

A notable characteristic of nutritional anthropology is its eclecticism. The ecological model leads investigators to draw from methods and theories in nutritional biochemistry, physiology, genetics, and epidemiology, as well as the social and policy sciences. At the same time, there are several commonalities in the research approach of nutritional anthropologists. These not only cut across the specific questions that are the topics of study but also reflect an anthropological approach to these questions. These commonalities include the following:

✦   Studies generally focus on a *population* rather than studying individual subjects without consideration of the population of which they are a part. Often the population is defined in terms of a specific *community*, although larger, geographically delimited units may also be utilized.

✦   Many studies select the *household* as the primary unit of analysis, which permits the investigation of nutrition and food use within the context of household organization.

✦   Most studies examine multiple aspects of family characteristics (for example, economic status, demographic and social characteristics), even when the focus is on a particular factor—that is, the approach tends to be "holistic."

✦   Most studies include both qualitative, descriptive data and quantitative data, which are obtained by utilizing several different data collection methods. These

range from informal and open-ended interviews and observations to highly structured formats for interviews and physical measurements, which yield data that are amenable to statistical analysis.

NUTRITIONAL ANTHROPOLOGY IN ACTION

The foregoing overview of the field has examined the main types of research issues that are addressed by nutritional anthropologists who conduct their work under the auspices of academic institutions and with funding from sources that support scientific investigation. Another aspect of nutritional anthropology is the work carried out by anthropologists who are working in applied settings and conducting studies that are intended to assist programs to function more effectively. Because this kind of work is designed to serve the immediate needs of an organization, agency, or other clients, it is usually more difficult to access through academically oriented publishing sources. Some of it appears in newsletters, project reports, and other similar media. The fact that some of this work is never presented in printed form and that much of it is in widely scattered sources makes it more difficult to characterize. However, the following three categories appear to be the main areas in which applied nutritional anthropologists are currently working:

✦   Formative research to obtain a better definition of a general nutritional problem that will be the focus of programs or other actions to improve that problem. For example, anthropologists have conducted community studies of infant and young child feeding in order to provide programs with information to better define the specific problems that families face in a community or region where a new program will be started. A related goal is to identify common problematic behaviors that are negatively affecting child health and growth.

✦   Research to improve communication strategies and the content of nutrition and health education. Applied nutritional anthropologists work with programs and community members to identify local concepts and beliefs and determine what methods are most appropriate for providing people with the information they need in a manner that will enable them to accept and use it. In the best situations, the anthropologists also provide information and advice from the community back to programs so that the agencies can learn and profit from community knowledge.

◆ Qualitative ethnographic evaluation of nutrition and health interventions. Some public health agencies have become interested in obtaining qualitative evaluations that provide insights into how communities are responding to their programs, including what community members perceive to be the goals, purposes, strengths, and weaknesses of the activities and services that have been introduced. For example, the United Nations University has sponsored many studies to "assess nutrition and primary health care programs from the household perspective, and to do so as rapidly and accurately as possible" (Scrimshaw, 1992:27).

In recent years, the number of anthropologists working in applied settings has greatly increased. Among this growing body of applied scientists are individuals who specialize in nutrition. Some of them have advanced training in the biological aspects of nutrition, while others come into food and nutrition programs with training in public health, in policy and program evaluation, or in cultural anthropology. As the opportunities for comparative analysis of their studies and experiences increase, applied nutritional anthropology will be in a strong position to make significant contributions to our understanding of human behavior related to food and nutrition. This, in turn, will help to create new knowledge for action to address the pressing problems that currently threaten the health and well-being of people all over the globe.

REFERENCES CITED

Cohen, M., & Armelagos, G. (Eds.). (1984). *Paleopathology at the origins of agriculture.* New York: Academic Press.

Franke, R. W. (1987). The effects of colonialism and neo-colonialism on the gastronomic patterns of the third world. In M. Harris & E. B. Ross (Eds.), *Food and evolution: Toward a theory of human food habits* (pp. 455–81). Philadelphia: Temple University Press.

Goldschmidt, W. (1968). Theory and strategy in the study of cultural adaptability. In Y. A. Cohen (Ed.), *Man in adaptation: The cultural present* (pp. 231–49). Chicago: Aldine.

Jelliffe, D. B., & Bennett, F. J. (1961). Cultural and anthropological factors in infant and maternal nutrition. *Federation Proceedings,* 20 (suppl. 7), 185–88.

Jerome, N. W., Kandel, R. F., & Pelto, G. H. (1980). An ecological approach to nutritional anthropology. In N. W. Jerome, R. F. Kandel, & G. H. Pelto (Eds.), *Nutritional anthropology: Contemporary approaches to diet and culture* (pp. 13–45). Pleasantville, NY: Redgrave Publishing Co.

McKay, D. A. (1971). Food, illness, and folk medicine: Insights from Ula, Trengganu, West Malaysia. *Ecology of Food and Nutrition,* 1, 67–78.

Pelto, G. H. (1996). Nutritional anthropology. In D. Levinson & M. Ember (Eds.), *Encyclopedia of cultural anthropology.* Vol. 3 (pp. 881–84). New York: Henry Holt and Co.

Scrimshaw, S. C. M. (1992). Adaptation of anthropological methodologies to rapid assessment of nutrition and primary care. In N. S. Scrimshaw & G. R. Gleason (Eds.), *Rapid assessment procedures: Qualitative methodologies for planning and evaluation of health related programmes* (pp. 25–38). Boston: International Nutrition Foundation for Developing Countries.

Wolf, E. R. (1966). *Peasants.* Englewood Cliffs, NJ: Prentice Hall.

PART I

A Taste of Nutritional Anthropology

Nutritional anthropology encompasses many types of studies. The three articles that follow illustrate some of these different interests, as well as some of the key issues in this area of inquiry. In his classic article, "Eating Christmas in the Kalahari," Richard Lee relates a lesson learned about humility in providing a gift of food. In "How Many Calories Are There in a 230-Calorie Dinner?" John Grossmann brings to life the process of determining the nutrient composition of a food. In "The Magic Bullet?" Lavinia Edmonds describes the often lethal synergy between disease and malnutrition. All three articles were written for a general audience. Together they provide a sense of some of the issues to be addressed in greater depth in the part introductions and articles to follow.

Richard Lee, the author of "Eating Christmas in the Kalahari," is a cultural anthropologist who undertook a long-term study of the economy of the !Kung San in the Kalahari Desert of southern Africa in the 1960s and 1970s (also see article 6). Lee relates a story of his own foibles in deciding to purchase an ox as a gift for his community of informants. Lee imparts a lesson about the power of food, the symbolism that is embedded in important "gifts" and other forms of exchange.

Lee's work with the !Kung San included an estimation of the energy and protein intake of individuals (article 6). Estimating nutrient intake is a typical task in studies by nutritional anthropologists. To do a dietary assessment, one generally records what an individual ate during a day (or a longer period of time) and then from this list of foods and portions calculates the nutrient content of the diet. The translation from food to nutrients is usually accomplished with the aid of a nutritional analysis program (such as Foodpro II or Nutritionist IV). The nutrient analysis program contains a database of the nutrient composition of many foods. For example, it contains information on the vitamin C content of a small apple and the magnesium content of a medium mango. But how did this database come about? And just how accurate is it?

These questions are the focus of John Grossmann's article. Grossmann lets us follow a package of Oriental-Style Shrimp with Rice through what is called "proximate analysis." In proximate analysis, a food is broken down into its major constituents: moisture (or water), fiber, protein, fat, carbohydrate, and ash. To figure out the micronutrient (vitamins and minerals) composition of this or any other meal, more detailed work would need to be done. Does the process of proximate nutrient analysis surprise you? Are you surprised that the dinner in question did not come out to be exactly 230 calories?

Understanding the causes and consequences of malnutrition, as well as finding solutions, is another concern of nutritional anthropologists. "The Magic Bullet?" by Lavinia Edmonds, describes one man's struggle to combat vitamin A deficiency in children. The man is Al Sommer, a physician. Vitamin A deficiency results in blindness and is a serious problem in many developing countries, especially in Asia and Africa. Blindness is not the only problem. Al Sommer also discovered that there is a deadly synergy between vitamin A deficiency and infection, especially measles. This means that for children who are vitamin A deficient, measles is a life-threatening disease and many die. The World Health Organization (WHO) estimates that some 14 million preschool children have suffered eye damage due to vitamin A deficiency, some 350,000 go blind or partially blind each year, and 60 percent of those who go blind die within a few months (WHO, 1999). These figures are astounding considering that Hippocrates, the Greek physician who lived between 460 and 377 B.C., knew that including liver (a good source of vitamin A) in the diet would cure night blindness, an early sign of vitamin A deficiency. The figures are even more astonishing in view of the fact that the vitamin deficiency can be cured by inexpensive vitamin A supplements, "magic bullets," and prevented by an adequate diet. So why aren't vitamin A supplements widely available in the areas where they are needed?

Ensuring that all children have an adequate diet is another solution. Is it a better one? A diet adequate in vitamin A is one that contains animal products, especially liver, dark green vegetables, and orange-colored

10

fruits and vegetables (carrots, yellow-fleshed sweet potatoes, mangos, and others). The vegetables do not actually contain vitamin A, but they do contain carotenes that are converted to vitamin A in the body. Why don't all people include those foods in their diets, or the diets of their children? These are questions nutritional anthropologists, working in a variety of different societies, have attempted to answer.

REFERENCES CITED

WHO. (April 1999). Vitamin A deficiency. http://www.who.int/gpv-dvacc/diseases/vitamin_a.htm.

2

Eating Christmas in the Kalahari

Richard Borshay Lee

The !Kung Bushmen's knowledge of Christmas is thirdhand. The London Missionary Society brought the holiday to the southern Tswana tribes in the early nineteenth century. Later, native catechists spread the idea far and wide among the Bantu-speaking pastoralists, even in the remotest corners of the Kalahari Desert. The Bushmen's idea of the Christmas story, stripped to its essentials, is "praise the birth of white man's god-chief"; what keeps their interest in the holiday high is the Tswana-Herero custom of slaughtering an ox for his Bushmen neighbors as an annual goodwill gesture. Since the 1930's, part of the Bushmen's annual round of activities has included a December congregation at the cattle posts for trading, marriage brokering, and several days of trance-dance feasting at which the local Tswana headman is host.

As a social anthropologist working with !Kung Bushmen, I found that the Christmas ox custom suited my purposes. I had come to the Kalahari to study the hunting and gathering subsistence economy of the !Kung, and to accomplish this it was essential not to provide them with food, share my own food. or interfere in any way with their food-gathering activities. While liberal handouts of tobacco and medical supplies were appreciated, they were scarcely adequate to erase the glaring disparity in wealth between the anthropologist, who maintained a two-month inventory of canned goods, and the Bushmen, who rarely had a day's supply of food on hand. My approach, while paying off in terms of data, left me open to frequent accusations of stinginess and hard-heartedness. By their lights, I was a miser.

The Christmas ox was to be my way of saying thank you for the cooperation of the past year; and since it was to be our last Christmas in the field, I determined to slaughter the largest, meatiest ox that money could buy, insuring that the feast and trance dance would be a success.

Through December I kept my eyes open at the wells as the cattle were brought down for watering. Several animals were offered, but none had quite the grossness that I had in mind. Then, ten days before the holiday, a Herero friend led an ox of astonishing size and mass up to our camp. It was solid black, stood five feet high at the shoulder, had a five-foot span of horns, and must have weighed 1,200 pounds on the hoof. Food consumption calculations are my specialty, and I quickly figured that bones and viscera aside, there was enough meat—at least four pounds—for every man, woman, and child of the 150 Bushmen in the vicinity of /ai/ai who were expected at the feast.

Having found the right animal at last, I paid the Herero £20 ($56) and asked him to keep the beast with his herd until Christmas day. The next morning word spread among the people that the big solid black one was the ox chosen by /ontah (my Bushman name; it means, roughly, "whitey") for the Christmas feast. That afternoon I received the first delegation. Ben!a, an outspoken sixty-year-old mother of five, came to the point slowly.

"Where were you planning to eat Christmas?"

"Right here at /ai/ai," I replied.

"Alone or with others?"

"I expect to invite all the people to eat Christmas with me."

"Eat what?"

"I have purchased Yehave's black ox, and I am going to slaughter and cook it."

"That's what we were told at the well but refused to believe it until we heard it from yourself."

"Well, it's the black one," I replied expansively, although wondering what she was driving at.

"Oh, no!" Ben!a groaned, turning to her group. "They were right." Turning back to me she asked, "Do you expect us to eat that bag of bones?"

"Bag of bones! It's the biggest ox at /ai/ai."

"Big, yes, but old. And thin. Everybody knows there's no meat on that old ox. What did you expect us to eat off it, the horns?"

Everybody chuckled at Ben!a's one-liner as they walked away, but all I could manage was a weak grin.

That evening it was the turn of the young men. They came to sit at our evening fire. /gaugo, about my age, spoke to me man-to-man.

"/ontah, you have always been square with us," he lied. "What has happened to change your heart? That sack of guts and bones of Yehave's will hardly feed one camp, let alone all the Bushmen around /ai/ai." And he proceeded to enumerate the seven camps in the /ai/ai vicinity, family by family. "Perhaps you have forgotten that we are not few, but many. Or are you too blind to tell the difference between a proper cow and an old wreck? That ox is thin to the point of death."

"Look, you guys," I retorted, "that is a beautiful animal, and I'm sure you will eat it with pleasure at Christmas."

"Of course we will eat it; it's food. But it won't fill us up to the point where we will have enough strength to dance. We will eat and go home to bed with stomachs rumbling."

That night as we turned in, I asked my wife, Nancy: "What did you think of the black ox?"

"It looked enormous to me. Why?"

"Well, about eight different people have told me I got gypped; that the ox is nothing but bones."

"What's the angle?" Nancy asked. "Did they have a better one to sell?"

"No, they just said that it was going to be a grim Christmas because there won't be enough meat to go around. Maybe I'll get an independent judge to look at the beast in the morning."

Bright and early, Halingisi, a Tswana cattle owner, appeared at our camp. But before I could ask him to give me his opinion on Yehave's black ox, he gave me the eye signal that indicated a confidential chat. We left the camp and sat down.

"/ontah, I'm surprised at you: you've lived here for three years and still haven't learned anything about cattle."

"But what else can a person do but choose the biggest, strongest animal one can find?" I retorted.

"Look, just because an animal is big doesn't mean that it has plenty of meat on it. The black one was a beauty when it was younger, but now it is thin to the point of death."

"Well I've already bought it. What can I do at this stage?"

"Bought it already? I thought you were just considering it. Well, you'll have to kill it and serve it, I suppose. But don't expect much of a dance to follow."

My spirits dropped rapidly. I could believe that Ben!a and /gaugo just might be putting me on about the black ox, but Halingisi seemed to be an impartial critic. I went around that day feeling as though I had bought a lemon of a used car.

In the afternoon it was Tomazo's turn. Tomazo is a fine hunter, a top trance performer (*see* "The Trance Cure of the !Kung Bushmen," *Natural History*, November, 1967), and one of my most reliable informants. He approached the subject of the Christmas cow as part of my continuing Bushmen education.

"My friend, the way it is with us Bushmen," he began, "is that we love meat. And even more than that, we love fat. When we hunt we always search for the fat ones, the ones dripping with layers of white fat; fat that turns into a clear, thick oil in the cooking pot, fat that slides down your gullet, fills your stomach and gives you a roaring diarrhea," he rhapsodized.

"So, feeling as we do," he continued, "it gives us pain to be served such a scrawny thing as Yehave's black ox. It is big, yes, and no doubt its giant bones are good for soup, but fat is what we really crave and so we will eat Christmas this year with a heavy heart."

The prospect of a gloomy Christmas now had me worried, so I asked Tomazo what I could do about it.

"Look for a fat one, a young one . . . smaller, but fat. Fat enough to make us //gom ('evacuate the bowels'), then we will be happy."

My suspicions were aroused when Tomazo said that he happened to know of a young, fat, barren cow that the owner was willing to part with. Was Toma working on commission, I wondered? But I dispelled this unworthy thought when we approached the Herero owner of the cow in question and found that he had decided not to sell.

The scrawny wreck of a Christmas ox now became the talk of the /ai/ai water hole and was the first news told to the outlying groups as they began to come in from the bush for the feast. What finally convinced me that real trouble might be brewing was the visit from u!au, an old conservative with a reputation for fierceness. His nickname meant spear and referred to an incident thirty years ago in which he had speared a man to death. He had an intense manner; fixing me with his eyes, he said in clipped tones:

"I have only just heard about the black ox today, or else I would have come here earlier. /ontah, do you honestly think you can serve meat like that to people and avoid a fight?" He paused, letting the implications sink in. "I don't mean fight you, /ontah; you are a white man. I mean a fight between Bushmen. There are many fierce ones here, and with such a small quantity of meat to distribute, how can you give everybody a fair share? Someone is sure to accuse another of taking too much or hogging all the choice pieces. Then you will see what happens when some go hungry while others eat."

The possibility of at least a serious argument struck me as all too real. I had witnessed the tension that surrounds the distribution of meat from a kudu or gemsbok kill, and had documented many arguments that sprang up from a real or imagined slight in meat distribution. The owners of a kill may spend up to two hours arranging and rearranging the piles of meat under the gaze of a circle of recipients before handing them out. And I also knew that the Christmas feast at /ai/ai would be bringing together groups that had feuded in the past.

Convinced now of the gravity of the situation, I went in earnest to search for a second cow; but all my inquiries failed to turn one up.

The Christmas feast was evidently going to be a disaster, and the incessant complaints about the meagerness of the ox had already taken the fun out of it for me. Moreover, I was getting bored with the wisecracks, and after losing my temper a few times, I resolved to serve the beast anyway. If the meat fell short, the hell with it. In the Bushmen idiom, I announced to all who would listen:

"I am a poor man and blind. If I have chosen one that is too old and too thin, we will eat it anyway and see if there is enough meat there to quiet the rumbling of our stomachs."

On hearing this speech, Ben!a offered me a rare word of comfort. "It's thin," she said philosophically, "but the bones will make a good soup."

At dawn Christmas morning, instinct told me to turn over the butchering and cooking to a friend and take off with Nancy to spend Christmas alone in the bush. But curiosity kept me from retreating. I wanted to see what such a scrawny ox looked like on butchering, and if there *was* going to be a fight, I wanted to catch every word of it. Anthropologists are incurable that way.

The great beast was driven up to our dancing ground, and a shot in the forehead dropped it in its tracks. Then, freshly cut branches were heaped around the fallen carcass to receive the meat. Ten men volunteered to help with the cutting. I asked /gaugo to make the breast bone cut. This cut, which begins the butchering process for most large game, offers easy access for removal of the viscera. But it also allows the hunter to spot-check the amount of fat on the animal. A fat game animal carries a white layer up to an inch thick on the chest, while in a thin one, the knife will quickly cut to bone. All eyes fixed on his hand as /gaugo, dwarfed by the great carcass, knelt to the breast. The first cut opened a pool of solid white in the black skin. The second and third cut widened and deepened the creamy white. Still no bone. It was pure fat; it must have been two inches thick.

"Hey /gau," I burst out, "that ox is loaded with fat. What's this about the ox being too thin to bother eating? Are you out of your mind?"

"Fat?" /gau shot back, "You call that fat? This wreck is thin, sick, dead!" And he broke out laughing. So did everyone else. They rolled on the ground, paralyzed with laughter. Everybody laughed except me; I was thinking.

I ran back to the tent and burst in just as Nancy was getting up. "Hey, the black ox. It's fat as hell! They were kidding about it being too thin to eat. It was a joke or something. A put-on. Everyone is really delighted with it!"

"Some joke," my wife replied. "It was so funny that you were ready to pack up and leave /ai/ai."

If it had indeed been a joke, it had been an extraordinarily convincing one, and tinged, I thought, with more than a touch of malice as many jokes are. Nevertheless, that it was a joke lifted my spirits considerably, and I returned to the butchering site where the shape of the ox was rapidly disappearing under the axes and knives of the butchers. The atmosphere had become festive. Grinning broadly, their arms covered with blood well past the elbow, men packed chunks of meat into the big cast-iron cooking pots, fifty pounds to the load, and muttered and chuckled all the while about the thinness and worthlessness of the animal and /ontah's poor judgment.

We danced and ate that ox two days and two nights; we cooked and distributed fourteen potfuls of meat and no one went home hungry and no fights broke out.

But the "joke" stayed in my mind. I had a growing feeling that something important had happened in my relationship with the Bushmen and that the clue lay in the meaning of the joke. Several days later, when most of the people had dispersed back to the bush camps, I raised the question with Hakekgose, a Tswana man who had grown up among the !Kung, married a !Kung girl, and who probably knew their culture better than any other non-Bushman.

"With us whites," I began, "Christmas is supposed to be the day of friendship and brotherly love. What I can't figure out is why the Bushmen went to such lengths to criticize and belittle the ox I had bought for the feast. The animal was perfectly good and their jokes and wisecracks practically ruined the holiday for me."

"So it really did bother you," said Hakekgose. "Well, that's the way they always talk. When I take my rifle and go hunting with them, if I miss, they laugh at me for the rest of the day. But even if I hit and bring one down, it's no better. To them, the kill is always too small or too old or too thin; and as we sit down on the kill site to cook and eat the liver, they keep grumbling, even with their mouths full of meat. They say things like, 'Oh this is awful! What a worthless animal! Whatever made me think that this Tswana rascal could hunt!'"

"Is this the way outsiders are treated?" I asked.

"No, it is their custom; they talk that way to each other too. Go and ask them."

/gaugo had been one of the most enthusiastic in making me feel bad about the merit of the Christmas ox. I sought him out first.

"Why did you tell me the black ox was worthless, when you could see that it was loaded with fat and meat?"

"It is our way," he said smiling. "We always like to fool people about that. Say there is a Bushman who has been hunting. He must not come home and announce like a braggard, 'I have killed a big one in the bush!' He must first sit down in silence until I or someone else comes up to his fire and asks, 'What did you see today?' He replies quietly, 'Ah, I'm no good for hunting. I saw nothing at all [pause] just a little tiny one.' Then I smile to myself," /gaugo continued, "because I know he has killed something big.

"In the morning we make up a party of four or five people to cut up and carry the meat back to the camp. When we arrive at the kill we examine it and cry out, 'You mean to say you have dragged us all the way out here in order to make us cart home your pile of bones? Oh, if I had known it was this thin I wouldn't have come.' Another one pipes up, 'People, to think I gave up a nice day in the shade for this. At home we may be hungry but at least we have nice cool water to drink.' If the horns are big, someone says, 'Did you think that somehow you were going to boil down the horns for soup?'

"To all this you must respond in kind. 'I agree,' you say, 'this one is not worth the effort; let's just cook the liver for strength and leave the rest for the hyenas. It is not too late to hunt today and even a duiker or a steenbok would be better than this mess.'

"Then you set to work nevertheless; butcher the animal, carry the meat back to the camp and everyone eats," /gaugo concluded.

Things were beginning to make sense. Next, I went to Tomazo. He corroborated /gaugo's story of the obligatory insults over a kill and added a few details of his own.

"But," I asked, "why insult a man after he has gone to all that trouble to track and kill an animal and when he is going to share the meat with you so that your children will have something to eat?"

"Arrogance," was his cryptic answer.

"Arrogance?"

"Yes, when a young man kills much meat he comes to think of himself as a chief or a big man, and he thinks of the rest of us as his servants or inferiors. We can't accept this. We refuse one who boasts, for some-day his pride will make him kill somebody. So we always speak of his meat as worthless. This way we cool his heart and make him gentle."

"But why didn't you tell me this before?" I asked Tomazo with some heat.

"Because you never asked me," said Tomazo, echoing the refrain that has come to haunt every field ethnographer.

The pieces now fell into place. I had known for a long time that in situations of social conflict with Bushmen I held all the cards. I was the only source of tobacco in a thousand square miles, and I was not incapable of cutting an individual off for noncooperation. Though my boycott never lasted longer than a few days, it was an indication of my strength. People resented my presence at the water hole, yet simultaneously dreaded my leaving. In short I was a perfect target for the charge of arrogance and for the Bushmen tactic of enforcing humility.

I had been taught an object lesson by the Bushmen; it had come from an unexpected corner and had hurt me in a vulnerable area. For the big black ox was to be the one totally generous, unstinting act of my year at /ai/ai, and I was quite unprepared for the reaction I received.

As I read it, their message was this: There are no totally generous acts. All "acts" have an element of calculation. One black ox slaughtered at Christmas does not wipe out a year of careful manipulation of gifts given to serve your own ends. After all, to kill an animal and share the meat with people is really no more than Bushmen do for each other every day and with far less fanfare.

In the end, I had to admire how the Bushmen had played out the farce—collectively straight-faced to the end. Curiously, the episode reminded me of the *Good Soldier Schweik* and his marvelous encounters with authority. Like Schweik, the Bushmen had retained a thoroughgoing skepticism of good intentions. Was it this independence of spirit, I wondered, that had kept them culturally viable in the face of generations of contact with more powerful societies, both black and white? The thought that the Bushmen were alive and well in the Kalahari was strangely comforting. Perhaps, armed with that independence and with their superb knowledge of their environment, they might yet survive the future.

3

How Many Calories Are There in a 230-Calorie Dinner?

John Grossmann

A bit foolish and slightly chilled. That's how I felt recently on a plane bound for Tennessee, a ten-ounce package of Benihana Oriental-Style Shrimp with Rice squeezed between my back and the seat. I'd forgotten to take it out of the freezer the night before, and I was helping it thaw, belatedly following the instruction of chemist Lars Reimann, who had agreed to let me watch as his technicians carefully destroyed it in the name of slimmer waistlines.

Reimann is vice-president of Woodson-Tenent Laboratories, among the most prominent of a couple dozen American labs that pick apart frozen dinners and other products turned out by some of the nation's largest food producers—ConAgra Frozen Foods, for example. What the companies get in return is a nutritional box score, a percentage breakdown that includes such key items as fat, carbohydrates, protein, and usually a calorie count.

"Under 300 calories." I'd seen this claim on all kinds of frozen entrees. But I had no idea how the calories were counted. So it was that I telephoned Reimann and arranged to fly my own sample down to Memphis. The package put the actual count at 230 calories. I wanted to know if it was true.

Reimann greeted me in a dazzlingly white, crisply starched lab coat, his name stitched in blue over the left breast pocket. He looked as though he'd been sent over from central casting: the Hollywood archetype of an executive chemist. His office, too, had the composed look of a movie set. On the wall left of the desk hung a periodic table of the elements; on the tidy adjacent bookshelves stood both a microscope and a balance.

The now-unfrozen package I handed Reimann was not much bigger than a paperback novel. The front of the box showed a mound of pink shrimp, some glossy pieces of green pepper with a few peas, a couple of water chestnuts, and a drizzling of translucent sauce—all atop a bed of fluffy white rice. Especially right then, just short of noon, the meal looked pretty good.

It looked considerably less appetizing after we'd walked it down to the lab, where Rosie Webber, a "sample preparation person," cut open the two "microwavable" pouches, emptied everything into the ten-cup bowl of a huge Cuisinart, and flicked the switch. In seconds it was thin, pale-green mush. Baby food.

It must be perfectly homogenized, Reimann said over the noise. First our technicians find the water and fat content, then the protein, fiber, carbohydrate, and so on. Don't worry about the calories, he said, we'll get around to them later.

Reimann introduced me to a meticulous young woman named Linda Littlejohn and described her as a "lipid chemist," a specialist in fats. Littlejohn shook my hand, pulled on a pair of gloves, reached for a couple of pie pans the size of mason jar lids, and weighed them.

"We add about two grams of the sample to each of these tin dishes and weigh them again," she said, starting right in on the water determination. Littlejohn pressed the dishes—literally—into service. After dabbing each with a blob of homogenized shrimp dinner, she carefully crimped them into sealed half moons. Why two samples? As a hedge against mistakes, Littlejohn said, recording one sample as 2.306 grams and the other as 2.1082 grams. "Now we put them in a vacuum oven at just less than boiling temperature for about five hours, and then transfer them to a desiccator till they cool. Then we weigh each sample again. The 'before' and 'after' difference in weight is the amount of moisture that's been removed."

Reimann saw my eyes glaze over at the word *desiccator*, and he pointed to a piece of equipment the size of a microwave oven. Inside, he explained, were moisture-loving silica crystals. "If you simply removed the samples from the oven, they might reabsorb moisture from the air—one percent or more—as they returned to room temperature."

With the tiny globs of my shrimp dinner roasting in the oven, Littlejohn turned to the fat. With a pipette she placed ten drops of the green mush into the bottom of an odd dumbbell-shaped flask with a valve in the middle, then repeated the procedure for a companion flask. Into a third she added a thin brown puree. I must have looked perplexed. "Rabbit food," she said. "This is the control sample. We already know exactly how much fat it has."

Littlejohn doused the samples with ten milliliters of hydrochloric acid and two milliliters of alcohol—the acid to free the fat from the rest of the blend, the alcohol to dissolve it—and gave each flask a shake. Finally she put the flasks on a long, built-in hot plate to boil, condense, and boil some more. "We'll come back in about 45 minutes," she said. "There's nothing fast about analytical chemistry."

◆ ◆ ◆

16

Ham Sandwich Digest

Calories. They sneak up on you. Take two slices of whole wheat bread, 140 calories; a couple of pieces of country ham, 105; two slices of Swiss cheese, 135; a tablespoon of mayonnaise, 100; a teaspoon of Dijon mustard, 5; and a leaf of lettuce, 1. What you have is one ham sandwich, 486 calories. But just where do those calories go?

Certainly not into a hollow leg. The sandwich, disintegrating as it goes, moves a smidgen at a time from the stomach into the small intestine, where enzymes turn it into things the body can absorb. Carbohydrates are converted to sugars, fats to fatty acids and glycerol, and proteins to a smattering of amino acids. These bits and pieces pass through the wall of the intestine and wend their way to the liver. The calories go along.

The liver transforms all the sugars into glucose, or blood sugar. But instead of flooding the blood-stream with glucose, the liver turns most of it into glycogen. The liver can store only about 340 calories worth of glycogen at a time, the muscles about 1,400. Any excess is turned into fat, and fat knows few bounds. The body has somewhere around 40 billion fat storage cells. In times of plenty, they blow up like balloons. The fat cells of a slender woman can easily stash away 74,000 calories; a man's, 95,000.

Unfortunately, glucose isn't the only sandwich by-product that can be diverted to the fat cells. Both fatty acids and surplus amino acids—those not made into enzymes, muscles, and such—can wind up as body fat. Clearly, eating too much of any food can add pounds.

So how much of that sandwich has been stored 24 hours after lunch, and how much has been burned? It all depends, of course, on what else you're eating and doing.

Around the house, you burn roughly equal amounts of carbohydrate and fat. If you maintain your weight on 2,000 calories a day, for example, about 1,300 will be spent just expanding the lungs, pumping blood, driving the nervous system, and otherwise sustaining life; the brain and nerves alone scarf down 400 to 600 calories each day. By doing nothing more than fidgeting you can burn an additional 100 to 800 calories a day.

Let's say the 486 calories in the sandwich are a part of your daily 2,000. About two thirds of the sandwich, or 316 calories, will go toward keeping body and soul together. The other third, 170 calories, will be burned by activities: work, play, fidgeting, fixing dinner.

But suppose you need just 2,000 calories a day and are eating 3,000—that's another story. Then less than half the sandwich will be used to keep the body running. Less than a quarter will go toward everyday exercise. The remainder—165 calories—will make a beeline for the fat cells. It takes only 3,500 extra calories to add one pound of body fat.

Suppose you decide to ditch that new body fat by jogging for an hour. After several minutes, your muscles will start calling more on the fat in your fat cells than on the carbohydrate stored in your muscles. If you're running for distance and not for speed, you'll continue to burn mostly fat.

Now suppose that Fang, your neighbor's German shepherd, comes charging out of his yard. You break into a sprint and are soon gasping for air. During this short-term burst, your lungs can't pump enough oxygen into your blood to let your body consume fat. Instead, your muscles switch to their carbohydrate stores, and you poop out.

Obviously, the best plan is to jog, bicycle, dance, walk, or work out in a way that pumps enough oxygen to the cells to burn fat. In other words, exercise aerobically. A 120-pound woman who jogs five miles in an hour will burn about 500 calories, most of it fat. So much for the ham sandwich.

Just how hard can you work out and still get the last laugh on your fat cells? Remember this rule of thumb: If you can't carry on a conversation while exercising, you're not shedding fat.—*Patricia Long*

Through the years, chemists have burned a lot of calories zeroing in on the energy in foods. The most precise method is to set the food on fire and measure the heat given off. That happens in a stainless steel gizmo about the size and shape of a loaf of Italian bread. Inside is a miniature heating coil that ignites the food.

This nifty piece of equipment, called a bomb calorimeter, introduced me to a terrific bet. Consider this: Food burned in a bomb calorimeter reveals its energy by warming the water in which the bomb is immersed. The energy needed to raise the temperature of one kilogram of water by 1°C equals one kilogram calorie, or one kilocalorie. This kilocalorie is exactly what you, I, and the frozen dinner makers call a calorie; technically, we're all off by a thousand. The 300-calorie Lean Cuisines in our freezers really contain 300,000 calories. Try it as a wager. Maybe you can win a meal from your dieting sister-in-law.

The person who made *calorie* a household word was a Wesleyan University professor of chemistry named Wilbur O. Atwater. Often called the father of American nutrition, Atwater counted calories at the turn of the century for the U.S. Department of Agriculture. He conducted hundreds of experiments. Some were completed in minutes, with bits of broccoli or bratwurst combusted in a bomb calorimeter; others lasted as long as five days, with student volunteers confined to a special four-by-eight-foot room. Atwater carefully prescribed and measured all food delivered into the room through an airlock, and he was equally precise about the output. He measured the rise in room temperature as the students converted food to heat, and he burned samples of bodily wastes in a bomb calorimeter to measure what the students didn't digest. His studies showed, among other things, that we're unable to get any energy out of fibers—cellulose, for example. We'd starve on a celery diet.

Atwater's work raised more than a little controversy, particularly when his newfound wisdom moved him to tell the world how to eat. Many scorned his advice that Americans cut down on fat in their diets. Teetotalers bristled when he served alcoholic beverages to students in his calorie room, and became outraged when he declared that alcohol could be considered an energy-bearing food.

In time, Atwater's efforts gave rise to a thick collection of tables published by the U.S. Department of Agriculture and now known as *USDA Handbook No. 8.* It's this book that reveals the caloric value of four cooked asparagus spears (15) or one slice of quiche lorraine (600)—2,500 items in all. Moreover, Atwater's studies provided nutritionists with a simple way to count calories. No need to burn food or lock students in a closet. Simply determine a food's proportions of fat, protein, and carbohydrate, then multiply: four calories for each gram of protein, four for each gram of carbohydrate, and nine for each gram of fat. These numbers, Atwater found, represent good averages no matter what food is on the fork. Scores of professional calorie counters now apply this 4-4-9 rule every day. And that's where things were headed at the Woodson-Tenent lab in Memphis.

✦ ✦ ✦

On schedule, three quarters of an hour later, Littlejohn returned to her trio of flasks. The mixtures were now the color of cola. To each she added a ten-milliliter squirt of alcohol and set them on the lab table to

cool. Later she dribbled 20 milliliters of two different kinds of ether into each flask and shook them one by one. "The fatty acids don't really want to be in with the alcohol," she said. "They prefer the ether." Already two layers were beginning to form: on top lay the ether containing the fat from my shrimp dinner. Littlejohn explained that she'd isolate the ether, then boil off the solvent to leave the fat, a step that would take the better part of an hour. I begged off to find Reimann, who had long since returned to his office.

He smiled at my attempts to dust off my high school chemistry and patiently described how my dinner's protein and fiber contents would be wrung from several more samples with the same exactitude. Cramped quarters at the lab in Memphis forced these projects over to a sister lab in Des Moines. In the final act of the drama, the Iowa lab would incinerate another dollop of shrimp mix in an oven hot enough to melt glass. The output would be a tiny bit of ash, the residue of salts—in this case an irrelevant statistic.

"If you're on a diet and you don't have high blood pressure," Reimann explained, "you can put all the salt you want on your food; it's not going to change the calories."

Calories? That's what I'd come for, after all. So far I'd seen nothing but stunning precision: samples cooling in a desiccator to keep measurements from drifting one percent out of line, a metric balance so accurate that in handling the samples Littlejohn wore gloves to keep the oil of even a single fingerprint from skewing the reading by a few thousandths of a gram.

And all that troubled me. The lab's four-decimal-point precision would soon give way to the whole-number averages of Atwater's 4-4-9 rule. It would be akin to a bank teller taking in money all day, carefully counting deposits of $13, $89, $137, and so on—and then totaling them by measuring the stacks of bills with a yardstick.

"It does seem kind of goofy," Reimann admitted. He then proceeded to inform me that, in analyzing animal feeds, Woodson-Tenent often spends an extra day or two to arrive at a truer measurement of the protein.

"You mean you're more precise with animal food than human food?"

"Sure. Many times animals get only one source of feed, so it had better be nutritionally complete."

But what about the last-stage loss of precision? Didn't that trouble him? Not really, Reimann said, except for a single wrinkle: Fiber contains no calories a human can use, but it's always counted with the carbohydrates. "The one big stinker is that fiber—whether you subtract it or not when figuring the calorie content of the carbohydrates." Oddly, the USDA doesn't require the fiber subtraction, so some labs don't bother with it. The result: inflated carbohydrate fig-

Calories: Grill Yourself

1. Which seafood has the most calories per ounce?
   a) Clam
   b) Oyster
   c) Lobster
   d) Squid
   e) Scallop

2. An ounce of which snack has the fewest calories?
   a) Plain popcorn
   b) Pickled pigs' feet
   c) Coleslaw
   d) Green olives

3. A California avocado has ____ more calories than a similar-size Florida avocado.
   a) 17%   c) 67%
   b) 27%   d) 100%

4. Match each with its fat content:
   a) Croissant   1) 32%
   b) Roasted peanuts 2) 50%
   c) Milk chocolate 3) 21%

5. Which has the most calories?
   a) Camembert cheese
   b) Cheesecake
   c) Cheddar cheese
   d) Vanilla ice cream

6. True or false: Roast leg of lamb has more calories per ounce than coconut.

7. Men ages 35 to 50 take in an average of ____ calories per day. Women the same age take in ____ calories.

8. Which three vegetables have measurable levels of fat?
   a) Carrots
   b) Sweet potatoes
   c) Summer squash
   d) Brussels sprouts
   e) Artichokes
   f) Lima beans

9. True or false: Grapefruits have more calories than strawberries.

10. Which has the most calories per ounce?
   a) Maple syrup
   b) Safflower oil
   c) Sirloin steak

11. True or false: An eight-ounce gin and tonic has about the same number of calories as an eight-ounce milkshake.

ANSWERS

1. *d*, squid. One ounce of oysters has 18 calories; clams, 21; lobster, 25; scallops, 25; and squid, 26. Oysters are actually fatter than squid, but they have half the protein and more water.

2. *b*, pickled pigs' feet. They're high in protein and low in fat.

3. *c*, 67%. California avocados have twice as much fat; Florida avocados, about 10% more water.

4. Croissant, 21%; roasted peanuts, 50%; milk chocolate, 32%.

5. *c*, cheddar cheese, with a hefty 32% fat. Camembert has 24% fat, cheesecake 20%, and vanilla ice cream only 11%.

6. *False.* Coconut, which is high in fat, contains 98 calories an ounce. The same amount of lamb, with less than half the fat, has 79 calories.

7. On average, men consume about 2,300 calories a day. A typical woman makes do on about 1,500.

8. *c*, summer squash, *d*, brussels sprouts, and *f*, lima beans all contain about 0.6 percent fat.

9. *True.* Grapefruits have slightly more, with 55 calories per six ounces, compared to 50 for strawberries.

10. *b*, safflower oil. This one's easy if you've read about the 4-4-9 rule in the main story. Maple syrup is mostly water and carbohydrate, steak is mostly water and protein, and safflower oil is all fat. The oil weighs in at 250 calories per ounce. An ounce of maple syrup has about 71; steak, 80.

11. *False.* Two ounces of 80 proof gin delivers about 125 calories; six ounces of tonic water, about 66. Total: 191. A milkshake with 4 ounces of milk and 4 ounces of ice cream totals 315 calories.

ures, and calorie counts that often run high. That could be good news for calorie-shaving dieters, because they might be getting even less than they paid for. Unfortunately, there's no way to know which products are which. Reimann pointed down the hall toward the lab. "With some of these frozen entrees you're talking about a difference of as much as 10 calories, just from the fiber."

But do 10 or 20 missing calories really matter? "Let's not make a big thing out of something that doesn't need to be that precise," Reimann said. "There's a guy here at work who can eat tremendous amounts of food and he doesn't gain an ounce, whereas others are on constant diets and are still chubby. People metabolize food differently. I admit, though, that I look at the calorie listings when I go shopping. They're a good indicator."

The USDA appears to be of like mind. The agency justifies its fiber policy and use of the 4-4-9 rule by pointing to a host of uncertainties: No two crops of beans are exactly the same, for example. Nor are any two sides of beef. And package weights may not be precise either.

Then there's the matter of rounding. According to the USDA, products containing more than 50 calories must be rounded to the nearest 10. Furthermore, allowing for batch differences and other imperfections, companies are given a 20 percent leeway. While claiming to weigh in at 230 calories, my shrimp dinner could legally be 276. Or 184.

Knowing all this, I look back enlightened and bemused at what I saw in the beakers Linda Littlejohn removed from the heating element late in my visit to the lab. All that remained was a thin film, not much bigger than a quarter and about as distinguished as a half swallow of coffee hardened in the bottom of a for-

gotten cup. This was the fat. Littlejohn precisely measured its weight, taking care to record the total to the third decimal place. In view of all the rounding to come, it seemed more a quaint gesture than a necessity.

And that was my parting shot at calorie counting. A few days later Reimann mailed me a Certificate of Analysis. It read:

Serving size: 10 ounces (282 grams)
Moisture: 78.2% = 220.5 grams
Protein: 3.53% = 9.955 grams
Fat: 1.28% = 3.61 grams
Fiber: 0.3% = 0. 846 grams
Ash: 1.03% = 2.905 grams
Carbohydrates: 15.96% = 45.01 grams

The package had pegged the calories at 230. But now that I knew all the ins and outs, I didn't expect a perfect match. I reached for my calculator and invoked the 4-4-9 rule (remembering to subtract the fiber from the carbohydrates).

Protein × 4 = 39.82 calories.
Carbohydrates × 4 = 176.656 calories.
Fat × 9 = 32.49 calories.

The sum? 248.966 calories—OK, call it 250. Not what the package said, but close enough for government work. I realized I'd done everything I could to learn about that dinner except to find out how it would taste. And that, I decided, was someone else's job.

4

The Magic Bullet?

Lavinia Edmonds

Al Sommer, in his polo shirt and khaki pants, pokes his head into the thatched hut to find the little boy, as he expected, sitting still in the shadows. Someone has placed bright blue toy cars around the dirt floor of the hut, but the 4-year-old hasn't noticed. Sommer asks the mother to bring the child out into the light. The Hopkins professor of ophthalmology and epidemiology has seen this ailment more times than he likes—in field work in Indonesia, Bangladesh, Tanzania, Guatemala, and here, as a camera from ABC-TV's "20/20" records in 1986, in a remote village in the Philippines.

Children going blind. The disease, known as xerophthalmia, usually starts with night blindness. Then the eyes cloud with tiny white foamy formations on the cornea. In the last stage, the surface of the cornea becomes dry and susceptible to infection, and

the eyes seem to melt away. Xerophthalmia is the major form of preventable blindness in the third world. In the tropics alone, it is estimated to blind about 500,000 young children annually; about half the children die of other diseases.

Sommer happens to have on hand a jar of yellow, tear-shaped vitamin A capsules reserved for occasions like this. He holds the squirming child in his arms and pushes the capsule quickly into his mouth, "Isn't that delicious?" And then he says to the mother, "He was a couple of days away from developing severe blindness." Given the capsule, containing 200,000 international units of vitamin A (about the amount in 10 carrots), the child's disintegrating vision will be completely reversed within hours. But most significant and controversial is Sommer's conclusion: "We just reduced the child's risk of dying by 20 percent."

Sommer has been internationally recognized for combatting blindness caused by lack of vitamin A. In a field guide and the definitive text *Nutritional Blindness,* he set the standards for diagnosis and treatment. Night blindness has been the earliest clinical sign of vitamin A deficiency; Sommer is refining a method of detecting it earlier.

But in the last decade the scope of Sommer's work has widened dramatically, with controversial results. In what has become a personal and scientific mission, Sommer now champions vitamin A not only to prevent nutritional blindness but also to reduce overall infection and mortality rates. Vitamin A, he believes, can reduce a good portion of the 12 million-plus children's deaths that occur annually in the developing world. And he has persuaded a number of important people to champion the vitamin with him, from members of Congress and officials of the U.S. Agency for International Development (AID) to "20/20" host Hugh Downs. (Moved by seeing children regain their sight through vitamin A, Downs told Barbara Walters on the air that he was tempted to quit his job and distribute vitamin A capsules.)

It was while looking at risk factors for xerophthalmia in Indonesia in 1982 that Sommer stumbled across the finding that would change his field. He found that children's risk of death correlated less strongly with their general nutritional status than with the severity of their vitamin A deficiency, as measured by their vision problems.

In a follow-up project in Aceh, on the northern tip of Sumatra, Sommer, his Hopkins colleagues, and Indonesian counterparts studied 29,939 children in 450 villages. Half were given vitamin A, half were not. The results were published May 24, 1986, in the British journal *Lancet.* Not surprisingly, the group given the nutrient had 85 percent less xerophthalmia. But it also had a much lower death rate—34 percent lower, the study reported. Among children aged 1 to 5, mortality in control villages was 49 percent greater. As Sommer seeks to replicate the finding in Nepal and Ethiopia, its repercussions are still reverberating throughout the scientific and international relief communities.

Few public health measures are claimed to reduce childhood mortality even by 10 percent. But 34 percent? "I wish he had not made such a high claim," says Chris Kjolhede, a former Sommer student who is now an assistant professor at the Institute for International Programs of the School of Public Health. "I don't think it's borne out in his study. A 10 percent claim would be more realistic. If his claims don't bear up in other studies, he could become the Linus Pauling of vitamin A."

Across Wolfe Street from Kjolhede, in a suite of offices at the Wilmer Eye Institute, Sommer directs the 48-person Dana Center for the Prevention of Blindness. The conference table surrounded by six plush green chairs contrasts with Sommer's field office in Nepal, where a week before he and his two associates had to hunt for electrical outlets to plug in their computers. A tall, athletic-looking man, seemingly younger than his 47 years, Sommer leans forward excitedly. He's earnest and efficient, making points with stories and a healthy dose of statistics from his studies.

In fact, he counters, the claims from the Aceh study were conservative, for the mortality rate of the vitamin A recipient group included those who died in the first three months—too soon for the capsule to have had any effect. "If you correct for that, it [the death rate difference] automatically goes to 48 percent." Nor should this seem incredible, Sommer says, pointing to a growing body of independent laboratory research suggesting that vitamin A bolsters the immune system and fights infection.

Nevertheless, Kjolhede's criticisms were echoed by a National Academy of Sciences committee that evaluated the Aceh study. It pointed to design flaws, such as the absence of a placebo (forbidden by the Indonesian government). "We felt we needed to take a close look, because there are so many policy implications," explains committee chair Reynaldo Martorell, of Stanford's Food Research Institute. "Providing two doses of vitamin A per year was so tantalizing to policy planners. We felt this needed to be replicated in other settings. It would be a really nice thing, but what if it's not true?"

At the same time, says NAS panel member Barbara Underwood, international programs director at the National Eye Institute, "none of us feel Al is wrong. He has done a great service. Sometimes you have to go overboard to get your point across to the people in policy positions."

Sommer is getting his point across. Vitamin A supplementation has become a high-profile project, with Sommer seizing the initiative in the tradition of vitamin pioneer E. V. McCollum. McCollum, known for identifying vitamins A and D, had a far-reaching role in changing the American diet. Like McCollum, Sommer advises governments, testifies in Congress, and otherwise promotes his ideas however he can. In large part because of Sommer, Congress has earmarked $8 million this year for vitamin A programs and UNICEF has bought millions of capsules for distribution in the third world. Some say UNICEF's child survival acronym GOBI (for growth monitoring, oral rehydration, breast feeding, and immunization) will be changed to GOBIA to include vitamin A once all the evidence is in.

Tackling practical problems in the field with zeal and creativity, Sommer is admired in the world of programs and politics. "He's the first to expand on and build on the knowledge about vitamin A," says Susan Pettiss, program director at the relief organization Helen Keller International. "He's been an inspiration to governments. Planning and development is so difficult in third world countries. He's provided the studies and a plan of action." That same zeal contributes to the caution some scientists express about Sommer's work. So does professional competition, no doubt.

But also underlying the disagreement is a philosophical debate: Can one little pill work such wonders? Kjolhede and others argue that while vitamin A is known to reverse blinding conditions, almost miraculously, it does not begin to address the multiple problems causing children to die in third world countries. They are suspicious of Sommer's work because of its "mindset that one can deliver a simple intervention with a big bang, that vitamin A is the ultimate magic bullet," says Robert Black, chair of international health in the School of Public Health. "For many, that philosophy is an anathema. We're dealing with very complex problems of inadequate services, poverty—structural problems. Any technology imposed from outside is more crippling. You have to attack the social position, access to goods and health."

Sommer knows the criticism well. "There is a camp that can't believe something this simple and inexpensive can have the effect it's had," he says. "There are lots of reasons to expect tremendous variation in impact. What is startling to me is how consistent the impact has seemed."

❖ ❖ ❖

It has long been known that vitamin A improves vision; what mother hasn't tried to feed carrots to a child with the bribe that it will help him to see? Hippocrates prescribed vitamin A–rich liver to cure night blindness.

But it was Elmer McCollum, then working at the Wisconsin Agricultural Experiment Station, who published his discovery of "fat-soluble A" in 1913. McCollum and his colleagues found that when rats were fed a diet in which lard, olive oil, or almond oil provided the sole sources of fat, they could not grow or remain in good health. The rats lost eyes and hair and died in extreme cases. Rats given butter fat, cod liver oil, or egg yolk fat remained healthy. The essential component of the latter fats McCollum called fat-soluble A. It's a very pale yellow substance stored in the liver and carried to mucous-secreting cells in the eye and the epithelial cells that cover the body and its organs. Just how the cells use it is still not understood.

Besides some fats, there is another source of vitamin A—cheaper and healthier, if less efficient: The yellow pigment, or carotene, of carrots and of many other vegetables and fruits is converted to fat-soluble A in the liver.

McCollum also saw that the deficiency weakened the immune system of rats, leading to its label as an "anti-infection" agent. Even in the 1930s vitamin A was known to be related to the growth of epithelial tissues. Without the nutrient, the skin becomes keratinized, or dry, and the mucous membranes may fail to secrete normally. The barriers to bacterial infection are let down, and infection enters through the digestive system, the respiratory tract, the mouth, or the surface of the eye.

Understanding of the nutrient's immunological powers is increasing now that scientists are beginning to grasp how the body's defense system works. Animal studies show that vitamin A deficiency harms the lymph nodes, thymus, and spleen. A-deficient rats have fewer lymphocytes to resist bacteria and viruses. In various experiments on humans, vitamin A inhibited growth of certain tumors, and even could change the type and function of the malignant cell, according to R. K. Chandra in a literature review of vitamin A and immunocompetence.

"There's been a slow trickle of research on the immune response and vitamin A," says Richard Semba, an instructor of ophthalmology at Wilmer. "Vitamin A–deficient children are easy to find, but in many parts of the world it's associated with protein-energy malnutrition. We know general malnutrition also depresses the immune system." In West Java, where A deficiency is not often accompanied by protein-energy malnutrition, Semba and colleagues are studying how the immune system responds to standard vaccinations in 120 vitamin A–deficient children and a control group. Experience suggests that the vaccinations don't work as well in the deficient children. Sommer is hopeful about the research's implications: "Maybe it could open doors to fighting other diseases, AIDS. Who the hell knows?"

According to Sommer, at least three properties distinguish vitamin A, making it so full of potential for curing ills beyond blindness. As a fat-soluble vitamin, it is stored for at least three months; so two capsules a year can fill the body's needs. It has amazing restorative power: Rubbed on the eye, it can literally dissolve the lesions causing early vision problems. And it's cheap, about one cent a dose.

But there is always the danger of overselling its miraculous healing power, as Wilmer researchers are well aware. Earlier this year former Wilmer director Edward Maumenee was temporarily stripped of his research privileges; he and colleagues were accused of violating research rules and of making unfounded claims in a 1985 paper about a vitamin A–based ointment's ability to cure dry eye, a condition common among older women in this country. Yet Maumenee maintains the fault lay in the study methods, not in vitamin A.

Maumenee was an adviser to Sommer during his residency at Wilmer, which began in 1973. A year earlier, during his fellowship in epidemiology at the School of Public Health, Sommer assembled a vitamin A interest group in the board room where E. V. McCollum's portrait hung. "He was a great inspiration," says Sommer. "McCollum was perhaps unique in recognizing and dedicating himself to the practical application of his discoveries."

Recruited to the Hopkins school in 1918, McCollum was a master of low-cost public education campaigns. He promoted the well-rounded diet full of nutrients and vitamins in more than 100 columns for *McCall's* magazine and speeches to home economists. Thanks in part to McCollum's testimony before Congress, vitamin A– and D–rich milk and fortified foods came to be staples of the American diet. Today the United States has only isolated cases of vitamin A deficiency.

"There are scientists who feel a real scientist should never dirty his hands," says Sommer. "But McCollum combined science with proselytizing. As a scientist, you've got a moral responsibility for the application of findings." This legacy, which Sommer has adopted, makes many scientists uneasy, just as conventional politicians mistrusted Jimmy Carter and his religion.

Sommer and those who carry out his studies talk of the collegiality, spirit, and adventure of "the field." Always around the corner loom crises—floods, famines, or coups. Certain situations call for on-the-spot creativity, such as how to ship dried sweet-pea leaves from Tanzania to Baltimore for testing without being dumped at U.S. Customs. (Answer: Use friends in the embassy to send the leaves via diplomatic pouch, as Sommer once arranged.) Beyond the adventure is the conviction that their work could lead to a revolution in child survival strategies.

❖ ❖ ❖

Sommer traces his public health interest to a stint in a cholera clinic in East Pakistan (now Bangladesh). After receiving his MD from Harvard in 1967, instead of joining the Army, he signed up to serve in the Center for Disease Control's cholera research laboratory in Dacca, East Pakistan. "He seemed the brightest of the lot," recalls the lab's chief, W. Henry Mosley, now director of the School of Public Health's Institute for International Programs.

Sommer recalls with a laugh that he read about East Pakistan in *National Geographic* and went "because I thought then it would be an interesting thing to do for two years. But seeing how much impact an individual can have, with appropriate resources, I saw how you could affect millions." Some of Sommer's sensitivity to the suffering he saw is conveyed in a group of black-and-white photographs that he took and displays now on the wall of his office: A bone-thin mother looks horrified as her two children, dying of cholera, lie crumpled in a cot behind her.

While working in the clinic, Sommer met Donald McCai, a Scottish physician who ran a health service in a remote corner of Pakistan. "We did collaborative studies. I remember one day he showed me a bunch of children with Bitot's spots" (white spots on the eye). "I can make them go away with vitamin A," Sommer recalls McCai saying. Sommer describes the encounter as "interesting and prophetic."

Sommer was soon absorbed in more immediate problems, when a cyclone swept inland from the Bay of Bengal in November 1970. "The cyclone left us stranded with soil that was incapable of growing food, because it was salty [from the tidal wave]. Relief efforts were chaotic. The Red Cross would drop bundles of rice from the sky. People fought over whatever was dropped," he recalls.

Surveying the network of islands by helicopter, Mosley could see bits of houses and human limbs swept up by the tidal wave into treetops. Sommer and others soon formed a health group for delivery of emergency supplies. They set up headquarters on a deserted island, cleared an airstrip, and detailed their needs.

Two months later, Sommer led 10 teams of two men apiece through villages devastated by the cyclone, selecting random houses in villages four miles apart to interview a total of 2,973 families. Mean mortality was 16.5 percent, representing a minimum of 224,000 deaths, and a million people were still dependent on outside food relief. More than 180,000 homes were destroyed, Sommer and Mosley reported. In their landmark study, reported in *Lancet* in May 1972, they established the importance of epidemiological studies at the site of disasters in getting an accurate picture of needs and target relief and recovery efforts. It was a story of loss that Sommer and Mosley told more accurately than the press or the government. And the experience tapped Sommer's epidemiological interests and fed his instinct to do important scientific studies with immediate practical application.

That same year, at Hopkins, Sommer postponed his residency at Wilmer to study epidemiology—what he was doing instinctively anyway. Then Susan Pettiss, director of blindness prevention programs at Helen Keller International, recruited him to help to set up prevalence studies of nutritional blindness in Central America, and his career in vitamin A began. "Everything kind of falls together," says Sommer, who had no plan to combine epidemiology and ophthalmology. "The only thing I knew was I wanted to be a doctor. From there, I followed my nose."

At the School of Public Health, Sommer filled the cubicle allotted to him with millions of punch cards from a project he'd started in a remote province of East Pakistan. "I came with a lot of data and a lot of papers." In the field, he had discovered it was difficult to get the height and weight of children—then used as the primary indicators of a child's nutritional status. Following the suggestion of a Quaker relief team, Sommer tested the use of arm measurements instead as an indication of malnutrition. The paper he wrote was rejected by journals for five years. Finally published in the *American Journal of Clinical Nutrition,* it's now recognized as a classic in the burgeoning field known as nutritional surveillance.

Sommer has always been eminently practical. In the late 1970s he demonstrated that vitamin A given by capsule was just as effective as an injection and far easier to give. "This is very important from a practical point of view," Sommer explains. "If a child is in a village where they don't have access to facilities and develops night blindness or Bitot's spots, anybody can give that child a dose of vitamin A by mouth. And in this day and age, with AIDS, you absolutely wouldn't want to use a needle and syringe."

But in the age of AIDS, it is hard to persuade developing countries to focus on blindness prevention. In a ward where physicians are trying to keep children alive, they can easily overlook xerophthalmia, Sommer explains. He recalls visiting hospital wards in Guatemala in 1980. "The ophthalmologist there said, 'No, no, we never see xerophthalmia.' Then they invited me to see the facilities. As soon as you get into the diarrhea ward, you walk over to a kid there with his eyes closed. You open the eyes, and the corneas have gone to rot, just melted away. Child's blind, always will be blind."

The low priority given to blindness can extend to the highest levels of government in developing countries, says Sommer. "We have spoken with ministers of health, primarily in Africa, who feel terrible that children are night blind and some children are going blind permanently, but say, 'One third of our children are going to die before the age of 5. Can we divert limited health resources from programs to promote child survival to programs that are merely going to prevent children from going blind?' That was a catch-22 situation and one that we couldn't do much about.

"What's happened since then is the discovery that vitamin A supplementation may be a very powerful way to reduce child mortality, and when we found that out, it had tremendous political repercussions."

❖ ❖ ❖

From 1976 to 1979, Sommer and his wife moved with their children to Indonesia, where the government wanted him to study regions with high levels of xeroph-thalmia. Sommer says he took along a list of questions: What are the earliest clinical signs of xerophthalmia? What is the range of symptoms? What is the most practical means of treating the disease? But he hadn't then thought much about the role of vitamin A deficiency in other diseases. Just the converse, in fact: In a survey of 3,481 preschool-aged children, he wanted to assess whether bouts of respiratory disease and diarrhea put children at risk for vitamin A deficiency and thus xerophthalmia.

Back home in Baltimore one weekend before the Christmas of 1982, Sommer was preparing for a talk to the American Ophthalmological Society on his Indonesian work. He was at his office, thumbing through the computer printouts of his results from examining the 3,481 children. "Holy cow!" Sommer recalls exclaiming. "Children seemed to be dropping out of the tables." Mortality increased in direct relation to the severity of xerophthalmia.

Sommer turned his original idea upside down. He realized that in his concentration on the eye, he had been blinded to other implications. In this study, he found mild vitamin A deficiency was associated with at least 16 percent of all deaths in children aged 1 to 6 years. The results, wrote Sommer, suggested that mild xerophthalmia "justifies vigorous community-wide intervention as much to reduce childhood mortality as to prevent blindness."

So much for that study. His talk at the association elicited "a big yawn," he recalls. But the Aceh study that followed—over six times the size—created the waves, finding that administration of vitamin A reduced mortality rates among children by 34 percent. It is still unbelievable to some who work in the field.

The NAS panel found problems in the Aceh data: an inordinately high number of boys affected by vitamin A versus few girls; too many in the 6-year-old category (due to the difficulties in locating birth certificates). These are the kinds of quirks that can come up in any field study. More fundamentally, complained both the NAS committee and a letter to the editor of *Lancet,* Sommer's data didn't break down the causes of death. Those who died from accidents were thrown in with those who had measles. Sommer concedes the study was not without its holes, as his original report pointed out. But cause of death was surplus information, he argues. "It's always great to say we would also like to know what the mothers ate that day. These are just picky things."

Already, a few independent studies have found the vitamin to have a similar dramatic impact on mortality. According to one, on the Indonesian island of Java, fortification of MSG with vitamin A in five villages reduced childhood mortality by a third, increased linear growth by an average of 1 centimeter a year, and raised hemoglobin levels by 10 percent.

"MSG Helps Build Strong Bodies . . ."

A child needs only about 2,000 International Units of vitamin A—a fourth of a carrot—a day. Most Americans get several times that much daily through all the foods fortified with the nutrient—including milk, bread, cereal, and cheese—not counting egg yolks and oils naturally rich with vitamin A. And fortifying widely eaten foods is the best means of supplementing diets because it provides small daily doses—unlike the capsules, containing 200,000 IUs, given to correct vitamin A deficiency.

Applying this American solution to developing countries, however, can run into unexpected obstacles. The case of Indonesia illustrates the point.

In 1979 the Indonesian government, finding that it had high levels of blindness caused by vitamin A deficiency, organized a workshop and hired two consultants to figure out what foods to fortify and how. They settled upon monosodium glutamate (MSG), used there as commonly as salt is in the United States. Alfred Sommer, who acted as an adviser, expected that in two years Indonesia would be fortifying MSG for everyone. But a number of wrinkles developed.

Indonesian producers, who prided themselves on the whiteness of their MSG, were aghast when fortification turned it yellow. "We spent a couple of years trying to figure out how to make a white vitamin A," says Sommer. Working with the U.S. Department of Agriculture, the Indonesian manufacturers developed a way to coat the fortified MSG particles with titanium dioxide, turning them white. The coating had the added benefit of sealing in the vitamin A and prolonging its potency.

The next problem arose when a consumer health group objected to the use of MSG, which it called a carcinogen. The group cited studies from the early 1970s, in which rats given massive doses of MSG developed brain lesions. The U.N.'s Joint Expert Committee on Food Additives reviewed the literature and established a minimum dose of MSG—which in fact is many times more than the average Indonesian's daily consumption. As a compromise, however, the manufacturer was forbidden from advertising that the MSG was "new and improved" with vitamin A to boost sales.

Without that incentive, manufacturers were not enthusiastic about shouldering the $4 million annual cost of adding vitamin A. Finally, the Indonesian government worked out a formula increasing the price of the fortified MSG by 6 percent over three years. "The increase is miniscule compared to inflation," notes Sommer.

Preliminary results indicate the fortification has had an impact. In a controlled trial, five villages received vitamin A–fortified MSG; the control group used plain MSG. Preschoolers given the fortified MSG had a 45 percent lower mortality rate; for infants mortality was 11 percent lower. Those children's growth rates were higher also.

Indonesian MSG manufacturers, meanwhile, have installed pharmaceutical blenders to mix MSG and vitamin A. The pharmaceutical Hoffman-La Roche has donated the vitamin A itself. And the fortified MSG is now being sold to three million people in three counties. If this trial proves to be commercially feasible, a nationwide program could follow.

Sommer grants that results from Indonesia do not necessarily apply in all conditions. So he has embarked on two similar but somewhat improved studies in Nepal and Ethiopia. Another, by Harvard public health researchers, will test the Sudan. In Africa alone, the incidence of nutritional blindness has been found to vary from 10 percent in desert regions, such as Chad, down to almost nothing in regions of West Africa, where red palm oil, rich in vitamin A, is commonly used for cooking. Sommer believes the results from Nepal could be applied to India, and that the Ethiopia results could be applied to most of Africa.

Those studies, expected to be completed within two years, will introduce placebos. But Sommer and

colleagues see no reason to detail the causes of death, as suggested by the NAS committee. "Causes of mortality are beyond the scope of the study," says epidemiologist Jim Tielsch, the project manager in Ethiopia.

As to the question of how vitamin A works, Tielsch finds it irrelevant to the results of the study. "We can't answer why it will work. We don't know why aspirin works. We don't how many things work, but that doesn't keep us from using them."

Dissatisfied with overall associations, Kjolhede and other researchers are trying to link vitamin A deficiency to specific diseases. He and his colleagues in the international health department are doing random trials in Indonesia to see if the vitamin alters the rates of respiratory infections and diarrhea. Results are expected by early 1991.

Sommer has studied the nutrient's relationship to another disease, measles, if only in a small group. "Measles is the major cause of blindness in children in Africa," explains Sommer. "Most of that is because the children are vitamin A–deficient and the measles makes that much worse so quickly that the eyes literally just dissolve within a matter of hours." That much is widely accepted, but not everyone is convinced by Sommer's finding at a hospital in Tanzania, reported in 1986, that vitamin A reduced mortality in children with measles by 50 percent. Within months after that report, WHO and UNICEF issued a joint recommendation that all measles patients receive high doses of the vitamin. Even Sommer was surprised at his impact.

"A lot of people said that was inappropriate to issue a global recommendation on the basis of one small study. I must say I was gratified, and somewhat surprised. But it was because that study came on top of the large studies we'd done in Asia where vitamin A supplementation reduced mortality rates by a third or more even when you didn't have measles."

✦ ✦ ✦

If Sommer's critics question his claims, they also envy his powers of persuasion. The emergence in Congress, for instance, of vitamin A supplementation as a popular child survival strategy owes much to serendipity, the Ethiopian famine, and Al Sommer, according to Anthony Gambino, staff member of the House Select Committee on Hunger.

In 1984 attention had been riveted to the civil war in Ethiopia and its devastating famine. In an article accompanying a 1985 cover story on Ethiopia's starvation and disease, *Newsweek* dubbed vitamin A capsules "golden bullets" and quoted Sommer as saying they are the "cheapest, most practical means of increasing childhood survival." "Many congressmen on the committee had been to Ethiopia and wanted to do something," says Gambino. And vitamin A—"inexpensive, practical to administer, cost-effective," in the words of Ohio Representative Tony Hall—was just the kind of solution Congress was looking for.

In testimony before the hunger committee, Sommer made a "phenomenal presentation," with scientific documentation—still understandable to the politicians—and slides that told the dramatic story. Gambino says Sommer's testimony was the main reason for the unprecedented earmarking of AID funds —$8 million this year—for vitamin A research and programs.

Sommer's political and promotional successes wouldn't be so galling to his rivals if he weren't so effective, taking money from other struggling programs, such as campaigns to increase breast-feeding.

"He has really put vitamin A on the map as an important factor in childhood survival," says Mosley, who has closely followed his old colleague's career. He admits to concern over some inconsistencies in the Aceh study and the magnitude of the effect Sommer claims. He laments that agricultural programs were cut back to provide funds for vitamin A. Even so, Mosley admires Sommer for actively campaigning for his ideas. Because the scientists who developed oral rehydration therapy did little to promote it, Mosley says, more than five years lapsed before it was widely applied to combat diarrheal diseases, the number one killer of children in developing countries.

Says Frances Davidson, an AID nutrition adviser who will oversee Sommer's study in Nepal, "Sommer has really galvanized a lot of people." One of the first agencies to incorporate vitamin A programs, AID sees it as an important part of its campaign against malnutrition. Sometimes, Davidson says, it takes someone like Sommer to highlight the micro to get to the macro, the bigger picture of malnutrition. Once he has secured the cooperation of his host countries to set up studies, Sommer writes memoranda of understanding, promising help to set up long-term vitamin A distribution programs, or whatever is appropriate to the needs and resources of the country after the study.

Programs and decrees of commitment are as varied as the countries, but they often can be traced to a health official's encounter with Sommer. R. P. Pokhrel, who has established a well-regarded network of ophthalmologists and eye hospitals in an effort to prevent all kinds of blindness in Nepal, met Sommer in Geneva. He happens to be influential as the king's ophthalmologist and opened the doors necessary for Sommer to set up his research there. Pokhrel sees capsules as emergency measures; he wants to change diets, beginning by cultivating vegetable gardens at eye hospitals. "When people come, we will try to give them a subsidy to grow vitamin A–rich vegetables in their own kitchen garden."

But Allen Foster, a British ophthalmologist and medical consultant who has worked in Tanzania for 10 years, doesn't see vitamin A as a top-priority investment in Africa as long as so many children are dying of AIDS. Other resistance filtered from the scientific community to a meeting of health administrators in Africa. One group was ready to find ways to get vitamin A capsules to children, while others expressed revulsion at such a simplistic solution to their complex problems.

Sommer says he's not sold on the capsules, either. "Ultimately we would like to move people onto a better diet, but it's not been easy over the years." Fortification would be the next best step *(see box)*. The best program would teach mothers to feed children leafy green vegetables—McCollum's lesson of the 1950s for the United States. "The problem is that most children everywhere do not like spinach," says Sommer. "One of the obvious things seems to be to chop up leafy vegetables into little pieces and then mix them up with rice, since children love rice. . . . I have watched children sit there and pick the little green pieces out of the rice. So you have to come up with ways to help them out."

Although changing minds about pills or foods is difficult, Sommer notes some positive signs. "Xerophthalmia seems to be disappearing in Indonesia. In some . . . regions of the country, it's gone down by 80 to 90 percent. We're not sure what to attribute that to," he says. Vitamin A supplementation has "been in the news; the government is pushing it. Maybe the word is getting out. . . ."

◆ ◆ ◆

But for a man on a mission, each piece of news merely pushes him onto the next step. In June he was back in Indonesia to discuss a new program for giving vitamin A to expectant mothers, among other things. And if the new studies confirm the Aceh results, he'll be forging ahead with international vitamin A programs.

Also on Sommer's agenda is detecting vitamin A deficiency earlier through a cytology impression kit. A piece of filter paper is used to collect mucous-secreting cells from the eye; examined under the microscope, they can reveal the deficiency before it shows up as night blindness. Preliminary trials of the new test suggest that there may be 10 times more cases of the deficiency in Indonesia than the 3 percent of the population estimated from eye symptoms.

Kjolhede has reported erratic results using the test in Guatemala; Sommer in turn criticizes that study. Eager for quicker interventions, Sommer is working to refine the test and has already developed a slick pamphlet full of pictures and easy-to-follow instructions for the field worker.

Sommer never stops promoting his projects. "I have no doubt I would make a reasonably good used car salesman," he muses. "People ask me how did I market my idea? I have no magic tricks. It's part of education. People are upset at a scientist out there beating the bushes. But if you don't, you leave everything to chance. Our end point is, 'How do I solve the problem where kids are going blind and die?' The thought of sitting back and waiting for it to happen sounds ludicrous."

PART II

The Quest for Food:
Evolutionary and Comparative Perspectives

The Biological Baseline

What foods did our ancestors eat? How did they manage to obtain an adequate supply of nutrients? Why should we contemporary humans care about the answer to these questions? The articles in this part explore the diet and nutrition of our ancestors from three sources of inference: our ancestors, our close primate cousins, and peoples who survived into the twentieth century with a foraging lifestyle.

Our protohuman ancestors separated from the evolutionary line leading to our closest living relatives, gorillas and chimpanzees, about 5 million years ago. From that time and until about 10,000 years ago, all humans obtained food by hunting, fishing, gathering, and, as Pat Shipman emphasizes in one of the following articles, scavenging (consumption of animals that died from causes unrelated to humans). Thus, for well over 99 percent of our time as an evolutionary lineage, we have subsisted by foraging—that is, hunting, gathering, fishing, and scavenging existing sources. Conversely, we adopted agriculture and became food producers in the last blink of an evolutionary eye. How did our ancestors' guts, hands, teeth, brains, and social behaviors evolve over this long history of foraging? What is our biobehavioral legacy?

Foods, and the nutrients they contain, were doubtlessly key regulators of the lives of animals now extinct, just as they are for living species. It is likely that preagricultural humans focused on foods that were both easily obtained and nutritious, and then their biology and behavior changed over time as they continued to utilize these foods. For example, the hominid line that includes individuals identified as *Australopithecus robustus* developed huge molar teeth (the relatively flat-surfaced teeth toward the back of the mouth). This anatomical change suggests an increased reliance on bulky and/or hard-to-chew foods, such as bamboo. These hominids may have been vegetarians. A contemporaneous group of hominids, identified as *Australopithecus africanus,* appears to have been less specialized in their food quest. It is this group that may have developed tools, perhaps to transport food, to dig for roots, or to kill and consume animals. Understanding the acquisition, distribution, and consumption of foods leads to knowledge about biology and culture.

But how can we know the past without written records? In general, there are three sources of data that one can use to make inferences. One is archaeological and paleontological information—that is, information from fossils and their ecological contexts. This is the most direct source of information. A second source is the information available from the study of nonhuman primates (and other closely related species), and a third source is information available from the study of the few remaining foragers. We call this information inferential because one must make the assumption or inference that the information is applicable to our ancestors. These three sources of information are utilized in the articles to follow. In different ways, these articles show how fascinating it is to try to reconstruct ancient foodways. The selections also highlight a number of fundamental issues, such as the relative importance of hunting and meat eating. As a group, they illustrate how behavior may be inferred from analogy and from the study of material remains (stones and bones).

Dr. Pat Shipman, the author of "Scavenger Hunt," is a human paleontologist/science writer who works at reconstructing the lives of prehistoric humans from fragmentary skeletal remains. Reconstruction involves putting the "flesh back on the bones" and building inferences about lives of individuals and groups. What did individuals look like, how big were they, how old were they when they died? Efforts to reconstruct behaviors, including what individuals ate (or what ate them!) are based on reconstructions of the environment, culture, and biology.

Dr. Shipman focuses on a group of prehistoric humans who lived around 2 to 3 million years ago. These prehistoric humans are typically referred to as Plio-Pleistocene hominids, simply marking the geological time during which they lived. They are best known from their remains found at sites in South Africa and East Africa such as Olduvai Gorge, where Shipman carried out her research.

An old and still dominant idea is that our ancestors were proficient hunters. Although smaller than we are, they were intelligent, worked cooperatively, and had crude stone tools to help make up for their small body size. This idea of humans as hunters took off in the 1940s and 1950s. Perhaps after the horror of World War II, many scientists began to think that we must be innately aggressive, and this may be a legacy of our hunting past. In this view of early humans, men (and only men) provisioned their families. The picture that emerged was of men who hunted cooperatively, did a great deal of male bonding in the process, and were the bread (or meat) winners of the primordial nuclear family. In retrospect, these images look a great deal like the 1950s suburban lifestyles of those who imagined them.

Shipman tested this interpretation by studying cut marks on fossil bones of the assumed prey of early humans using a scanning electron microscope (SEM) and found that the bones often have two distinct sets of marks. The deepest and first set of marks seems to have been made by the teeth of predatory cats or dogs. On top of these tooth marks are scratches that she infers were caused by the stone tools of our ancestors. Shipman's interpretation is not of a kill by these early humans, but one by efficient African carnivores. By evidence of their later involvement, and the location of cut marks on the less meaty parts of the bone, Shipman suggests that the humans were scavengers. At best, they scared off hyenas. They got what the big cats did not want: they ate leftovers.

Shipman's article highlights the study of fossils, the most direct source of evidence for reconstructing past lifeways. Although the fossil evidence is direct, Shipman shows that what the evidence means is not always obvious. Our preconceived ideas often affect what we see. Our visions of life before the advent of agriculture have oscillated between two extreme views. On one side is the vision of life before civilization as a sort of Garden of Eden. This perspective is captured well in the highly romanticized work and ideas of Rousseau. On the other side is the idea of progress: life was disorderly and has gotten progressively better with civilization. In the words of Thomas Hobbes, life was "nasty, brutish and short."

What is the reality of life in the past? Which view is closer to the truth? Is there a general truth? One way to address these questions is by directly studying the remains of hunters and gatherers for evidence of the stresses of life. This is what Goodman and Armelagos do in their article, "Disease and Death at Dr. Dickson's Mounds" (article 8). Another means is to make inferences from studies of contemporary foragers such as the work that cultural anthropologist Richard Lee reports on in "What Hunters Do for a Living, or, How to Make Out on Scarce Resources."

In "Eating Christmas in the Kalahari" (article 2), Lee recounts his lessons learned about symbolic meanings associated with food exchange among the Dobe !Kung San of the Kalahari. In the primary research article to follow, Lee aims to answer the question "How difficult is it for the San to meet their daily food needs?" Lee's work was a pioneering energy input-output analysis. He observed and measured the amount of time expended in subsistence activities and calculated the amounts of energy and protein that were obtained. To the surprise of many, the time that the !Kung San spent foraging for plant foods averaged only a couple of hours a day and energy return was high relative to energy expended. Lee particularly highlights the importance of mongongo nuts as sources of energy and protein. Finally, Lee estimated that vegetable rather than animal products provided the majority of nutrients. Are Lee's results true for most or all foragers? His observation that the San "eat as much vegetable food as they need and as much meat as they can" gives us another perspective on "Eating Christmas in the Kalahari."

Katharine Milton is a primatologist and biological anthropologist who has studied the dietary habits of South American monkeys. In her article entitled "Diet and Primate Evolution," she summarizes and synthesizes a third source of inference, study of nonhuman primates. Dr. Milton shows how difficult it is for primates to exploit the tropical canopy. A nutritious meal is not "just for the taking": leaves are bulky and hard to digest, insects are found sporadically, and primates must compete with other species to find ripe fruits. Thus, primates coevolved with a wide variety of "feeding niches." Under what circumstances did Milton study her primates? What techniques did she exploit?

Milton also introduces the theme of "Darwinian medicine" (this theme is the focus of article 9, "Paleolithic Nutrition," by Eaton and Konner). According to Darwinian medicine (also called evolutionary medicine), many of our present health and nutritional problems are the results of a poor fit between our evolved capacities and the situations we now face. For example, primates have excellent sources of ascorbic acid, and thus have lost their ability to make (synthesize) this vitamin. Milton suggests that our guts evolved to handle bulky foods. Could it be that some gastrointestinal problems today are a direct result of the low-fiber diet typical of most Americans?

In summary, this part provides speculations, insights, and much "food for thought." Shipman provides an excellent example of archaeological data used to make inferences about the means by which food was obtained. By combining experimental and observational studies, Milton summarizes the variety of means by which primates exploit the forest canopy. Lee provides a clear illustration of a number of key issues in the lives of contemporary foragers. Shipman speculates that our Paleolithic forebears were not the fierce hunters they are often thought to be, and Lee's data call into question the importance placed on hunting over gathering, meat over fruits and vegetables, male-centered activities over female-centered activities.

How much of the diet of our ancestors was based on hunting, gathering, or scavenging? How much came from meats, vegetables, and fruits? Do we have the guts, teeth, and brains of an omnivore and the psychology of a carnivore? Although the precise mix remains unknown, what seems certain is that the methods of procurement and the types of foods changed over time and place. Thankfully, we are a flexible species.

SUGGESTIONS FOR THINKING AND DOING NUTRITIONAL ANTHROPOLOGY

1. Compare teeth. Look in a mirror at the chewing surfaces of your teeth. Compare your teeth to those of your cat or dog. Go to a local natural history museum (or any place you might be able to observe the teeth of different animals) and describe the differences. What are the functions of teeth? How are variations in typical diets reflected in variations in size and shape?

2. Write an essay on the importance of meat in human evolution. Were we born to be meat eaters, vegetarians, or omnivores? What data can be brought to this question? A variety of sources may be used, such as evidence from human anatomy and physiology (lengths of intestines) and epidemiological studies of diet and health. In class, compose essays and debate the importance of meat. A useful first source is *Food and Evolution* (Harris and Ross, 1987).

3. Study your own food quest using the techniques of observation that are employed by Lee and by Milton. Over the course of a week, record the amount of time you spend in your quest for food. How much time do you spend "shopping" and "preparing" food? Calculate the amount that your food costs. How long did it take you or your parents to earn that money? Did you spend more or less time than the San?

SUGGESTED READINGS

Harris, M., & Ross, E. (Eds.). (1987). *Food and evolution.* Philadelphia: Temple University Press. (Selections by Katharine Milton and others further explore the significance of the diet of hominids and nonhuman primates.)

Hill, K., & Hertardo, M. (1996). *Ache life history: The ecology and demography of a foraging people.* Hawthorne, NY: Aldine de Gruyter. (An exceptional comparative analysis of South American foragers based on a long-term study.)

Lee, R. (1979). *The !Kung San: Men, women, and work in a foraging society.* Cambridge: Cambridge University Press. (An update and expansion of Lee's seminal work.)

Lee, R., & DeVore, I. (Eds.). (1968). *Man the hunter.* Chicago: Aldine. (A classic book, and the source of the article by Richard Lee.)

Rodman, P. (Ed.). (1984). *Adaptations for foraging in nonhuman primates.* New York: Columbia University Press.

5

Scavenger Hunt

Pat Shipman

In both textbooks and films, ancestral humans (hominids) have been portrayed as hunters. Small-brained, big-browed, upright, and usually mildly furry, early hominid males gaze with keen eyes across the golden savanna, searching for prey. Skillfully wielding a few crude stone tools, they kill and dismember everything from small gazelles to elephants, while females care for young and gather roots, tubers, and berries. The food is shared by group members at temporary camps. This familiar image of Man the Hunter has been bolstered by the finding of stone tools in association with fossil animal bones. But the role of hunting in early hominid life cannot be determined in the absence of more direct evidence.

I discovered one means of testing the hunting hypothesis almost by accident. In 1978, I began documenting the microscopic damage produced on bones by different events. I hoped to develop a diagnostic key for identifying the post-mortem history of specific fossil bones, useful for understanding how fossil assemblages were formed. Using a scanning electron microscope (SEM) because of its excellent resolution and superb depth of field, I inspected high-fidelity replicas of modern bones that had been subjected to known events or conditions. (I had to use replicas, rather than real bones, because specimens must fit into the SEM's small vacuum chamber.) I soon established that such common events as weathering, root etching, sedimentary abrasion, and carnivore chewing produced microscopically distinctive features.

In 1980, my SEM study took an unexpected turn. Richard Potts (now of Yale University), Henry Bunn (now of the University of Wisconsin at Madison), and I almost simultaneously found what appeared to be stone-tool cut marks on fossils from Olduvai Gorge, Tanzania, and Koobi Fora, Kenya. We were working almost side by side at the National Museums of Kenya, in Nairobi, where the fossils are stored. The possibility of cut marks was exciting, since both sites preserve some of the oldest known archeological materials. Potts and I returned to the United States, manufactured some stone tools, and started "butchering" bones and joints begged from our local butchers. Under the SEM, replicas of these cut marks looked very different from replicas of carnivore tooth scratches, regardless of the species of carnivore or the type of tool involved. By comparing the marks on the fossils with our hundreds of modern bones of known history, we were able to demonstrate convincingly that hominids using stone tools had processed carcasses of many different animals nearly two million years ago. For the first time, there was a firm link between stone tools and at least some of the early fossil animal bones.

This initial discovery persuaded some paleoanthropologists that the hominid hunter scenario was correct. Potts and I were not so sure. Our study had shown that many of the cut-marked fossils also bore carnivore tooth marks and that some of the cut marks were in places we hadn't expected—on bones that bore little meat in life. More work was needed.

In addition to more data about the Olduvai cut marks and tooth marks, I needed specific information about the patterns of cut marks left by known hunters performing typical activities associated with hunting. If similar patterns occurred on the fossils, then the early hominids probably behaved similarly to more modern hunters; if the patterns were different, then the behavior was probably also different. Three activities related to hunting occur often enough in peoples around the world and leave consistent enough traces to be used for such a test.

First, human hunters systematically disarticulate their kills, unless the animals are small enough to be eaten on the spot. Disarticulation leaves cut marks in a predictable pattern on the skeleton. Such marks cluster near the major joints of the limbs: shoulder, elbow, carpal joint (wrist), hip, knee, and hock (ankle). Taking a carcass apart at the joints is much easier than breaking or cutting through bones. Disarticulation enables hunters to carry food back to a central place or camp, so that they can share it with others or cook it or even store it by placing portions in trees, away from the reach of carnivores. If early hominids were hunters who transported and shared their kills, disarticulation marks would occur near joints in frequencies comparable to those produced by modern human hunters.

Second, human hunters often butcher carcasses, in the sense of removing meat from the bones. Butchery marks are usually found on the shafts of bones from the upper part of the front or hind limb, since this is where the big muscle masses lie. Butchery may be carried out at the kill site—especially if the animal is very large and its bones very heavy—or it may take place at the base camp, during the process of sharing food with others. Compared with disarticulation, butchery leaves relatively few marks. It is hard for a hunter to locate an animal's joints without leaving cut marks on the bone. In contrast, it is easier to cut the meat away from the midshaft of the bone without making such marks. If early hominids shared their food, however, there ought to be a number of cut marks located on the midshaft of some fossil bones.

Finally, human hunters often remove skin or tendons from carcasses, to be used for clothing, bags, thongs, and so on. Hide or tendon must be separated from the bones in many areas where there is little flesh, such as the lower limb bones of pigs, giraffes, antelopes, and zebras. In such cases, it is difficult to cut the skin without leaving a cut mark on the bone. Therefore, one expects to find many more cut marks on such bones than on the flesh-covered bones of the upper part of the limbs.

Unfortunately, although accounts of butchery and disarticulation by modern human hunters are remarkably consistent, quantitative studies are rare. Further, virtually all modern hunter-gatherers use metal tools, which leave more cut marks than stone tools. For these reasons I hesitated to compare the fossil evidence with data on modern hunters. Fortunately, Diane Gifford of the University of California, Santa Cruz, and her colleagues had recently completed a quantitative study of marks and damage on thousands of antelope bones processed by Neolithic (Stone Age) hunters in Kenya some 2,300 years ago. The data from Prolonged Drift, as the site is called, were perfect for comparison with the Olduvai material.

Assisted by my technician, Jennie Rose, I carefully inspected more than 2,500 antelope bones from Bed I at Olduvai Gorge, which is dated to between 1.9 and 1.7 million years ago. We made high-fidelity replicas of every mark that we thought might be either a cut mark or a carnivore tooth mark. Back in the United States, we used the SEM to make positive identifications of the marks. (The replication and SEM inspection was time consuming, but necessary: only about half of the marks were correctly identified by eye or by light microscope.) I then compared the patterns of cut mark and tooth mark distributions on Olduvai fossils with those made by Stone Age hunters at Prolonged Drift.

By their location, I identified marks caused either by disarticulation or meat removal and then compared their frequencies with those from Prolonged Drift. More than 90 percent of the Neolithic marks in these two categories were from disarticulation, but to my surprise, only about 45 percent of the corresponding Olduvai cut marks were from disarticulation. This difference is too great to have occurred by chance; the Olduvai bones did not show the predicted pattern. In

fact, the Olduvai cut marks attributable to meat removal and disarticulation showed essentially the same pattern of distribution as the carnivore tooth marks. Apparently, the early hominids were not regularly disarticulating carcasses. This finding casts serious doubt on the idea that early hominids carried their kills back to camp to share with others, since both transport and sharing are difficult unless carcasses are cut up.

When I looked for cut marks attributable to skinning or tendon removal, a more modern pattern emerged. On both the Neolithic and Olduvai bones, nearly 75 percent of all cut marks occurred on bones that bore little meat; these cut marks probably came from skinning. Carnivore tooth marks were much less common on such bones. Hominids were using carcasses as a source of skin and tendon. This made it seem more surprising that they disarticulated carcasses so rarely.

A third line of evidence provided the most tantalizing clue. Occasionally, sets of overlapping marks occur on the Olduvai fossils. Sometimes, these sets include both cut marks and carnivore tooth marks. Still more rarely, I could see under the SEM which mark had been made first, because its features were overlaid by those of the later mark, in much the same way as old tire tracks on a dirt road are obscured by fresh ones. Although only thirteen such sets of marks were found, in eight cases the hominids made the cut marks *after* the carnivores made their tooth marks. This finding suggested a new hypothesis. Instead of hunting for prey and leaving the remains behind for carnivores to scavenge, perhaps hominids were scavenging from the carnivores. This might explain the hominids' apparently unsystematic use of carcasses: they took what they could get, be it skin, tendon, or meat.

Man the Scavenger is not nearly as attractive an image as Man the Hunter, but it is worth examining. Actually, although hunting and scavenging are different ecological strategies, many mammals do both. The only pure scavengers alive in Africa today are vultures; not one of the modern African mammalian carnivores is a pure scavenger. Even spotted hyenas, which have massive, bone-crushing teeth well adapted for eating the bones left behind by others, only scavenge about 33 percent of their food. Other carnivores that scavenge when there are enough carcasses around include lions, leopards, striped hyenas, and jackals. Long-term behavioral studies suggest that these carnivores scavenge when they can and kill when they must. There are only two nearly pure predators, or hunters—the cheetah and the wild dog—that rarely, if ever, scavenge.

What are the costs and benefits of scavenging compared with those of predation? First of all, the scavenger avoids the task of making sure its meal is dead: a predator has already endured the energetically costly business of chasing or stalking animal after animal until one is killed. But while scavenging may be cheap, it's risky. Predators rarely give up their prey to scavengers without defending it. In such disputes, the larger animal, whether a scavenger or a predator, usually wins, although smaller animals in a pack may defeat a lone, larger animal. Both predators and scavengers suffer the dangers inherent in fighting for possession of a carcass. Smaller scavengers such as jackals or striped hyenas avoid disputes to some extent by specializing in darting in and removing a piece of a carcass without trying to take possession of the whole thing. These two strategies can be characterized as that of the bully or that of the sneak: bullies need to be large to be successful, sneaks need to be small and quick.

Because carcasses are almost always much rarer than live prey, the major cost peculiar to scavenging is that scavengers must survey much larger areas than predators to find food. They can travel slowly, since their "prey" is already dead, but endurance is important. Many predators specialize in speed at the expense of endurance, while scavengers do the opposite.

The more committed predators among the East African carnivores (wild dogs and cheetahs) can achieve great top speeds when running, although not for long. Perhaps as a consequence, these "pure" hunters enjoy a much higher success rate in hunting (about three-fourths of their chases end in kills) than any of the scavenger-hunters do (less than half of their chases are successful). Wild dogs and cheetahs are efficient hunters, but they are neither big enough nor efficient enough in their locomotion to make good scavengers. In fact, the cheetah's teeth are so specialized for meat slicing that they probably cannot withstand the stresses of bone crunching and carcass dismembering carried out by scavengers. Other carnivores are less successful at hunting, but have specializations of size, endurance, or (in the case of the hyenas) dentition that make successful scavenging possible. The smaller carnivores seem to have a somewhat higher hunting success rate than the large ones, which balances out their difficulties in asserting possession of carcasses.

In addition to endurance, scavengers need an efficient means of locating carcasses, which, unlike live animals, don't move or make noises. Vultures, for example, solve both problems by flying. The soaring, gliding flight of vultures expends much less energy than walking or cantering as performed by the part-time mammalian scavengers. Flight enables vultures to maintain a foraging radius two to three times larger than that of spotted hyenas, while providing a better vantage point. This explains why vultures can scavenge all of their food in the same habitat in which it is impossible for any mammal to be a pure scavenger. (In fact, many mammals learn where carcasses are located from the presence of vultures.)

Since mammals can't succeed as full-time scavengers, they must have another source of food to provide the bulk of their diet. The large carnivores rely on hunting large animals to obtain food when scavenging doesn't work. Their size enables them to defend a carcass against others. Since the small carnivores—jackals and striped hyenas—often can't defend carcasses successfully, most of their diet is composed of fruit and insects. When they do hunt, they usually prey on very small animals, such as rats or hares, that can be consumed in their entirety before the larger competitors arrive.

The ancient habitat associated with the fossils of Olduvai and Koobi Fora would have supported many herbivores and carnivores. Among the latter were two species of large saber-toothed cats, whose teeth show extreme adaptations for meat slicing. These were predators with primary access to carcasses. Since their teeth were unsuitable for bone crushing, the saber-toothed cats must have left behind many bones covered with scraps of meat, skin, and tendon. Were early hominids among the scavengers that exploited such carcasses?

All three hominid species that were present in Bed I times (*Homo habilis, Australopithecus africanus, A. robustus*) were adapted for habitual, upright bipedalism. Many anatomists see evidence that these hominids were agile tree climbers as well. Although upright bipedalism is a notoriously peculiar mode of locomotion, the adaptive value of which has been argued for years (see Matt Cartmill's article, "Four Legs Good, Two Legs Bad," *Natural History*, November 1983), there are three general points of agreement.

First, bipedal running is neither fast nor efficient compared to quadrupedal gaits. However, at moderate speeds of 2.5 to 3.5 miles per hour, bipedal *walking* is more energetically efficient than quadrupedal walking. Thus, bipedal walking is an excellent means of covering large areas slowly, making it an unlikely adaptation for a hunter but an appropriate and useful adaptation for a scavenger. Second, bipedalism elevates the head, thus improving the hominid's ability to spot items on the ground—an advantage both to scavengers and to those trying to avoid becoming a carcass. Combining bipedalism with agile tree climbing improves the vantage point still further. Third, bipedalism frees the hands from locomotor duties, making it possible to carry items. What would early hominids have carried? Meat makes a nutritious, easy-to-carry package; the problem is that carrying meat attracts scavengers. Richard Potts suggests that carrying stone tools or unworked stones for toolmaking to caches would be a more efficient and less dangerous activity under many circumstances.

In short, bipedalism is compatible with a scavenging strategy. I am tempted to argue that bipedalism evolved because it provided a substantial advantage to scavenging hominids. But I doubt hominids could scavenge effectively without tools, and bipedalism predates the oldest known stone tools by more than a million years.

Is there evidence that, like modern mammalian scavengers, early hominids had an alternative food source, such as either hunting or eating fruits and insects? My husband, Alan Walker, has shown that the microscopic wear on an animal's teeth reflects its diet. Early hominid teeth have microscopic wear more like that of chimpanzees and other modern fruit eaters than that of carnivores. Apparently, early hominids ate mostly fruit, as the smaller, modern scavengers do. This accords with the estimated body weight of early hominids, which was only about forty to eighty pounds —less than that of any of the modern carnivores that combine scavenging and hunting but comparable to the striped hyena, which eats fruits and insects as well as meat.

Would early hominids have been able to compete for carcasses with other carnivores? They were too small to use a bully strategy, but if they scavenged in groups, a combined bully-sneak strategy might have been possible. Perhaps they were able to drive off a primary predator long enough to grab some meat, skin, or marrow-filled bone before relinquishing the carcass. The effectiveness of this strategy would have been vastly improved by using tools to remove meat or parts of limbs, a task at which hominid teeth are poor. As agile climbers, early hominids may have retreated into the trees to eat their scavenged trophies, thus avoiding competition from large terrestrial carnivores.

In sum, the evidence on cut marks, tooth wear, and bipedalism, together with our knowledge of scavenger adaptation in general, is consistent with the hypothesis that two million years ago hominids were scavengers rather than accomplished hunters. Animal carcasses, which contributed relatively little to the hominid diet, were not systematically cut up and transported for sharing at base camps. Man the Hunter may not have appeared until 1.5 to 0.7 million years ago, when we do see a shift toward omnivory, with a greater proportion of meat in the diet. This more heroic ancestor may have been *Homo erectus*, equipped with Acheulean-style stone tools and, increasingly, fire. If we wish to look further back, we may have to become accustomed to a less flattering image of our heritage.

6

What Hunters Do for a Living, or, How to Make Out on Scarce Resources

Richard B. Lee

The current anthropological view of hunter-gatherer subsistence rests on two questionable assumptions. First is the notion that these peoples are primarily dependent on the hunting of game animals, and second is the assumption that their way of life is generally a precarious and arduous struggle for existence.

Recent data on living hunter-gatherers (Meggitt, 1964b; Service, 1966) show a radically different picture. We have learned that in many societies, plant and marine resources are far more important than are game animals in the diet. More important, it is becoming clear that, with a few conspicuous exceptions, the hunter-gatherer subsistence base is at least routine and reliable and at best surprisingly abundant. Anthropologists have consistently tended to underestimate the viability of even those "marginal isolates" of hunting peoples that have been available to ethnographers.

The purpose of this article is to analyze the food getting activities of one such "marginal" people, the !Kung Bushmen of the Kalahari Desert. Three related questions are posed: How do the Bushmen make a living? How easy or difficult is it for them to do this? What kinds of evidence are necessary to measure and evaluate the precariousness or security of a way of life? And after the relevant data are presented, two further questions are asked: What makes this security of life possible? To what extent are the Bushmen typical of hunter-gatherers in general?

BUSHMAN SUBSISTENCE

The !Kung Bushmen of Botswana are an apt case for analysis.[1] They inhabit the semi-arid northwest region of the Kalahari Desert. With only six to nine inches of rainfall per year, this is, by any account, a marginal environment for human habitation. In fact, it is precisely the unattractiveness of their homeland that has kept the !Kung isolated from extensive contact with their agricultural and pastoral neighbors.

Field work was carried out in the Dobe area, a line of eight permanent waterholes near the South-West Africa border and 125 miles south of the Okavango River. The population of the Dobe area consists of 466 Bushmen, including 379 permanent residents living in independent camps or associated with Bantu cattle posts, as well as 87 seasonal visitors. The Bushmen share the area with some 340 Bantu pastoralists largely of the Herero and Tswana tribes. The ethnographic present refers to the period of field work: October, 1963–January, 1965.

The Bushmen living in independent camps lack firearms, livestock, and agriculture. Apart from occasional visits to the Herero for milk, these !Kung are entirely dependent upon hunting and gathering for their subsistence. Politically they are under the nominal authority of the Tswana headman, although they pay no taxes and receive very few government services. European presence amounts to one overnight government patrol every six to eight weeks. Although Dobe-area !Kung have had some contact with outsiders since the 1880's, the majority of them continue to hunt and gather because there is no viable alternative locally available to them.[2]

Each of the fourteen independent camps is associated with one of the permanent waterholes. During the dry season (May–October) the entire population is clustered around these wells. Table 1 shows the numbers at each well at the end of the 1964 dry season. Two wells had no camp resident and one large well supported five camps. The number of camps at each well and the size of each camp changed frequently during the course of the year. The "camp" is an open aggregate of cooperating persons which changes in size and composition from day to day. Therefore, I have avoided the term "band" in describing the !Kung Bushman living groups.[3]

Each waterhole has a hinterland lying within a six-mile radius which is regularly exploited for vegetable and animal foods. These areas are not territories in the zoological sense, since they are not defended against outsiders. Rather they constitute the resources that lie within a convenient walking distance of a waterhole. The camp is a self-sufficient subsistence unit. The members move out each day to hunt and gather, and return in the evening to pool the collected foods in such a way that every person present receives an equitable share. Trade in foodstuffs between camps is minimal; personnel do move freely from camp to camp, however. The net effect is of a population constantly in motion. On the average, an individual spends a third of his time living only with close relatives, a third visiting other camps, and a third entertaining visitors from other camps.

Because of the strong emphasis on sharing, and the frequency of movement, surplus accumulation of storable plant foods and dried meat is kept to a minimum. There is rarely more than two or three days' supply of food on hand in a camp at any time. The result of this lack of surplus is that a constant subsistence

Table 1. Numbers and distribution of resident Bushmen and Bantu by waterhole*

Name of Waterhole	No. of Camps	Population of Camps	Other Bushmen	Total Bushmen	Bantu
Dobe	2	37	—	37	—
!angwa	1	16	23	39	84
Bate	2	30	12	42	21
!ubi	1	19	—	19	65
!gose	3	52	9	61	18
/ai/ai	5	94	13	107	67
!xabe	—	—	8	8	12
Mahopa	—	—	23	23	73
Total	14	248	88	336	340

*Figures do not include 130 Bushmen outside area on the date of census.

Table 2.   The Bushman annual round

	Jan.	Feb.	Mar.	April	May	June	July	Aug.	Sept.	Oct.	Nov.	Dec.
Season	Summer Rains			Autumn Dry			Winter Dry			Spring Dry		First Rains
Availability of Water	Temporary summer pools everywhere		Large summer pools			Permanent waterholes only						Summer pools developing
Group Moves	Widely dispersed at summer pools		At large summer pools			All population restricted to permanent waterholes						Moving out to summer pools
Men's Subsistence Activities	1. Hunting with bow, arrows, and dogs (Year-round) 2. Running down immatures 3. Some gathering (Year-round)						Trapping small game in snares			Running down newborn animals		
Women's Subsistence Activities	1. Gathering of mongongo nuts (Year-round) 2. Fruits, berries,						Roots, bulbs, melons			Roots, leafy resins greens		
Ritual Activities	Dancing, trance performances, and ritual curing (Year-round) Boys' initiation*											†
Relative Subsistence Hardship	Water-food distance minimal					Increasing distance from water to food				Water-food distance minimal		

*Held once every five years; none in 1963–64.

†New Year's: Bushmen join the celebrations of their missionized Bantu neighbors.

effort must be maintained throughout the year. Unlike agriculturalists who work hard during the planting and harvesting seasons and undergo "seasonal unemployment" for several months, the Bushmen hunter-gatherers collect food every third or fourth day throughout the year.

Vegetable foods comprise from 60–80 per cent of the total diet by weight, and collecting involves two or three days of work per woman per week. The men also collect plants and small animals but their major contribution to the diet is the hunting of medium and large game. The men are conscientious but not particularly successful hunters; although men's and women's work input is roughly equivalent in terms of man-day of effort, the women provide two to three times as much food by weight as the men.

Table 2 summarizes the seasonal activity cycle observed among the Dobe-area !Kung in 1964. For the greater part of the year, food is locally abundant and easily collected. It is only during the end of the dry season in September and October, when desirable foods have been eaten out in the immediate vicinity of the waterholes that the people have to plan longer hikes of 10–15 miles and carry their own water to those areas where the mongongo nut is still available. The important point is that food is a constant, but distance required to reach food is a variable; it is short in the summer, fall, and early winter, and reaches its maximum in the spring.

This analysis attempts to provide quantitative measures of subsistence status including data on the following topics: abundance and variety of resources, diet selectivity, range size and population density, the composition of the work force, the ratio of work to leisure time, and the caloric and protein levels in the diet. The value of quantitative data is that they can be used comparatively and also may be useful in archeological reconstruction. In addition, one can avoid the pitfalls of subjective and qualitative impressions; for example, statements about food "anxiety" have proven to be difficult to generalize across cultures (see Holmberg, 1950; and Needham's critique, 1954).

Abundance and Variety of Resources

It is impossible to define "abundance" of resources absolutely. However, one index of *relative* abundance is whether or not a population exhausts all the food available from a given area. By this criterion, the habitat of the Dobe-area Bushmen is abundant in naturally occurring foods. By far the most important food is the Mongongo (mangetti) nut (*Ricinodendron rautanenii* Schinz). Although tens of thousands of pounds of these nuts are harvested and eaten each year, thousands more rot on the ground each year for want of picking.

The mongongo nut, because of its abundance and reliability, alone accounts for 50 per cent of the vegetable diet by weight. In this respect it resembles a cultivated staple crop such as maize or rice. Nutritionally it is even more remarkable, for it contains five times the calories and ten times the proteins per cooked unit of the cereal crops. The average daily per-capita consumption of 300 nuts yields about 1,260 calories and 56 grams of protein. This modest portion, weighing only about 7.5 ounces, contains the caloric equivalent of 2.5 pounds of cooked rice and the protein equivalent of 14 ounces of lean beef (Watt and Merrill, 1963).

Furthermore the mongongo nut is drought resistant and it will still be abundant in the dry years when cultivated crops may fail. The extremely hard outer shell protects the inner kernel from rot and allows the nuts to be harvested for up to twelve months after they have fallen to the ground. A diet based on mongongo nuts is in fact more reliable than one based on cultivated foods, and it is not surprising, therefore, that when a Bushman was asked why he hadn't taken to agriculture he replied: "Why should we plant, when there are so many mongongo nuts in the world?"

Apart from the mongongo, the Bushmen have available 84 other species of edible food plants, including 29 species of fruits, berries, and melons and 30 species of roots and bulbs. The existence of this variety allows for a wide range of alternatives in subsistence strategy. During the summer months the Bushmen have no problem other than to choose among the tastiest and most easily collected foods. Many species, which are quite edible but less attractive, are bypassed, so that gathering never exhausts *all* the available plant foods of an area. During the dry season the diet becomes much more eclectic and the many species of roots, bulbs, and edible resins make an important contribution. It is this broad base that provides an essential margin of safety during the end of the dry season when the mongongo nut forests are difficult to reach.

In addition, it is likely that these rarely utilized species provide important nutritional and mineral trace elements that may be lacking in the more popular foods.

Diet Selectivity

If the Bushmen were living close to the "starvation" level, then one would expect them to exploit every available source of nutrition. That their life is well above this level is indicated by the data in Table 3. Here all the edible plant species are arranged in classes according to the frequency with which they were observed to be eaten. It should be noted, that although there are some 85 species available, about 90 per cent of the vegetable diet by weight is drawn from only 23 species. In other words, 75 per cent of the listed species provide only 10 per cent of the food value.

In their meat-eating habits, the Bushmen show a similar selectivity. Of the 223 local species of animals known and named by the Bushmen, 54 species are classified as edible, and of these only 17 species were hunted on a regular basis.[4] Only a handful of the dozens of edible species of small mammals, birds, reptiles, and insects that occur locally are regarded as food. Such animals as rodents, snakes, lizards, termites, and grasshoppers, which in the literature are included in the Bushman dietary (Schapera, 1930), are despised by the Bushmen of the Dobe area.

Range Size and Population Density

The necessity to travel long distances, the high frequency of moves, and the maintenance of populations at low densities are also features commonly associated with the hunting and gathering way of life. Density estimates for hunters in western North America and Australia have ranged from 3 persons/square mile to as low as 1 person/100 square miles (Kroeber, 1939; Radcliffe-Brown, 1930). In 1963–65, the resident and visiting Bushmen were observed to utilize an area of about 1,000 square miles during the course of the annual round for an effective population density of 41 persons/100 square miles. Within this area, however, the amount of ground covered by members of an individual camp was surprisingly small. A day's round-trip of twelve miles serves to define a "core" area six miles in radius surrounding each water point. By fanning out in all directions from their well, the members of a camp can gain access to the food resources of well over 100 square miles of territory within a two-hour hike. Except for a few weeks each year, areas lying

Table 3. !Kung Bushman plant foods

Food Class	Part Eaten								Totals (Percentages)		
	Fruit and Nut	Bean and Root	Fruit and Stalk	Root, Bulb	Fruit, Berry, Melon	Resin	Leaves	Seed, Bean	Total Number of Species in Class	Estimated Contribution by Weight to Vegetable Diet	Estimated Contribution of Each Species
I. *Primary* Eaten daily throughout year (mongongo nut)	1	—	—	—	—	—	—	—	1	c. 50	c. 50*
II. *Major* Eaten daily in season	1	1	1	1	4	—	—	—	8	c. 25	c. 3
III. *Minor* Eaten several times per week in season	—	—	—	7	3	2	2	—	14	c. 15	c. 1
IV. *Supplementary* Eaten when classes I–III locally unavailable	—	—	—	9	12	10	1	—	32	c. 7	c. 0.2
V. *Rare* Eaten several times per year	—	—	—	9	4	—	—	—	13	c. 3	c. 0.1
VI. *Problematic* Edible but not observed to be eaten	—	—	—	4	6	4	1	2	17	nil	nil
Total species	2	1	1	30	29	16	4	2	85	100	—

*1 species constitutes 50 per cent of the vegetable diet by weight.

†23 species constitute 90 per cent of the vegetable diet by weight.

‡62 species constitute the remaining 10 per cent of the diet.

beyond this six-mile radius are rarely utilized, even though they are no less rich in plants and game than are the core areas.

Although the Bushmen move their camps frequently (five or six times a year) they do not move them very far. A rainy season camp in the nut forests is rarely more than ten or twelve miles from the home waterhole, and often new campsites are occupied only a few hundred yards away from the previous one. By these criteria, the Bushmen do not lead a free-ranging nomadic way of life. For example, they do not undertake long marches of 30 to 100 miles to get food, since this task can be readily fulfilled within a day's walk of home base. When such long marches do occur they are invariably for visiting, trading, and marriage arrangements, and should not be confused with the normal routine of subsistence.

Demographic Factors

Another indicator of the harshness of a way of life is the age at which people die. Ever since Hobbes characterized life in the state of nature as "nasty, brutish and short," the assumption has been that hunting and gathering is so rigorous that members of such societies are rapidly worn out and meet an early death. Silberbauer, for example, says of the Gwi Bushmen of the central Kalahari that "life expectancy . . . is difficult to calculate, but I do not believe that many live beyond 45" (1965, p. 17). And Coon has said of the hunters in general:

> The practice of abandoning the hopelessly ill and aged has been observed in many parts of the world. It is always done by people living in poor environments where it is necessary to move about frequently to obtain food, where food is scarce, and transportation difficult. . . . Among peoples who are forced to live in this way the oldest generation, the generation of individuals who have passed their physical peak is reduced in numbers and influence. There is no body of elders to hand on tradition and control the affairs of younger men and women, and no formal system of age grading (1948, p. 55).

The !Kung Bushmen of the Dobe area flatly contradict this view. In a total population of 466, no fewer than 46 individuals (17 men and 29 women) were determined to be over 60 years of age, a proportion that compares favorably to the percentage of elderly in industrialized populations.

The aged hold a respected position in Bushman society and are the effective leaders of the camps. Senilicide is extremely rare. Long after their productive years have passed, the old people are fed and cared for by their children and grandchildren. The blind, the senile, and the crippled are respected for the special ritual and technical skills they possess. For instance, the four elders at !gose waterhole were totally or partially blind, but this handicap did not prevent their active participation in decision-making and ritual curing.

Another significant feature of the composition of the work force is the late assumption of adult responsibility by the adolescents. Young people are not expected to provide food regularly until they are married. Girls typically marry between the ages of 15 and 20, and boys about five years later, so that it is not unusual to find healthy, active teenagers visiting from camp to camp while their older relatives provide food for them.

As a result, the people in the age group 20–60 support a surprisingly large percentage of non-productive young and old people. About 40 per cent of the population in camps contribute little to the food supplies. This allocation of work to young and middle-aged adults allows for a relatively carefree childhood and adolescence and a relatively unstrenuous old age.

Leisure and Work

Another important index of ease or difficulty of subsistence is the amount of time devoted to the food quest.[5] Hunting has usually been regarded by social scientists as a way of life in which merely keeping alive is so formidable a task that members of such societies lack the leisure time necessary to "build culture."[6] The !Kung Bushmen would appear to conform to the rule, for as Lorna Marshall says:

> It is vividly apparent that among the !Kung Bushmen, ethos, or "the spirit which actuates manners and customs," is survival. Their time and energies are almost wholly given to this task, for life in their environment requires that they spend their days mainly in procuring food (1965, p. 247).

It is certainly true that getting food is the most important single activity in Bushman life. However this statement would apply equally well to small-scale agricultural and pastoral societies too. How much time is *actually* devoted to the food quest is fortunately an empirical question. And an analysis of the work effort of the Dobe Bushmen shows some unexpected results. From July 6 to August 2, 1964, I recorded all the daily activities of the Bushmen living at the Dobe waterhole. Because of the coming and going of visitors, the camp population fluctuated in size day by day, from a low of 23 to a high of 40, with a mean of 31.8 persons. Each day some of the adult members of the camp went out to hunt and/or gather while others stayed home or went visiting. The daily recording of all personnel on hand made it possible to calculate the number of man-days of work as a percentage of total number of man-days of consumption.

Although the Bushmen do not organize their activities on the basis of a seven-day week, I have divided the data this way to make them more intelligible. The work-week was calculated to show how many days out of seven each adult spent in subsistence activities (Table 4, Column 7). Week II has been eliminated from the totals since the investigator contributed food. In week I, the people spent an average of 2.3 days in subsistence activities, in week III, 1.9 days, and in week IV, 3.2 days. In all, the adults of the Dobe camp worked about two and a half days a week. Since the average working day was about six hours long, the fact emerges that !Kung Bushmen of Dobe, despite their harsh environment, devote from twelve to nineteen hours a week to getting food. Even the hardest working individual in the camp, a man named ≠oma who went out hunting on sixteen of the 28 days, spent a maximum of 32 hours a week in the food quest.

Table 4. Summary of Dobe work diary

Week	(1) Mean Group Size	(2) Adult-Days	(3) Child-Days	(4) Total Man-Days of Consumption	(5) Man-Days of Work	(6) Meat (lbs.)	(7) Average Work Week/Adult	(8) Index of Subsistence Effort
I (July 6–12)	25.6 (23–29)	114	65	179	37	104	2.3	.21
II (July 13–19)	28.3 (23–27)	125	73	198	22	80	1.2	.11
III (July 20–26)	34.3 (29–40)	156	84	240	42	177	1.9	.18
IV (July 27–Aug. 2)	35.6 (32–40)	167	82	249	77	129	3.2	.31
4-wk. total	30.9	562	304	866	178	490	2.2	.21
Adjusted total*	31.8	437	231	668	156	410	2.5	.23

* See text.

KEY: Column 1: Mean group size = $\dfrac{\text{total man-days of consumption}}{7}$.

     Column 7: Work week = the number of work days per adult per week.

     Column 8: Index of Subsistence Effort = $\dfrac{\text{man-days of work}}{\text{man-days of consumption}}$ (e.g., in Week I, the value of "S" = .21, i.e., 21 days of work/ 100 days of consumption or 1 work day produces food for 5 consumption days).

Because the Bushmen do not amass a surplus of foods, there are no seasons of exceptionally intensive activities such as planting and harvesting, and no seasons of unemployment. The level of work observed is an accurate reflection of the effort required to meet the immediate caloric needs of the group. This work diary covers the mid-winter dry season, a period when food is neither at its most plentiful nor at its scarcest levels, and the diary documents the transition from better to worse conditions (see Table 2). During the fourth week the gatherers were making overnight trips to camps in the mongongo nut forests seven to ten miles distant from the waterhole. These longer trips account for the rise in the level of work, from twelve or thirteen to nineteen hours per week.

If food getting occupies such a small proportion of a Bushman's waking hours, then how *do* people allocate their time? A woman gathers on one day enough food to feed her family for three days, and spends the rest of her time resting in camp, doing embroidery, visiting other camps, or entertaining visitors from other camps. For each day at home, kitchen routines, such as cooking, nut cracking, collecting firewood, and fetching water, occupy one to three hours of her time. This rhythm of steady work and steady leisure is maintained throughout the year.

The hunters tend to work more frequently than the women, but their schedule is uneven. It is not unusual for a man to hunt avidly for a week and then do no hunting at all for two or three weeks. Since hunting is an unpredictable business and subject to magical control, hunters sometimes experience a run of bad luck and stop hunting for a month or longer. During these periods, visiting, entertaining, and especially dancing are the primary activities of men. (Unlike the Hadza, gambling is only a minor leisure activity.)

The trance-dance is the focus of Bushman ritual life; over 50 per cent of the men have trained as trance-performers and regularly enter trance during the course of the all-night dances. At some camps, trance-dances occur as frequently as two or three times a week and those who have entered trances the night before rarely go out hunting the following day. Accounts of Bushman trance performances have been published in Lorna Marshall (1962) and Lee (1967). In a camp with five or more hunters, there are usually two or three who are actively hunting and several others who are inactive. The net effect is to phase the hunting and non-hunting so that a fairly steady supply of meat is brought into a camp.

Caloric Returns

Is the modest work effort of the Bushmen sufficient to provide the calories necessary to maintain the health of the population? Or have the !Kung, in common

Table 5.   Caloric and protein levels in the !Kung Bushman dietary, July–August, 1964

		Per-Capita Consumption			
Class of Food	**Percentage Contribution to Diet by Weight**	**Weight in Grams**	**Protein in Grams**	**Calories per Person per Day**	**Percentage Caloric Contribution of Meat and Vegetables**
Meat	37	230	34.5	690	33
Mongongo nuts	33	210	56.7	1,260 ⎫	
Other vegetable foods	30	190	1.9	190 ⎭	67
Total all sources	100	630	93.1	2,140	100

with some agricultural peoples (see Richards, 1939), adjusted to a permanently substandard nutritional level?

During my field work I did not encounter any cases of kwashiorkor, the most common nutritional disease in the children of African agricultural societies. However, without medical examinations, it is impossible to exclude the possibility that subclinical signs of malnutrition existed.[7]

Another measure of nutritional adequacy is the average consumption of calories and proteins per person per day. The estimate for the Bushmen is based on observations of the weights of foods of known composition that were brought into Dobe camp on each day of the study period. The per-capita figure is obtained by dividing the total weight of foodstuffs by the total number of persons in the camp. These results are set out in detail elsewhere (Lee, in press) and can only be summarized here. During the study period 410 pounds of meat were brought in by the hunters of the Dobe camp, for a daily share of nine ounces of meat per person. About 700 pounds of vegetable foods were gathered and consumed during the same period. Table 5 sets out the calories and proteins available per capita in the !Kung Bushman dietary from meat, mongongo nuts, and other vegetable sources.

This output of 2,140 calories and 93.1 grams of protein per person per day may be compared with the Recommended Daily Allowances (RDA) for persons of the small size and stature but vigorous activity regime of the !Kung Bushmen. The RDA for Bushmen can be estimated at 1,975 calories and 60 grams of protein per person per day (Taylor and Pye, 1965, pp. 45–48, 463). Thus it is apparent that food output exceeds energy requirements by 165 calories and 33 grams of protein. One can tentatively conclude that even a modest subsistence effort of two or three days' work per week is enough to provide an adequate diet for the !Kung Bushmen.

THE SECURITY OF BUSHMAN LIFE

I have attempted to evaluate the subsistence base of one contemporary hunter-gatherer society living in a marginal environment. The !Kung Bushmen have available to them some relatively abundant high-quality foods, and they do not have to walk very far or work very hard to get them. Furthermore this modest work effort provides sufficient calories to support not only the active adults, but also a large number of middle-aged and elderly people. The Bushmen do not have to press their youngsters into the service of the food quest, nor do they have to dispose of the oldsters after they have ceased to be productive.

The evidence presented assumes an added significance because this security of life was observed during the third year of one of the most severe droughts in South Africa's history. Most of the 576,000 people of Botswana are pastoralists and agriculturalists. After the crops had failed three years in succession and over 100,000 head of cattle had died on the range for lack of water, the World Food Program of the United Nations instituted a famine relief program which has grown to include 180,000 people, over 30 per cent of the population (Government of Botswana, 1966). This program did not touch the Dobe area in the isolated northwest corner of the country and the Herero and Tswana women there were able to feed their families only by joining the Bushman women to forage for wild foods. Thus the natural plant resources of the Dobe area were carrying a higher proportion of population than would be the case in years when the Bantu harvested crops. Yet this added pressure on the land did not seem to adversely affect the Bushmen.

In one sense it was unfortunate that the period of my field work happened to coincide with the drought, since I was unable to witness a "typical" annual subsistence cycle. However, in another sense, the coincidence was a lucky one, for the drought put the Bushmen and their subsistence system to the acid test and, in terms of adaptation to scarce resources, they passed with flying colors. One can postulate that their subsistence base would be even more substantial during years of higher rainfall.

What are the crucial factors that make this way of life possible? I suggest that the primary factor is the Bushmen's strong emphasis on vegetable food sources. Although hunting involves a great deal of effort and prestige, plant foods provide from 60–80 per cent of the annual diet by weight. Meat has come to be regarded as a special treat; when available, it is welcomed as a break from the routine of vegetable foods, but it is never depended upon as a staple. No one ever goes hungry when hunting fails.

The reason for this emphasis is not hard to find. Vegetable foods are abundant, sedentary, and predictable. They grow in the same place year after year, and the gatherer is guaranteed a day's return of food for a day's expenditure of energy. Game animals, by contrast, are scarce, mobile, unpredictable, and difficult to catch. A hunter has no guarantee of success and may in fact go for days or weeks without killing a large mammal. During the study period, there were eleven men in the Dobe camp, of whom four did no hunting at all. The seven active men spent a total of 78 man-days hunting, and this work input yielded eighteen animals killed, or one kill for every four man-days of hunting. The probability of any one hunter making a kill on a given day was 0.23. By contrast, the probability of a woman finding plant food on a given day was 1.00. In other words, hunting and gathering are not equally felicitous subsistence alternatives.

Consider the productivity per man-hour of the two kinds of subsistence activities. One man-hour of hunting produces about 100 edible calories, and of gathering, 240 calories. Gathering is thus seen to be 2.4 times more productive than hunting. In short, hunting is a *high-risk, low-return* subsistence activity, while gathering is a *low-risk, high-return* subsistence activity.

It is not at all contradictory that the hunting complex holds a central place in the Bushman ethos and that meat is valued more highly than vegetable foods (Marshall, 1960). Analogously, steak is valued more highly than potatoes in the food preferences of our own society. In both situations the meat is more "costly" than the vegetable food. In the Bushman case,

the cost of food can be measured in terms of time and energy expended. By this standard, 1,000 calories of meat "costs" ten man-hours, while the "cost" of 1,000 calories of vegetable foods is only four man-hours. Further, it is to be expected that the less predictable, more expensive food source would have a greater accretion of myth and ritual built up around it than would the routine staples of life, which rarely if ever fail.

Eskimo-Bushman Comparisons

Were the Bushmen to be deprived of their vegetable food sources, their life would become much more arduous and precarious. This lack of plant foods, in fact, is precisely the situation among the Netsilik Eskimo, reported by Balikci (Chapter 8, R. Lee and I. DeVore, 1968, *Man the Hunter*). The Netsilik and other Central Arctic peoples are perhaps unique in the almost total absence of vegetable foods in their diet. This factor, in combination with the great cyclical variation in the numbers and distribution of Arctic fauna, makes Eskimo life the most precarious human adaptation on earth. In effect, *the kinds of animals that are "luxury goods" to many hunters and gatherers, are to the Eskimos, the absolute necessities of life.* However, even this view should not be exaggerated, since most of the Eskimos in historic times have lived south of the Arctic Circle (Laughlin, Chapter 25a, R. Lee and I. DeVore, 1968, *Man the Hunter*) and many of the Eskimos at all latitudes have depended primarily on fishing, which is a much more reliable source of food than is the hunting of land and sea mammals.

WHAT HUNTERS DO FOR A LIVING: A COMPARATIVE STUDY

I have discussed how the !Kung Bushmen are able to manage on the scarce resources of their inhospitable environment. The essence of their successful strategy seems to be that while they depend primarily on the more stable and abundant food sources (vegetables in their case), they are nevertheless willing to devote considerable energy to the less reliable and more highly valued food sources such as medium and large mammals. The steady but modest input of work by the women provides the former, and the more intensive labors of the men provide the latter. It would be theoretically possible for the Bushmen to survive entirely on vegetable foods, but life would be boring indeed without the excitement of meat feasts. The totality of their subsistence activities thus represents an outcome of two individual goals; the first is the desire to live well with adequate leisure time, and the second is the desire to enjoy the rewards, both social and nutritional, afforded by the killing of game. In short, *the Bushmen of the Dobe area eat as much vegetable food as they need, and as much meat as they can.*

It seems reasonable that a similar kind of subsistence strategy would be characteristic of hunters and gatherers in general. Wherever two or more kinds of natural foods are available, one would predict that the population exploiting them would emphasize the more reliable source. We would also expect, however, that the people would not neglect the alternative means of subsistence. The general view offered here is that gathering activities, for plants and shellfish, should be the most productive of food for hunting and gathering man, followed by fishing, where this source is available. The hunting of mammals is the least reliable source of food and should be generally less important than either gathering or fishing.

In order to test this hypothesis, a sample of 58 societies was drawn from the *Ethnographic Atlas* (Murdock, 1967). The basis for inclusion in the sample was a 100 per cent dependence on hunting, gathering and fishing for subsistence as rated in Column 7–11 of the Atlas (Murdock, 1967, pp. 154–55).[8,9]

The *Ethnographic Atlas* coding discusses "Subsistence Economy" as follows:

> A set of five digits indicates the estimated relative dependence of the society on each of the five major types of subsistence activity. The first digit refers to the gathering of wild plants and small land fauna; the second, to hunting, including trapping and fowling; the third, to fishing, including shell fishing and the pursuit of large aquatic animals; the fourth, to animal husbandry; the fifth, to agriculture (Murdock, 1967, pp. 154–55).

Two changes have been made in the definitions of subsistence. First, the participants at the symposium on Man the Hunter agreed that the "pursuit of large aquatic animals" is more properly classified under hunting than under fishing. Similarly, it was recommended that shellfishing should be classified under gathering, not fishing. These suggestions have been followed and the definitions now read: *Gathering*—collecting of wild plant, small land fauna and shellfish; *Hunting*—pursuit of land and sea mammals; *Fishing*—obtaining of fish by any technique. In 25 cases, the subsistence scores have been changed in light of these definitions and after consulting ethnographic sources.[10]

The percentage dependence on gathering, hunting, and fishing, and the most important single source of food for each society . . . can be at best only rough approximations; however, the results are so striking that the use of these scores seems justified. In the Old World and South American sample of 24 societies, sixteen depend on gathering, five on fishing, while only three depend primarily on mammal hunting: the Yukaghir of northeast Asia, and the Ona and Shiriana of South America. In the North American sample, thirteen societies have primary dependence on gathering, thirteen on fishing, and eight on hunting. Thus for the world as a whole, half of the societies (29 cases) emphasize gathering, one-third (18 cases) fishing, and the remaining one-sixth (11 cases) hunting.

On this evidence, the "hunting" way of life appears to be in the minority. The result serves to underline the point made earlier that mammal hunting is the least reliable of the subsistence sources, and one would expect few societies to place primary dependence on it. As will be shown, most of the societies that rely primarily on mammals do so because their particular habitats offer no viable alternative subsistence strategy.

The Relation of Latitude to Subsistence

The peoples we have classified as "hunters" apparently depend for most of their subsistence on sources *other* than meat, namely, wild plants, shellfish and fish. In fact the present sample over-emphasizes the incidence of hunting and fishing since some three-fifths of the cases (34/58) are drawn from North America (north of the Rio Grande) a region which lies entirely within the temperate and arctic zones. Since the abundance and species variety of edible plants decreases as one moves out of the tropical and temperate zones, and approaches zero in the arctic, it is essential that the incidence of hunting, gathering, and fishing be related to latitude.

Table 6 shows the relative importance of gathering, hunting, and fishing within each of seven latitude divisions. Hunting appears as the dominant mode of subsistence *only* in the highest latitudes (60 or more degrees from the equator). In the arctic, hunting is primary in six of the eight societies. In the cool to cold temperate latitudes, 40 to 59 degrees from the equator, fishing is the dominant mode, appearing as primary in 14 out of 22 cases. In the warm-temperate, subtropical, and tropical latitudes, zero to 39 degrees from the equator, gathering is by far the dominant mode of subsistence, appearing as primary in 25 of the 28 cases.

Table 6.   Primary subsistence source by latitude

Degrees from the Equator	Primary Subsistence Source			
	Gathering	Hunting	Fishing	Total
More than 60°	—	6	2	8
50°–59°	—	1	9	10
40°–49°	4	3	5	12
30°–39°	9	—	—	9
20°–29°	7	—	1	8
10°–19°	5	—	1	6
0°–9°	4	1	—	5
World	29	11	18	58

For modern hunters, at any rate, it seems legitimate to predict a hunting emphasis only in the arctic, a fishing emphasis in the mid-high latitudes, and a gathering emphasis in the rest of the world.[11]

The Importance of Hunting

Although hunting is rarely the primary source of food, it does make a remarkably stable contribution to the diet. Fishing appears to be dispensable in the tropics, and a number of northern peoples manage to do without gathered foods, but, with a single exception, *all* societies at all latitudes derive at least 20 per cent of their diet from the hunting of mammals. Latitude appears to make little difference in the amount of hunting that people do. Except for the highest latitudes, where hunting contributes over half of the diet in many cases, hunted foods almost everywhere else constitute 20 to 45 per cent of the diet. In fact, the mean, the median, and the mode for hunting all converge on a figure of 35 per cent for hunter-gatherers at all latitudes. This percentage of meat corresponds closely to the 37 per cent noted in the diet of the !Kung Bushmen of the Dobe area. It is evident that the !Kung, far from being an aberrant case, are entirely typical of the hunters in general in the amount of meat they consume.

CONCLUSIONS

Three points ought to be stressed. First, life in the state of nature is not necessarily nasty, brutish, and short.

The Dobe-area Bushmen live well today on wild plants and meat, in spite of the fact that they are confined to the least productive portion of the range in which Bushman peoples were formerly found. It is likely that an even more substantial subsistence base would have been characteristic of these hunters and gatherers in the past, when they had the pick of African habitats to choose from.

Second, the basis of Bushman diet is derived from sources other than meat. This emphasis makes good ecological sense to the !Kung Bushmen and appears to be a common feature among hunters and gatherers in general. Since a 30 to 40 per cent input of meat is such a consistent target for modern hunters in a variety of habitats, is it not reasonable to postulate a similar percentage for prehistoric hunters? Certainly the absence of plant remains on archeological sites is by itself not sufficient evidence for the absence of gathering. Recently abandoned Bushman campsites show a similar absence of vegetable remains, although this article has clearly shown that plant foods comprise over 60 per cent of the actual diet.

Finally, one gets the impression that hunting societies have been chosen by ethnologists to illustrate a dominant theme, such as the extreme importance of environment in the molding of certain cultures. Such a theme can be best exemplified by cases in which the technology is simple and/or the environment is harsh. This emphasis on the dramatic may have been pedagogically useful, but unfortunately it has led to the assumption that a precarious hunting subsistence base was characteristic of all cultures in the Pleistocene. This view of both modern and ancient hunters ought to be reconsidered. Specifically I am suggesting a shift in focus away from the dramatic and unusual cases, and toward a consideration of hunting and gathering as a persistent and well-adapted way of life.

NOTES

1. These data are based on fifteen months of field research from October, 1963, to January, 1965. I would like to thank the National Science Foundation (U.S.) for its generous financial support. This article has been substantially revised since being presented at the symposium on Man the Hunter.

2. The Nyae Nyae !Kung Bushmen studied by Lorna Marshall (1957, 1960, 1965) have been involved in a settlement scheme instituted by the South African government. Although closely related to the Nyae Nyae !Kung, the Dobe !Kung across the border in Botswana have not participated in the scheme.

3. Bushman group structure is discussed in more detail in Lee (1965, pp. 38–53; and Chapter 17c, R. Lee & I. DeVore (eds.) (1968). *Man the Hunter.* Chicago: Aldine).

4. Listed in order of their importance, the principal species in the diet are: wart hog, kudu, duiker, steenbok, gemsbok, wildebeeste, springhare, porcupine, ant bear, hare, guinea fowl, francolin (two species), korhaan, tortoise, and python.

5. This and the following topic are discussed in greater detail in Lee, "!Kung Bushman Subsistence: An Input-Output Analysis" (in press).

6. Lenski, for example, in a recent review of the subject, states: "Unlike the members of hunting and gathering societies [the horticulturalists] are not compelled to spend most of their working hours in the search for food and other necessities of life, but are able to use more of their time in other ways" (1966, p. 121). Sahlins (Chap. 9b, R. Lee and I. DeVore, 1968, *Man the Hunter*) offers a counter-argument to this view.

7. During future field work with the !Kung Bushmen, a professional pediatrician and nutritionist are planning to examine children and adults as part of a general study of hunter-gatherer health and nutrition sponsored by the U.S. National Institutes of Health and the Wenner-Gren Foundation for Anthropological Research.

8. Two societies, the Gwi Bushmen and the Walbiri of Australia, were not coded by the *Ethnographic Atlas.* Their subsistence base was scored after consulting the original ethnographies (for the Gwi, Silberbauer, 1965; for the Walbiri, Meggitt, 1962, 1964).

9. In order to make more valid comparisons, I have excluded from the sample mounted hunters with guns such as the Plains Indians, and casual agriculturalists such as the Gê and Siriono. Twenty-four societies are drawn from Africa, Asia, Australia and South America. This number includes practically all of the cases that fit the definition. North America alone, with 137 hunting societies, contains over 80 per cent of the 165 hunting societies listed in the *Ethnographic Atlas.* The sampling procedure used here was to choose randomly one case from each of the 34 "clusters" of North American hunter-gatherers.

10. For their useful suggestions, my thanks go to Donald Lathrap, Robin Ridington, George Silberbauer, Hitoshi Watanabe, and James Woodburn. Special thanks are due to Wayne Suttles for his advice on Pacific coast subsistence.

11. When severity of winter is plotted against subsistence choices, a similar picture emerges. Hunting is primary in three of the five societies in very cold climates (annual temperature less than 32° F.); fishing is primary in 10 of the 17 societies in cold climates (32°–45° F.); and gathering is primary in 27 of the 36 societies in mild to hot climates (over 50° F.).

7

Diet and Primate Evolution

Katharine Milton

As recently as 20 years ago, the canopy of the tropical forest was regarded as an easy place for apes, monkeys and prosimians to find food. Extending an arm, it seemed, was virtually all our primate relatives had to do to acquire a ready supply of edibles in the form of leaves, flowers, fruits and other components of trees and vines. Since then, efforts to understand the reality of life for tree dwellers have helped overturn that misconception.

My own field studies have provided considerable evidence that obtaining adequate nutrition in the canopy—where primates evolved—is, in fact, quite difficult. This research, combined with complementary work by others, has led to another realization as well: the strategies early primates adopted to cope with the dietary challenges of the arboreal environment profoundly influenced the evolutionary trajectory of the primate order, particularly that of the anthropoids (monkeys, apes and humans).

Follow-up investigations indicate as well that foods eaten by humans today, especially those consumed in industrially advanced nations, bear little resemblance to the plant-based diets anthropoids have favored since their emergence. Such findings lend support to the suspicion that many health problems common in technologically advanced nations may result, at least in part, from a mismatch between the diets we now eat and those to which our bodies became adapted over millions of years. Overall, I would say that the collected evidence justifiably casts the evolutionary history of primates in largely dietary terms.

The story begins more than 55 million years ago, after angiosperm forests spread across the earth during the late Cretaceous (94 to 64 million years ago). At that time, some small, insect-eating mammal, which may have resembled a tree shrew, climbed into the trees, presumably in search of pollen-distributing insects. But its descendants came to rely substantially on edible plant parts from the canopy, a change that set the stage for the emergence of the primate order.

Natural selection strongly favors traits that enhance the efficiency of foraging. Hence, as plant foods assumed increasing importance over evolutionary time (thousands, indeed millions, of years), selection gradually gave rise to the suite of traits now regarded as characteristic of primates. Most of these traits facilitate movement and foraging in trees. For instance, selection yielded hands well suited for grasping slender branches and manipulating found delicacies.

Selective pressures also favored considerable enhancement of the visual apparatus (including depth perception, sharpened acuity and color vision), thereby helping primates travel rapidly through the three-dimensional space of the forest canopy and easily discern the presence of ripe fruits or tiny, young leaves. And such pressures favored increased behavioral flexibility as well as the ability to learn and remember the identity and locations of edible plant parts. Foraging benefits conferred by the enhancement of visual and cognitive skills, in turn, promoted development of an unusually large brain, a characteristic of primates since their inception.

As time passed, primates diverged into various lineages: first prosimians, most of which later went extinct, and then monkeys and apes. Each lineage arose initially in response to the pressures of a somewhat different dietary niche; distinct skills are required to become an efficient forager on a particular subset of foods in the forest canopy. Then new dietary pressures placed on some precursor of humans paved the way for the development of modern humans. To a great extent, then, we are truly what we eat.

✦ ✦ ✦

My interest in the role of diet in primate evolution grew out of research I began in 1974. While trying to decide on a topic for my doctoral dissertation in physical anthropology, I visited the tropical forest on Barro Colorado Island in the Republic of Panama. Studies done on mantled howler monkeys (*Alouatta palliata*) in the 1930s at that very locale had inadvertently helped foster the impression that primates enjoyed the "life of Riley" in the canopy.

Yet, during my early weeks of following howlers, I realized they were not behaving as expected. Instead of sitting in a tree and eating whatever happened to be growing nearby, they went out of their way to seek specific foods, meanwhile rejecting any number of seemingly promising candidates. Having found a preferred food, they did not sate themselves. Instead they seemed driven to obtain a mixture of leaves and fruits, drawn from many plant species.

The old easy-living dogma was clearly far too simplistic. I decided on the spot to learn more about the problems howlers and other anthropoids face meeting their nutritional needs in the tropical forest. I hoped, too, to discern some of the strategies they had evolved to cope with these dietary difficulties.

The challenges take many forms. Because plants cannot run from hungry predators, they have developed other defenses to avoid the loss of their edible components. These protections include a vast array of chemicals known as secondary compounds (such as tannins, alkaloids and terpenoids). At best, these chemicals taste awful; at worst, they are lethal.

Also, plant cells are encased by walls made up of materials collectively referred to as fiber or roughage: substances that resist breakdown by mammalian digestive enzymes. Among the fibrous constituents of the cell wall are the structural carbohydrates—cellulose and hemicellulose—and a substance called lignin; together these materials give plant cell walls their shape, hardness and strength. Excessive intake of fiber is troublesome, because when fiber goes undigested, it provides no energy for the feeder. It also takes up space in the gut. Hence, until it can be excreted, it prevents intake of more nourishing items. As will be seen, many primates, including humans, manage to extract a certain amount of energy, or calories, from fiber despite their lack of fiber-degrading enzymes. But the process is time-consuming and thus potentially problematic.

The dietary challenges trees and vines pose do not end there. Many plant foods lack one or more nutrients required by animals, such as particular vitamins or amino acids (the building blocks of protein), or else they are low in readily digestible carbohydrates (starch and sugar), which provide glucose and therefore energy. Usually, then, animals that depend primarily on plants for meeting their daily nutritional requirements must seek out a variety of complementary nutrient sources, a demand that greatly complicates food gathering.

For instance, most arboreal primates focus on ripe fruits and leaves, often supplementing their mostly herbivorous intake with insects and other animal matter. Fruits tend to be of high quality (rich in easily digested forms of carbohydrate and relatively low in fiber), but they provide little protein. Because all animals need a minimal amount of protein to function, fruit eaters must find additional sources of amino acids. Furthermore, the highest-quality items in the forest tend to be the most scarce. Leaves offer more protein and are more plentiful than fruit, but they are of lower quality (lower in energy and higher in fiber) and are more likely to include undesirable chemicals.

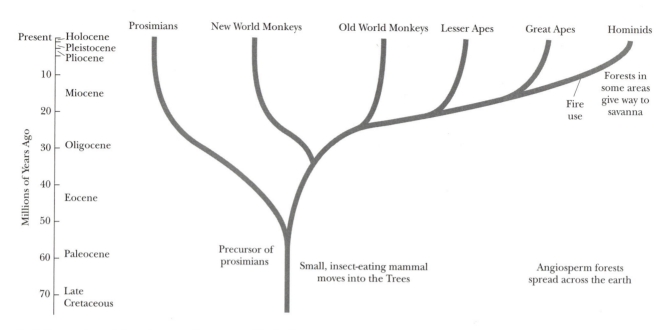

Present — Holocene
— Pleistocene
— Pliocene

10 —

Miocene

20 —

Millions of Years Ago

30 — Oligocene

40 —

50 — Eocene

60 — Paleocene

70 — Late
Cretaceous

Prosimians   New World Monkeys   Old World Monkeys   Lesser Apes   Great Apes   Hominids

Forests in
some areas
give way to
savanna

Fire
use

Precursor of
prosimians

Small, insect-eating mammal
moves into the Trees

Angiosperm forests
spread across the earth

Evolutionary tree of the primate order is rooted in the late Cretaceous, when a small, insect-eating mammal climbed into the trees to take advantage of feeding opportunities presented by the spread of angiosperm forests. As the descendants of this mammal (artist's representation to left of tree) adapted to a new dietary niche in the canopy, they developed traits now regarded as characteristic of primates, such as a rounded snout and nails (instead of claws). These descendants gave way to true primates, beginning with the prosimians. Our own genus, *Homo,* emerged during the Pliocene. Exact dates of radiations are debatable.

The need to mix and match plant foods is further exacerbated by the large distance between trees of the same species in tropical forests, which include hundreds of tree species. An animal that concentrated on eating food from a single species would have to exert great effort going from one individual of that species to another. What is more, trees exhibit seasonal peaks and valleys in the production of the fruits and young leaves primates like to eat, again making reliance on a single food species untenable.

❖ ❖ ❖

From an evolutionary perspective, two basic strategies for coping with these many problems are open to a nascent plant eater. In one, morphology reigns supreme: over long time spans, natural selection may favor the acquisition of anatomic specializations—especially of the digestive tract—that ease the need to invest time and energy searching for only the highest-quality dietary items. That is, morphological adaptations enable animals to depend on plant parts that are ubiquitous, such as on mature leaves (which are readily available but not of particularly high quality).

Colobine monkeys, one of the Old World primate groups in Africa and Asia, offer an excellent example of this strategy. Unlike the typical primate digestive tract (including that of humans), with its simple acid stomach, that of colobines includes a compartmental-

ized, or sacculated, stomach functionally analogous to that of cows and other ruminants. This anatomic specialization enables colobines to process fiber extremely efficiently.

Chewed leaves flow through the esophagus into the forestomach, one of the two stomach compartments in colobines. In this alkaline forestomach, microbes known as cellulolytic bacteria do what digestive enzymes of the monkeys cannot do: degrade fiber. In a process known as fermentation, the bacteria break down the cellulose and hemicellulose in plant cell walls, using those substances as an energy source to fuel their own activities. As the bacteria consume the fiber, they release gases called volatile fatty acids. These gases pass through the stomach wall into the colobine bloodstream, where they provide energy for body tissues or are delivered to the liver for conversion into glucose. Some researchers think the colobine forestomach may also aid in the detoxification of harmful secondary compounds in plant foods.

Efficiency of nutrient extraction from fibrous foods is enhanced in another way in colobine monkeys. As cellulolytic bacteria die, they pass out of the forestomach into the second compartment, a simple acid stomach similar to our own. Here special enzymes (lysozymes) cleave the bacterial cell walls. In consequence, protein and other nutritious materials that compose the cellulolytic bacteria become available for digestion by the monkeys. (In a sense, then, once leaves are chewed and swallowed, colobine monkeys do not interact directly with their food; they live on products of the fermentation process and on the nutrients provided by the fermenters.)

In contrast to colobines, humans and most other primates pass fiber basically unchanged through their acid stomach and their small intestine (where most nutrients are absorbed) and into the hindgut (the cecum and colon). Once fiber reaches the hindgut, cellulolytic bacteria may be able to degrade some of it. But, for most primates, eating copious amounts of fiber does not confer the same benefits as it does for the digestively specialized colobines.

Another morphological change that can facilitate survival on lower-quality plant parts is to grow larger over time. Compared with small animals, big ones must consume greater absolute amounts of food to nourish their more extensive tissue mass. But, for reasons that are imperfectly understood, the bigger animals can actually attain adequate nourishment by taking in less energy per unit of body mass. This relatively lower energy demand means larger animals can meet their energy requirements with lower-quality foods. Growing bigger has been only a limited option for most primates, however. If arboreal animals grow too massive, they risk breaking the branches underneath their feet and falling to the ground.

❖ ❖ ❖

The second basic strategy open to plant eaters is more behavioral than morphological. Species can opt to feed selectively on only the highest-quality plant foods. But because quality items are rare and very patchily distributed in tropical forests, this strategy requires the adoption of behaviors that help to minimize the costs of procuring these resources. The strategy would be greatly enhanced by a good memory. For example, an ability to remember the exact locations of trees that produce desirable fruits and to recall the shortest routes to those trees would enhance foraging efficiency by lowering search and travel costs. So would knowledge of when these trees were likely to bear ripe fruits. Reliance on memory, with its attendant benefits, might then select for bigger brains having more area for storing information.

Of course, these two basic evolutionary strategies —the morphological and behavioral—are not mutually exclusive, and species vary in the extent to which they favor one or the other. As a group, however, primates have generally depended most strongly on selective feeding and on having the brain size, and thus the wit, to carry off this strategy successfully. Other plant-eating orders, in contrast, have tended to focus heavily on morphological adaptations.

I gained my first insights into the evolutionary consequences of selective feeding in primates in the mid-1970s, when I noticed that howler monkeys and black-handed spider monkeys (*Ateles geoffroyi*)—two New World primate species—favored markedly different diets. Howler and spider monkeys, which diverged from a common ancestor, are alike in that they are about the same size, have a simple, unsacculated stomach, are totally arboreal and eat an almost exclusively plant-based diet, consisting for the most part of fruits and leaves. But my fieldwork showed that the foundation of the howler diet in the Barro Colorado forest was immature leaves, whereas the foundation of the spider monkey diet was ripe fruits.

Most of the year howlers divided their daily feeding time about equally between new leaves and fruits. But during seasonal low points in overall fruit availability, they ate virtually nothing but leaves. In contrast, spider monkeys consumed ripe fruits most of the year, eating only small amounts of leaves. When fruits became scarce, spider monkeys did not simply fill up on leaves as the howlers did. Their leaf intake did increase, but they nonetheless managed to include considerable quantities of fruit in the diet. They succeeded by carefully seeking out all fruit sources in the forest; they even resorted to consuming palm nuts that had not yet ripened.

These observations raised a number of questions. I wanted to know how howlers obtained enough energy during months when they lived exclusively on leaves. As already discussed, much of the energy in leaves is bound up in fiber that is inaccessible to the digestive enzymes of primates. Further, why did howlers eat considerable foliage even when they had abundant access to ripe fruits? By the same token, why did spider monkeys go out of their way to find fruit during periods of scarcity; what stopped them from simply switching to leaves, as howlers did? And how did spider monkeys meet daily protein needs with their fruit-rich diet? (Recall that fruits are a poor source of protein.)

Because howler and spider monkeys are much alike externally, I speculated that some internal feature of the two species—perhaps the structure of the gut or the efficiency of digestion—might be influencing these behaviors. And, indeed, studies in which I fed fruits and leaves to temporarily caged subjects revealed that howler monkeys digested food more slowly than did spider monkeys. Howlers began eliminating colored plastic markers embedded in foods an average of 20 hours after eating. In contrast, spider monkeys began eliminating these harmless markers after only four hours. Examining the size of the digestive tract in the two species then revealed how these different passage rates were attained. In howler monkeys the colon was considerably wider and longer than in spider monkeys, which meant food had a longer distance to travel and that significantly more bulk could be retained.

Collectively, these results implied that howlers could survive on leaves because they were more adept at fermenting fiber in the cecum and colon. They processed food slowly, which gave bacteria in the capacious hindgut a chance to produce volatile fatty acids in quantity. Experiments I later carried out with Richard McBee of Montana State University confirmed that howlers may obtain as much as 31 percent of their required daily energy from volatile fatty acids produced during fermentation.

In contrast, spider monkeys, by passing food more quickly through their shorter, narrower colons, were less efficient at extracting energy from the fiber in their diet. This speed, however, enabled them to move masses of food through the gastrointestinal tract each day. By choosing fruits, which are highly digestible and rich in energy, they attained all the calories they needed and some of the protein. They then supplemented their basic fruit-pulp diet with a few very select young leaves that supplied the rest of the protein they required, without an excess of fiber.

Hence, howler monkeys never devote themselves exclusively to fruit, in part because their slow passage rates would probably prevent them from processing all the fruit they would need to meet their daily energy requirement. And the amount of fruit they could consume certainly would not provide enough protein. Conversely, spider monkeys must eat fruit because their digestive tract is ill equipped to provide great amounts of energy from fermenting leaves; efficient fermentation requires that plant matter be held in the gut for some time.

◆ ◆ ◆

By luck, I had chosen to study two species that fell at opposite ends of the continuum between slow and rapid passage of food. It is now clear that most primate species can be ranked somewhere along this continuum, depending on whether they tend to maximize the efficiency with which they digest a given meal or maximize the volume of food processed in a day. This research further shows that even without major changes in the design of the digestive tract, subtle adjustments in the size of different segments of the gut can help compensate for nutritional problems posed by an animal's dietary choices. Morphological compensations in the digestive tract can have their drawbacks, however, because they may make it difficult for a species to alter its dietary habits should environmental conditions change suddenly.

These digestive findings fascinated me, but a comparison of brain size in the two species yielded one of those "eurekas" of which every scientist dreams. I examined information on the brain sizes of howler and spider monkeys because the spider monkeys in Panama seemed "smarter" than the howlers—almost human. Actually, some of them reminded me of my friends. I began to wonder whether spider monkeys behaved differently because their brains were more like our own. My investigations showed that, indeed, the brains of howler and spider monkeys do differ, even though the animals are about the same size. (Same-sized animals generally have like-sized brains.) The spider monkey brain weighs about twice that of howlers.

Now, the brain is an expensive organ to maintain; it usurps a disproportionate amount of the energy (glucose) extracted from food. So I knew natural selection would not have favored development of a large brain in spider monkeys unless the animals gained a rather pronounced benefit from the enlargement. Considering that the most striking difference between howler and spider monkeys is their diets, I proposed that the bigger brain of spider monkeys may have been favored because it facilitated the development of mental skills that enhanced success in maintaining a diet centered on ripe fruit.

A large brain would certainly have helped spider monkeys to learn and, most important, to remember, where certain patchily distributed fruit-bearing trees were located and when the fruit would be ready to eat. Also, spider monkeys comb the forest for fruit by dividing into small, changeable groups. Expanded mental capacity would have helped them to recognize members of their particular social unit and to learn the meaning of the different food-related calls through which troop members convey over large distances news of palatable items. Howler monkeys, in contrast, would not need such an extensive memory, nor would they need so complex a recognition and communication system. They forage for food as a cohesive social unit, following well-known arboreal pathways over a much smaller home range.

If I was correct that the pressure to obtain relatively difficult-to-find, high-quality plant foods encourages the development of mental complexity (which is paid for by greater foraging efficiency), I would expect to find similar differences in brain size in other primates. That is, monkeys and apes who concentrated on ripe fruits would have larger brains than those of their leaf-eating counterparts of equal body size. To pursue this idea, I turned to estimates of comparative brain sizes published by Harry J. Jerison of the University of California at Los Angeles. To my excitement, I found that those primate species that eat higher-quality, more widely dispersed foods generally have a larger brain than do their similar-sized counterparts that feed on lower-quality, more uniformly distributed resources.

	Readily Accessible Calories	Protein	Fiber	Chemical Defenses	Availability on a Given Tree
Flowers	Moderate	Moderate to high	Low to moderate	Variable	Fewer than three months
Fruits	High	Low	Moderate	Low	Fewer than three months
Young Leaves	Low	High	Moderate	Moderate	Half the year
Mature Leaves	Low	Moderate	High	Moderate	Almost year-round

Many challenges can deter primates in the tropical forest from obtaining the calories and mix of nutrients they need from plant foods. Because most such foods are inadequate in one way or another, animals must choose a variety of items each day. The chart loosely reflects the relative abundance of desirable (*green*) and problematic (*yellow*) components in a mouthful of common foods. It also indicates the typical availability of these foods on any given tree.

As I noted earlier, primates typically have larger brains than do other mammals of their size. I believe the difference arose because primates feed very selectively, favoring the highest-quality plant parts—for instance, even primates that eat leaves tend to choose very immature leaves or only the low-fiber tips of those leaves.

✦ ✦ ✦

Having uncovered these links between dietary pressures and evolution in nonhuman primates, I became curious about the role of such pressures in human evolution. A review of the fossil record for the hominid family—humans and their precursors—provided some intriguing clues.

Australopithecus, the first genus in our family, emerged in Africa more than 4.5 million years ago, during the Pliocene. As is true of later hominids, they were bipedal, but their brains were not appreciably larger than those of today's apes. Hence, selection had not yet begun to favor a greatly enlarged brain in our family. The fossil record also indicates *Australopithecus* had massive molar teeth that would have been well suited to a diet consisting largely of tough plant material. Toward the end of the Pliocene, climate conditions began to change. The next epoch, the Pleistocene (lasting from about two million to 10,000 years ago), was marked by repeated glaciations of the Northern Hemisphere. Over both epochs, tropical forests shrank and were replaced in many areas by savanna woodlands.

As the diversity of tree species decreased and the climate became more seasonal, primates in the expanding savanna areas must have faced many new dietary challenges. In the Pleistocene the last species of *Australopithecus*—which by then had truly massive jaws and molars—went extinct. Perhaps those species did so, as my colleague Montague W. Demment of the University of California at Davis speculates, because they were outcompeted by the digestively specialized ungulates (hoofed animals).

The human, or *Homo,* genus emerged during the Pliocene. The first species of the genus, *H. habilis,* was similar in body size to *Australopithecus* but had a notably larger brain. This species was replaced by the even larger-brained *H. erectus* and then, in the Pleistocene, by *H. sapiens,* which has the biggest brain of all. In parallel with the increases in brain size in the *Homo* genus, other anatomic changes were also occurring. The molar and premolar teeth became smaller, and stature increased.

To me, the striking expansion of brain size in our genus indicates that we became so successful because selection amplified a tendency inherent in the primate order since its inception: that of using brain power, or behavior, to solve dietary problems. Coupled with the anatomic changes—and with the associations in living primates between larger brains and a high-quality diet—this increase also points to the conclusion that the behavioral solution was to concentrate on high-quality foods. In fact, I suspect early humans not only maintained dietary quality in the face of changing environmental conditions but even improved it.

Expansion of the brain in combination with growth in body size and a reduction in the dentition supports the notion of a high-quality diet for a couple of reasons. When one examines present-day orangutans and gorillas, it becomes clear that in our superfamily, Hominoidea (apes and humans), an increase in

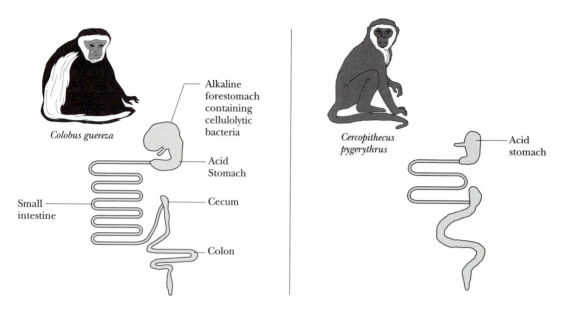

Digestive tract of colobine monkeys, such as that in *Colobus guereza* (*left*), is specialized: the stomach consists of two distinct compartments instead of the single chamber found in vervet monkeys (*right*) and most other primates. One of those compartments—the forestomach—is designed to extract more energy from fiber than would normally be obtainable. Colobine monkeys can thus survive on a more fibrous diet than can other primates of similar size.

body size combined with *decreased* dietary quality leads to a slow-moving, fairly sedentary and unsociable ape. Yet our *Homo* ancestors apparently were mobile and sociable—more resembling the lively, social and communicative chimpanzee. Unlike orangutans and gorillas, chimpanzees feed preferentially on high-quality, energy-rich ripe fruits.

Likewise, the reduction in the molars and premolars shows that the texture of foods we ate had somehow been altered such that the dentition no longer had so much work to do. In other words, either these early humans were eating different (less fibrous, easier-to-chew) foods than was *Australopithecus,* or they were somehow processing foods to remove material that would be hard to chew and digest. Indeed, stone tools found with fossil remains of *H. habilis* indicate that even the earliest members of our genus were turning to technology to aid in the preparation of dietary items.

The probability that hominids persisted in seeking energy-rich foods throughout their evolution suggests an interesting scenario. As obtaining certain types of plant foods presumably became more problematic, early humans are thought to have turned increasingly to meat to satisfy their protein demands. One can readily envision their using sharp stone flakes to cut through tough hides and to break bones for marrow. To incorporate meat into the diet on a steady basis and also to amass energy-rich plant foods, our ancestors eventually developed a truly novel dietary approach.

They adopted a division of labor, in which some individuals specialized in the acquisition of meat by hunting or scavenging and other individuals specialized in gathering plants. The foods thus acquired were saved instead of being eaten on the spot; they were later shared among the entire social unit to assure all members of a balanced diet.

Survival of the individual thus came to depend on a number of technological and social skills. It demanded not only having a brain able to form and retain a mental map of plant food supplies but also having knowledge of how to procure or transform such supplies. In addition, survival now required an ability to recognize that a stone tool could be fashioned from a piece of a rock and a sense of how to implement that vision. And it required the capacity to cooperate with others (for instance, to communicate about who should run ahead of a hunted zebra and who behind), to defer gratification (to save food until it could be brought to an agreed site for all to share) and both to determine one's fair portion and to ensure that it was received. Such demands undoubtedly served as selective pressures favoring the evolution of even larger, more complex brains.

Similarly, spoken communication may at first have helped facilitate the cooperation needed for efficient foraging and other essential tasks. Gradually, it became elaborated to smooth the course of social interactions.

◆ ◆ ◆

SPIDER MONKEY (*Ateles geoffroyi*)	HOWLER MONKEY (*Alouatta palliata*)
TYPICAL DIET Fruits: 72 percent Leaves: 22 percent Flowers: 6 percent	TYPICAL DIET Fruits: 42 percent Leaves: 48 percent Flowers: 10 percent
WEIGHT Six to eight kilograms	WEIGHT Six to eight kilograms
BRAIN SIZE 107 grams	BRAIN SIZE 50.3 grams
DAY RANGE 915 meters	DAY RANGE 443 meters
DIGESTIVE FEATURES Small colon Fast passage of food through colon	DIGESTIVE FEATURES Large colon Slow passage of food through colon

Spider monkey is a fruit specialist, whereas the howler monkey eats large quantities of leaves. The author proposes that diet played a major role in shaping the different traits of the two like-sized species, which shared a common ancestor. Natural selection favored a larger brain in spider monkeys, in part because enhanced mental capacity helped them remember where ripe fruits could be found. And spider monkeys range farther each day because in any patch of forest, ripe fruits are less abundant than leaves. The digestive traits of spider and howler monkeys promote efficient extraction of nutrition from fruits and leaves, respectively.

In other words, I see the emergence and evolution of the human line as stemming initially from pressures to acquire a steady and dependable supply of very high quality foods under environmental conditions in which new dietary challenges made former foraging behaviors somehow inadequate. Specialized carnivores and herbivores that abound in the African savannas were evolving at the same time as early humans, perhaps forcing them to become a new type of omnivore, one ultimately dependent on social and technological innovation and thus, to a great extent, on brain power. Edward O. Wilson of Harvard University has estimated that for more than two million years (until about 250,000 years ago), the human brain grew by about a tablespoon every 100,000 years. Apparently each tablespoonful of brain matter added in the genus *Homo* brought rewards that favored intensification of the trend toward social and technological advancement.

Although the practice of adding some amount of meat to the regular daily intake became a pivotal force in the emergence of modern humans, this behavior does not mean that people today are biologically suited to the virtually fiber-free diet many of us now consume. In fact, in its general form, our digestive tract does not seem to be greatly modified from that of the common ancestor of apes and humans, which was undoubtedly a strongly herbivorous animal.

Yet as of the mid-1980s no studies had been done to find out whether the gut functions of modern humans were in fact similar to those of apes. It was possible that some functional differences existed, because anatomic evidence had shown that despite similarity in the overall form of the digestive tract, modern humans have a rather small tract for an animal of their size. They also differ from apes in that the small intestine accounts for the greatest fraction of the volume of the human digestive tract; in apes the colon accounts for the greatest volume.

To better understand the kind of diet for which the human gut was adapted, Demment and I decided to compare human digestive processes with those of the chimpanzee, our closest living relative. We hoped to determine whether, over the course of their respective evolutionary histories, humans and chimpanzees had diverged notably in their abilities to deal with fiber. (We were greatly encouraged in this effort by the late Glynn Isaac, who was then at the University of California at Berkeley.)

The feeding habits of chimpanzees are well known. Despite their skill in capturing live prey (particularly monkeys), these apes actually obtain an estimated 94 percent of their annual diet from plants, primarily ripe fruits. Even though the fruits chimpanzees eat tend to be rich in sugar, they contain far less pulp and considerably more fiber and seeds than do the domesticated fruits sold in our supermarkets. Hence, I calculated that wild chimpanzees take in hundreds of grams of fiber each day, much more than the 10 grams or less the average American is estimated to consume.

Various excellent studies, including a fiber project at Cornell University, had already provided much information about fiber digestion by humans. At one time, it was believed that the human digestive tract did not possess microbes capable of degrading fiber. Yet bacteria in the colons of 24 male college students at Cornell proved quite efficient at fermenting fiber found in a variety of fruits and vegetables. At their most effective, the microbial populations broke down as much as three quarters of the cell-wall material that the subjects ingested; about 90 percent of the volatile fatty adds that resulted were delivered to the bloodstream.

Following the example of the Cornell study, Demment and I assessed the efficiency of fiber breakdown in chimpanzees fed nutritious diets containing varying amounts of fiber. Demment handled the statistical analyses, and I collected raw data. How dry that sounds in comparison to the reality of the experience! At the Yerkes Primate Center in Atlanta, I whiled away the summer with six extremely cross chimpanzees that never missed an opportunity to pull my hair, throw fecal matter and generally let me know they were underwhelmed by our experimental cuisine.

✦ ✦ ✦

Our results showed that the chimpanzee gut is strikingly similar to the human gut in the efficiency with which it processes fiber. Moreover, as the fraction of fiber in the diet rises (as would occur in the wild during seasonal lulls in the production of fruits or immature leaves), chimpanzees and humans speed the rate at which they pass food through the digestive tract.

These similarities indicate that as quality begins to decline in the natural environment, humans and chimpanzees are evolutionarily programmed to respond to this decrease by increasing the rate at which food moves through the tract. This response permits a greater quantity of food to be processed in a given unit of time; in so doing, it enables the feeder to make up for reduced quality by taking in a larger volume of food each day. (Medical research has uncovered another benefit of fast passage. By speeding the flow of food through the gut, fiber seems to prevent carcinogens from lurking in the colon so long that they cause problems.)

If the human digestive tract is indeed adapted to a plant-rich, fibrous diet, then this discovery lends added credence to the commonly heard assertion that people in highly technological societies eat too much refined carbohydrate and too little fiber. My work offers no prescription for how much fiber we need. But certainly the small amount many of us consume is far less than was ingested by our closest human ancestors.

More recently, my colleagues and I have analyzed plant parts routinely eaten by wild primates for their content of various constituents, including vitamin C and pectin. Pectin, a highly fermentable component of cell walls, is thought to have health benefits for humans. Our results suggest that diets eaten by early humans were extremely rich in vitamin C and contained notable pectin. Again, I do not know whether we need to take in the same proportions of these substances as wild primates do, but these discoveries are provocative.

To a major extent, the emergence of modern humans occurred because natural selection favored adaptations in our order that permitted primates to focus their feeding on the most energy-dense, low-fiber diets they could find. It seems ironic that our lineage, which in the past benefited from assiduously avoiding eating too much food high in fiber, may now be suffering because we do not eat enough of it.

FURTHER READING

Ecology of Arboreal Folivores. Edited by G. Gene Montgomery. Smithsonian Institution Press, 1978.

Distribution Patterns of Tropical Plant Foods as an Evolutionary Stimulus to Primate Mental Development. K. Milton in *American Anthropologist*, Vol. 83, No. 3, pages 534–548; September 1981.

Food Choice and Digestive Strategies of Two Sympatric Primate Species. K. Milton in *American Naturalist*, Vol. 117, No. 4, pages 496–505; April 1981.

Primate Diets and Gut Morphology: Implications for Hominid Evolution. K. Milton in *Food and Evolution: Toward a Theory of Human Food Habits*. Edited by Marvin Harris and Eric B. Ross. Temple University Press, 1987.

Digestion and Passage Kinetics of Chimpanzees Fed High and Low-Fiber Diets and Comparison with Human Data. K. Milton and M. W. Demment in *Journal of Nutrition*, Vol. 118, No. 9, pages 1082–1088; September 1988.

Foraging Behaviour and the Evolution of Primate Intelligence. K. Milton in *Machiavellian Intelligence: Social Expertise and the Evolution of Intellect in Monkeys, Apes, and Humans*. Edited by Richard Byrne and Andrew Whiten. Oxford University Press, 1988.

Agriculture: The Great Revolution

By evolutionary standards, the adoption of agriculture happened very quickly. The available archaeological evidence points to the first domesticated crops and animals appearing around 12,000 years ago. The Middle East was the first home to domesticated animals—dogs, sheep, goats, and cattle—and crops such as barley, wheat, peas, and lentils (Figure 1). Following soon after, and probably as independent inventions, other domesticates appeared in other areas: rice, millet, and pigs in China; peppers, squash, beans, and corn in Mesoamerica; the potato in the Andes; sugarcane in the Pacific Islands. Wherever these crops thrived, agriculture and agricultural peoples increased in numbers and spread themselves and their lifestyle across the continents. Agriculture may now seem to be humdrum and mundane, yet after agriculture human life would never be the same. We domesticated crops and our crops domesticated us.

The archaeologist V. Gordon Childe wrote in the 1930s that agriculture was the most important of human revolutions. First, it is implicit that agriculture changed what individuals do: Instead of looking for food, farmers and herders tend to their crops and animals. As obvious as this might seem, the consequences for biology and culture are dramatic. Changes in activity patterns lead to new diseases, new selective pressures, and a reorganization of social life. Second and equally implicit, what individuals eat changed. Wild fruits, nuts, leaves, and wild animals were replaced with domesticated grains and meats of domesticated animals. Do agricultural foods provide more or less energy, protein, and micronutrients? What is the consequence of the aforementioned changes in activity patterns?

Agriculture has a number of obvious advantages over foraging. First, crops may be eaten or destroyed, but they are invariably to be found where they were planted. Agriculture brings a sense, if not necessarily a reality, of stability, regularity, predictability, and control. Second, the amount of time and energy put into growing food is generally less than that spent foraging for food. Therefore, in addition to providing for a family, a successful farmer can produce a surplus that can be traded for other goods. The result is that time is freed up for others to pursue secondary tasks: make works of beauty, build monuments, fight battles, give tribute.

The second revolution of agriculture is a revolution in demography, ecology, and culture. Because agriculture is based on maintaining fixed fields, mobility is decreased. Groups develop greater attachment and sense of "ownership" of lands, and the way people think about the land changes. Also, agriculture, by providing a greater density of food per unit area, permitted more people to live in a given area. In fact, population increase and agricultural intensification almost always occur simultaneously. Population increase may have forced humans to adopt agriculture, and agriculture, by providing more food, may have allowed populations to increase.

With agriculture, the first cities developed. With agriculture came food surpluses. Roles were invented to harness agricultural surpluses, and social classes developed in relationship to production. Agriculture, then, appears to have been a mixed blessing. It allowed for a quickened pace of technological, social, and ideological development, but at what cost? On one side are progressivists such as Hobbes. Agriculture made all things possible from the Parthenon and the B-minor Mass to the computer with which we write and the cup of coffee by its side, no less the coffeemaker and the electricity to run it. It is hard to imagine a foraging society that would have invented any of these things! On the other hand, the central compromise of agriculture, greater food quantity, may have come with costs. Because agriculture changed ecology and culture, it is the root cause of a great deal of social ills, such as warfare and inequality between the sexes and classes.

Biological anthropologists Alan Goodman and George Armelagos are experts in paleopathology, reading signs of undernutrition and poor health from the bones and teeth of past groups. They wondered what the health and nutritional consequences would be of the shift to an agricultural economy, and it is this question that they explore in "Disease and Death at Dr. Dickson's Mounds." To answer the question, they studied the bones and teeth of more than 500 individuals who were buried at Dickson Mounds near Lewiston, Illinois. They were able to identify individuals who grew up before and after people began practicing agriculture (an analysis of the location and manner of burial made this possible). By comparing the rates of

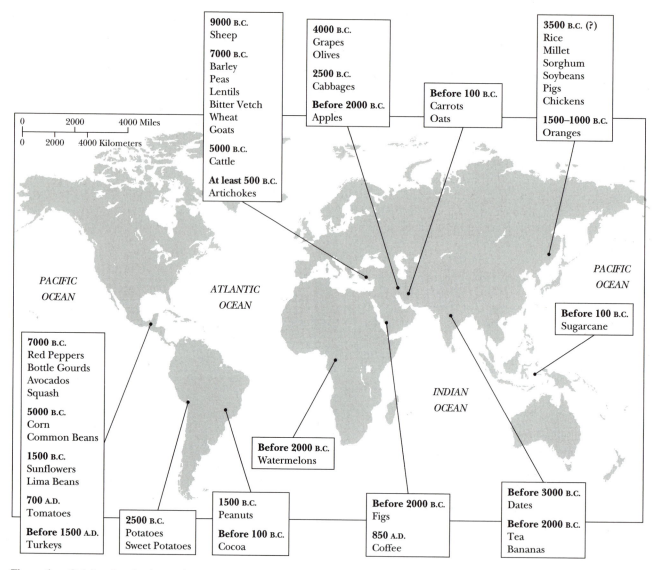

Figure 1.   Origin of main domesticates.

disease and malnutrition in the pre- and postagricultural groups, they were able to conduct a naturalistic study of the consequences of agriculture.

Goodman and Armelagos discovered that those who lived before the transition to agriculture exhibited fewer signs of disease and poor nutrition and that they lived longer. What is their evidence? Why would agriculture lead to a decline in health and nutrition? Is it simply that agriculture does not provide a healthy diet? Can one separate the effect of population increase from the effects of agriculture? Finally, is the decline in health related to socio-economic changes (such as increasing classlike differentiation) that tend to follow agricultural intensification?

The benefits of agriculture, then, may have come with a nutritional cost for the first horticulturists. But are there also costs to you and me? In the next article, the radiologist Boyd Eaton and the medical doctor and anthropologist Melvin Konner discuss the diet of Paleolithic peoples and suggest that many current maladies are due to our lifestyles being out of tune with our Stone Age physiologies.

In "Paleolithic Nutrition: A Consideration of Its Nature and Current Implications," Drs. Eaton and Konner consider what Paleolithic humans may have eaten and what their diet may portend for individuals today. In contrast to the previous article, which was intended for a general readership, this article first appeared in the *New England Journal of Medicine*, a widely read and highly prestigious medical journal. The authors assess the diets of contemporary foragers, such as the !Kung San (articles 2 and 6), and prehistoric hunter-gatherers such as those studied by Goodman and Armelagos. They estimated that the diet of Paleolithic humans consisted of about 35 percent animal product.

How secure is this generalization? Is it likely that meat consumption, for example, was as high as they proposed? How constant was the food supply? Is any generalization possible given the diversity of forager lifestyles and diets? Lastly, is it any more valid to think we are adapted to a Paleolithic rather than an Eocene primate's insect-rich diet? Might we just as easily point to the healthiness of eating fruits or low-fat insects, as our primate cousins do? How do we reconcile Eaton and Konner with Milton (article 7)? Specifics notwithstanding, the form of the argument is solidly evolutionary anthropology. Subsistence strategies and food consumption have changed more quickly than our digestive tracts. The result is that our culture and biology are "out of sync" and we suffer biologically.

"Junk Food Monkeys" is a lighthearted follow-up to "Paleolithic Nutrition" with a serious point. Robert Sapolsky, a neuroendocrinologist who usually studies the etiology and consequences of physiological stress in primates, reports on his chance observations of the changing diet, behavior, and health of a group of olive baboons who live on the Serengeti Plain in Kenya. His insights are the result of his recognizing that an important "natural experiment" was taking place before his eyes.

One of the baboon troops had a garbage dump placed in the middle of its territory. As Sapolsky relates, this changed everything. Like switching from foraging to farming, less work was needed to find food, and what the animals ate also changed dramatically. Perhaps it is more like the monkeys skipped over all of the early agricultural phases and were jettisoned to postindustrial consumption: eating all manner of leftovers. On the whole, was the change for the better or worse? Is there a lesson for us humans in this story?

Today, in this postagricultural/postindustrial world of mass transportation and "McDonald's-ization" of the far corners of the world, fewer families grow the foods they consume. The closest most of us will come to foraging occurs when we exercise our power to choose among the 100-plus varieties of breakfast cereals in the safe and well-lighted confines of the local supermarket. But what we eat is still based on agriculture. What did agriculture bring us? Knowing how our ancestors managed to get their daily supplies of vegetables, fruits, and meats and the social and biological consequences of

this "struggle for food" can provide a window into their lives. Perhaps, too, it can tell us much about ourselves.

SUGGESTIONS FOR THINKING AND DOING NUTRITIONAL ANTHROPOLOGY

1.   Cohen and Armelagos (1984) include nearly twenty case studies of the health and nutritional consequences of the change from foraging to farming. Using this book or other sources, what generalizations about the consequences of agriculture can be supported? Under what conditions does agriculture appear to do the greatest harm to human health?

2.   After the publication of *The Paleolithic Prescription* (Eaton et al., 1988), a cartoon was published showing a group of hunters roasting their recent kill. One hunter asks, "Why is our life expectancy so short if our diet is so healthy?" Can you answer this apparent paradox?

3.   Eat a Paleolithic diet for a day. How was it different from your usual diet? Was it difficult to find suitable food?

SUGGESTED READINGS

Cohen, M., & Armelagos, G. (Eds.). (1984). *Paleopathology at the origins of agriculture.* New York: Academic Press. (This edited volume includes a large number of examples of the skeletal evidence for change in health and nutrition with agriculture.)

Eaton, B., Shostak, M., & Konner, M. (1988). *The paleolithic prescription.* New York: Harper & Row. (A recommended follow-up to the article by Eaton and Konner. This book helped to launch the field of Darwinian medicine.)

Heiser, C. (1990). *Seed to civilization.* Cambridge: Harvard University Press. (Easy-to-read overview of agricultural developments in different parts of the world.)

Larsen, C. S. (1997). *Bioarchaeology: Interpreting behavior from the human skeleton.* New York: Cambridge University Press. (Excellent summary of methods of reconstructing behavior, diet, nutrition, and health from bones and teeth.)

Nesse, R., & Williams, G. (1994). *Why we get sick: The new science of Darwinian medicine.* New York: Times Books. (An easy-to-read summary of Darwinian medicine from two of its founding fathers.)

Sobolik, K. (Ed.). (1994). *Paleonutrition: The diet and health of prehistoric Americans.* Carbondale: Southern Illinois University Press. (An excellent compilation of articles on the variety of methods and sources of information used to infer past diets.)

8

Disease and Death at Dr. Dickson's Mounds

Alan H. Goodman and George J. Armelagos

Clustered in west-central Illinois, atop a bluff near the confluence of the Illinois and Spoon rivers, are twelve to thirteen poorly defined earthen mounds. The mounds, which overlap each other to some extent, cover a crescent-shaped area of about an acre. Since at least the middle of the nineteenth century, local residents have known that prehistoric Native Americans built these mounds to bury their dead. But it was not until the late 1920s that Don Dickson, a chiropractor, undertook the first systematic excavation of the mounds, located on farmland owned by his father. Barely into his thirties at the time, Dickson became so involved in the venture that he never returned to his chiropractic practice. Apparently, he was intrigued by the novel undertaking of unearthing skeletons and trying to diagnose the maladies of long-dead individuals. Later on, he became more concerned with the patterns of disease and death in this extinct group in order to understand how these people lived and why they often died at an early age.

The "Dickson Mounds" (the site also includes two early, unmounded burial grounds) quickly attracted the attention of professional anthropologists. In the early 1930s, a team of University of Chicago archeologists exposed about 200 of the estimated 3,000 burials and identified a number of settlement sites in a 100-square-mile area. A second phase of excavation at Dickson began in the 1960s under the direction of Alan Harn, an archeologist working for the state of Illinois, whose crew excavated many of the local living sites and more than 800 additional burials. The archeological research revealed that these prehistoric people had taken part in an important transition, from hunting and gathering to an agricultural way of life.

About A.D. 950, hunter-gatherers lived along the Illinois River valley area near Dickson, subsisting on a wide range of local plants and animals, including grasses and seeds, fruits and berries, roots and tubers, vines, herbs, large and small mammals, migratory waterfowl and riverine birds, and fish. The moderate climate, copious water supply, and rich soil made this a bountiful and attractive area for hunter-gatherers. Groups occupied campsites that consisted of a few small structures, and the debris scattered around these sites suggests seasonal use. The population density was low, perhaps on the order of two to three persons per square mile. Then, about 1050, broken hoes and other agricultural tools, as well as maize, began to form part of village refuse, evidence of the introduction of maize agriculture. At the same time, the population grew. By 1200 the population density may have increased by a factor of ten, to about twenty-five persons per square mile. Living sites became larger and more permanent. The largest settlement in the area, Larson, was a residential and ceremonial center where some 1,000 inhabitants lived, many behind a palisaded wall.

Trade also flourished. Dickson became part of what archeologists call the Mississippian tradition, a network of maize-growing, mound-building societies that spread throughout most of the eastern United States. More and more, items used at the village sites or deposited as grave offerings were not of local origin. Some, such as marine shell necklaces, came from as far away as the Gulf of Mexico and Florida, one thousand miles to the south. Everyday objects such as spoons and jars were received from peoples of the eastern plains and the western prairies, while luxury items of ceremonial or decorative value arrived in trade from the south, probably coming upriver to Dickson through Cahokia, a Mississippian center some 110 miles away. Cahokia is a massive site that includes some 120 mounds within a six-square-mile area. As many as 30,000 persons lived at Cahokia and in the surrounding villages.

What we know about Dickson might have ended at this point, but continues because the skeletal remains that Harn excavated have been used to evaluate how the health of these prehistoric people fared following the adoption of agriculture and other changes in their life style. Interest in this issue stems from the writings of the eminent British archeologist V. Gordon Childe (1892–1957), who believed that the development of agriculture prompted the first great revolution in human technology, ushering in fundamental changes in economy, social organization, and ideology. Archeologists continue to debate the causes of agricultural revolutions. For example, some believe that in various regions of the world, increased population pressure, leading to food shortages and declining health, spurred the switch to agricultural food production. Others believe population increase was one of the consequences of agricultural revolutions. More important to us are the effects of an agricultural revolution on the health of people who lived at the time of such change.

Three circumstances have made it possible to test the effects agriculture had upon health at Dickson. First, Harn and those working with him valued the potential information to be gained from skeletons and therefore paid close attention to their excavation. Ultimately, the skeletal remains were sent to the University of Massachusetts at Amherst for analysis by George Armelagos and many of his graduate students (this is how we became involved). Second, the recovered remains include both individuals who lived before the development of maize agriculture (Late Woodland, or pre-Mississippian) and after (Mississippian). The two groups of individuals could be distinguished according to the mounds they were buried in, their placement within each mound, and their burial position (in earlier burials the bodies tend to be in a flexed or semi-flexed position; in later burials they tend to be extended). The third enabling condition was provided by Janice Cohen, one of Armelagos's graduate students. Her analysis of highly heritable dental traits showed that although Dickson was in contact with persons from outside the central Illinois River valley area during the period of rapid cultural change, outside groups did not replace or significantly merge with the local groups. It is therefore possible to follow the health over time of a single population that, for all intents and purposes, was genetically stable.

As a doctoral student working under Armelagos in the early 1970s, John Lallo, now at Cleveland State University, set out to test whether health at Dickson improved, got worse, or remained the same with the advent of agriculture and its accompanying changes. Lallo argued that intensification of maize agriculture most likely resulted in a poorer diet. Although a common assumption is that the adoption of agriculture should have provided a prehistoric people with a better diet, there are good reasons to predict just the opposite. Heavy reliance on a single crop may lead to nutritional problems. Maize, for example, is deficient in lysine, an essential amino acid. Furthermore, agricultural societies that subsist on a few foodstuffs are more vulnerable to famines brought about by drought and other disasters. Finally, increased population density, a more sedentary life style, and greater trade, all of which are associated with agriculture, provide conditions for the spread and maintenance of infectious diseases.

The skeletons of individuals who lived before and after the introduction of maize agriculture were examined for a number of different health indicators, in order to provide a balanced picture of the pattern of stress, disease, and death that affected the Dickson population. The indicators that proved most sensitive to health differences were: bone lesions (scars) due to infection, nutritional deficiencies, trauma, and degen-

erative conditions; long bone growth; dental developmental defects; and age at death. To avoid unconscious bias, we and the other researchers involved measured these seven traits without knowing in advance which skeletons came from each of the two cultural periods.

Persistent bacterial infection leaves its mark on the outer, or periosteal, layer of bone. Tibias (shinbones) are the most frequently affected bones because they have relatively poor circulation and therefore tend to accumulate bacteria. Toxins produced by bacteria kill some of the bone cells; as new bone is produced, the periosteal bone becomes roughened and layered. Lallo and his co-workers found that following the introduction of agriculture there was a threefold increase in the percentage of individuals with such lesions. Eighty-four percent of the Mississippian tibias had these "periosteal reactions," as compared with only 26 percent of pre-Mississippian tibias. The lesions also tended to be more severe and to show up in younger individuals in the Mississippian population.

A second type of lesion, more easily seen in the thinner bones of the body (such as those of the skull), is a sign of anemia. In response to anemia, the body steps up its production of red blood cells, which are formed in the bone marrow. To accomplish this the marrow must expand at the expense of the outer layer of bone. In severe cases, this expansion may cause the outer layer of bone to disappear, exposing the porous, sievelike inner bone. This lesion, called porotic hyperostosis, can occur with any kind of anemia. In the Dickson Mounds populations, the lesions are not severe, are restricted to the eye sockets and crania, and occur mainly in children and young adult females. This pattern suggests anemia resulting from a nutritional deficiency, specifically an iron deficiency. (A hereditary anemia, such as sickle-cell anemia, would have been more severe in its manifestation and would have affected all ages and both sexes in the population.)

There is a significant increase in the frequency of porotic hyperostosis during the Mississippian period. Half the Mississippian infants and children had porotic hyperostosis, twice the rate found for pre-Mississippian infants and children. Individuals with both periosteal reactions and porotic hyperostosis tend to have suffered more severely from each condition. This may be evidence of a deadly synergism of malnutrition and infection, like that often reported among contemporary populations.

Traumatic lesions were measured by diagnosis of healed fractures of the long bones of the legs and arms. Adult males had the highest frequency of such fractures. Approximately one out of three Mississippian males had at least one fracture, twice the frequency of their predecessors. These fractures often occurred at the midshaft of the ulna and radius, the bones of the lower arm. Fractures at this location are called parry fractures because they are typically the result of efforts to ward off a blow.

The frequency of degenerative pathologies, including arthritic conditions found on joints and the contacting surfaces of the vertebral column, also increased through time. One or more degenerative conditions were diagnosed in 40 percent of pre-Mississippian adults but in more than 70 percent of Mississippian adults.

In addition to the studies of the changing pattern of disease and trauma, we, along with Lallo and Jerome Rose, now at the University of Arkansas, assessed differences in skeletal growth and developmental timing. Skeletal growth and development are susceptible to a wide variety of stressful conditions and therefore reflect overall health. We found that in comparison to pre-Mississippians of the same age, Mississippian children between the ages of five and ten had significantly shorter and narrower tibias and femurs (the major long bones of the legs). This difference may be explained by a decreased rate of growth before the age of five. The Mississippians apparently were able to catch up in growth after age ten, however, since adult Mississippians are only slightly smaller than pre-Mississippians.

A more detailed exploration of developmental changes came from studying defects in enamel, the hard white coating of the crowns of teeth. Ameloblasts, the enamel-forming cells, secrete enamel matrix in ringlike fashion, starting at the biting surface and ending at the bottom of the crown. A deficiency in enamel thickness, called a hypoplasia, may result if the individual suffers a systemic physiological stress during enamel formation. Since the timing of enamel secretion is well known and relatively stable, the position of such a lesion on a tooth corresponds to an individual's age at the time of stress.

We examined the permanent teeth—teeth that form between birth and age seven. For skeletons with nearly complete sets of permanent teeth, 55 percent of pre-Mississippians had hypoplasias, while among Mississippians the figure rose to 80 percent. In both groups, hypoplasias were most frequently laid down between the ages of one and one-half and four. However, the hypoplasias in the Mississippian group peak at age two and one-half, approximately one-half year earlier than the pre-Mississippian peak. The peak is also more pronounced. This pattern of defects may indicate both an earlier age at weaning and the use of cereal products as weaning foods.

The repeated occurrence of hypoplasias within individuals revealed an annual cycle of stress. Most likely there was a seasonal food shortage. This seems to have worsened in the period just before the population becomes completely "Mississippianized," suggesting that it provided a rationale for intensifying agriculture.

All the above six indicators point toward a decrease in health associated with cultural change at Dickson. However, they are not meaningful apart from an analysis of the pattern of death in these populations. Healthy-looking skeletons, for example, may be the remains of young individuals who died outright because their bodies were too weak to cope in the face of disease, injury, and other forms of stress. Conversely, skeletons that show wear and tear may be those of individuals who survived during stressful times and lived to a ripe old age.

At Dickson, however, the trend is unambiguous. Individuals whose skeletons showed more signs of stress and disease (for example, enamel hypoplasias) also lived shorter lives, on average, than individuals with fewer such indications. For the population as a whole, life expectancy at birth decreased from twenty-six years in the pre-Mississippian to nineteen years in the Mississippian. The contrast in mortality is especially pronounced during the infant and childhood years. For example, 22 percent of Mississippians died during their first year as compared to 13 percent of the pre-Mississippians. Even for those who passed through the dangerous early years of childhood, there is a differential life expectancy. At fifteen years of age, pre-Mississippians could expect to live for an average of twenty-three more years, while Mississippians could expect to live for only eighteen more years.

What caused this decline in health? A number of possibilities have been proposed. Lallo and others have emphasized the effect of agriculture on diet. Most of the health trends may be explained by a decline in diet quality. These include the trends in growth, development, mortality, and nutritional disease, all four of which have obvious links to nutrition. The same explanation may be offered for the increase in infectious diseases, since increased susceptibility may be due to poor nutrition. Furthermore, a population subject to considerable infectious disease would be likely to suffer from other conditions, including increased rates of anemia and mortality and decreased growth rates.

The link between diet and infectious disease is bolstered by an analysis of trace elements from tibial bone cores. Robert Gilbert found that the Mississippian bones contain less zinc, an element that is limited in maize. Building on this research, Wadia Bahou, now a physician in Ann Arbor, Michigan, showed that the skeletons with the lowest levels of zinc had the highest frequency of infectious lesions. This is strong evidence that a diet of maize was relied on to a point where health was affected.

The population increase associated with the changeover to agriculture probably also contributed to the decline in health. We do not believe that the population ever threatened to exceed the carrying capacity of the bountiful Dickson area (and there are no signs of the environmental degradation one would expect to find if resources were overexploited). However, increased population density and sedentariness, coupled with intensification of contact with outsiders, create opportunities for the spread of infectious disease. George Milner of the University of Kentucky, while still a graduate student at Northwestern University, argued this point in comparing Dickson with the Kane Mounds populations. Kane is located near Cahokia, the major center south of Dickson. Despite Kane's proximity to this large center, its population density was much lower than at Larson, the major agricultural village of the Dickson population. Of the two, Kane had the lower rate of infectious diseases.

While the "agricultural hypothesis," including the effects of population pressure, offers an explanation for much of the health data, it doesn't automatically account for the two remaining measures: degenerative and traumatic pathologies. Poor nutrition and infectious disease may make people more susceptible to degenerative disease. However, the arthritic conditions found in the Dickson skeletons, involving movable joints, were probably caused by strenuous physical activity. The link, then, is not with the consumption of an agricultural diet but, if anything, with the physically taxing work of agricultural production. An explanation for the increase in traumatic injuries is harder to imagine. Possibly, the increased population density caused social tension and strife to arise within communities, but why should this have happened?

A curious fact makes us think that explanations based only on agricultural intensification and population increase are missing an important contributing factor. Recent archeological research at Dickson suggests that hunting and gathering remained productive enterprises and were never completely abandoned. Many of the local Mississippian sites have a great concentration of animal bones and projectile points used for hunting. A balanced diet apparently was available. The health and trace element data, however, suggest that the Mississippian diet was deficient. There is a disparity between what was available and what was eaten.

At present our search for an explanation for this paradox centers on the relationship between Dickson and the Cahokia population. The builders of the Dickson Mounds received many items of symbolic worth from the Cahokia region, such as copper-covered ear spools and marine shell necklaces. Much of the health data would be explained if Dickson had been trading perishable foodstuffs for these luxury items. In particular, the diversion of meat or fish to Cahokia would explain the apparent discrepancy between diet and resources.

To have a food surplus to trade, individuals from the Dickson area may have intensified their agricultural production while continuing to hunt and gather. The increase in degenerative conditions could have resulted from such a heavy workload. The system may also have put social strain on the community, leading to internal strife. And the accumulation of wealth in terms of ceremonial or other luxury items may have necessitated protection from outside groups. This would explain why the Larson site was palisaded. Both internal and external strain may have led to the increase in traumatic pathologies.

To test the validity of this scenario, we are hoping to gather additional evidence, concentrating on an analysis of trade. The flow of perishable goods such as meat is hard to trace, but we can study the sets of animal bones found at Cahokia and at Dickson village and butchering sites. The distribution of animal bones at the archeological sites can then be compared with examples of bone distributions in areas where trading has been ethnographically recorded. Further evidence is provided by data such as Milner's, which showed that health at Kane—a community that shared in Cahokia's power—was better than at Dickson.

The trading of needed food for items of symbolic value, to the point where health is threatened, may not seem to make sense from an objective, outsider's perspective. But it is a situation that has been observed in historic and modern times. An indigenous group learns that it can trade something it has access to (sugar cane, alpacas, turtles) for something it greatly admires but can only obtain from outside groups (metal products, radios, alcohol). The group's members do not perceive that the long-term health and economic results of such trade are usually unfavorable. Nor are all such arrangements a result of voluntary agreement. The pattern of health observed at Dickson is seen in most situations where there is a decline in access to, and control over, resources. For example, lower classes in stratified societies live shorter lives and suffer more from nearly all major diseases.

Agriculture is not invariably associated with declining health. A recent volume edited by Mark N. Cohen and George J. Armelagos, *Paleopathology and the Origins of Agriculture,* analyzed health changes in twenty-three regions of the world where agriculture developed. In many of these regions there was a clear, concurrent decline in health, while in others there was little or no change or slight improvements in health. Perhaps a decline is more likely to occur when agriculture is intensified in the hinterland of a political system. Groups living far away from the centers of trade and power are apt to be at a disadvantage. They may send the best fruits of their labors to market and receive little in return. And during times of economic hardship or political turmoil, they may be the ones to suffer the most, as resources are concentrated on maintaining the central parts of the system.

ADDITIONAL READING

Paleopathology and the Origins of Agriculture, edited by Mark N. Cohen and George J. Armelagos (New York: Academic Press, 1984), compares the health of prehistoric farmers with their hunter-gatherer forebears. A chapter by Alan H. Goodman et al., "Health Changes at Dickson Mounds, Illinois (A.D. 950–1300)," chronicles the effects of economic and cultural change on the health of prehistoric populations in this area. Robert Gilbert, Jr., and James Mielke edited *Analysis of Prehistoric Diets* (New York: Academic Press, 1985), a report on the methods used to interpret prehistoric nutritional stress. For a review of humankind's first three million years, see Robert J. Wenke's *Patterns in Prehistory* (New York: Oxford University Press, 1980).

9

Paleolithic Nutrition:
A Consideration of Its Nature and Current Implications

S. Boyd Eaton and Melvin Konner

Humanity has existed as a genus for about 2 million years, and our prehuman hominid ancestors, the australopithecines, appeared at least 4 million years ago (Table 1). This phase of evolutionary history made definitive contributions to our current genetic composition, partly in response to dietary influences at that time. The foods available to evolving hominids varied widely according to the paleontological period, geographical location, and seasonal conditions, so that our ancestral line maintained the versatility of the omnivore that typifies most primates. Natural selection has provided us with nutritional adaptability; however, human beings today are confronted with diet-related health problems that were previously of minor importance and for which prior genetic adaptation has poorly prepared us. Chronic illnesses affecting older, postreproductive persons could have had little selective influence during evolution, yet such conditions are now the paramount cause of morbidity and mortality in Western nations.

The human genetic constitution has changed relatively little since the appearance of truly modern human beings, *Homo sapiens sapiens,* about 40,000 years ago.[2,3] Even the development of agriculture 10,000 years ago has apparently had a minimal influence on our genes. Certain hemoglobinopathies and retention of intestinal lactase into adulthood are "recent" genetic evolutionary trends, but very few other examples are known. Such developments as the Industrial Revolu-

tion, agribusiness, and modern food-processing techniques have occurred too recently to have had any evolutionary effect at all. Accordingly, the range of diets available to preagricultural human beings determines the range that still exists for men and women living in the 20th century—the nutrition for which human beings are in essence genetically programmed.[4]

Differences between the dietary patterns of our remote ancestors and the patterns now prevalent in industrialized countries appear to have important implications for health, and the specific pattern of nutritional disease is a function of the stage of civilization.[5] Physicians and nutritionists are increasingly convinced that the dietary habits adopted by Western society over the past 100 years make an important etiologic contribution to coronary heart disease, hypertension, diabetes, and some types of cancer. These conditions have emerged as dominant health problems only in the past century and are virtually unknown among the few surviving hunter-gatherer populations whose way of life and eating habits most closely resemble those of preagricultural human beings.[6] The longer life expectancy of people in industrialized countries is not the only reason that chronic illnesses have assumed new importance. Young people in the Western world commonly have developing asymptomatic forms of these conditions, but hunter-gatherer youths do not.[7–10] Furthermore, the members of technologically primitive cultures who survive

Table 1.   The main events of human evolution*

Millions of Years Ago	Epoch	Development	
0.0002		Industrial revolution	
	Holocene		
0.01		Agricultural revolution	
	Latest Pleistocene		
0.045		*Homo sapiens sapiens* (anatomically modern) appears	Paleolithic period (from first manufacture of stone tools to shortly before the development of agriculture)
	Late Pleistocene		
0.080		*H. sapiens neanderthalensis* appears	
	Middle Pleistocene		
0.400		Archaic *H. sapiens* appears	
1.6	Early Pleistocene	*H. erectus* present	
2.0		*H. habilis* present	
	Pliocene	Australopithecine divergence	
4.5		Bipedal *Australopithecus afarensis* present	
	Late Miocene		
7.5		Hominid–pongid divergence (inferred from molecular data)	
11			
	Middle Miocene	African and Asian hominoids diverge	
17			
	Early Miocene	Hominoid radiation begins	
24			

*Modified slightly from the "1984 consensus" of paleontologists, as presented by Pilbeam.[1]

to the age of 60 years or more remain relatively free from these disorders, unlike their "civilized" counterparts.[9,11,12]

NUTRITIONAL EVOLUTION

The ancestral mammals were insectivores, and invertebrate predation was thus the basis from which primate feeding behavior evolved.[13] However, as the primate order expanded and body size increased, vegetable foods became increasingly important for most species. During the Miocene era (from about 24 to about 5 million years ago) fruits appear to have been the main dietary constituent for hominids,[14] but their fossilized dental remains seem suitable for mastication of both animal and vegetable material.[15] After the divergence of the human and ape lines (now thought to have occurred between 7.5 and 4.5 million years ago)[1] our ancestral feeding pattern included increasing amounts of meat, although it is uncertain whether this change reflects hunting, scavenging, or both.[16,17] It is now thought that *Homo habilis* began to manufacture stone

tools about 2 million years ago and that the succeeding species, *Homo erectus,* began to consume a much larger amount of meat between 1.8 and 1.6 million years ago.[18–20] It is clear that thereafter early human beings consumed a considerable amount of meat: large accumulations of animal remains are found where they lived, the tools they used were mainly geared toward processing game, and their living sites were selectively located in areas where there was a relatively substantial biomass of large grazing animals. The importance of vegetable foods is harder to assess, since plant remains are poorly preserved. Fossilized fruit pits and nuts are commonly found, but tools for processing plant foods are conspicuously absent in comparison with their widespread proliferation in later prehistory.[21] Shells and fish bones are unknown in archaeological material dating from before 130,000 years ago[22] and are found infrequently in material dating from before 20,000 years ago, so that, in paleontological terms, widespread use of aquatic foods is a recent phenomenon.[23]

Several authorities have estimated that *Homo erectus* and early *Homo sapiens* obtained over 50 per cent of their diet from plant sources.[24,25] However, when the Cro-Magnons and other truly modern human beings appeared, concentration on big-game hunting increased; techniques and equipment were fully developed while the human population was still small in relation to the biomass of available fauna.[26] In some areas during this time meat probably provided over 50 per cent of the diet.[27] But because of overhunting, climate changes, and population growth, the period shortly before the inception of agriculture and animal husbandry was marked by a shift away from big-game hunting and toward a broader spectrum of subsistence activities. Remains of fish, shellfish, and small game are all more common at sites dating from this period, as well as tools that are useful for processing plant foods, such as grindstones, mortars, and pestles.[23] In at least two Middle Eastern sites, trace-element analysis for strontium levels in bone reveals a definite increase in the amount of vegetable material in the diet together with decreased meat consumption at this time.[28] Modern hunter-gatherers most closely resemble the human beings of this relatively recent period.

Agriculture markedly altered human nutritional patterns: over the course of a few millennia the proportion of meat declined drastically while vegetable foods came to make up as much as 90 per cent of the diet.[27] This shift had prominent morphologic consequences: early European *Homo sapiens sapiens*, who enjoyed an abundance of animal protein 30,000 years ago, were an average of six inches taller than their descendants who lived after the development of farming.[29] The same pattern was repeated later in the New World: the Paleoindians were big-game hunters 10,000 years ago, but their descendants in the period just before European contact practiced intensive food production, ate little meat, were considerably shorter,[30] and had skeletal manifestations of suboptimal nutrition,[31–34] which apparently reflect both the direct effects of protein–calorie deficiency and the synergistic interaction between malnutrition and infection.[35] Since the Industrial Revolution, the animal-protein content of Western diets has become more nearly adequate, as indicated by increased average height: we are now nearly as tall as were the first biologically modern human beings. However, our diets still differ markedly from theirs, and these differences lie at the heart of what has been termed "affluent malnutrition."[6]

RECENT HUNTER-GATHERER NUTRITION

Over 50 hunter-gatherer societies have been studied extensively enough to justify some nutritional generalizations about them,[36–38] but only a handful have survived into the second half of the 20th century and have

had their diets thoroughly analyzed. In general, groups of hunter-gatherers who, like the earliest human beings, live in an inland, semitropical habitat derive between 50 and 80 per cent of their food (by weight) from plants, with animal sources providing between 20 and 50 per cent.[38] These generalizations hold true for the Hadza of Tanzania[39] (who obtain 20 per cent of their diet from animals), the !Kung[37] (37 per cent) and ≠Kade[40] (20 per cent) San (Bushmen) of the Kalahari, and the Philippine Tasaday[41] (42 per cent), though before contact with Western civilization, the Tasaday were probably less successful hunters. The recently investigated Aché of Paraguay[42] (80 per cent) represent a possible exception, but their setting is so unusual and so affected by contact with more modern economies that they are very unlikely to be representative. Coastal and riverine peoples derive from 10 to 50 per cent of their food from fishing; for example, the Australian Aborigines of Arnhem Land get about 40 per cent of their total intake from fish and shellfish, whereas only a quarter comes from plants.[43,44] Because of their harsh environment, Arctic hunters, such as the aboriginal Eskimos, obtain less than 10 per cent of their food from vegetation.[45] In comparison with the majority of paleolithic human beings, existing hunter-gatherers occupy marginal habitats,[26] and their lives differ in many ways from those of people living before the advent of agriculture. Nevertheless, the range and content of foods they consume are similar (in the sense that they represent wild game and uncultivated vegetable foods) to those that our ancestors ate for up to 4 million years. Thus, an analysis of the nutritional content of these foods can provide a rational basis for estimating what human beings are genetically "programmed" to eat, digest, and metabolize.

MEAT

Paleolithic populations obtained their animal protein from wild game, especially gregarious ungulate herbivores, such as deer, bison, horses, and mammoths. The nutritional quality of such meat differs considerably from that of meat available in the modern American supermarket; the latter has much more fat—in subcutaneous tissue, in fascial planes, and as marbling within the muscle itself.[46] Domesticated animals have always been fatter than their wild ancestors because of their steady food supply and reduced physical activity, but recent breeding and feeding practices have further increased the proportion of fat to satisfy our desire for tender meat.[47–49] These efforts have succeeded: modern high-fat carcasses are 25 to 30 per cent fat or even more.[47] In contrast, a survey of 15 different species of free-living African herbivores revealed a mean carcass fat content of only 3.9 per cent.[50] Not only is there more fat in domesticated animals, its composition is different; wild game contains over five times more polyunsaturated fat per gram than is found in domestic livestock.[51,52] Furthermore, the fat of wild animals contains an appreciable amount (approximately 4 per cent) of eicosapentaenoic acid (C20:5), a long-chain, polyunsaturated, ω3 fatty acid currently under investigation because of its apparent antiatherosclerotic properties.[53,54] Domestic beef contains almost undetectable amounts of this nutrient.[53]

Meat from free-living animals has fewer calories and more protein per unit of weight than meat from domesticated animals,[40,51,55,56] but the amino acid composition of muscle tissue from each source is similar.[51] Since the cholesterol content of fat is roughly equivalent to that of lean tissue,[57] the cholesterol content of game would not be expected to differ substantially from that of commercially available meat. A detailed list of selected nutritional characteristics of 25 wild animal species is available from us.

VEGETABLE FOODS

Except for Eskimos and other high-latitude peoples, hunter-gatherers typically use many species of wild plants for food.[36,39,40] Roots, beans, nuts, tubers, and fruits are the most common major dietary constituents, but others, ranging from flowers to edible gums, are occasionally consumed. Small cereal grains, which have been staples for "civilized" peoples since the Agricultural Revolution, make a surprisingly minor contribution overall; however, the wide range of vegetable foods eaten by foragers contrasts with the relatively narrow variety of crops produced by horticulturists and traditional agriculturalists. Furthermore, many domesticated food plants have higher ratios of starch to protein than do their wild forms.[58] The nutrient composition of the wild vegetable foods most commonly consumed by the !Kung,[59] and ≠Kade[40] San, Hadza,[60] Australian Aborigines,[61–63] and Tasaday[41] has been determined. A detailed list of the individual nutritional contents of all 44 items is available from us; average values of selected nutrients are shown in Table 2.

PROBABLE DAILY NUTRITION FOR PALEOLITHIC HUMAN BEINGS

Representative nutrient values for wild game and vegetable foods consumed by recent hunter-gatherers

Table 2. Nutritional values (mean ± S.E.) of 44 wild vegetable foods* consumed by the !Kung[59] and ≠ Kade[40] San, Hadza,[60] Tasaday,[41] and Australian Aborigines[61–63]

Content	Nutritional Value
Protein (g/100 g)	4.13 ± 1.04
Fat (g/100 g)	2.84 ± 1.54
Carbohydrate (g/100 g)	22.79 ± 3.15
Fiber (g/100 g)	3.12 ± 0.62
Energy (kcal)	128.76 ± 21.17

*The foods include 2 beans, 2 nuts, 11 roots, 1 rhizome, 2 leaf buds, 1 stalk, 2 melons, 1 seed pod, 2 berries, 1 truffle, 7 tubers, 11 fruits, and 1 corm

can be derived from the literature.[40,41,50,51,55,56,59–71] In turn, these figures can be used to estimate the daily nutrient intake for paleolithic human beings. Estimates of energy intake and various animal:vegetable ratios in subsistence patterns can be generated. Although the specific dietary constituents used by any particular group of preagricultural human beings must have varied with ambient conditions, average nutrient values should reflect central tendencies transcending these effects.

Energy Sources

Game and wild plants yield an average of 1.41 and 1.29 kcal per gram, respectively.[40,41,50,51,55,56,59–71] We can estimate the weight of animal and plant food consumed by assuming a daily energy intake of, say, 3000 kcal,[72] and a subsistence pattern of 35 per cent meat[36,73] and calculating as follows. The daily weight of animal food, in grams, multiplied by 1.41 kcal per gram plus the daily weight of plant food multiplied by 1.29 kcal per gram must equal 3000 kcal. In this model, animal food is 35 per cent and plant food is 65 per cent of the total weight of food eaten. If x is the total weight of food, then:

$$1.41(0.35x) + 1.29(0.65x) = 3000$$
$$x = 2252 \text{ g}$$

(These figures suggest a degree of precision that is of course unwarranted. They are presented simply as the results generated by this particular model.) Under these idealized and probably intermittent isocaloric conditions, the total daily food intake of 2252 g would have been provided by 788.2 g of game and 1463.8 g of vegetable food. On the basis of these calculations and

Table 3. Proposed average daily macronutrient intake for late paleolithic human beings consuming a 3000-kcal diet containing 35 per cent meat and 65 per cent vegetable foods

	Intake (g)
Protein	**251.1**
Animal	190.7
Vegetable	60.4
Fat	**71.3**
Animal	29.7
Vegetable	41.6
Carbohydrate	333.4.6
Fiber	45.7

mean nutrient values, the average daily nutrient intake for paleolithic human beings can be reconstructed as shown in Table 3.

Fat and Fatty Acids

The fat from Cape buffalo is 30 per cent polyunsaturated, 32 per cent monounsaturated, and 38 per cent saturated.[51] Assuming a similar ratio for wild game in general, the animal fat in a reconstructed paleolithic diet would provide 8.91 g of polyunsaturated fatty acids and 11.29 g of saturated fatty acids. The fat in 36 wild vegetable foods used by the Hadza,[60] San (Bushmen),[74] and other African tribal groups[75] is 38.7 per cent polyunsaturated, on average. If a similar figure can be assumed for wild vegetable fat generally, then the plant foods in this paleolithic dietary example would yield 16.1 g of polyunsaturated fatty acids. In 24 American vegetable foods saturated fatty acids constitute 15.6 per cent of total fat.[56] If the proportion in wild plants is similar, then a paleolithic diet containing 35 per cent meat and 65 per cent vegetables would contribute 6.49 g of saturated vegetable fat, and the overall ratio of polyunsaturated to saturated fats for a day's total (animal and vegetable) fat intake would be 1.41.

Cholesterol

Meat from modern domesticated animals has an average of 75 mg of cholesterol in each 100-g portion.[56] The cholesterol content of meat from wild game should be similar, since the proportion of cholesterol in meat is surprisingly unaffected by the fat content.[57] Thus, pa-

leolithic human beings consuming 788.2 g of meat in a day would have ingested 591.2 mg of cholesterol.

Sodium and Potassium

The sodium and potassium content for 14 vegetable foods used by recent hunter-gatherers is known.[40,41,59] These foods have an average of 10.1 mg of sodium and 550 mg of potassium, respectively, for each 100-g portion. If these values are representative, the daily average of 1463.8 mg of paleolithic vegetable food would have yielded 147.8 mg of sodium. Data on the sodium and potassium content of wild game are unavailable, but if the average values for beef, lamb, pork, and veal (68.75 mg of sodium and 387.5 mg of potassium per 100 g)[56] are assumed to be comparable to those for meat from wild animals, then the 788.2 g of meat in a 35:65 (meat:vegetable) paleolithic diet would have provided 541.9 mg of sodium, for a daily total of 689.7 mg. The overall ratio of dietary potassium to sodium would have been 16.1 to 1.0.

Calcium

The calcium content of 37 plant foods consumed by recent foragers averages 102.5 mg for each 100 g,[40,59,61,62] so the daily provision of calcium from vegetable sources would have been 1500.4 mg in the paleolithic diet. Venison and the meat of most domesticated animals contain about 10 mg of calcium per 100 g of tissue,[56] so meat in a 35:65 paleolithic diet would have yielded an additional 78.8 mg, for a daily grand total of 1579.2 mg of calcium.

Ascorbic Acid

The mean ascorbic acid content of 27 vegetables eaten[40,59–62] by recent hunter-gatherers is 26.8 mg per 100 g, so that the average vitamin C intake would have been 392.3 mg each day in paleolithic diets conforming to this pattern. (This calculation excludes the Australian green plum,[62] which has the highest known vitamin C content [3150 mg per 100 g] and would tend to inflate the estimate.)

Other Nutrients

Even at the lowest estimate of the ratio of meat to plant food (20:80), by modern standards, the estimated paleolithic diet would have been adequate in animal protein, iron, vitamin B_{12}, and folate, whereas agricultural populations of the underdeveloped world in the 20th century have widespread deficiencies in these nutrients.

Because of seasonal and local variation, among other factors, populations that subsist by collecting food invariably have a greater variety of plant foods than is typical for agricultural populations.[13] This variety would have ensured a gradual accumulation of most of the necessary trace elements found in plant foods, despite differing concentrations in different sources. However, the possibility of geographically limited deficiencies in certain nutrients (e.g., iodine) cannot be ruled out.

Fiber

Because of the relatively high proportion of vegetable foods and the primitive character of food processing, paleolithic diets must have included substantially more nondigestible fiber than do typical Western diets. The average fiber content of 37 wild plant foods for which information on fiber content is available is 3.12 ± 0.62 g per 100 g (mean $\pm$S.E.). For a paleolithic diet containing 65 per cent vegetable foods, the estimated fiber content would have been 45.7 g.

Shortages

The majority of preindustrial societies, including those based on hunting and gathering, experience seasonal nutritional stress and occasional (less frequent than annual) severe shortages. Although the paleolithic period was almost certainly characterized by conditions of greater abundance, both in game and plant foods, than those experienced by recent hunter-gatherers,[26] it is nevertheless likely that paleolithic populations experienced infrequent shortages sufficient to produce weight loss and to threaten survival in persons with inadequate adipose reserves. It would have been adaptive to consume more calories than the minimal daily requirement and to store fat during periods of relative abundance. This pattern is in fact observed among recent hunter-gatherers,[76,77] although its magnitude is not known.[37]

Subsistence data from 58 technologically primitive societies reveal that the mean, median, and mode for recent foragers converge on a dietary ratio of 35 per cent meat and 65 per cent vegetable foods.[36,73] Of course, the paleolithic diet was not fixed; it varied in its individual components, as well as in its relative proportions of animal and vegetable foodstuffs. For these rea-

Table 4. Estimated nutritional characteristics for various animal:vegetable subsistence patterns

	Animal:Vegetable Ratio			
	20:80	40:60	60:40	80:20*
Total dietary energy (%)				
Protein	24.5	37	49	61
Carbohydrate	55	41	28	14
Fat	20.5	22	23	25
P:S ratio†	1.72	1.33	1.08	0.91
Cholesterol (mg)	343	673	991	1299

*For a 3000-kcal diet, an 80:20 subsistence pattern would require an intake of 437 g of protein per day. Urea synthesis and its accompanying obligate water loss place an approximate upper limit of about 400 g of protein per day for a steady diet. This suggests that with animal:vegetable subsistence patterns of this magnitude, the animals eaten were probably fatter (e.g., for hibernation or cold insulation) than those described in the text. This inference, in turn, is consistent with high proportions of meat consumed only by hunter-gatherers in the higher latitudes.

†P:S denotes polyunsaturated:saturated fats.

sons, the use of average nutrient values derived from items used by different groups of contemporary hunter-gatherers is more helpful than an analysis of any one group's diet. The mean values can be used to estimate nutritional characteristics for widely varying subsistence patterns (Table 4).

THE PALEOLITHIC DIET IN MODERN PERSPECTIVE

Whether based on as much as 80 per cent or as little as 20 per cent meat, the paleolithic diet differed substantially from the typical diet in the United States today, and it also differed, although much less so, from that currently advocated by nutritionists and by the U.S. government[78] (Table 5). The foods we eat are usually divided into four basic groups: meat and fish, vegetables and fruit, milk and milk products, and breads and cereals. Two or more daily servings from each are now considered necessary for a balanced diet, but adults living before the development of agriculture and animal husbandry derived all their nutrients from the first two food groups; they apparently consumed cereal grains rarely, if at all, and they had no dairy foods whatsoever. Nevertheless, with a diet containing 35 per cent meat, their calcium intake would have far exceeded the highest estimate of the minimal daily requirement. Neanderthals and Cro-Magnons who inhabited subarctic Eurasia and whose diet is considered to have been

Table 5. Comparison of the late paleolithic diet,* the current American diet, and U.S. dietary recommendations

	Late Paleolithic Diet	Current American Diet[78]	U.S. Senate Select Committee Recommendations[78]
Total dietary energy (%)			
Protein	34	12	12
Carbohydrate	45	46	58
Fat	21	42	30
P:S ratio[†]	1.41	0.44	1.00
Cholesterol (mg)	591	600	300
Fiber (g)	45.7	19.7[‡]	30–60[79]
Sodium (mg)	690	2300–6900[80]	1100–3300[80]
Calcium (mg)	1580	740[§]	800–1200[¶]
Ascorbic acid (mg)	392.3	87.7[§]	45[¶]

*Assuming the diet contained 35 per cent meat and 65 per cent vegetables.

†P:S denotes polyunsaturated:saturated fats.

‡British National Food Survey, 1976.

§U.S. Department of Agriculture Food Consumption Survey, 1977–1978.

¶Recommended Daily Dietary Allowance, Food and Nutrition Board, National Academy of Sciences–National Research Council.

most like that of the Eskimos, among recent populations, had massive bones, indicating that they obtained sufficient calcium. The probable paleolithic intake of dietary fiber was much higher than ours and approached that common in rural Africa, where disease conditions linked with deficient dietary fiber rarely occur,[79] although paleolithic human beings obtained their fiber predominantly from fruits and vegetables rather than grain. A paleolithic diet consisting of 35 per cent meat would have contained only a sixth of the sodium in the typical American diet—a third of the level most recently recommended.[80] Even in a diet with 80 per cent meat, the sodium intake would have just reached the lowest recommended level and would have been markedly below the lowest estimate of current intake. Given the typically wide variety of collected plant foods and assuming ascorbic acid to be representative, the vitamin intake of paleolithic human beings would have substantially exceeded ours, irrespective of the proportion of meat in the diet.

In the hunting society of our ancestors meat provided a large fraction of each day's food, ensuring high iron and folate levels. Protein contributed twice to nearly five times the proportion of total calories that it does for Americans. Their high-meat diet contained a high level of cholesterol—similar to or even higher than the level in our diet; most paleolithic human beings must have greatly exceeded the U.S. Senate Select Committee's recommended cholesterol level.[78] Conversely, they ate much less fat than we do, and the fat they ate was substantially different from ours.

Whether subsistence was based predominantly on meat or on vegetable foods, the paleolithic diet had less total fat, more essential fatty acids, and a much higher ratio of polyunsaturated to saturated fats than ours does. In comparison with us, our paleolithic ancestors consumed more structural and less depot fat.

The extent to which some of the major chronic diseases of industrialized society are related to the typical Western diet is controversial, but evidence for an important linkage is steadily accumulating. Medical researchers in diverse fields are beginning to define a generally preventive diet—one of benefit against conditions ranging from atherosclerosis to cancer. Such investigations are converging in several ways with the studies of paleontologists and anthropologists. Ultimately, of course, only experimental and clinical studies can confirm hypotheses about the medical consequences of dietary choices. Nevertheless, it is both intellectually satisfying and heuristically valuable to estimate the typical diet that human beings were adapted to consume during the long course of our evolution. Points of convergence between this estimate and modern recommendations are encouraging, and points of divergence suggest new lines of research. The diet of our remote ancestors may be a reference standard for modern human nutrition and a model for defense against certain "diseases of civilization."

♦ ♦ ♦

We are indebted to Denis Burkitt, George Cahill, Irven DeVore, Richard Lee, John R. K. Robson, Margaret J. Schoeninger, Pat Shipman, Marjorie Shostak, and Alan Walker for helpful comments, and to Debra Fey for assistance in preparing it.

REFERENCES

1. Pilbeam D. The descent of hominoids and hominids. Sci Am 1984; 250:84–96.
2. Rendel JM. The time scale of genetic change. In: Boyden SV, ed. The impact of civilization on the biology of man. Canberra, Australia: Australian National University Press, 1970:27–47.
3. Cavalli-Sforza, LL. Human evolution and nutrition. In: Walcher DN, Kretchmer N, eds. Food, nutrition and evolution: food as an environmental factor in the genesis of human variability. New York: Masson, 1981:1–7.
4. Yudkin J. Archaeology and the nutritionist. In: Ucko PJ, Dimbley GW, eds. The domestication and exploitation of plants and animals. Chicago: Aldine, 1969:547–52.
5. Mayer J. Nutrition and civilization. Trans NY Acad Sci 1967; 29:1014–32.
6. Trowell H. Hypertension, obesity, diabetes mellitus and coronary heart disease. In: Trowell HC, Burkitt DP, eds. Western diseases: their emergence and prevention. Cambridge, Mass.: Harvard University Press, 1981:3–32.
7. Enos WF, Holmes RH, Beyer J. Coronary disease among United States soldiers killed in action in Korea. JAMA 1953; 152:1090–3.
8. Schaefer O. Medical observations and problems in the Canadian arctic. Can Med Assoc J 1959; 81:386–93.
9. Moodie PM. Aboriginal health. Canberra, Australia: Australian National University Press, 1973:92.
10. Velican D, Velican C. Atherosclerotic involvement of the coronary arteries of adolescents and young adults. Atherosclerosis 1980; 36:449–60.
11. Truswell AS, Hansen JDL. Medical research among the !Kung. In: Lee RB, DeVore I, eds. Kalahari hunter-gatherers. Cambridge, Mass.: Harvard University Press, 1976:166–94.
12. Arthaud JB. Cause of death in 339 Alaskan natives as determined by autopsy. Arch Pathol 1970; 90:433–8.
13. Hladik CM. Diet and the evolution of feeding strategies among forest primates. In: Harding RSO, Teleki G. Omnivorous primates: gathering and hunting in human evolution. New York: Columbia University Press, 1981:215–54.
14. Kay R. Diets of early Miocene African hominoids. Nature 1977; 268:628–30.
15. Stini WA. Body composition and nutrient reserves in evolutionary perspective. In: Walcher DN, Kretchmer N, eds. Food, nutrition, and evolution: food as an environmental factor in the genesis of human variability. New York: Masson, 1981:107–20.
16. Hill K. Hunting and human evolution. J Hum Evolut 1982; 11:521–44.
17. Shipman P. Early hominid lifestyle: hunting and gathering or foraging and scavenging? In: Clutton-Brock J, Grigson C, eds. Animals and archaeology: hunters and their prey. Oxford: BAR, 1983:31–49.
18. Bunn HT. Archaeological evidence for meat-eating by Plio-Pleistocene hominids from Koobi Fora and Olduvai Gorge. Nature 1981; 291:574–7.
19. Potts R, Shipman P. Cutmarks made by stone tools on bones from Olduvai Gorge, Tanzania. Nature 1981; 291:577–80.
20. Walker A, Zimmerman MR, Leakey REF. A possible case of hypervitaminosis A in Homo erectus. Nature 1982; 296:248–50.
21. Kraybill N. Preagricultural tools for the preparation of foods in the old world. In: Reed CA, ed. Origins of agriculture. The Hague: Mouton, 1977:485–521.
22. Klein RG. Stone age exploitation of animals in Southern Africa. Am Sci 1979; 67:151–60.
23. Cohen MN. The food crisis in prehistory: over population and origins of agriculture. New Haven, Conn.: Yale University Press, 1977.
24. Howell FC, Clark JD. Acheulian hunter-gatherers of sub-Saharan Africa. In: Howell FC, Bourliere F, eds. African ecology and human evolution. Chicago: Aldine, 1963:458–533.
25. Isaac GLI, Crader DC. To what extent were early hominids carnivorous?: an archaeological perspective. In: Harding RSO, Teleki G, eds. Omnivorous primates: gathering and hunting in human evolution. New York: Columbia University Press, 1981:37–103.
26. Foley R. A reconsideration of the role of predation on large mammals in tropical hunter-gatherer adaptation. Man 1982; 17:393–402.
27. MacNeish RS. A summary of the subsistence. In: Byers DS, ed. The prehistory of the Tehuacan Valley. Vol. 1. Austin. Tex.: University of Texas Press, 1967:290–309.
28. Schoeninger MJ. Diet and the evolution of modern human form in the Middle East. Am J Phys Anthropol 1982; 58:37–52.
29. Angel JL. Paleoecology, paleodemography and health. In: Polgar S, ed. Population, ecology and social evolution. The Hague: Mouton, 1975:167–90.
30. Nickens PR. Stature reduction as an adaptive response to food production in Mesoamerica. J Archaeol Sci 1976; 3:31–41.
31. Buikstra JE. Biocultural dimensions of archaeological study: a regional perspective. In: Blakely RL, ed. Biocultural adaptations in prehistoric America. Athens, Ga.: University of Georgia Press, 1977:67–84.
32. Larsen CS. Skeletal and dental adaptations to the shift to agriculture on the Georgia coast. Curr Anthropol 1981; 22:422–3.
33. Cassidy CM. Nutrition and health in agriculturalists and hunter-gatherers: a case study of two prehistoric populations. In: Jerome RF, Pelto GH, eds. Nutritional anthropology: contemporary approaches to diet and culture. Pleasantville, N.Y.: Redgrave, 1980:117–45.
34. Cook DC. Subsistence base and health in prehistoric Illinois Valley: evidence from the human skeleton. Med Anthropol 1979; 3:109–24.
35. Scrimshaw NS, Taylor CE, Gordon JE. Interactions of nutrition and infection. Am J Med Sci 1959; 237:367–403.

36. Lee RB. What hunters do for a living, or, how to make out on scarce resources. In: Lee RB, DeVore I, eds. Man the hunter. Chicago: Aldine, 1968:30–48.

37. *Idem.* The !Kung San: men, women, and work in a foraging society. New York: Cambridge University Press, 1979.

39. Gaulin SJC, Konner M. On the natural diet of primates, including humans. In: Wurtman RJ, Wurtman JJ, eds. Nutrition and the brain. Vol. 1. New York: Raven Press. 1977:1–86.

39. Woodburn J. An introduction to Hadza ecology. In: Lee RB, DeVore I, eds. Man the hunter. Chicago: Aldine, 1968:49–55.

40. Tanaka J. The San, hunter-gatherers of the Kalahari: a study in ecological anthropology. New York: Columbia University Press, 1980.

41. Robson JRK, Yen DE. Some nutritional aspects of Philippine Tasaday diet. In: Robson JRK, ed. Food, ecology and culture. New York: Gordon Breech, 1980:1–7.

42. Hawkes K, Hill K, O'Connell JF. Why hunters gather: optimal foraging and the Aché of eastern Paraguay. Am Ethnol 1982; 9:379–98.

43. McArthur M. Food consumption and dietary levels of groups of Aborigines living on naturally occurring foods. In: Mountford CP, ed. Records of the American-Australian scientific expedition to Arnhem Land. Vol. 2. Melbourne: Melbourne University Press, 1960:90–135.

44. Meehan B. Hunters by the seashore. J Hum Evolut 1977; 6:363–70.

45. Draper HH. The aboriginal Eskimo diet in modern perspective. Am Anthropol 1977; 79:309–316.

46. Wittwer SH. Altering fat content of animal products through genetics, nutrition, and management. In: National Research Council. Fat content and composition of animal products. Washington, D.C.: National Academy of Sciences, 1976:80–4.

47. Byerly TC. Effects of agricultural practices on foods of animal origin. In: Harris RS, Karmas E, eds. Nutritional evaluation of food processing. 2nd ed. Westport, Conn.: Avi, 1975:58–97.

48. Smith GC, Carpenter ZL. Eating quality of meat animal products and their fat content. In: National Research Council. Fat content and composition of animal products. Washington, D.C.: National Academy of Sciences, 1976:147–82.

49. Allen CE, Mackey MA. Compositional characteristics and the potential for change in foods of animal origin. In: Beitz DC, Hansen RG, eds. Animal products in human nutrition. New York: Academic Press, 1982:199–224.

50. Ledger HP. Body composition as a basis for a comparative study of some East African mammals. Symp Zool Soc Lond 1968; 21:289–310.

51. Crawford MA. Fatty-acid ratios in free-living and domestic animals. Lancet 1968; 1:1329–33.

52. Wo CKW, Draper HH. Vitamin E status of Alaskan Eskimos. Am J Clin Nutr 1975; 28:808–13.

53. Crawford MA, Gale MM, Woodford MH. Linoleic acid and linolenic acid elongation products in muscle tissue of *Syncerus caffer* and other ruminant species. Biochem J 1969; 115:25–7.

54. Dyerberg J, Bank HO, Stoffersen E, Moncada ES, Vane JR. Eicosapentaenoic acid and prevention of thrombosis and atherosclerosis? Lancet 1978; 2:117–9.

55. Deethardt D. The best of bison. Brookings, S.D.: South Dakota State University Press, 1973.

56. Watt BK, Merrill AL. Composition of foods. (Agriculture handbook no. 8). Washington, D.C.: United States Department of Agriculture, 1975.

57. Feeley RM, Criner PE, Watt BK. Cholesterol content of foods. J Am Diet Assoc 1972; 61:134–49.

58. Harris RS. Effects of agricultural practices on foods of plant origin. In: Harris RS, Karmas, E., eds. Nutritional evaluation of food processing. 2nd ed. Westport, Conn.: Avi, 1975:33–57.

59. Wehmeyer AS, Lee RB, Whiting M. The nutrient composition and dietary importance of some vegetable foods eaten by the !Kung Bushmen. S Afr Med J 1969; 43:1529–30.

60. Wehmeyer AS. The nutrient composition of some edible wild fruits found in the Transvaal. S Afr Med J 1966; 40:1102–4.

61. Fysch CF, Hodges KJ, Siggins LY. Analysis of naturally occurring foodstuffs of Arnhem Land. In: Mountford CP, ed. Records of the American-Australian scientific expedition to Arnhem Land. Vol. 2. Melbourne: Melbourne University Press, 1960:136–9.

62. Brand JC, Cherikoff V, Lee A, McDonnel J. Nutrients in important bush foods. Proc Nutr Soc Austr 1982; 7:50–4.

63. Harris DR. Subsistence strategies across Torres Strait. In: Allen J, Jones R, eds. Sunda and Sahul: prehistoric studies in Southeast Asia, Melanesia and Australia. London: Academic Press, 1977:421–63.

64. Crawford MA, Gale MM, Woodford MH. Muscle and adipose tissue lipids of the warthog, *Phacohoerus aethiopicus*. Int J Biochem 1970; 1:654–8.

65. Ashbrook FG. Butchering, processing, and preservation of meat. New York: Van Nostrand Reinhold, 1955:37.

66. Cook BB, Witham LE, Olmstead M, Morgan AF. The influence of seasonal and other factors on the acceptability and food value of meat of two subspecies of California deer and of antelope. Hilgardia 1949; 19:265–84.

67. Berkes F, Farkas CS. Eastern James Bay Cree Indians: changing patterns of wild food use and nutrition. Ecol Food Nutr 1978; 7:155–72.

68. Wilber CG, Gorski TW. The lipids in *Bison bison.* J Mammol 1955; 36:305–8.

69. Morris EA, Witkind WM, Dix RL, Jacobson J. Nutritional contents of selected aboriginal foods in northeastern Colorado: buffalo (*Bison bison*) and wild onions (*Allium spp.*) J Ethnobiol 1981; 1:213–20.

70. Smith NS. Appraisal of condition estimation methods for East African ungulates. East Afr Wildlife J 1970; 8:123–9.

71. McCulloch JSG, Talbot LM. Comparison of weight estimation methods for wild animals and domestic livestock. J Appl Ecol 1965; 2:59–69.

72. Montgomery E. Towards representative energy data: the Machiguenga Study. Fed Proc 1978; 37:61–4.

73. Hayden B. Subsistence and ecological adaptations of modern hunter-gatherers. In: Harding RDS, Teleki G, eds. Omnivorous primates: gathering and hunting in human evolution. New York: Columbia University Press, 1981:344–421.

74. Engelter C, Wehmeyer AS. Fatty acid composition of oils of some edible seeds of wild plants. J Agric Food Chem 1970; 18:25–6.

75. Busson F. Plantes alimentaires de l'Ouest Africain. Marseilles: Lecont, 1965.

76. Wilmsen EN. Seasonal effects of dietary intake on Kalahari San. Fed Proc 1978; 37:65–72.

77. Speth JD, Spielmann KA, Energy source, protein metabolism, and hunter-gatherer subsistence strategies. J Anthropol Archaeol 1983; 2:1–31.

78. Select Committee on Nutrition and Human Needs, United States Senate. Dietary goals for the United States. Washington, D.C.: Government Printing Office, 1977.

79. Mendeloff AI. Dietary fiber and human health. N Engl J Med 1977; 297:811–4.

80. Marsh AC, Klippstein RN, Kaplan SD. The sodium content of your food. Washington, D.C.: United States Department of Agriculture, 1980.

10

Junk Food Monkeys

Robert M. Sapolsky

Few of us think much about Jean-Jacques Rousseau these days. We remember his noble savage, his idealized view of mankind in its primordial splendor, when life was gentle, innocent, and natural. Not that most of us reject Rousseau's thinking; it's just that amid the bustle and ambition of the Me Generation and Reagan's eighties, it no longer seems fashionable to ponder the possibly superior moral state of primordial humans.

Their possibly superior physical state, however, is an issue of more than passing concern, and here a Rousseauean view of sorts continues to hold sway—a view, that is, with an eighties spin. As a society that spends billions of dollars on medical care, health clubs, and looking good, what we want to know is: How was the physical health of primordial humans? What was their secret workout regimen for achieving their beautiful precivilized bodies? What were cholesterol levels like in the Garden of Eden?

Many think that in certain respects early humans fared better than we do. When you subtract the accidents, infections, and infantile diseases that beset them, our forebears might not have had it so bad. In a 1985 article in the *New England Journal of Medicine,* physician-anthropologists S. Boyd Eaton and Melvin Konner did an ingenious job of reconstructing the likely diet of our Paleolithic ancestors, and they concluded that there was much to be said for the high-fiber, low-salt, low-fat diet their evidence suggested.

Anthropologists studying the hunter-gatherers in the Kalahari Desert, a group that's believed to retain the way of life of earlier humans, have come to similar conclusions. Among the !Kung, for example, some maladies that we view as a normal part of human aging are proving not to be obligatory after all: hearing acuity is not lost, blood pressure and cholesterol levels do not rise, degenerative heart disease doesn't seem to develop. As we sit here amid our ulcers and hypertension and hardening arteries, it is getting harder for us to avoid the uncomfortable suspicion that we have fallen from a state of metabolic grace.

For the past decade I have been observing a group of some of our closest relatives as they fell from their own primordial metabolic grace into something resembling our nutritional decadence. My subjects are olive baboons living in the Masai Mara National Reserve in the Serengeti Plain of Kenya.

Chiefly I'm interested in the relationships between their social behavior and dominance rank, the amount of social stress the baboons experience, and how their bodies react to it. Certainly I didn't set out to investigate the relevance of eighteenth-century French philosophy to twentieth-century American life by looking at a timeless primate society in the African plains. But to study the questions I am interested in, I have to combine extensive behavioral observations with some basic lab work: drawing the animals' blood, measuring hormones, monitoring blood pressure, and conducting other clinical tests to find out how their bodies are functioning. And in this context Rousseau reared his worrisome head.

Masai Mara is a wonderful place to be a researcher. It's a fairly idyllic place to be a baboon: a vast untouched landscape of savannas and woodlands and one of the last great refuges for wild animals left on Earth. Herds of wildebeest roam on the open plains, lions lounge beneath the flat-topped acacia trees, giraffes and zebras drink side by side at the watering places. Inevitably Masai Mara has also become an attractive place to tourists, resulting in all the usual problems that occur when large fluxes of people descend on previously virgin wilderness.

◆ ◆ ◆

One of the biggest problems here, as in our own national parks, is what to do with the garbage. The solution so far has been to dump much of it into large pits, 5 feet deep by 30 feet wide, hidden among trees in out-of-the-way areas. Brimming with food and refuse rotting in 100-degree heat, infested with flies and circled by vultures and hyenas, the pits look like a scene from a Hieronymus Bosch painting. One of the baboon troops I study had such a garden of earthly delights dumped right in the middle of its territory.

For the baboons this was a major change in fortune, the primatological equivalent, perhaps, of winning the lottery. A major concern in any wild animal's life is getting sufficient food, and an average baboon in the Serengeti spends 30 to 40 percent of each day foraging —climbing trees to reach fruits and leaves, digging laboriously in the ground to unearth tubers, walking five or ten miles to reach sources of food. Their diet is Spartan: figs and olives, grass and sedge parts, corms, tubers, and seedpods. It's unusual for them to hunt or scavenge, and meat accounts for less than one percent of the food they consume. So the typical baboon diet teems with fiber and is very low in fat, sugar, and cholesterol.

For the nouveau riche Garbage Dump troop, life changed dramatically. When I started observing them, in 1978, they had recently discovered the dump's existence and were making an occasional food run. By 1980 the entire group—some 80 animals, ranging from 25-year-old adults to newborn infants—had moved into new sleeping quarters in the trees surrounding the dump. Instead of stirring at dawn, these animals would typically stay in the trees, snoozing and grooming, and only rouse themselves in time to meet the 9 A.M. garbage tractor. The day's feeding would be finished after half an hour of communal frenzy over the pickings. But it was the pickings themselves that made the biggest difference in the baboons' lives.

Once, in the name of science, I donned lab gloves, held my breath, and astonished the tractor driver by methodically sifting through his moldering garbage. The refuse was certainly a far cry from tubers and leaves: fried drumsticks or a slab of beef left over by a tourist with eyes bigger than his stomach; fruit salad gone a bit bad, perhaps left too long on the sun-

drenched buffet table; fragments of pies and cakes, and alarming yellow dollops of custard pudding, nibbled at by a disciplined dieter—processed sugars, fat, starch, and cholesterol, our modern Four Horsemen of the Apocalypse.

And what were the physiological consequences for these baboons in Utopia? First the good news: Young baboons grew faster, reaching developmental landmarks such as puberty at earlier ages. These beneficial changes were exactly what one would expect of humans switching from a lean subsistence diet to a more affluent Westernized fare. In the countries of the West the age of first menstruation has declined from an estimated 15 years during the 1800s to our current average of about 12 and a half.

The trend in baboons has been particularly well documented by Jeanne Altmann of the University of Chicago, a biologist studying both foraging and garbage-eating troops in another park in Kenya. Among her animals, eating garbage has led to the onset of puberty at age three and a half instead of age five. Females now typically give birth for the first time at age five, a year and a half earlier than before. Moreover, because the infants develop faster, they are weaned earlier; consequently, females start menstruating again that much sooner, and once they resume, they conceive more quickly. Indeed, Altmann's garbage eaters have had something of a baby boom compared with their foraging cousins.

Another advantage of garbage eating became clear during the tragic East African drought of 1984. During that period wild game found life extremely difficult. The luckier animals merely spent more time and covered more distance in search of food. The less lucky starved and succumbed to diseases previously held in check. However, tourists did not starve, and neither did baboons living off their detritus.

So, at first glance, from the evolutionary standpoint of reproductive fitness, some daily custard pudding appears to do wonders, increasing reproductive rates and buffering the troop from famine. But now here's the bad news: some of the same lousy changes seen in humans eating Westernized fare also occurred in baboons.

Your average wild baboon eating a natural diet has cholesterol levels that would shame the most ectomorphic triathlete. University of Texas pathologist Glen Mott and I have studied a number of troops and found cholesterol levels averaging 66 milligrams in 100 cubic centimeters of blood among adult males. Not only that, but more than half the total cholesterol was in the form of high-density lipoproteins, the "good" type. In humans, cholesterol levels less than 150 with a third of the total in the high-density form are grounds for bragging at the health club.

But when we studied the Garbage Dump baboons, a different picture emerged. Cholesterol levels were nearly a third higher, and most of the increase was attributable to a rise in damaging low-density lipoproteins, the type that builds up plaque on artery walls.

Joseph Kemnitz, a primatologist at the Wisconsin Regional Primate Research Center, analyzed blood samples from these animals and found that levels of insulin were more than twice as high in the Garbage Dumpers as in those eating a natural diet. This hormone is secreted by the pancreas in response to eating, especially eating rich, sugary food, and its function is to tell cells to store glucose for future use as energy.

If insulin levels rise too high, however, cells become inured to its message; instead of being stored, glucose is left circulating in the bloodstream. It's this state of affairs that can eventually lead to adult-onset diabetes, a distinctly Western malady. Since the Garbage Dumpers came from gene stocks similar to those of the natural foragers, genetic differences couldn't account for their much higher insulin levels. The most likely suspect was their junk-food diet and their relative inactivity.

Are the Garbage Dumpers now at risk for diabetes and heart disease, candidates for celebrity diets and coronary bypasses? It is hard to tell; no one has ever reported adult-onset diabetes in wild baboons, but, then, no one has ever looked. Surprisingly, people have looked at the cardiovascular systems of wild baboons and found fatty deposits in their blood vessels and heart. Garbage Dumpers presumably run a higher risk of depositing fat in their arteries, but whether it will affect their health and life spans remains to be seen.

One major impact on the health of Garbage Dumpers became clear in a grim way, however. If you are going to spend your time around human garbage, you are going to have to deal with whatever that garbage has become infected with. And if these infectious agents are new to you, your immunological defenses are not likely to be very good.

A few years ago my Garbage Dump animals began to become dramatically ill. They wasted away, coughing up blood, losing the use of their limbs. Three veterinarians from the Institute of Primate Research in Nairobi—Ross Tarara, Mbaruk Suleman, and James Else—investigated the outbreak and traced it to bovine tuberculosis, probably from eating contaminated meat. It was the first time the disease had been reported in wild primates, and by the time it abated it had killed half the Garbage Dump troop. For them, there had been no free lunch after all.

Has the Westernization of these animals' diets thus been good or bad? This is much the same as questioning the benefits of our own Westernization. Toxic wastes and automatic weapons strike me as bad developments; on the other hand, vaccines, thermal underwear, and 70-year life expectancies seem like marvelous improvements upon the Middle Ages. All things considered, we seem to have benefited, at least from a health perspective.

For the baboons, too, the answer must be carefully considered. Growing fat is unwise if you plan to sit in an arboreal armchair but very wise if you're about to face a dry season. Similarly, a nice piece of meat is a fine thing during a famine, but not such a hot idea if it's contaminated.

It is platitudinous to say that this is a complicated issue, but it is clear that life for the foraging baboon is not one of pure Rousseauean ease, nor life for the garbage eaters one of unambiguous decline. My bias is that the latter's health has, on the whole, suffered from their garbage trove. But what has struck me in these studies is that there are also benefits and the judgment is somewhat difficult to make. It seems that for the baboon, just as for us, there are few unambiguous rules for figuring out what to do with the choices life throws in our lap.

Variation in Contemporary Food Systems: Pluses and Minuses

Anthropologists are interested in what our ancestors foraged for lunch, as well as how contemporary peoples living in different parts of the world obtain an adequate diet. Obtaining adequate food, in both the short and long terms, is fundamental to the survival of all animals, humans included. How do Turkana pastoralists living in an area of East Africa with so little rainfall that it is virtually a desert find enough to eat? How do Indians in small villages deep in the rain forests of the Amazon find enough to eat? There are no markets to buy food. What is their diet like? How could it be that small farmers in some developing countries do not get enough to eat? How could that happen when they are the ones growing the crops? These kinds of questions are fundamental to our understanding of how human populations adapt to their environment, and precisely the kinds of questions nutritional anthropologists are particularly interested in.

The following articles include examples of food acquisition and diet in groups living in different places and making a living in different ways. Together with the article by Lee (article 6), the following three articles provide a glimpse of some of the food procurement strategies in the late twentieth century and what they mean for human diets. The strategies we have chosen include subsistence agriculture (food production using primarily domesticated plants, and sometimes animals) and pastoralism (primary reliance on domesticated animals for food or to trade for food) as practiced by people who produce all or almost all of their own food, and subsistence agriculture embedded in a market economy. The sequence in which we present these food procurement systems parallels their appearance in archaeological and historic time; subsistence agriculture in a nonmarket economy is the oldest.

Dufour's article, "Use of Tropical Rainforests by Native Amazonians," focuses on Tukanoan Indians in Northwest Amazonia. The Tukanoans are subsistence agriculturists, who produce food for their own consumption, and do it with human labor. The system they use is called swidden or shifting cultivation. Basically, it involves cutting down forest, burning it, and planting food crops in soil enriched by the newly deposited ash. It is an ancient agricultural system, and one still prominent in the tropics. Tukanoans supplement their agri-

cultural production with hunting and fishing and some collecting of wild plants and small animals such as insects and crustaceans(crayfish). Interestingly, although Tukanoans live in one of the most diverse ecosystems on the planet, their diet is not very diverse. It is based on cassava (manioc, a root crop) that is prepared primarily as a bread, and fish. Some 80 percent or more of all the food energy in the diet comes from cassava. For an average adult woman or man living in the United States, that would be equivalent to eating 1.5 to 2 pounds of bread a day.

The article by Galvin, Coppock, and Leslie, "Diet, Nutrition, and the Pastoral Strategy," focuses on pastoralists in East Africa who derive most of their sustenance (milk, blood, meat) from herds of domesticated animals. They also sell some animals and animal products to obtain grains. The Turkana pastoralists live in a hot grassland environment with too little rainfall to support agriculture. The animals they herd are Old World ungulates (hoofed animals): cattle, sheep, goats, and camels. Herd owners keep mixed herds that have feeding requirements similar to those of the wild ungulates of the region; they move frequently within their territory to find adequate pasture and water for their herds and water for themselves. In essence, the pastoral system functions as a system to convert plant foods unsuitable for people (grasses and shrubs) to milk and meat. From the point of view of human nutrition, this is a conversion of low-quality plant food to high-quality animal foods.

Kathleen Galvin, an anthropologist, and her co-authors, part of a large multidisciplinary study of Turkana pastoralists, provided some of the first detailed data on pastoral diets. In the article presented here, they compare the Turkana with another pastoral group, the Borana, who live not far away, but in a considerably moister (mesic) and more productive (in terms of vegetation) region. Livestock provides the basis of the economy of both groups, and milk is the major source of food. On an annual basis, they obtain about 60 percent of food energy from milk and about 20 percent from cereal grains (principally maize meal). At some times of the year, the Turkana obtain almost 80 percent of their food energy (calories) from milk. For the average adult female in the United States, a similar diet would be provided by 2.2 quarts of milk and 1.5 cups of cooked maize meal (such as grits or *polenta*), and for males 2.9 quarts of milk and 2 cups of cooked maize meal—clearly not a very diverse diet.

Gretel Pelto's article, "Social Class and Diet in Contemporary Mexico," compares the diet of a rural family who cultivates some of their own food with that of an urban middle-class family who purchase all of their food. The differences in the variety of foods consumed is striking, and Pelto's analysis makes it abundantly clear that in situations in which food must be purchased, higher income leads to a more diverse and nutritionally adequate diet. Although the data she draws on and her analysis reflect conditions of the 1970s and 1980s, the conditions and patterns she describes are essentially the same today. It is one of the great ironies of the world we live in that the rural poor who cultivate food for the market sometimes do not have enough to eat.

How does the current food procurement system of the United States compare with those of other peoples and with our own past? The present system is complex. It is a highly industrialized system in which the principal raw material is actually the fossil fuel used to drive the farm machinery and manufacture the fertilizers, herbicides, and pesticides (Pimentel et al., 1973). Little food makes it directly from farm field to table. Most food passes through a complex and highly industrialized processing system, which often takes foods apart and remakes them in novel ways. Then, before food is sold, it is packaged. Packaging tends to be more elaborate than necessary to conveniently hold a given amount of food together, or to provide it with protection from the elements, and sometimes even provides containers to cook the food in and eat it from. Manufacturing the packages themselves requires additional fossil fuel. Finally, the packaged foods are transported (which also requires fossil fuel) to markets throughout the country.

A typical breakfast for someone in Colorado might include orange juice from Florida, sausage made from turkeys raised in Iowa, a cereal made from maize grown in Nebraska but "puffed" and sugarcoated in the General Mills factory in Illinois, and coffee imported from Kenya but packaged in Seattle. All of this is available at the local supermarket, which has a floor area of some 6,200 square meters (54,000 square feet), almost the size of an American-style football field. This area is bigger than most of the gardens used by Tukanoan Indians (gardens range from 0.15 to 0.78 hectare, or 1,500 to 7,800 square meters). The supermarket shelves hold some 10,000 to 12,000 different food items. Even if these include essentially similar items in different size packages and produced by different manufacturers, it is still a lot of different food

items, and many, many more than the number of different food plants in a Tukanoan garden.

A plus of the industrialized food procurement system of the United States is that the large, highly mechanized farms can produce very large amounts of food, and people with the money to purchase food can have a varied and nutritious diet. A minus is energy cost: It is not an efficient system in terms of the amount of energy used to produce the food energy to feed one person. Another minus may actually be the great diversity of foods available to consumers. This is counterintuitive because we assume that a diet based on a wide variety of foods is better than a low-diversity diet. However, recent evidence suggests that the great diversity of foods available in the United States may encourage people to eat more than they need, and hence contribute to the current problem of obesity. The Tukanoan and Turkana food procurement systems, on the other hand, are more efficient in terms of energy used, but they produce much less food. They do provide diets that are adequate over the long term, even though they have little diversity. A real plus for the Tukanoan and Turkana food procurement systems is that they are probably sustainable over the long term. Whether our industrialized system is sustainable over the long term is highly questionable.

SUGGESTIONS FOR THINKING AND DOING NUTRITIONAL ANTHROPOLOGY

1. Recall the foods you ate yesterday. How many different types of foods did you eat? How many of these foods did you grow yourself? How many did you prepare yourself?

2. Before you take out the trash, spend a few minutes looking through it. How much discarded food does it contain? Is it enough for one meal? Open the refrigerator and remove all the food items that have been there longer than a week and are probably no longer suitable to eat. How many meals' worth of food are there?

3. Take a walk around your local supermarket. How many types of foods look like they came directly from a farmer's field or dairy barn? What percentage are they of all foods in the supermarket?

SUGGESTED READINGS AND REFERENCES

Hames, R. B., & Vickers, W. (Eds.). (1983). *Adaptive responses of native Amazonians.* New York: Academic Press. (An edited volume with articles on the subsistence patterns of native Amazonians.)

Pimentel, D., Hurd, L. E., Bellotti, A. C., Forster, M. J., Okra, I. N., Sholea, O. D., & Whitman, R. J. (1973). Food production and the energy crisis. *Science, 182*, 433–449.

Pimentel, D., & Pimentel, M. (1979). *Food energy and society.* London: Edward Arnold.

Southwick, C. H. (1985). *Global ecology in human perspective.* New York: Oxford University Press.

Steinhart, J. S., & Steinhart, C. E.. (1974). Energy use in the U.S. food system. *Science, 184*, 307–316.

11

Use of Tropical Rainforests by Native Amazonians

Darna L. Dufour

Indigenous peoples have lived in the rainforests of Amazonia for a long time, probably thousands of years. They were once more numerous and occupied more of Amazonia than they do today. Those groups known ethnographically live in interfluvial regions and share a broadly similar subsistence pattern based on horticulture, hunting, fishing, and collecting. They provide the best example of sustainable use of tropical rainforests under low population densities.

Of the ways in which Amerindians use the rainforest, the best documented are their diverse, multistoried agricultural plots, or swiddens. More recently studied is their management of swidden fallows, in which annual crops are combined with perennial tree crops and the natural process of reforestation. Some groups also modify what appears to be primary forest by planting along trailsides and campsites. The result of their agricultural practices is a mosaic of vegetational patches in different stages of succession and under differing degrees of management. This vegetational mosaic is then used for food, materials, and medicinals, as well as for hunting game animals.

The objectives of this article are briefly to summarize the history of indigenous peoples, describe some of the contributions anthropology and allied disciplines have made to understanding how these peoples use tropical rainforests, and, finally, to compare this knowledge briefly with patterns of use characteristic of other populations. Many examples are drawn from the Tukanoan Indians in the Colombian Vaupes region in Northwest Amazonia, the area with which I am most familiar.

HISTORY OF NATIVE AMAZONIANS

When the Europeans arrived, the indigenous population of Amazonia was much greater than it is today. One estimate is that the Amerindians numbered approximately 6.8 million in an area of almost 10 million km^2 (Denevan 1976).[1] Population density was highest in the floodplains of the major rivers, or what is referred to as *várzea,* and along the Atlantic coast. Early explorers such as G. Carvajal and F. Orellana reported dense settlements along the banks of the

Amazon in the 1540s and a level of social organization referred to as a chiefdom (Roosevelt 1989). The remains of large middens (refuse heaps), as well as the extent and depth of *terra preta do indio*[2] (Indian black earth) provide additional evidence that the riparian zones of major rivers were heavily populated (Roosevelt 1989, Smith 1980). The interior forests and savannas, or *terra firme,* appear to have been much more sparsely populated (Denevan 1976).

The indigenous population in the floodplain declined rapidly, and, by only 150 years after Orellana's expedition, the chiefdoms were extinct (Roosevelt 1989). The severe depopulation that followed this contact is assumed to have been the result of a combination of disease, slavery, and warfare. The rate of population decline in the more isolated interior forest areas was probably lower than in the floodplain, because many of these groups had only sporadic contact with outsiders until well into this century (Denevan 1976).

In the early 1970s, the indigenous population of Amazonia was estimated at less than 500,000 (Denevan 1976). In Brazil alone, the population dropped between 1900 and 1957 from approximately 1 million to less than 200,000 (Ribeiro 1967). Amerindians are now confined to interior forests and savannas, and the once densely populated floodplain is home to *caboclos,* the descendants of detribalized Indians and early European immigrants (Moran 1974, Parker et al. 1983). However, even in *terra firme,* it is clear that no present-day indigenous villages are as large as some of the villages were in the past (Nimuendajú 1939, Smith 1980). Understanding of indigenous use of Amazonian ecosystems is limited to *terra firme* forests, and these forests themselves may have been more heavily used in the past.

AMERINDIAN USE OF FORESTS FOR AGRICULTURE

Swidden Plots

The traditional indigenous agricultural system is based on swidden cultivation (also known as slash-and-burn or shifting cultivation). In essence, this system involves felling and burning a patch of forest, cultivating and harvesting crops for a period of several years, and then allowing the forest to regrow for 15 years or more before the site is cleared again (Beckerman 1987). The felling and burning releases the nutrients stored in the forest biomass and makes them available to cultivated crops. The long fallow restores soil fertility, protects the physical properties of the soil, allows time for nutrient accumulation in the biomass, and helps control agricultural pest populations.

Amerindian swiddens are typically small, 0.4–0.6-hectare (Beckerman 1987), polycultural plots (i.e., they are planted in more than one crop simultaneously). Multiple varieties of the staple crops are planted in each swidden. Most groups of Amerindians also have monocrop swidden plots devoted to the dietary staple. The predominate staples are cassava (*Manihot esculenta* Crantz) and plantains and bananas (*Musa* sp.).

Cassava, or manioc, is a perennial shrub grown for its starchy roots. It is native to the neotropics, and well adapted to the low-fertility, acidic soils common in *terra firme* (Cock 1985). Cassava is cyanogenic, and varieties are recognized as being either bitter or sweet (i.e., containing high or low amounts of cyanide). The bitter-sweet distinction determines culinary use: bitter varieties are elaborately processed to reduce cyanide levels before being consumed, whereas the sweet ones can simply be peeled and boiled (Dufour 1988).

The agricultural plots of Tukanoan Indians in northwestern Amazonia provide a good example of traditional swidden cultivation. Swidden plots are felled by individual households in well-drained soils in both primary and successional forests. Most households fell swiddens in both types of forest. Bitter cassava, the dietary staple, is densely planted over nearly the entire garden surface. Other crops, such as taro (*Colocasia* spp.), sweet potato (*Ipomoea* sp.), arrowroot (*Maranta ruiziana*), pineapple (*Anana sativa*), chili peppers (*Capsicum annuum*), mafafa (*Xanthosoma mafafa*), lulo (*Solanum* sp.), bananas, and plantains, are interplanted where microenvironmental conditions (such as drainage and ash concentration) are deemed most suitable. They are planted toward the center of the garden where the regrowth of the forest will be most easily delayed by weeding. Coca (*Erythroxylum coca*), which is a shrub, and tree crops such as guama (*Inga* sp.), uvilla (*Pourouma cercropiaefolia*), and peach-palm (*Bactris gasipaes*) are also interplanted with cassava toward the center of the garden.

Tukanoan swidden plots are polycultural. They are polyvarietal as well, but the diversity of cassava varieties is much greater than the diversity of the other crop species. For example, in identifying cultivated plants in subsample units in four Tukanoan swiddens[3] (Table 1), we found that each contained between 2 and 16 dif-

Tukanoan woman sieving grated cassava roots to extract the starch. This extraction is part of the process used to make cassava bread, the dietary staple in Northwest Amazonia.

ferent crops, but as many as 17 to 48 different cassava varieties. On average, the four most common cassava varieties in each swidden accounted for only 38% of all cassava plants identified. We also found that, of all the cassava varieties reported, only the one or two sweet ones in each swidden were planted in a recognizable patch. The remaining ones were all interplanted. We found 4 to 17 bitter varieties per sampling unit (12.57 m^2), with a mean of 7.8 ± 3.72 (Figure 1).

Tukanoan swiddens are most intensively used and managed from approximately the 12th through the 24th month after burning. During this time, the first cassava crop is being harvested and some areas of the swidden are weeded for replanting. A second, smaller cassava crop is planted in swiddens with good yields as the first is being harvested, so that cassava harvesting continues through approximately the 36th month. Other crops are harvested as they mature and are needed. Tree crops such as uvilla and peach palm mature in approximately three years and are harvested until forest regrowth dominates the plot.

Table 1. Number of crop species, cassava varieties, and varieties of other crops in sample units of four Tukanoan swidden plots in Northwest Amazonia.

Swidden	Size (ha)	Sample Units	Crop Species	Cultivars Cassava	Cultivars Other
Primary forest*	0.35	20	17	48	25
Primary forest	0.15	10	2	17	1
Rastrojo† (60-year)	0.78	29	10	39	11
Rastrojo (25-year)	0.70	25	6	37	5

Unpublished data from 1986. Sampling units were randomly selected circles of 2-meter radius. All plants in each circle were tagged and then identified by the garden owner. Names of cassava cultivars were systematically checked for overlap with each garden owner, but naming of cultivars between swidden plots was not cross-checked.

*Tall forest, not cut in the memory of current inhabitants, is assumed to be primary forest.

†*Rastrojo* is local Spanish for successional forest. Ages are estimated from informants' histories of use.

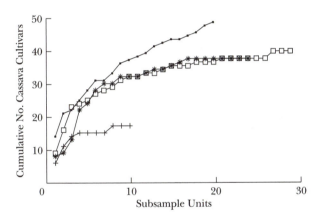

Figure 1. Cumulative number of cassava varieties in subsample units in four Tukanoan swiddens. Subsample units were randomly placed circles, 2 meters in radius.

Households establish one or two new swidden plots each year, and therefore they have access to a number of swiddens in different stages at any time: a newly planted swidden with immature crops, a cassava-producing swidden, and one or more older swiddens or fallows with fruit trees, fish poisons, and medicinal plants. Some of the plots are contiguous and form a mosaic of patches of successional vegetation. Others are widely dispersed to take advantage of areas of particularly good agricultural soil and/or serve as bases for hunting and fishing.

Swidden Fallows

The transition between a swidden and a swidden fallow is not sharp, and, certainly from the Amerindian point of view, the plot is not abandoned after the principal

Tukanoan woman harvesting cassava roots in a representative swidden in Northwest Amazonia. The palmate-leafed plant at lower left is cassava.

crop has been harvested. Denevan and Padoch (1988) examined the swiddens of Bora Indians living in the humid tropical rainforests of Peru at different stages of regrowth from the time of cutting. They found a continuum from a swidden dominated by cultivated grasses, forbs, and shrubs; to an orchard fallow phase, in which there was a combination of fruit trees, smaller cultigens, and natural vegetation; to a forest fallow that

Table 2.   Harvestable plants found in Bora fields and fallows at different stages of regrowth after cutting (Adapted from Denevan et al. 1984.)

Stage	Cultigens	Other Useful Plants
Newly planted field (0–3 mo)	None	Dry firewood
New field (3–9 mo)	Maize, rice, cowpeas	Various useful early successional species
Mature field (9 mo–2 yr)	Manioc, some tubers,* bananas, cocona, other quick-maturing crops	Some useful vines and herbs in abandoned edge
Transitional field (1–5 yr)	Replanted manioc, peanuts, pineapple, guava, caimito, uvilla, avocado, cashew, coca, barbasco, chili peppers, miscellaneous tubers	Useful medicinals and other plants within field; on edges, seedlings of useful trees appear; saplings of *Cercropia* and *Ochroma lagopus* in abandoned edges
Transitional fruit field (4–6 yr)	Peach palm, bananas, uvilla, caimito, guava, annatto, coca, some tubers, propagules of pineapple, other crops	Many useful soft construction woods and firewoods, palms (including *Astrocaryum*), useful vines, and understory aroids
Orchard fallow (6–12 yr)	Peach palm, some uvilla, macambo, propages	Useful plants as above and self-seeding *Inga*
Forest fallow (12–30 yr)	Macambo, umari, breadfruit, copal	Self-seeding macambo and umari; high forest successional species appearing; some hardwoods becoming harvestable (e.g., *Iriartea* sp.); many large palms (*Astrocarym hunicungo, Euterpe* sp., *Jessenia bataua*)
Old fallow (30+ yr)	Macambo, umari	Numerous construction, medicinal, handicraft, and food plants

Plant identifications are as follows: Annatto (*Bixa orellana*), avocado (*Persea americana*), banana (*Musa* sp.), barbasco (*Lonchocarpus* sp.), breadfruit (*Artocarpus incisa*), caimito (*Pouteria caimito*), cashew (*Anacardium occidentale*), chili pepper (*Capsicum* sp.), coca (*Erythroxylon coca*), cocona (*Solanum* sp.), copal (*Hymenaea courbaril*), cowpeas (*Vigna unguiculata*), guava (*Inga* sp.), macambo (*Theobroma bicolor*), maize (*Zea mays*), manioc (*Manihot esculenta*), peach palm (*Bactris gasipaes*), peanut (*Arachis hypogaea*), pineapple (*Ananas comosus*), rice (*Oryza sativa*), umari (*Poraqueilba sericea*), uvilla (*Pourouma cercropiaefolia*).

*These tubers include cocoyams (*Xanthosoma* sp.), sweet potatos (*Ipomoea batatas*), and yams (*Dioscorea trifida macrocarpa*).

still contained economically useful plants, but became progressively more and more like the surrounding forest (Table 2). Some of the useful plants were non-domesticated plants that appeared in the natural reforestation sequence and were protected.

The Bora, therefore, practice a form of agroforestry in which perennial tree crops are combined with natural forest regrowth (Denevan et al. 1984). Similar practices have been reported for other Amerindians and appear to be widespread (Balée and Gély 1989, Eden and Andrade 1987, Harris 1971, Posey 1984).

Forest-Fields and Trailside Plantings

Posey (1984) has documented among Kayapo Indians in Brazil a much broader system of forest management, which he refers to as *nomadic agriculture*. Traditionally the Kayapo were seminomadic and spent much of the year trekking along an extensive system of trails between the Tocantins and Araguaya rivers and the north-south limits of the Planalto and Amazon rivers.

Anthropologists had assumed that the Kayapo lived by hunting and collecting wild plant foods during these treks. However, Posey (1984) found that the trailsides and campsites were actually planted with "numerous varieties of yams, sweet potatoes, Marantacea, Cissus, Zingiberaceae, Araceae, Cannaceae, and other unidentified, edible, tuberous plants," as well as fruit trees and medicinal plants. This planting was a conscious attempt to replicate naturally occurring concentrations of resources in primary forest. The plants used included both domesticates and semidomesticates (i.e., plants transplanted from primary and successional forest). These semidomesticates were also transplanted to old swiddens and naturally occurring forest gaps.

Ecological Effects of Traditional Agricultural Practices

The ecological effects of traditional Amerindian agricultural practices are still poorly understood. Swidden cultivation, as practiced by Amerindians with short cropping and long fallows, is considered a relatively benign disturbance (Herrera et al. 1981), and it does not seriously impair ecosystem function (Uhl 1987).

At the level of the individual swidden plot, a number of traditional farming practices are considered beneficial. For example, the use of shade trees, mixed cropping of species that differ in phenology, dense spacing of crops, and fallowing all help preserve soil organic matter, which is a critical factor in the maintenance of soil fertility in the deeply weathered and leached soils common in Amazonia (Ewel 1986). The species richness of the plots is assumed to confer pest protection and decrease the risk of complete crop failure (Ewel 1986; c.f. Brown and Ewel 1987). Planting many varieties of a staple crop may fulfill the same functions (Balée and Gély 1989, Beckerman 1983, Boster 1983, Parker et al. 1983).

Forest regeneration during the fallow is considered a key to the sustainability of swidden systems (Ewel 1986). Amerindian management of the successional process, by the selective weeding out of certain trees and the protecting and planting of others, appears to have a greater impact on species diversity than it does on forest regrowth in stature and biomass (Uhl 1987). Uhl (1983) has suggested that heavily managed successions in areas such as house gardens may grow to forest stature as fast or faster than natural ones (Uhl 1983).

Recovery to primary forest in terms of biomass and species diversity, however, is slow. Current estimates are that in areas like San Carlos de Rio Negro it will take 100 years or more for traditionally farmed sites to return to primary forest, and sites suffering greater disturbance will take even longer (Saldarriaga 1985, Uhl and Murphy 1981).

Given this long period of recovery, and the practice of cutting swidden plots yearly, it is clear that human settlements will be surrounded by a complex mosaic of agricultural and agroforestry plots, as well as forest in various stages of regrowth. In addition, in some areas, the species composition of the forests themselves will be the result of human endeavors to increase the density of useful plants. Such vegetational mosaics may offer advantages in terms of pest protection and be a way of risk spreading (Eden and Andrade 1987, Ewel 1986). For indigenous populations, these landscapes offer clear advantages in hunting and collecting.

AMERINDIAN USE OF FORESTS FOR HUNTING, FISHING, AND COLLECTING

Hunting, fishing, and collecting are integral components of the subsistence pattern of Amerindians that cannot be considered apart from swidden agriculture (Balée and Gély 1989). In nutritional terms, these activities provide the sources of dietary protein, fat, and other nutrients that are critical supplements to the high-carbohydrate staples.

Faunal Resources

Amerindians hunt a wide variety of animals, the numerically most important of which are primates and rodents (Redford and Robinson 1987). One of the explicitly recognized functions of swidden plots is to attract game animals for hunting. The roots, tubers, and low-successional vegetation of swidden are attractive to such game animals as rodents, peccary, and deer.

Crop losses due to predation are routinely compensated for by overplanting (Balée and Gély 1989, Carneiro 1983). Tukanoan women, for example, plant extra sweet-cassava for a small rodent, boo (*Dasyprocta punctada,* which averages approximately 2 kg in weight), and only complain when "he" seems to be eating more than "his" share. This rodent accounted for more than 20% of all animals killed during three-month-long observation periods in 1977, and women hunting in gardens with dogs were responsible for almost half of all kills (Dufour 1981).

The fruit trees in swidden fallows are attractive to a number of large game animals, especially tapir (*Tapirus terrestris*) and peccary (*Tayassu* spp.; Balée and Gély 1989, Chagnon and Hames 1979, Denevan et al. 1984, Dufour 1981, Posey 1984). The Kayapo purposefully disperse their gardens so as to attract game animals over a large area (Parker et al. 1983, Posey 1982, 1983, 1984). For this reason, Posey (1984) suggests that old swiddens be called "game-farm-orchards."

The effect of indigenous hunting practices on animal biomass and diversity is a complex question. Posey (1982) has argued that certain game species would not occur in forest unmodified by humans, and several of the important mammals such as deer, tapir, and collared peccary may reach higher densities in modified areas. Further, not all animals that frequent the swiddens are taken for food (Ross 1978), and researchers have described a number of ways in which the Amerindians may be regulating their hunting of game animals (Balée 1985, Beckerman 1980, Reichel-Dolmatoff 1976).

The only long-term study of the effects of indigenous hunting is Vickers' (1988) documentation of the hunting returns in a Siona-Secoya village in northeastern Ecuador over a 10-year period. His data suggest that some species were being depleted locally. These included the woolly monkey (*Lagothrix lagotricha*), a large forest understory bird called the curassow (*Mitu salvini*), and a large ground-dwelling bird, the trumpeter (*Psophia crepitans*). Other species, such as pec-

Oblique aerial view of swidden plots of different ages in Northwest Amazonia.

caries, tapir, deer, other primates, other birds, rodents, and reptiles, did not, however, show evidence of depletion. These data support the suggestion that the patches of successional vegetation created in swidden cultivation may allow some game species to survive near human settlements (Redford and Robinson 1987).

Fishing. The majority of the Amerindians in Amazonia rely on fish, rather than game, as their principal source of animal protein. In blackwater areas where rivers are small, such as northwestern Amazonia, fish can be considered part of the forest ecosystem, because nonpredatory fish feed primarily on forest products (Knöppel 1970). Tukanoan Indians recognize the importance of forests to fish (Chernela 1985, Dufour 1981). The flood forest, or igapo, is an important feeding ground for fish. The Indians have protected it from deforestation (Chernela 1985).

Other Tukanoan practices, such as the use of fish poisons, may negatively affect the local fish populations, but it is not clear to what extent. The fish poisons are the crushed roots, stems, and/or leaves of a variety of wild and cultivated plants. Their use was traditionally controlled by the village shaman (Reichel-Dolmatoff 1976) and typically restricted to small forest streams that could be temporarily dammed. The effects of these poisons appear to be temporary (several hours) and highly localized.

Collecting. Small vertebrates, such as frogs, as well as invertebrates, are important faunal resources that are collected. The use of insects for food is widespread (Dufour 1987, Posey 1978). The more commonly collected and consumed insects appear to be ants (especially *Atta* spp.), termites, and larvae of both Coleoptera (especially Buprestidae, Curculionidae, and Scarabaeidae) and Lepidoptera. Tukanoans harvest ants and termites at low but constant rates. Nests are never destroyed, and some colonies in favorable locations are actively protected. Palm grubs (Curculionidae) are a managed resource: palms are cut with the expectation that they will be invaded by weevils and the larvae can be harvested at a later date.

Floral Resources

Amerindians collect a wide range of plants and plant products as food and for use in housing, tool manufacture, craft production, and medicine. The role of collected plant foods in the diet ranges from trail snacks and emergency foods to important sources of nutrients. Palm fruits and Brazil nuts are well-known examples of wild plant foods. Less well-known are oil seeds such as *Erisma japura* and the legume *Monopteryx angustifolia*, which are seasonally important in the diets of some groups (Dufour and Zarucchi 1979).

Tukanoan boy fishing with hook and line from a small dugout canoe.

because the predominance of these trees in the forest is associated with evidence of human settlement. Babassu palms tend to be the dominant, or at least an important species in burned forest clearings because of the manner in which they germinate: the apical meristem grows downward, rather than upward, and remains protected underground for a year or more (Anderson and Anderson 1985, Balée 1989). Brazil nut forests, at least in some areas, appear on or near *terra preta* sites (Balée 1989). Furthermore, Kayapo actually plant Brazil nuts as a source of food for themselves and the game they hunt (Posey 1985). Balée (1989) estimates that at least 11.8% of *terra firme* in the Brazilian Amazon is covered by anthropogenic forests.

CONTRASTS WITH NONINDIGENOUS FARMERS

Indigenous peoples are not the only ones who have a detailed knowledge of the local Amazonian ecosystems in which they live. The long-term residents of Amazonia, the *caboclos* (also *riberenos, mestizos,* or *campesinos*), do as well. The *caboclos* are the rural peasantry of Amazonia, and they are now the principal inhabitants of the *várzea,* the narrow but productive floodplain of Amazonian rivers (Parker et al. 1983). Their use of resources resembles that of Amerindians, from whom many are descended, but they are more oriented to market economies and typically quick to respond to market opportunities (Padoch 1988, Parker et al. 1983).

For example, the *caboclos,* studied by Padoch (1988) along the Ucayali River in Peru, recognized a complex set of ecological zones in the riparian environment and used them to advantage. They cash-cropped rice on the seasonally flooded mud flats of the river and cultivated subsistence and market crops on the *restingas* (river levees). On the poorer soils of the higher areas, they had intensively managed for subsistence crops the swidden plots, which gradually turned into orchards and then forest fallows. Some orchards were used for as long as 30 years, and the forest fallows were weeded selectively to maintain a high proportion of useful species.

Like Amerindians, *caboclos* use a wide variety of forest products as food, medicinals, fiber, and building materials. They also collect nontimber forest products such as palm fruits, Brazil nuts, and rubber for commercial sale (Padoch 1988, Parker et al. 1983). At least for Brazil nuts and rubber, their collection practices are productive and environmentally conservative, and they provide examples of the sustainable use of Amazonian forests (Fearnside 1988).

Plant foods are collected from the entire range of successional vegetation types, from nondomesticated herbs such as *Phytolacca rivinoides,* which grow in newly burnt swiddens, to the seeds of the rubber trees, *Hevea* sp., which grow in primary forests (Dufour 1981). In collecting plant parts (fruits, nuts, and seeds) from the litter on the forest floor or from living trees, humans are competing with other herbivores, but the impact of their activity on the forest is minimal. When trees are felled to harvest fruit or other parts, the impact is greater. Localized depletion of products such as cedar (*Cedrela odorata*) for canoes and palms for roof thatch has been documented (Vickers 1988).

Some of the more important collected plant foods appear to be from anthropogenic forests, that is, forests that are the result of human disturbance. Balée (1989) has argued that babassu palm (*Orbignya phalerata*) forests and Brazil nut (*Bertholletia excelsa*) forests, among others, should be considered anthropogenic,

Seeds of *Monopteryx angustifolia*, a seasonally important wild plant food in Northwest Amazonia.

The newest immigrants to Amazonian rainforests are the *colonos*, or colonists. *Colonos* are the subsistence farmers who went and still go to the Amazon as part of resettlement schemes promoted by government agencies (Moran 1988). The majority see the rainforest for the first time when they arrive in the Amazon, and, understandably, they have little knowledge of how to make a living in it.

In his study of Brazil's Transamazon Resettlement Scheme in the 1970s, Moran (1988) found that the *colonos* treated the forest as an enemy rather than a resource. They cleared more land per year, but cultivated less, and they were less successful agriculturally than *caboclos* living in the same area. They gradually learned, however, to clear less land, work it more intensively, and use some of the resources of the forest.

CHANGING VIEWS OF NATIVE AMAZONIAN RESOURCE USE

Recent studies have considerably refined understanding of the ways in which Amerindians use the tropical rainforest. Originally anthropologists and ecologists envisioned swiddens, fallows, and forests as more or less separate entities. Now, however, we understand more clearly the process of swiddens becoming forests, the length of time involved, and the degree to which human management is part of the transition.

The distinctions between domesticated and wild plants, or natural and managed forest, are also not as sharp as we thought they were. Much of what has been considered natural forest in Amazonia is probably the result of hundreds of years of human use and management (Posey 1984, Smith 1980). We are not certain how specific human activities may have changed Amazonian ecosystems over the long term, but they were certainly an essential component. Future research will have to take into account the long history of occupation and use of these forests by Amerindians.

The agricultural systems of Amerindians and *caboclos* have proven to be more sophisticated and complex than we imagined. There is a growing recognition that these agricultural systems have a great deal to offer in the design of sustainable agroecosystems (Denevan et al. 1984, Ewel 1986, Hart 1980). Further study of these systems that explicitly recognizes and incorporates the detailed knowledge and long experience of Amerindians and *caboclos* is needed. Such study will require the collaboration of anthropologists and ecologists.

ACKNOWLEDGMENTS

Funding for research in the Northwest Amazon was provided by the National Science Foundation (BSN-8519490). I am very grateful to R. Wilshusen for his invaluable assistance in mapping and sampling

Tukanoan swiddens and his helpful comments on the manuscript. W. Balée kindly provided prepublication copies of two of his papers.

NOTES

1. The use of Amazonia in this article follows that of Denevan (1976). It refers to greater Amazonia, which includes the tropical lowlands and plateaus east of the Andes and north of the Tropic of Capricorn, except for the Gran Chaco region. It is an area considerably larger than the drainage of the Amazon and its tributaries.

2. *Terra preta do indio* is a soil darkened by the residue of repeated fires. It characterizes ceramics and other remains of human activity (Smith 1980).

3. D. L. Dufour and R. Wilshusen, 1986, unpublished data.

REFERENCES

Anderson, A., and S. Anderson. 1985. A "tree of life" grows in Brazil. *Nat. Hist.* 94(12): 40–47.

Balée, W. 1985. Ka'apor ritual hunting. *Hum. Ecol.* 13: 485–510.

———. 1989. The culture of Amazon forests. In D. A. Posey and W. Balée, eds. Special issue: *Resource Management in Amazonia: Indigenous and Folk Strategies. Adv. Econ. Bot.* 7: 1–21.

Balée, W., and A. Gély. 1989. Managed forest succession in Amazonia: the Ka'apor case. In D. A. Posey and W. Balée, eds. *Resource Management in Amazonia: Indigenous and Folk Strategies. Adv. Econ. Bot.* 7: 129–158.

Beckerman, S. 1980. Fishing and hunting by the Barí of Colombia. Pages 67–109 in R. B. Hames, ed. *Studies in Hunting and Fishing in the Neotropics.* Bennington College, VT.

———. 1983. Barí swidden gardens: crop segregation patterns. *Hum. Ecol.* 11: 85–101.

———. 1987. Swidden in Amazonia and the Amazon rim. Pages 55–94 in B. L. Turner and S. B. Brush, eds. *Comparative Farming Systems.* Guilford Press, New York.

Boster, J. 1983. A comparison of the diversity of Jivaroan gardens with that of the tropical forest. *Hum. Ecol.* 11: 47–68.

Brown, B. J., and J. J. Ewel. 1987. Herbivory in complex and simple tropical successional ecosystems. *Ecology* 68: 108–116.

Carneiro, R. 1983. The cultivation of manioc among the Kuikuru of the upper Xingu. Pages 65–111 in R. B. Hames and W. T. Vickers, eds. *Adaptive Responses of Native Amazonians.* Academic Press, New York.

Chagnon, N., and R. B. Hames. 1979. Protein deficiency and tribal warfare in Amazonia: new data. *Science* 20: 910–913.

Chernela, J. 1985. Indigenous fishing in the neotropics: the Tukanoan Uanano of the blackwater Uaupés River basin in Brazil and Colombia. *Interciencia* 10: 78–86.

Cock, J. H. 1985. *Cassava: New Potential for a Neglected Crop.* Westview Press, Boulder, CO.

Denevan, W. M. 1976. The aboriginal population of Amazonia. Pages 205–234 in W. M. Denevan, ed. *The Native Population of the Americas.* University of Wisconsin Press, Madison.

Denevan, W. M., and C. Padoch. 1988. The Bora agroforestry project. In W. M. Denevan and C. Padoch, eds. Special issue: *Swidden-Fallow Agroforestry in the Peruvian Amazon. Adv. Econ. Bot.* 5: 1–7.

Denevan, W. M., J. M. Treacy, J. B. Alcorn, C. Padoch, J. Denslow, and S. F. Paitan. 1984. Indigenous agroforestry in the Peruvian Amazon: Bora Indian management of swidden fallows. *Interciencia* 9: 346–357.

Dufour, D. L. 1981. Household variation in energy flow in a population of tropical forest horticulturalists. Ph.D. dissertation, State University of New York, Binghamton.

———. 1987. Insects as food. *Am. Anthropol.* 89: 383–397.

———. 1988. Cyanide content of Cassava (*Manihot esculenta,* Euphorbiaceae) cultivars used by Tukanoan Indians in Northwest Amazonia. *Econ. Bot.* 42: 255–266.

Dufour, D. L., and J. L. Zarucchi. 1979. Monopteryx Angustifolia and Erisma Japura: their use by indigenous peoples in the northwest Amazon. *Bot. Mus. Leaf. Harv. Univ.* 27: 69–91.

Eden, M. J., and A. Andrade. 1987. Ecological aspects of swidden cultivation among the Andoke and Witoto Indians of the Colombian Amazon. *Hum. Ecol.* 15: 339–359.

Ewel, J. J. 1986. Designing agricultural ecosystems for the humid tropics. *Annu. Rev. Ecol. Syst.* 17: 245–271.

Fearnside, P. M. 1989. Extractive reserves in Brazilian Amazonia. *BioScience* 39: 387–393.

Hames, R. B. 1979. A comparison of the efficiencies of the shotgun and the bow in neotropical forest hunting. *Hum. Ecol.* 7: 219–252.

Harris, D. R. 1971. The ecology of swidden cultivation in the Upper Orinoco rain forest, Venezuela. *Geogr. Rev.* 61: 475–495.

Hart, R. D. 1980. A natural ecosystem analog approach to the design of a successional crop system for tropical forest environments. *Biotropica* 12: 73–83.

Herrera, R., C. F. Jordan, E. Medina, and H. Klinge. 1981. How human activities disturb the nutrient cycles of a tropical rainforest in Amazonia. *Ambio* 10: 109–114.

Knöppel, H. 1970. Food of central Amazonian fishes: contribution to the nutrient ecology of Amazonian rain forest streams. *Kiel Amazoniana* 2: 257–352.

Moran, E. F. 1974. The adaptive system of the Amazonian Caboclo. Pages 136–159 in C. Wagley, ed. *Man in the Amazon.* University of Florida Press, Gainsville.

———. 1988. Following the Amazon highways. Pages 155–162 in J. S. Denslow and C. Padoch, eds. *People of the Tropical Rainforest.* University of California Press, Berkeley.

Nimuendajú, C. 1939. *The Apinaye.* Anthropological series no. 8. Catholic University of America, Washington, DC.

Padoch, C. 1988. People of the floodplain and forest. Pages 127–140 in J. S. Denslow and C. Padoch, eds. *People of the Tropical Rainforest.* University of California Press, Berkeley.

Parker, E., D. A. Posey, J. Frechione, and L. F. Da Silva. 1983. Resource exploitation in Amazonia: ethnoecological examples from four populations. *Ann. Carnegie Mus.* 52: 163–203.

Posey, D. A. 1978. Ethnoentomological survey of Amerind groups in lowland Latin America. *Fla. Entomol.* 61: 225–229.

———. 1982. Keepers of the forest. *Garden* 6: 18–24.

———. 1983. Indigenous ecological knowledge and development of the Amazon. Pages 225–256 in E. Moran, ed. *The Dilemma of Amazonian Development.* Westview Press, Boulder, CO.

———. 1984. A preliminary report on diversified management of tropical forest by the Kayapó Indians of the Brazilian Amazon. In G. T. Prance and J. A. Kallunki, eds. *Ethnobotany in the Neotropics. Adv. Econ. Bot.* 1: 112–126.

———. 1985. Indigenous management of tropical forest ecosystems: the case of the Kayapó Indians of the Brazilian Amazon. *Agroforestry Systems* 3: 139–158.

Posey, D. A., J. Frechione, J. Eddins, L. Francelino da Silva, D. Myers, D. Case, and P. Macbeath. 1984. Ethnoecology as applied anthropology in Amazon development. *Hum. Organ.* 43: 95–107.

Redford, K. H., and J. G. Robinson. 1987. The game of choice: patterns of Indian and colonist hunting in the neotropics. *Am. Amthropol.* 89: 650–667.

Reichel-Dolmatoff, G. 1976. Cosmology as ecological analysis: a view from the forest. *Man* 11: 307–318.

Ribeiro, D. 1967. Indigenous cultures and languages of Brazil. Pages 69–76 in J. H. Hopper, ed. *Indians of Brazil in the Twentieth Century.* Institute for Cross-Cultural Research, Washington, DC.

Roosevelt, A. 1989. Lost civilizations of the lower Amazon. *Nat. Hist.* 98(2): 75–83.

Ross, E. 1978. Food taboos, diet, and hunting strategy: the adaptation to animals in Amazon cultural ecology. *Curr. Anthropol.* 19: 1–19.

Saldarriaga, J. G. 1985. Forest succession in the upper Rió Negro of Colombia and Venezuela. Ph.D. dissertation, University of Tennessee, Knoxville.

Smith, N. J. H. 1980. Anthrosols and human carrying capacity in Amazonia. *Annals of the Association of American Geographers* 70: 553–566.

Uhl, C. 1983. You can keep a good forest down. *Nat. Hist.* 92(4): 71–79.

———. 1987. Factors controlling succession following slash and burn agriculture in Amazonia. *Ecology* 75: 377–407.

Uhl, C., and P. Murphy. 1981. A comparison of productivities and energy values between slash and burn agriculture and secondary succession in the upper Rió Negro region of the Amazon. *Agro-Ecosystems* 7: 63–83.

Vickers, W. T. 1988. Game depletion hypothesis of Amazonian adaptation: data from a native community. *Science* 239: 1521–1522.

12

Diet, Nutrition, and the Pastoral Strategy

Kathleen A. Galvin, D. Layne Coppock, and Paul W. Leslie

The resource-exploitation strategy of African pastoralists has been the subject of speculation and debate since Herskovits (1926) proclaimed his cattle-complex hypothesis (Schneider 1984). Today there is general agreement that pastoralists attempt to maintain large herds of livestock or to maximize livestock numbers, but there are different disciplinary interpretations about the rationale and implications of this aspect of the pastoral strategy. Anthropological analyses such as this one tend to emphasize the prestige values and subsistence values of large herds; numerous livestock are needed to assure status and power within the pastoral community and to provide an adequate supply of food to the pastoral population (Coppock 1992a; Galvin 1992; Jahnke 1982). However, some calculations show that African livestock production on a per capita basis is usually low and highly variable. These figures are interpreted to suggest that few existing pastoral populations have enough livestock to assure an adequate and continuous food supply at all times (Dahl and Hjort 1976; Fratkin 1991; Galvin 1992). Similar sorts of calculations have been used to demonstrate that the pastoralist exploitation strategy is particularly inefficient and therefore requires more livestock for subsistence than a more "rational" strategy would require (Brown 1971; Prins 1992; Semple 1971).

Economic perspectives focus on the nonnutritional utility of large livestock herds, recognizing the investment value of livestock both as perceived wealth and as potentially liquidatable assets. A point of interest among economists involves the pricing and land-tenure policies or conditions that pastoralists use in deciding whether to sell livestock or to increase their investment portfolio via herd expansion (Ariza-Nino and Shapiro 1984; Doran et al. 1979; Evangelou 1984; Jarvis 1986; Schneider 1957, 1984).

Ecologists and those concerned about land degradation often suggest that large herds of pastoral livestock are environmentally destructive (Lamprey 1983; Stiles 1983). However, keeping large herds of adult animals, rather than producing and selling younger animals, may be interpreted as a viable ecological strategy. Biomass maintenance strategies are said to characterize mature or stable ecological systems, whereas maximization of production tends to occur in early successional ecosystems or in those recovering from disturbance (Margalef 1968; Odum 1969). Another ecological-economic interpretation of the pastoral strategy emphasizes the value of large herds as a means of risk avoidance (Swift 1977, 1982). This is particularly important in unstable or nonequilibrial systems in which livestock populations are controlled largely by externally generated stresses like droughts rather than by cybernetic or steady-state feedbacks (Ellis and Swift 1988; Sandford 1983).

A recent analysis of the pastoral strategy based on nutritional considerations as well as herding patterns suggests that the goal is actually to maintain a large and growing human population for personal, political, and territorial motives. Livestock herds must be correspondingly large to support the subsistence and cultural needs of a large (at least relative to livestock biomass) and growing human population (Galvin 1992).

Despite differing disciplinary emphases, all of these perspectives recognize, explicitly or implicitly, the fundamental subsistence role of large livestock herds, where commercial offtake is limited or absent. Each perspective also sees investment value in large livestock herds although interpretations vary about the primary motive for the investment (i.e., whether for social prestige, risk avoidance or some other strategic purpose). Thus, there seems to be some consensus that there are multiple values in the maintenance of large livestock herds for pastoralists. However, long-term or large-scale changes in economic, ecological, or social conditions may lead to changes in the pastoral strategy, such as trade-offs between biomass and investment versus production and sales. How do such changes influence the underlying subsistence role of livestock in pastoral societies and the diet and nutritional status of pastoral people? Conversely, what can we surmise about the pastoral strategy and population welfare from changes in diet and nutritional status?

Nutritional status is measured by the sum of the quality of food procurement activities and dietary intake levels, mediated by disease. It reflects these factors, integrated over some extended time period, and is a nonspecific indicator of nutritional state (Haas

and Pelletier 1989). Nutritional status is most often assessed through the evaluation of dietary intake and/or growth, body size, and composition (Huss-Ashmore and Johnston 1985). Diet composition and food consumption tell us about the subsistence strategy, food preferences, and food availability of a particular human group, whereas anthropometric measures of growth, body size, and body composition reflect how well the subsistence strategy works. Diet and nutrition can be interpreted as an index of population welfare or well-being (Huss-Ashmore and Curry 1989). Thus, variations in diet composition, diet intake, and body size and composition over time or space may reveal something about how subsistence activities respond to changing economic or ecological conditions.

A CONCEPTUAL FRAMEWORK

It is proposed here that diet and nutrition reflect tactics used and decisions made by pastoralists in support of the overall pastoral strategy. Livestock are an important source of food, providing milk, meat, and blood, with some seasonal variation based on the type of livestock species exploited and the duration and/or severity of the season. Nonpastoral foods such as cereals are consumed when pastoral foods are in short supply. Because the core of the diet is often formed by livestock products, the diet is high in protein. However, diets are also low in energy because of low total consumption of foods. Nutritional status is generally low because of the low concentration of energy in the diet.

How might this traditional diet and resultant nutritional status vary across environments and in response to changes in economic developmental status? First, the ecological aspects. In this [article], variation in pastoral diets and nutritional status across environmental conditions is evaluated. We address the question: What aspects of diet composition and nutritional status change across environments? Second, dietary and nutritional responses to changes in economic conditions or developmental status are explored. If a goal of pastoral development is to decrease herd size and to increase production and offtake, it might be expected that this sort of change would move pastoralists away from their strategy of investment in livestock toward greater production and consumption, thereby changing diet and nutritional status. By the same reasoning, economic disruption, rather than progressive development, might also lead to changes in diet and nutrition if the fundamental strategy is altered. Diet and nutritional data from East African Turkana and Borana pastoralists are used to examine this conceptual framework in conjunction

Table 1.   Ecosystem characteristics of the Turkana and Borana regions

	Turkana	Borana
Rainfall (mm)	150–600	500–900
Elevations (m)	500–1,000	1,000–1,600
Temperatures (°C)		
Annual range	28–32	19–43
Diurnal range	19–24	—

SOURCES: Turkana data are from Coughenour et al. (1985) and Little and Johnson (1985). Borana data are from Bille (1983) and Holden et al. (1991).

with contrasts among other pastoral societies (Maasai, Ariaal, and Rendille).[1] The pastoral groups discussed in this [article] occupy different environments and are involved in market economies to various degrees.

ENVIRONMENT AND ECONOMY AMONG PASTORALISTS

The Borana and Turkana ecosystems may be near the two environmental extremes for pastoralism in arid and semiarid regions of East Africa. Turkana is quite dry and Borana is relatively mesic. Turkana territory is located in the Gregory Rift Valley of northern Kenya, where elevations range from 550 m to over 1000 m on the mountain peaks (Table 1). Temperatures are hot: Mean annual ambient temperature is about 30°C, with little seasonal variation; diurnal temperatures may range between 19°C and 43°C. Rainfall averages between 150 and 600 mm but is spatially and temporally unpredictable. A weak bimodal rainfall pattern causes a pulse of plant production from April to June. The growing season usually lasts from sixty to ninety days in most years, leaving a nine- to ten-month dry season with little or no plant growth unless the short rains occur in September–November. Regional vegetation consists of annual grasses, dwarf shrubs, shrubs, and trees. Vegetation types include bushland, savanna, and dwarf shrub grassland interspersed with many riparian woodlands dominated by Acacia trees.

In contrast to the Turkana ecosystem, that of Borana is more mesic and productive. The Borana live on the southern Ethiopian Plateau between an elevation of 1000 and 1600 m. Rainfall averages between 500 and 900 mm. Sixty percent of the rains fall from March to mid-May, and the remainder usually fall between October and November (Bille 1983). This bimodal distribution of rainfall is important in stretching out the growing season, which is about one and a

Table 2.   Human and livestock densities for Turkana and Borana

	Turkana	Borana
Area (km²)	9,000	15,475
Humans/km²	1.3	7.3
Cattle/km²	1.4	20.9
Small stock/km²	11.3	6.6
Camels/km²	1.3	0.2
TLU/km²	4.4	21.7
TLU/person	3.5	3.2

SOURCES: Turkana data are from Coughenour et al. (1985) and Ecosystems Ltd. (1983). Borana data are from Milligan (1983) and Upton (1986).

Note: One tropical livestock unit (TLU) = 1 cow; 1 camel = 1.25 TLUs; 1 goat or sheep = 0.125 TLU (from FAO 1967).

half to two times as long as in Turkana (mean—132 days; range—113 to 151 days) (Cossins and Upton 1988). This region supports savanna, woodland, and bush thicket, with varying amounts of perennial grasses. Unlike Turkana, Borana can get cold, with ambient temperatures ranging from 19°C to 24°C.

The two pastoral ecosystems are different in climate, growing season, livestock composition, livestock density, and human density (Table 2). The Ngisonyoka Turkana occupy an area of approximately 9,000 km², which supports a low population density of 1.3 persons per km². The Borana territory supports a population density almost six times as great. Livestock densities (in terms of tropical livestock units [TLUs]/km²) are five times greater in Borana than in Turkana. However, though the Borana are more productive than the Turkana and support between five and six times as many livestock and people, it is noteworthy that the livestock-to-human ratio is very similar (Turkana 3.5 TLUs per person, Borana 3.2). These ratios are similar to that for the whole of the southern Maasai region of Kenya, 3.7 TLUs (Bekure et al. 1991), but much lower than those in the Maasai group ranches, 13.4 TLUs/person (Bekure et al. 1991).[2] However, it appears that the Borana population is growing rapidly, at approximately 2.5 percent per annum (B. Lindtjørn, unpublished data, cited in Coppock [1993] and in Coppock et al. [1993]). The Borana probably have few economic opportunities in urban areas, so their livestock-to-human ratio may decline more in the future.[3]

The economies of both the Turkana and Borana are based on the exploitation of domestic livestock (Behnke 1990; Cossins and Upton 1987, 1988; Ellis et al. 1987; Galvin 1992). Herds of camels, cattle, and small ruminants are raised for home consumption in Turkana, with little commercial marketing of livestock. Sometimes in the late dry season and in years of poor rainfall, livestock are sold to offset shortfalls in subsistence production. When rainfall is low, the numbers of livestock sold tend to increase, and most of the money obtained in the sale is used for the purchase of food. This pattern may be modified depending on the condition of the pastoral economy at the time of a particular drought or dry period (Behnke 1990; Ellis et al. 1987; Galvin 1985). Surplus livestock products, principally milk, are sold by pastoral households living close to settlements in the wet season, when production is high but prices are low.

Trade in small stock (sheep and goats) is more prevalent in Turkana than trade of cattle; annual offtake rates for small ruminants in the 1980s ranged between 1 percent and 4 percent (Behnke 1990). Turkana camels are seldom sold outside the district. Cattle trade is risky because of the potential of livestock raiding and other losses en route to market (principally to Nairobi) and the unpredictable nature of pricing. When cattle are sold, the Turkana prefer selling adult steers. When adult males are not available to sell, animals are bartered within the pastoral community and between pastoralists and traders. A pastoralist may exchange a two-year-old bull for three male goats with another pastoralist, then sell the goats for cash. Immature camels or donkeys can also be traded for goats. At the end of the dry season, pastoralists may barter animals to a trader for food. The trader then sells those livestock during the rainy season, when food is plentiful and herders are looking for breeding and milking stock.

Despite these diverse exchange patterns, participation in the market economy through livestock marketing is small, and wage labor is virtually nonexistent for the Turkana (Ellis et al. 1987). In contrast, the Borana appear to be diversifying their formerly subsistence-dominated economy by marketing livestock and livestock products (Cossins and Upton 1987).

Livestock form the basis of the Borana economy, but marketing plays a greater role than among the Turkana. Subsistence production (primarily milk) still provides the major portion of household foodstuffs, but livestock marketing is vitally important to household economics. Borana livestock sales are dominated by mature male cattle, but sales of small stock are on the increase in recent years. The Borana have begun keeping more sheep and goats in response to increasing market opportunities and household need. In the past, small stock were utilized mainly during dry periods; when cattle production declined, offtake from small stock increased (Belete Dessalegn 1985; Cossins and Upton 1987).

It has been estimated that nearly 40 percent of the proceeds obtained through the sale of Borana livestock is expended on food, with 17 percent spent on grain and the remainder on tea, coffee, sugar, and other foodstuffs. The other 60 percent of this income is allocated to the purchase of livestock and household items, especially clothing, which accounts for approximately 75 percent of the income spent on nonfood items (Negussie Tilahun 1984). Although we do not have systematic data for the Turkana, we estimate that most of the proceeds from the sale of livestock in Turkana go to purchase foodstuffs, primarily maizemeal (K. A. Galvin, personal observation).[4]

Cultivation is increasing in the mesic areas close to Borana urban centers. Approximately 1.4 percent of the land area was cultivated in 1986, and although this is a small percentage of the total area, the area under cultivation appears to have increased during the 1980s (Cossins and Upton 1988). Poorer pastoralists seem to make up the majority of new farmers who live near villages on the edge of the pastoral areas (D. L. Coppock, personal observation). Cultivation seems to be increasing in Turkana, too, but its viability and profitability is unknown (P. W. Leslie, personal observation).

In summary, both the Turkana and Borana still operate in largely pastoral economies. However, there are signs that the Borana, and to a lesser extent the Turkana, are increasing crop production, and the Borana are increasing the holdings and sales of small ruminants. Both groups sell livestock, principally older male animals in the dry season, when terms of trade are poor. Whereas the Borana occupy a mesic ecosystem with some market interactions, the Turkana inhabit a very dry environment with very few marketing opportunities. In southern Kenya some Maasai groups live in an environment that is intermediate in rainfall (300–600 mm) but much advanced in marketing opportunities, in part because of their proximity to Nairobi.

Like the Borana, the Maasai have a production system based on cattle, although small stock are important for slaughter and sales. As the human population in Maasailand has increased, livestock sales and the purchase of grain have increased, but milk production for home consumption still dominates the production strategy. Nevertheless, livestock marketing and wage labor both contribute significant cash flows to Maasai households. Household cash income ($560 to $1,242 per household per year in 1981–1983, based on an exchange rate of 15 Ksh/$) is derived principally from livestock sales (76 percent) and wage labor (8 percent) whereas sales of milk, cattle hides, goat skins, home-brewed beer, and other miscellaneous transactions account for 16 percent of cash income (Bekure et al. 1991).

Greater participation in the national market economy and considerably more disposable cash put the Maasai in a position to use their income for consumption; they could consume a more diverse and nutritious diet than the Borana (who have a cash income of $45 to $382 per household per year in 1987, based on an exchange rate of 2.05 birr Eth/$ [Holden and Coppock 1992]) or the Turkana. In fact, though, food purchases account for only 36 percent of Maasai expenditures, and most of this is spent on maizemeal rather than the more exotic products available near Nairobi. Instead of using their considerable cash income for food and nutrition or other forms of consumption most cash (40 percent) is reinvested in their livestock through the purchase of veterinary drugs, equipment, or additional animals. Borana cash income is lower than that of the Maasai, and allocation of income differs (approximately 40 percent for food, 45 percent for household items, mostly clothing, and 15 percent for livestock expenditures). The Turkana, with very little cash income, spend the majority of that cash for food. These examples show that as pastoral income increases, the proportion spent for food appears to decline, and the proportion reinvested in livestock may increase. How much proximity to markets (or lack thereof) accounts for this pattern is unknown.

ENVIRONMENTAL AND ECONOMIC EFFECTS ON PASTORAL DIETS AND NUTRITION

Diet Composition

Pastoral diets change seasonally and interannually with changing climatic and socioeconomic circumstances. Figure 1 shows mean annual and seasonal diet composition for Turkana and Borana pastoralists. In a 1982 dietary study it was shown that Turkana pastoralists subsist primarily from their livestock; milk provided 62 percent of annual dietary energy, 89 percent in the wet season and 30 percent in the dry season (Galvin 1992). In two later surveys of Turkana diets (the wet seasons of 1989 and 1990), not surprisingly, milk was the most important food among women (91 percent in 1989, 94 percent in 1990).[5] However, other foods (cereals, blood, and meat) were much more important in 1989 than in 1990, when blood was a distant second to milk . . . . nce. By the 1990 early dry season, diet com- . . . ly 65 percent milk for Turkana women. Cere-

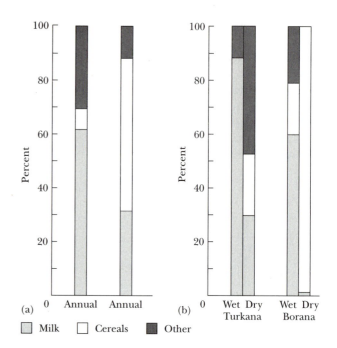

Figure 1.   Percent contribution of foods in the diets of Turkana and Borana, (a) annually and (b) seasonally. Turkana dietary data were derived from a measured diet intake study in 1982. Diet data were obtained from 28 individuals whose diets were repeatedly measured one day for four seasons (over 12 months). A total of 103 days of diet intake data were collected (Galvin 1985). Data on Borana diets were collected in a 24-hour diet-recall study and through retrospective interviews in 1988. Twenty-nine households comprising 136 individuals were visited once to assess the relative contribution of different foods in the diet of household members in the present season (through 24-hour recall) and each of the previous four seasons (covering 12 months) through interviews.

als made up 15 percent, and the remaining 20 percent of the diet was composed of meat (10 percent), blood (7 percent), and tea and wild foods (3 percent).

Milk is also the preferred food of Borana pastoralists (Figure 1). We see both great seasonal variability in the diet and perhaps a trend in diet composition as the Borana become more involved in market interactions through the 1980s. Early in the decade (1982) milk contributed 55 percent of diet energy intake, whereas cereals provided 33 percent of dietary energy. The remainder was made up of meat, blood, sugar, and other items (Cossins and Upton 1988). During the drought year of 1984–1985, milk made up only 19 percent of the dietary energy in the long dry season but 54 percent in the wet season, and following the rains (short dry season) milk provided 32 percent of caloric intake. Cereals contributed 73 percent, 27 percent, and 61 percent in the long dry season, the wet season, and the short dry season, respectively (Donaldson

1986). These figures show a major replacement of livestock products by market-purchased cereals when compared to the 1982 data. This substitution could have been strictly drought-related. However, in 1987 diets of women in periurban settings were composed mainly of cereals (92 percent of dietary energy) during the cool dry season (September), indicating that milk was being sold in local markets (Holden et al. 1991).[6] This dietary trend indicates that grain consumption was commonly high in the 1980s and was probably exacerbated by drought and proximity to market. This trend may also signify a change in the Borana pastoral strategy to incorporate more market interactions, limited adoption of cultivation, and other changes resulting from population and ecological causes as well as from greater market access (Holden and Coppock 1992; ILCA 1990).

Nestel (1985, 1986) reported annual diets of Kenyan Maasai (women and children) at one group ranch to consist of 64 percent milk, 16 percent grains, and 20 percent other food, whereas at another group ranch diets consisted of 31 percent milk, 34 percent grains, and 45 percent other foods.[7] However, at both group ranches milk made the largest contribution to total dietary energy in the wet season. Conversely, cereals were the main contributors to the diet in the dry season for these two Kenyan Maasai groups. The diet of the Maasai of the Ngorongoro Conservation Area in Tanzania has also been estimated. Cereals made up most of the dietary energy in the dry season of 1981 (Arhem et al. 1981; Homewood et al. 1987; Homewood and Rogers 1991).

Other pastoralists also rely on milk as the dietary staple whenever possible. Fratkin (1991) estimated that 66 percent of total Ariaal per capita caloric consumption was derived (in 1985) from milk, whereas cereals provided 11 percent of total energy. For the pastoral Rendille, milk may have provided up to 75 percent of dietary energy, in the early 1980s (Field and Simpkin 1985).

Diet Intake

Measured diet-intake studies have been conducted only among the Maasai and the Turkana, and estimates of caloric intake were similar but low in the two populations (Galvin 1992; Nestel 1986). Turkana energy intake was 1,340 kcal per person per day, whereas for Maasai women and children, caloric intake was 1,080 kcal per day (mean intake for Turkana women and children only was 1,009 kcal/day), reflecting in part the high proportion of young people in each population (Galvin 1985, 1992; Nestel 1985).[8]

Maasai caloric intake was lower in the wet season (832 kcal/person/day) than in the dry season (1,248 kcal/person/day), revealing a Maasai cultural preference for milk when it is abundant. Opposite seasonal patterns exist for the Turkana, whose dry-season intake was 1,308 kcal/person/day (979 kcal excluding men), whereas the wet-season energy intake was 1,434 kcal/person/day (1,103 excluding men). The wet-season difference between Turkana and Maasai energy intake shows the Turkana subsistence-oriented economy to be dependent on a diversity of livestock for milk, especially camels, who are prolific milk producers (Galvin 1985). Milk for Maasai consumption is derived only from cattle.

In summary, these data demonstrate the fluctuating diet composition of East African pastoralists, depending on season, year, and location. Diets remain very simple and center around milk as the staple whenever possible. The intra- and interannual changes in diet composition seem to occur in contexts where economic change is slight, as in Turkana, and where the change in diet is linked more to economics, as among the Borana and Maasai. Energy intake is low across environments and regardless of the state of economic development.

Nutritional Status

Although Turkana and Borana ecosystems, pastoral population levels, and livestock populations differ, levels of nutrition are similar in these two populations (Table 3). Anthropometric measures show no differences in weight, mid-upper-arm circumference (UAC), or triceps skinfolds (TSF) in men, but there is a significant difference in height, with Turkana men being taller than Borana.[9] Men's body mass indices (BMI) were not different. Turkana and Borana women, however, showed significant differences in height, UAC, and BMI. The difference in mid-upper-arm circumference may be caused by the different work patterns of women in these two populations. Turkana women water livestock and may do heavier work than do Borana women (Little et al. 1983, but also see Coppock 1992b). However, the difference in women's BMI is likely associated with the fact that the Borana are, on average, shorter and heavier than the Turkana.

In an attempt to define adult nutritional state with measures of weight and height, James et al. (1988) specified levels of chronic energy deficiency based on BMI scores. According to this scheme, approximately 23 percent of Turkana adults showed BMI of 16.9 or below, indicating chronic or severe energy deficiency.

Table 3.   Anthropometric measurements and body mass index (BMI) scores for Turkana and Borana adults

	n	**HT**	**WT**	**UAC**	**TSF**	**BMI**
Females						
Turkana	42	163.3 ± 6.5	46.8 ± 6.3	24.0 ± 2.4	12.6 ± 5.2	17.5 ± 1.8
Borana	53	159.1 ± 6.0	47.5 ± 6.4	22.8 ± 8.2	10.9 ± 3.4	18.7 ± 1.9
T-value		3.26	−0.50	2.28	1.56	−3.03
p		0.002	0.618	0.025	0.122	0.003
Males						
Turkana	40	173.9 ± 8.0	56.1 ± 7.3	24.0 ± 1.9	5.7 ± 2.1	18.5 ± 1.5
Borana	50	169.9 ± 6.1	54.7 ± 6.8	23.4 ± 1.9	4.9 ± 1.4	19.0 ± 1.7
T-value		2.70	0.94	1.45	1.65	−1.50
p		0.008	0.351	0.150	0.104	0.138

Note: Population differences were tested for mean height, weight, mid-upper-arm circumference (UAC), and triceps skinfold (TSF) using independent t-tests. Body mass index (BMI) = wt(kg)/ht^2 (m) (Najjar and Rowland 1987).

Fifteen percent of Borana adults displayed BMI scores of 16.9 or below. Body mass index scores of 18.5 or higher, indicating substantial energy reserves, were found in 35 percent of Turkana adults and 53 percent of the adult Borana sample. The remainder of the Turkana sample (42 percent) and the Borana sample (32 percent) may or may not have adequate energy reserves (classification may only occur after more information is available on physical activities).

When compared to BMI references for black Americans, both the Turkana and Borana demonstrated very low BMI scores. All but two Turkana women were at or below the tenth percentile, and 81 percent were at or below the fifth percentile (18.8) (Najjar and Rowland 1987). Eighty-one percent of the Borana sample of women were at or below the fifteenth percentile, and 58 percent were at or below the fifth percentile. Ninety-three percent of Turkana men had a BMI at or below the tenth percentile for black American BMIs, and 70 percent were at or below the fifth percentile (19.3). The sample of Borana men showed that 84 percent had BMIs at or below the fifteenth percentile, and 62 percent were at or below the fifth percentile.

Again using references for black Americans, all Turkana and Borana men, save three, had UACs at or below the fifth percentile. Ninety percent of Turkana women were at or below the twenty-fifth percentile, and 52 percent were at or below the fifth percentile. Ninety-two percent of the sample of Borana women showed UACs at or below the fifteenth percentile, and 70 percent were at or below the fifth percentile.

Triceps skinfold and weight measurements stan- ... (Z-scores) against the Health and Nutritional ... on Survey (HANES) standards are shown in ... (Najjar and Rowland 1987). Turkana wom-

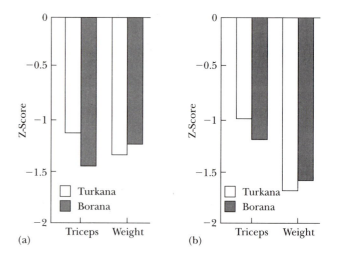

Figure 2.   Triceps skinfold and weight measurements for (a) women and (b) men compared with the U.S. national health and nutrition survey (NHANES) (Najjar and Rowland 1987).

en's triceps skinfolds are about 1.1 standard deviations (Z = −1.06) less than those of U.S. women of the same age; Borana TSFs are 1.3 standard deviations below those of U.S. women (Z = −1.34). Weights for Turkana and Borana women are 1.4 and 1.2 standard deviations, respectively, below those of U.S. women of the same age (Z = −1.36, Z = −1.22) (Figure 2a). Turkana and Borana men's triceps skinfolds are, on average, 1.1 standard deviations below those of U.S. men of the same age (Z = −1.01, Z = −1.15); weights are, on average, 1.7 standard deviations lower than those of U.S. men (Z = −1.75, Z = 1.65) (Figure 2b).

Regardless of measures of nutritional status, there are few differences between populations, and both populations show extremely low indicators of nutritional status compared to North American references. Thus, despite major differences in environmental conditions and economic development, the measures of body mass and composition suggest that the nutritional states of these two pastoral populations are similar.[10]

DISCUSSION AND CONCLUSIONS

What does this analysis tell us about diet and nutritional status as a fundamental aspect of the pastoral ecological/economic strategy? Is nutritional status a reliable indicator of the well-being of the population? The analysis shows that the Turkana and Borana livestock biomass densities are similar (3.5 TLUs/person in Turkana and 3.2 TLUs/person in Borana, Table 2). These figures are also similar to other pastoral regions in Kenya, where TLUs per person range from 3.4 in the northeast section of the country to 3.7 for the whole of the southern Maasai region. These ratios are similar regardless of environment. However, TLU ratios on two Maasai group ranches are very high— (11.3 TLUs/person on one group ranch, 15.9 TLUs/person on another) (Nestel 1986). These figures likely reflect a response to market opportunities and perhaps migration out of the Maasai area into neighboring urban centers. Maasai herd offtake ranges between 12 and 22 percent per annum, largely as a result of sales (Bekure et al. 1991). Turkana offtake may be a fraction of this (1 to 4 percent). Estimates of Borana sales offtake range between 9 and 12 percent, with an additional 6 to 8 percent for home consumption and exchange (Negussie Tilahun 1984). Household expenditures for the Maasai show that the largest amount of income goes into livestock reinvestment (Bekure et al. 1991). Likewise, most of Borana income goes back into the purchase of livestock and clothes (Negussie Tilahun 1984). A smaller proportion goes into food purchases, suggesting that pastoralists' diets (fluctuating composition and low energy intake) and nutritional status are not very responsive to environmental or economic differences. Grains are extremely important to the diet as populations increase, but the increase in grain consumption may not be indicative of a change in the overall pastoral strategy.

Comparison of the diets of the Turkana, Borana, and Maasai shows a cultural preference for pastoral products. Seasonality affects pastoral production, so those groups who rely on cattle, the Borana and Maasai, must consume grains in the dry seasons, when milk production decreases. The Turkana can consume milk for a greater part of the year because camel milk production is more consistent through the year (Galvin 1985). Year-to-year variation in diets also occurs and can be quite dramatic.

The Turkana and Borana data show nutritional status to be similar to one another and below reference norms. Over 50 percent of both populations showed BMIs below adequate levels, and BMIs were also very low when compared with those of black Americans. The marginal nutritional state of pastoralists found here seems to point to several conclusions. Prevailing nutritional status is a product of trade-offs associated with the pastoral subsistence strategy. Pastoralists may be trying to maintain and encourage high human population numbers. They are also trying to keep large herds dominated by reproductive females.

Diet and nutrition, at least in these societies, are conservative aspects of the pastoral strategy and do not respond greatly to changes in development, market access, and cash income. Therefore, an observed change in diet that is associated with changes in market access, "modernization," or development should not automatically be interpreted as a response to those changes. Diet and (presumably) nutrition are expected to change somewhat in the absence of such processes. Both seasonal and longer-term fluctuations in diet and nutrition have to be kept in mind when evaluating the impact of change.

Based on the cases examined here, it is hard to argue that East African pastoralists are in the process of "modernizing" their production and consumption strategies in ways that are immediately reflected in nutritional status and health. It seems likely that East African pastoralists are trying to maintain their traditional strategy of population persistence and herd maintenance, selling stock only when needed to make up shortages of milk.

NOTES

Part of this research was conducted during KAG's tenure as a National Science Foundation Post-Doctoral Research Fellow in Environmental Biology (BNR-8700206). The International Livestock Center for Africa (ILCA) facilitated work by KAG in Ethiopia. Shewangizaw Bekele helped with data collection in Borana. Research on Turkana 1989 and 1990 diets was conducted by P. W. Leslie with support from National Science Foundation grant BNS-8718477.

1. The data on Turkana and Borana nutritional status and Borana diets were collected between March and June 1988 as part of a study to assess the nutritional ecology of pastoralists.

2. The Maasai group ranch concept was conceived as a means to transform the Maasai nomadic subsistence economy into a sedentary, commercial economy. Maasai group ranches resulted from the adjudication of Maasai land into "ranches" whose membership was to be permanent and whose livestock would be limited by the local carrying capacity. Maasai acceptance stemmed from farmers' encroachment and a government promise to develop ranch infrastructure (Bekure et al. 1991).

3. The population of Maasai is also growing (3 percent annually) (Bekure et al. 1991; Nestel 1986). However, with their proximity to Nairobi and other urban areas, Maasai may have increased opportunities for human migration out of the Maasai area. By doing this they are able to maintain high livestock-to-human ratios.

4. It is interesting to note that Borana men and women wear purchased cloth, but among Turkana pastoral women, clothes made from animal skins are still the rule, with few exceptions. Turkana men do wear purchased clothes. This cultural difference probably decreases the expense Turkana have for clothing.

5. Qualitative data on Turkana diets were collected in two surveys. The first was in the 1989 wet season (mid-June to mid-July) for 106 women, and the second was in the 1990 wet season for 98 women. In each survey women were asked what foods were of primary and then secondary importance. The proportion of women in each survey who reported particular foods as being of either primary or secondary importance were calculated. In addition, dietary data for 98 Turkana women were collected by the twenty-four-hour-recall method from mid-July to mid-August 1990. Contribution of each food (by percent energy) to the diet was calculated for each woman and then averaged over all women. Paul W. Leslie collected these data with help from Sandra Gray, Michael A. Little, and Lewis Lama.

6. The contribution of the amount of cereal to the diet may have been overestimated, as women's mean daily caloric intake was estimated at 3,664 kcal, an average adult woman's intake unheard of in an African pastoral population and not supported by the nutritional data presented in this [article] (see also Galvin 1992).

7. Maasai diet composition and energy intake were assessed by the twenty-four-hour dietary recall method on 127 households (579 people), each of which was visited one day every two months for two years.

8. See note 7 on Maasai diet intake assessment. A measured dietary intake study was used to determine Turkana diets. Diets of twenty-eight people were repeatedly measured one day each of four seasons (twelve months).

9. The upper-arm circumference measurement is used to assess muscle mass and thereby protein stores. Triceps skinfold measurements provide an estimate of the size of the subcutaneous fat deposit, which in turn provides an indirect measure of body fat (Gibson 1990). Body mass index measures the leanness of individuals (Gibson 1990) and in turn provides an indirect assessment of chronic energy deficiency ... adults (James et al. 1988).

... litional work conducted among the Turkana suggests ... systematic difference between nomadic and set- ... na with regard to body mass or composition (Little ...). This suggests that even a major change in subsis-

tence strategy has not affected nutritional state, at least for the Turkana.

REFERENCES

Arhem, K., K. Homewood, and A. Rodgers 1981 *A Pastoral Food System.* The Ngorongoro Maasai in Tanzania Bureau of Resource Assessment and Land Use Planning (BRALUP) Research Paper No. 70. University of Dar es Salaam, Tanzania.

Ariza-Nino, E., and K. H. Shapiro 1984 Cattle as Capital, Consumables and Cash: Modelling Age-of-Sale Decisions in African Pastoral Production. In J. R. Simpson and P. Evangelou (eds.), *Livestock Development in Subsaharan Africa. Constraints, Prospects, Policy,* pp. 317–334. Boulder: Westview Press.

Behnke, R. H. 1990 *Livestock Marketing in Turkana District.* Draft report. Overseas Development Institute, London.

Bekure, S., P. N. de Leeuw, B. E. Grandin, and P. J. H. Neate (eds.). 1991 *Maasai Herding. An Analysis of the Livestock Production System of Maasai Pastoralists in Eastern Kajiado District, Kenya.* ILCA Systems Study 4. Addis Ababa: International Livestock Centre for Africa.

Belete Dessalegn 1985 *Smallstock and Camel Research in the Southern Rangelands.* Joint Ethiopian Pastoral Systems Study (JEPSS) interim research report. Addis Ababa: International Livestock Centre for Africa (ILCA).

Bille, J. C. 1983 *The Climatic Risks to Livestock Production in the Ethiopian Rangelands.* Joint Ethiopian Pastoral Systems Study (JEPSS) Research Report No. 4. Addis Ababa: International Livestock Centre for Africa (ILCA).

Brown, L. H. 1971 The Biology of Pastoral Man as a Factor in Conservation. *Biological Conservation* 3(2): 93–100.

Coppock, D. L. 1992a *Observations on the Traditional Logic of Pastoral Livestock Marketing in Southern Ethiopia.* Current Natural Resources Development Activities in Developing Nations. Proceedings of the International Rangeland Development Symposium, Society for Range Management, pp. 31–42.

Coppock, D. L. 1992b Ethiopian Pastoral Development. *National Geographic Research and Exploration* 8(3): 296–307.

Coppock, D. L. 1993 Constraints to Development of Extensive Livestock Systems: Experiences from Southern Ethiopia. In M. Gill, E. Owen, G. E. Pollott, and T. L. J. Lawrence (eds.), *Animal Production in Developing Countries.* Occasional Publication No. 16, British Society of Animal Production.

Coppock, D. L., S. J. Holden, and C. O'Connor 1993 *Milk Processing and Periurban Dairy Marketing in Semiarid Ethiopia and Prospects for Development Intervention.* Unpublished manuscript.

Cossins, N. J., and M. Upton 1987 The Borana Pastoral System of Southern Ethiopia. *Agricultural Systems* 25: 199–218.

Cossins, N. J., and M. Upton 1988 The Impact of Climatic Variation on the Borana Pastoral System. *Agricultural Systems* 27: 117–135.

Coughenour, M. B., J. E. Ellis, D. M. Swift, D. L. Coppock, K. Galvin, J. T. McCabe, and T. C. Hart 1985 Energy Extraction and Use in Nomadic Pastoral Ecosystem. *Science* 230: 619–625.

Dahl, G., and A. Hjort 1976 *Having Herds. Pastoral Herd Growth and Household Economy.* Stockholm Studies in Social Anthropology. Department of Social Anthropology, University of Stockholm, Sweden.

Donaldson, J. J. 1986 *Pastoralism and Drought: A Case Study of the Borana of Southern Ethiopia.* Master's thesis. Department of Agriculture and Horticulture, University of Reading, Reading, UK.

Doran, M. H., A. R. C. Low, and R. L. Kemp 1979 Cattle as a Store of Wealth in Swaziland: Implications for Livestock Development and Overgrazing in Eastern and Southern Africa. *American Journal of Agricultural Economics* 61: 41–47.

Ecosystems Ltd. 1983. *Turkana District Resource Survey.* Turkana Rehabilitation Program Draft Final Report. Ministry of Energy and Regional Development. Nairobi: Government of Kenya.

Ellis, J. E., K. Galvin, J. T. McCabe, and D. M. Swift 1987 *Pastoralism and Drought in Turkana District, Kenya.* Report to the Norwegian Agency for International Development (NORAD), Nairobi.

Ellis, J. E., and D. M. Swift 1988 Stability of African Pastoral Ecosystems: Alternate Paradigms and Implications for Development. *Journal of Range Management* 41(6): 450–459.

Evangelou, P. 1984 Cattle Marketing Efficiency in Kenya's Maasailand. In J. R. Simpson and P. Evangelou (eds.), *Livestock Development in Subsaharan Africa: Constraints, Prospects, Policy,* pp. 123–142. Boulder: Westview Press.

Field, C. R., and S. P. Simpkin 1985 *The Importance of Camels to Subsistence Pastoralists in Kenya.* Integrated Project in Arid Lands (IPAL) Technical Report E-7. Nairobi: UNESCO.

Food and Agriculture Organization 1967 *FAO Production Yearbook.* Rome: Food and Agriculture Organization.

Fratkin, E. 1991 *Surviving Drought and Development: Ariaal Pastoralists of Northern Kenya.* Boulder: Westview Press.

Galvin, K. A. 1985 *Food Procurement, Diet and Nutrition of Turkana Pastoralists in an Ecological and Social Context.* Ph.D. dissertation, State University of New York at Binghamton.

Galvin, K. A. 1992 Nutritional Ecology of Pastoralists in Dry Tropical Africa. *American Journal of Human Biology* 4(2): 209–221.

Gibson, R. S. 1990 *Principles of Nutritional Assessment.* New York: Oxford University Press.

Haas, J. D., and D. L. Pelletier 1989 Nutrition and Human Population Biology. In M. A. Little and J. D. Haas (eds.), *Human Population Biology: A Transdisciplinary Science,* pp. 152–170. New York: Oxford University Press.

Herskovits, M. J. 1926 The Cattle Complex in East Africa. *American Anthropologist* 28: 230–272, 361–388, 494–528, 633–664.

Holden, S. J., and D. L. Coppock 1992 Effects of Distance to Market, Season and Family Wealth on Pastoral Dairy Marketing in Ethiopia. *Journal of Arid Environments* 23: 321–334.

Holden, S. J., D. L. Coppock, and M. Assefa 1991 Pastoral Dairy Marketing and Household Wealth Interactions and Their Implications for Calves and Humans in Ethiopia. *Human Ecology* 19(1): 35–59.

Homewood, K. M., and W. A. Rodgers 1991 *Maasailand Ecology: Pastoralist Development and Wildlife Conservation in Ngorongoro, Tanzania.* New York: Cambridge University Press.

Homewood, K., W. A. Rodgers, and K. Arhem 1987 Ecology of Pastoralism in Ngorongoro Conservation Area, Tanzania. *Journal of Agricultural Science, Cambridge* 108: 47–72.

Huss-Ashmore, R., and J. J. Curry 1989 Diet, Nutrition and Agricultural Development in Swaziland. 1. Agricultural Ecology and Nutritional Status. *Ecology of Food and Nutrition* 23: 189–209.

Huss-Ashmore, R., and F. E. Johnston 1985 Bioanthropological Research in Developing Countries. *Annual Reviews of Anthropology* 14: 475–528.

ILCA 1990 *Annual Report and Programme Highlights.* International Livestock Centre for Africa, Addis Ababa.

Jahnke, H. E. 1982 *Livestock Production Systems and Livestock Development in Tropical Africa.* Kieler Wissenschaftsverlag Vauk, Kiel.

James, W. P. T., A. Ferro-Luzzi, and J. C. Waterlow 1988 Definition of Chronic Energy Deficiency in Adults. *European Journal of Clinical Nutrition* 42: 969–981.

Jarvis, L. S. 1986 *Supply Response in the Cattle Industry: The Argentine Case. Giannini Foundation of Agricultural Economics.* Special Report. Division of Agriculture and Natural Resources, University of California.

Lamprey, H. F. 1983 Pastoralism Yesterday and Today: The Overgrazing Problem. In F. Bourliere (ed.), *Tropical Savannas: Ecosystems of the World, Vol. 13,* pp. 643–666. Amsterdam: Elsevier.

Little, M. A., K. Galvin, and M. Mugambi 1983 Crosssectional Growth of Nomadic Turkana Pastoralists. *Human Biology* 55(4): 811–830.

Little, M. A., and B. R. Johnson 1985 Weather Conditions in South Turkana. Appendix 1. In Rada Dyson-Hudson and J. Terrence McCabe, *South Turkana Nomadism: Coping with an Unpredictably Varying Environment,* pp. 298–314. New Haven, CT: Human Relations Area Files.

Little, M. A., P. W. Leslie, and K. L. Campbell 1992 Energy Reserves and Parity of Nomadic and Settled Turkana Women. *American Journal of Human Biology* 4(6): 729–738.

Margalef, R. 1968 *Perspectives in Ecological Theory.* Chicago: University of Chicago Press.

Milligan, K. 1983 *An Aerial Reconnaissance of Livestock and Human Populations in Relation to Land Use and Ecological Conditions in the SORDU Project Area of Southern Ethiopia.* Joint Ethiopian Pastoral Systems Study (JEPSS): Research Report No. 5. Addis Ababa: International Livestock Center for Africa (ILCA).

Najjar, M. F., and M. Rowland 1987 *Anthropometric Reference Data and Prevalence of Overweight.* Vital and Health Statistics, Series 11-No. 238. Hyattsville, MD: U.S. Department of Health and Human Services.

Negussie, Tilahun 1984 *Household Economics Study in Borana.* Joint Ethiopian Pastoral System Study (JEPSS) Research Report No. 15b. Addis Ababa: International Livestock Centre for Africa (ILCA).

Nestel, P. 1985 *Nutrition of Maasai Women and Children in Relation to Subsistence Food Production.* Ph.D. dissertation. Nutrition Department, University of London.

Nestel, P. 1986 A Society in Transition: Developmental and Seasonal Influences on the Nutrition of Maasai Women and Children. *Food Nutrition Bulletin* 8: 2–18.

Odum, E. P. 1969 The Strategy of Ecosystem Development. *Science* 164: 262–270.

Prins, H. H. T. 1992 The Pastoral Road to Extinction: Competition Between Wildlife and Traditional Pastoralism in East Africa. *Environmental Conservation* 19(2): 117–123.

Sandford, S. 1983 *Management of Pastoral Development in the Third World.* New York: John Wiley and Sons.

Schneider, H. K. 1957 The Subsistence Role of Cattle Among the Pakot in East Africa. *American Anthropologist* 59: 278–300.

Schneider, H. K. 1984 Livestock in African Culture and Society: A Historical Perspective. In J. R. Simpson and P.

Evangelou (eds.), *Livestock Development in Subsaharan Africa: Constraints, Prospects, Policy,* pp. 187–200. Boulder: Westview Press.

Semple, A. T. 1971 Grassland Improvement in Africa. *Biological Conservation* 3: 173–180.

Stiles, D. N. 1983 Camel Pastoralism and Desertification in Northern Kenya. *Desertification Control* 8: 2–8.

Swift, J. 1977 Sahelian Pastoralists: Underdevelopment, Desertification, and Famine. *Annual Reviews of Anthropology* 6: 457–478.

Swift, J. 1982 The Future of African Hunter-Gatherer and Pastoral Peoples. *Development and Change* 13: 159–181.

Upton, M. 1986 Production Policies for Pastoralists: The Borana Case. *Agricultural Systems* 20: 17–35.

13

Social Class and Diet in Contemporary Mexico

Gretel H. Pelto

In contemporary Mexico there are sharp contrasts between the diets of the great masses of poor families and those of the (largely urban) middle and upper classes. The contrasts are demonstrable in data on "habitual diet," "amounts spent weekly on food," "degree of dependence on purchased foods," "variety of foods consumed," and "provenience of food items." Less obvious, but highly important, are the contrasts in "per capita nutrients consumed." Total energy costs, as well as other costs involved in the production and distribution of foods, also differ sharply when one compares the mass of low-income families with the more affluent sectors of the Mexican population. At yet another level of comparison, more fine-grained analysis would demonstrate important differences in bacterial and parasitic contamination, which are in part the result of differing conditions of food conservation and preparation.

Many of the dietary contrasts between rich and poor are closely linked to rural-urban differences, and it is difficult to disentangle the effects of social class from rural-urban factors. Although the complex mosaic of food-use patterns in Mexico must be viewed in the light of long-term processes of cultural evolution, the velocity of these processes has increased greatly in the latter part of the 20th century. The difficulty of analyzing such changes, with their multiple effects on the diets of rich and poor alike, is compounded by the fact that cultural change in modern

nations takes on different forms in rural, economically marginal regions and continually modernizing urban centers. The consequences of these differences can be examined at the individual, community, and national levels, including the consequences for individual health, for mortality and population structure, and for national resource utilization.

I will begin this discussion with a brief sketch of food use in two families in order to describe dietary differences in a qualitative fashion. I will then present statistical data concerning differentials in dietary patterns and nutrient intakes, followed by analysis of the consequences of these patterns.

DIETARY PATTERNS: TWO CASE STUDIES

Javier and Guadalupe Maria Lopez and their five children live in a small mountain village in the state of Mexico. They eke out a meager living through a combination of activities. They grow maize; Javier works occasionally as a day laborer; they sell foods such as squash blossoms, mushrooms, and maize fungus from their small fields; and periodically Javier travels to Mexico City to find temporary (unskilled) construction work.

Early morning in the Lopez household starts with coffee, laced with a couple of heaping tablespoons of sugar per mug. After several hours of work, Guadalupe Maria and the children gather for a mid-morning breakfast of tortillas and beans (cooked with onion, garlic, and salt), served with a sauce of coarsely chopped onion and chili. Javier's food is brought to him in the field during the agricultural season. His tortillas and beans are augmented by a liter of pulque, the moderately alcoholic beer made from the sap of the maguey plant (*Agave atrovirens*).

The main meal of the day (the *comida*), served after 3:00 P.M., when nine-year-old Danielo (the eldest son) returns from school, includes tortillas and a pasta (macaroni), prepared as a dry *sopa* with onion, garlic, salt, tomatoes, and a commercial soup concentrate for extra flavor. Sometimes rice replaces the macaroni, and sometimes beans are the main dish. The children drink water flavored with sugar and lime juice. Javier and Guadalupe Maria drink pulque—for Javier his third liter of the day.

In the early evening Guadalupe prepares tortillas, with "something" to put inside, wrapped to make a taco. In March and April that "something" is likely to be *nopales* (cactus leaves), chopped and fried with onion and chili. Fried potatoes, scrambled with an egg, beans, squash blossoms, or leftovers from the *comida* are likely alternatives. Sometimes the family has nothing available for the evening meal and goes to bed without eating.

Sunday is different. Sunday is market day in the nearby town. Often the family buys a little chicken, occasionally beef, to be prepared as a stew with squash, cabbage, or a few carrots. White bread rolls and sweet bread are also purchased. These are saved for breakfast and supper in the days following market day. Other special foods are purchased in the market to be eaten on the spot—frozen ices, smoked fish, and candy are favorites.

Young Danielo has his own resources for obtaining treats. Whenever he can acquire a few extra pesos, he buys gum, candy, factory-made "Gansitos," or other "Twinkies"-like cakes, filled with jelly or vegetable-based "creme" and sold by vendors near the school.

Special holidays—weddings, christenings, saints' days—provide a welcome departure from the usual fare at the Lopez household. The meals on such occasions are highly predictable: turkey in a sauce of chili and chocolate (*mole*), with rice, cake, or sweet bread; brandy or rum with Coca Cola for the adults, plus beer; and Coca Cola and other soft drinks for the children. Although the Lopez family is poor, they have relatives in several households and can count on being guests at several such special holiday feasts every year.

The town to which the Lopez family goes to market has a much wider repertory of foods than one finds in the Lopez house. In the weekly outdoor market, one sees the seasonal ebb and flow of tropical fruits from the (hot) lowlands—mounds of pineapples, papayas, mangoes, bananas, guayava, and others. Highland fruits and vegetables are also abundant. Cheese, fish, beef, pork, chicken, and a considerable array of canned goods can be purchased in the local stores. Commercial products, such as pancake mix and cornflakes, are readily available, but imported foods are only found in the city, where one also finds such specialty items as peanut butter, pizza, and whole wheat biscuits enriched with soy.

In Mexico City a great many foods practically unknown to the Lopez family find their way regularly to the table of the Villalba household. For Juan Villalba Mendez, many years of education and more than a modicum of good connections have brought a comfortable existence. Juan is trained as an electrical engineer and has a well-paid administrative position in the multinational computer corporation he joined some 10 years ago. Before her marriage, Carmen worked as a travel agent, and she expects to start her own travel firm in a few years, when her children are older.

On weekdays breakfast in the Villalba household is a simple affair: orange juice, toast, and coffee. Often the children have cereal and milk. Eggs are sometimes served on weekday mornings, and are nearly always prepared for weekend breakfasts, along with ham or bacon.

Mid-morning coffee, with a generous amount of sugar, sustains Juan until the 2:00 P.M. lunch break. This is his main meal of the day, taken in the company cafeteria or in one of the many restaurants in the vicinity of his office. Usually he has soup, salad, meat, chicken or fish, plus rice and bread. Juan wants to avoid the middle-aged paunch he associates with the onset of his father's diabetes, so he often forgoes the pie, custard, or ice cream offered with the mid-day *comida*.

Carmen is also concerned about dieting. She works hard to maintain a svelte figure, so she lunches at home on fruit and yoghurt, or salad and cheese. Once or twice a week she joins her friends for shopping or other activities, and that generally means a more substantial meal, similar to Juan's usual *comida*.

Evening meals in the Villalba household are quite variable. Sometimes Juan picks up a pizza, which is the children's favorite. Occasionally they have waffles or crepes, or perhaps an omelette. Frequently the evening meal parallels the afternoon *comida*, though it may be slightly less elaborate.

In the Villalba household there are always bowls of fresh fruit on the table (foods rarely seen in the Lopez family); but the children usually prefer to help themselves to potato chips, candied nuts, and other snack foods, along with the soft drinks that are practically always available in the refrigerator.

Sundays are also special in the Villalba family, but the weekend and weekday diets are not as noticeably different as they are in the Lopez household. Sunday meals are often no more elaborate than the meals of the rest of the week, and there is little difference in meat consumption. On the other hand, they may be different when the family goes out to picnic or enjoys an outing to the countryside or to Chapultepec Park. On those occasions there will be more snacks, soft drinks, and perhaps a pizza, hamburgers, or a special "family meal" at Burger Boy, Shakey's, or Kentucky Fried Chicken. In addition to these "international" versions of commercial meals, the Villalba family has a wide range of choices among the local specialties, sold by vendors of "typical" Mexican foods (tacos, sandwiches, ice cream, gelatins, corn on the cob, etc.), and roadside food stands. Often they purchase extra quantities of the special breads, candies, and fruits offered at roadside stands and shops to add to their weekday repasts.

The Villalba family frequently entertains guests and relatives and (unless they go out to a restaurant) their cook is asked to prepare an elegant evening meal. As gracious hosts, Juan and Carmen serve cocktails before dinner, and a fine domestic wine from Baja California is offered with the main dish. Domestic wines are considered nearly as good as imports these days, and the imports generally cost four times as much as the best domestic vintages.

The food pattern in our middle-class "sample case" resembles that of middle-class North Americans and Europeans in many ways. In comparison with many Euro-American households, the Mexican middle-class family is perhaps somewhat less "international" in its home cooking in the sense that Chinese and other Asian cuisines, for example, are not represented. Certain aspects of "typical Mexican" cooking and eating are preserved in the middle-class style, though the tortillas sold in supermarkets are usually made from wheat rather than maize.

THE FOOD AND DIET OF THE POOR

The example of the Lopez family illustrates many features of the diet of rural, low-income populations in Mexico.[1] The basic diet, reflected in the vignette of the Lopez household, relies heavily on maize. In many rural families 60 to 80 percent of the caloric intake comes from maize (Ramirez et al. 1975:161). The maize kernels are usually ground into *masa* (a clay-like dough), after being soaked in water and calcium carbonate to loosen the tough outer husk. At present the grinding is usually done in local family-owned mills, for a small fee. The *masa* is usually made into the familiar tortillas. Other, less frequently utilized ways of preparing maize include a thin gruel called *atole,* and tamales, an elongated "package" of cornmeal dough filled with meat or some other stuffing and steamed in cornhusks or leaves.

In terms of their caloric contributions, the other important foods of the rural poor are beans, sugar, and fats (lard or vegetable oils). The beans are generally boiled, with fat added for extra flavor when financial resources permit. Fat is also used to reheat previously cooked beans and to saute the flavoring ingredients (including onions and garlic) in mixed dishes. Sugar is consumed in coffee and lime-flavored water and is occasionally added to fruit juice in families with somewhat better resources. These four foods —maize, beans, sugar, and fat—are the principal sources of calories in most areas of rural Mexico (Ramirez et al. 1977:161). Together they account for an average of 80 percent of the total calories in individuals' diets (Chavez, Madrigal, and Moreno 1980: 22). Some exceptions to these patterns include the greater use of fruit in lowland warm areas.

Table 1 shows the contribution, by weight, of the main foods in the diet of the rural poor. The data are based on an extensive survey in one of the poorest rural regions in the state of Oaxaca.[2]

Maize is not only a critical source of calories; it is also the major source of protein, followed in importance by beans and animal products. About 80 percent of protein comes from vegetable products, and the other 20 percent from milk, eggs, and meat. The potential problem presented by the fact that maize is an "incomplete protein" is offset by the use of beans, which has a complementary amino acid pattern, providing a "complete protein" when the two foods are eaten together. Unfortunately, many families today are frequently substituting pasta and rice in increasing quantities in place of the relatively more costly beans. This practice, which reduces protein quality (utilizability), is probably not significant for adult nutrition, but recent studies suggest that protein quality does affect child growth (Torun, Young, and Rand 1981). Thus, the change from beans to pasta may compromise growth in poor children, particularly affecting the possibilities for "catch-up growth" following illness.

Table 1. Daily food consumption in rural Oaxaca (grams per person per day)

Food	Per Capita (Adult)	Per Capita (Pre-School)
Maize	394	143
Bread	21	24
Pasta	6	3
Rice	8	3
Wheat	1	4
Beans	40	9
Potatoes	7	3
Green vegetables	14	6
Yellow vegetables	34	7
Bananas	23	18
Citrus fruit	13	9
Other fruit	11	11
Milk	7	13
Meat	26	12
Eggs	19	20
Sugar	29	13
Soft drinks	31	29
Fats	9	3

SOURCE: Adapted from Chavez et al. (1980:120).

Table 2. Animal protein intake in various regions of Mexico (grams per person per day)

Region	Milk	Meat	Eggs	Total
Texas border	215	73	54	342
Sonora	115	80	57	252
Guerrero	69	51	16	136
Chiapas	10	57	24	91
Oaxaca	4	26	19	49

SOURCE: Adapted from Chavez et al. (1980:44).

The consumption of vegetables and fruits is highly variable from one rural region to another, although it is generally quite low throughout the entire country. For a number of reasons, including changes in farming practices (especially the increased use of herbicides in the maize fields), there appears to be a sharp decline in the use of wild greens (Messer 1977). Regional differences in fruit and vegetable consumption among rural people reflect not only differences in the availability of particular products but also differences in poverty levels. Mexico is a large country with significant resource differentials from region to region. Differentials in food consumption in the various regions are dramatically apparent in comparisons of animal protein intake, as illustrated in Table 2.

Some of the regions with the lowest average food intakes are characterized by high dependence on subsistence farming; however, the 1979 national survey showed no rural regions in which the percentage of subsistence farmers (those capable of self-provisioning of staple foods) exceeded 60 percent. Moreover, in the entire national sample of rural households, only 37 percent of families were full-time *campesinos* (small farmers), while an additional 27 percent reported that they gained their livelihood from a combination of farming and working part-time as artisans or in other non-farm work. Thirty-six percent of the households in the national sample were landless, with the men working as day laborers in farm and non-farm activities. Thus, many poor families have to buy all or most of their food, which partially helps to explain their low levels of intake.

In situations of high dependence on subsistence farming, the relationship of food intake to food costs may be attenuated. However, contemporary rural Mexico is not, by any means, a subsistence-based economy, as the previous figures indicate. The relationship of food consumption to food costs is documented by an analysis of consumption in relation to family food expenditure. Table 3 shows the average per capita consumption (for a national rural sample) of selected foods in relation to the level of weekly expenditures for food. There is a positive linear relationship between food consumption and total food expenditure for all food categories, except for the staples—maize and beans. Maize consumption is negatively related to income, and beans show no relationship.

Despite the fact that total expenditures for food and level of income are both affected by family size (larger families earn more and spend more), there is a very close correlation between per capita nutrient intake and these monetary measures. When food consumption patterns among rural families are analyzed for nutrients, the "nutritional meaning" of these diets begins to emerge. Table 4 presents the mean intakes (per capita) of a number of nutrients, by level of income.

Tables 3 and 4, which are based on surveys in rural regions of Mexico, document the direct effects of socioeconomic status on nutrition. The two top income categories may be regarded as comprising the relatively more affluent sector of the rural population, though only a small fraction of these households could be regarded as "middle class." The more affluent rural

Table 3.   Food consumption by food expenditure per week (consumption in grams per person per day)

Weekly Expenditure (Pesos)	Milk	Meat	Eggs	Sugar	Soft Drinks	Fat	Beans	Maize
Less than 250	46	32	18	34	43	19	35	373
250–500	106	58	28	40	82	28	36	326
500–1,000	176	93	39	49	131	36	32	257
1,000 plus	249	119	48	55	166	44	32	194

SOURCE: Adapted from Chavez et al. (1980:64–65).

Table 4.   Weekly income and nutrient intake per capita in rural Mexico

Income (Pesos)	Kcal.	Protein (grams)	Vitamin C (mg.)	Calcium (mg.)	Vitamin A (Retinol Equivalent)	Niacin (mg.)	Riboflavin (mg.)
Less than 250	1,604	42	25	639	230	13	0.7
250–500	1,813	49	35	494	259	15	0.8
500–1,000	1,927	53	52	719	395	18	1.2
1,000 plus	2,086	58	68	790	478	20	1.4

SOURCE: Adapted from Chavez et al. (1980).

families have taken on some urban patterns—for example, their shift from maize tortillas to wheat bread and the sharply increased use of milk in daily diets.

The casual traveler in rural Mexico, who sees large numbers of cattle, sheep, poultry, and other animals in all agricultural areas, might be surprised to learn that most of the families who own these meat animals have very low levels of meat and milk consumption, compared with urban people. In developing countries such as Mexico, meat and other animal products are too expensive for regular consumption. The meat, milk, and other products are better sold to urban dwellers for much-needed cash to buy less costly staples, including beans, pastas, and rice.

One of the most poignant ironies of life in the Third World is that the rural poor, living in the midst of food production resources, go hungry, while the inhabitants of poor urban communities appear to have somewhat better diets. This is not to say that malnutrition does not exist in urban slums, including the poverty-stricken slums of Mexican cities. But in comparison with the poorer rural regions, the low-income sectors in the cities appear to consume more food and to have a more varied diet, on average.

A study carried out during the late 1960s in the border city of Agua Prieta and in a nearby rural com-munity in the state of Sonora (one of the richest regions in the nation) provides detailed documentation of differences in food patterns and nutrient consumption between the urban and the rural poor. Table 5 presents data on differences in foods, while Table 6 shows the differences in nutrient intake.

As with the rural poor, we would expect the diets of urban poor people to vary from one part of the country to another, and the food patterns of the border town of Agua Prieta undoubtedly differ in many respects from those of towns in other parts of Mexico. The data from various urban low-income populations can also be expected to differ because of variations in the degree of poverty in specific neighborhoods and sub-communities.

Recent studies carried out by the Instituto Nacional de la Nutricion in working-class and lower-class barrios of Mexico City provide a fuller picture of diet in the metropolis (Batrouni et al. 1981). The areas selected for data gathering in this study were *barrios populares,* all of which were considered to be "less than middle class" neighborhoods. Squatter settlements, or *"areas de mise-ria marginales,"* were not included. The neighborhoods were selected to represent three levels of income, the top category comprising working-class families. By North American standards these are all very poor households. From the perspective of most rural Mexi-

Table 5. Food consumption among rural and urban poor in Sonora (grams per person per day)

Food	Urban Sample	Rural Sample
Milk	83	51
Eggs	29	14
Meat	37	38
Fats	40	8
Vegetables	49	44
Fresh fruit	37	4
Sugar/sweets	52	15
Tortillas/maize	37	41
Tortillas/wheat	246	252
Beans	74	92
Pasta/rice	17	15

SOURCE: Adapted from Arroyo et al. (1969:41).

Table 6. Nutrient consumption among urban and rural poor in Sonora (per person per day)

Nutrient	Urban	Rural
Calories	2,098.0	1,726.0
Protein (grams)	59.0	57.0
Calcium (milligrams)	692.0	536.0
Iron (milligrams)	21.0	22.0
Vitamin A (Retinol equivalent)	500.0	287.0
Thiamine (milligrams)	1.6	1.8
Vitamin C (milligrams)	21.0	13.0

SOURCE: Adapted from Arroyo et al. (1969:44).

Table 7. Food consumption in a working-class barrio area of Mexico City, 1979 (grams per person per day)

Food Item	Neighborhood Income Level		
	High	Middle	Low
Bread/baked goods	67	83	87
Tortillas (maize/wheat)	198	224	243
Pasta	27	28	28
Beans	39	43	48
Milk	323	292	200
Meat	80	74	60
Eggs	57	51	50
Fruit	62	50	34
Vegetables	36	28	27
Soft drinks	235	201	220

SOURCE: Adapted from Batrouni et al. (1981:17).

The sharpest dietary contrasts between the low-income city-dweller and the rural poor can be seen in the consumption of dairy products (milk and cheese), meat, and eggs. Even the lowest stratum of the Mexico City sample consumes more than twice as many eggs, twice as much meat, and fifty times as much milk as the rural poor in Oaxaca (see Table 2). Although the contrast with the diets in Sonora (see Table 5) is somewhat less striking, the time difference of more than 10 years is an important factor in this comparison.

When the diets of the low-income urban families are analyzed for nutrient content, one finds that most of the common deficiencies of rural populations have been eliminated, except in the poorest neighborhoods. Table 8 presents these data for the three urban strata.

These data suggest that the urban poor also have low intake of some nutrients, especially vitamin A and vitamin C. In reading these statistics we must keep in mind that these are averages. If members of a population are, on average, meeting 100 percent of their caloric needs, it is quite possible that approximately half of the households in that population fall below the recommended daily allowances, while the other half exceed the 100 percent mark. Thus, it should be clear from Table 8 that there are considerable numbers of malnourished people in the low-income populations sampled in Mexico City.

The magnitudes of the differences between the urban and rural poor vary from region to region within Mexico, with the southernmost regions generally worse than the areas along the Texas border. Table 9 documents the observation that, nationally, urban working-class families are on average better off than

can families, on the other hand, the "working poor" in Mexico City had substantial cash income in 1979–80.

From the dietary survey in the barrios, it appears that tortillas continue to be important items in the diet, although the urban dwellers often prefer wheat tortillas in place of the traditional maize (Table 7). However, they are consumed at about 60 percent of the rate reported for rural regions such as Oaxaca.

Compared with low-income rural people, city-dwelling working-class families eat more rice and beans and a great deal more bread and other baked goods. In most of these families the consumption of fruits and vegetables remains comparatively low, only slightly higher than that of their rural counterparts. Bananas, oranges, limes, mangos, tomatoes, onions, chilis, carrots, and peas are the most frequently consumed fruits and vegetables.

Table 8. Average percentage of recommended daily allowances consumed in three lower-class strata in Mexico City, 1979

Nutrients	Lower Socioeconomic Strata		
	High	Medium	Low
Calories	102	99	88
Protein	125	123	101
Calcium	172	178	137
Iron	144	142 -	123
Thiamine	149	152	124
Riboflavin	105	102	75
Niacin	117	177	90
Vitamin C	126	130	66
Vitamin A	68	69	46

SOURCE: Batrouni et al. (1981:20).

rural families even in the most favored rural regions. However, the very poorest urban populations fall well below the average food consumption reported for rural families in areas of good resources, in part because such regions include modest numbers of affluent families, which serve to inflate the overall averages.

The National Nutrition Survey statistics, averaged across the regions, are also informative (Table 10). These data show that the threat of malnutrition is greater for rural schoolchildren than for urban children. To appreciate the significance of these figures, we need to remind ourselves that when the mean intake falls below recommended allowances, considerable numbers of individuals are experiencing severe deficits.

THE FOOD AND DIET OF THE MIDDLE AND UPPER CLASSES

Until very recently there has been little interest in the food-intake patterns of middle- and upper-class families in Mexico. To a large extent the lack of information reflects research priorities in a situation of limited resources and the pressing need to describe and understand the nature and consequences of undernutrition. At the same time, there has been a tendency among Mexican nutritionists, like professionals everywhere, to ignore diet and nutrition patterns in their own social class.

The dearth of data on middle- and upper-class diet in Mexico, and in many developing countries, is likely to be remedied in the next few years. There is growing concern about the "diet of affluence" and increasing recognition of the role of diet in the "diseases of civi-

lization." Moreover, there is increasing sensitivity about the effects of middle- and upper-class dietary patterns on the overall availability of foods and the commercial production and distribution of agricultural products. These factors, as well as the need to develop more adequate national consumption data for forecasting future requirements, call for increased study of dietary patterns in the middle and upper socioeconomic sectors.

A recent study analyzing variation in garbage in Mexico City sheds light on the contrasts between upper- and lower-class diets (Restrepo and Phillips 1982). Based on careful examination of garbage samples from selected neighborhoods, the study by the National Consumers' Institute showed dramatic contrasts in the estimated frequencies of consumption of many foods (Table 11).

The relationships between consumption patterns and socioeconomic status are clearly evident in the differential utilization of major food products. Consumption of milk and milk products is approximately five times higher in the upper classes than in the lower socioeconomic strata (INN 1983). Fruit and vegetable consumption is three to four times higher; consumption of meat is more than three times higher, and the consumption of cereals (other than maize) is four times higher. Bean consumption drops slightly in the higher-income groups, whereas maize, the traditional mainstay of the diet of the poor, drops to less than 50 percent of the lower-class consumption level.

Historically, one of the most striking differences between the diets of the elite and those of the rest of the population has been the role of wheat bread. The Spaniards brought wheat to Mexico in the early 16th century. According to the historian Fernandez del Castillo, "by 1923 the sacred land of the Mexicans was covered with beautiful fields of wheat" (CulturaSep 1983). The Indians were forced to cultivate wheat on the lands confiscated by the Spanish crown, and milling and baking were also controlled by the Spaniards. Baking activities were concentrated in cities and towns, where, as in many parts of Europe, the price and weight of bread were carefully controlled. From its inception in Mexico, wheat and wheat products have been controlled by the elite and have presented considerable opportunities for profit, particularly with the expansion of the Spanish population.

With the advent of industrialized baking in the early part of this century, followed later by the introduction of new "green revolution" wheat strains, the Mexican baking industry has expanded greatly. Government subsidies for wheat and the growth of cities, which facilitated distribution, contributed further to its profitability.

Not surprisingly in a situation in which a particular type of food becomes associated with the privileged

Table 9. Protein and calorie consumption by region and income

Regions/Populations	Total Calories	Total Protein (grams)	Total Animal Protein (grams)
Urban			
Working-class	2,380	86.1	45.8
Lower-class	2,320	67.1	23.5
Peripheral	2,030	59.0	14.3
Rural			
Areas of good nutrition	2,330	69.0	20.0
Areas of fair nutrition	2,120	60.0	15.1
Areas of poor nutrition	2,060	56.1	10.0
Areas of very poor nutrition	1,890	50.2	7.9

SOURCE: Adapted from Ramirez et al. (1975:163).

Table 10. Nutrient intakes of rural and urban poor in percentages of recommended daily allowances (combined mean values for all regions of Mexico)

Groups	Protein	Calories
Rural		
Family	94	92
Schoolchildren	62	68
Pre-schoolers	65	73
Urban		
Family	108	99
Schoolchildren	102	83
Pre-schoolers	83	93

SOURCE: Adapted from Ramirez et al. (1975:51).

Table 11. Food consumption patterns in lower- and upper-income neighborhoods (number of days per year foods were consumed)

Foods	Lower-Class	Upper-Class
Rice	28	183
Cheese	16	183
Fish	13	91
Shrimp, molluscs	17	36
Canned, dehydrated vegetables	30	183
Canned, dried fruit	15	91
Potatoes	41	122
Bacon	0	91
Baby foods, juices	0	122
"T.V. dinners"	0	122
Fruit, vegetable juices	17	61
Breakfast cereals	15	26

SOURCE: Adapted from Restrepo and Phillips (1982:99).

class, bread was first incorporated into the diets of the poor as ceremonial food. In addition to its importance in the Catholic mass, the consumption of special breads is an integral part of both public and private ceremonials, including betrothals, weddings, and saints' days, of which All Saints Day (November 1) has the most elaborated bread and bread symbolism (CulturaSep 1983). As revealed in the dietary data summarized above, bread and other wheat products have become increasingly important in the diets of the poor, particularly the urban poor. Nonetheless, the differential consumption of wheat products by members of different social classes remains a noticeable feature of Mexican dietary patterns.

CONSEQUENCES OF DIETARY PATTERNS FOR HEALTH AND MORTALITY

Having reviewed the major dimensions of dietary patterns, we will now turn to an examination of the implications of these patterns, first in relation to health and mortality, then in relation to national resource utilization.

The diet of Mexican farmers and unskilled, poor workers, derived from the centuries-old diet of pre-Hispanic times, is not without its strong points from a nutritional perspective. It is high in fiber, low in cholesterol, high in complex carbohydrates—all characteristics that are currently recommended to populations in the industrialized countries as preventive of heart disease, high blood pressure, diabetes, and some forms of cancer. People consuming the Mexican peasant diet should be at lower risk of experiencing these debilitating and life-threatening diseases.

However, most of the victims of cardiovascular disease, diabetes, and cancer are adults; thus, to be "at risk" for these diseases one had to live to adulthood. The major hazards of the dietary patterns of the poor in Mexico affect infants and young children. The low nutrient density of the diet (the ratio of other nutrients to calories) means that infants and children often cannot eat enough food to meet their nutrient needs. The result is retarded growth, increased susceptibility to disease, and inadequate energy for activity. In an environment of poor sanitation, with high levels of exposure to pathogens, children (and adults) face recurrent illness, which causes further deterioration in nutritional status. If unchecked, the vicious cycle of disease and malnutrition leads to death; the synergistic relationship between them underlies the mortality statistics for Third World countries (see Mata 1978; Scrimshaw, Taylor, and Gordon 1966).

A low-fat, high-bulk diet also affects the health and well-being of the pregnant woman and her fetus. Food intake during pregnancy is one of the factors that affects pregnancy weight gain and infant birth weight. Like other poor women in Third World countries, Mexican rural women typically experience low pregnancy weight gains and often deliver babies whose weight at birth is well below birth weights in industrialized nations. Throughout the world birth weight is a primary factor associated with neonatal mortality (Habicht et al. 1973).

Inadequate caloric and nutrient consumption also affects a woman's ability to produce adequate breast milk over an extended period of time. Data from a careful longitudinal study in Tezonteopan, in the state of Puebla, demonstrated that poor rural women, consuming typical quantities of the basic rural diet, could not sustain a sufficient level of milk production to support their infants' growth, although there was considerable variability in the point at which milk production fell to seriously low levels (Chavez and Martinez 1979). Thus begins a pattern in which the undernourished infant, born at a low birth weight, cannot maintain an adequate growth trajectory. With increased disease experience as he or she grows older, malnutrition takes a progressively heavy toll. For some children this means death, but for many others it means low energy, poor physical development, and reduced opportunities to develop intellectually and emotionally (ibid.).

Although the link between malnutrition and mortality is most significant during infancy and early childhood, poor nutritional status affects the mortality risk during illness at all ages. Through its effects on mortality, nutrition affects population structure by two mechanisms: directly by eliminating individuals from the population, and indirectly by influencing fertility decision making.

In rural Mexico infant and young child mortality have declined in recent decades, partly as a function of improved access to medical care and modern drugs. However, mortality rates remain high compared with those of industrialized countries. Poor rural families can still expect to suffer the loss of children. For example, in the small town of Solis, in the state of Mexico (an area with greater resources than many other parts of the country), 39 percent of families interviewed in the early 1970s reported the death of at least one child (DeWalt, Bee, and Pelto 1972). In the Indian communities of the region, more than 60 percent of families had lost a child, and many had lost several.

The role of child loss in decision making about reproductive behavior has received a good deal of attention in recent decades (see, for example, Salo and Valimaki 1981). The "child replacement hypothesis" postulates that parents are motivated to "replace" a child's death with a new birth for a complex of emotional and economic reasons. Although infant and child mortality is not necessarily the primary factor in decisions to use or reject contraception, when mortality is high it is probable that people will be less receptive to family planning services. Thus, malnutrition may have an indirect effect on population structure through its effect on contraceptive decision making.

Examining the health consequences of the peasant diet, it is important to remember that this diet is far from the one that sustained pre-Columbian Mexico. Refined sugar, consumed in coffee by both adults and children, as well as in soft drinks and candy, has taken a toll on the dental health of farmers and workers. Moreover, in the same communities in which one finds undernutrition, obesity is beginning to appear (Chavez and Diaz 1964). Ironically, poor people in Mexico are in danger of at least some of the diseases of affluence, at the same time that they are suffering from the consequences of a nutritionally inadequate diet.

The positive aspects of the middle-class diet, from the perspective of health and nutrition, are relatively obvious. Adequate protein and calorie intake during pregnancy and childhood promote growth, with energy left for various kinds of productive and leisure activities. People have adequate nutritional reserves to recover from illness and greater resistance to disease. Intake of vitamins and minerals is superior to that of the poor, thus further increasing the probability of good health.

On the other hand, the diet of the Mexican middle class, like that of middle-class people the world over, predisposes individuals to several of the major killer diseases. High saturated-fat intake, although it has not definitively been shown to be a primary cause of cardiovascular disease, is widely regarded as a contributing factor. High protein intake is associated with problems of calcium retention and may be associated with the development of osteoporosis. Diets high in refined carbohydrate have been postulated to increase the risk of diabetes, while low-fiber diets have been associated with increased risk of intestinal cancer. Thus, to the extent that the diets of the Mexican middle class come to resemble diets in countries that have been industrialized for a longer period of time, one can expect that the morbidity and mortality patterns will also approximate those of the United States and Western Europe.

The health impact of commercially processed food, with its high levels of flavoring, stabilizing, and coloring agents, remains a controversial subject. It is probable that the Mexican middle and upper classes have higher exposure to such agents than do the rural poor. Again, to the extent that these products of modern industry affect health, we can expect that the health risk is currently greater for city-dwellers than for rural peoples, and for the middle class than for poorer classes. On the other hand, the food preparation practices of middle-class families reduce the risk of exposure to bacterial contamination. Disinfecting agents, which are added to water and used to soak fresh fruits and vegetables, are now widely available in Mexico City supermarkets. The use of these products greatly reduces exposure to amoebas and other protozoa, as well as to bacteria.

In summary, the deficiencies in the diets of the most impoverished sectors of the Mexican population cause considerable suffering. Although the incidences of severe deficiency diseases are low compared with those in many other Third World countries, it is estimated that nutritional deficiencies still account directly for a quarter of the deaths of pre-school children (Chavez 1969). Mild and moderate levels of malnutrition take a heavy toll as well, not only on physical health, but also on growth, development, and personal well-being. Undernutrition, in conjunction with disease, poor sanitation, and limited access to health care, produces a social-physical environment in which children do not grow to their full potential: "Just as in war, malnutrition casualties should be counted not only by death, but also by the 'wounded' people, especially the permanently disabled" (Chavez et al. 1971).

At the other end of the economic spectrum, the diets of the affluent are not without their own risks. The maintenance of healthy eating patterns in the midst of plenty is apparently not easy in the modern world. The long-term health consequences of middle-class diets are not as obviously negative as the conse-

quences of undernutrition, but they are not an unmixed blessing. Together with the other stresses of urban life, the high consumption of saturated fats, refined sugars and grains, and other products of modern, industrial food production pose significant health threats to the people who are affluent enough to maintain such diets.

DIETARY PATTERNS AND NATIONAL RESOURCE UTILIZATION

Since the startling and disturbing revelations of the Club of Rome in its analysis of the limits of growth (Meadows et al. 1972), it has become increasingly clear that the industrialized countries use a grossly disproportionate share of the world's resources. This applies not only to raw materials and fossil fuels, but to food supplies as well. The widening gap in wealth and lifestyles between poor and affluent nations is increasingly reflected in the contrasts in resources, dietary patterns, and lifestyles between the poor and the affluent classes within the developing nations.

Consumption of Animal Products

As a basic comparison, we note the difference in caloric consumption between the poor and the affluent. The average differential of 400 to 500 calories per day is not insignificant when projected to a national level. However, this is but the tip of the iceberg. The energy costs of producing animal food products (which are disproportionately consumed by middle- and upper-income families) are very great compared with the costs of producing vegetable foods (Borgstrom 1972). When caloric intake is calculated in terms of "primary calories," which include the calories consumed by animals, the daily per capita caloric consumption by affluent people in the world exceeds 10,000 calories. The "gap" between recorded caloric intakes (averaging 2,500 to 3,000 kilocalories) and the actual caloric costs in food value is about 7,000. In contrast, according to Borgstrom's calculations, the estimated "calorie gap" for a peasant in India is only 1,000 kilocalories (Borgstrom 1972:31).

Taking this analysis a step further, Martinez and colleagues (1976) have calculated that a Mexican middle-class diet that includes 100 grams of animal protein per day costs 14,000 "agricultural calories" and a half million "industrial calories" (fuel, transport,

Table 12. Increases in the production and per capita consumption of animals in Mexico, 1972–79 (in percentages)

	Production	Consumption
Beef	52	31
Pork	104	65
Chicken	70	35
Eggs	50	22
Milk	34	22

SOURCE: Adapted from DeWalt (1985).

equipment, etc.). On the other hand, they estimate that the diets of poor families, based mainly on maize, beans, and other vegetable foods, require only about 2,000 "agricultural calories" and 8,000 "industrial calories" per day (Martinez et al. 1976:245).

The inequities in food consumption are clear from dietary intake data, expressed as per capita consumption rates. When these are transposed to food dollar figures, as Gonzalez Casanova has done (1980), we see that the 15 percent of Mexicans with the most purchasing power purchase 50 percent of the total value of foods in the Mexican food system, while the poorest 30 percent in income purchase only 10 percent of the total (Gonzalez Casanova 1980:202). The calculations of Martinez and colleagues (1976) make it clear that the energy inequities are much greater than even the food consumption and food expenditure data demonstrate.

Much of the increased demand for animal products in Mexico is being met by increased domestic production. Table 12 shows the increase over the seven-year period from 1972 to 1979. It should be noted that the per capita consumption increases are less than the production increases, reflecting both the rapid increase in the Mexican population during the same period and the export of a portion of the animal food produced.

The demand for milk and other dairy products, although commendable from certain nutritional standpoints, also has important implications. Dairying is an energy-intensive industry and is becoming increasingly so with the adoption of modern dairying techniques. Processing, transportation, and preservation costs are high, not only placing large-scale consumption of milk products out of the reach of the rural poor, but also demanding significant fossil fuel and other material resources for the manufacture and maintenance of equipment and transportation facilities.

Grains for Human Consumption and Animal Feed

Of great concern is the fact that during the recent period of increase in consumption of animal foods, the production of basic grains has dropped sharply (DeWalt 1985). In 1965 the annual per capita production of food grains was 280 kilograms. By 1979 it had dropped to 169 kilograms—60 percent of the 1965 figures. This decline is particularly dramatic when we consider that the "green revolution" was supposed to have saved the Mexican food grain situation in the 1960s. The decline in per capita grain production was not due primarily to population increases; rather, it resulted from government policies that encouraged the production of sorghum and discouraged basic grain production. Although sorghum is preferred for animal feeding, some of the basic grains (wheat, barley, and maize) have also been diverted to feed livestock.

The shift in the allocation of land from foods intended for direct human consumption to animal feed is not limited to large commercial farms. The small farmers have also converted a portion of their crops to fodder. For example, in the Solis Valley in central Mexico, it appears that many of the wheat and barley fields that can be seen among the fields of maize are planted to provide grains for animal consumption, "because it makes them grow faster." The majority of the meat animals fattened from these fields find their way to the tables of the middle and upper classes in Mexico City. Ramirez and associates (1975) estimate that nearly 50 percent of the increase in animal product production since 1960 is consumed in Mexico City. Thus, the consumption patterns of the affluent, which feature meat as a central component of the diet, have diverted scarce resources from food grain to livestock production—a far less efficient use of land and water resources.

The Hidden Costs of Contemporary Food Patterns

Other energy expenditures and environmental costs are associated with the dietary patterns of the middle and upper classes. The development of supermarkets, food-processing plants, and other components of the food industry not only increase the input of "agricultural" and "industrial" calories; they also increase the amount of solid waste (Restrepo and Phillips 1982:52). The containers—bags, boxes, cans, and bottles—that are used to transport and store foods contribute, perhaps, only a small portion to the total problem of solid waste, but the collective impacts of the new modes of obtaining and consuming food that characterize the more affluent sectors of the population not only contribute to the problem of "visual pollution," but carry other hidden costs in environmental degradation and the energy necessary for the management of waste disposal.

A number of years ago the Mexican anthropologist Rudolfo Stavenhagen used the term "internal colonialism" to refer to the relationship between marginal rural areas and the urban power centers (Stavenhagen 1967). The flow of food resources from the rural areas to the cities of Mexico, and beyond to other wealthy populations, can be seen as yet another manifestation of this process. Class differences in food patterns in contemporary Mexico go far beyond the dramatic differences in nutrient intakes. In addition to the hidden costs of malnutrition in the poorer sectors, the carnivorous appetites of affluence place an immense burden of energy costs on an already strained ecological system.

ACKNOWLEDGMENTS

The reader scanning the bibliography will quickly note the frequency with which A. Chavez's name appears. As director of the Division of Community Nutrition of the National Institute of Nutrition, he has been responsible for a large share of the research projects that collectively provide a picture of nutrition in contemporary Mexico.

Beyond his prodigious efforts as a researcher and research administrator, his depth of understanding about the nature of malnutrition has influenced researchers all over the world. I am greatly indebted to him for whatever insights this [article] may contain. I also want to thank Pertti J. Pelto and Lindsay H. Allen for their thoughtful and critical commentary.

NOTES

1. The dietary patterns of the rural poor have been exceedingly well documented, primarily as a result of the massive efforts of the National Institute of Nutrition (INN) and other research groups. Available materials include large-scale surveys, which present statistical, descriptive data on food consumption and nutritional status (usually expressed as mean values for large population segments), and detailed longitudinal studies using small samples.

2. The reader unfamiliar with food weights might find it useful to note that an egg weighs 60 grams. In Table 1 the average per capita consumption of 26 grams of meat per day compares with an average North American consumption of 300 to 400 grams of meat per day.

REFERENCES

Arroya, P. A., et al. 1969 *Alimentacion en una Region Fronteriza: Agua Prieta y Esqueda, Sonora.* Publicacion L-15. Mexico City: Division de Nutricion, Instituto Nacional de la Nutricion.

Batrouni, L., et al. 1981 *La Alimentacion y la Nutricion de los Barrios Populares de la Ciudad de Mexico.* Publicacion L-42. Mexico City: Division de Nutricion, Instituto Nacional de la Nutricion.

Borgstrom, Georg 1972 *The Hungry Planet.* New York: Macmillan.

Chavez, A. 1969 El Problema de la Nutricion Infantil. *Revista Technica de Alimentos Mexicanos* 4:22.

Chavez, A., and D. M. Diaz 1964 Frequencia de Obesidad en Algunas Zonas de la Republica Mexicana. *Publicacion de la Sociedad Mexicàna de Endrocronologia* 5:119–29.

Chavez, A., et al. 1971 Ecological Factors in the Nutrition and Development of Children in Poor Rural Areas. *Proceedings of the Western Hemisphere Nutrition Congress III.* 265–80.

Chavez, A.; H. Madrigal; and O. Moreno 1980 *La Alimentacion en el Medio Rural.* Publicacion L-33. Mexico City: Division de Nutricion, Instituto Nacional de la Nutricion.

Chavez, A., and C. Martinez 1979 *Nutricion y Desarrallo Infantil.* Mexico City: Nueva Editorial Interamericana.

CulturaSep 1983 *La Cosa Esta Del Cocol y Otros Panes Mexicanos.* Mexico City: Museo Nacional de Culturas Populares.

DeWalt, B. R. 1985 Mexico's Second Green Revolution: Food for Feed. *Estudios Mexicanos* 1:29–60.

DeWalt, B.; R. Bee; and P. J. Pelto 1972 *The People of Temascalcingo: A Regional Study of Modernization.* Monograph. Storrs, Conn.: Department of Anthropology, University of Connecticut.

Gonzalez Casanova, P. 1980 The Economic Development of Mexico. *Scientific American.* 243(4):192–204.

Habicht, J.-P., et al. 1973 Relationships of Birthweight, Maternal Nutrition and Infant Mortality. *Nutrition Reports International* 7:533–46.

INN (Instituto Nacional de la Nutricion) 1983 Unpublished Data.

Martinez, C., et al. 1976 *La Estructura del Consumo de Alimentos en el Medio Rural Pobre.* Publicacion L-29. Mexico City: Division de Nutricion, Instituto Nacional de la Nutricion.

Mata, Leonardo 1978 *The Children of Santa Maria Cauque.* Cambridge, Mass.: MIT Press.

Meadows, D. H., et al. 1972 *The Limits to Growth.* New York: New American Library.

Messer, E. 1977 The Ecology of Vegetarian Diet in a Modernizing Mexican Community. In *Nutrition and Anthropology in Action,* T. K. Fitzgerald, ed., pp. 117–24. Amsterdam: Van Gorcum.

Ramirez Hernandez, J., et al. 1975 Problematica y Perspectivas de las Disponibilidades de Alimentos en Mexico. *Revista del Comercio External Mexicano* 25:559–66.

Restrepo, I., and D. Phillips 1982 *La Basura: Consumo y Desperdicio en Distrito Federal.* Mexico City: Instituto Nacional del Consumidor.

Salo, M., and H. Valimaki 1981 Infant Mortality, Birth Interval and Economic Development: An Example From Rural Finland. *Medical Anthropology* 5:507–22.

Scrimshaw, N.; C. Taylor; and J. Gordon 1966 *Interactions of Nutrition and Infection.* WHO Monograph Series, No. 57. Geneva: World Health Organization.

Stavenhagen, R. 1967 Social Aspects of Agrarian Structure in Mexico. In *Agrarian Problems and Peasant Movements in Latin America,* R. Stavenhagen, ed. Garden City, N.Y.: Anchor Books.

Torun, B.; V. R. Young; and W. Rand 1981 Protein-Energy Requirements of Developing Countries: Evaluation of New Data. *Food and Nutrition Bulletin Supplement.* No. 5. Tokyo: United Nations University.

PART III
Why Do We Eat What We Eat?

Explaining Foodways #1: Materialist Approaches

Why do we eat what we eat? Are the means by which foods are chosen, processed, and combined simply a matter of what tastes good, or of cultural idiosyncrasy, or are they somehow related to nutritional needs? How these questions are answered provides insight into theoretical approaches used in anthropology.

Food is rich with social and ideological meaning, and food systems reflect larger systems of thought, power, and control. As omnivores, there are many things we could eat, but every human group defines a limited number of items as food, and makes even more choices at each meal. How do we choose the meal from a menu of possibilities? Is the logic of choice based on some deep bodily or ecological need? If so, what is the process by which desire and needs are linked? Moreover, what needs are fulfilled?

The cultural anthropologist Marvin Harris is well known for his development of a perspective called *cultural materialism,* in which cultural systems and behaviors are viewed as evolved adaptations to material needs (Harris, 1979; 1985). Extending the argument to food, Harris hypothesizes that food systems have evolved to efficiently meet nutritional needs and to be sustainable within particular ecological limits. Simply put, we do the things we do, including growing, preparing, and eating specific foods, because they meet inescapable material needs. Harris considers purely ideological or religious explanations of food taboos to be circular: they do not lead to a deeper understanding of the taboo. His objective is to understand what is *behind* ideology and religion. For Harris, what is dismissed by some as mere ideology or religious belief had, and may still have, an evolved logic.

In a well-known example in his book *Good to Eat* (1985), Harris considers the Jewish and Muslim prohibition against eating pig. He feels certain that the prohibition against eating pig, which for Jews is from the book of Leviticus, circa 450 B.C., is a law that makes some materialist sense. The challenge is to discover why eating pig is materially as well as morally wrong.

Moses Maimonides, a physician to the Islamic emperor Saladin, provided one explanation in the twelfth century. He wrote that the filthy and loathsome pig was forbidden because it was unwholesome. Seven centuries later, an association was discovered between trichinosis and undercooked pork, thus providing scientific support for Maimonides' idea.

Harris considers Maimonides to be on the right track, but wrong in the particulars of his argument. He points out that had Maimonides been correct, the decree should have been against undercooked pork rather than all pig products. Harris offers a more ecological explanation. He notes that pigs do not efficiently gain weight on a diet of grasses. Thus, unlike cows and goats, which do well on grasses, pigs often end up needing to compete with humans for food. Thus, the prohibition is basically a way of saying that pigs do not make good ecological and economic sense.

In "India's Sacred Cow," the first article of this part, Harris similarly notes that many have been struck by the seeming contradiction between starving Hindus and cows that seem to run free throughout India. Why is this food source not eaten? If cows were considered food, wouldn't this help to meet important nutritional needs?

Harris wishes to demolish the stereotype that Hindu law is irrational and that Hindus would rather starve to death than eat their sacred cows. He shows how a live Indian cow contributes in a number of useful ways to the local economy. Cows are used for plowing and hauling, their milk is drunk, their dung is used for fertilizer, and when they die their leather is put to a variety of uses, while non-Hindus consume the meat. Harris concludes that, by comparison, the U.S. system of cattle production is inefficient and perhaps a bit irrational. How satisfying is Harris's explanation? Does it have the ring of a deeper explanation? Can you think of another explanation?

Michael Harner presents a style of argument similar to that of Harris, but for a very different and even more controversial subject: Aztec cannibalism. Cannibalism is considered to be one of the most widespread of taboos (Arens, 1979). Harner, nonetheless, clearly argues that the Aztecs practiced cannibalism and that they did so to meet nutritional needs. He makes two related points that can be viewed as hypotheses to consider.

◆ The Aztecs of central Mexico frequently practiced human sacrifice and cannibalism in the fifteenth century.

◆ Aztecs consumed human flesh in order to obtain a high-quality source of much-needed protein.

Harner's article is one that is particularly useful to discuss and debate because it hits on a number of key issues having to do with the quality of anthropological data and explanation. While he vigorously portrays Aztecs as cannibals, think about the perspective of the European chroniclers. What are the potential biases of his sources? (It is interesting to note that at this time Africans sometimes thought that European explorers were cannibals.) On the other hand, just because they might be biased, does this mean that the observations were incorrect? Finally, might our inability to accept cannibalism say more about us and our taboo than it does about the Aztecs?

The potential answers to the "Why cannibalism?" question are particularly interesting. As a matter of religion, sacrifice and cannibalism might be seen as a way to "appease the gods." A frequent political explanation is that sacrifice is an extreme form of social control. Having the ultimate power, the power to kill, is something that would keep the masses in line. Other explanations might be more ecological. Sacrifice is a form of killing, and this might help to limit population growth. And, finally, eating victims might provide a key source of sustenance. How can one choose among these explanations?

We may never know the truth of the extent of cannibalism and the needs it fulfilled. What would you like to know in order to judge whether Harner's hypothesis might be correct? Is the needed information knowable? In the face of incomplete data, what would convince you? What other types of information would provide support for the argument, and what might weaken it?

The work of Harris and Harner is interesting and speculative. In some cases the data are not available, and in other cases it would require an inordinate amount of time to put together a stronger test. A more multidisciplinary model for an unusual dietary practice is provided by Timothy Johns in "Well-Grounded Diet." Clay eating has frequently been observed and reported. Why eat clay? To answer this question, Johns has looked for a number of clues. What clays are selected, and what compounds do they include? What do we know about the properties of these clays? Who eats clays? Do individuals with particular food cravings eat clays? Are clays eaten by certain age or sex classes of individuals? With what are clays eaten?

Johns suggests that the clay eating is mostly done to detoxify compounds and to make foods more palatable. The earth itself is the world's oldest medicinal. Through detailed work—in the field and the laboratory—Johns develops his argument that clays are especially good at binding toxic compounds. How convinced are you of his explanation? How does his research and explanation compare to those of Harner and Harris? Having read Johns, have some sources of information come to light that could be used by Harner or Harris?

SUGGESTIONS FOR THINKING AND DOING NUTRITIONAL ANTHROPOLOGY

1. Reexamine the evidence for Aztec cannibalism. Identify the availability of other protein sources (including unusual sources such as algae and insects). Locate reference sources on Aztec population, ecology and food production, and human protein requirements. Does cannibalism still make sense as a protein source?

2. Explanations have consequences for action. Imagine that project VACA has assigned you to India to solve the problem of endemic undernutrition in that country. You have read Harris and you agree with him. How would this understanding guide your actions? Conversely, what different actions might be suggested if you are not convinced by Harris?

3. Food cravings are commonly thought to reflect biological needs. A desire for salt reflects a need for sodium, and a desire for ice cream might reflect a deficiency in calcium. Think of an example of a food craving, and investigate current understanding of whether or not it reflects physiological need.

SUGGESTED READINGS

Arens, W. (1979). *The man-eating myth: Anthropology and anthropophagy.* Oxford University Press: Oxford. (Easy reading on the quality of ethnographic data, especially as it pertains to rumors of cannibalism.)

Durham, W. H. (1991). *Coevolution: Genes, culture, and human diversity.* Stanford, Calif.: Stanford University Press. (Durham presents theory and examples of "memes," or how cultural traits may be selected and evolved.)

Etkin, N. L. (Ed.). (1994). *The pharmacologic, ecologic, and social implications of using noncultigens.* Tucson: University of Arizona Press. (Excellent compilation of cross-cultural data on plants as medicines.)

Harris, M. (1979). *Cultural materialism: The struggle for a science of culture.* New York: Random House. (Harris presents in detail his theory of cultural materialism.)

————. (1985). *Good to eat: Riddles of food and culture.* New York: Simon and Schuster. (A popular book on the material and adaptive significance of cultural behaviors.)

Johns, T. (1996). *The origins of human diet and medicine.* Tucson: University of Arizona Press. (A wealth of interesting examples of how foods are detoxified and used for medicinal purposes.)

14

India's Sacred Cow

Marvin Harris

News photographs that came out of India during the famine of the late 1960s showed starving people stretching out bony hands to beg for food while sacred cattle strolled behind them undisturbed. The Hindu, it seems, would rather starve to death than eat his cow or even deprive it of food. The cattle appear to browse unhindered through urban markets eating an orange here, a mango there, competing with people for meager supplies of food.

By Western standards, spiritual values seem more important to Indians than life itself. Specialists in food habits around the world like Fred Simoons at the University of California at Davis consider Hinduism an irrational ideology that compels people to overlook abundant, nutritious foods for scarcer, less healthful foods.

What seems to be an absurd devotion to the mother cow pervades Indian life. Indian wall calendars portray beautiful young women with bodies of fat white cows, often with milk jetting from their teats into sacred shrines.

Cow worship even carries over into politics. In 1966 a crowd of 120,000 people, led by holy men, demonstrated in front of the Indian House of Parliament in support of the All-Party Cow Protection Campaign Committee. In Nepal, the only contemporary Hindu kingdom, cow slaughter is severely punished. As one story goes, the car driven by an official of a United States agency struck and killed a cow. In order to avoid the international incident that would have occurred when the official was arrested for murder, the Nepalese magistrate concluded that the cow had committed suicide.

Many Indians agree with Western assessments of the Hindu reverence for their cattle, the zebu, or *Bos indicus,* a large-humped species prevalent in Asia and Africa. M. N. Srinivas, an Indian anthropologist, states: "Orthodox Hindu opinion regards the killing of cattle with abhorrence, even though the refusal to kill the vast number of useless cattle which exists in India today is detrimental to the nation." Even the Indian Ministry of Information formerly maintained that "the large animal population is more a liability than an asset in view of our land resources." Accounts from many different sources point to the same conclusion: India, one of the world's great civilizations, is being strangled by its love for the cow.

The easy explanation for India's devotion to the cow, the one most Westerners and Indians would offer, is that cow worship is an integral part of Hinduism. Religion is somehow good for the soul, even if it sometimes fails the body. Religion orders the cosmos and explains our place in the universe. Religious beliefs, many would claim, have existed for thousands of years and have a life of their own. They are not understandable in scientific terms.

But all this ignores history. There is more to be said for cow worship than is immediately apparent. The earliest Vedas, the Hindu sacred texts from the Second Millennium B.C., do not prohibit the slaughter of cattle. Instead, they ordain it as a part of sacrificial rites. The early Hindus did not avoid the flesh of cows and bulls; they ate it at ceremonial feasts presided over by Brahman priests. Cow worship is a relatively recent development in India; it evolved as the Hindu religion developed and changed.

This evolution is recorded in royal edicts and religious texts written during the last 3,000 years of Indian history. The Vedas from the First Millennium B.C. contain contradictory passages, some referring to ritual slaughter and others to a strict taboo on beef consumption. A. N. Bose, in *Social and Rural Economy of Northern India, 600 B.C.–200 A.D.,* concludes that many of the sacred-cow passages were incorporated into the texts by priests of a later period.

By 200 A.D. the status of Indian cattle had undergone a spiritual transformation. The Brahman priesthood exhorted the population to venerate the cow and forbade them to abuse it or to feed on it. Religious feasts involving the ritual slaughter and consumption of livestock were eliminated and meat eating was restricted to the nobility.

By 1000 A.D., all Hindus were forbidden to eat beef. Ahimsa, the Hindu belief in the unity of all life, was the spiritual justification for this restriction. But it is difficult to ascertain exactly when this change occurred. An important event that helped to shape the modern complex was the Islamic invasion, which took place in the Eighth Century. All Hindus may have found it politically expedient to set themselves off from the invaders, who were beefeaters, by emphasizing the need to prevent the slaughter of their sacred animals. Thereafter, the cow taboo assumed its modern form and began to function much as it does today.

The place of the cow in modern India is every place—on posters, in the movies, in brass figures, in stone and wood carvings, on the streets, in the fields. The cow is a symbol of health and abundance. It provides the milk that Indians consume in the form of yogurt and ghee (clarified butter), which contribute subtle flavors to much spicy Indian food.

This, perhaps, is the practical role of the cow, but cows provide less than half the milk produced in India. Most cows in India are not dairy breeds. In most regions, when an Indian farmer wants a steady, high-quality source of milk he usually invests in a female water buffalo. In India the water buffalo is the specialized dairy breed because its milk has a higher butterfat content than zebu milk. Although the farmer milks his zebu cows, the milk is merely a by-product.

More vital than zebu milk to South Asian farmers are zebu calves. Male calves are especially valued because from bulls come oxen, which are the mainstay of the Indian agricultural system.

Small, fast oxen drag wooden plows through late-spring fields when monsoons have dampened the dry, cracked earth. After harvest, the oxen break the grain from the stalk by stomping through mounds of cut wheat and rice. For rice cultivation in irrigated fields, the male water buffalo is preferred (it pulls better in deep mud), but for most other crops, including rainfall rice, wheat, sorghum, and millet, and for transporting goods and people to and from town, a team of oxen is preferred. The ox is the Indian peasant's tractor, thresher and family car combined; the cow is the factory that produces the ox.

If draft animals instead of cows are wanted, India appears to have too few domesticated ruminants, not too many. Since each of the 70 million farms in India requires a draft team, it follows that Indian peasants should use 140 million animals in the fields. But there are only 40 million oxen and male water buffalo in the subcontinent, a shortage of 30 million draft teams.

In other regions of the world, joint ownership of draft animals might overcome a shortage, but Indian agriculture is closely tied to the monsoon rains of late spring and summer. Field preparation and planting must coincide with the rain, and a farmer must have his animals ready to plow when the weather is right. When the farmer without a draft team needs bullocks most, his neighbors are all using theirs. Any delay in turning the soil drastically lowers production.

Because of this dependence on draft animals, loss of the family oxen is devastating. If a beast dies, the farmer must borrow money to buy or rent an ox at interest rates so high that he ultimately loses his land. Every year foreclosures force thousands of poverty-stricken peasants to abandon the countryside for the overcrowded cities.

If a family is fortunate enough to own a fertile cow, it will be able to rear replacements for a lost team and thus survive until life returns to normal. If, as sometimes happens, famine leads a family to sell its cow and ox team, all ties to agriculture are cut. Even if the family survives, it has no way to farm the land, no oxen to work the land, and no cows to produce oxen.

The prohibition against eating meat applies to the flesh of cows, bulls, and oxen, but the cow is the most sacred because it can produce the other two. The peasant whose cow dies is not only crying over a spiritual loss but over the loss of his farm as well.

Religious laws that forbid the slaughter of cattle promote the recovery of the agricultural system from the dry Indian winter and from periods of drought. The monsoon, on which all agriculture depends, is erratic. Sometimes it arrives early, sometimes late, sometimes not at all. Drought has struck large portions of India time and again in this century, and Indian farmers and the zebus are accustomed to these natural disasters. Zebus can pass weeks on end with little or no food and water. Like camels, they store both in their humps and recuperate quickly with only a little nourishment.

During droughts the cows often stop lactating and become barren. In some cases the condition is permanent but often it is only temporary. If barren animals were summarily eliminated, as Western experts in animal husbandry have suggested, cows capable of recovery would be lost along with those entirely debilitated. By keeping alive the cows that can later produce oxen, religious laws against cow slaughter assure the recovery of the agricultural system from the greatest challenge it faces—the failure of the monsoon.

The local Indian governments aid the process of recovery by maintaining homes for barren cows. Farmers reclaim any animal that calves or begins to lactate. One police station in Madras collects strays and pastures them in a field adjacent to the station. After a small fine is paid, a cow is returned to its rightful owner when the owner thinks the cow shows signs of being able to reproduce.

During the hot, dry spring months most of India is like a desert. Indian farmers often complain they cannot feed their livestock during this period. They maintain the cattle by letting them scavenge on the sparse grass along the roads. In the cities cattle are encouraged to scavenge near food stalls to supplement their scant diet. These are the wandering cattle tourists report seeing throughout India.

Westerners expect shopkeepers to respond to these intrusions with the deference due a sacred animal; instead, their response is a string of curses and the crack of a long bamboo pole across the beast's back or a poke at its genitals. Mahatma Gandhi was well aware of the treatment sacred cows (and bulls and oxen) received in India. "How we bleed her to take the last drop of milk from her. How we starve her to emaciation, how we ill-treat the calves, how we deprive them of their portion of milk, how cruelly we treat the oxen, how we castrate them, how we beat them, how we overload them."

Oxen generally receive better treatment than cows. When food is in short supply, thrifty Indian peasants feed their working bullocks and ignore their cows, but rarely do they abandon the cows to die. When cows are sick, farmers worry over them as they would over members of the family and nurse them as if they were children. When the rains return and when the fields are harvested, the farmers again feed their cows regularly and reclaim their abandoned animals. The prohibition against beef consumption is a form of disaster insurance for all India.

Western agronomists and economists are quick to protest that all the functions of the zebu cattle can be improved with organized breeding programs, cultivated pastures, and silage. Because stronger oxen would pull the plow faster, they could work multiple plots of land, allowing farmers to share their animals. Fewer healthy, well-fed cows could provide Indians with more milk. But pastures and silage require arable land, land needed to produce wheat and rice.

A look at Western cattle farming makes plain the cost of adopting advanced technology in Indian agriculture. In a study of livestock production in the United States, David Pimentel of the College of Agriculture and Life Sciences at Cornell University found that 91 percent of the cereal, legume, and vegetable protein suitable for human consumption is consumed by livestock. Approximately three quarters of the arable land in the United States is devoted to growing food for livestock. In the production of meat and milk, American ranchers use enough fossil fuel to equal more than 82 million barrels of oil annually.

Indian cattle do not drain the system in the same way. In a 1971 study of livestock in West Bengal, Stewart Odend'hal of the University of Missouri found that Bengalese cattle ate only the inedible remains of subsistence crops—rice straw, rice hulls, the tops of sugar cane, and mustard-oil cake. Cattle graze in the fields after harvest and eat the remains of crops left on the ground; they forage for grass and weeds on the roadsides. The food for zebu cattle costs the human population virtually nothing. "Basically," Odend'hal says, "the cattle convert items of little direct human value into products of immediate utility."

❖ ❖ ❖

In addition to plowing the fields and producing milk, the zebus produce dung, which fires the hearths and fertilizes the fields of India. Much of the estimated 800 million tons of manure produced annually is collected by the farmers' children as they follow the family cows and bullocks from place to place. And when the children see the droppings of another farmer's cattle along the road, they pick those up also. Odend'hal reports that the system operates with such high efficiency that the children of West Bengal recover nearly 100 percent of the dung produced by their livestock.

From 40 to 70 percent of all manure produced by Indian cattle is used as fuel for cooking; the rest is returned to the fields as fertilizer. Dried dung burns slowly, cleanly, and with low heat—characteristics that satisfy the household needs of Indian women. Staples like curry and rice can simmer for hours. While the meal slowly cooks over an unattended fire, the women of the household can do other chores. Cow chips, unlike firewood, do not scorch as they burn.

It is estimated that the dung used for cooking fuel provides the energy-equivalent of 43 million tons of coal. At current prices, it would cost India an extra 1.5 billion dollars in foreign exchange to replace the dung with coal. And if the 350 million tons of manure that are being used as fertilizer were replaced with commercial fertilizers, the expense would be even greater. Roger Revelle of the University of California at San Diego has calculated that 89 percent of the energy used in Indian agriculture (the equivalent of about 140 million tons of coal) is provided by local sources. Even if foreign loans were to provide the money, the capital outlay necessary to replace the Indian cow with tractors and fertilizers for the fields, coal for the fires, and transportation for the family would probably warp international financial institutions for years.

Instead of asking the Indians to learn from the American model of industrial agriculture, American farmers might learn energy conservation from the Indians. Every step in an energy cycle results in a loss of energy to the system. Like a pendulum that slows a bit with each swing, each transfer of energy from sun to plants, plants to animals, and animals to human beings involves energy losses. Some systems are more efficient than others; they provide a higher percentage of the energy inputs in a final, useful form. Seventeen percent of all energy zebus consume is returned in the form of milk, traction and dung. American cattle raised on Western range land return only 4 percent of the energy they consume.

But the American system is improving. Based on techniques pioneered by Indian scientists, at least one commercial firm in the United States is reported to be building plants that will turn manure from cattle feedlots into combustible gas. When organic matter is broken down by anaerobic bacteria, methane gas and carbon dioxide are produced. After the methane is cleansed of the carbon dioxide, it is available for the

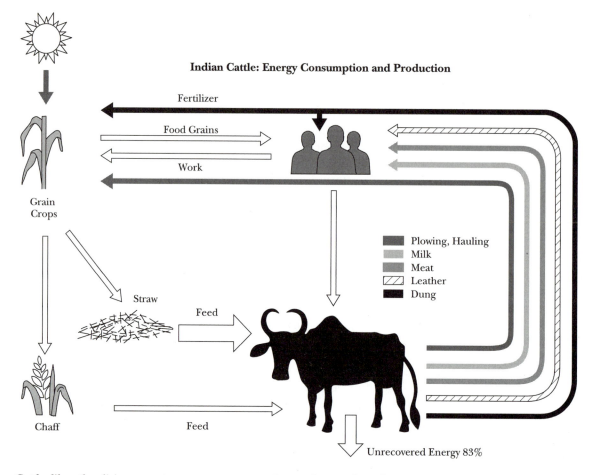

Indian Cattle: Energy Consumption and Production

Cattle, like other living organisms, consume energy in one form and produce it in another. The diagrams above trace the consumption and production of energy by Indian and American cattle. The size of the shaded arrows reflects the proportion of energy flow; the gray arrows indicate unmeasured quantities. Indian cattle transform 17 percent of the food they eat into useful goods. American cattle transform only 4 percent of the energy used in their production into useful forms. Indian cattle eat agricultural waste products unfit for human consumption. In America, cattle eat grain that could feed people, and beef and dairy farming require fossil fuels that could be put to more efficient use.

same purposes as natural gas—cooking, heating, electricity generation. The company constructing the biogasification plant plans to sell its product to a gas-supply company, to be piped through the existing distribution system. Schemes similar to this one could make cattle ranches almost independent of utility and gasoline companies, for methane can be used to run trucks, tractors, and cars as well as to supply heat and electricity. The relative energy self-sufficiency that the Indian peasant has achieved is a goal American farmers and industry are now striving for.

Studies like Odend'hal's understate the efficiency of the Indian cow, because dead cows are used for purposes that Hindus prefer not to acknowledge. When a cow dies, an Untouchable, a member of one of the lowest ranking castes in India, is summoned to haul away the carcass. Higher castes consider the body of the

dead cow polluting; if they do handle it, they must go through a rite of purification.

Untouchables first skin the dead animal and either tan the skin themselves or sell it to a leather factory. In the privacy of their homes, contrary to the teachings of Hinduism, untouchable castes cook the meat and eat it. Indians of all castes rarely acknowledge the existence of these practices to non-Hindus, but most are aware that beefeating takes place. The prohibition against beefeating restricts consumption by the higher castes and helps distribute animal protein to the poorest sectors of the population that otherwise would have no source of these vital nutrients.

Untouchables are not the only Indians who consume beef. Indian Muslims and Christians are under no restriction that forbids them beef, and its consumption is legal in many places. The Indian ban on cow

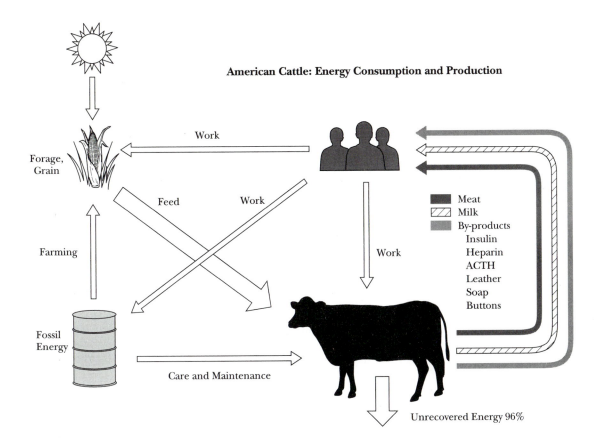

American Cattle: Energy Consumption and Production

Forage, Grain

Work

Feed   Work

Farming

Meat
Milk
By-products
Insulin
Heparin
ACTH
Leather
Soap
Buttons

Work

Fossil Energy

Care and Maintenance

Unrecovered Energy 96%

slaughter is state, not national, law and not all states restrict it. In many cities, such as New Delhi, Calcutta, and Bombay, legal slaughterhouses sell beef to retail customers and to the restaurants that serve steak.

If the caloric value of beef and the energy costs involved in the manufacture of synthetic leather were included in the estimates of energy, the calculated efficiency of Indian livestock would rise considerably.

As well as the system works, experts often claim that its efficiency can be further improved. Alan Heston, an economist at the University of Pennsylvania, believes that Indians suffer from an overabundance of cows simply because they refuse to slaughter the excess cattle. India could produce at least the same number of oxen and the same quantities of milk and manure with 30 million fewer cows. Heston calculates that only 40 cows are necessary to maintain a population of 100 bulls and oxen. Since India averages 70 cows for every 100 bullocks, the difference, 30 million cows, is expendable.

What Heston fails to note is that sex ratios among cattle in different regions of India vary tremendously, indicating that adjustments in the cow population do take place. Along the Ganges River, one of the holiest shrines of Hinduism, the ratio drops to 47 cows for every 100 male animals. This ratio reflects the preference for dairy buffalo in the irrigated sectors of the Gangetic Plains. In nearby Pakistan, in contrast, where

cow slaughter is permitted, the sex ratio is 60 cows to 100 oxen.

Since the sex ratios among cattle differ greatly from region to region and do not even approximate the balance that would be expected if no females were killed, we can assume that some culling of herds does take place; Indians do adjust their religious restrictions to accommodate ecological realities.

They cannot kill a cow but they can tether an old or unhealthy animal until it has starved to death. They cannot slaughter a calf but they can yoke it with a large wooden triangle so that when it nurses it irritates the mother's udder and gets kicked to death. They cannot ship their animals to the slaughterhouse but they can sell them to Muslims, closing their eyes to the fact that the Muslims will take the cattle to the slaughterhouse.

These violations of the prohibition against cattle slaughter strengthen the premise that cow worship is a vital part of Indian culture. The practice arose to prevent the population from consuming the animal on which Indian agriculture depends. During the First Millennium B.C., the Ganges Valley became one of the most densely populated regions of the world.

Where previously there had been only scattered villages, many towns and cities arose and peasants farmed every available acre of land. Kingsley Davis, a population expert at the University of California at

Berkeley, estimates that by 300 B.C. between 50 million and 100 million people were living in India. The forested Ganges Valley became a windswept semidesert and signs of ecological collapse appeared; droughts and floods became commonplace, erosion took away the rich topsoil, farms shrank as population increased, and domesticated animals became harder and harder to maintain.

It is probable that the elimination of meat eating came about in a slow, practical manner. The farmers who decided not to eat their cows, who saved them for procreation to produce oxen, were the ones who survived the natural disasters. Those who ate beef lost the tools with which to farm. Over a period of centuries, more and more farmers probably avoided beef until an unwritten taboo came into existence.

Only later was the practice codified by the priesthood. While Indian peasants were probably aware of the role of cattle in their society, strong sanctions were necessary to protect zebus from a population faced with starvation. To remove temptation, the flesh of cattle became taboo and the cow became sacred.

The sacredness of the cow is not just an ignorant belief that stands in the way of progress. Like all concepts of the sacred and the profane, this one affects the physical world; it defines the relationships that are important for the maintenance of Indian society.

Indians have the sacred cow; we have the "sacred" car and the "sacred" dog. It would not occur to us to propose the elimination of automobiles and dogs from our society without carefully considering the consequences, and we should not propose the elimination of zebu cattle without first understanding their place in the social order of India.

Human society is neither random nor capricious. The regularities of thought and behavior called culture are the principal mechanisms by which we human beings adapt to the world around us. Practices and beliefs can be rational or irrational, but a society that fails to adapt to its environment is doomed to extinction. Only those societies that draw the necessities of life from their surroundings, without destroying those surroundings, inherit the earth. The West has much to learn from the great antiquity of Indian civilization, and the sacred cow is an important part of that lesson.

FOR FURTHER INFORMATION

Gandhi, Mohandas K. *How to Serve the Cow*. Navajivan Publishing House, 1954.

Harris. Marvin. *Cows, Pigs, Wars and Witches: The Riddles of Culture*. Random House, 1974.

Heston, Alan, et al. "An Approach to the Sacred Cow of India." *Current Anthropology*, Vol. 12, 1971, pp. 191–209.

Odend'hal, Stewart. "Gross Energetic Efficiency of Indian Cattle in Their Environment." *Journal of Human Ecology*, Vol. 1, 1972, pp. 1–27.

Raj, K. N. "Investment in Livestock in Agrarian Economies: An Analysis of Some Issues Concerning 'Sacred Cows' and 'Surplus Cattle.'" *Indian Economic Review*, Vol. 4. 1969, pp. 1–33.

15

The Enigma of Aztec Sacrifice

Michael Harner

On the morning of November 8, 1519, a small band of bearded, dirty, exhausted Spanish adventurers stood at the edge of a great inland lake in central Mexico, staring in disbelief at the sight before them. Rising from the center of the lake was a magnificent island city, shining chalk white in the early sun. Stretching over the lake were long causeways teeming with travelers to and from the metropolis, Tenochtitlán, the capital of the Aztec empire, now known as Mexico City.

The Spaniards, under the command of Hernán Cortés, were fresh from the wars of the Mediterranean and the conquest of the Caribbean. Tough and ruthless men, numbering fewer than four hundred, they had fought their way up from the eastern tropical coast of Mexico. Many had been wounded or killed in battles with hostile Indians on the long march. Possibly all would have died but for their minuscule cavalry of fifteen horses—which terrified the Indians, who thought the animals were gods—and the aid of a small army of Indian allies, enemies of the Aztecs.

Reprinted with permission from *Natural History* Magazine, April 1977. Copyright © 1977 by The American Museum of Natural History. Revisions by the author, 1978.

The panorama of the Aztec citadel across the water seemed to promise the Spaniards the riches that had eluded them all their lives. One of them, Bernal Díaz del Castillo, later wrote: "To many of us it appeared doubtful whether we were asleep or awake . . . never yet did man see, hear, or dream of anything equal to our eyes this day." For the Spaniards, it was a vision of heaven.

Slightly more than a year and a half later, in the early summer of 1521, it was a glimpse of hell. Again the Spaniards found themselves on the lakeshore, looking toward the great capital. But this time they had just been driven back from the city by the Aztec army. Sixty-two of their companions had been captured, and Cortés and the other survivors helplessly watched a pageant being enacted a mile away across the water on one of the major temple-pyramids of the city. As Bernal Díaz later described it,

> The dismal drum of Huichilobos sounded again, accompanied by conches, horns, and trumpetlike instruments. It was a terrifying sound, and when we looked at the tall *cue* [temple-pyramid] from which it came we saw our comrades who had been captured in Cortés' defeat being dragged up the steps to be sacrificed. When they had hauled them up a small platform in front of the shrine where they kept their accursed idols we saw them put plumes on the heads of many of them; and then they made them dance with a sort of fan in front of Huichilobos. Then, after they had danced the *papas* [Aztec priests] laid them down on their backs on some narrow stones of sacrifice and, cutting open their chests, drew out their palpitating hearts which they offered to the idols before them.

Cortés and his men were the only Europeans to see the human sacrifices of the Aztecs, for the practice ended shortly after the successful Spanish conquest of the Aztec empire. But the extremity of Aztec sacrifice has long persisted in puzzling scholars. No human society known to history approached that of the Aztecs in the quantities of people offered as religious sacrifices: 20,000 a year is a common estimate.

A typical anthropological explanation is that the religion of the Aztecs required human sacrifices; that their gods demanded these extravagant, frequent offerings. This explanation fails to suggest why that particular form of religion should have evolved when and where it did. I suggest that the Aztec sacrifices, and the cultural patterns surrounding them, were a natural result of distinctive ecological circumstances.

Some of the Aztecs' ecological circumstances were common to ancient civilizations in general. Recent theoretical work in anthropology indicates that the rise of early civilizations was a consequence of the pressures that growing populations brought to bear on natural resources. As human populations slowly multiplied, even before the development of plant and animal domestication, they gradually reduced the wild flora and fauna available for food and disrupted the ecological equilibriums of their environments. The earliest strong evidence of humans causing environmental damage was the extinction of many big game species in Europe by about 10,000 B.C., and in America north of Mexico by about 9,000 B.C. Simultaneously, human populations in broad regions of the Old and New Worlds had to shift increasingly to marine food resources and small-game hunting. Finally, declining quantities of wild game and food plants made domestication of plants and animals essential in most regions of the planet.

In the Old World, domestication of herbivorous mammals, such as cattle, sheep, and pigs, proceeded apace with that of food plants. By about 7,200 B.C. in the New World, however, ancient hunters had completely eliminated herbivores suitable for domestication from the area anthropologists call Mesoamerica, the region of the future high civilizations of Mexico and Guatemala. Only in the Andean region and southern South America did some camel-related species, especially the llama and the alpaca, manage to survive hunters' onslaughts, and thus could be domesticated later, along with another important local herbivore, the guinea pig. In Mesoamerica, the guinea pig was not available, and the Camelidae species became extinct several thousand years before domesticated food production had to be seriously undertaken. Dogs, such as the Mexican hairless, and wildfowl, such as the turkey, had to be bred for protein. The dog, however, was a far from satisfactory solution because, as a carnivore, it competed with its breeders for animal protein.

The need for intensified domesticated food production was felt early, as anthropologist Robert Carneiro has pointed out, by growing populations in fertile localities circumscribed by terrain poorly suited to farming. In such cases, plants always became domesticated, climate and environment permitting, but herbivorous mammals apparently could not, unless appropriate species existed. In Mesoamerica, the Valley of Mexico, with its fertile and well-watered bottom lands surrounded by mountains, fits well Carneiro's environmental model. In this confined area, population was increasing up to the time of the Spanish conquest, and the supply of wild game was declining. Deer were nearly gone from the Valley by the Aztec period.

The Aztecs responded to their increasing problems of food supply by intensifying agricultural production with a variety of ingenious techniques, including the reclamation of soil from marsh and lake bottoms in the chinampa, or floating garden, method. Unfortunately, their ingenuity could not correct their lack of a suitable domesticable herbivore that could provide animal protein and fats. Hence, the ecological situation of the Aztecs and their Mesoamerican neighbors was unique among the world's major civilizations. I have recently proposed the theory that large-scale cannibalism, disguised as sacrifice, was the natural consequence of these ecological circumstances.

The contrast between Mesoamerica and the Andes, in terms of the existence of domesticated herbivores, was also reflected in the numbers of human victims sacrificed in the two areas. In the huge Andean Inca empire, the other major political entity in the New World at the time of the conquest, annual human sacrifices apparently amounted to a few hundred at most. Among the Aztecs, the numbers were incomparably greater. The commonly mentioned figure of 20,000, however, is unreliable. For example, one sixteenth-century account states that 20,000 were sacrificed yearly in the capital city alone, another reports this as 20,000 infants, and a third claims the same number as being slaughtered throughout the Aztec empire on a single particular day. The most famous specific sacrifice took place in 1487 at the dedication of the main pyramid in Tenochtitlán. Here, too, figures vary: one source states 20,000, another 72,344, and several give 80,400.

In 1946 Sherburne Cook, a demographer specializing in American Indian populations, estimated an overall annual mean of 15,000 victims in a central Mexican population reckoned at two million. Later, however, he and his colleague Woodrow Borah revised his estimate of the total central Mexican population upward to 25 million. Recently, Borah, possibly the leading authority on the demography of Mexico at the time of the conquest, has also revised the estimated number of persons sacrificed in central Mexico in the fifteenth century to 250,000 per year, equivalent to one percent of the total population. According to Borah, this figure is consistent with the sacrifice of an estimated 1,000 to 3,000 persons yearly at the largest of the thousands of temples scattered throughout the Aztec Triple Alliance. The numbers, of course, were fewer at the lesser temples, and may have shaded down to zero at the smallest.

These enormous numbers call for consideration of what the Aztecs did with the bodies after the sacrifices. Evidence of Aztec cannibalism has been largely ignored or consciously or unconsciously covered up. For example, the major twentieth-century books on the Aztecs barely mention it; others bypass the subject completely. Probably some modern Mexicans and anthropologists have been embarrassed by the topic: the former partly for nationalistic reasons; the latter partly out of a desire to portray native peoples in the best possible light. Ironically, both these attitudes may

represent European ethnocentrism regarding cannibalism—a viewpoint to be expected from a culture that has had relatively abundant livestock for meat and milk.

A search of the sixteenth-century literature, however, leaves no doubt as to the prevalence of cannibalism among the central Mexicans. The Spanish conquistadores wrote amply about it, as did several Spanish priests who engaged in ethnological research on Aztec culture shortly after the conquest. Among the latter, Bernardino de Sahagún is of particular interest because his informants were former Aztec nobles, who supplied dictated or written information in the Aztec language, Nahuatl.

According to these early accounts, some sacrificial victims were not eaten, such as children offered by drowning to the rain god, Tlaloc, or persons suffering skin diseases. But the overwhelming majority of the sacrificed captives apparently were consumed. A principal—and sometimes only—objective of Aztec war expeditions was to capture prisoners for sacrifice. While some might be sacrificed and eaten on the field of battle, most were taken to home communities or to the capital, where they were kept in wooden cages to be fattened until sacrificed by the priests at the temple-pyramids. Most of the sacrifices involved tearing out the heart, offering it to the sun and, with some blood, also to the idols. The corpse was then tumbled down the steps of the pyramid and carried off to be butchered. The head went on the local skull rack, displayed in central plazas alongside the temple-pyramids. At least three of the limbs were the property of the captor if he had seized the prisoner without assistance in battle. Later, at a feast given at the captor's quarters, the central dish was a stew of tomatoes, peppers, and the limbs of his victim. The remaining torso, in Tenochtitlán at least, went to the royal zoo where it was used to feed carnivorous mammals, birds, and snakes.

Recent archeological research lends support to conquistadores' and informants' vivid and detailed accounts of Aztec cannibalism. Mexican archeologists excavating at an Aztec sacrificial site in the Tlatelolco section of Mexico City between 1960 and 1969 uncovered headless human rib cages completely lacking the limb bones. Associated with these remains were some razorlike obsidian blades, which the archeologists believe were used in the butchering. Nearby they also discovered piles of human skulls, which apparently had been broken open to obtain the brains, possibly a choice delicacy reserved for the priesthood, and to mount the skulls on a ceremonial rack.

Through cannibalism, the Aztecs appear to have been attempting to reduce very particular nutritional deficiencies. Under the conditions of high population pressure and class stratification that characterized the Aztec state, commoners or lower-class persons rarely had the opportunity to eat any game, even the domesticated turkey, except on great occasions. They often had to content themselves with such creatures as worms and snakes and an edible lake-surface scum called "stone dung," which may have been algae fostered by pollution from Tenochtitlán. Preliminary research seems to indicate that although fish and waterfowl were taken from the lakes, most of the Aztec poor did not have significant access to this protein source and were forced to be near-vegetarians, subsisting mainly on domesticated plant foods such as maize and beans.

The commoners theoretically could get the eight essential amino acids necessary for building body tissues from maize and beans. (A combination of the two foods complement each other in their essential amino acid components.) However, recent nutritional research indicates that in order to assure that their bodies would use the eight essential amino acids to rebuild body tissues, and not simply siphon off the dietary protein as energy, the Aztec commoners would have had to consume large quantities of maize and beans simultaneously or nearly simultaneously year-round. But crop failures and famines were common. According to Duran, a sixteenth-century chronicler, poor people often could not obtain maize and beans in the same season, and hence could not rely upon these plants as a source of the essential amino acids. How did the Aztecs know they needed the essential amino acids? Like other organisms perfected under natural selection, the human body is a homeostatic system that, under conditions of nutritional stress, tends to seek out the dietary elements in which it is deficient. Without this innate capacity, living organisms could not survive.

Another Aztec dietary problem was the paucity of fats, which were so scarce in central Mexico that the Spaniards resorted to boiling down the bodies of Indians killed in battle in order to obtain fat for dressing wounds and tallow for caulking boats. While the exact amount of fatty acids required by the human body remains a subject of uncertainty among nutritionists, they agree that fats, due to their slower rate of metabolism, provide a longer-lasting energy source than carbohydrates. Fatty meat, by providing not only fat, which the body will use as energy, but also essential proteins, assures the utilization of the essential amino acids for tissue building. Interestingly, prisoners confined by the Aztecs in wooden cages prior to sacrifice could be fed purely on carbohydrates to build up fat.

In contrast to the commoners, the Aztec elite normally had a diet enriched by wild game imported from the far reaches of the empire where species had not been so depleted. But even nobles could suffer from famines and sometimes had to sell their children into slavery in order to survive. Not surprisingly, the Aztec elite apparently reserved for themselves the right to eat human flesh, and conveniently, times of famine meant that the gods demanded appeasement through many human sacrifices.

At first glance, this prohibition against commoners eating human flesh casts doubt on cannibalism's potential to mobilize the masses of Aztec society to engage in wars for prisoners. Actually, the prohibition was, if anything, a goad to the lower class to participate in these wars since those who single-handedly took captives several times gained the right to eat human flesh. Successful warriors became members of the Aztec elite and their descendants shared their privileges. Through the reward of flesh-eating rights to the group most in need of them, the Aztec rulers assured themselves an aggressive war machine and were able to motivate the bulk of the population, the poor, to contribute to state and upper-class maintenance through active participation in offensive military operations. Underlying the war machine's victories, and the resultant sacrifices, were the ecological extremities of the Valley of Mexico.

With an understanding of the importance of cannibalism in Aztec culture, and of the ecological reasons for its existence, some of the Aztecs' more distinctive institutions begin to make anthropological sense. For example, the old question of whether the Aztecs' political structure was or was not an "empire" can be reexamined. One part of this problem is that the Aztecs frequently withdrew from conquered territory without establishing administrative centers or garrisons. This "failure" to consolidate conquest in the Old World fashion puzzled Cortés, who asked Moctezuma to explain why he allowed the surrounded Tlaxcalans to maintain their independence. Moctezuma reportedly replied that his people could thus obtain captives for sacrifice. Since the Aztecs did not normally eat people of their own polity, which would have been socially and politically disruptive, they needed nearby "enemy" populations on whom they could prey for captives. This behavior makes sense in terms of Aztec cannibalism: from the Aztec point of view, the Tlaxcalan state was preserved as a stockyard. The Aztecs were unique among the world's states in having a cannibal empire. Understandably, they did not conform to Old World concepts of empire, based on economies with domesticated herbivores providing meat or milk.

The ecological situation of the Aztecs was probably an extreme case of problems general to the high population pressure societies of Mesoamerica. Cannibalism encouraged the definition of the gods as eaters of human flesh and led almost inevitably to emphasis on fierce, ravenous, and carnivorous deities, such as the jaguar and the serpent, which are characteristic of Mesoamerican pantheons. Pre-Columbian populations could, in turn, rationalize the more grisly aspects of large-scale cannibalism as consequences of the gods' demands. Mesoamerican cannibalism, disguised as propitiation of the gods, bequeathed to the world some of its most distinctive art and architecture. The temple-pyramids of the Maya and the Toltecs, and of the pre-Aztec site at Teotihuacán in the Valley of Mexico, resemble those of the Aztecs in appearance and probably had similar uses. Even small touches, such as the steepness of the steps on pyramids in Aztec and other Mesoamerican ruins, become understandable given the need for efficiently tumbling the bodies from the sacrificial altars to the multitudes below. Perhaps those prehistoric scenes were not too dissimilar from that which Bernal Díaz described when his companions were sacrificed before his eyes in Tenochtitlán:

Then they kicked the bodies down the steps, and the Indian butchers who were waiting below cut off their arms and legs and flayed their faces, which they afterwards prepared like glove leather, with their beards on, and kept for their drunken festivals. Then they ate their flesh with a sauce of peppers and tomatoes.

Gruesome as these practices may seem, an ecological perspective and population pressure theory render the Aztec emphasis on human sacrifice understandable as a natural and rational response to the material conditions of their existence. In *Tristes Tropiques,* the French anthropologist Claude Levi-Strauss described the Aztecs as suffering from "a maniacal obsession with blood and torture." A materialist ecological approach reveals the Aztecs to be neither irrational nor mentally ill, but merely human beings who, faced with unusual survival problems, responded with unusual behavior.

16

Well-Grounded Diet

Timothy Johns

Famines prompt the most desperate forms of human behavior. In such bleak episodes of history people have eaten almost everything, even the earth itself. In 1911 the French anthropologist F. Gaud reported that in periods of famine the Manja peoples of what is now the Republic of Congo "gather the earth of termites' nests and consume it mixed with water and powdered tree-bark." The technique bears a remarkable similarity to methods that once were practiced in Europe, where clay, euphemistically referred to as mountain meal, was eaten in times of war and deprivation. In his 1930 treatise on clay eating the American ethnographer Berthold Laufer notes that residents of rural Finland survived the famine of 1832 by eating "foodstuffs [containing] a meal-like siliceous earth mixed with real flour and tree-bark." In his 1975 study, *Hunger as a Factor in Human Affairs,* the Soviet anthropologist Pitirim A. Sorokin reports that during famines in Russia and western Europe "the people have been brought to eating . . . all sorts of roots, grass, hay, bark, earth with a small addition of flour, [and] clay."

But the practice of geophagy, or clay eating, is by no means limited to episodes of hardship, or even to the distant past. A wide range of peoples around the world continue to eat clay in a broad array of contexts.

The residents of many regions including New Guinea, the Philippines, Guatemala and parts of West Africa and the Amazon basin consume various kinds of clay as spices, condiments or relishes. Pregnant women often consume clay. Perhaps best known is the tradition of earth eating among poor African-American women in the southern United States [see Dennis A. Frate's "Last of the Earth Eaters," *The Sciences,* November/December 1984]. Those women are veritable connoisseurs of soil, collecting dirt from select roadside sites and later sprinkling it on ice cream or eating it by the spoonful.

Many learned studies have tried to explain this far-reaching taste for earth. Observers in the nutritional sciences have often proposed that clay eating is a response to a dietary deficiency of iron, calcium or some other mineral. But attractive as such theories are conceptually, there is not enough hard evidence to support them; for example, whereas clays are eaten by pregnant women, who may require mineral supplements, they are also eaten by men and children, who probably do not need additional nutrients. The more usual academic response to clay eating is simply to dismiss it as aberrant and unnatural. The medical literature treats it as a pathology, lumping it with other compulsive consumptive behaviors including the ingestion of starch, paint, cigarette butts or burnt matches.

In my own encounters with clay eating, however, I have found the practice to be a rational behavior with a sound biological basis. I more or less stumbled upon the phenomenon in the early 1980s, while I was investigating the agricultural and culinary habits of the Aymara and Quechua peoples in the Andes Mountains of Bolivia and Peru. These peoples have domesticated and incorporated bitter potatoes into their diet. What is unusual is their method of consumption: edible clays, excavated from specific local sites, are mixed with water to form a slurry into which the potatoes are dipped before they are eaten. When asked about their preference, respondents noted that the so-called potato clays eliminate the bitterness of the potatoes.

Similar chronicles that tell of Andean natives consuming specific clays with potatoes date from the sixteenth century. Spanish explorers of the time reported that edible clays were commonly traded among South American villages; remnants of that trade persist in Bolivia and southern Peru. And the association of clay with potatoes extends well beyond the Andes. The Hopi, Navajo, Zuñi and other tribes of the American Southwest and neighboring Mexico traditionally gathered potatoes from the wild and consumed them with edible clays that were distinct from the clays traditionally employed in pottery making and white wash. (Nowadays those tribes ingest potato clays almost exclusively on ceremonial occasions.) Practitioners noted that the clay helped prevent the nausea that resulted when large amounts of potatoes were eaten without clays.

As it happens, all the kinds of potato in question contain toxins called glycoalkaloids, chemicals known to induce stomach pains, vomiting and even death when they are consumed in large quantities. Yet the chemistry of the clays detoxifies the potatoes, offsetting what would otherwise be an unpleasant gustatory experience. Thus for many people, the habit of eating clay appears to be not aberrant at all but adaptive, a natural means of countering gastrointestinal distress.

But are such cases merely isolated ones, lone examples of a cultural behavior derived from an older and more basic nutritional need for clays? Or do they signal a general trend, an adaptive response with evolutionary value? The evidence points to the latter explanation. Throughout human history naturally occurring toxins have placed constraints on the kinds of plants people could eat. Clay eating provides the consumer with a certain degree of protection, allowing greater flexibility of choice in the diet—an especially important adaptation in times of famine. That many animals, including chimpanzees and gorillas, regularly

eat clay supports the idea that the detoxifying effects of clay eating confer an evolutionary advantage. It may be that the world's oldest medicine is the earth itself.

◆ ◆ ◆

The chemical basis for the detoxifying effect of clay is no mystery. Clays bind well with organic compounds, in part because clays are made up of fine particles and thus have large surface areas. Moreover, all clays are crystalline in structure and are essentially made up of stacked layers of silicon and aluminum (or magnesium) sheets. The individual silicon and aluminum atoms can trade places with cations, or positively charged particles, from nearby compounds. Often the substitute cations carry an electric charge different from the one carried by the molecules in the clay; for instance, an aluminum cation with a charge of +3 might be replaced with a nearby iron cation with a charge of +2. Such substitutions give rise to a net electric charge in the clay, causing the clay to absorb additional cations, of the same or different variety, in order to restore its electrical neutrality.

When clays are ingested with food, the cations associated with the clays can be exchanged with cations in the food or in digestive fluids. The interchange can lead to a net gain or loss in mineral nutrition, depending on the food, the diet and the necessity of the mineral to the ingestor. The addition of calcium, for instance, might be nutritionally beneficial, whereas a loss of dietary zinc or iron could prove detrimental. More important, though, clays are capable of binding to toxic substances, including the glycoalkaloids in bitter potatoes.

Indeed, in many respects glycoalkaloids appear to be ideal targets for adsorption by clays. Glycoalkaloids contain nitrogen, which is normally a neutral atom; when placed under the acidic conditions found in the stomach, however, the nitrogen—and thus the glycoalkaloid as a whole—takes on a positive charge, which enables the toxic molecule to take part in cation exchange. The toxins also possess a relatively large surface area, which increases the likelihood that they will interact with clay particles. Thus bound, the toxins pass through the digestive tract without causing discomfort. In fact, in my studies of glycoalkaloid binding by clays, I found the glycoalkaloid molecules to be bound to a degree that would easily account for the detoxifying capacity attributed by Amerindians to potato clays.

◆ ◆ ◆

At the same time the potato clays themselves seem to be particularly suited to their task. In the early 1980s I collected several edible clays from the Andes and from Arizona: two, known as *ch'aqo* and *p'asalla*, from Peru; *p'asa,* from Bolivia; and a Navajo clay called *dleesh.* All of them happen to contain smectite, a mineral comparable to charcoal—the recommended clinical remedy in cases of drug overdose—in its capacity to counter the effects of toxins. The molecular bonds in such clays are relatively weak, allowing water, cations and organic molecules to become fixed between adjacent layers of clay. This arrangement increases the surfaces available for adsorption—the binding of foreign cations by the clay—and so enhances the effectiveness of the clays in detoxifying organic toxins. One result of in vitro experiments is worth highlighting: the amount of clay needed to reduce glycoalkaloids in the average wild potato to a nontoxic level is minuscule compared with the amount consumed at a typical meal.

The culinary practices of Andeans and Native Americans of the Southwest also appear to promote the adsorption of glycoalkaloids. Aymara meals are simple: potatoes are usually eaten as the sole or dominant constituent of a meal, and salt is used sparingly. The practice leads to fewer compounds in the gut that can compete with clay as a binding substance. Furthermore, glycoalkaloids tend to concentrate in the outermost part of the potato, near its surface; when a potato is dipped into slurry (as it is in the Andean and Hopi practices), the glycoalkaloids readily come into contact with the clay particles. In fact, the slurry may detoxify the potato before it even reaches the consumer's mouth, thus eliminating the bitter taste.

❖ ❖ ❖

Many disparate cultures have practiced equally complex customs involving the ingestion of clay. Consider the Pomo of northern California, who baked and ate acorn bread as a traditional part of their diet. Before the acorns were baked they contained high levels of bitter, acidic chemicals called tannins. To eliminate the astringency the Pomo mixed a certain red clay with the ground meal of the acorns. Water was added to make a dough, and small loaves were baked in an earthen oven for twelve hours; the black bread thus produced was regarded as sweet. Natives of Sardinia, in the Mediterranean, once practiced an almost identical custom: they boiled acorns along with a traditional acorn clay known as *trocco* or *torco* and baked the mixture into bread. In each instance the clay was added explicitly to make the nuts more palatable.

Clearly the clay plays an active role in rendering the tannins ineffective. Martin Duquette, a colleague of mine at McGill University, and I measured the tannic acid available for digestion both before and after the bread was baked in the traditional manner. We found that the acorns were only one-fourth as toxic when clays were added. But the acorn clays of California and Sardinia do not reduce the toxicity of the tannins by adsorbing them, as the potato clays do with the glycoalkaloids; in fact, acorn clays do not bind well with tannins at all. Instead, when the breads are heated, the clays appear to act as catalysts, helping alter the structure of the tannin molecules and rendering them incapable of binding to gut cells. The baking of clays, then, detoxifies tannins and demonstrates, in a way more sophisticated than simple ingestion, the use of clay in culinary technology.

It is tempting to extrapolate from the potato and acorn examples and explain clay eating solely as an adaptive cultural response to toxins in the raw materials of food. But one cannot readily dispose of the idea that clays are eaten for their nutritional value. For example, the acorn clays in California and Sardinia contain large amounts of calcium as the exchangeable cation; acorn breads made with those clays can therefore provide much of the recommended daily allowance of calcium.

Duquette and I made a similar discovery when we analyzed eight edible clays collected from Africa. Seven of them are still eaten on that continent, primarily by pregnant women. The eighth was from a site in Zambia occupied by early humans between 100,000 and 200,000 years ago and excavated in the 1950s by J. Desmond Clark, an anthropologist at the University of California at Berkeley. The presence of the clay is an anomaly there, and it may well have been eaten by the area's residents. When Duquette and I examined the samples, we found that several of them contained large amounts of important dietary minerals such as calcium, copper, iron, magnesium or manganese. But that finding by itself was not enough to prove the nutritional value of the minerals in the clays. In addition, minerals must be available in a useful form: they must occur as exchangeable cations. In the clays we tested many of the minerals were chemically unavailable; in samples from Nigeria the only cation available in any quantity was aluminum, a mineral of no nutritional value. Moreover, no single mineral was available in appreciable amounts from any of the clays.

The finding becomes significant when nutrition scientists try to explain why people eat clay and why the custom ever caught on in the first place. Although certain edible clays provide nutrients, not all of them do; thus from a nutritional point of view clay eating does not confer a clear evolutionary advantage to its practitioners. Once clay is seen as a valuable detoxifier, however, the virtues of eating it become almost self-evident.

❖ ❖ ❖

Like many other animals, people are omnivores: they consume a wide range of plants and animals and are able to adapt to changes in the availability of food in the environment. But novel foods can also be of unpredictable quality; it is impossible to tell just by looking at them whether they are safe to eat. Fortunately, people and other animals have various physiological and behavioral mechanisms for dealing with toxins. Nausea and vomiting are obvious examples: both mechanisms quickly remove offending foods from the gastrointestinal tract, thereby preventing toxins from being absorbed into the body. They also warn the consumer—rather harshly—not to eat more of that food. Not surprisingly, toxins are the main line of defense for many plants.

Clay eating appears to be a similar mechanism in that it allows animals to make their way through an uncertain and potentially threatening dietary environment. Rats provide an intriguing case in point. As a species rats are notoriously difficult to poison; when they encounter a novel flavor that they associate with poison, they develop a conditioned aversion to the flavor. In the 1970s the psychobiologist Denis Mitchell and his colleagues at the University of Southern California undertook experimental studies of rats to investigate the response. Mitchell found that when rats are poisoned, they eat clay if it is available. He then exposed rats to poison in conjunction with a novel flavor; true to form, when the rats were subsequently exposed to the flavor without the toxin, they avoided the flavor. When offered no food alternative except the novel flavor, however, the rats ate it along with clay. Evidently rats have adopted clay eating as a defense against a hostile dinner, perhaps to circumvent their physiological inability to vomit.

Clay eating also has been observed in many non-human primates that include toxic plants in their diets. For example, gorillas in the mountains of Rwanda eat clay. And chimpanzees seasonally, sometimes daily, eat specific clays, often from termite mounds. Gorillas in the mountains of Rwanda also eat clay. The behavior, in its context, has led some primate ecologists to suggest, as I have, that the chimpanzees eat clays to detoxify their diet. That suggestion is difficult to test experimentally, though the activity would hardly be surprising. Chimpanzees have been reported to consume a number of African plants that are used medicinally by people, often for stomach and intestinal problems. Many people are familiar with the rudimentary forms of pharmacophagy, or self-medication, that are often seen in other animals. Dogs and cats induce vomiting by eating grass and other uncustomary substances, perhaps after eating contaminated food. In fact, when animals ingest plant or inorganic materials for some benefit other than basic nutrition, they usually seem to be countering problems of the gastrointestinal tract.

As practiced by people, though, clay eating is much more than merely an innate behavior. In many regions of the world it plays a part in sophisticated techniques of food preparation, and the details of the practice are passed along from generation to generation. In numerous, often intricate ways the practice is embedded in culture itself.

Indeed, the use of clays as minor but regular additives to food is likely a relic of a past in which the consumption of clay was of much greater importance than it is today: an atavistic behavior from the days when our hominid ancestors foraged in a resource-limited, chemically threatening environment. No doubt the adaptation continued to be evolutionarily advantageous in periods when food was scarce. During famines, of course, people—as well as higher primates and other animals—must subsist on foods they are not used to eating. Often such foods are only marginally edible: bitter potatoes and acorns are prime examples. The Navajo, Hopi, Zuñi and other tribes of the Southwest are known to have gathered wild tubers in seasonal periods of scarcity and as a famine food.

◆ ◆ ◆

Clay eating thus persisted as a kind of buffer, or protective device, for quelling gastrointestinal stress induced by barely tolerable wild plants or pangs of hunger. Perhaps the largely symbolic nature of clay eating in some cultures—such as in Guatemala, where the practice takes on religious overtones—serves as a means of maintaining knowledge essential for survival in time of famine. Since clay would already be classified as a food, the onset of famine requires only that the culture alter the proportion of food items in its diet rather than consume an item regarded as inedible.

At the same time the adoption of geophagy as a general response to toxins allowed people to make wider use of natural resources and led to the domestication of certain plants. Wild potatoes were presumably a minor dietary constituent or a famine resource under primitive conditions of exploitation, but eventually they came to provide a subsistence base for complex prehistoric civilization in the central Andes. Clay eating may thus have provided a spark for the development of early agriculture.

Over the millennia, human culture has transformed geophagy into a medical practice with a plethora of manifestations and applications. Consider clay eating by pregnant women. Nausea and vomiting are common in pregnancy, the result of hormonal metabolites released through the bile into the small intestine. Not surprisingly, many pregnant women who eat clay say they do so to settle their stomachs. The clay sample from Zambia that Duquette and I analyzed was sold in that country as a stomach medicine and was purchased primarily by expectant women. Likewise, the persistence of clay eating by women in the southern U.S. can be understood to a large extent as a continuation of what is considered in Africa to be a beneficial and culturally acceptable practice.

Although attitudes toward geophagy may have changed in the modern world, the practice has not disappeared; it has simply been altered by new ways of processing foods and medicines. If ever there was a case of old wine in new bottles, for instance, it is Kaopectate, that remedy for diarrhea sold in most North American drugstores. The active ingredient is kaolinite, the same mineral in the clays prescribed by traditional healers in Africa. In fact, in 1985 Donald E. Vermeer and R. G. Ferrell of Louisiana State University concluded that the kaolinite clays from Nigeria such as the ones Duquette and I examined are best regarded as antidiarrheal medicines.

Like any behavior geophagy can be inappropriate when engaged in to excess. In this country, at least one person is known to have died of a perforated colon after eating too much clay in one sitting. Nor is all earth good earth: dirt scooped up from the backyard or basement may contain contaminants such as lead that can harm the ingestor or a fetus. In addition, some people who no longer have access to their accustomed delicacy have switched to eating starch or baking soda, which contain high levels of sodium that contribute directly to high blood pressure. Taken in proper context, however, geophagy can be beneficial and should be appreciated as normal behavior. Earth may not be to everyone's taste, but it is one of the oldest tastes known to humankind.

Explaining Foodways #2:
Ideology, Symbolism, and Social Power

In the Yucatán Peninsula, the Maya drink nearly a bottle of Coca-Cola™ per person per day. When asked why they drink so much Coke, many respond that Coke is strong and sweet and tastes good. Some say it is healthy. Coca-Cola was virtually unknown to the Maya two decades ago, but now one can purchase Coca-Cola at nearly every family-operated little store in the most isolated of Mayan towns. Signs on the sides of these *tiendas* and on ubiquitous billboards extol the flavor and healthiness of Coca-Cola. Television commercials also exalt these same virtues. When a guest is invited into a Mayan home, a child may be sent to fetch soft drinks. It is a matter of etiquette to offer soft drinks to visitors, especially North Americans, and Coca-Cola is high status and Western. Coke is urban, cosmopolitan, and white.

Food is "good to think." Food reflects identity and who we are: gender, age, social class, political persuasion, and personal style. Ethnic groups are often associated linguistically with foods (Italians = macaroni), conversations are sprinkled with food terms (bread = money), and the very definition of a meal (versus a snack) changes depending on circumstance and the presence of a core food. Some of these linguistic associations may seem trivial, but in many situations they subtly define self and other. Every social group sets limits on what constitutes food and how foods should be obtained, prepared, served, and consumed. Food provides a window through which one can better understand ideology, social organization, control, and power.

In every culture, there are items that could be defined as "food" but are not considered edible. In the United States, dogs and horses are pets, and most of us would not consider consuming them. Yet there is little revulsion to the idea of eating pigs or cows, as there is in other parts of the world (article 14). Cannibalism is a widespread taboo, yet in some historical instances it appears that cannibalism was practiced and may have even been an act of great ritual importance (article 15). Under famine conditions, what is usually defined as nonfood may be consumed. Abhorrence of eating insects may be reduced by coating them in something familiar, like chocolate.

Foods typically occupy a number of ideological places in the ever-changing universe of cultural meaning. For example, in North America beef was generally considered a high-status food, often associated with manliness, an association that may hark back to the rugged image of the cowboy and cattleman. Slowly, however, the widespread availability of inexpensive hamburgers and information on the relationship between red meat consumption and adult diseases has tainted beef's image. For some, beef is now symbolic of ecological destruction and personal pollution.

Foods are often associated with important events. A meal of "steak and potatoes" reminds us of the 1950s. In the United States, turkey is the main dish of the Thanksgiving Day meal. White cake is a symbol of marriage. In New England, a pumpkin on a porch is a sign of Halloween. The manner in which foods are prepared has changing meaning. A decade ago sushi was almost unknown outside of Japanese enclaves. Eating raw, "uncooked" fish was considered wrong. Now sushi has become cosmopolitan. What will be the "in" foods of the twenty-first century?

In most societies, a "meal" typically includes a staple food. Anne Allison (article 19) writes about how the Japanese often feel that they have not eaten unless they have eaten rice. In the United States, some individuals still feel uncomfortable with a "meal" that does not include meat, but this is decreasing. Eating from another's plate is accepted in many societies, whereas in ours it would be considered very poor manners. In many societies, the male head of the household is fed first; in others he is fed last. What are the cultural rules that govern the definition of food and proper eating behaviors? Where do these rules come from, and how do they change? How universal are rules and the processes by which rules are formed? Are rules meant to be resisted and broken?

A useful distinction can be made between the "substance" of food—its chemical constituents—and the "circumstance" of food (Farb and Armelagos, 1980). The circumstances are the social and ecological context in which food is embedded. For example, one could bake a cake for a friend or buy the same kind of cake for a friend. The substance is the same, but the circumstance—the mode of preparation—is not. One could serve a lavish dinner consisting of shrimp cocktail, T-bone steak, baked potato, salad, rolls and butter, coffee, wine, dessert, and condiments. Or one could save time and money by providing one's guests with portions of liquid protein, salt, sugar, lard, water, and so on. The nutrient composition may be the same, but the meal would not taste the same and the meaning would be very different (Farb and Armelagos, 1980).

The four articles in this part provide examples of some of the social structural and symbolic issues associated with food. In "The Social and Symbolic Uses of Ethnic/Regional Foodways: Cajuns and Crawfish in South Louisiana," C. Paige Gutierrez explores the symbolic role of crawfish in forming and maintaining Cajun identity. In 1755, the British ousted a group of French speakers, called Acadians, from Nova Scotia, and after some time many of the Acadian refugees settled in southern Louisiana, where they eventually came to be called Cajuns. The original Acadians intermingled and intermarried with an assortment of other ethnic groups in the area so that today, Cajun is both an ethnic and a regional identity.

Somewhat as the lobster is to the state of Maine, the crawfish has developed as a symbol of Cajun culture. Cajuns are seen to take on some of the characteristics of crawfish as animal and as food. Crawfish are feisty, as are the Cajuns. Crawfish separate Cajuns (who live behind the "crawfish curtain"!) from non-Cajun Louisiana.

Gutierrez also examines the symbolic dynamics of social class and Cajun food. Crawfish are typically associated with the lower class. They are "mudbugs" and perceived as dirty. Eating crawfish with one's hands is also considered dirty. On the other hand, there is an allure of exoticness that has not been lost on the Louisiana tourist industry. Finally, eating crawfish cuts across social classes and further solidifies pan-Cajun identity.

In "The Children Cry for Bread: Hegemony and the Transformation of Consumption," Mary J. Weismantel discusses the symbolic importance of the substitution of wheat bread for barley gruel in the morning meal of indigenous, highland Ecuadorians. This seemingly simple substitution, one with minimal nutritional ramifications, is also a sign of increased involvement of rural areas in international exchange, what Pelto and Pelto refer to as delocalization (article 31), and reflects divisions within families, across genders and generations, and between white Ecuadorians and indigenous Ecuadorians.

In the parish of Zumbagua, the typical morning meal is called *café*. Like the *café* of white Ecuadorians, this meal starts with boiled water. To the water is added not sugar and breads but heaping spoonfuls of *machica*, finely ground and toasted barley meal. In recent years, children have begun to ask for bread, a luxury, store-bought item, instead of *machica*. Weismantel explains that in "crying for bread," the children are asking for a food purchased in the market by their father while simultaneously rejecting the homegrown and processed food provided by their mother.

Beyond the family, the distinction between dry bread and wet barley gruel reflects the extension of the state into indigenous affairs. To most of us, the two staples, wheat bread and barley gruel, seem much the same symbolically. But to the adults of Zumbagua, bread conjures up images of conquest, economic exploitation, and racism, mixed with the lure of whiteness, cities, and the modern.

Identity is also a main theme of Anne Allison's article, "Japanese Mothers and *Obentōs*." *Obentōs* are boxed lunches that are made for nursery school children by Japanese mothers. They typically consist of a variety of about six small and separately wrapped foods that are placed in the lunch box, or *obentō*. There is pervasive social pressure on mothers to prepare appealing and nutritious *obentōs* and on children to eat them quickly. A wealth of magazines and other sources of information are devoted to guiding mothers as to how to prepare an *obentō* that will be enjoyed and quickly consumed.

Allison, a cultural anthropologist who lived in Japan, where her son went to nursery school, places her study within a theoretical perspective that focuses on how symbols and power are interrelated and within the broader context of Japanese food rules. The presentation of food is important, and the focus of presentation is on contrast and opposition. Allison is particularly interested in how power is wielded. She argues that *obentōs* are a form of ideological control by the state. In particular, women are responsible for feeding their children. If a child does not eat, the problem is seen more as the result of the mother's failure to prepare an appealing *obentō* than as the child's poor appetite. Teachers will alert mothers when children fail to eat their *obentōs*, clearly suggesting that the problem resides with the maker of the meal. Friends will give suggestions and help to make *obentōs*. Women and children, however, are not totally powerless. They willfully play the game because there is enjoyment in the challenge of making aesthetically appealing *obentōs*, and surely in eating them, too!

Turning back to the United States, we see a different set of symbols in action. In "Rituals at McDonald's," cultural anthropologist Conrad P. Kottak explores some of what may be behind the all-too-familiar experience of eating at a McDonald's restaurant. Kottak's "fieldwork" took place at his local McDonald's in Ann Arbor, Michigan. He first traces the rapid rise and spread of McDonald's up to 1978. The spread has continued, and according to the McDonald's Corporation Web site (www.mcdonalds.com), there were over 24,500 McDonald's restaurants serving hamburgers in 114 countries in 1997.

Kottak focuses on why McDonald's has been so widely embraced and how this might relate to advertising (the rituals, meanings, and symbols McDonald's tries to associate with its products). How much has McDonald's come to define what is American and to provide a sense of unity (as American)? Is this sort of "ritual at work" any different from making *obentōs* in Japan or eating crawfish in Cajun country? What or who is being manipulated? Who ultimately profits?

Having a sense of what foods symbolize—the complexities of interactions of symbols, meanings and markers of status that go along with the foods themselves, how the foods were obtained, and how they were prepared—can provide valuable insights into culture and cultural change. As the French anthropologist Claude Levi-Strauss once wrote, food is "good to think."

THINKING AND DOING NUTRITIONAL ANTHROPOLOGY

1.   How often do you eat alone? Write about what you do when you eat alone. Are there situations in which you feel embarrassed about eating alone? Interview family, friends, and fellow students. What patterns do you detect?

2.   Food sharing is a marker of social boundaries. Write about times in which you share food or drinks. What are the levels of food sharing? To whom would you give a taste of a soft drink? With whom would you feel comfortable sharing a plate of French fries, a piece of cake, a pasta primavera?

3.   Holidays are often associated with specific foods. For example, Thanksgiving is a time to eat turkey. What did you eat last Thanksgiving? With whom did you eat? Interview others. How common is it, in reality, to eat turkey on Thanksgiving? What ethnic and class patterns do you find?

4.   Reflect on your own food history. Select a food that you grew up with. What images does it conjure up? What do you associate with this food? Did you ever refuse to eat this food? Was this an act of empowerment? Was this food ever withheld from you?

5.   Choose a food that is associated with a region or culture. Investigate how this association seems to have come about. Is the food now a staple or now only symbolic? What images does the food conjure up? Do some of these images color how you think of people from the region or ethnic group?

SUGGESTED READINGS

Counihan, C., & Van Esterik, P. (Eds). (1997). *Food and culture: A reader.* New York: Routledge. (A set of readings on symbolic, cultural, and political economics aspects of food and eating.)

Curtin, D. W., & Heldke, L. M. (Eds). (1992). *Cooking, eating and thanking: Transformative philosophies of food.* Bloomington: Indiana University Press. (Interesting essays on thinking about food philosophically.)

Douglas, M. (Ed.). (1984). *Food in the social order: Studies of food and festivities in three American communities.* New York: Russell Sage Foundation. (Detailed essays on ethnic foodways in the United States.)

Farb, P., & Armelagos, G. (1980). *Consuming passions: The anthropology of eating.* Boston: Houghton Mifflin. (Easy-to-read overview of the anthropology of food.)

Goody, J. (1982). *Cooking, cuisine, and class: A study in comparative sociology.* New York: Cambridge University Press. (A seminal book on food in relationship to symbolism and social class.)

Mussell, L., & Brown, K. (Eds.). (1984). *Ethnic and regional foodways in the United States.* Knoxville: University of Tennessee Press. (Similar to Douglas [1984] and, as the title suggests, a compendium of information and analyses of foodways. Gutierrez's article (17) was originally published here.)

17

The Social and Symbolic Uses of Ethnic/Regional Foodways: Cajuns and Crawfish in South Louisiana

C. Paige Gutierrez

A tourist, stepping off the plane at the New Orleans International Airport, is confronted with an array of commercial products found in no other part of the United States. Airport gift shops sell the city's heritage in the form of freeze-dried gumbo mix, plastic-wrapped pralines, voodoo paraphernalia, Dixieland jazz records, and dark-skinned "quadroon" dolls dressed in ruffled antebellum hoop skirts. Scattered among these New Orleans artifacts are souvenirs of a different kind—those that are more properly associated with Cajun country, which lies to the southwest, west, and northwest of the city. Prominent among the Cajun-oriented products is the image of the crawfish (or "crayfish" or "crawdad" to the unacculturated tourist). A visitor leaving New Orleans and venturing into Cajun country will find even more commercial crawfish iconography: plastic crawfish key chains and combs, real crawfish frozen into clear acrylic paperweights shaped like the state of Louisiana, children's books featuring anthropomorphized crawfish as main characters, and expensive gold or silver crawfish pendants. The tourist will also notice that these emblematic crawfish are frequently juxtaposed with verbal expressions of ethnic/regional consciousness. The words "Cajun," "Acadian," "Cajun Country," and "Louisiana" often appear in conjunction with crawfish imagery; for example, a popular local license plate and T-shirt show an upraised fist holding a crawfish, with the accompanying slogan "Cajun Power."

Even though these souvenirs are commercial products that have appeared as a response to a rise in tourism during the past two decades, they are also indicative of a strong symbolic association involving Cajuns, crawfish, and region that reaches beyond the walls of the souvenir store. The crawfish—both as animal and as food—is the predominant ethnic and regional emblem for Cajuns and for southern Louisiana.

The word "Cajun" implies both an ethnic and a regional identity. The French who settled in Nova Scotia in the seventeenth century became known as Acadians. They prospered in Canada until 1755, when the British destroyed their holdings and ousted them from Acadia. After three decades of wandering, large numbers of Acadian refugees settled permanently in southern Louisiana, where they eventually became known as

"Cajuns." Cajun lifeways in Louisiana developed in response to a physical environment that included swamps, bayous, marshes, and prairies, and a social environment that commingled continental and Caribbean French peoples, Germans, Spaniards, Blacks, Indians, Anglo-Americans and others.[1] Cajuns adapted successfully to the various physical environments of the area and acculturated much of the non-Cajun population to the Cajun lifestyle. Thus, there are many people in southern Louisiana today, who, though not descended from the Acadians, call themselves Cajuns and/or participate widely in Cajun culture.[2]

Although it is impossible to define fully the word "Cajun," it has been suggested that "a Cajun is most emphatically identifiable as an individual who is typically Roman Catholic, is rural or of rural extraction, emphasizes kinship relations over those of nonkin-based associations, and who speaks or understands both English and Louisiana French languages or has close relatives who do so."[3] In addition, south Louisiana remains the homeland even for a Cajun residing elsewhere. Cajun culture has shaped and has been shaped by geographic region. Despite the incursions of the modern world (which sometimes actually strengthen regional identity, as is the case with the oil industry and its contribution to the growth of new Cajun occupations such as roustabouting and petroleum engineering), Cajun Louisiana in many ways still conforms to Zelinsky's definition of a traditional region:

> These regions are relatively self-contained, endoga-
> mous, stable, and of long duration. . . . An intimate
> symbiotic relationship between man and land develops
> over many centuries, one that creates indigenous
> modes of thought and action, a distinctive visible land-
> scape, and a form of human ecology specific to the
> locality. Although the usual processes of random cul-
> tural mutation, the vagaries of history, and some slight
> intermixture of peoples, and the diffusion of innova-
> tions of all sorts prevents the achievement of total stasis
> or equilibrium, or complete internal uniformity, it
> would not be unfair to characterize such a traditional
> region as one based on blood and soil. In the extreme,
> it becomes synonymous with a particular tribe or ethnic
> group.[4]

◆ ◆ ◆

The interplay of ethnicity and region, of "blood and soil," is implicitly recognized in the Louisiana state legislature's designation of a twenty-two-parish area of southern Louisiana as "Acadiana"—a term derived from the fusion of the words "Acadian" and "Louisiana."

When mainstream America came to Acadiana in the twentieth century in the form of forced English-language education, the mass media, the petrochemical industry, and World War II, the Cajuns found themselves in a position not unlike that of the newly arrived Old World immigrants to the United States. Although this "new world" of the outsider offered many opportunities for a better life, it also threatened to destroy that which was traditional and meaningful in the old life. Local customs were often ridiculed by the more "sophisticated" outsiders, and the use of the French language in advertising, legal documents, and in public schools was forbidden by state law. Many outsiders, and insiders as well, associated Cajun culture with ignorance and poverty.

However, the minority and ethnic revival movements which occurred throughout the United States in the 1960s and 1970s have parallels in southern Louisiana. The Council for the Development of French in Louisiana (CODOFIL) was founded in 1968 and has since sought to strengthen the French component of Cajun identity through language education programs, heritage festivals, publications, and cultural exchanges between Louisiana and France, Quebec, and other French-speaking parts of the world. CODOFIL and related organizations best represent the "Genteel Acadians," the wealthier or more formally educated Cajuns, who have chosen the speaking of standard French as a key rallying symbol for their ethnic revival movement.[5] These Genteel Acadians are opposed by the less organized, but equally verbal, "Proud Coonasses," who often speak a nonstandard Louisiana French dialect or no French at all, and who emphasize the playful and sometimes rowdy side of Cajun life, with its heavy drinking and eating, gambling, cockfighting, and barroom brawls.[6] A popular bumper sticker sums up the Coonass philosophy: "Happiness in Cajun Land is Gumbo, Go-Go, and Do-Do"—food, sex, and sleep. The Proud Coonasses have taken a term once used by outsiders as an ethnic slur and transformed it into a symbol of ethnic regional consciousness. The Genteel Acadians strongly oppose the use of the term Coonass (or its pictorial equivalent) as vulgar and do not identify with the lifestyle that the term represents. On the other hand, the Proud Coonasses have little interest in learning to speak standard French and sometimes see the Genteel Acadians as elitist or hypocritical.

The conflict centering around these two symbolic acts—the use of standard French and the use of the term Coonass—is reminiscent of Barth's observation that ethnic revivalism often brings with it a struggle between different segments of the group over the "selection of signals for identity and the assertion of value for these cultural diacritica, and the suppression or denial of relevance of other differentiae."[7] Although the struggle between the Genteel Acadians and the Proud Coonasses continues, neither group is likely to succeed in having its chosen "signal for identity" become *the* Cajun ethnic/regional symbol.[8] That role has been quietly assumed by the crawfish, which is flexible enough to represent both Genteel Acadians and Proud Coonasses, and the majority of Cajuns who fit in between these two extremes. The crawfish unites Cajuns to each other and to their land, while it also successfully highlights the boundaries between Cajuns and outsiders.

Each year between December and May the streams, ponds, swamps, and ditches of southern Louisiana produce an abundance of crawfish. It is estimated that the Atchafalaya Basin Swamp, a half-million-acre area located in central Acadiana, produces almost 6 million kilograms of wild crawfish annually, while manmade crawfish ponds produce another 5.5 million kilograms.[9] There is no way of reliably estimating the amount of additional crawfish obtained by noncommercial, Sunday crawfishermen who scour roadside ditches and swampy areas for personal consumption. Yet elderly locals claim that the supply of crawfish has dwindled over the years and look back to a time when crawfish were so numerous that hordes of them crossing the highways created traffic hazards, and housewives in low-lying areas could scoop up a bucketful for dinner from their own backyards. Crawfish farming has helped to offset the decline in the natural supply of crawfish. Both the farms and the major natural crawfish-producing areas are restricted primarily to Cajun-dominated parishes, and almost ninety percent of the crawfish harvest is consumed in Acadiana and New Orleans.[10] Some locals joke that French Louisiana lies "behind the crawfish curtain," separated gastronomically from Anglo-American north Louisiana, where crawfish are often ignored or even scorned as food.

Not only do south Louisianians monopolize the cooking and consumption of crawfish, but they also dominate the entire industry, from trapping and processing to distribution. The Cajun is the primary heir to the cultural and technological knowledge pertinent to crawfish foodways in the United States. Thus a strong association between Cajuns and crawfish is understandable. A popularized summary of crawfish legendry, sold locally as a souvenir, states that "when a bayou baby is nine days old, his mother sticks his finger in a crawfish hole, and that makes him a Cajun."[11] A similar acknowledgment of the close association between the two is expressed in the folksong below, *Cribisse! Cribisse!* ("Crawfish! Crawfish!"), collected in the 1930s. (The term "Frenchmen" is commonly used in southern Louisiana to refer to Cajuns.)

Crawfish, crawfish, got no show, baby,
Crawfish, crawfish, got no show,
The Frenchman ketch 'im fer to make gumbo, baby.

Get up in the morning you find me gone, baby,
Get up in the morning you find me gone,
I'm on my way to the crawfish pond, baby.

Frenchman, Frenchman, only nine days old, baby,
Frenchman, Frenchman, only nine days old,
Broke his arm in a crawfish hole, baby.

Crawfish ain't skeered of a six-mule team, baby,
Crawfish ain't skeered of a six-mule team,
But run from a Frenchman time he see 'im, baby.

Look all 'round a Frenchman's bed, baby,
Look all 'round a Frenchman's bed,
You don' find nothin' but crawfish heads, baby.[12]

The folk song portrays the crawfish as both a living animal with a personality and as a prepared food. In Louisiana, the crawfish exists both as part of nature, in the form of a living animal, and as part of culture, when it is transformed by cooking into food. The dual role of the crawfish-as-animal and the crawfish-as-food in Cajun life is partly responsible for the creature's success as an ethnic emblem. The crawfish can be manipulated symbolically both as animal and as food, and the meaning expressed by the image of crawfish-as-animal is different from the meaning expressed by crawfish-as-food. Thus the crawfish possesses a broad range and flexibility as an ethnic/regional emblem.

The Cajun and the crawfish-as-animal thrive together in the south Louisiana environment. This camaraderie has not gone unnoticed in Cajun popular lore, where the identities of the human and the animal are playfully allowed to blur. A local legend claims that the lobsters which accompanied the Acadian refugees in their trek from Canada to Louisiana shrunk into crawfish during the exhausting journey. These crawfish remained loyal friends to the Louisiana Cajuns, even modeling their chimneyed mud burrows after the mud chimneys on early Cajun houses.[13] Such personification of the animal is not uncommon in Louisiana lore. For example, in a joke told by local comedian Justin Wilson and also found in oral tradition, a mother crawfish, speaking in a Cajun English dialect, calms her offsprings' fears of horses and cows, but tells them to "run lak de devil" when they see a Cajun, because "he'll eat anyt'ing."[14] Sometimes the personification process is reversed, and the Cajun is pictured as taking on the characteristics of the crawfish. Several informants have remarked, after eating large quanti-

ties of crawfish, "I'll be walking backwards for a week" (referring to the animals' usual form of locomotion).

There is another aspect of the animal's behavior that makes it an especially appropriate ethnic emblem: its pugnaciousness and tenacity in seemingly hopeless situations. Crawfish with claws outstretched threaten revenge on their human captors all the way from the trap to the cooking pot. Local jokes portray a crawfish sitting on a railroad track, aggressively snapping its claws at an oncoming locomotive. Cajuns view the crawfish's feistiness with respect as well as humor. Hallowell suggests that "Cajuns have taken the animal's courage as a symbol for their own cultural revival."[15] Although it would be more precise to say that the animal's courage is only one of several factors that make it an appropriate Cajun symbol, the fighting spirit of the crawfish nevertheless certainly contributes to the effectiveness of the symbol. The intrepidity and persistence of the crawfish are paralleled in the Cajuns' own image of themselves as a people who have managed to fight and survive in the face of deportation, economic hardship, social oppression, and a sometimes hostile environment.

The modern media in Acadiana are constantly finding new applications for the crawfish-as-animal emblem. For example, an outdoor urban mural in the Cajun city of Lafayette has as its focus a giant crawfish holding an oil rig in one claw. Bicentennial notecards featured a crawfish fife-and-drum corps, and 1980 presidential campaign bumper stickers pictured crawfish waving GOP flags. At the 1980 Breaux Bridge Crawfish Festival, where crawfish iconography is carried to the limit, there were T-shirts for sale illustrated with a Cajun-style band made up of crawfish musicians, and cardboard crawfish holding Dixie beer cans in their claws advertised a favorite local beverage. A local author has recently published a series of children's books about Crawfish-Man, a part-human and part-crawfish "superhereaux" whose goal it is to "keep the peace, justice and the Cajun Way."[16] A simple Cajun fisherman under ordinary circumstances, Crawfish-Man is transformed into a powerful, claw-snapping savior of Cajuns who are in trouble. Crawfish-Man is the perfect example of the personified, pugnacious crawfish.

The physical nature of the crawfish-as-animal enhances the power of the crawfish-as-food as an ethnic marker. Like other hard-shelled crustaceans, the crawfish must be boiled or steamed alive, after which the edible parts may be extracted by a rather complicated peeling process. The meat may be eaten immediately after peeling, or it may be used as an ingredient in more complicated dishes. When boiled crawfish are served, each diner is responsible for peeling his or her own crawfish. Thus participation in a crawfish boil requires special cultural knowledge in order to eat the food as served. In addition, a diner's reaction to the sight of the rather "life-like" boiled crawfish may separate the insider from the outsider at a crawfish boil. Therefore this food event is especially efficacious in highlighting ethnic boundaries.

Crawfish boils are common spring social events in southern Louisiana. They are held at private homes or at "camps" (second homes used primarily for parties or for fishing and hunting bases) and are attended by large numbers of relatives and friends. The event requires the presence of a group of people; boiling crawfish for one or two would hardly be worth the trouble. A crawfish boil begins with the acquisition of live crawfish. In the past, the crawfish were obtained directly from the environment, thus requiring that someone in the group know how to catch crawfish. Today, however, many people simply buy live crawfish by the sack at local seafood markets.

Once the crawfish arrive at the site of the boil, the proceedings become a community project. The preparations and cooking take place out of doors; it would be very messy indeed to have a crawfish boil indoors. The job of boiling the crawfish is men's work. (Cajun men are proud of their culinary skills and often do the cooking at large-scale food events.) The men first sort the live crawfish from any dead ones that may be in the sacks. This process requires dexterity if one is to avoid being pinched by the animals' claws, and care must be taken to prevent the escape of any of the animals. The live crawfish are placed in a container of water to "clean themselves out."

Meanwhile, the guests drink beer and comment on the quality of the crawfish, and the men prepare the cooking pot. They may use a large metal container, specially designed for boiling seafood, or perhaps a large metal garbage can that serves the purpose equally well. Today, the source of heat is usually a butane burner connected to a portable butane tank. The pot rests over the fire on a heavy metal tripod. The task of setting up the pot and the butane burner requires a degree of physical strength and is potentially a dangerous job. To make this task easier, Cajuns who can afford it may have complete outdoor crawfish-boil facilities, with a moveable suspended pot, a permanent butane source, and a built-in cooler that holds a keg of beer.

After the water in the pot begins to boil, the seasoning is added. A commercial seasoning mix may be used, or the host may combine the seasonings himself. Red pepper and salt are the predominant seasonings, but other items, such as onions or lemons, may be added as well. New red potatoes or corn on the cob may also be boiled with the crawfish. The water is allowed to boil until the crawfish have been sorted and cleaned, and the seasoned water is frequently tasted,

discussed, and added to. When it is agreed that the seasoning is "right," the crawfish are lowered into the pot in a large metal basket. Some people prefer to steam crawfish in a lesser amount of water with a lid, although most people boil them. The "correct" way to cook them may be a topic of considerable conversation. After about ten minutes the crawfish are tested for doneness. This, too, may be a point of slight disagreement, with each man putting in his opinion.

Meanwhile, the people who are not directly involved in the cooking process (often women) have prepared the table by covering it with newspapers and laying out drinks, bread, napkins, and perhaps trays for the discarded shells. Sometimes knives or nutcrackers are provided for cracking the claws of especially large crawfish. The crawfish are served by the men, who lift the heavy basket from the pot and pour the crawfish in a great mound down the center of the table. There are usually no clearly defined "places" at the table—people simply sit down and reach for the nearest crawfish in the pile in front of them. No attempt is made to divide the crawfish into equal amounts for each person; each diner is on his own and may eat as many crawfish as possible until the supply runs out.

Because of the large number of newcomers in Acadiana, it is not unusual for a non-Cajun co-worker or friend to be invited to a crawfish boil. An outsider attending his first crawfish boil potentially faces two problems. First, a non-Cajun may take one look at a boiled crawfish and decide that it is inedible. To a Cajun, of course, crawfish are quite edible; in fact, they are highly desired as food. But to many outsiders, the crawfish, by its very nature, is inedible or even repulsive. Today in the United States, our animal foods usually bear little resemblance to the living animal by the time they reach the kitchen or the table. A hamburger does not look or act like a cow. But crawfish must be alive when first cooked, and, being alive, the main course makes every attempt to escape or pinch the fingers of the cook (or guests). In addition, crawfish, whether alive or boiled, bear a strong resemblance to insects. Live crawfish in a container squirm and crawl over each other and make hissing and bubbling sounds, and boiled crawfish still retain their small, segmented bodies, hard shells, multiple legs, antennas, and protruding eyes. Indeed, crawfish are often called "mudbugs." Since few people in the United States eat insects, it is not uncommon for an outsider to avoid eating what he perceives to be an insect-like creature. Also, some outsiders erroneously believe that crawfish are unsanitary animals, because they live in the mud at the bottom of streams and ditches. One outsider remarked, "I can't believe my eyes when I drive along the interstate and see all those people digging up vermin from the scum in the drainage ditches, and taking them home to eat." Cajuns, of course, are likely to be insulted by such sentiments. A person who is too afraid or too squeamish to eat crawfish is either pitied or resented, and he is certainly not invited back to the next crawfish boil.

If a newcomer decides to eat the boiled crawfish, he faces a second problem: learning *how* to eat the crawfish. The locals, of course, know that the only edible portions of a crawfish are its tail meat, its fat, and, in large crawfish, the claw meat. The tail is broken from the "head" (actually the head and thorax) and the tail meat is quickly removed in one piece from the shell by a twisting and pinching process that is difficult to master. The intestinal vein is separated from the meat and discarded. The fat is extracted from the open end of the head by a finger or by simply sucking the head. The meat is removed from large claws after cracking them with a knife or the teeth; however, the claws of smaller crawfish are discarded.

The speed and dexterity with which a person peels crawfish determines the number of crawfish that a person consumes. Not only does a person who cannot peel crawfish end up with a very light meal, but such a person looks very silly indeed. Cajuns joke about outsiders who try to eat the head of the crawfish, or who tear up the meat in removing it from the shell, or who take a full five minutes to peel and eat a single crawfish, or who eat the intestinal vein by mistake, or who absent-mindedly rub an eye with a pepper-covered finger. Of course, if an outsider is a guest at a Cajun crawfish boil, the hosts will be most helpful in teaching the newcomer to eat the crawfish properly. In such a situation, the Cajun is in control and holds the situationally relevant knowledge. Those who know how to eat crawfish seem to enjoy, in a non-malicious way, the ignorance of others, and take pride in being able to teach a novice how to eat properly. Sometimes an insider will peel a number of crawfish and give the meat to the guest. This is a gesture of high regard; people do not usually take time from their own peeling and eating to peel for others, unless there is a special relationship between the two people. A mother will help her child, for example, or a husband or wife who has finished eating will help the other. A high status is attached to the person who eats a great number of crawfish, as indicated by the size of the pile of discarded shells at his place. The ability to consume many crawfish is a reflection of the person's peeling skill and robust appetite, both of which are highly regarded by Cajuns. It is said in Acadiana that a newcomer can become a local only if he can learn to eat crawfish and drink dark roast coffee.

Cajun country has gained international fame in gourmet circles, and many outsiders are eager to become acquainted with the "exotic" local foodways.

Although few tourists have the opportunity to attend a local crawfish boil, numerous tourist-oriented restaurants give newcomers a gentle introduction to Cajun cooking in a thoroughly American commercial setting. In such establishments, the pepper content is kept to a minimum (relative to home cooking), and boiled crawfish may be served in relatively small quantities by waitresses who graciously explain the peeling process. Or a customer may order a crawfish dinner that includes several different dishes: gumbo or stew, etoufee with rice, patties, pie, fried crawfish tails, bisque, and the familiar American tossed green salad. In the more expensive restaurants, dishes are available that would rarely if ever grace the table of the average local: avocado stuffed with crawfish dressing, crawfish casserole made with cream sauce, crawfish Newburgh, crawfish cocktail, crawfish and lettuce salad. Non-Cajun ethnic restaurants provide crawfish pizza and Chinese-style crawfish dishes. In all these dishes, the crawfish comes in the form of peeled tail meat. As such, it closely resembles shrimp in appearance, and, of course, does not require the technical knowledge necessary to eat boiled crawfish. Thus, in the heavily advertised Cajun restaurants, where tourists and their dollars are welcome, the loosening of ethnic boundaries is reflected in the setting and the food. To the outsider, these restaurants are "different" enough to be interesting, but not so different as to be threatening or unenjoyable. Smaller, out-of-the-way restaurants also exist in Acadiana, where the clientele is more local, French is more commonly spoken, the food is more highly seasoned, the menu is relatively limited, and the atmosphere is less plush and formal (boiled crawfish are served on newspaper or cardboard, for example). Although such restaurants welcome outsiders who happen by, only the more adventurous are apt to feel comfortable in what is obviously the "insiders'" territory.

People throughout Acadiana display pride in their local foodways. Dozens of major festivals and countless smaller fairs feature Cajun cuisine for the benefit of both tourists and locals. The town of Breaux Bridge sponsors the biennial Crawfish Festival, "the world's biggest crawfish boil," during which tons of crawfish are cooked and consumed. A historical marker in the town reads in part: "Breaux Bridge: Long recognized for its culinary artistry in the preparation of crawfish. The 1958 Louisiana Legislature officially designated Breaux Bridge 'La Capitale Mondiale de l'Ecrivisse' in honor of its centennial year." However, the more elderly residents of Breaux Bridge claim that crawfish-eating was not always something to brag about. Crawfish were "poor people's food," provided freely by the swamps and streams. A story is told in Breaux Bridge about an old crawfisherman who used to take the long way home with his catch from the Atchafalaya Swamp in order to avoid the humiliation of being seen with crawfish by the Lafayette "city folk" picnicking on the levee. Today, he still must take the long way home to avoid the city folk, who now deluge him with offers to buy his crawfish. A local woman in her eighties says, "Now the big shots eat crawfish, and the poor can't afford to. I wish I had eaten more back then; now I can't afford to buy them." An item that was once free for the taking has become an expensive food with "gourmet" overtones.

The development in Louisiana of what might be called "crawfish chic" is widely felt, even in high-level international business circles, as this recent news item illustrates:

> Lafayette's fame as a garden city, a mecca for gourmet food and a "can do" community of decision-makers in the oil industry is well-known in Abu Dhabi, United Arab Emirates.
>
> One of Acadiana's ambassadors of good will and international trade development is Huey Lambert, vice-president of AMASAR (American Associates of Arabia), and he provides this latest report. The Mansoori Oil Field Division held its second annual "Louisiana Crawfish Dinner Beach Party" in Abu Dhabi on May 24. It was a huge success.
>
> Huey brought 120 pounds of crawfish for the party; next year he'll have to increase the figure to 300 pounds. Around 200 people attended, 50 from Louisiana, others from France and the Middle East. They loved the food seasoned with south Louisiana pepper sauce.
>
> Huey met a Texan in London who offered $500 for one of the two containers of live Louisiana crawfish. The AMASAR exec turned him down.[17]

This reversal of status of the crawfish-as-food is undoubtedly related to its effectiveness as an ethnic emblem. Today people are proud to be Cajuns and proud to eat crawfish, and the memory of past humiliations can only serve to strengthen this pride.

The new role of the crawfish as gourmet food partially explains the acceptance of the crawfish as ethnic symbol by the Genteel Acadians. Tail meat may be combined with cream, wine, mushrooms, or other relatively expensive ingredients to produce any number of refined dishes appropriate for posh occasions. Even a crawfish boil may be "dressed up"; a south Louisiana department store sells special napkins, napkin rings, place mats, trays, utensils, and glasses for formal crawfish boils. The store also offers a complete set of crawfish-emblazoned fine Bavarian china for serving all types of crawfish dishes.

On the other hand, Cajuns today are aware of the food's past low status and of the fact that some outsiders still see the crawfish as repulsive. The Proud

Coonasses draw on this awareness in their own application of the crawfish as ethnic emblem. A popular bumper sticker in south Louisiana bears a message for those people who still disdain crawfish (and Cajuns): "Coonasses make better lovers because they eat anything." A similar attitude toward criticism of Cajun food habits is reflected by T-shirts that bear the words "I suck heads." In addition, a crawfish boil may be as rowdy as the hosts and guests wish it to be. A crawfish boil can provide an occasion for heavy eating, drinking, and "partying," and as such is a perfect reflection of the self-professed Coonass lifestyle.

Today, live crawfish are available only in southern Louisiana and in a few other nearby market cities. Marketing experts realize that the sales of live crawfish in non-Cajun areas would be low, but attempts are being made to expand the market area for frozen, peeled tail meat.[18] But for now, the consumption of crawfish is limited largely to south Louisiana, where one small-town poet has expressed her gratitude for the animal's presence in "Grace Before a Crawfish Meal":

> Bless us O Lord and bless these
> Crawfish which we are about to enjoy.
> Bless those who caught them, those who prepare them
> And give crawfish to those who have none.
>
> We thank you O God for this wonderful world
> And for all that you have put on it.
> And we give You special thanks O God
> For having put the Cajuns and the crawfish
> Down in the same place. Amen.[19]

NOTES

1. Nicholas Spitzer, "Cajuns and Creoles: The French Gulf Coast," *Southern Exposure* 5, nos. 2–3 (1977):140–55.

2. Jon L. Gibson and Steven Del Sesto, "The Culture of Acadiana: An Anthropological Perspective," in *The Culture of Acadiana: Tradition and Change in South Louisiana,* ed. Jon L. Gibson and Steven Del Sesto (Lafayette: Univ. of Southwestern Louisiana, 1975), 3.

3. Ibid.

4. Wilbur Zelinsky, *The Cultural Geography of the United States* (Englewood Cliffs, N.J.: Prentice-Hall, 1973), 110–11.

5. Patricia K. Rickels, "The Folklore of the Acadians," in *The Cajuns: Essays on Their History and Culture,* ed. Glenn R. Conrad (Lafayette: Univ. of Southwestern Louisiana, 1978), 251.

6. According to CODOFIL research, the word "coonass" was not used in Louisiana prior to World War II. When Cajun soldiers with their "peculiar" French dialect were stationed in France, the French locals referred to them as "conasse"—a word originally used for a bumbling prostitute and later for a stupid person or country bumpkin. The word was apparently

brought back to the United States by Cajuns and their Texas neighbors. According to CODOFIL, the unfamiliar French term was heard as "coonass," and has since been interpreted pictorially as the rear view of a raccoon with tail upraised. The term was first used as an ethnic slur against Cajuns, but in the past two decades it has been used in a positive sense by some Cajuns themselves. It has been my observation that the word is now so commonly used by many Cajuns (despite the fact that some Cajuns abhor the term) that the word is quickly losing both its negative and positive connotations and is becoming a simple synonym for the word Cajun.

7. Frederik Barth, "Introduction," in *Ethnic Groups and Boundaries,* ed. Frederik Barth (Boston: Little, Brown, 1969), 35.

8. See the editorial "We Are Not Coonasses!" *Louisiane Francaise* 32 (March 1980):5.

9. Holland C. Blades, Jr., *The Distribution of South Louisiana Crawfish,* Department of Publications Research Series No. 32 (Lafayette: Univ. of Southwestern Louisiana, 1974), 5.

10. Milton B. Newton, Jr., *Atlas of Louisiana* (Baton Rouge: School of Geoscience, Louisiana State Univ., 1972), 94.

11. Leona Martin Guirard, "Talk About Crawfish," printed souvenir (1973).

12. Irene Therese Whitfield, *Louisiana French Folk Songs* (Baton Rouge: Louisiana State Univ. Press, 1939), 138.

13. Guirard.

14. Howard Jacobs, "The Cajun Palate," *Acadiana Profile: A Magazine for Bi-Lingual Louisiana* 2, no. 3 (Sept./Oct. 1971):21.

15. Christopher Hallowell, *People of the Bayou: Cajun Life in Lost America* (New York: Dutton, 1979), 114.

16. Tim Edler, *The Adventures of Crawfish-Man* (Baton Rouge: Little Cajun Books, 1979), and *Crawfish-Man Rescues Ron Guidry* (Baton Rouge: Little Cajun Books, 1980).

17. Bob Angers, "Anecdotes and Antidotes," *Acadiana Profile: A Magazine for Bi-Lingual Louisiana* 7, no. 4 (July/August, 1979):13.

18. James C. Carroll and Holland C. Blades, "A Quantitative Analysis of the Amounts of South Louisiana Crawfish that Move to Market through Selected Channels of Distribution," Department of Publications Research Series No. 35 (Lafayette: Univ. of Southwestern Louisiana, 1974), 14.

19. Leona Martin Guirard, "Grace Before a Crawfish Meal," printed souvenir (undated).

18

The Children Cry for Bread: Hegemony and the Transformation of Consumption

Mary J. Weismantel

INTRODUCTION

In this [article], I discuss the substitution of wheat bread for barley gruel in the early morning meal in Zumbagua, an indigenous parish of highland Ecuador. While at the macroscopic level such changes in consumption may appear to be part of an inevitable, unilinear progression from subsistence to market systems, they are experienced by households actually undergoing them as a contradictory and conflict-filled process in which ideological and cultural issues play an important part. Wheat bread for barley gruel in the early morning seems like an insignificant change, the substitution of one carbohydrate for another, but because bread enters the indigenous kitchen as part of a complex of cultural, ideological and social transformations, its significance can be greater than the effects on family nutrition or the household budget would suggest. In indigenous Andean communities today, there is a symbolic association of leavened white bread with the dominant culture; this association has historical

and material aspects that relate it to general transformations in the political economy at a regional level.

Not only does purchase of breads by indigenous peasants raise social and ideological questions, but close study of this phenomenon highlights issues within the realm of economic analysis as well. As I hope to show in this [article], use of the household as an analytical unit of consumption and production can disguise very real differences between household members as economic actors. In Zumbagua, the household as a whole is involved in a combination of subsistence, commercial and wage labor activities, but the involvement of individuals in these spheres of activity is determined by their age and gender. Conflicts of interest between household members are frequently exposed and exacerbated by everyday consumption issues such as dietary innovations. These conflicts of interest between household members in turn reveal the contradictory pressures and forces at work in the nation as a whole.

Zumbagua is a rural parish of the province of Cotopaxi, in the western cordillera of the Andes. The parish today is relatively isolated and unimportant politically and economically, but this was not always the case. Zumbagua first entered the historical record as an Augustinian hacienda during the colonial period, at which time it was an important and lucrative land-holding, where enormous flocks of sheep produced wool for the textile workshops of the intermontane valley. In the republican era, these Church-owned lands were taken over by the state, which used proceeds from the hacienda to fund social services in urban areas. Thus production within the parish has for several centuries been directed by national-level organizations that channelled profits from the zone into investments in the urban economy.

Because the hacienda of Zumbagua belonged to the state, it is one of the few highland areas which was directly and radically affected by the national agrarian reform law enacted in 1964. In the mid-1960s, the hacienda was dissolved and title to the land distributed among parish residents. Inequalities in land distribution quickly developed, with white[1] hacienda employees establishing themselves as an economic and social elite. However, some indigenous families have succeeded in challenging white control, although many then take on the trappings of ethnic whiteness themselves, and simply reproduce the existing system of exploitation once they attain elite status. Ethnic whiteness in Zumbagua, as in much of the Andes, is largely inseparable from integration into the cash economy. Storekeepers, busdrivers and schoolteachers are "white," even if the individuals who presently hold these jobs were "Indians" ten years ago.

At the present, most of Zumbagua's residents are both much poorer and much more ethnically indigenous in language, dress and custom than is common in Ecuador today. The population lives in widely dispersed rural households scattered over the parish's 10,000 hectares. Most of the parish is of an unusually high altitude for Ecuador, ranging from 3500–4000 meters in elevation, well above the upper limits of maize cultivation at that latitude. Residents of the parish utilize several production zones, the most important being high valley lands, used for barley, fava bean and potato cultivation, and the still higher paramo grasslands, used for sheep and llama pastoralism and as a source of grass fuel. But although the people of Zumbagua have a strong emotional commitment to farming, it is in fact impossible for households to support themselves purely through agriculture and pastoralism. Every household is also involved in a variety of other activities, which in fact tie them to the national economy to a far greater degree than is immediately apparent. One important strategy is to send some males outside the parish as temporary wage laborers. Older workers typically find employment in small sugarcane fields and mills located in the lowlands immediately to the west of the parish, but younger men tend to go to the capital city of Quito to find work, usually in construction.

The rapid change in the relations of production of the parish in the last several decades has had a profound effect on social relations at the household level. The biggest schism is between young adults, who have come of age since the dissolution of the hacienda, and an older generation who lived under the hacienda system. The problems revealed by the issue of bread and gruel, however, do not highlight this generation gap, but rather bring to light divisions within younger families.

The proletarianization of males is creating a gender gap among young adults, which does not exist in the older generation. Males typically begin work in Quito between the ages of ten and fourteen, so that by the time a man marries at the age of twenty he has had a very different socialization than his bride. He is at home in an urban environment, speaks Spanish, listens to the radio, knows something of national sports and politics, music and slang. She, in contrast, has rarely if ever left the parish, speaks only Quichua, wears indigenous clothing, and knows the mythology, songs and elaborate Quichua riddle games of indigenous culture. She is a subsistence farmer and pastoralist, having taken over almost all the agricultural duties of the farmstead, while he is a wage laborer. Since Andean marriage does not entail a merging of financial assets and earnings, there is frequently an economic disparity between the two as well: he has money and she does not.

There is also a generation gap within these young families, between parents and children. Unlike their parents, many Zumbagua children today go to school. The children thus are becoming acculturated to national Ecuadorian society: schoolchildren understand Quichua but hardly speak it, and spend their time tearing photographs of cars, airplanes and motorcycles out of any scrap of Spanish-language magazines they can lay their hands on. The lessons they learn in the classroom, which include the rule that white, urban and professional is good and Indian, rural and peasant is bad, hardly encourage them to learn farming from their mothers and grandparents. Although their labor is very important to the family farm, most children do not look to farming as their future, regardless of whether they attend school or not.

In the above description, I have presented the roles of male and female, adult and child as fixed and predictable. In fact, however, although these descriptions are not inaccurate, they not only gloss over individual variation but also fail to reveal the conflicting attitudes individuals often feel towards the social and productive roles they play. There are few individuals, of any age or sex, who do not feel the attraction of both agricultural and proletarian lifeways, and fewer still who have not cursed the inadequate livelihood provided by both economic strategies. The fact that men who work in Quito have had to adopt more "white" cultural traits than their wives does not necessarily mean that they value "whiteness" more. The glamor of urban life and purchased goods can appeal more to women, for whom they represent an exotic and unknown world, than for their husbands, who frequently characterize the time they spend in the city as a painful exile from indigenous life.

In hacienda days, ethnic identity and productive role were determined for the people of Zumbagua by forces beyond their control. Exploitation of this work force by the national economy was then made possible by a rigid caste system in which distinctive customs preserved social boundaries. Today a new political economy prevails, and national ideologies call for the rapid assimilation of indigenous peoples. But the issue of whether such assimilation is in fact desirable is one on which the parish itself remains divided.

In Zumbagua, where ethnicity is largely a matter of socially recognized markers such as language, dress and custom, consumption choices become a major arena in which individuals and groups establish their ethnic identity. Consumption decisions thus involve a complex of issues beyond financial capacity and individual psychology. In the parish today, issues which are ultimately of a political and ideological nature, such as choices in productive strategy and cultural identity, are being argued not so much through overt debate, speechmaking and confrontations in the political arena of the parish, but rather through everyday consumption decisions being made at the household level. The pressure to assimilate does not remain at the level of abstract ideology, but pervades the textures of everyday life.

The people of Zumbagua are constantly bombarded from within and without by images of their cultural practices as being backwards and wrong. The imposition of these labels of inadequacy is part of a political and economic process which is hegemonic in nature. The erosion of the subsistence economy is inevitably occurring, an overdetermined process in which ecological degradation, overpopulation, and drastic changes in the national economy have all played a part. But the erosion of people's faith in the validity of the food and clothing, language and celebrations they grew up with is also the product of a multiplicity of forces. In an isolated rural area like Zumbagua, this message filters through in small ways, but the pressure is unrelenting. I refer to it as hegemonic because, to quote Raymond Williams, the impo-

sition of a political order is hegemonic when it is not . . . "expressed in directly political forms . . . by direct or effective coercion . . ." but rather through ". . . a complex interlocking of political forms, and active social and cultural forms. . . . What is decisive is not only the conscious system of ideas and beliefs but the whole lived social process as practically organized by specific and dominant meanings and values" (Raymond Williams 1977:108–109).

The transformation of indigenous practice occurs not only when the schoolchild is taught to salute the Ecuadorian flag, but also when his mother hesitates over what foods to serve her family, fearful that there is something inadequate in a meal of homegrown foods unembellished by purchased foodstuffs or condiments. Even women who have little interaction with white outsiders, separated from them by the language barrier, learn the lessons of cultural and social inferiority. Children so young that they have scarcely ever left the farmstead have already begun to learn them too. These messages of inferiority color private consumption rituals within the household, as well as more public actions.

FOOD AND IDENTITY

My research in Zumbagua was directed towards uncovering the semiotic system that underlies the cooking of foods, a system that I refer to as cuisine. This study necessitated analysis of the relationship of Zumbagua ways of cooking to those of other Ecuadorians, the semiotic systems of people who, for the most part, are richer and whiter than those who live in the parish. For heuristic purposes, it would be possible to study Zumbagua cuisine in isolation from other cuisines that surround it, but the parish has never existed in such isolation. The cuisine of the parish has evolved as a system which, like its people, exists in a certain ethnic and class relation to other cuisines.

The people of Zumbagua are poor, rural, indigenous, and they live in the Sierra. In addition, they live above the zone of maize cultivation. All of these facts about them are reflected in their cuisine; in fact, as I discuss below, at times one food, *machica*, symbolizes all of these facts within its fan (Turner 1967) of referential meanings. Not only the diet of Zumbagua but its cuisine differs from that of the nation as a whole. Zumbagua people eat "Indian" foods in "Indian" ways: not only elements and techniques but the very syntagmatic chains by which they are combined into meals are not the same as even the stereotypical highland Ecuadorian cuisine. This difference is significant: it signifies not simply a particular way of life but one which is stigmatized.

Perhaps the quintessential *plato tipico* or traditional dish in Ecuador is the kind of dish referred to as a *seco*. In the typical *seco,* the plate holds a piece of meat (beef, chicken, goat) cooked using one of a rather limited repertoire of techniques, condiments and vegetables. At the side are perhaps some fried potatoes and another vegetable, or a relish of marinated, finely sliced onions and tomatoes with lemon and *cilantro*. The dominant element on the plate, however, is the large, unseasoned pile of white rice.

In the full midday meal or *almuerzo,* the *seco* is flanked by a preceding soup and terminal sweet *colada,* dishes that evoke a meal structure descended from pre-Hispanic patterns. But as *caldo de pata* and other Ecuadorian soups are increasingly replaced by imports like canned cream of mushroom soup, and fruit *coladas* by a soft drink or a dish of canned peaches, the earlier heritage becomes less visible even though the sequence of courses still bears its mark. The sequence of meals also continues to resist North American influences: the light, continental-style morning *cafe* is followed by the main meal, the heavy, multi-course *almuerzo* in the early afternoon, and a light meal in the evening.

To wealthy Ecuadorians whose repertoire of foods includes European and North American dishes, the *seco* and the *colada* are nostalgic reminders of the past. For most Ecuadorians, however, these dishes remain standard everyday fare. For the well-to-do, *platos tipicos* such as *seco* remain important because they symbolize the country's heritage. Unlike pizzas or sandwiches made of Wonder Bread, American cheese and bologna (*pan de miga, queso americano y pastel mexicano*), the glamorous fast foods, processed foods and snack foods that are modish among the young and the nouveaux riches, students and professional classes, *platos tipicos* are substantial, solid: bland and starchy, they reach their full flower in the traditional *almuerzo,* the heavy midday meal at which the entire family gathers. *Platos tipicos* stand for the strength of the family, that primary virtue of traditional Ecuadorian society. The ideological importance of *platos tipicos* for Ecuador is problematic, however, in a way which characterizes an Ecuadorian dilemma in seeking an autonomous identity through emphasizing the nation's heritage. For *platos tipicos* carry other messages besides "family" and "nation." They also stand for the poor, the ignorant, and the non-white: people with whom the elite, for the most part, do not wish to identify.

This opposition between the full *almuerzo* and the fast-food snack, though real, obscures a more complex hierarchy of cuisines. Shrimps *ceviches* and tropical fruits like the *grenadilla* and *chirimoya* certainly stand on the Ecuadorian side of the two rival American cuisines, North American and national, found in Quito today. But although "Ecuadorian cuisine" appears as a unified entity when opposed to sandwiches or pizzas, Ecuador in fact contains many cuisines. For example, the long-standing rivalry between highlands and coast is symbolized by potatoes vs. rice, by *locros* (stews) vs. *secos* (dry meals), by blandness vs. spiciness. This is true even though the *seco* made with rice is found throughout Ecuador, including the highlands. The *seco* dominates Ecuadorian cuisine; this dominance reflects a certain historical relationship between coast and sierra.

The *seco* also evokes the provinces rather than the capital city. In small towns and even provincial capitals, the restaurants all serve the same fare: *churrascos* and *apanados, pollo dorado, seco de chivo* (all of which are types of *secos*) appear on every menu and all are assembled on the plate in the same way. But while for Quitenos such dishes signify provincialism and a native heritage being left behind by the modern world, to the people of Zumbagua the same menu represents that outside, urban, modern world from which they feel disenfranchised.

In Zumbagua cuisine, like that of white Sierrans, there are two basic categories of dishes, *sopas* and *secos*. But in contrast to the white *almuerzo,* where *sopa* and *colada* flank a central, validating *seco,* in Zumbagua the *sopa* has a clear predominance.[2] The role of the *sopa* in Zumbagua cuisine is similar to that which Mary Douglas describes when she speaks of the power of the familiar dish to arouse in people "the flash of recognition and confidence which welcomes an ordered pattern" (Mary Douglas 1971:80). There is no doubt that the presence of the *sopa* validates most Zumbagua meals. It is the most important and most typical syntagm (dish/meal) of Zumbagua cuisine. Generally speaking, most main meals eaten in the parish consist of *sopas*. Each person sharing the meal is expected to eat at least two bowls full of soup, and more is always offered. The heavy starch content makes it a very filling meal.

The basis of these meals is boiled water. The word for "to cook," *yanuna,* itself means "to boil." Boiling is absolutely central to Zumbagua cooking practice. The essential wetness of Zumbagua dishes, which are served in bowls and eaten with spoons, contrasts sharply with the *seco;* the word *seco* itself means dry, highlighting its opposition to the water-based *sopa*. There is a strong disinclination in Zumbagua against eating any foods during a meal that have not first been immersed in hot water. Raw or dry foods are snacks meant to be eaten away from home or between mealtimes; they should not be eaten during a meal.

Beyond this underlying process of boiling in water, it is hard to write a minimal definition of a *sopa*. Unlike most peasant cuisines, everyday meals in Zumbagua may be based on any one of a variety of starches; no single complex carbohydrate predominates. It is the manner of cooking, the "ordered pattern" used, that characterizes the Zumbagua *almuirsu* (cf. Mintz 1985: 8–9).

Sopas can be divided into two basic categories, *colada* and *caldo*. The first are thick, the latter clear soups. (This distinction is not absent from our own cuisine, although it is not clearly distinguished linguistically. Cream soups, bisques, chowders and bean soups are *coladas;* consommes, broths, noodle and vegetable soups are *caldos*.) Note that potatoes, while important, do not play the role of fundamental thickener in *coladas*. While North American cuisine frequently uses potatoes as the thickening agent for a *colada*-style soup, in Zumbagua potatoes are never allowed to cook long enough to disintegrate in this fashion.[3] Other starches are used as the base of *coladas*, potatoes never. They are present in both *caldo* and *colada*, but are the validator for neither. A *colada* is validated by its thickening starch food, a *caldo* by its broth.

Whereas a *colada* must have a flour or meal of some sort used to thicken it, *caldos* may be without any starch. It is possible to make a meat broth for the sick which contains no starches at all, or only potatoes. Sick people frequently decide that they have no stomach for one or another starch, aversions which are always heeded; the extremely ill may only be able to eat pure broths. These clear broths in fact represent the quintessential *caldo*. However, neither meat broth nor its substitute, small amounts of purchased processed vegetable fat dissolved in boiling water, need to be present to make *caldo*. Hot water, noodles and salt make a perfectly acceptable *caldo*, one which cash-poor people consider somewhat desirable.

Overall, *coladas* are more common than *caldos* in everyday cuisine. A good, substantial *sopa*, the kind of meal an average family eats on a regular basis, consists of hot water thickened with home-ground barley or purchased wheat flour, cooked with a spoonful of fat, some salt, and three to five chopped onions. On most but not all days, a *sopa* also contains some extras: pieces of mutton, perhaps, or cabbage. A *sopa* should always contain enough potatoes so that each bowl served contains several, although in many households it often does not.

If potatoes are beyond many household's budget today, rice, the staple element of small-town "white" cuisine, is a rarely eaten treat. Like the sophisticated Ecuadorian confronted with emblems of popular culture from the U.S., the people of Zumbagua view dishes such as the rice-based *seco* with both hatred and desire.

Secos contrast with everyday meals in Zumbagua not only in ingredients and in their non-soup nature

but in other ways as well. These include aesthetic principles about color, texture, temperature, and consistency. In the parish, it is held that to be appealing food should be liquid, thick, uniform, and barely lukewarm. This is an ideal which women strive for in their cooking. The contrast between this ideal and the norms found in "white" cuisine is clearest in the *almuerzo*, the largest and most important meal of the day, but it can be found in the lighter meals eaten in peasant households before dawn and after dusk as well.[4]

BREAD AND HEGEMONY

Throughout Ecuador, the early-morning meal is referred to as *cafe*. For most "white" Ecuadorians, *cafe* consists of a cup of hot water, served with a saucer and a spoon, into which the individual consumer mixes instant coffee and sugar. It is served with two bread rolls. This meal is familiar to indigenous residents of the parish, since it is served in the early morning in restaurants and market stalls in the "white" towns Zumbagua people frequent. In most households within Zumbagua, however, the early morning meal takes quite a different form. Although still called *cafe*, it does not contain any coffee at all. The main component is *machica*, finely ground toasted barley meal. This *cafe*, like the "white" one, involves the serving of hot water, but there are no cups or saucers in evidence. Like most other meals in Zumbagua, this one is served in deep enamel bowls.

Water is heated to boiling, and sugar is dissolved into the water. Each person is handed a bowl of this sugar-water along with a spoon. At the same time, a container filled with *machica* is placed on the ground within everyone's reach, and everyone is invited to have some: *chapuvay, chapuilla,* "go ahead and mix yourself some." There is some range in personal tastes, but most people put about an equal amount of *machica* to sugar water in their bowl. This is frequently done gradually, with leisurely actions interspersed with morning conversations. At first the hot sweet water is sipped, then bit by bit spoonfuls of *machica* are added, producing a warm sweet gruel. Sometimes a cooked gruel of sweetened, coarsely ground barley (*arroz de cebada*) is served instead of water and *machica*.

Although most households consider *machica* an absolute necessity, a substance one simply cannot live without, an alternative construction of *cafe*, familiar to everyone, substitutes bread for *machica*. Despite being a quite different form of a starch food than *machica*, in the actual consumption bread, a "dry" food which does not require immersion in water, becomes somewhat similar to other indigenous starches: as people drink spoonfuls of coffee, they break the breads into pieces and mash them into the cup, producing a sweet soupy mass not unlike a gruel.

This act of making "white" breads similar to "indigenous" gruels in the actual consumption does not negate the implied threat to indigenous identity that eating bread in the early morning contains. This threat is especially felt because of the intimate, familiar nature of *cafe,* a meal which is only shared by household members. There is a tendency in Zumbagua for special-occasion meals to be served and eaten according to rules borrowed from white cuisine, and some indigenous households self-consciously try to model even their everyday eating habits according to white forms, behavior which quickly earns them the criticism of their neighbors. But controversy over whether to adopt white forms for everyday use, such as eating *cafe* according to the white pattern where carbohydrates are eaten as dry breads, also exists within households.

Many of the early morning quarrels I witnessed in Zumbagua homes erupted over the question of bread. This conflict arises between young children and their parents. Pre-school children, especially, demand bread as their right, and refuse to accept *mishqui,* sweet gruels, or *machica* in its place. Refusal is difficult for parents, since young children, especially the youngest child, are commonly indulged a great deal. Quichua-speaking mothers mimic their children's Spanish cries for bread: "Sulu tandata munan pan, pan, pan, 'nin. Sulu wakan." They only want bread [*tanda,* Q.]. "Bread, bread, bread" they say [*pan,* Sp.]. They just cry.

In current practice, bread is definitely a member of the *wanlla* set of foods, which also includes bananas, oranges and other fruits, hard candies and cookies. It is a snack food, and is frequently given as a gift. As such, bread is a necessity in certain circumstances: it is included among the offerings to the dead on *Finados,*[5] the gifts exchanged during marriage negotiations or when asking someone to be a godparent, or as part of the redistributive flow surrounding fiesta sponsorship. Unless they are very poor, most families also buy some bread on Saturday as a treat for the children and for gift-giving in the web of *wanlla* presentations. Some of this bread is stored in the kitchen for any special occasions that might arise during the week. Many battles of will take place as mothers struggle to dole out the breads bought on Saturday as special treats, while the children demand them as daily fare. Fathers who witness these scenes seem to feel shame at their own inadequacy, their inability to fill their children's hands with bread. They may react with anger towards the child for his unreasonable demand, or towards the mother for denying the request. Often men shout that they will

buy more tomorrow, as though resenting the implication that they in fact cannot.

What seems to be taking place is a struggle on the children's part to redefine what had been a treat *(wanlla),* a luxury good which most families can afford to buy but not for every day, into a staple, a necessary part of the morning meal. This is the process which Mintz describes as intrinsic to the needs of capitalism: demand must be created, new foods must be ". . . transformed into the ritual of daily necessity and even into images of daily decency" (Mintz 1979:65). The children desire bread as the validation of a meal, that which seals it and marks it as satisfactory. They are pushing to redefine the role of bread in the domestic economy, not as a snack or treat but as something without which a meal would be incomplete. This redefinition implies an enlargement of the role of purchased foods in the household economy, and a preference for masculine over feminine contributions to consumption.

The change being suggested here is not the introduction of a new food into Zumbagua. Bread is already well established as a *wanlla* food, a snack or luxury food which nonetheless is a necessity in certain social interchanges. The substitution being urged by the children simply implies a change in the particular role played by bread. The significance of this change becomes clearer if we examine the meanings surrounding bread and those surrounding *machica,* the food which bread may supplant. Although other starches are important in the diet, barley, and especially *machica,* is a kind of core cultural symbol for Zumbagua. It is referred to by terms such as *bien calienticu,* food that warms you up when you eat it or *abrigaditu,* warm and comforting; people say that it is as filling as meat (although they don't mean this literally, but are using the comparison to highlight *machica*'s positive attributes). Those who have listened to the public health nurses' lectures on nutrition use the phrase *Buena alimentacion* to describe its goodness, while others simply insist that it is *alli alli mikuna* [Q.], a very good food. It is the food that is given to kittens and baby puppies, and the first solid food given to human babies. Mothers give little bags full of sweetened *machica* to their children when they send them off herding, and worry all day if a careless youngster leaves his behind.

Because it is the essential symbol of the home, *machica* is the quintessential symbol of hospitality. Some is always kept on hand to offer to visitors. It is not offered to formal guests, and certainly not to the white nurse, schoolteacher or priest, for whom, after much frantic searching, the crusty year-old jar of instant coffee is unearthed while a child is sent racing downhill to buy bread. *Machica* is for the familiar guest, for the *comadre* who always comes to help harvest or the neighbor who has come to castrate your pig. A woman loves to bring out the *machica* when her family visits from her *natal comuna*, or when sisters visit from the *comunas* into which they have married. It is as though with this single act she can recreate the disbanded family home.

The meanings attached to *machica* derive partially from the way it is made. Ideally, it is entirely produced on the farmstead. Cultural ideals demand that barley sown by a family be seed from its own stores, not purchased; the sowing, care, harvest and threshing of the crop is done by extended family members; lastly, the sifting, grinding and toasting of the grain to make *machica* is done by the women of the family. Mothers make *machica* for their children, and in-marrying women prove their allegiance to the family, and their obedience to their mother-in-law, by grinding barley in the cold hours before dawn. Where the traditional extended family is still maintained, daughters-in-law creep into their mother-in-law's kitchen at four in the morning to start making *machica*. In the newer family structure, where wage labor gives a young couple independence from parents and in-laws, couples may pay to have barley ground in the town mill. This is socially disapproved, however. Machine-ground *machica* isn't *mishqui*, sweet or tasty, people say, and older women cluck with disapproval over a house where dawn finds a cold hearth, that is, where *machica* is not being toasted in the morning. Because of this association of *machica* with female productive and social roles, women react very emotionally to their children's rejection of barley gruels. It is not only the demand for precious purchased food over abundant home-grown grains that troubles them. In demanding bread, children reject their mother's contribution to the household and reach for foods that their fathers provide.

Zumbagua adults do not feel that bread is appropriate for everyday meals because it is part of a class of food defined as *wanlla*. *Wanlla* is anything that is not part of a meal. In this sense, it could be translated as "snack," "treat," "junk food" or "dessert food," and *wanlla* can be all of these. But the second meaning of *wanlla* is "gift." All of the foods called *wanlla* are primarily purchased in order to be redistributed. The motivation is not so much altruism as the exercise of power: giving *wanlla* is a critically important social and political action in Zumbagua; no one can be a successful social actor without understanding how to give and to manipulate others into giving. Any food given as a gift can be called *wanlla*. Hence in certain contexts rice, onions, noodles, milk or any other food could be *wanlla*. Some foods, however, are always *wanlla* in nature: they do not form part of regular meals and their primary purpose, in Zumbagua eyes, is as gifts. Since eating in Zumbagua always takes the form of

offering and receiving food, these goods are still *wanlla* even when bought by members of a household and consumed within that household.

Bread is the *wanlla* par excellence. It is the universally appropriate gift, the favorite treat. In Zumbagua minds, bread has none of the qualities of a staple. It is truly a *golosina*, a treat, a luxury. More so than perhaps any other food, consumption of bread is directly dependent on a family's disposable cash income. It is the one special food that everyone would like to have on hand all the time, while at the same time it is recognized that no one ever needs bread. Potatoes and barley are necessities; bread is for enjoyment.

In households where men are absent wageworkers, the relationship of husband and wife entails certain exchanges of food. Whatever the husband's job, one of the obligations of a wife is to have food ready for him when he returns home. In households where he comes home only on weekends, every other week or even only once a month, this offering on her part becomes increasingly important symbolically. She cooks the best food she has, and the form she uses is strictly indigenous, using locally produced foods like *machica* to welcome him back home. While she presents him with these boiled grain soups or gruels, he brings *wanlla*: raw foods and treats from the city. These may include noodles, flour, cookies, candies and fruit, but bread is an important component.

The relative importance of her contribution compared to his depends on the financial situation of the household. If the young couple is part of a large, landholding extended family, he may return bearing only treats and goodies. But if they are a relatively isolated, land-poor couple, she and the children may have been subsisting on nothing but *machica* and water awaiting his return, and he will then bring in a substantial supply of groceries. In treating purchased foods like bread as part of everyday meals, the children seem in some ways to be making a prediction that the latter kind of household will become more common as they grow up, a prediction that seems more likely than not. Whatever the future may be, they certainly are expressing a preference for a male-provided, purchased commodity, bread, over the female-produced complex of cooked grains. And in defining bread as part of everyday meals, they are proposing a substantial shift in the role bread plays in Zumbagua cuisine.

GRUEL AND HISTORY

This contrast between two starch food forms, one of which is produced by and represents the local economy, while the other is part of a state-level economy and so enters the local community with all the prestige and symbolic power of the state behind it, is reminiscent of the relationship between maize and potatoes described by John Murra (1975) for Inca times. According to Murra, potatoes were the humble food of humble people, while maize, the cultivation of which necessitated systems of irrigation, was associated with the imperial power of the Inca state. The ability of the Inca state to make maize into a prestige item is suggested in the fragments of myths and stories cited by Murra in which the superiority of maize over potatoes is implicitly suggested.

According to Murra, the Spanish chroniclers were blind to the competition between maize and potatoes because, coming from a grain-based economy themselves, they never considered the possibility that tubers could be a staple. I find this observation to be very pertinent to the question of breads and gruels today, since our own predisposition towards bread as a basic food, as seen in its description as the "staff of life," can prevent us from perceiving the alien nature of leavened wheat breads to household economies based on boiled foods. As Americans, we all carry with us the mythic image of home-baked bread, but in areas of the world where fuel is precious, bread baking is beyond the scope of the individual household.

Our own prejudice towards leavened bread, which can be seen in the unpleasant associations that the word "gruel" has in English, is an artifact of what Raymond Sokolov (1984:108) has called "the inexorable march of wheat." As he points out, our disdain for boiled grain dishes is not just a matter of taste but is the product of specific political and economic processes in Europe and, later, in the Americas as well. The hegemonic nature of the contrast between gruels and breads played a part in the changes in taste that accompanied the spread of the Roman Empire, for example, where Tannahill says that "Bread . . . was established as being more desirable than grain-pastes and porridges" (Tannahill 1973:57). According to Goody, "In Europe . . . the northern extension of bread from the Mediterranean was associated with its use by the conquering Romans and by the missionizing Christians, who sacralized this high-status food through its use in the Mass" (1982:180). In Zumbagua, the intonation by European priests during the Mass of "Give us this day our daily bread" has similar connotations of white validation of a high-prestige food to indigenous listeners.

Oats and barley, and the porridges and unleavened breads that are made from them, symbolized the provincialism of the Scots to the eighteenth-century writer Samuel Johnson. According to Sokolov, Johnson's jibes on the subject of Scottish culinary tradition, with its emphasis on such gruel-based dishes as haggis and flummery, are revealing of the relationship between London and the hinterlands of the British Isles.

"[Johnson's] . . . complete insensitivity to the real situation that condemned the Celtic fringe (and the north of England) to oats and barley . . . is an unappealing, but, once again, typical expression of the imperial status of London" (1984:110).

In this century, Goody cites the opposition between porridges and breads as one facet of the colonized/colonizer dichotomy in Ghana, where rising black elites, who previously made much of their familiarity with European culinary habits, have only recently begun to publicly eat porridge as an affirmation of their ethnicity (Goody 1982:177, passim). Goody's comments on the production aspects of this opposition are very relevant to the Andean case. He points out that the early success of bread among European foods introduced into the area can perhaps be attributed to the possibility of producing it on a small, localized scale (1982:180). In Ecuador, bread baking and sales figure importantly among the entrepreneurial possibilities open to the lower-class "white" and cholo populations whose livelihood is based on products which appeal to and are affordable for people from the small towns and rural hinterlands of the Sierra.

As Goody points out, the contrast between leavened breads and gruels or toasted grain products is one of technology; baking bread implies use of an oven, a technology which contrasts with that of the rural household where techniques are limited to boiling and toasting (1977:180–181). Because of the high energy input required for their use, ovens in turn require some type of commercial or communal organization of production in low energy consuming economies such as that of rural Ecuador.[6]

In conclusion, then, bread in Zumbagua has for some time now been a high-status food which contrasts with local products, although its specific role in local cuisine may be changing. Family arguments over the introduction of bread into the early-morning meal involve issues larger and more complex than worries over the family budget. In addition, the roles of children and parents, men and women in these conflicts indicates the heterogeneous nature of family members both as producers and as consumers, a heterogeneity which household-level economic analysis can overlook. As to the resolution of the conflict, it remains to be seen whether the children's cries for bread and the continued erosion of the household's ability to sustain itself through subsistence agriculture will succeed in transforming everyday practice.

NOTES

1. Race and ethnicity in the Ecuadorian Sierra, as in much of Latin America, is determined primarily by socio-

economic class, "Indian" and "peasant," "white" and "elite" being practically synonymous. In Zumbagua, ethnicity for permanent residents is bipolar, *blanco* (white) referring to the small local elite and *longo/a* (a derogatory term similar in connotation to the English "nigger") labeling the indigenous majority. Zumbagua "whites" would not be considered white at all by urban or upper-middle class Ecuadorians, while the metaphorical nature of these terms is demonstrated by the presence in the parish of green-eyed, fair-haired, freckled "longos," the product of the institutionalized miscegenation of hacienda days, as well as by the membership among the parish "whites" of a family of coastal blacks. Terms for people of mixed blood, such as *mestizo, cholo,* or *misti* are infrequently heard in the parish and never refer to those who were born there. The word *cholo* identifies market sellers, while professionals such as the staff of the Catholic Church or the government-sponsored clinic are referred to as *gringos,* foreigners, even when Ecuadorian. Everyone born in the parish is categorized as *blanco* or *longo,* although local gossip identifies those who are "trying to be *blanco*" or "trying to be both."

2. I use terms—*sopa* and *seco, caldo* and *colada*—which come from Ecuadorian national cuisine, but are here applied to categories used within the parish. These are not words that people of the parish themselves use. Although more acculturated and Spanish-speaking residents of the parish may use these terms to apply to Zumbagua dishes, monolingual Quichua speakers do not. Soups are commonly referred to simply as *almuirsu,* from the Spanish *almuerzo,* lunch. I have borrowed these terms to label certain implicit categories used by Zumbagua women when cooking: they refer to specific types of syntagmatic chains I discovered in their practice. I use the Ecuadorian Spanish terms because they most closely approximate native categories (not surprisingly, given the common cultural roots, European and Native American, of both cuisines) and to avoid meanings implicit in English cooking terminology.

3. Local farmers prefer varieties which retain form after boiling and consider those which break down (*deshacerse*) as inferior.

4. The Zumbagua sequence of meals is similar in concept to the typical Ecuadorian pattern, in that meals eaten after dark are light while daytime meals are heavy. As I describe elsewhere (Weismantel 1987) among current con-

flicts over cuisine in the parish is the issue as to whether to eat three times a day, the national pattern, or four (*cafe* {5 A.M.}, *almuirsu* {10 A.M.}, *almuirsu* {3 P.M.}, *cafe* {8 P.M.}). The latter meal structure is suited to the schedules of women who must both cook and herd sheep, but it cannot be sustained if the children attend public schools that send them home at noon for a meal.

5. Finados is the November 1–2 celebration for the dead, observed throughout the Andes. Many of the rituals of the holiday, which syncretize indigenous and Hispanic elements, suggest the symbolic significance of food and eating, and especially of starchy foods; the *colada morada* or *yana api* is in fact a gruel, made of maize in maize-producing areas, but in Zumbagua it is more frequently made of *machica.* For food symbolism in Finados, see Weismantel 1983; Hartman 1973, 1974 provides the best data on contemporary Ecuadorian practice.

6. There are communities in the Sierra that have ovens, however; these are frequently owned as money-making enterprises by certain families who undertake the roasting of pigs or the baking of quantities of breads for weddings and other special occasions.

REFERENCES

Douglas, Mary. 1971. Deciphering a Meal. In *Myth, Symbol and Culture.* Clifford Geertz, ed. New York: W. W. Norton and Co., pp. 61–82.

Goody, Jack. 1982. *Cooking, Cuisine and Class: A Study of Comparative Sociology.* Cambridge: Cambridge University Press.

Mintz, Sidney. 1979. Time, Sugar and Sweetness. *Marxist Perspectives* 2:56–73.

———. 1985. *Sweetness and Power: The Place of Sugar in Modern History.* NY: Viking Press.

Sokolov, Raymond. 1984. Oat Cuisine. *Natural History* 93 (4):108–111.

Tannahill, Reay. 1972. *Food in History.* NY: Stein and Day.

Turner, Victor. 1967. *The Forest of Symbols.* Ithaca: Cornell University Press.

Williams, Raymond. 1977. *Marxism and Literature.* Cambridge: Cambridge University Press.

19

Japanese Mothers and *Obentō*s:
The Lunch-Box as Ideological State Apparatus

Anne Allison

*Obentō*s *are boxed lunches Japanese mothers make for their nursery school children. Following Japanese codes for food preparation—multiple courses that are aesthetically arranged—these lunches have a cultural order and meaning. Using the* obentō *as a school ritual and chore—it must be consumed in its entirety in the company of all the children—the nursery school also endows the* obentō *with ideological meanings. The child must eat the* obentō; *the mother must make an* obentō *the child will eat. Both mother and child are being judged; the subjectivities of both are being guided by the nursery school as an institution. It is up to the mother to make the ideological operation entrusted to the* obentō *by the state-linked institution of the nursery school, palatable and pleasant for her child, and appealing and pleasurable for her as a mother. [food, mother, Japan, education, ideology]*

INTRODUCTION

Japanese nursery school children, going off to school for the first time, carry with them a boxed lunch (*obentō*) prepared by their mothers at home. Customarily these *obentō*s are highly crafted elaborations of food: a multitude of miniature portions, artistically designed and precisely arranged, in a container that is sturdy and cute. Mothers tend to expend inordinate time and attention on these *obentō*s in efforts both to please their children and to affirm that they are good mothers. Children at nursery school are taught in turn that they must consume their entire meal according to school rituals.

Food in an *obentō* is an everyday practice of Japanese life. While its adoption at the nursery school level may seem only natural to Japanese and unremarkable to outsiders, I will argue in this article that the *obentō* is invested with a gendered state ideology. Overseen by the authorities of the nursery school, an institution which is linked to, if not directly monitored by, the state, the practice of the *obentō* situates the producer as a woman and mother, and the consumer, as a child of a mother and a student of a school. Food in this context is neither casual nor arbitrary. Eaten quickly in its entirety by the student, the *obentō* must be fashioned by the mother so as to expedite this chore for the child. Both mother and child are being watched, judged, and

constructed; and it is only through their joint effort that the goal can be accomplished.

I use Althusser's concept of the Ideological State Apparatus (1971) to frame my argument. I will briefly describe how food is coded as a cultural and aesthetic apparatus in Japan, and what authority the state holds over schools in Japanese society. Thus situating the parameters within which the *obentō* is regulated and structured in the nursery school setting, I will examine the practice both of making and eating *obentō* within the context of one nursery school in Tokyo. As an anthropologist and mother of a child who attended this school for fifteen months, my analysis is based on my observations, on discussions with other mothers, daily conversations and an interview with my son's teacher, examination of *obentō* magazines and cookbooks, participation in school rituals, outings, and Mothers' Association meetings, and the multifarious experiences of my son and myself as we faced the *obentō* process every day.

I conclude that *obentō*s as a routine, task, and art form of nursery school culture are endowed with ideological and gendered meanings that the state indirectly manipulates. The manipulation is neither total nor totally coercive, however, and I argue that pleasure and creativity for both mother and child are also products of the *obentō*.

CULTURAL RITUAL
AND STATE IDEOLOGY

As anthropologists have long understood, not only are the worlds we inhabit symbolically constructed, but also the constructions of our cultural symbols are endowed with, or have the potential for, power. How we see reality, in other words, is also how we live it. So the conventions by which we recognize our universe are also those by which each of us assumes our place and behavior within that universe. Culture is, in this sense, doubly constructive: constructing both the world for people and people for specific worlds.

The fact that culture is not necessarily innocent, and power not necessarily transparent, has been revealed by much theoretical work conducted both inside and outside the discipline of anthropology. The scholarship of the neo-Marxist Louis Althusser (1971), for example, has encouraged the conceptualization of power as a force which operates in ways that are subtle, disguised, and accepted as everyday social practice. Althusser differentiated between two major structures of power in modern capitalist societies. The first, he called (Repressive) State Apparatus (SA), which is power that the state wields and manages primarily through the threat of force. Here the state sanctions the usage of power and repression through such legitimized mechanisms as the law and police (1971: 143–5).

Contrasted with this is a second structure of power—Ideological State Apparatus(es) (ISA). These are institutions which have some overt function other than a political and/or administrative one: mass media, education, health and welfare, for example. More numerous, disparate, and functionally polymorphous than the SA, the ISA exert power not primarily through repression but through ideology. Designed and accepted as practices with another purpose—to educate (the school system), entertain (film industry), inform (news media), the ISA serve not only their stated objective but also an unstated one—that of indoctrinating people into seeing the world a certain way and of accepting certain identities as their own within that world (1971: 143–7).

While both structures of power operate simultaneously and complementarily, it is the ISA, according to Althusser, which in capitalist societies is the more influential of the two. Disguised and screened by another operation, the power of ideology in ISA can be both more far-reaching and insidious than the SA's power of coercion. Hidden in the movies we watch, the music we hear, the liquor we drink, the textbooks we read, it is overlooked because it is protected and its protection—or its alibi (Barthes 1957: 109–11)—allows the terms and relations of ideology to spill into and infiltrate our everyday lives.

A world of commodities, gender inequalities, and power differentials is seen not therefore in these terms but as a naturalized environment, one that makes sense because it has become our experience to live it and accept it in precisely this way. This commonsense acceptance of a particular world is the work of ideology, and it works by concealing the coercive and repressive elements of our everyday routines but also by making those routines of the everyday familiar, desirable, and simply our own. This is the critical element of Althusser's notion of ideological power: ideology is so potent because it becomes not only ours but us—the terms and machinery by which we structure ourselves and identify who we are.

JAPANESE FOOD AS CULTURAL MYTH

An author in one *obentō* magazine, the type of medium-sized publication that, filled with glossy pictures of *obentō*s and ideas and recipes for successfully recreating them, sells in the bookstores across Japan, declares, ". . . the making of the *obentō* is the one most worrisome concern facing the mother of a child going off to school for the first time (*Shufunotomo* 1980: inside cover). Another *obentō* journal, this one heftier and packaged in the encyclopedic series of the prolific women's publishing firm, *Shufunotomo*, articulates the same social fact: "first-time *obentō*s are a strain on both parent and child" (*"hajimete no obentō wa, oya mo ko mo kinchōshimasu"*) (*Shufunotomo* 1981: 55).

An outside observer might ask: What is the real source of worry over *obentō*? Is it the food itself or the entrance of the young child into school for the first time? Yet, as one look at a typical child's *obentō*—a small box packaged with a five or six-course miniaturized meal whose pieces and parts are artistically arranged, perfectly cut, and neatly arranged—would immediately reveal, no food is "just" food in Japan. What is not so immediately apparent, however, is why a small child with limited appetite and perhaps scant interest in food is the recipient of a meal as elaborate and as elaborately prepared as any made for an entire family or invited guests.

Certainly, in Japan much attention is focussed on the *obentō*, investing it with a significance far beyond that of the merely pragmatic, functional one of sustaining a child with nutritional foodstuffs. Since this investment beyond the pragmatic is true of any food prepared in Japan, it is helpful to examine culinary codes for food preparation that operate generally in the society before focussing on children's *obentō*s.

As has been remarked often about Japanese food, the key element is appearance. Food must be organized, re-organized, arranged, re-arranged, stylized, and re-stylized to appear in a design that is visually attractive. Presentation is critical: not to the extent that taste and nutrition are displaced, as has been sometimes attributed to Japanese food, but to the degree that how food looks is at least as important as how it tastes and how good and sustaining it is for one's body.

As Donald Richie has pointed out in his eloquent and informative book *A taste of Japan* (1985), presentational style is the guiding principle by which food is prepared in Japan, and the style is conditioned by a number of codes. One code is for smallness, separation, and fragmentation. Nothing large is allowed, so portions are all cut to be bite-sized, served in small amounts on tiny individual dishes, and are arranged on a table (or on a tray, or in an *obentō* box) in an array of small, separate containers.[1] There is no one big dinner plate with three large portions of vegetable, starch, and meat as in American cuisine. Consequently the eye is pulled not toward one totalizing center but away to a multiplicity of de-centered parts.[2]

Visually, food substances are presented according to a structural principle not only of segmentation but also of opposition. Foods are broken or cut to make contrasts of color, texture, and shape. Foods are meant to oppose one another and clash: pink against green, roundish foods against angular ones, smooth substances next to rough ones. This oppositional code operates not only within and between the foodstuffs themselves, but also between the attributes of the food and those of the containers in or on which they are placed: a circular mound in a square dish, a bland colored food set against a bright plate, a translucent sweet in a heavily textured bowl (Richie 1985: 40–1).

The container is as important as what is contained in Japanese cuisine, but it is really the containment that is stressed, that is, how food has been (re)constructed and (re)arranged from nature to appear, in both beauty and freshness, perfectly natural. This stylizing of nature is a third code by which presentation is directed; the injunction is not only to retain, as much as possible, the innate naturalness of ingredients—shopping daily so food is fresh and leaving much of it either raw or only minimally cooked—but also to recreate in prepared food the promise and appearance of being "natural." As Richie writes, ". . . the emphasis is on presentation of the natural rather than the natural itself. It is not what nature has wrought that excites admiration but what man has wrought with what nature has wrought" (1985: 11).

This naturalization of food is rendered through two main devices. One is by constantly hinting at and appropriating the nature that comes from outside—decorating food with seasonal reminders, such as a maple leaf in the fall or a flower in the spring, serving in-season fruits and vegetables, and using season-coordinated dishes such as glassware in the summer and heavy pottery in the winter. The other device, to some degree the inverse of the first, is to accentuate and perfect the preparation process to such an extent that the food appears not only to be natural, but more nearly perfect than nature without human intervention ever could be. This is nature made artificial. Thus, by naturalization, nature is not only taken in by Japanese cuisine, but taken over.

It is this ability both to appropriate "real" nature (the maple leaf on the tray) and to stamp the human reconstruction of that nature as "natural" that lends Japanese food its potential for cultural and ideological manipulation. It is what Barthes calls a second order myth (1957: 114–7): a language which has a function people accept as only pragmatic—the sending of roses to lovers, the consumption of wine with one's dinner, the cleaning up a mother does for her child—which is taken over by some interest or agenda to serve a different end—florists who can sell roses, liquor companies who can market wine, conservative politicians who campaign for a gendered division of labor with women kept at home. The first order of language ("language-object"), thus emptied of its original meaning, is converted into an empty form by which it can assume a new, additional, second order of signification ("meta-language" or "second-order semiological system"). As Barthes points out however, the primary meaning is never lost. Rather, it remains and stands as an alibi, the cover under which the second, politicized meaning can hide. Roses sell better, for example, when lovers view them as a vehicle to express love rather than the means by which a company stays in business.

At one level, food is just food in Japan—the medium by which humans sustain their nature and health. Yet under and through this code of pragmatics, Japanese cuisine carries other meanings that in Barthes' terms are mythological. One of these is national identity: food being appropriated as a sign of the culture. To be Japanese is to eat Japanese food, as so many Japanese confirm when they travel to other countries and cite the greatest problem they encounter to be the absence of "real" Japanese food. Stated the other way around, rice is so symbolically central to Japanese culture (meals and *obentō*s often being assembled with rice as the core and all other dishes, multifarious as they may be, as mere complements or side dishes) that Japanese say they can never feel full until they have consumed their rice at a particular meal or at least once during the day.[3]

Embedded within this insistence on eating Japanese food, thereby reconfirming one as a member of the culture, are the principles by which Japanese food is customarily prepared: perfection, labor, small distinguishable parts, opposing segments, beauty, and the stamp of nature. Overarching all these more detailed codings are two that guide the making and ideological appropriation of the nursery school *obentō* most directly: 1) there is an order to the food: a right way to do things, with everything in its place and each place coordinated with every other, and 2) the one who prepares the food takes on the responsibility of producing food to the standards of perfection and exactness that Japanese cuisine demands. Food may not be casual, in other words, nor the producer casual in her production. In these two rules is a message both about social order and the role gender plays in sustaining and nourishing that order.

SCHOOL, STATE, AND SUBJECTIVITY

In addition to language and second order meanings I suggest that the rituals and routines surrounding *obentō*s in Japanese nursery schools present, as it were, a third order, manipulation. This order is a use of a currency already established—one that has already appropriated a language of utility (food feeds hunger) to express and implant cultural behaviors. State-guided schools borrow this coded apparatus: using the natural convenience and cover of food not only to code a cultural order, but also to socialize children and mothers into the gendered roles and subjectivities they are expected to assume in a political order desired and directed by the state.

In modern capitalist societies such as Japan, it is the school, according to Althusser, which assumes the primary role of ideological state apparatus. A greater segment of the population spends longer hours and more years here than in previous historical periods. Also education has now taken over from other institutions, such as religion, the pedagogical function of being the major shaper and inculcator of knowledge for the society. Concurrently, as Althusser has pointed out for capitalist modernism (1971: 152, 156), there is the gradual replacement of repression by ideology as the prime mechanism for behavior enforcement. Influenced less by the threat of force and more by the devices that present and inform us of the world we live in and the subjectivities that world demands, knowledge and ideology become fused, and education emerges as the apparatus for pedagogical and ideological indoctrination.

In practice, as school teaches children how and what to think, it also shapes them for the roles and positions they will later assume as adult members of the society. How the social order is organized through vectors of gender, power, labor, and/or class, in other words, is not only as important a lesson as the basics of reading and writing, but is transmitted through and embedded in those classroom lessons. Knowledge thus is not only socially constructed, but also differentially acquired according to who one is or will be in the political society one will enter in later years. What precisely society requires in the way of workers, citizens, and parents will be the condition determining or influencing instruction in the schools.

This latter equation, of course, depends on two factors: 1) the convergence or divergence of different interests in what is desired as subjectivities, and 2) the power any particular interest, including that of the state, has in exerting its desires for subjects on or through the system of education. In the case of Japan, the state wields enormous control over the systematization of education. Through its Ministry of Education (Monbushō), one of the most powerful and influential ministries in the government, education is centralized and managed by a state bureaucracy that regulates almost every aspect of the educational process. On any given day, for example, what is taught in every public school follows the same curriculum, adheres to the same structure, and is informed by textbooks from the prescribed list. Teachers are nationally screened, school boards uniformly appointed (rather than elected), and students institutionally exhorted to obey teachers given their legal authority, for example, to write secret reports (*naishinsho*), that may obstruct a student's entrance into high school.[4]

The role of the state in Japanese education is not limited, however, to such extensive but codified authorities granted to the Ministry of Education. Even more powerful is the principle of the "*gakureki shakkai*" (lit. academic pedigree society) by which careers of adults are determined by the schools they attend as youth. A reflection and construction of the new economic order of post-war Japan,[5] school attendance has become the single most important determinant of who will achieve the most desirable positions in industry, government, and the professions. School attendance is itself based on a single criterion: a system of entrance exams which determines entrance selection and it is to this end—preparation for exams—that school, even at the nursery school level, is increasingly oriented. Learning to follow directions, do as one is told, and "*ganbaru*" (Asanuma 1987) are social imperatives, sanctioned by the state, and taught in the schools.

NURSERY SCHOOL AND IDEOLOGICAL APPROPRIATION OF THE *OBENTŌ*

The nursery school stands outside the structure of compulsory education in Japan. Most nursery schools are private; and, though not compelled by the state, a greater proportion of the three to six-year old population of Japan attends pre-school than in any other industrialized nation (Tobin 1989; Hendry 1986; Boocock 1989).

Differentiated from the *hoikuen*, another pre-school institution with longer hours which is more like daycare than school,[6] the *yochien* (nursery school) is widely perceived as instructional, not necessarily in a formal curriculum but more in indoctrination to attitudes and structures of Japanese schooling. Children learn less about reading and writing than they do about how to become a Japanese student, and both parts of this formula—Japanese and student—are equally stressed. As Rohlen has written, "social order is generated" in the nursery school, first and foremost, by a system of routines (1989: 10, 21). Educational routines and rituals are therefore of heightened importance in *yochien*, for whereas these routines and rituals may be the format through which subjects are taught in higher grades, they are both form and subject in the *yochien*.

While the state (through its agency, the Ministry of Education) has no direct mandate over nursery school attendance, its influence is nevertheless significant. First, authority over how the *yochien* is run is in the hands of the Ministry of Education. Second, most parents and teachers see the *yochien* as the first step to the system of compulsory education that starts in the first grade and is closely controlled by Monbushō. The principal of the *yochien* my son attended, for example, stated that he saw his main duty to be preparing children to enter more easily the rigors of public education soon to come. Third, the rules and patterns of "group living" (*shūdanseikatsu*), a Japanese social ideal that is reiterated nationwide by political leaders, corporate management, and marriage counselors, is first introduced to the child in nursery school.[7]

The entry into nursery school marks a transition both away from home and into the "real world," which is generally judged to be difficult, even traumatic, for the Japanese child (Peak 1989). The *obentō* is intended to ease a child's discomfiture and to allow a child's mother to manufacture something of herself and the home to accompany the child as s/he moves into the potentially threatening outside world. Japanese use the cultural categories of *soto* and *uchi*; *soto* connotes the outside, which in being distanced and other, is dirty and hostile; and *uchi* identifies as clean and comfortable what is inside and familiar. The school falls initially and, to some degree, perpetually, into a category of *soto*. What is ultimately the definition and location of *uchi*, by contrast, is the home, where family and mother reside.[8] By producing something from the home, a mother both girds and goads her child to face what is inevitable in the world that lies beyond. This is the mother's role and her gift; by giving of herself and the home (which she both symbolically represents and in reality manages[9]), the *soto* of the school is, if not transformed into the *uchi* of home, made more bearable by this sign of domestic and maternal hearth a child can bring to it.

The *obentō* is filled with the meaning of mother and home in a number of ways. The first is by sheer labor. Women spend what seems to be an inordinate amount of time on the production of this one item. As an experienced *obentō* maker, I can attest to the intense attention and energy devoted to this one chore. On the average, mothers spend 20–45 minutes every morning cooking, preparing, and assembling the contents of one *obentō* for one nursery school-aged child. In addition, the previous day they have planned, shopped, and often organized a supper meal with leftovers in mind for the next day's *obentō*. Frequently women[10] discuss *obentō* ideas with other mothers, scan *obentō* cookbooks or magazines for recipes, buy or make objects with which to decorate or contain (part of) the *obentō*, and perhaps make small food portions to freeze and retrieve for future *obentō*.[11]

Of course, effort alone does not necessarily produce a successful *obentō*. Casualness was never indulged, I observed, and even mothers with children who would eat anything prepared *obentō*s as elaborate as anyone else's. Such labor is intended for the child but also the mother: it is a sign of a woman's commitment as a mother and her inspiring her child to being similarly committed as a student. The *obentō* is thus a representation of what the mother is and what the child should become. A model for school is added to what is gift and reminder from home.

This equation is spelled out more precisely in a nursery school rule—all of the *obentō* must be eaten. Though on the face of it this is petty and mundane, the injunction is taken very seriously by nursery school teachers and is one not easily realized by very small children. The logic is that it is time for the child to meet certain expectations. One of the main agendas of the nursery school, after all, is to introduce and indoctrinate children into the patterns and rigors of Japanese education (Rohlen 1989; Sano 1989; Lewis 1989). And Japanese education, by all accounts, is not about fun (Duke 1986).

Learning is hard work with few choices or pleasures. Even *obentō*s from home stop once the child enters first grade.[12] The meals there are institutional: largely bland, unappealing, and prepared with only nutrition in mind. To ease a youngster into these upcoming (educational, social, disciplinary, culinary) routines, *yochien obentō*s are designed to be pleasing and personal. The *obentō* is also designed, however, as a test for the child. And the double meaning is not unintentional. A structure already filled with a signification of mother and home is then emptied to provide a new form: one now also written with the ideological demands of being a member of Japanese culture as well as a viable and successful Japanese in the realms of school and later work.

The exhortation to consume one's entire *obentō*[13] is articulated and enforced by the nursery school teacher. Making high drama out of eating by, for example, singing a song; collectively thanking Buddha (in the case of Buddhist nursery schools), one's mother for making the *obentō,* and one's father for providing the means to make the *obentō;* having two assigned class helpers pour the tea, the class eats together until everyone has finished. The teacher examines the children's *obentō*s, making sure the food is all consumed, and encouraging, sometimes scolding, children who are taking too long. Slow eaters do not fare well in this ritual, because they hold up the other students, who as a peer group also monitor a child's eating. My son often complained about a child whose slowness over food meant that the others were kept inside (rather than being allowed to play on the playground) for much of the lunch period.

Ultimately and officially, it is the teacher, however, whose role and authority it is to watch over food consumption and to judge the person consuming food. Her surveillance covers both the student and the mother, who in the matter of the *obentō,* must work together. The child's job is to eat the food and the mother's to prepare it. Hence, the responsibility and execution of one's task is not only shared but conditioned by the other. My son's teacher would talk with me daily about the progress he was making finishing his *obentō*s. Although the overt subject of discussion was my child, most of what was said was directed to me: what I could do in order to get David to consume his lunch more easily.

The intensity of these talks struck me at the time as curious. We had just settled in Japan and David, a highly verbal child, was attending a foreign school in a foreign language he had not yet mastered; he was the only non-Japanese child in the school. Many of his behaviors during this time were disruptive: for example, he went up and down the line of children during morning exercises hitting each child on the head. Hamada-sensei (the teacher), however, chose to discuss the *obentō*s. I thought surely David's survival in and adjustment to this environment depended much more on other factors, such as learning Japanese. Yet it was the *obentō* that was discussed with such recall of detail ("David ate all his peas today, but not a single carrot until I asked him to do so three times") and seriousness that I assumed her attention was being misplaced. The manifest reference was to box-lunches, but was not the latent reference to something else?[14]

Of course, there was another message, for me and my child. It was an injunction to follow directions, obey rules, and accept the authority of the school system. All of the latter were embedded in and inculcated through certain rituals: the nursery school, as any school (except such non-conventional ones as Waldorf and Montessori) and practically any social or institutional practice in Japan, was so heavily ritualized and

ritualistic that the very form of ritual took on a meaning and value in and of itself (Rohlen 1989: 21, 27–8). Both the school day and school year of the nursery school were organized by these rituals. The day, apart from two free periods, for example, was broken by discrete routines—morning exercises, arts and crafts, gym instruction, singing—most of which were named and scheduled. The school year was also segmented into and marked by three annual events—sports day (*undōkai*) in the fall, winter assembly (*seikatsu happyōkai*) in December, and dance festival (*bon odori*) in the summer. Energy was galvanized by these rituals, which demanded a degree of order as well as a discipline and self-control that non-Japanese would find remarkable.

Significantly, David's teacher marked his successful integration into the school system by his mastery not of the language or other cultural skills, but of the school's daily routines—walking in line, brushing his teeth after eating, arriving at school early, eagerly participating in greeting and departure ceremonies, and completing all of his *obentō* on time. Not only had he adjusted to the school structure, but he had also become assimilated to the other children. Or restated, what once had been externally enforced now became ideologically desirable; the everyday practices had moved from being alien (*soto*) to familiar (*uchi*) to him, from, that is, being someone else's to his own. My American child had to become, in some sense, Japanese, and where his teacher recognized this Japaneseness was in the daily routines such as finishing his *obentō.* The lesson learned early, which David learned as well, is that not adhering to routines such as completing one's *obentō* on time leads to not only admonishment from the teacher, but rejection from the other students.

The nursery school system differentiates between the child who does and the child who does not manage the multifarious and constant rituals of nursery school. And for those who do not manage there is a penalty which the child learns either to avoid or wish to avoid. Seeking the acceptance of his peers, the student develops the aptitude, willingness, and in the case of my son —whose outspokenness and individuality were the characteristics most noted in this culture—even the desire to conform to the highly ordered and structured practices of nursery school life. As Althusser (1971) wrote about ideology: the mechanism works when and because ideas the world and particular roles in that world that serve other (social, political, economic, state) agendas become familiar and one's own.

Rohlen makes a similar point: that what is taught and learned in nursery school is social order. Called *shūdanseikatsu* or group life, it means organization into a group where a person's subjectivity is determined by group membership and not "the assumption of choice and rational self-interest" (1989: 30). A child learns in nursery school to be with others, think like others, and act in tandem with others. This lesson is taught primarily through the precision and constancy of basic routines: "Order is shaped gradually by repeated practice of selected daily tasks . . . that socialize the children to high degrees of neatness and uniformity" (p. 21). Yet a feeling of coerciveness is rarely experienced by the child when three principles of nursery school instruction are in place: 1) school routines are made "desirable and pleasant" (p. 30), 2) the teacher disguises her authority by trying to make the group the voice and unit of authority, and 3) the regimentation of the school is administered by an attitude of "intimacy" on the part of the teachers and administrators (p. 30). In short, when the desires and routines of the school are made into the desires and routines of the child, they are made acceptable.

MOTHERING AS GENDERED IDEOLOGICAL STATE APPARATUS

The rituals surrounding the *obentō*'s consumption in the school situate what ideological meanings the *obentō* transmits to the child. The process of production within the home, by contrast, organizes its somewhat different ideological package for the mother. While the two sets of meanings are intertwined, the mother is faced with different expectations in the preparation of the *obentō* than the child is in its consumption. At a pragmatic level the child must simply eat the lunch box, whereas the mother's job is far more complicated. The onus for her is getting the child to consume what she has made, and the general attitude is that this is far more the mother's responsibility (at this nursery school, transitional stage) than the child's. And this is no simple or easy task.

Much of what is written, advised, and discussed about the *obentō* has this aim explicitly in mind: that is making food in such a way as to facilitate the child's duty to eat it. One magazine advises:

> The first day of taking *obentō* is a worrisome thing for mother and "*boku*" (child[15]) too. Put in easy-to-eat foods that your child likes and is already used to and prepare this food in small portions (*Shufunotomo* 1980: 28).

Filled with pages of recipes, hints, pictures, and ideas, the magazine codes each page with "helpful" headings:

+ First off, easy-to-eat is step one.
+ Next is being able to consume the *obentō* without leaving anything behind.
+ Make it in such a way for the child to become proficient in the use of chopsticks.
+ Decorate and fill it with cute dreams (*kawairashi yume*).
+ For older classes (*nenchō*), make *obentō* filled with variety.
+ Once he's become used to it, balance foods your child likes with those he dislikes.
+ For kids who hate vegetables. . . .
+ For kids who hate fish. . . .
+ For kids who hate meat. . . . (pp. 28–53).

Laced throughout cookbooks and other magazines devoted to *obentō*, the *obentō* guidelines issued by the school and sent home in the school flier every two weeks, and the words of Japanese mothers and teachers discussing *obentō*, are a number of principles: 1) food should be made easy to eat: portions cut or made small and manipulable with fingers or chopsticks, (child-size) spoons and forks, skewers, toothpicks, muffin tins, containers, 2) portions should be kept small so the *obentō* can be consumed quickly and without any left-overs, 3) food that a child does not yet like should be eventually added so as to remove fussiness (*sukikirai*) in food habits, 4) make the *obentō* pretty, cute, and visually changeable by presenting the food attractively and by adding non-food objects such as silver paper, foil, toothpick flags, paper napkins, cute handkerchiefs, and variously shaped containers for soy sauce and ketchup, and 5) design *obentō*-related items as much as possible by the mother's own hands including the *obentō* bag (*obentōfukuro*) in which the *obentō* is carried.

The strictures propounded by publications seem to be endless. In practice I found that visual appearance and appeal were stressed by the mothers. By contrast, the directive to use *obentō* as a training process—adding new foods and getting older children to use chopsticks and learn to tie the *furoshiki*[16]—was emphasized by those judging the *obentō* at the school. Where these two sets of concerns met was, of course, in the child's success or failure completing the *obentō*. Ultimately this outcome and the mother's role in it was how the *obentō* was judged in my experience.

The aestheticization of the *obentō* is by far its most intriguing aspect for a cultural anthropologist. Aesthetic categories and codes that operate generally for Japanese cuisine are applied, though adjusted, to the nursery school format. Substances are many but petite, kept segmented and opposed, and manipulated intensively to achieve an appearance that often changes or disguises the food. As a mother insisted to me, the creation of a bear out of miniature hamburgers and rice, or a flower from an apple or peach, is meant to sustain a child's interest in the underlying food. Yet my child, at least, rarely noticed or appreciated the art I had so laboriously contrived. As for other children, I observed that even for those who ate with no obvious "fussiness," mothers' efforts to create food as style continued all year long.

Thus much of a woman's labor over *obentō* stems from some agenda other than that of getting the child to eat an entire lunch-box. The latter is certainly a consideration and it is the rationale as well as cover for women being scrutinized by the school's authority figure—the teacher. Yet two other factors are important. One is that the *obentō* is but one aspect of the far more expansive and continuous commitment a mother is expected to make for and to her child. *"Kyōiku mama"* (education mother) is the term given to a mother who executes her responsibility to oversee and manage the education of her children with excessive vigor. And yet this excess is not only demanded by the state even at the level of the nursery school; it is conventionally given by mothers. Mothers who manage the home and children, often in virtual absence of a husband/father, are considered the factor that may make or break a child as s/he advances towards that pivotal point of the entrance examinations.[17]

In this sense, just as the *obentō* is meant as a device to assist a child in the struggles of first adjusting to school, the mother's role generally is perceived as being the support, goad, and cushion for the child. She will perform endless tasks to assist in her child's study: sharpen pencils and make midnight snacks as the child studies, attend cram schools to verse herself in subjects her child is weak in, make inquiries as to what school is most appropriate for her child, and consult with her child's teachers. If the child succeeds, a mother is complimented; if the child fails, a mother is blamed.

Thus at the nursery school level, the mother starts her own preparation for this upcoming role. Yet the jobs and energies demanded of a nursery school mother are, in themselves, surprisingly consuming. Just as the mother of an entering student is given a book listing all the pre-entry tasks she must complete, for example, making various bags and containers, affixing labels to all clothes in precisely the right place and with the size exactly right, she will be continually expected thereafter to attend Mothers' Association meetings, accompany children on fieldtrips, wash the clothes and indoor shoes of her child every week, add required items to a child's bag on a day's notice, and generally be available. Few mothers at the school my son attended could afford to work in even part-time or temporary jobs. Those women who did tended either to keep their outside work a secret or be reprimanded by a teacher for insufficient devotion to their child. Motherhood, in other words, is institutionalized through the child's school and such routines as making the *obentō* as a full-time, kept-at-home job.[18]

The second factor in a woman's devotion to over-elaborating her child's lunch-box is that her experience doing this becomes a part of her and a statement, in some sense, of who she is. Marx writes that labor is the most "essential" aspect to our species-being and that the products we produce are the encapsulation of us and therefore our productivity (1970: 71–76). Likewise, women are what they are through the products they produce. An *obentō* therefore is not only a gift or test for a child, but a representation and product of the woman herself. Of course, the two ideologically converge, as has been stated already, but I would also suggest that there is a potential disjoining. I sensed that the women were laboring for themselves apart from the agenda the *obentō* was expected to fill at school. Or stated alternatively, in the role that females in Japan are highly pressured and encouraged to assume as domestic manager, mother, and wife, there is, besides the endless and onerous responsibilities, also an opportunity for play. Significantly, women find play and creativity not outside their social roles but within them.

Saying this is not to deny the constraints and surveillance under which Japanese women labor at their *obentō*. Like their children at school, they are watched by not only the teacher but each other, and perfect what they create, partially at least, so as to be confirmed as a good and dutiful mother in the eyes of other mothers. The enthusiasm with which they absorb this task then is like my son's acceptance and internalization of the nursery school routines; no longer enforced from outside it becomes adopted as one's own.

The making of the *obentō* is, I would thus argue, a double-edged sword for women. By relishing its creation (for all the intense labor expended, only once or twice did I hear a mother voice any complaint about this task), a woman is ensconcing herself in the ritualization and subjectivity (subjection) of being a mother in Japan. She is alienated in the sense that others will dictate, inspect, and manage her work. On the reverse side, however, it is precisely through this work that the woman expresses, identifies, and constitutes herself. As Althusser pointed out, ideology can never be totally abolished (1971: 170); the elaborations that women work on "natural" food produce an *obentō* which is creative and, to some degree, a fulfilling and personal statement of themselves.

Minami, an informant, revealed how both restrictive and pleasurable the daily rituals of motherhood can be. The mother of two children—one, aged three and one, a nursery school student, Minami had been a professional opera singer before marrying at the relatively late age of 32. Now, her daily schedule was organized by routines associated with her child's nursery school: for example, making the *obentō*, taking her daughter to school and picking her up, attending Mothers' Association meetings, arranging daily play dates, and keeping the school uniform clean. While Minami wished to return to singing, if only on a part-time basis, she said that the demands of motherhood, particularly those imposed by her child's attendance at nursery school, frustrated this desire. Secretly snatching only minutes out of any day to practice, Minami missed singing and told me that being a mother in Japan means the exclusion of almost anything else.[19]

Despite this frustration, however, Minami did not behave like a frustrated woman. Rather she devoted to her mothering an energy, creativity, and intelligence I found to be standard in the Japanese mothers I knew. She planned special outings for her children at least two or three times a week, organized games that she knew they would like and would teach them cognitive skills, created her own stories and designed costumes for afternoon play, and shopped daily for the meals she prepared with her children's favorite foods in mind. Minami told me often that she wished she could sing more; but never once did she complain about her children, the chores of child-raising, or being a mother. The attentiveness displayed otherwise in her mothering was exemplified most fully in Minami's *obentō*s. No two were ever alike, each had at least four or five parts, and she kept trying out new ideas for both new foods and new designs. She took pride as well as pleasure in her *obentō* handicraft; but while Minami's *obentō* creativity was impressive, it was not unusual.

Examples of such extraordinary *obentō* creations from an *obentō* magazine include: 1) ("donut *obentō*"): two donuts, two wieners cut to look like a worm, two cut pieces of apple, two small cheese rolls, one hard-boiled egg made to look like a rabbit with leaf ears and pickle eyes and set in an aluminum muffin tin, cute paper napkin added, 2) (wiener doll *obentō*): a bed of rice with two doll creations made out of wiener parts (each consists of eight pieces comprising hat, hair, head, arms, body, legs), a line of pink ginger, a line of green parsley, paper flag of France added, 3) (vegetable flower and tulip *obentō*): a bed of rice laced with chopped hard-boiled egg, three tulip flowers made out of cut wieners with spinach precisely arranged as stem and leaves, a fruit salad with two raisins, three cooked peaches, three pieces of cooked apple, 4) (sweetheart doll *obentō*—*abekku ningyō no obentō*): in a two-section *obentō* box there are four rice balls on one side, each with a different center, on the other side are two dolls made of quail's eggs for heads, eyes and mouth added, bodies of cucumber, arranged as if lying down with two raw carrots for the pillow, covers made of one flower—cut cooked carrot, two pieces of ham, pieces of cooked spinach, and with different colored plastic skewers holding the dolls together (*Shufunotomo* 1980: 27, 30).

The impulse to work and re-work nature in these *obentō* is most obvious perhaps in the strategies used to transform, shape, and/or disguise foods. Every mother I knew came up with her own repertoire of such techniques, and every *obentō* magazine or cookbook I examined offered a special section on these devices. It is important to keep in mind that these are treated as only flourishes: embellishments added to parts of an *obentō* composed of many parts. The following is a list from one magazine: lemon pieces made into butterflies, hard-boiled eggs into *daruma* (popular Japanese legendary figure of a monk without his eyes), sausage cut into flowers, a hard-boiled egg decorated as a baby, an apple piece cut into a leaf, a radish flaked into a flower, a cucumber cut like a flower, a *mikan* (nectarine orange) piece arranged into a basket, a boat with a sail made from a cucumber, skewered sausage, radish shaped like a mushroom, a quail egg flaked into a cherry, twisted *mikan* piece, sausage cut to become a crab, a patterned cucumber, a ribboned carrot, a flowered tomato, cabbage leaf flower, a potato cut to be a worm, a carrot designed as a red shoe, an apple cut to simulate a pineapple (pp. 57–60).

Nature is not only transformed but also supplemented by store-bought or mother-made objects which are precisely arranged in the *obentō*. The former come from an entire industry and commodification of the *obentō* process: complete racks or sections in stores selling *obentō* boxes, additional small containers, *obentō* bags, cups, chopstick and utensil containers (all these with various cute characters or designs on the front), cloth and paper napkins, foil, aluminum tins, colored ribbon or string, plastic skewers, toothpicks with paper flags, and paper dividers. The latter are the objects mothers are encouraged and praised for making themselves: *obentō* bags, napkins, and handkerchiefs with appliqued designs or the child's name embroidered. These supplements to the food, the arrangement of the food, and the *obentō* box's dividing walls (removable and adjustable) furnish the order of the *obentō*. Everything appears crisp and neat with each part kept in its own place: two tiny hamburgers set firmly atop a bed of rice; vegetables in a separate compartment in the box; fruit arranged in a muffin tin.

How the specific forms of *obentō* artistry—for example, a wiener cut to look like a worm and set within a muffin tin—are encoded symbolically is a fascinating subject. Limited here by space, however, I will only offer initial suggestions. Arranging food into a scene recognizable by the child was an ideal mentioned by many mothers and cookbooks. Why those of animals, human beings, and other food forms (making a pineapple out of an apple, for example) predominate may have no other rationale than being familiar to children and easily re-produced by mothers. Yet it is also true that this tendency to use a trope of realism—casting food into realistic figures—is most prevalent in the meals Japanese prepare for their children. Mothers I knew created animals and faces in supper meals and/or *obentō*s made for other outings, yet their impulse to do this seemed not only heightened in the *obentō* that were sent to school but also played down in food prepared for other age groups.

What is consistent in Japanese cooking generally, as stated earlier, are the dual principles of manipulation and order. Food is manipulated into some other form than it assumes either naturally or upon being cooked: lines are put into mashed potatoes, carrots are flaked, wieners are twisted and sliced. Also, food is ordered by some human rather than natural principle; everything must have neat boundaries and be placed precisely so those boundaries do not merge. These two structures are the ones most important in shaping the nursery school *obentō* as well, and the inclination to design realistic imagery is primarily a means by which these other culinary codes are learned by and made pleasurable for the child. The simulacrum of a pineapple recreated from an apple therefore is less about seeing the pineapple in an apple (a particular form) and more about reconstructing the apple into something else (the process of transformation).

The intense labor, management, commodification, and attentiveness that goes into the making of an *obentō* laces it, however, with many and various meanings. Overarching all is the potential to aestheticize a certain social order, a social order which is coded (in cultural and culinary terms) as Japanese. Not only is a mother making food more palatable to her nursery school child, but she is creating food as a more aesthetic and pleasing social structure. The *obentō*'s message is that the world is constructed very precisely and that the role of any single Japanese in that world must be carried out with the same degree of precision. Production is demanding; and the producer must both keep within the borders of her/his role and work hard.

The message is also that it is women, not men, who are not only sustaining a child through food but carrying the ideological support of the culture that this food embeds. No Japanese man I spoke with had or desired the experience of making a nursery school *obentō* even once, and few were more than peripherally engaged in their children's education. The male is assigned a position in the outside world where he labors at a job for money and is expected to be primarily identified by and committed to his place of work.[20] Helping in the management of home and raising of children has not become an obvious male concern or interest in Japan, even as more and more women enter what was previously the male domain of work. Females have remained at and as the center of home in Japan and this message too is explicitly transmitted in both the production and consumption of entirely female-produced *obentō*.

The state accrues benefits from this arrangement. With children depending on the labor women devote to their mothering to such a degree, and women being pressured as well as pleasurized in such routine maternal productions as making the *obentō*—both effects encouraged and promoted by institutional features of the educational system heavily state-run and at least ideologically guided at even the nursery school level—a gendered division of labor is firmly set in place. Labor from males, socialized to be compliant and hard-working, is more extractable when they have wives to rely on for almost all domestic and familial management. And females become a source of cheap labor, as they are increasingly forced to enter the labor market to pay domestic costs (including those vast debts incurred in educating children) yet are increasingly constrained to low-paying part-time jobs because of the domestic duties they must also bear almost totally as mothers.

Hence, not only do females, as mothers, operate within the ideological state apparatus of Japan's school system that starts semi-officially, with the nursery school, they also operate as an ideological state apparatus unto themselves. Motherhood *is* state ideology, working through children at home and at school and through such mother-imprinted labor that a child carries from home to school as with the *obentō*. Hence the post–World War II conception of Japanese education as being egalitarian, democratic, and with no agenda of or for gender differentiation, does not in practice stand up. Concealed within such cultural practices as culinary style and child-focussed mothering is a worldview in which the position and behavior an adult will assume has everything to do with the anatomy s/he was born with.

At the end, however, I am left with one question. If motherhood is not only watched and manipulated by the state but made by it into a conduit for ideological indoctrination, could not women subvert the political order by redesigning *obentō*? Asking this question, a Japanese friend, upon reading this [article], recalled her own experiences. Though her mother had been conventional in most other respects, she made her children *obentō*s that did not conform to the prevailing conventions. Basic, simple, and rarely artistic, Sawa also noted, in this connection, that the lines of these *obentō*s resembled those by which she was generally raised: as gender-neutral, treated as a person not "just as a girl," and being allowed a margin to think for herself. Today she is an exceptionally independent woman who has created a life for herself in America, away from homeland and parents, almost entirely on her own. She loves Japanese food, but the plain *obentō*s her mother made for her as a child, she is newly appreciative of now, as an adult. The *obentō*s fed her, but did not keep her culturally or ideologically attached. For this, Sawa says today, she is glad.

NOTES

Acknowledgments: The fieldwork on which this article is based was supported by a Japan Foundation Postdoctoral Fellowship. I am grateful to Charles Piot for a thoughtful reading and useful suggestions for revision and to Jennifer Robertson for inviting my contribution to this issue. I would also like to thank Sawa Kurotani for her many ethnographic stories and input, and Phyllis Chock and two anonymous readers for the valuable contributions they made to revision of the manuscript.

1. As Dorinne Kondo has pointed out, however, these cuisinal principles may be conditioned by factors of both class and circumstance. Her *shitamachi* (more traditional area of Tokyo) informants, for example, adhered only casually to this coding and other Japanese she knew followed them more carefully when preparing food for guests rather than family and when eating outside rather than inside the home (Kondo 1990: 61–2).

2. Rice is often, if not always, included in a meal; and it may substantially as well as symbolically constitute the core of the meal. When served at a table it is put in a large pot or electric rice maker and will be spooned into a bowl, still no bigger or predominant than the many other containers from which a person eats. In an *obentō* rice may be in one, perhaps the largest, section of a multi-sectioned *obentō* box, yet it will be arranged with a variety of other foods. In a sense rice provides the syntactic and substantial center to a meal yet the presentation of the food rarely emphasizes this core. The rice bowl is refilled rather than heaped as in the preformed *obentō* box, and in the *obentō* rice is often embroidered, supplemented, and/or covered with other foodstuffs.

3. Japanese will both endure a high price for rice at home and resist American attempts to export rice to Japan in order to stay domestically self-sufficient in this national food *qua* cultural symbol. Rice is the only foodstuff in which the Japanese have retained self-sufficient production.

4. The primary sources on education used are Horio 1988; Duke 1986; Rohlen 1983; Cummings 1980.

5. Neither the state's role in overseeing education nor a system of standardized tests is a new development in post–World War II Japan. What is new is the national standardization of tests and, in this sense, the intensified role the state has thus assumed in overseeing them. See Dore (1965) and Horio (1988).

6. Boocock (1989) differs from Tobin *et al.* (1989) on this point and asserts that the institutional differences are insignificant. She describes extensively how both *yōchien* and *hoikuen* are administered (*yōchien* are under the authority of Monbushō and *hoikuen* are under the authority of the Kōseishō, the Ministry of Health and Welfare) and how both feed into the larger system of education. She emphasizes diversity: though certain trends are common amongst preschools, differences in teaching styles and philosophies are plentiful as well.

7. According to Rohlen (1989), families are incapable of indoctrinating the child into this social pattern of *shūdan-seikatsu* by their very structure and particularly by the relationship (of indulgence and dependence) between mother and child. For this reason and the importance placed on group structures in Japan, the nursery school's primary objective, argues Rohlen, is teaching children how to assimilate into groups. For further discussion of this point see also Peak 1989; Lewis 1989; Sano 1989; and the *Journal of Japanese Studies* issue [15(1)] devoted to Japanese preschool education in which these articles, including Boocock's, are published.

8. For a succinct anthropological discussion of these concepts, see Hendry (1987: 39–41). For an architectural study of Japan's management and organization of space in terms of such cultural categories as *uchi* and *soto*, see Greenbie (1988).

9. Endless studies, reports, surveys, and narratives document the close tie between women and home; domesticity and femininity in Japan. A recent international survey conducted for a Japanese housing construction firm, for example, polled couples with working wives in three cities, finding that 97% (of those polled) in Tokyo prepared breakfast for their families almost daily (compared with 43% in New York and 34% in London); 70% shopped for groceries on a daily basis (3% in New York, 14% in London), and that only 22% of them had husbands who assisted or were willing to assist with housework (62% in New York, 77% in London) (quoted in *Chicago Tribune* 1991). For a recent anthropological study of Japanese housewives in English, see Imamura (1987). Japanese sources include *Juristo zōkan sōgō tokushu* 1985; *Mirai shakan* 1979; *Ohirasōri no seifu kenkyūkai* 3.

10. My comments pertain directly, of course, to only the women I observed, interviewed, and interacted with at the one private nursery school serving middle-class families in urban Tokyo. The profusion of *obentō*-related materials in the press plus the revelations made to me by Japanese and observations made by other researchers in Japan (for example, Tobin 1989; Fallows 1990), however, substantiate this as a more general phenomenon.

11. To illustrate this preoccupation and consciousness: during the time my son was not eating all his *obentō* many fellow mothers gave me suggestions, one mother lent me a magazine, his teacher gave me a full set of *obentō* cookbooks (one per season), and another mother gave me a set of small frozen food portions she had made in advance for future *obentō*s.

12. My son's teacher, Hamada-sensei, cited this explicitly as one of the reasons why the *obentō* was such an important training device for nursery school children. "Once they

become *ichinensei* (first-graders) they'll be faced with a variety of food, prepared without elaboration or much spice, and will need to eat it within a delimited time period."

13. An anonymous reviewer questioned whether such emphasis placed on consumption of food in nursery school leads to food problems and anxieties in later years. Although I have heard that anorexia is a phenomenon now in Japan, I question its connection to nursery school *obentō*s. Much of the meaning of the latter practice, as I interpret it, has to do with the interface between production and consumption, and its gender linkage comes from the production end (mothers making it) rather than the consumption end (children eating it). Hence while control is taught through food, it is not a control linked primarily to females or bodily appearance, as anorexia may tend to be in this culture.

14. Fujita argues, from her experience as a working mother of a daycare (*hoikuen*) child, that the substance of these daily talks between teacher and mother is intentionally insignificant. Her interpretation is that the mother is not to be overly involved in nor too informed about matters of the school (1989).

15. "*Boku*" is a personal pronoun that males in Japan use as a familiar reference to themselves. Those in close relationships with males—mothers and wives, for example—can use *boku* to refer to their sons or husbands. Its use in this context is telling.

16. In the upper third grade of the nursery school (*nenchō* class; children aged five to six) my son attended, children were ordered to bring their *obentō* with chopsticks and not forks and spoons (considered easier to use) and in the traditional *furoshiki* (piece of cloth which enwraps items and is double tied to close it) instead of the easier-to-manage *obentō* bags with drawstrings. Both *furoshiki* and chopsticks (*o-hashi*) are considered traditionally Japanese and their usage marks not only greater effort and skills on the part of the children but their enculturation into being Japanese.

17. For the mother's role in the education of her child, see, for example, White (1987). For an analysis, by a Japanese, of the intense dependence on the mother that is created and cultivated in a child, see Doi (1971). For Japanese sources on the mother-child relationship and the ideology (some say pathology) of Japanese motherhood, see Yamamura (1971); Kawai (1976); Kyūtoku (1981); *Sorifu seihonen taisaku honbuhen* (1981); *Kadeshobo shinsha* (1981). Fujita's account of the ideology of motherhood at the nursery school level is particularly interesting in this connection (1989).

18. Women are entering the labor market in increasing numbers yet the proportion to do so in the capacity of part-time workers (legally constituting as much as thirty-five hours per week but without the benefits accorded to full-time workers) has also increased. The choice of part-time over full-time employment has much to do with a woman's simultaneous and almost total responsibility for the domestic realm (Juristo 1985; see also Kondo 1990).

19. As Fujita (1989: 72–79) points out, working mothers are treated as a separate category of mothers, and non-working mothers are expected, by definition, to be mothers full time.

20. Nakane's much quoted text on Japanese society states this male position in structuralist terms (1970).

Though dated, see also Vogel (1963) and Rohlen (1974) for descriptions of the social roles for middle-class, urban Japanese males. For a succinct recent discussion of gender roles within the family, see Lock (1990).

REFERENCES

Althusser, Louis. 1971. *Ideology and ideological state apparatuses (Notes toward an investigation in Lenin and philosophy and other essays)*. New York: Monthly Review.

Asanuma, Kaoru. 1987. *"Ganbari" no kozo (Structure of "Ganbari")*. Tokyo: Kikkawa Kobunkan.

Barthes, Roland. 1957. *Mythologies*. Trans. by Annette Lavers. New York: Noonday Press.

Boocock, Sarane Spence. 1989. Controlled diversity: An overview of the Japanese preschool system. *The Journal of Japanese Studies* 15(1): 41–65.

Chicago Tribune. 1991. Burdens of working wives weigh heavily in Japan. January 27, Section 6, p. 7.

Cummings, William K. 1980. *Education and equality in Japan*. Princeton NJ: Princeton University Press.

Doi, Takeo. 1971. *The anatomy of dependence: The key analysis of Japanese behavior*. Trans. by John Becker. Tokyo: Kodansha Int'l. Ltd.

Dore, Ronald P. 1965. *Education in Tokugawa Japan*. London: Routledge and Kegan Paul.

Duke, Benjamin. 1986. *The Japanese school: Lessons for industrial America*. New York: Praeger.

Fallows, Deborah. 1990. Japanese women. *National Geographic* 177(4): 52–83.

Fujita, Mariko. 1989. "It's all mother's fault": Childcare and the socialization of working mothers in Japan. *The Journal of Japanese Studies* 15(1): 67–91.

Greenbie, Barrie B. 1988. *Space and spirit in modern Japan*. New Haven CT: Yale University Press.

Hendry, Joy. 1986. *Becoming Japanese: The world of the pre-school child*. Honolulu: University of Hawaii Press.

———. 1987. *Understanding Japanese society*. London: Croom Helm.

Horio, Teruhisa. 1988. *Educational thought and ideology in modern Japan: State authority and intellectual freedom*. Trans. by Steven Platzer. Tokyo: University of Tokyo Press.

Imamura, Anne E. 1987. *Urban Japanese housewives: At home and in the community*. Honolulu: University of Hawaii Press.

Juristo zōkan Sōgōtokushu. 1985. Josei no Gensai to Mirai (The present and future of women). 39.

Kadeshobo shinsha. 1981. *Hahaoya (Mother)*. Tokyo: Kadeshobo shinsha.

Kawai, Hayao. 1976. *Basei shakai nihon no Byōri (The pathology of the mother society—Japan)*. Tokyo: Chūō koronsha.

Kondo, Dorinne K. 1990. *Crafting selves: Power, gender, and discourses of identity in a Japanese workplace*. Chicago IL: University of Chicago Press.

Kyūtoku, Shigemori. 1991. *Bogenbyō (Disease rooted in motherhood)*. Vol. II. Tokyo: Sanma Kushuppan.

Lewis, Catherine C. 1989. From indulgence to internalization: Social control in the early school years. *Journal of Japanese Studies* 15(1): 139–57.

Lock, Margaret. 1990. Restoring order to the house of Japan. *The Wilson Quarterly* 14(4): 42–49.

Marx, Karl and Frederick Engels. 1970 (1947). *Economic and philosophic manuscripts*, ed. C. J. Arthur. New York: International Publishers.

Mirai shakan. 1979. Shufu to onna (Housewives and women). Kunitachishi Komininkan Shimindaigaku Semina—no Kiroku. Tokyo: Miraisha.

Mouer, Ross and Yoshio Sugimoto. 1986. *Images of Japanese society. A study in the social construction of reality*. London: Routledge and Kegan.

Nakane, Chie. 1970. *Japanese society*. Berkeley: University of California Press.

Ohirasōri no Seifu kenkyūkai. 1980. Katei kiban no jujitsu (The fullness of family foundations). (Ohirasōri no Seifu kenkyūkai—3). Tokyo: Okurashō Insatsukyōku.

Peak, Lois. 1989. Learning to become part of the group: The Japanese child's transition to preschool life. *The Journal of Japanese Studies* 15(1): 93–123.

Richie, Donald. 1985. *A taste of Japan: food fact and fable, customs and etiquette, what the people eat*. Tokyo: Kodansha International Ltd.

Rohlen, Thomas P. 1974. *The harmony and strength: Japanese white-collar organization in anthropological perspective*. Berkeley: University of California Press.

———. 1983. Japan's high schools. Berkeley: University of California Press.

———. 1989. Order in Japanese society: attachment, authority, and routine. *The Journal of Japanese Studies* 15(1): 5–40.

Sano, Toshiyuki. 1989. Methods of social control and socialization in Japanese day-care centers. *The Journal of Japanese Studies* 15(1): 125–38.

Shufunotomo Besutoserekushon shiri-zu. 1980. Obentō 500 sen. Tokyo: Shufunotomo Co., Ltd.

Shufunotomohyakka shiri-zu. 1981. 365 nichi no obentō hyakka. Tokyo: Shufunotomo Co.

Sōrifu Seihonen Taisaku Honbuhen. 1981. Nihon no kodomo to hahaoya (Japanese mothers and children): kokusai-hikaku (international comparisons). Tokyo: Sōrifu Seishonen Taisaku Honbuhen.

Tobin, Joseph J., David Y. H. Wu, and Dana H. Davidson. 1989. *Preschool in three cultures: Japan, China, and the United States.* New Haven CT: Yale University Press.

Vogel, Erza. 1963. *Japan's new middle class: The salary man and his family in a Tokyo suburb.* Berkeley: University of California Press.

White, Merry. 1987. *The Japanese educational challenge: a commitment to children.* New York: Free Press.

Yamamura, Yoshiaki. 1971. *Nihonjin to haha: Bunka toshite no haha no kannen ni tsuite no kenkyu (The Japanese and mother: Research on the conceptualization of mother as culture).* Tokyo: Toyo-shuppansha.

20

Rituals at McDonald's

Conrad P. Kottak

The world is blessed each day, on the average, with the opening of a new McDonald's restaurant. They now number more than 4,000 and dot not only the United States but also such countries as Mexico, Japan, Australia, England, France, Germany, and Sweden. The expansion of this international web of franchises and company-owned outlets has been fast and efficient; a little more than twenty years ago McDonald's was limited to a single restaurant in San Bernardino, California. Now, the number of McDonald's outlets has far outstripped the total number of fast-food chains operative in the United States thirty years ago.

McDonald's sales reached $1.3 billion in 1972, propelling it past Kentucky Fried Chicken as the world's largest fast-food chain. It has kept this position ever since. Annual sales now exceed $3 billion. McDonald's is the nation's leading buyer of processed potatoes and fish. Three hundred thousand cattle die each year as McDonald's customers down another three billion burgers. A 1974 advertising budget of $60 million easily made the chain one of the country's top advertisers. Ronald McDonald, our best-known purveyor of hamburgers, French fries, and milkshakes, rivals Santa Claus and Mickey Mouse as our children's most familiar fantasy character.

How does an anthropologist, accustomed to explaining the life styles of diverse cultures, interpret these peculiar developments and attractions that influence the daily life of so many Americans? Have factors other than low cost, taste, fast service, and cleanliness—all of which are approximated by other chains—contributed to McDonald's success? Could it be that in consuming McDonald's products and propaganda, Americans are not just eating and watching television but are experiencing something comparable in some respects to a religious ritual? A brief consideration of the nature of ritual may answer the latter question.

Several key features distinguish ritual from other behavior, according to anthropologist Roy Rappaport. Foremost are formal ritual events—stylized, repetitive, and stereotyped. They occur in special places, at regular times, and include liturgical orders—set sequences of words and actions laid down by someone other than the current performer.

Rituals also convey information about participants and their cultural traditions. Performed year after year, generation after generation, they translate enduring messages, values, and sentiments into observable action. Although some participants may be more strongly committed than others to the beliefs on which rituals are based, all people who take part in joint public acts signal their acceptance of an order that transcends their status as individuals.

In the view of some anthropologists, including Rappaport himself, such secular institutions as McDonald's are not comparable to rituals. They argue that rituals involve special emotions, nonutilitarian intentions, and supernatural entities that are not characteristic of Americans' participation in McDonald's. But other anthropologists define ritual more broadly. Writing about football in contemporary America, William Arens (see "The Great American Football Ritual," *Natural History,* October 1975) points out that behavior can simultaneously have sacred as well as secular aspects. Thus, on one level, football can be interpreted simply as a sport, while on another, it can be viewed as a public ritual.

While McDonald's is definitely a mundane, secular institution—just a place to eat—it also assumes some of the attributes of a sacred place. And in the context of comparative religion, why should this be surprising? The French sociologist Emile Durkheim long ago pointed out that some societies worship the ridiculous as well as the sublime. The distinction between the two does not depend on the intrinsic qualities of the sacred symbol. Durkheim found that Australian aborigines often worshiped such humble and nonimposing creatures as ducks, frogs, rabbits, and grubs—animals whose inherent qualities hardly could have been the origin of the religious sentiment they inspired. If frogs and grubs can be elevated to a sacred level, why not McDonald's?

I frequently eat lunch—and, occasionally, breakfast and dinner—at McDonald's. More than a year ago, I began to notice (and have subsequently observed more carefully) certain ritual behavior at these fast-food restaurants. Although for natives, McDonald's seems to be just a place to eat, careful observation of what goes on in any outlet in this country reveals an astonishing degree of formality and behavioral uniformity on the part of both staff and customers. Particularly impressive is the relative invariance in act and

utterance that has developed in the absence of a distinct theological doctrine. Rather, the ritual aspect of McDonald's rests on twentieth-century technology—particularly automobiles, television, work locales, and the one-hour lunch.

The changes in technology and work organization that have contributed to the chain's growth in the United States are now taking place in other countries. Only in a country such as France, which has an established and culturally enshrined cuisine that hamburgers and fish fillets cannot hope to displace, is McDonald's expansion likely to be retarded. Why has McDonald's been so much more successful than other businesses, than the United States Army, and even than many religious institutions in producing behavioral invariance?

Remarkably, even Americans traveling abroad in countries noted for their distinctive food usually visit the local McDonald's outlet. This odd behavior is probably caused by the same factors that urge us to make yet another trip to a McDonald's here. Wherever a McDonald's may be located, it is a home away from home. At any outlet, Americans know how to behave, what to expect, what they will eat, and what they will pay. If one has been unfortunate enough to have partaken of the often indigestible pap dished out by any turnpike restaurant monopoly, the sight of a pair of McDonald's golden arches may justify a detour off the highway, even if the penalty is an extra toll.

In Paris, where the French have not been especially renowned for making tourists feel at home, McDonald's offers sanctuary. It is, after all, an American institution, where only Americans, who are programmed by years of prior experience to salivate at the sight of the glorious hamburger, can feel completely at home. Americans in Paris can temporarily reverse roles with their hosts; if they cannot act like the French, neither can the French be expected to act in a culturally appropriate manner at McDonald's. Away from home, McDonald's, like a familiar church, offers not just hamburgers but comfort, security, and reassurance.

An American's devotion to McDonald's rests in part on uniformities associated with almost all McDonald's: setting, architecture, food, ambience, acts, and utterances. The golden arches, for example, serve as a familiar and almost universal landmark, absent only in those areas where zoning laws prohibit garish signs. At a McDonald's near the University of Michigan campus in Ann Arbor, a small, decorous sign—golden arches encircled in wrought iron—identifies the establishment. Despite the absence of the towering arches, this McDonald's, where I have conducted much of my fieldwork, does not suffer as a ritual setting. The restaurant, a contemporary brick structure that has been nominated for a prize in architectural design, is best known for its stained-glass windows, which incorporate golden arches as their focal point. On bright days, sunlight floods in on waiting customers through a skylight that recalls the clerestory of a Gothic cathedral. In the case of this McDonald's, the effect is to equate traditional religious symbols and golden arches. And in the view of the natives I have interviewed, the message is clear.

When Americans go to a McDonald's restaurant, they perform an ordinary, secular, biological act—they eat, usually lunch. Yet, immediately upon entering, we can tell from our surroundings that we are in a sequestered place, somehow apart from the messiness of the world outside. Except for such anomalies as the Ann Arbor campus outlet, the town house McDonald's in New York City, and the special theme McDonald's of such cities as San Francisco, Saint Paul, and Dallas, the restaurants rely on their arches, dull brown brick, plate-glass sides, and mansard roofs to create a setting as familiar as home. In some of the larger outlets, murals depicting "McDonaldland" fantasy characters, sports, outdoor activities, and landscapes surround plastic seats and tables. In this familiar setting, we do not have to consider the experience. We know what we will see, say, eat, and pay.

Behind the counter, McDonald's employees are differentiated into such categories as male staff, female staff, and managers. While costumes vary slightly from outlet to outlet and region to region, such apparel as McDonald's hats, ties, and shirts, along with dark pants and shining black shoes, are standard.

The food is also standard, again with only minor regional variations. (Some restaurants are selected to test such new menu items as "McChicken" or different milkshake flavors.) Most menus, however, from the rolling hills of Georgia to the snowy plains of Minnesota, offer the same items. The prices are also the same and the menu is usually located in the same place in every restaurant.

Utterances across each spotless counter are standardized. Not only are customers limited in what they can choose but also in what they can say. Each item on the menu has its appropriate McDonald's designation: "quarter pounder with cheese" or "filet-O-fish" or "large fries." The customer who asks, "What's a Big Mac?" is as out of place as a southern Baptist at a Roman Catholic Mass.

At the McDonald's that I frequent, the phrases uttered by the salespeople are just as standard as those of the customers. If I ask for a quarter pounder, the ritual response is "Will that be with cheese, sir?" If I do not order French fries, the agent automatically incants, "Will there be any fries today, sir?" And when I pick up my order, the agent conventionally says, "Have a nice day, sir," followed by, "Come in again."

Nonverbal behavior of McDonald's agents is also programmed. Prior to opening the spigot of the drink machine, they fill paper cups with ice exactly to the bottom of the golden arches that decorate them. As customers request food, agents look back to see if the desired item is available. If not, they reply, "That'll be a few minutes, sir (or ma'am)," after which the order of the next customer is taken.

McDonald's lore of appropriate verbal and nonverbal behavior is even taught at a "seminary," Hamburger University, located in Elk Grove Village, Illinois, near Chicago's O'Hare airport. Managers who attend choose either a two-week basic "operator's course" or an eleven-day "advanced operator's course." With a 360-page *Operations Manual* as their bible, students learn about food, equipment, and management techniques—delving into such esoteric subjects as buns, shortening, and carbonization. Filled with the spirit of McDonald's, graduates take home such degrees as bachelor or master of hamburgerology to display in their outlets. Their job is to spread the word—the secret success formula they have learned—among assistant managers and crew in their restaurants.

The total McDonald's ambience invites comparison with sacred places. The chain stresses clean living and reaffirms those traditional American values that transcend McDonald's itself. Max Boas and Steve Chain, biographers of McDonald's board chairman, Ray Kroc, report that after the hundredth McDonald's opened in 1959, Kroc leased a plane to survey likely sites for the chain's expansion. McDonald's would invade the suburbs by locating its outlets near traffic intersections, shopping centers, and churches. Steeples figured prominently in Kroc's plan. He believed that suburban churchgoers would be preprogrammed consumers of the McDonald's formula—quality, service, and cleanliness.

McDonald's restaurants, nestled beneath their transcendent arches and the American flag, would enclose immaculate restrooms and floors, counters and stainless steel kitchens. Agents would sparkle, radiating health and warmth. Although to a lesser extent than a decade ago, management scrutinizes employees' hair length, height, nails, teeth, and complexions. Long hair, bad breath, stained teeth, and pimples are anathema. Food containers also defy pollution; they are used only once. (In New York City, the fast-food chain Chock Full O' Nuts foreshadowed this theme long ago and took it one step further by assuring customers that their food was never touched by human hands.)

Like participation in rituals, there are times when eating at McDonald's is not appropriate. A meal at McDonald's is usually confined to ordinary, everyday life. Although the restaurants are open virtually every day of the year, most Americans do not go there on Thanksgiving, Easter, Passover, or other religious and quasi-religious days. Our culture reserves holidays for family and friends. Although Americans neglect McDonald's on holidays, the chain reminds us through television that it still endures, that it will welcome us back once our holiday is over.

The television presence of McDonald's is particularly obvious on holidays, whether it be through the McDonald's All-American Marching Band (two clean-cut high school students from each state) in a nationally televised Thanksgiving Day parade or through sponsorship of sports and family entertainment programs.

Although such chains as Burger King, Burger Chef, and Arby's compete with McDonald's for the fast-food business, none rivals McDonald's success. The explanation reflects not just quality, service, cleanliness, and value but, more importantly, McDonald's advertising, which skillfully appeals to different audiences. Saturday morning television, for example, includes a steady dose of cartoons and other children's shows sponsored by McDonald's. The commercials feature several McDonaldland fantasy characters, headed by the clown Ronald McDonald, and often stress the enduring aspects of McDonald's. In one, Ronald has a time machine that enables him to introduce hamburgers to the remote past and the distant future. Anyone who noticed the shot of the McDonald's restaurant in the Woody Allen film *Sleeper,* which takes place 200 years hence, will be aware that the message of McDonald's as eternal has gotten across. Other children's commercials gently portray the conflict between good (Ronald) and evil (Hamburglar). McDonaldland's bloblike Grimace is hooked on milkshakes, and Hamburglar's addiction to simple burgers regularly culminates in his confinement to a "patty wagon," as Ronald and Big Mac restore and preserve the social order.

Pictures of McDonaldland appear on cookie boxes and, from time to time, on durable plastic cups that are given away with the purchase of a large soft drink. According to Boas and Chain, a McDonaldland amusement park, comparable in scale to Disneyland, is planned for Las Vegas. Even more obvious are children's chances to meet Ronald McDonald and other McDonaldland characters in the flesh. Actors portraying Ronald scatter their visits, usually on Saturdays, among McDonald's outlets throughout the country. A Ronald can even be rented for a birthday party or for Halloween trick or treating.

McDonald's adult advertising has a different, but equally effective, theme. In 1976, a fresh-faced, sincere young woman invited the viewer to try breakfast—a new meal at McDonald's—in a familiar setting. In still other commercials, healthy, clean-living Americans gambol on ski slopes or in mountain pastures. The sin-

gle theme running throughout all the adult commercials is personalism. McDonald's, the commercials tell us, is not just a fast-food restaurant. It is a warm, friendly place where you will be graciously welcomed. Here, you will feel at home with your family, and your children will not get into trouble. The word *you* is emphasized—"You deserve a break today"; "You, you're the one"; "We do it all for you." McDonald's commercials say that you are not simply a face in a crowd. At McDonald's, you can find respite from a hectic and impersonal society—the break you deserve.

Early in 1977, after a brief flirtation with commercials that harped on the financial and gustatory benefits of eating at McDonald's, the chain introduced one of its most curious incentives—the "Big Mac attack." Like other extraordinary and irresistible food cravings, which people in many cultures attribute to demons or other spirits, a Big Mac attack could strike anyone at any time. In one commercial, passengers on a jet forced the pilot to land at the nearest McDonald's. In others, a Big Mac attack had the power to give life to an inanimate object, such as a suit of armor, or restore a mummy to life.

McDonald's advertising typically de-emphasizes the fact that the chain is, after all, a profit-making organization. By stressing its program of community projects, some commercials present McDonald's as a charitable organization. During the Bicentennial year, commercials reported that McDonald's was giving 1,776 trees to every state in the union. Brochures at outlets echo the television message that, through McDonald's, one can sponsor a carnival to aid victims of muscular dystrophy. In 1976 and 1977 McDonald's managers in Ann Arbor persuaded police officers armed with metal detectors to station themselves at restaurants during Halloween to check candy and fruit for hidden pins and razor blades. Free coffee was offered to parents. In 1976, McDonald's sponsored a radio series documenting the contributions Blacks have made to American history.

McDonald's also sponsored such family television entertainment as the film *The Sound of Music,* complete with a prefatory, sermonlike address by Ray Kroc. Commercials during the film showed Ronald McDonald picking up after litterbugs and continued with the theme, "We do it all for you." Other commercials told us that McDonald's supports and works to maintain the values of American family life—and went so far as to suggest a means of strengthening what most Americans conceive to be the weakest link in the nuclear family, that of father–child. "Take a father to lunch," kids were told.

Participation in McDonald's rituals involves temporary subordination of individual differences in a social and cultural collectivity. By eating at McDonald's, not only do we communicate that we are hungry, enjoy hamburgers, and have inexpensive tastes but also that we are willing to adhere to a value system and a series of behaviors dictated by an exterior entity. In a land of tremendous ethnic, social, economic, and religious diversity, we proclaim that we share something with millions of other Americans.

Sociologists, cultural anthropologists, and others have shown that social ties based on kinship, marriage, and community are growing weaker in the contemporary United States. Fewer and fewer people participate in traditional organized religions. By joining sects, cults, and therapy sessions, Americans seek many of the securities that formal religion gave to our ancestors. The increasing cultural, rather than just economic, significance of McDonald's, football, and similar institutions is intimately linked to these changes.

As industrial society shunts people around, church allegiance declines as a unifying moral force. Other institutions are also taking over the functions of formal religions. At the same time, traditionally organized religions—Protestantism, Catholicism, and Judaism—are reorganizing themselves along business lines. With such changes, the gap between the symbolic meaning of traditional religions and the realities of modern life widens. Because of this, some sociologists have argued that the study of modern religion must merge with the study of mass culture and mass communication.

In this context, McDonald's has become one of many new and powerful elements of American culture that provide common expectations, experience, and behavior—overriding region, class, formal religious affiliation, political sentiments, gender, age, ethnic group, sexual preference, and urban, suburban, or rural residence. By incorporating—wittingly or unwittingly—many of the ritual and symbolic aspects of religion, McDonald's has carved its own important niche in a changing society in which automobiles are ubiquitous and where television sets outnumber toilets.

Adapting Foods to People and People to Foods

Not only do people eat different kinds of foods, but foods themselves contain many different sorts of chemical compounds and elements, only some of which are nutrients. How a particular food is prepared for consumption affects the presence, and even the availability, of some compounds and elements. For example, the amount of vitamin C is less in cooked than in raw foods because vitamin C is heat sensitive. Therefore, the duration and temperature of cooking affect the vitamin C content of the food. How people process and prepare foods is especially important when those foods in question provide most of the energy in the diet—that is, when those foods are the staple foods. Some peoples have developed food processing and preparation techniques that have truly significant consequences for the quality of their diets. One good example is the food processing techniques used by Amazonian Indians to eliminate a toxic compound, cyanide, in cassava (manioc). Another classic example is how the processing of maize (corn in U.S. English) alters the biological availability of the vitamin niacin.

The cyanide story is developed by Dufour in the article "A Closer Look at the Nutritional Implications of Bitter Cassava Use." Dufour, a biological anthropologist, lived for almost two years with Tukanoan Indians in the Amazon Basin and became fascinated by the idea that these people routinely consumed a root that they themselves considered highly toxic in a raw state. This root, cassava (visualize a long sweet potato–like root with a bark-like peel), is their dietary staple. Cassava was probably domesticated thousands of years ago somewhere in South America and has been the dietary staple of many Amazonian Indians for a very long time. What is the cyanide doing there in the root in the first place? Who knows, but cyanide is a compound found in many wild plants, and we hypothesize that it is produced by the plant as a protection against predation—a kind of natural insecticide. It is not found in many domesticated plants, or at least in the parts of the plant normally eaten. Humans can tolerate small amounts of cyanide in the foods they eat and the air they breathe (cigarette smoke contains cyanide) because they can detoxify it metabolically. Large amounts of cyanide, however, can overpower the detoxification process and lead to illness, and sometimes death. The amount of cyanide present in the cassava cultivated by Tukanoan Indians is large enough to cause illness and

death. So how can they use it as a dietary staple? This is the question Dufour attempts to answer.

The processing of maize is an example of another strategy that improves the nutritional values of plants. Maize does not contain a toxin; it is an ordinary grain in terms of its chemical composition. But curiously enough, the niacin (a B vitamin) in maize is not as biologically available to humans as one would assume looking at the chemical composition of the raw grain itself. What Katz, Hediger, and Valleroy demonstrate in their article, "Traditional Maize Processing Techniques in the New World," is that the maize processing techniques developed by native peoples in Central America for making tortillas (the traditional flat bread) increase the biological availability of niacin to human consumers. This processing is quite unique in that the maize kernels are soaked in an alkaline solution before being ground into flour. The soaking does two things. First, it softens and loosens the fibrous outer peel of the kernel. Second, it increases the biological availability (bioavailability) of niacin.

Does this make a difference nutritionally? Yes, it definitely does for people who live on a maize-based diet. A good example of how important it can be is the problem of niacin deficiency that developed among sharecroppers in the southern United States in the early twentieth century (Roe, 1973). The sharecroppers lived in poverty on a diet that was largely maize, pork fat, and molasses, and they developed high rates of the disease called pellagra, one of the symptoms of which is dementia. This occurred before much was known about vitamins and before niacin had been discovered, and unfortunately many people with pellagra were put in mental hospitals before nutritional scientists figured out they were suffering from a nutritional disorder!

Not only does the way people process and prepare foods alter foods' chemical composition, but humans also vary in how they digest and metabolize some of the compounds and elements in foods. How could that be? Food is taken into the mouth, where it is chopped, mashed, and mixed with saliva. It goes to the stomach, where it is mixed with acid to further its breakdown into small particles, and then into the small intestine, where enzymes complete the breakdown of food particles into compounds and elements that can be absorbed through the wall of the intestine. We call this enzymatic breakdown digestion, and it is here where problems can occur because one needs a particular enzyme for each type of compound. Peptidase works on the chemical bonds in proteins (peptide bonds), sucrase works on the chemical bonds of sucrose (plant sugar), lactase works on the chemical bonds of lactose (milk sugar), and so on. The production of enzymes is a function of one's genetic code and normal diet. Most people produce sufficient quantities and types of enzymes to digest the foods in their normal diet, but there are some interesting exceptions. Some Inuit (formerly called Eskimos) do not produce the sucrase to digest sucrose. We assume this is because plants have become a significant part of their diet only in the past 50 years or so.

A classic example is that of lactose (milk sugar). Not all people, *as adults,* produce sufficient lactase to digest lactose (milk sugar). Why that might be and who these people are is the subject of Kretchmer's article, "Genetic Variability and Lactose Tolerance." The paper was published in 1975, and although some of the language may seem dated, it is well worth reading because it was one of the first explanations for population differences in lactose tolerance.

Lactose, like other common sugars in our diet, tastes sweet, and like other sugars it is actually two sugars in one, a molecule of glucose bound to a molecule of galactose. To digest it requires splitting the chemical bond holding the glucose and galactose molecules together. This is done by an enzyme, conveniently named lactase (the name of the milk sugar, with the "ase" indicating an enzyme). Lactose itself cannot be absorbed by the small intestine; if lactase is not available, the lactose passes on intact into the large intestine, where it causes bloating, flatulence (gas), and diarrhea—painful and rather inconvenient.

The last article in this part, "The Tall *and* the Short of It," by Barry Bogin, adds a new twist. It emphasizes how malleable humans are in responding to environmental forces. Bogin, a biological anthropologist, has spent many years studying the growth of Mayan Indian children in Guatemala, some of the shortest people in the world. When some Mayan families immigrated to the United States, Bogin continued studying their children. The migration set up a classic natural experiment: members of a single biological population living in two very different environments. Bogin finds that the Mayan children in the United States grew taller and faster than those in Guatemala, a good example of body size as a "plastic" characteristic. Bogin also argues that we can think about the relationship between body size and environment in another way. The shortness of the Maya in Central America is an indicator that the Central American environment is less than optimal for human growth than is the U.S. environment (growth is also used as an indicator of environmental conditions in articles 27–30).

What have we learned from the articles in this part? People adapt or manipulate the chemical composition of foods in ways that make them more suitable. The reverse can also occur. People also adapt to food, in the sense that they are able to digest, metabolize, and detoxify common compounds in their diets. Lastly, we learned from Bogin that human growth responds to the quality, especially the nutritional quality, of the whole environment. That is a plastic response, and we can also consider it a way of adapting.

SUGGESTIONS FOR THINKING AND DOING NUTRITIONAL ANTHROPOLOGY

1. Make a list of all the foods you consume today that contain maize (corn) or some product derived from maize. Read labels and look for ingredients such as corn oil, hydrogenated corn oil, cornstarch, corn syrup, high-fructose corn syrup (HFCS), cornmeal, corn flour, hominy, grits. What percentage of all the foods you ate contained some form of maize?

2. What kinds of special foods and food products are available at your local supermarket for lactose-intolerant people? Find out what kinds of dairy foods lactose-intolerant people can *usually* tolerate. The key here is *usually*, because although Kretchmer portrays lactose intolerance as an all-or-none condition, we now know that lactase production depends to some extent on usual diet.

3. Find out why artificial sweeteners such as Nutrasweet and Equal, and "sugar-free" products such as Diet Pepsi, contain a warning: PHENYLKETONURICS: CONTAINS PHENYLALANINE. What is phenylalanine? Who are phenylketonurics, and why do they need to avoid phenylalanine?

SUGGESTED READINGS

Foster, N., & Cordell, L. S. (1992). *Chilis to chocolates: Food the Americas gave the world.* Tucson: University of Arizona Press.

Hames, R. B., & Vickers, W. (Eds.). (1983). *Adaptive responses of native Amazonians.* New York: Academic Press. (An edited volume with articles on the subsistence patterns of native Amazonians that highlight the importance of cassava in traditional diets.)

Roe, D. (1973). *A plague of corn: The social history of pellagra.* Ithaca, NY: Cornell University Press.

21

A Closer Look at the Nutritional Implications
of Bitter Cassava Use

Darna L. Dufour

Cassava, or manioc (*Manihot esculenta* Crantz), is the traditional dietary staple of many native Amazonians. Although it is very productive on the *tierra firme* soils of Amazonia, it is one of the few food crops in which the content of cyanide can create problems of toxicity, and therefore its use is a potential source of nutritional stress.

In the last 20 years there has been a tremendous increase in the research on cassava (for reviews, see Cock 1985; Okezie and Kosikowski 1982). This research has been stimulated by the growing importance of cassava in both human and animal diets. Cassava is now the fourth most important source of food energy in the tropics worldwide (Cock 1982), and its use is expected to double before the year 2000 (Okezie and Kosikowski 1982). The potential toxicity of cassava is considered one of the major limiting factors in its use for both culinary purposes and animal feed (Okezie and Kosikowski 1982), and some researchers consider the "bitter," or high-cyanide, cultivars unsuitable for human food (Gomez et al. 1984). Cyanide toxicity associated with cassava consumption has been linked to a number of health problems in Africa (Nestel and MacIntyre 1973; Ermans et al. 1980; Osuntokun 1981; Rosling 1987).

Among indigenous peoples in Amazonia, the high-cyanide, or so-called "bitter," cassava appears to have been the staple crop in the Amazon basin, northeastern South America, and the Antilles (Nordenskiold 1924; Steward and Faron 1959). Low-cyanide, or "sweet," cassava was more widely distributed (Nordenskiold 1924) but tended to be part of a crop complex dominated by either maize or bitter cassava (Renvoize 1972). The exception to this is on the eastern slopes of the Andes where sweet cassava was the staple crop (Steward 1959). The elaborate processing systems associated with "bitter" varieties have long attracted the attention of anthropologists and other observers, but their actual effectiveness in reducing toxicity has received little attention. Other important questions regarding the toxicity of the cultivars used, the distribution of bitter and sweet cultivars, and the roles of bitter and sweet

cassava in the adaptation of native peoples have gone unanswered.

The purpose of this [article] is to report the results of recent research on the use of bitter cassava by Tukanoan Indians in northwest Amazonia, and in doing so to focus attention on the use of cassava by native Amazonians. In addition I would like to reconsider some of the commonly cited disadvantages of cassava use. These disadvantages are, first, that it is a crop with low nutrient density and hence is a relatively poor source of dietary protein and minerals. Second, the "bitter" varieties of cassava require extensive processing, which further reduces protein and mineral content. The third disadvantage, proposed by Spath (1981), is that the residual toxicity, i.e., cyanide, in a cassava-based diet increases the need for the amino acids methionine and cystine, which are generally more abundant in animal than in plant proteins. This last disadvantage is part of the broader question of the toxicity of cassava.

The fieldwork reported here was done in 1984–86 with Tukanoan Indians in the Colombian Vaupés, primarily in the village of Yapu on the Papuri River.[1] The characteristics of this group have been discussed previously (Dufour 1983). Ecologically the Vaupés is an area of low elevation covered with dense tropical rain forest broken with patches of *caatinga* (a type of low forest occurring on white sand) and drained by black-water rivers. In climatic terms the area is humid to very humid. Precipitation averages 3,500 mm a year, and temperatures average 26°C. During the long "dry" season from about November to February, precipitation averages between 150 and 200 mm per month (PRO-RADAM 1979:13).

Yapu is a village settlement of Tatuyo-speaking Tukanoan Indians. Like other traditional Tukanoans, those at Yapu are swidden horticulturalists whose principal crop is cassava. Secondary crops include plants such as taro (*Colocasia* spp.), sweet potato (*Ipomoea* sp.), arrowroot *(Maranta ruiziana)*, bananas, plantains, and a number of fruits. Animal foods are obtained from fishing, hunting, and gathering (Dufour 1983).

CASSAVA

Cassava is a perennial woody shrub belonging to the family Euphorbiaceae. It is native to the Neotropics and well adapted to the low fertility, highly acid soils that are common in Amazonia (Rogers 1965; Moran 1973; Cock 1985; Howeler 1985). It is tolerant of drought as well as high rainfall, so long as drainage is good (Cock 1985:18). It is grown primarily for its starchy storage roots, but the leaves are also used as food.

The plant and the edible roots are referred to as both cassava and manioc. Cassava is now the more widely used term in English, and it is the one I will use here. It is probably derived from *casabe, cazabe,* or *kasabi,* the Taino (Arawak) word for cassava bread (Carrizales 1984; Jones 1959:29). Manioc is from the Tupí-Guararí *mandioca* (Sauer 1950), and is also the word for the plant in French.[2]

The toxicity of cassava results from the presence of cyanogenic glucosides that break down into glucose and hydrogen cyanide (prussic acid) upon hydrolysis. Hydrolysis results from contact between the glucosides and the endogenous enzyme linamarase; it occurs when plant tissues lose their physiological integrity or are damaged by processes such as harvesting, peeling, or grating. All cassava cultivars contain cyanogenic glucosides, but the concentrations vary greatly between cultivars and with season, climate, and edaphic conditions (Coursey 1973; Bourdoux et al. 1980). The distinction between sweet and bitter cassava is common throughout Amazonia, and indeed throughout the world. In general it refers to roots that can simply be peeled, boiled, and eaten, as opposed to those that are considered bitter or toxic and require additional processing before being consumed. In a more precise way, *sweet* is used to refer to cassava roots with cyanide concentrations of less than 100 ppm, and *bitter* is used for those with concentrations of greater than 100 ppm fresh weight (FW). This is the sense in which the terms are used here.

CASSAVA IN
NORTHWEST AMAZONIA

Tukanoans at Yapu maintain about 100 named cassava cultivars, all but two of which they classify as *kii* and consider "bitter." These are the dietary staples. The remaining two are referred to by the Geral term *makasera* and are considered "sweet." A sample of common kii cultivars from Yapu had cyanide concentrations ranging from 280 to 531 ppm FW, with a mean of 454 ppm FW. Hence, they are properly considered

"very bitter," or high-cyanide containing (Dufour 1988a). There is no information on the cyanide content of the cultivars used by other native Amazonians, but in comparison to those of other areas of the world, the average cyanide concentration of the Yapu cultivars is the highest of any reported.

In the northwest Amazon, cassava appears in the diet in a number of forms, the most important of which are *casabe,* a bread, and *fariña,* a toasted meal. Casabe is a uniquely Amazonian use of cassava and traditionally was the most widespread mode of preparation (Schwerin 1971:12). Among Tukanoans, casabe is a thick, soft bread made fresh daily from white-fleshed roots. It is the preferred accompaniment to fish, game, and insects, and when those are not available, it is eaten after being dipped in a "pepper pot." Fariña is the basis of meals when people are traveling or working away from the village, and it is most commonly consumed as a drink—a small amount swirled in water.

The Tukanoan processing technique for casabe is elaborate and has been described previously (Dufour 1985, 1989; Hugh-Jones 1979). It is shown schematically in Figure 1. First, the roots are rasped to remove the outermost layer of peel, and then they are washed and grated. Grating reduces the roots to a fine, watery mash, which is then separated into three fractions: liquids, starch, and fiber. The separation is accomplished by washing (with water and extracted juices) and squeezing the mash in a basketry strainer to remove the starch and liquids from the more fibrous portion, and then allowing the starch to settle out of the wash water. Once the starch has settled, the supernatant is decanted off and boiled immediately to make the beverage *manicuera*. The other two products, starch and fiber, are stored at least overnight but preferably for 48 hours, and then are recombined and baked as a casabe. To prepare casabe, the fiber is dewatered in a *tipiti* (basketry sleeve press), lightly toasted, and then mixed with the starch. The starch is also used to thicken beverages (*mingao*) and fish porridges (*puné*).

Casabe can also be prepared by simply dewatering and baking the freshly grated mash. This type of casabe is not very commonly consumed in Yapu and is referred to here as "fresh casabe." It is a denser bread and lacks the fermented taste of ordinary casabe. When baked as a cracker-thin cake it is used as an ingredient in beer. Other types of casabe include those made from plain starch, in either a thick or a thin form, and those made from the raw, fermented mash destined for fariña.

Fariña is prepared from yellow-fleshed roots that are trimmed of the stem end and soaked in stream water until softened (two to four days), then peeled, grated, allowed to ferment for a minimum of three days, dewatered with a tipiti, sifted to produce an even

(a)   (b)

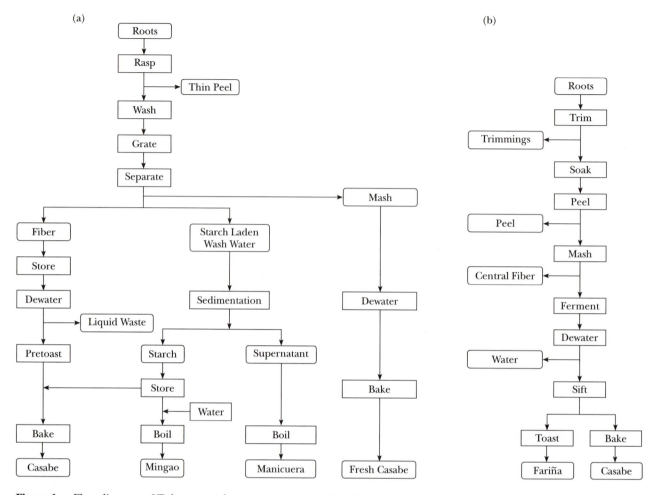

Figure 1.   Flow diagram of Tukanoan-style cassava processing for (a) casabe and related products and (b) fariña.

EFFECTIVENESS OF PROCESSING TECHNIQUES

The effectiveness of the processing techniques used to prepare casabe and fariña in detoxifying roots was assessed in a series of experiments conducted at the Centro Internacional de Agricultura Tropical (CIAT) in Cali, Colombia, and is discussed in detail in Dufour (1989). In these experiments we measured the loss of free cyanide, or HCN, and total cyanide, which includes both HCN and cyanogenic glucosides. Cyanide in the form of cyanogenic glucosides is also referred to as bound cyanide, i.e., cyanide bound to glucose.

The changes in total and free cyanide that occurred during processing for casabe are shown in Table 1. There was only a modest reduction in total cyanide with rasping and grating. The grated mash,

however, showed a dramatic increase in free cyanide, indicating that the grating resulted in the conversion of cyanogenic glucosides to the free form. Since free cyanide is water soluble, most of the remainder was concentrated in the wash water and then volatilized with cooking. The boiled juice, manicuera, contained only 0.8 percent (FW basis) of the initial concentration of total cyanide.

The cyanide levels in the starch and fiber continued to decline slowly during storage and with cooking. The casabes made with starch and fiber that had been stored for 48 hours contained less than 4 percent of the initial total cyanide. Those made with starch and fiber stored 24 hours contained more than twice as much, as did the fresh casabes.

The effectiveness of the Tukanoan technique in reducing cyanide levels in cassava is due to several factors. First, grating causes extensive disintegration of the plant tissues, and the subsequent mixing ensures maximal contact between the enzyme and the glucosides, a process that maximizes the conversion of bound to free cyanide. Second, the inner peel is grated

texture, and toasted (see Fig. 1). The type of fariña prepared by Tukanoans is called *farinha d'agua* in Brazil.

Table 1.   Changes in total and free cyanide in cassava roots processed for casabe. Values are the average of three processing runs with MCOL1684 and three with MVEN25 on a fresh weight basis (FW). Dry matter values in parentheses.

Day	Process Stage	Moisture %	Cyanide, ppm FW		F/T %	Total Cyanide % Initial
			Total	Free		
Day 1	Whole roots	64	528 (1,441)	76 (211)	14	100.0
	Rasped roots	65	411 (1,158)	72 (227)	18	77.8
	Mash (grated roots)	64	416 (1,136)	289 (789)	69	78.8
	Fiber, fresh	74	103 (396)	54 (215)	52	19.5
	Starch, fresh	49	91 (182)	75 (148)	82	17.2
	Wash water[a]	92	153 (3,229)	130 (3,138)	85	29.0
	Manicuera	82	4 (19)	3 (10)	75	0.8
	Mash, dewatered	50	236 (451)	173 (330)	73	44.7
	Casabe, fresh	29	40 (58)	10 (15)	25	7.6
Day 2	Fiber, sour	73	80 (290)	56 (206)	70	15.1
	Fiber, sour, dewatered	56	68 (153)	44 (96)	65	12.9
	Starch, sour	48	62 (120)	50 (99)	81	11.7
	Casabe, ordinary	26	39 (55)	25 (35)	64	7.4
Day 3	Fiber, sour	72	60 (209)	37 (129)	62	11.4
	Fiber, sour, dewatered	58	40 (96)	28 (68)	70	7.6
	Starch, sour	45	39 (72)	35 (64)	90	7.4
	Casabe, ordinary	25	17 (22)	7 (10)	41	3.2

[a]Dry matter values are for a single processing run.

along with the pulp. This facilitates hydrolysis because enzymatic activity in the peel is higher than in the pulp (Bruijn 1973; Nambisan and Sundaresan 1985). This practice of including the inner peel has been reported only for Tukanoans and Karinya (Karl Schwerin, personal communication). Third, the washing of the mash concentrates most of the free cyanide in the wash water, where it can be effectively volatilized by boiling.

Cyanide losses during the processing of fariña are shown in Table 2. The roots showed a gradual decline in total cyanide with trimming and soaking, and when softened (day 6), contained only 21 percent of the initial total cyanide. The loss of cyanide can be attributed to enzyme hydrolysis and volatilization of HCN, as well as to fermentation (Ayernor 1985:94). The roots showed additional small decreases in cyanide content with peeling and mashing, and in the first days of fermentation. The fermented mash on day 10 contained only 2.4 percent of the initial total cyanide. Total and free cyanide content was further reduced by toasting (see values on a dry matter basis).

The values for total and free cyanide obtained in the processing experiment are comparable to those found in fariña samples collected in the Colombian Vaupés region. These had concentrations of 8.3 ± 2.59

ppm total cyanide and 6.2 ± 0.48 ppm free cyanide on a fresh weight basis (n = 24).

ROLE OF PROCESSING STEPS IN DETOXIFICATION

The results of these processing experiments challenge some of the assumptions held by anthropologists regarding the role of Amazonian processing techniques in detoxification. Three common assumptions are that the peeling, the use of the tipiti, and the application of heat are the important steps in detoxification. A fourth assumption is that processing significantly reduces the nutritional value of cassava (Sponsel 1986).

First, peeling, which was assumed to remove a large portion of the cyanide (Dole 1978), does not really achieve that in the "bitter" varieties, although it certainly does in the "sweet." Rather, when very bitter cultivars are used, leaving the inner peel intact when the roots are grated facilitates hydrolysis.

Second, the tipiti, that famous and unique basketry sleeve press, has been assumed to play a key role in detoxification (Carrizales 1984). However, as Dole (1978) pointed out, the tipiti's principal function is

Table 2.   Changes in total and free cyanide in cassava roots processed for fariña. Values are for one processing run with MCOL1684 on a fresh weight basis (FW). Dry matter values in parentheses.

Day	Stage	Moisture %	Cyanide, ppm FW				F/T %	Total Cyanide % Initial
			Total		Free			
Day 1	Whole roots	67	328	(972)	42	(124)	13	100.0
Day 2	Soaked roots	67	247	(758)	18	(56)	7	75.3
Day 3	Soaked roots	70	222	(744)	34	(113)	15	67.7
Day 4	Soaked roots	73	175	(642)	63	(232)	36	53.3
Day 5	Soaked roots	73	104	(338)	40	(149)	38	31.7
Day 6	Soaked roots	69	68	(251)	36	(116)	53	20.7
	Peeled-grated	68	35	(109)	18	(55)	51	10.6
Day 7	Fermented mash	66	11	(32)	10	(29)	92	3.4
Day 8	Fermented mash	66	10	(30)	8	(23)	80	3.0
Day 9	Fermented mash	66	8	(22)	7	(20)	75	2.4
Day 10	Fermented mash	66	6	(16)	4	(11)	67	1.8
	Fariña	3	8	(8)	4	(4)	50	2.4

dewatering. It can function in detoxification because both the glucosides and free cyanide are water soluble, but its role depends on when in the processing sequence it is used. In the Tukanoan processing sequence used for casabe, dewatering is done after there has been adequate time for hydrolysis and volatilization of free cyanide; hence it plays a very minimal role in detoxification. The use of the tipiti would be most important when freshly grated roots were used for casabe and when cooking was done shortly after grating. This method of preparing casabe, however, does not appear to be very common. Other groups that make casabe without extracting the starch typically let the mash set overnight before baking it (Lancaster et al. 1982; Seigler and Pereira 1981). This should allow adequate time for both hydrolysis and volatilization of HCN, even if the mash is dewatered before it is stored.

The key tool in detoxification is the one that precedes the tipiti in the processing sequence—the grating board. This instrument macerates the plant material and in doing so allows hydrolysis to proceed rapidly. In the preparation of fariña, the long period of soaking is the most effective part of the process in detoxifying the roots. Again the tipiti is not very important because the total cyanide content has already been reduced more than 98 percent before it is used.

A third assumption is that because heat volatilizes free cyanide, the application of heat results in detoxification (Schwerin 1985). A corollary of this is that simple methods of processing, such as boiling and baking, are adequate for detoxification (Roosevelt 1980:129). But in elaborate processing systems such as that of the Tukanoans, the application of heat is of only minimal

importance because most of the glucosides have been converted to free cyanide and released before heat is applied. The application of heat in this type of processing system is probably most important in gelatinizing the starches and producing the desired texture in foods. Further, although the application of heat will volatilize HCN, it usually stops hydrolysis because the enzyme linamarase is deactivated at 72°C. Therefore, if heat is applied before hydrolysis has been completed, the food can retain significant amounts of bound cyanide, which is thermally stable up to 150°C (Nambisan and Sundaresan 1985).

It follows that simple cooking techniques such as boiling and roasting can eliminate free cyanide but will not be as effective in removing cyanogenic glucosides (Cooke and Maduagwu 1978). In boiling, free cyanide is lost to the air through volatilization, but bound cyanide goes into solution and can be found in the cooking water. Thus, cooked dishes, such as stews, in which the cooking water is consumed retain as much as 88 percent of the total cyanide (Bruijn 1971, cited in Cooke and Maduagwu 1978; Cooke and Maduagwu 1978). In areas such as India, where bitter cultivars are boiled, the cooking water is not consumed and is actually changed two or three times during cooking (Nambisan and Sundaresan 1985). This practice of changing the cooking water has not been reported for indigenous groups in Amazonia.

The roasting of whole cassava roots by burying them in hot ashes is done in the northwest Amazon with sweet cultivars and has been reported for a number of groups in Amazonia (Schwerin 1971). Cyanide loss under these kinds of conditions has not been studied, but it is probably similar to that observed during the baking of cassava chips in ovens, which has been shown to be a relatively ineffective method of reducing cyanide levels, again because the enzyme linamarase is inactivated at 72°C and linamarin is heat stable to 150°C (Cooke and Maduagwu 1978). It is doubtful that in normal roasting, as done by indigenous peoples, the root tissues reach 150°C, since they are thoroughly cooked at less than 100°C. Thus the roasting of whole tubers in ashes would probably remove little of the total cyanide.

In summary, the simpler methods of processing such as boiling and roasting are not very effective in reducing cyanide concentration and are only suitable for use with low-cyanide roots. This finding suggests that the exclusive use of these techniques will be confined to populations using low-cyanide cultivars. It does not follow, however, that groups using more complex processing techniques are necessarily using high-cyanide cultivars.

The fourth common assumption is that processing significantly reduces the nutritional value of cassava (Sponsel 1986). This is not a valid generalization; nutritional loss depends on the type of processing done. In some processing systems the loss of minerals in soaking, washing, and dewatering can be as high as 40 to 70 percent, and the loss of soluble proteins as high as 50 percent (Meuser and Smolnik 1980). The processing technique used for casabe, however, is nutritionally conservative. Waste is limited to the outer peel (<2 percent fresh weight), and the consumption of manicuera makes available the minerals and soluble proteins that would otherwise be lost. This advantage can only be gained if processing is done in small batches and the liquids boiled and consumed shortly afterward, because they deteriorate rapidly in both raw and cooked states. Retention of the peel also increases the nutritional value of cassava products because the peel fraction is higher in both minerals and protein than the pulp.

CYANIDE EXPOSURE AND THE INCREASED NEED FOR AMINO ACIDS

To estimate the exposure to dietary, cassava-borne cyanide in Yapu we determined food intake for 24 adults (12 males and 12 females) using the 3-day weighed intake method during November 1986. Energy and protein values for Tukanoan foods were taken from food composition tables, principally those of Wu Leung and Flores (1961) and Dufour (1988b). Cyanide values for cassava-based foods were taken

Table 3. Sources of energy and protein in the diets of 24 Yapu adults (means ± SD)

	Energy, % Total	Protein, % Total
Cultigens: Manioc	79.8 ± 9.00	20.9 ± 13.41
Other	9.0 ± 7.91	14.6 ± 16.28
Wild vegetable products	1.4 ± 4.04	0.8 ± 2.39
Wild animal products	8.5 ± 7.05	61.4 ± 28.73
Store foods	2.1 ± 4.46	2.4 ± 9.63

Table 4. Mean daily energy, protein, and cyanide intakes of 24 Yapu adults

	Mean ± SD
Energy, kcal	2272 ± 746.4
kcal/kg	42.9 ± 12.7
Protein, g	43.3 ± 23.12
g/kg	0.82 ± 0.43
Total Cyanide, mg	20.0 ± 8.29
mg/kg	0.4 ± 0.11
Free Cyanide, mg	9.1 ± 3.24
mg/kg	0.2 ± 0.04

from the processing done in the present study and samples collected in Yapu.

Results of the food intake study are shown in Tables 3 and 4. The overall composition of the diet is similar to that reported previously for this population (Dufour 1983). Total cyanide intakes were on the order of 20 mg/day (0.4 mg/kg/day), and free cyanide intakes were approximately half that value, 9 mg/day (0.18 mg/kg/day).

The metabolic detoxification of dietary cyanide occurs principally via the conversion of cyanide to thiocyanate, which is then excreted in urine. The key enzyme in this reaction contains sulphur, which is derived from sulphur-containing amino acids, methionine and cystine. Reliance on this metabolic pathway increases the need for these two amino acids. For the Yapu diet, cyanide detoxification would require about 2 mg/kg/day of methionine. This estimate may be high, however, as the toxicity of intact cyanogenic glucosides has not been established. If only free cyanide, which definitely requires detoxification, is considered, the methionine requirement would be about 1 mg/kg/day.

What does this imply in terms of the adequacy of the current Yapu diet? The dietary data indicate that

Table 5. Yapu diet compared to FAO/WHO/UNU suggested pattern (preschoolers) for critical amino acids

Amino Acid	FAO	Yapu Diet
Lysine	58	70
Methionine + Cystine	25	34
Threonine	34	40
Tryptophan	11	11

adults' crude protein intakes average 0.85 grams per kilogram of body weight per day. This is 96 to 102 percent of the FAO/WHO/UNU Safe Level (1985), depending on how the digestibility of the diet is estimated. Energy intake is 45 kilocalories per kilogram of body weight and appears to be adequate, so we can assume that dietary protein is probably not being used to supply energy. The amino acid pattern of the Yapu diet is compared to the FAO/WHO/UNU suggested pattern requirement for preschool children in Table 5. The FAO/WHO/UNU requirement for methionine and cystine is 25 mg/kg/day, and the Yapu diet provides approximately 34 mg/kg/day. Thus, even if the additional requirements for detoxification of 2 mg/kg/day are considered, sulphur-containing amino acids do not appear to be limiting in this diet. This is noteworthy inasmuch as Yapu protein intakes are barely adequate by FAO/WHO/UNU (1985) standards.

Spath's (1981) contention that the reliance on cassava as a dietary staple increases the minimum daily requirement for methionine is valid, but the Yapu data indicate that this increase in need is quite small. I think that given this small increase in need and the limited nature of our understanding of human amino acid requirements, it would be difficult to support Spath's (1971) argument that methionine alone may be acting as a limiting factor in Amazonia.

CONCLUSIONS AND IMPLICATIONS FOR FUTURE RESEARCH

The results presented here indicate that cassava may not be quite so poor a source of protein and minerals as we have assumed, but as is true of other staple foods, its nutritional value is a function of processing. Although Tukanoans cultivate very bitter varieties of cassava, their processing system is effective in detoxifying the roots. The residual cyanide in food products is low, and the current diet of adults appears to provide adequate quantities of the sulfur-containing amino acids used in the metabolic detoxification of dietary cyanide.

What are the implications of these results for future research? I would like to make two suggestions. First, a number of the health problems associated with cassava use in Africa are the direct result of inadequate processing. Given the preference for high-cyanide cassava varieties in Amazonia, the potential for these same sorts of problems is clearly present if less efficient processing techniques are adopted in the future. Presently, in the more traditional villages like Yapu, cassava processing is highly constrained culturally and there is almost no variation between women or over time in how products are prepared. Cassava processing is, however, an extremely time-consuming activity. As women's expectations change with acculturation, cassava processing techniques may also change. In more acculturated areas like Mitu, there has been a shift to fariña and a virtual abandonment of casabe and associated products. The quality of the fariña for sale suggests that the traditional long fermentation period is being shortened.

Further, since metabolic detoxification of cassava-borne cyanide is dependent on sulfur-containing amino acids, a decrease in the quantity or quality of protein in the current high-cassava diet would increase the risk of cyanide-related health problems. The general assumption is that dietary quality, including animal protein consumption, decreases with acculturation, but there are few empirical data available.

I believe that the strong cultural preference for bitter cassava varieties by at least some native Amazonians deserves more attention. To my knowledge, it is the only example of selection for the more toxic varieties of a given crop. In the Yapu area this selection does not appear to be related to productivity differences between the bitter and sweet cultivars, but it does appear to be related to qualitative differences in the food products made from bitter and sweet cultivars (Dufour 1993).

NOTES

1. This research was supported by NSF grant number BNS-8519490, a Fulbright research grant, and an Early Career Development Award from the University of Colorado. I thank Felipa and Cándido Muñoz of Yapu, Vaupés, Colombia, for the processing work at CIAT; T. Salcedo of CIAT for the laboratory analyses; and the Instituto Colombiano de Antropología for its collaboration. I also thank Paul N. Patmore and Richard Wilshusen for their assistance with the fieldwork, and J. Cock, R. Best, and C. Wheatley of CIAT for their support.

2. In Central America and northern parts of South America the plant is referred to as *yuca,* also a Taino word (Carrizales 1984). In Brazil, Paraguay, and Argentina it is referred to as *mandioca* (Albuquerque 1969), and in parts of Colombia, as *mañoco.*

REFERENCES CITED

Albuquerque, M. de
1969   *A mandioca na Amazonia.* Belém, Brazil: Superintendencia do Desenvolvimento da Amazonia.

Ayernor, G. S.
1985   Effects of the Retting of Cassava on Product Yield and Cyanide Detoxification. *Journal of Food Technology* 20:89–96.

Bourdoux, P., A. Mafuta, A. Hanson, and A. M. Ermans
1980   Cassava Toxicity: The Role of Linamarian. In *Role of Cassava in the Etiology of Endemic Goitre and Cretinism,* edited by A. M. Ermans, N. M. Mbulamoko, F. Delange, and R. Ahluwalia, pp. 15–28. Ottawa: International Development Research Centre Monograph IDRC-136e.

Bruijn, G. H. de
1973   The Cyanogenic Character of Cassava *(Manihot esculenta).* In *Chronic Cassava Toxicity,* edited by B. Nestle and R. MacIntyre, pp. 43–48. Ottawa: International Development Research Centre Monograph IDRC-010e.

Carrizales, V.
1984   Evolución histórica de la tecnología del cazabe. *Interciencia* 9(4):206–13.

Cock, J. H.
1982   Cassava: A Basic Energy Source in the Tropics. *Science* 218:755–62.
1985   *Cassava: New Potential for a Neglected Crop.* Boulder, Colo.: Westview Press.

Cooke, R. D., and E. N. Maduagwu
1978   The Effects of Simple Processing on the Cyanide Content of Cassava Chips. *Journal of Food Technology* 13:299–306.

Coursey, D. G.
1973   Cassava as Food: Toxicity and Technology. In *Chronic Cassava Toxicity,* edited by B. Nestel and R. MacIntyre, pp. 27–36. Ottawa: International Development Research Centre Monograph IDRC-010e.

Dole, G. E.
1978   The Use of Manioc Among the Kuikuru: Some Interpretations. In *The Nature and Status of Ethnobotany,* edited by R. I. Ford, pp. 217–49. Ann Arbor: Museum of Anthropology, University of Michigan.

Dufour, D. L.
1983   Nutrition in the Northwest Amazon: Household Dietary Intake and Time-Energy Expenditure. In *Adaptive Responses of Native Amazonians,* edited by R. Hames and W. Vickers, pp. 329–55. New York: Academic Press.

1985   Manioc as a Dietary Staple: Implications for the Budgeting of Time and Energy in the Northwest Amazon. In *Food Energy in Tropical Ecosystems,* edited by D. J. Cattle and K. H. Schwerin, pp. 1–20. New York: Gordon and Breach.

1988a   Cyanide Content of Cassava *(Manihot esculenta, Euphorbiacae)* Cultivars Used by Tukanoan Indians in Northwest Amazonia. *Economic Botany* 42 (2):255–66.

1988b   The Composition of Some Foods Used in Northwest Amazonia. *Interciencia* 13(2):83–86.

1989   Effectiveness of Cassava Detoxification Techniques Used by Indigenous Peoples in Northwest Amazonia. *Interciencia* 14(2):88–91.

1993   The Bitter Is Sweet: A Case Study of Bitter Cassava *(Manihot esculenta)* Use in Amazonia. In *Tropical Forests, People and Food: Biocultural Interactions and Applications to Development,* edited by C. M. Hladik, A. Hladik, O. F. Linares, H. Pagezy, A. Semple, and M. Haldey, pp. 575–88. Paris: UNESCO/Parthenon.

Ermans, A. M., N. M. Mbulamoko, F. Delange, and R. Ahluwalia, eds.
1980   *Role of Cassava in the Etiology of Endemic Goitre and Cretinism.* Ottawa: International Development Research Centre Monograph IDRC-136e.

FAO/WHO/UNU
1985   *Energy and Protein Requirements.* Geneva: World Health Organization.

Gomez, G., et al.
1984   Effect of Variety and Plant Age on the Cyanide Content of Whole-root Cassava Chips and Its Reduction by Sun-drying. *Animal Feed Science and Technology* 11:57–65.

Howeler, R. H.
1985   Mineral Nutrition and Fertilization of Cassava: A Review of Recent Research. In *Cassava Research, Production and Utilization,* edited by J. H. Cock and J. A. Reyes, pp. 249–320. Cali, Colombia: CIAT.

Hugh-Jones, C.
1979   *From the Milk River.* Cambridge: Cambridge University Press.

Jones, W. O.
1959   *Manioc in Africa.* Stanford, Calif.: Stanford University Press.

Lancaster, P. A., J. S. Ingram, M. Y. Lim, and D. G. Coursey
1982   Traditional Cassava-based Foods: Survey of Processing Techniques. *Economic Botany* 36:12–45.

Meuser, F., and H. D. Smolnik
1980   Processing of Cassava to Gari and Other Foodstuffs. *Starch/Starke* 32:116–22.

Moran, E. F.
1973   Energy Flow Analysis and the Study of *Manihot esculenta* Crantz. *Acta Amazonica* 3(3):29–39.

Nambisan, B., and S. Sundaresan
1985   Effect of Processing on the Cyanoglucoside Content of Cassava. *Journal of Science of Food and Agriculture* 36:1197–1203.

Nestel, B., and R. MacIntyre, eds.
1973   *Chronic Cassava Toxicity.* Ottawa: International Development Research Centre Monograph IDRC-010e.

Nordenskiold, E.
1924   *The Ethnography of South America Seen from Mojos in Brazil.* Goteborg: Erlanders Boktryckeri Aktiebolag.

Okezie, B. O., and F. V. Kosikowski
1982   Cassava as Food. *Critical Reviews in Food Science and Nutrition* 17(3):259–75.

Osuntokun, B. O.
1981   Cassava Diet, Chronic Cyanide Intoxification and Neuropathy in Nigerian Africans. *World Review of Nutrition and Dietetics* 36:141–73.

PRORADAM (Proyecto Radargrametrico del Amazonas)
1979   *La Amazonia y sus recursos.* Bogotá: Republica de Colombia.

Renvoize, B. S.
1972   The Area of Origin of *Manihot esculenta* as a Crop Plant: A Review of the Evidence. *Economic Botany* 26:352–60.

Rogers, D. J.
1965   Some Botanical and Ethnological Considerations of *Manihot esculenta. Economic Botany* 19(4):369–77.

Roosevelt, A. C.
1980   *Parmana: Prehistoric Maize and Manioc Subsistence Along the Amazon and Orinoco.* New York: Academic Press.

Rosling, H.
1987   *Cassava Toxicity and Food Security.* Uppsala, Sweden: Tryck kontakt.

Sauer, C. O.
1950   Cultivated Plants of Central and South America. In *Handbook of South American Indians,* edited by J. H.

Steward, pp. 507–33. Washington, D.C.: United States Government Printing Office.

Schwerin, K. H.
1971   The Bitter and the Sweet: Some Implications of the Traditional Techniques for Preparing Manioc. Paper presented at the annual meeting of the American Anthropological Association.
1985   Food Crops in the Tropics. In *Food Energy in Tropical Ecosystems,* edited by D. J. Cattle and K. H. Schwerin. New York: Gordon and Breach.

Seigler, D. S., and J. F. Pereira
1981   Modernized Preparation of Casave in the Llanos Orientales of Venezuela. *Economic Botany* 35(3): 356–62.

Spath, C. D.
1981   Getting to the Meat of the Problem: Some Comments on Protein as a Limiting Factor in Amazonia. *American Anthropologist* 83(2):377–79.

Sponsel, L. E.
1986   Amazon Ecology and Adaptation. *Annual Review of Anthropology* 15:67–97.

Steward, J. H., and L. C. Faron
1959   *Native Peoples of South America.* New York: McGraw-Hill.

Wu Leung, W. T., and M. Flores
1961   *Food Composition Table for Use in Latin America.* Bethesda, Md.: Interdepartmental Committee on Nutrition for National Defense, National Institutes of Health.

22

Traditional Maize Processing Techniques in the New World

Solomon H. Katz, M. L. Hediger, and L. A. Valleroy

Three major agricultural revolutions, each closely associated with the origins of great civilizations, have occurred within the last 10,000 years. These subsistence changes, marking the beginning of a dependency on cereal crops, have had a profound effect on the evolutionary course of modern humans. They have allowed, among other things, considerable shifts in diet, rapid increases in population size, major changes in the social and cultural organizations of various populations, and the laying of the developmental foundations for modern technology. In many respects, these changes are associated with both the biological and cultural evolution of modern man. Each of these revolutions was associated with particular cultigens. Wheat and other cereal grains were first domesticated in the Middle East, rice in Western Asia, and maize (Indian corn)[1] in the Western Hemisphere.

The earliest reported archeological evidence of maize dates back to the wild precursors that existed some 7000 years ago in central Mexico.[2] By 1500 to 2000 years later, maize was already under cultivation and was very much involved in the subsequent rise of the great Mesoamerican civilizations. In South America, maize[3] was also involved, along with other major cultigens, in the rise of the Andean civilizations. However, it did not have as important a role as in Mesoamerica. Over this period of time, maize became an obligatory cultigen, which in modern times has been hybridized to produce strains of corn capable of yielding a variety of characteristics of nutritional and agricultural value. Corn is still the largest single crop in the United States, and it is still the largest source of calories and protein for many of the people of Central America.[4]

Each of the plants domesticated in the various geographical areas has its nutritional limitations, and maize is no exception, especially in terms of the quantity and quality of its essential amino acids and niacin. In fact, unless corn is prepared by specific techniques, its nutritional value as a dietary source is at best marginal, and any human population that attempted to depend on it as a major staple would suffer some degree of malnutrition. To demonstrate the precise role of alkali cooking techniques in the freeing of otherwise unavailable nutrients in corn, we give a brief description of the biology and biochemistry of corn, and discuss the effects of alkali treatment upon its indigestible protein fractions. We also describe some hypotheses concerning the use of alkali for cooking corn, and provide cultural data from 51 societies recorded in the Human Relations Area Files (HRAF)[5] to test these hypotheses. Finally, we discuss the cultural, evolutionary, and other anthropological implications of the data.

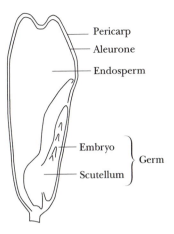

Figure 1. Longitudinal section of corn kernel

THE BIOLOGY AND BIOCHEMISTRY OF CORN

The importance of corn in the Western Hemisphere and elsewhere around the world has led to thorough studies of the nutritional value of this plant food and, especially, of its implications in Mexico and Central America where it predominates as a chief source of nutrition. In general, studies in Mexico and Central America have paid particular attention to the extensive use of tortillas, a food made from corn cooked with alkali, as the major dietary staple of the people.[6,7] A number of experiments with rats[8,9] and pigs have demonstrated that diets consisting of tortillas yield better growth patterns than diets of raw corn.[10] Nevertheless, it has been demonstrated by chemical analyses that, in the process of preparing tortillas, a certain amount of the nutritional value of the corn is lost.[7] This has led investigators to question how the preparation of tortillas enhances the biologically effective nutritional value of corn while simultaneously reducing its total nutritional content. Since the nutritional value of corn is limited chiefly by the quality and quantity of its proteins, it is necessary to identify the composition and nutritional characteristics of corn proteins.

The corn kernel has several anatomical parts. These include the outer covering, consisting of the pericarp and aleurone; the endosperm, comprising the largest fraction of the kernel; and the germ consisting of the embryo and scutellum (see Fig. 1). The dried corn kernel contains approximately 6.8 to 12.0 percent protein by weight, 74.5 percent starch, 12.0 percent water, 3.4 percent fat, and 1 percent ash and

crude fibers.[11] Proteins of several different classes, categorized on the basis of solubility, have been identified in corn, principally in the endosperm and germ portions of the kernel. Together, these two portions contain 90 to 95 percent of the protein in corn.[12] Within these two portions, there are four classes of proteins: (i) albumins and (ii) globulins, extractable in dilute saline solutions; (iii) zein, a heterogeneous protein with a molecular weight of 20,000 to 50,000, which is classed as a prolamine and is extractable in an ethanol solution; and (iv) glutelin, a heterogeneous protein varying in molecular weight from 20,000 to 1,000,000 and extractable in alkali solution (see Table 1).[12] This wide range of the glutelin's molecular weight is due to the extensive disulfide linkages between cysteine residues which account for the protein's tertiary structure and its particular sensitivity to denaturation in dilute alkali.[13]

In general, corn is deficient in the essential amino acids lysine and tryptophan, and in niacin, a member of the vitamin B complex. Approximately two-thirds of the lysine is within the glutelin fractions of the endosperm and germ, and in many nonruminant animals, including humans, the glutelin fractions are normally indigestible. Even under ideal laboratory conditions, the quantity of lysine that can be extracted from corn is nutritionally inadequate relative to the other essential amino acids that corn contains. Thus, any way of increasing the availability of the lysine in corn would enhance its nutritional value.

In the case of tryptophan, a precursor to niacin, Aguirre et al.[14] demonstrated in some 23 varieties of Guatemalan corn that the average daily intake of 500 grams supplies only 88 percent of the estimated adult requirement for this amino acid. On the other hand, the niacin content of the same corn varieties would supply only 59 percent of the dietary intake recommended by the National Research Council,[15] based on

Table 1.   Lysine, leucine, and isoleucine in the protein fractions of the endosperm and embryo of corn. Data are expressed as percentages of total nitrogen.[12] The measurements were made by Mertz et al.[12] according to a copper extraction-fractionation method. The acid soluble fraction is similar to, but not exactly the same as, the albumins and globulins. The data were obtained from the normal type of corn. New varieties of corn, such as opaque-2, have a higher lysine content and a more favorable isoleucine to leucine ratio.[12] Values for tryptophan were not obtained. Tryptophan and niacin comprise 0.044 percent and 0.0018 percent of the protein in the corn kernel.[14]

Amino Acid	Endosperm				Embryo			
	Acid Soluble Fraction	Zein	Glutelin	Total Endosperm	Acid Soluble Fraction	Zein	Glutelin	Total Endosperm
Lysine	1.8	0.3	3.6	2.0				6.1
Leucine	10.1	20.3	8.6	14.3				6.5
Isoleucine	3.0	4.2	3.4	3.8				3.1
Total nitrogen	16–26	41–60	17–31	98 (residue, 2–11)	30–40	5–10	49–54	98 (residue, 0–11)

a daily consumption of 500 grams. Because the metabolism of tryptophan is associated with the endogenous production of niacin, a population whose diet consisted mainly of maize would be likely to develop pellagra as a result of niacin deficiency, if other dietary constituents were not present on a seasonal basis to supplement the tryptophan or niacin, or both.[16,17] Indeed, pellagra was rampant in the southern United States through the Depression[18] and is still a major disease in South Africa and India. The disease has a very low rate of occurrence in Mesoamerica.[19,20]

There is evidence to suggest that pellagra can also be induced by an unfavorable isoleucine to leucine ratio, that is, by an excessive amount of leucine in the diet. Such is the case in a diet heavily dependent on corn.[16,21] In 500 grams of corn there is approximately twice the recommended adult intake of leucine, and the leucine to isoleucine ratio is nearly three times greater than that which is considered optimal.[22] Since the antagonistic effect of leucine on the conversion of tryptophan to niacin is ameliorated by increases in isoleucine, then any rise in the ratio of isoleucine to leucine as a result of cooking with alkali would help to minimize the effects of niacin deficiency.

Two important experiments by Bressani and his co-workers[7,22] demonstrated the effects of the alkali cooking processes on corn, with particular reference to the changes that take place with respect to low levels of lysine, tryptophan, and niacin, as well as the high levels of leucine. In the first experiment, Bressani et al.[7] documented overall losses of significant quantities of thiamin, riboflavin, niacin, nitrogen, fat, and crude fiber resulting from the preparation of tortillas from raw corn.[23] Tortillas are made in Central America by heating dried corn to almost boiling in a 5 percent solution of lime in water for 30 to 50 minutes; the mixture is then cooled, the supernatant is discarded, and the corn is washed thoroughly, and drained. The remaining corn is finely ground into a dough called *masa,* which is subsequently formed into pancake shapes and cooked on a hot clay griddle for approximately 2 minutes on each side. The effect of the lime is to yield a dilute calcium hydroxide solution which is basic or alkaline. While this cooking process, and particularly the lime treatment, clearly decreases the overall nutrient content of the corn, Bressani and Scrimshaw[22] demonstrated that cooking with lime selectively enhances the nutritional quality of corn. This qualitative change probably results from a relative decrease in the solubility of the zein portion of the corn proteins. The zein portion is deficient in lysine and tryptophan compared to the glutelin fraction, which is rich in proteins that yield essential amino acids.

Because the chemical procedures, used in determining amino acid content, are more effective than digestion in vivo, Bressani and Scrimshaw[22] subjected alkali cooked and uncooked corn samples to both chemical extraction and in vitro digestion with pepsin for 12 hours to determine whether the outcome of the two procedures differed. The results of the chemical procedures on the two samples showed no differences in the amounts of amino acids, expressed in milligrams per gram of nitrogen, except for the lowering of the leucine content in both samples. However, the results (Table 2), which are calculated from the data of Bressani and Scrimshaw,[22] indicate that there are a number of relative changes in the alkali-treated corn digested with pepsin, which improve its overall nutritional quality. These results are expressed as ratios of

Table 2. Ratios of essential amino acids in cooked (alkali-treated) and uncooked (raw) corn subjected to chemical hydrolysis and enzymatic digestion in vitro with pepsin for 12 hours. Computed from data of Bressani and Scrimshaw.[22] The raw data were expressed as milligrams of amino acid per gram of nitrogen in raw corn and tortillas.

	Ratio* of Amino Acid in Cooked and Uncooked Corn	
Amino Acid	Chemical Hydrolysis (cooked: uncooked)	Enzyme Digestion in Vitro (cooked: uncooked)
Histidine	0.86	2.33
Isoleucine	0.79	2.14
Leucine	0.43	1.16
Lysine	1.04	2.80
Methionine	0.71	2.09
Phenylalanine	0.42	1.14
Threonine	0.96	2.63
Tryptophan	0.50	1.29
Valine	0.38	1.02

*While chemical hydrolysis yields the absolute quantities of essential amino acids, for purposes of constructing these ratios, it is perhaps more significant to point out that the enzymatic digestion in vitro more closely parallels the ratios that would be obtained after digestion in vivo.

the amounts of amino acids in alkali-treated tortillas to the amounts extracted from raw corn.

When expressed on the basis of grams of amino acids per 100 grams of corn, the data indicate that in the lime-treated tortillas there is absolute lowering of most of the essential amino acids, with the exception of lysine. However, this is not unexpected because there are considerable losses of total nitrogen during the cooking process. What is most interesting is the relative enhancement of the ratios when the data are calculated on the basis of milligrams of amino acid per gram of nitrogen. Any increase in the ratios obtained on this basis would indicate that cooking with lime selectively enhances the quality of the corn protein that is available for enzymatic digestion. Under these conditions, the relative amount of lysine is increased 2.8 times, tryptophan is increased slightly, and both the relative and absolute ratios of isoleucine to leucine are increased 1.8 times. Other essential amino acids such as histidine, methionine, and threonine are also relatively doubled in concentration. Not only are the relative amounts of essential amino acids significantly improved by this process, but also the availability in vivo of both the precursors to niacin and niacin itself appear to be enhanced.[9] Thus, as long as maize is the

major component of the diet, then cooking techniques in which alkali and heat are used clearly enhance the balance of essential amino acids and free the otherwise almost unavailable niacin.

SIGNIFICANCE OF ALKALI COOKING TECHNIQUES

In effect, without alkali processing of corn, there would be a considerable degree of malnutrition in societies where corn is the major part of the diet; this malnutrition could only be avoided if the diet were supplemented with foods rich in essential amino acids. While it is conceivable that increases in the quantity of corn consumed might enable adults to overcome some of the problems of malnutrition,[24] it is unlikely that young children during phases of rapid growth and development could eat enough corn to compensate for its nutritional deficiencies. Such children would therefore suffer from significant effects of malnutrition. Societies whose cooking techniques did not include the use of alkali must either have adopted patterns of nutrition that included supplements to the maize diet, thereby decreasing its agricultural potential, or have become decimated by malnutrition, especially among the young children. We therefore hypothesized that all societies that depend on maize as a major dietary staple practice alkali cooking techniques.

Cultural Data

To test our hypothesis, we selected from the New World a large number of societies, that are described extensively in the ethnographic literature, and determined the extent to which they cultivate and consume maize, and whether or not they use some form of alkali treatment in the preparation of corn for consumption.

The 51 societies that we investigated are represented in the HRAF[5] and are located within defined cultural and geographical areas between 47°N and 43°S[25–27] where ecological conditions are suitable for the cultivation of corn. We restricted our investigation in this way because we assumed that maize cannot become a dietary staple of a society unless that society either cultivates its own corn or is in direct contact with another society that cultivates corn. The areas in which these societies are located include, for North and Central America, Kroeber's[26] (i) East and North, (ii) Intermediate and Intermountain, (iii) Southwest, and (iv) Mexico and Central America. Excluded from the North and Central American sample are those societies in the Arctic Coast and Northwest Coast areas. For South America, the relevant areas are Murdock's[27] larger ones that he terms (i) the Andean, encompassing the Isthmus, Colombian, Peruvian, and Chilean coasts and highlands, as well as the Caribbean, and (ii) the central western portion of the Tropical Forest area, excluding the Amazon basin, steppe-hunting area. Populations in the smaller peripheral hunting and fishing areas were not included in our studies because in these areas little or no maize was cultivated aboriginally.

In conducting our investigation, two researchers jointly rated the societies (see Table 3) according to (i) the extent to which they practice maize cultivation, (ii) the relative percentage of maize in their diets, and (iii) whether or not they use alkali when preparing maize for consumption. In these ratings the alkali used for cooking could include lime, which yields calcium hydroxide in solution; wood ashes, which yield potassium hydroxide; or lye, which yields sodium hydroxide. We used the HRAF categories that relate to tillage, cereal agriculture, diet, and food preparation. The ratings could only be inferred from the files since no absolute figures are available, and therefore our quantitative estimates were divided into only four categories including the designation "none," indicating that corn was neither cultivated nor consumed. As corroborative evidence, we consulted Murdock's[28] coding of subsistence economies for measures of dependence on agriculture (see Table 3 and Fig. 3).

There is a seasonal dimension to the processing and preparing of maize for consumption which our results in Table 3 do not indicate, but they bear mentioning in conjunction with the cultural explanations of alkali processing. With few exceptions, societies that use alkali cooking techniques as well as societies that do not use such techniques roast some of their maize. However, this roasting is done principally when the maize is green or not fully ripened, and it is done under ashes with the maize still in the husk. Although such roasting might have important effects on the corn, these effects have not been fully investigated.[8,23] Furthermore, the roasting is done only in those seasons when crops of all sorts are being harvested, wild flora is abundant, and a variety of foods are available for consumption. It is the fully ripened or stored maize that is generally processed with alkali, the treatment usually being described as a way of softening the tough outer kernel.[17]

Of the 51 societies that we rated, 7 that are classified as both high consumers and high cultivators of maize also use alkali in preparing it for consumption. Conversely, none of the 12 societies classified as both low cultivators and consumers use alkali. Table 4 indicates the overall mean difference between users and nonusers of alkali at the levels of both cultivation and consumption. Data are shown only for those societies that either consume or cultivate some maize. Those societies where maize is a potential cultigen but is neither cultivated nor consumed (rated 0 for consumption and 0 for cultivation) were excluded from the statistical analyses. On this basis, the mean difference between users and nonusers was highly significant ($P \ll .001$) for both consumption and cultivation. Figure 2 shows that there is a striking, almost one-to-one relationship between those societies that both consume and cultivate large amounts of maize and those that use alkali treatment. On the other hand, those societies consuming and cultivating smaller quantities of maize almost invariably do not use alkali cooking techniques.

Figure 3 shows the ratings for maize cultivation and consumption for each of the societies investigated and indicates whether or not each society uses alkali. It is important to note that not all of the 51 societies studied either consume or cultivate maize. For example, the seven Indian tribes in California gather vast quantities of acorns, and this seems to reduce their need for a staple such as corn. Note also that lime use is restricted to Mesoamerica and the southwestern United States. As well as being an important source of alkali, lime is also an excellent source of calcium.[22] This is unlike the high concentrations of potassium in wood ashes or sodium in lye. Finally, the overall lack of alkali treatments in most Andean populations may have implications for the history of maize cultivation.

DISCUSSION

We have attempted to explain the use of alkali for cooking maize as a necessary concomitant of intensive maize agriculture and high maize consumption. We will now show that this simple cooking technique for maize may have important implications for certain anthropological theories. For example, the data we have presented might help to substantiate a number of theories about the origins, development, and spread of maize cultivation in the New World, and about various sociocultural systems that are associated with the cultivation of maize.

One question that is of considerable interest is whether or not the lower rates of maize production and consumption in South America can be attributed directly to the lack of the discovery of alkali cooking techniques. Since alkali treatment is not used, and apparently has not been used in that area, one can postulate that it was necessary for other crops to be developed to supplement the otherwise inadequate maize diet. Such crops might not have been as successful, in terms of production, as maize. In Yucatan maize is the

Table 3. Summary of cultural information.[49] Names of subgroups of societies are shown in parentheses when appropriate. The designations from the HRAF are those indicated by Murdock.[28] For maize cultivation, the ratings 0, 1, 2, and 3 represent the estimated relative amount of maize cultivation practiced by each society in relation to the total crop production obtained by means of cultivation. The ratings are defined as follows: 0, none; 1, there are other major cultigens whose produce contributes to diet, and maize plays an insignificant role in the agricultural effort; 2, maize is cultivated intensively, but there is also substantial or comparable cultivation of other crops; 3, maize is cultivated intensively as the major subsistence item with little or no cultivation of other crops. For maize consumption, the ratings represent the estimated relative amount of maize in each society's total diet. It does not account for seasonal variation but only dietary intake within a yearly span. The ratings are defined as follows: 0, none; 1, in conjunction with the rating 1 for maize cultivation, or maize is not cultivated but obtained as a trade item from other peoples; 2, maize may be the major agricultural crop, but there is also dietary dependency on other forms of subsistence, such as hunting or gathering; 3, maize, being the major cultigen, is also the major food staple with only minor supplementation by other crops, wild plants, or animal produce. The column for alkali treatment indicates the presence (plus) or absence (minus) of alkali treatment during the processing of corn. This can include lime, wood ash, or lye in soaking or boiling. It does not include the process of exclusively roasting or baking under ashes because its value for alkali hydrolysis would be questionable. The digits in the column for Murdock's subsistence economy have values that were assigned by Murdock.[50] Each digit represents the relative dependency of the society on the five major types of subsistence economy: 1st digit, the gathering of wild plants and small land fauna; 2nd digit, hunting, including trapping and fowling; 3rd digit, fishing, including shellfishing and the pursuit of large aquatic animals; 4th digit, animal husbandry; 5th digit, agriculture. The digits in each column are defined on the basis of dependence, and the values are percentages: 0, 0 to 5; 1, 6 to 15; 2, 16 to 25; 3, 26 to 35; 4, 36 to 45; 5, 46 to 55; 6, 56 to 65; 7, 66 to 75; 8, 76 to 85; 9, 86 to 100. The comments are brief notes on the major subsistence staples of each society, and on how maize is obtained by those who utilize it in their diets but do not cultivate it. References are for the ethnographic sources consulted in the HRAF.[49]

Name of Society	HRAF Designation	Maize Cultivation	Maize Consumption	Alkali Treatment	Murdock Subsistence Economy	Comments	References[49]
Eastern and Northern North America							
1. Ojibwa (Chippewa)	NG 6	2	1	+ (soda, lye)	22402	Gather wild rice; equally cultivate beans, squash, pumpkins	Densmore 1929
2. Micmac	NJ 5	0	0	–	15400	Hunting, gathering, fishing	Parsons 1928; Speck and Dexter 1951; Wallis and Wallis 1955
3. Delaware (Munsee)	NM 7	3	2	+ (hardwood ashes)	22204	Hunting, fishing, gathering	Heckewelder 1819; Tantaquidgeon 1942; Kinietz 1946; Newcomb 1956
4. Iroquois (Seneca)	NM 9	3	2	+ (lye, ashes)	13204	Hunting, fishing, gathering	Morgan 1901 (1850); Waugh 1916; Quain 1937; Lyford 1945; Speck 1945
5. Comanche	NO 6	0	1	–	19000	Buffalo hunters; maize obtained as trade item from Kiowas, Witchitas, and other eastern tribes	Wallace and Hoebel 1934; Hoebel 1940
6. Natchez	NO 8	3	2	+ (ashes)	03205	Hunting, fishing	Swanton 1911

Table 3. *(continued)*

Name of Society	HRAF Designation	Maize Cultivation	Maize Consumption	Alkali Treatment	Murdock Subsistence Economy	Comments	References[49]
7. Winnebago	NP 12	3	2	+ (ashes)	23203	Hunting, fishing, gathering	Radin 1915/1916; Lurie 1961
8. Crow	NQ 10	0	1	+ (ashes)	28000	Maize obtained as trade item from the Hidatsa; buffalo hunters	Lowie 1935; Morgan 1959
9. Dhegiha (Omaha)	NQ 12	3	2	+ (ashes)	14104	Hunting, fishing, gathering	Dorsey 1881/1882; Fletcher and La Flesche 1905/1906
10. Gros Ventre	NQ 13	0	0	-	28000	Buffalo hunters	Kroeber 1908; Flannery 1953
11. Mandan	NQ 17	3	2	+ (ashes)	03205	Tubers mainly cultivated	Will and Spinden 1906; Will and Hyde 1917
12. Pawnee	NQ 18	3	2	+ (ashes)	14005	Gathering, buffalo hunting	Lesser 1933; Wedel 1936; Weltfish 1965
Intermediate and Intermountain North America							
13. Northern Paiute (Paviotso)	NR 13	0	0	-	52300	Acorn gatherers	Lowie 1924
14. S. E. Salish (Coeur d'Alene)	NR 19	0	0	-	34300	Acorn gatherers	Teit 1927/1928
15. Pomo (Eastern Pomo)	NS 18	0	0	-	43300	Acorn gatherers	Loeb 1926
16. Tübatulabal	NS 22	0	0	-	53200	Acorn gatherers	Wheeler-Voegelin 1938
17. Yokuts	NS 29	0	0	-	43300	Acorn gatherers	Gayton 1948
18. Yurok	NS 31	0	0	-	41500	Acorn gatherers	Heizer and Mills 1952
19. Washo	NT 20	0	0	-	43300	Acorn gatherers	Barrett 1917; d'Azevedo et al. 1963
Southwestern North America							
20. E. Apache (Chiricahua)	NT 8	0	0	-	64000	Hunting, gathering	Opler 1941
21. Navaho	NT 13	3	2	+ (ashes)	21304	Pastoralists	Hill 1938; Leighton and Leighton 1944; Kluckhohn and Leighton 1946; Reichard 1950
22. Plateau Yumans (Havasupai)	NT 14	3	2	+ (ashes)	32005	Maize is major crop	Curtis 1908; Spier 1928; Smithson 1959

Name of Society	HRAF Designation	Maize Cultivation	Maize Consumption	Alkali Treatment	Murdock Subsistence Economy	Comments	References[49]
23. River Yumans	NT 15	2	2	+ (lye, ashes)	41203	Shifting to wheat cultivation	Spier 1933
24. Tewa	NT 18	3	3	+ (ashes, lime)	01018	Maize is major crop	Robbins et al. 1916; Whitman 1940; Laski 1958
25. Zuñi	NT 23	3	3	+ (ashes, lime)	11008	Maize is major crop	Stevenson 1901/1902; Cushing 1920; Bunzel 1929/1930
26. Papago	NU 28	2	2	–	32005	Shifting to wheat cultivation	Castetter and Underhill 1935; Castetter and Bell 1942; Pijoan et al. 1943*
27. Seri	NU 31	0	0	–	22600	Hunting, gathering, fishing	McGee 1895/1896
Mexico and Central America							
28. Aztec	NU 7	3	3	+ (ashes, lime)	01207	Maize is major crop	Bandelier 1876/1879; Vaillant 1941; Sahagún 1957
29. Tarahumara	NU 33	3	3	+ (ashes, lime)	01207	Maize is major crop	Bennett and Zingg 1935; Fried 1953; Pennington 1963; Champion 1963
30. Tarasco	NU 34	3	3	+ (ashes, lime, soda)	01207	Maize is major crop	Beals and Hatcher 1943; Beals 1946; West 1948
31. Tzeltal	NV 9	3	3	+ (lime)	Not coded	Maize is major crop	Brom and LaFarge 1927; Villa Rojas 1969; Nash 1970
32. Yucatec Maya	NV 10	3	3	+ (lime)	01207	Maize is major crop	Gann 1918; Redfield and Villa Rojas 1934; Villa Rojas 1945
33. Mosquito	SA 15	1	1	–	32212	Plantain is major crop	Conzemius 1932
Andean and Tropical Forest							
34. Talamanca	SA 19	1	1	–	11215	Tubers mainly cultivated	Gabb 1876; Stone 1962
35. Cuna	SB 5	1	1	–	01306	Plantain is major crop	Densmore 1926; Wafer 1934; McKim 1947
36. Cagaba	SC 7	2	2	–	00028	Also cultivate beans and yuca extensively	Bolinder 1925; Reichel-Dolmatoff 1949/1950

Table 3. (*continued*)

Name of Society	HRAF Designation	Maize Cultivation	Maize Consumption	Alkali Treatment	Murdock Subsistence Economy	Comments	References[49]
37. Goajiro	SC 13	1	1	–	01171	Pastoralists	Armstrong and Métraux 1948: Santa Cruz 1960
38. Páez	SC 15	3	2	+ (ashes)	11026	Maize is major crop	Bernal Villa 1954
39. Cayaba	SD 6	2	2	–	11215	Also cultivate potatoes extensively	Barrett 1925; Murra 1948; Altschuler 1965
40. Jivaro	SD 9	1	1	–	12106	Maize is major crop	Karsten 1935; Sterling 1938
41. Inca	SE 13	2	2	–	01027	Also cultivate potatoes and guinea	Rowe 1946
42. Aymara	SF 5	1	1	–	00136	Cultivate potatoes and guinea	Tschopik 1946; La Barre 1948
43. Chiriguano	SF 10	2	2	–	11215	Cultivate variety of crops as well	Schmidt 1938; Métraux 1948
44. Ura (Chippewa)	SF 24	0	0	–	Not coded	Cultivate pumpkins and guinea	Métraux 1935; Métraux 1935/1936; LaBarre 1946
45. Araucanians (Mapuche)	SG 4	1	1	–	10126	Wheat is major crop	Titiev 1951; Hilger 1957
46. Mataco	S 17	1	1	–	22411	Cultivate pumpkins and watermelons	Pelleschi 1896
47. Choroti	SK 6	1	1	–	43201	Principally hunters	Rosen 1924
48. Callinago	ST 13	1	1	–	01504	Cultivate bitter and sweet manioc	Rouse 1948; Hodge and Taylor 1957
49. Puerto Rico	SU 1	1	1	–	Not coded	Variety of crops	Steward et al. 1956
50. Haiti	SV 3	1	1	–	Not coded	Cultivate yams	Courlander 1960
51. Jamaica	SY 1	2	2	+ (ashes)	Not coded	Corn is major crop along with cassava	Beckwith 1929

Pijoan et al.[51] have noticed subclinical signs of avitaminoses among the Papago, which are caused by dietary deficiencies.

Table 4. Results of statistical analyses of data from societies that consume or cultivate maize, or both. Societies that were rated zero for consumption were not included in the Student's *t*-test because they would have to consume corn in order to use alkali cooking methods. A similar consideration was made for cultivation.

Items	Consumption		Cultivation	
	Alkali $N = 21$	No Alkali $N = 18$	Alkali $N = 20$	No Alkali $N = 17$
Mean rating	2.24	1.28	2.85	1.29
Standard deviation	±0.63	±0.46	±0.37	±0.47
Student's *t*-test	5.52		11.11	
P	≤.001		≤.001	

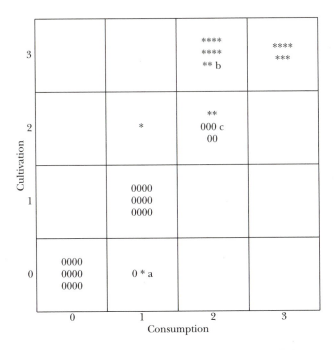

Figure 2. The relationship between the use of alkali for processing maize and the extent to which societies cultivate or consume maize. An asterisk indicates a society that uses alkali to process maize; a zero indicates that a society does not use alkali. The degrees of cultivation and consumption were rated: 0, none; 1, low, less than one-third of crops, or diet, respectively; 2, moderate, one-third to two-thirds; 3, high, more than two-thirds. The symbols *a*, *b*, and *c* indicate the Crow, Páez, and Papago societies, respectively.

predominant crop, and the ratio of nonagricultural to agricultural workers is reported to be 12:1.[29,30] However, it is difficult to test such hypotheses at this time, since this would involve complicated assumptions about ecological variables, the timing of discovery and the use of other cultigens, and other socioeconomic factors.

The data from our statistical analyses are strongly supported by descriptive historical data. Descriptive

data are available that explain and account for several important exceptions (see the Papago, Crow, and Páez societies in Table 3) to the almost universal relationship between the production and consumption of maize and the use of alkali cooking techniques.

The Papago of the southwestern United States were classified as moderate producers and consumers of maize aboriginally but, unlike the remaining societies of the Southwest, there is no evidence that they processed corn with alkali. The Crow do use alkali, but they cultivate no corn and only sporadically consume it, obtaining it as a trade item from the neighboring Hidatsa, who are agriculturists. The Páez, on the other hand, deviate from the apparent South American pattern by cultivating maize as their major subsistence item and processing it with alkali.

The lack of alkali cooking techniques among the Papago can be explained on an ecological basis. According to Castetter and Bell[31] the Papago are seminomadic, living in an arid environment that prohibits year-round cultivation and sedentism. The land is not fertile enough to allow large harvests. Because food is scarce during most seasons, and because of their nomadism during the dry seasons, the Papago do not store their maize nor do they allow it to fully ripen. They eat most of it roasted in the husk during seasons when supplementary foods are available.

The use of an alkali processing technique by the Crow bears a simple historical explanation. The Crow once formed a single people with the Hidatsa,[32] splitting off from that society to take up existence as nomadic buffalo hunters on the plains. This is supported both ethnohistorically and linguistically. Like the other sedentary village farmers of the upper Missouri River, the Mandan and the Arikara, the Hidatsa process maize by using alkali.[33] The Crow continued to have contact with the Hidatsa, trading their buffalo meat for maize, and it follows that they merely continued their tradition from sedentary days of processing maize with alkali.

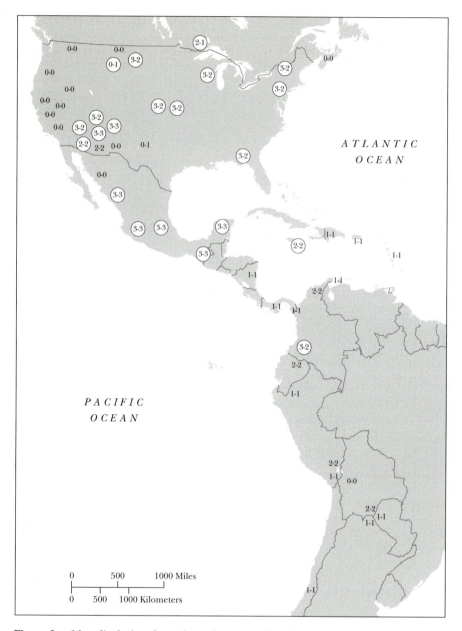

Figure 3. Map displaying the ratings given to each society for maize cultivation and consumption and the use of alkali for cooking corn. For each society, two numbers are shown. The first indicates the rating for maize cultivation as in Table 3. The second indicates the rating for maize consumption. Societies utilizing alkali processing techniques have circled numbers.

To explain the cultivation of maize by the Páez, and their use of alkali, it is necessary to utilize archeological data. The Páez are Chib-chan speakers, living in the highland basins of Colombia. Archeological evidence supports the theory[34] that there was a late introduction of maize in Colombia, and that the maize came not from the Andes, but from Mesoamerica. Maize arrived simultaneously with other Mesoamerican cultigens as a fully developed complex, probably with an actual influx of peoples from Mesoamerica.

The alkali processing technique most probably came into Colombia in conjunction with the cultigen.

Evidence for the use of alkali cooking techniques by certain societies may provide us with further insight into questions surrounding the origin of these techniques and enable us to determine whether they were invented independently by different societies or diffused along with maize cultivation in the Americas. It is interesting that the Páez are the only South American society in our sample that process maize with alkali, and that for this purpose they use wood ashes. Evidence in this instance points to a late introduction of maize, probably from Mesoamerica.[34] Thus it is likely that the maize processing technique was introduced in conjunction with a cultigen complex. This is further suggested by the fact that all the North American producers and consumers of maize obtain alkali for maize preparation from wood ashes whereas none, except the Páez, do so in South America (see Fig. 3). The evidence from North America also favors diffusion of the alkali cooking technique, since all moderate (and heavy) cultivators and consumers use the same process. While this is not proof of independent domestication and invention of maize agriculture in the Andean areas, or elsewhere in South America, it does seem to raise new questions about these theories. Lime, as a source of alkali, is found predominantly in Mesoamerica and sporadically in the southwestern United States. Ashes and lye as sources of alkali are used elsewhere. This fact may have ecological significance regarding the presence and availability of limestone.

Since our evidence indicates that maize becomes an extensive part of the diet only when alkali cooking techniques are used, it should also be possible to obtain further archeological evidence to support this hypothesis. There is evidence[35] that lime-soaking pots were already in use by 100 B.C. at Teotihuacan, the first urban center in Mesoamerica. The economic implications of the early utilization of lime suggest important questions about its production, distribution, sale,[36] and trade throughout Mesoamerica.

While most of the societies in our sample use either lime, lye, or wood ashes as a source of alkali, it has recently been observed that the Lacandon Maya of Chiapas, Mexico, after eating fresh water mussels, cremate the shells and use the ashes as a source of alkali.[37] This practice may have important archeological implications in other lowland jungle areas of Yucatan and Guatemala, where natural sources of limestone are available but may not be used because alkali made from shells is preferred. With this evidence it is interesting to juxtapose the reports of plentiful supplies of fresh water shells from snails during the Pre-Classic period (ending in A.D. 250) in Copan[38] and in the Mayan Belize River valley.[39] However, Longyear[38] has also noted that, by the Classic period, a steady and sharp decline had occurred in the abundance of shells and small animal bones in Copan.

Elsewhere in the Mayan region, Haviland[40] has documented from human skeletal remains at Tikal both a reduction in stature from Pre-Classic through Late Classic times (A.D. 550 to 900) and an increasing problem of malnutrition as demonstrated by radiological analyses of long bones. He attributed these findings to malnutrition stemming from increasing population density and decreasing sources of high quality protein from wild game. Similar malnutrition and high population densities occurred in the Belize River valley.[30]

As a whole, the evidence from small animal bones and snail shells suggests that there was a parallel decline in these two protein resources and that this decline was probably due to overconsumption in the regions where the population densities were rising beyond the capacities of the ecosystems to support them. If the decrease in snails was also associated with a decrease in the availability of shells for alkali production in those areas where other alkali resources such as limestone were unused or scarce, then such developments could have had serious implications for those societies that might have become dependent on maize as the major part of their diet. Of course, these suggestions must be investigated further, because to our knowledge there are no published reports on the use of shells in the preparation of alkali for the treatment of maize during these times.

It is important to consider the nature of previous explanations of alkali cooking techniques for corn, since these techniques have been described extensively in the ethnographic literature. The explanation that most anthropologists and their informants have offered for the significance of this treatment in each society is that alkali softens and "hulls" the tough pericarp of the maize. At one level, this explanation is both accurate and plausible, and it may be for these reasons that only a few ethnographers have extended the explanation further, postulating, for example, that alkali treatment aids in the general digestive process. According to Beals,[41] the Tarascans grind maize on the *metate* with bicarbonate of soda in order to prevent constipation. Tantaquidgeon[42] notes that the Delaware utilize hominy as the appropriate food for the sick. In describing the practices of the same society, Lindestrom[43] states that the ashes in which bread is baked function, as sand does for birds, "to clean their stomachs." However, among the Yucatec Maya the maize which is offered to the gods during various ceremonies is never treated with alkali, varying in this respect from the usual preparation of maize for human consumption.[44] Bennett and Zingg[45] are among the few anthropologists who mention the cross-cultural significance of alkali treatment. They comment that boiling with alkali "is an essential corn preparation technique" which has migrated northward with the diffusion of maize.

What emerges from this brief review of anthropological explanations of the alkali processing of corn is the lack of a significant biological dimension in the conceptual paradigm of the ethnographic anthropologist.[46,47] By juxtaposing the latent biological dimension with the cross-cultural literature, alkali processing techniques assume highly significant proportions by apparently setting a type of critical limit on the consumption of maize. This concept of a critical limit can be used to enhance our understanding of the past and present distribution of maize agriculture and to suggest ways by which we can examine all aspects of such basic anthropological theories as those concerned with independent invention and diffusion.

ADAPTIVE AND EVOLUTIONARY IMPLICATIONS

It is evident that in studies of human adaptability and evolution the sciences of man must consider in greater detail the interacting relationships of human biology and culture. The importance of these relationships has been well demonstrated from the genetic level in studies of diseases such as sickle cell anemia.[48] Yet, in the case presented here, if the alkali cooking techniques used by societies consuming large quantities of maize are examined in the cultural context alone, then they would seem only to be innocuous methods for softening the outer kernel and would carry no adaptive or evolutionary significance. However, the evidence presented here implies that without these cooking techniques a high degree of dependence on corn produces serious malnutrition. Alternatively, if one considers the implications of raw maize for genetic evolution, it is unlikely that specific adaptations to diets of maize cooked without alkali would occur because any genetic change would have to involve the biosynthetic pathways of many essential nutrients.

Instead, one of the chief adaptations which allowed for the intensification of maize agriculture was a cultural one associated with the technology of food processing. In turn, the intensification of maize agriculture allowed for the evolution of further social complexity based on the reliability of subsistence, the concomitant residential stability, and the ability to support nonagricultural producing members of the society. This evolving social complexity undoubtedly affected adaptation at a variety of other demographic, ecological, and social levels which probably influenced the genetic composition of the population. Although the possible evolutionary changes that this example suggests may not be necessarily the same as one which might have occurred at the genetic level, such as sickle cell anemia, their implications for human adaptability may be no less important. This suggests that it is increasingly difficult to accept evolutionary studies where biological and cultural adaptation are treated independently.

REFERENCES AND NOTES

1. Throughout this article, the term "corn" refers collectively to both the modern hybrid and aboriginal races of *Zea mays*, while "maize" refers specifically to the aboriginal races.

2. R. MacNeish, in *The Prehistory of the Tehuacan Valley*, D. Byers, Ed. (Univ. of Texas Press, Austin, 1967). vol. 1, pp. 3–33, 114–131, and 290–310.

3. There is a long-standing controversy over the question of whether domesticated Andean maizes diffused into the Andes from Mesoamerica, or whether there was an independent focus of domestication in this area.

4. H. G. Wilkes, *Science* 177, 1071 (1972).

5. Human Relations Area Files, Inc. (New Haven, Conn., 1949).

6. R. O. Cravioto, R. K. Anderson, E. R. Lockhart, F. de Miranda, R. S. Harris, *Science* 102, 91 (1945).

7. R. Bressani, R. Paz y Paz, N. S. Scrimshaw, *J. Agric. Food Chem.* 6, 770 (1958).

8. It should be noted that experiments with rats have not been as definitive as those with pigs. For example, W. N. Pearson [*J. Nutr.* 62, 445 (1957)] reported that rats fed boiled corn thrived almost as well as rats fed alkali-treated corn. Two other reports also indicate that rats eating raw corn had the same growth rate as those on a diet of alkali-treated corn [see McDaniel and Hundley (n. 9); W. A. Krehl et al., *J. Biol. Chem.* 166, 1531 (1946)]. This discrepancy is probably due to the fact that rats are more efficient in the conversion of tryptophan to niacin than man [E. Kodicek, R. Braude, S. K. Kon, K. G. Mitchell, *Br. J. Nutr.* 10, 51(1956)].

9. E. G. McDaniel and J. M. Hundley, *Fed. Proc.* 17, 484 (1958).

10. J. Laguna and K. Carpenter, *J. Nutr.* 45, 21 (1951).

11. H. J. Heinz Company, *Nutritional Data* (H. J. Heinz Company, Pittsburgh, Pa., 1963).

12. E. T. Mertz, O. E. Nelson, L. S. Bates, in *Adv. Chem. Ser.* 57 (1966).

13. J. W. Paulis, C. James, J. S. Wall, *J. Agric. Food Chem.* 17, 1301 (1969).

14. F. Aguirre, R. Bressani, N. S. Scrimshaw, *Food Res.* 18, 273 (1953).

15. *WHO Tech. Rep. Ser.* 477 (World Health Organization, Geneva, 1971).

16. L. V. Hanken, J. E. Leklern, R. R. Brown, R. C. Mekel, *Am. J. Clin. Nutr.* 24, 730 (1971).

17. Another important nutritional supplement to the marginally deficient status of tryptophan in maize is the rather plentiful supply that occurs in beans. Thus a reciprocal relationship frequently exists with respect to beans or squash and the effective utilization of corn. However, it should be pointed out that corn tends to be more stable with respect to production and storage. On this basis, there could have been more seasonal variation in the availability of these important supplements. It is interesting in this context, that beans were domesticated considerably after maize in Mesoamerica, but this does not seem to be the case in Peru.

18. This can probably be associated with the extensive consumption of corn grits which were not treated with alkali.

19. J. M. May and D. L. McClellan, *The Ecology of Malnutrition in Mexico and Central America* (Hafner, New York, 1972). Since this manuscript was submitted, an excellent review of this problem has been published by D. A. Roe [*A Plague of Corn: The Social History of Pellagra*, Cornell Univ. Press, Ithaca, N.Y., 1973].

20. In various contemporary Latin American countries, such as Guatemala, the high consumption of coffee, which is rich in niacin, and the consumption of beans, which have a high tryptophan content, probably explain the apparent absence of pellagra.

21. C. Gopalan, *Nutr. Rev.* 26, 323 (1968).

22. R. Bressani and N. S. Scrimshaw, *J. Agric. Food Chem.* 6, 774 (1958).

23. While it is not our intent to discuss the benefits of cooking with lime as opposed to other alkali yielding salts, it is important to point out that Bressani and Scrimshaw (n. 22) reported a very significant increase in the calcium content of maize that occurred as a result of the lime treatment [See S. H. Katz and E. Foulks, *Am. J. Phys. Anthropol.* 32, 299 (1970)].

24. It is important to point out, however, that the leucine to isoleucine ratio would continue to rise in uncooked corn (n. 22) and, therefore, would tend to nullify the effects of the increased quantity of tryptophan consumed.

25. H. Driver, *Indians of North America* (Univ. of Chicago Press, Chicago, ed. 2, 1969).

26. A. L. Kroeber, *Cultural and Natural Areas of Native North America* (Univ. of California Publications in American Archaeology and Ethnology. No. 48, Berkeley, 1939).

27. G. P. Murdock, *Southwest J. Anthropol.* 7, 415 (1951).

28. ———, *Ethnographic Atlas* (Univ. of Pittsburgh Press, Pittsburgh, Pa., 1967).

29. M. D. Coe, *The Maya* (Praeger, New York, 1966).

30. J. Marcus, *Science* 180, 911 (1973).

31. E. F. Castetter and W. H. Bell, *Pima and Papago Indian Agriculture* (Univ. of New Mexico Press, Albuquerque, 1942).

32. R. H. Lowie, *The Crow Indians* (Farrar and Rinehart, New York, 1935).

33. G. F. Will and G. E. Hyde, *Corn among the Indians of the Upper Missouri* (Univ. of Nebraska Press, Lincoln, 1917).

34. G. Reichel-Dolmatoff, *Excavationes Archeologias en Puerto Hormiga* (Ediciones de la Universidad de los Andes, Bogotá, 1965).

35. C. C. Kolb, personal communication.

36. That there were specific agents who sold lime in urban centers is well documented for Aztec times [B. de Sahagún, *Florentine Codex Books 4 and 5*, C. E. Dibble and A. J. Anderson, Translators, School of American Research and Univ. of Utah, Santa Fe, (1957)].

37. S. H. Katz, unpublished data.

38. J. M. Longyear, *Copan Ceramics: A Study of Southeastern Maya Pottery* (Carnegie Institution of Washington, Publ. 597, Washington. D.C., 1951).

39. G. R. Willey, W. R. Bullard, J. B. Glass, J. C. Gifford, *Prehistoric Maya Settlements in the Belize Valley* (Peabody Museum Series 54, Harvard Univ. Press, Cambridge, Mass., 1965).

40. W. A. Haviland, *Am. Antiquity* 32, 316 (1967).

41. R. L. Beals, *Cherán: A Sierran Tarascan Village* (Smithsonian Institution, Washington, D.C., 1946).

42. G. Tantaquidgeon, *A Study of Delaware Indian Medicine Practice and Folk Belief* (Pennsylvania Historical Commission, Harrisburg, 1942).

43. P. Lindestrom, *Geographica Americae with an Account of the Delaware Indians* (Swedish Colonial Society, Philadelphia, 1925).

44. R. Redfield and A. Villa Rojas, *Chan Kom; A Maya Village* (Univ. of Chicago Press, Chicago, 1934).

45. W. C. Bennett and R. M. Zingg, *The Tarahumara: An Indian Tribe of Northern Mexico* (Univ. of Chicago Press, Chicago, 1935).

46. For a review of this concept see Katz (n. 47); M. Winton [*Am. J. Phys. Anthropol.* 32, 293 (1970)] has also reviewed this problem as it relates to the ethnographic literature on the Colombian Indians.

47. S. H. Katz, paper presented at an international seminar, under the auspices of the Centre International d'Etudes de Bio-Anthropologie et d'Anthropologie Fondamentale, on the "Unity and Diversity of Man from the Point of View of Social and Cultural Anthropology," Paris, 1972.

48. ———, in *Methods and Theories in Anthropological Genetics*, M. Crawford and P. Workman, Eds. (Univ. of New Mexico Press, Albuquerque, 1973).

49. References for the societies in Table 3 may be found in the *Bibliography of Sources Processed for the Files* (Human Relations Area Files, Inc., New Haven, Conn., 1961). The following sources that are not in the Human Relations Area Files were also consulted: J. R. Swanton, *Indian Tribes of the Lower Mississippi Valley and Adjacent Gulf Coast of Mexico* (Bureau of American Ethnology, Washington, D.C., 1911); N. Lurie, Ed., *Mountain Wolf Woman, Sister of Crashing Thunder* (Univ. of Michigan Press, Ann Arbor, 1961); G. Weltfish, *The Lost Universe* (Basic Books, New York, 1965).

50. G. P. Murdock, *Outline of World Cultures* (Yale Univ. Press, New Haven, Conn., 1972).

51. M. Pijoan, C. A. Elkin, C. O. Eslinger, *J. Nutr.* 25, 491 (1943).

23

Genetic Variability and Lactose Tolerance

Norman Kretchmer

Throughout eons of evolutionary history, milk has been the chief food of young mammals, and the milk sugar lactose has been their prime source of carbohydrate. Yet it is only among certain subgroups of one species (*Homo sapiens*), and only in the last 6 to 10 thousand years, that milk and lactose have played a role in adult nutrition. The Neolithic discovery of domestication of plants and animals, followed by the adoption of dairying, allowed certain human groups to extend the consumption of milk into a phase of the life span in which there had previously been no need for the enzymatic capacity to digest lactose. This [article] will describe the response of individuals and populations to the nutritional challenge of adult lactose consumption, insofar as we have been able to discern it from our own studies and a review of the world literature (Johnson et al. 1974).

The individual response of greatest concern to the clinician, of course, is lactose intolerance; or, to use a more generally applicable term, lactose malabsorption. There are three basic forms of lactose malabsorption, each associated with low activity of the intestinal enzyme lactase, which is specific for the substrate lactose. The three forms of lactose malabsorption are distinguishable from one another by etiology and time of onset.

CONGENITAL MALABSORPTION

This condition is rarely observed in humans. A few cases of infantile diarrhea resulting from congenital lactose malabsorption have been reported in the medical literature, including several by Holzel in England (1967) and two by Durand in Italy (1958). Congenital malabsorption of lactose is universal at all ages among the seals, sea lions and walruses (*Pinnipedia*) of the Pacific Basin. These sea mammals have no lactase in their intestines at any age, and no lactose in their milk. This does not hold true, however, for the pinnipeds of the Atlantic Basin, which follow the typical mammalian pattern with respect to synthesis of lactase and lactose. It has been suggested that the two groups of seal mammals may have evolved from different ancestors—the Pacific *Pinnipedia* from a bear-like progenitor, and their Atlantic counterparts from some sort of ancient land otter (Kretchmer and Sunshine 1967).

SECONDARY LACTOSE MALABSORPTION

This phenomenon occurs rather frequently among infants or adults who have been subjected to gastrointestinal stress. It may be observed in association with specific or nonspecific diarrhea, postoperative reactions, the use of various drugs, etc. In each case, the inciting agent has caused the enzyme lactase to be obliterated from the intestine. Activity of lactase generally reappears within one to two months, as the cells of the villi regenerate. Secondary lactose malabsorption often appears in infants suffering from diarrhea (Sunshine and Kretchmer 1964), and has been familiar to pediatricians since it was first described by Abraham Jacobi in 1898.

HEREDITARY (POST-WEANING) MALABSORPTION

This form of lactose malabsorption is common among persons older than 3 to 5 years of age, and represents the typical mammalian pattern with respect to lactase activity.

In the vast majority of mammalian species, lactase activity is at its highest during the perinatal period; thereafter it decreases to very low values. Figure 1 shows the developmental profile of lactase activity in the intestine of the rat, with the characteristic elevation at about the time of birth, and a gradual decline with increasing maturity of the animal (Doell and Kretchmer 1962). In most species, there are about 10 units of lactase activity per g of intestinal mucosa in the perinatal period for every 1 unit per g of material in the adult animal. For example, the newborn kitten exhibits 4 units of enzymic activity per g of intestinal material, as compared with 0.5 units per g in the adult cat. In the dog, there are 6 units per g of intestinal material at birth, and 0.7 units in adulthood.

One exception to the general rule is the guinea pig, which is known for its early maturation; in this case, lactase activity remains almost constant from birth to maturity. The Pacific pinnipeds are also atypical, as mentioned earlier. But the most remarkable exception to the typical mammalian pattern of lactase

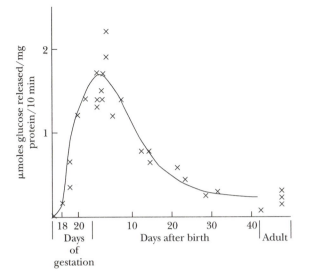

Figure 1. Lactose activity in the intestine of the rat

activity is found in the human species, some of whose adult members exhibit little or none. Although the enzyme is present in high activity (29 ± 6 units per g of intestinal mucosa) in all healthy infants, the value decreases to 2.7 ± 2 units for the adult malabsorber, as compared with 17 ± 7 units for the adult absorber.

In recent years there has been a steady accumulation of evidence, which demonstrates that lactose malabsorption in otherwise healthy adults is not only hereditary, but closely correlated with ethnic origin. Johnson et al. (1974) have surveyed the world literature on lactose malabsorption in adults and have divided the populations for which data is available into three major groups:

(1) Populations in which lactose absorbers predominate. This group includes the Danes, the Finns, the Dutch and the French, together with Poles, Czechs, Northern Italians and those Greeks living in the vicinity of Athens. In general, Northern European populations show a malabsorption rate of about 10 to 15%. A recent study of Hungarians indicates that their rate of malabsorption is about the same as that of the Finns, to whom they are linguistically related. Also included among the ethnic groups composed predominantly of absorbers are three African tribes—the Fulani of the Western sub-Saharan region, the Tussi of Uganda and Rwanda, and the Masai of Kenya and Tanzania.

(2) Populations in which the majority of adults are lactose malabsorbers. This category may well include most of the peoples of the earth. Known examples are populations of the Mediterranean Basin, Southeastern Europe, the Orient, Polynesia and Micronesia, together with a number of African tribes, Eskimos, and the Pima and Apache Indians of Arizona. Among the Yoruba of Western Nigeria, Ransome-Kuti et al. (1975)

found a malabsorption rate of 99%, while the Ibo of Eastern Nigeria attained a perfect 100%. Although few populations exhibit a 100% malabsorption rate (among the rare examples are the New Guineans, the Fijians, and those Italians in the area of Naples), the world literature indicates that major regions of the globe are inhabited by peoples who cannot digest lactose (Fig. 2).

(3) Populations formed by recent admixture between lactose-absorbing and nonabsorbing ethnic groups. These mixed populations exhibit frequencies of malabsorption intermediate between those of the parent groups. Among the mixed populations, the author has had the most experience with the Fulani-Hausa of Northern Nigeria. The Fulani, who are thought to be descendants of ancient Saharan cattle herders, are predominantly lactose absorbers. The Hausa, who are descended from ancient Berbers, are malabsorbers. In the population formed by intermarriage between the two groups, 60–70% of the adults are malabsorbers. American Negroes exhibit a malabsorption rate of approximately 80%, but the average for mixed populations is about 70%.

The data summarized above indicate that the capacity for adult lactose absorption is not randomly distributed among the peoples of the world. Populations in which absorbers predominate seem to be derived exclusively from those portions of the Old World in which dairying has been practiced for centuries. Figure 3 illustrates the extent of dairying as of 1500 A.D. At that time, there was a single large region of milk-using peoples extending from Tibet and Mongolia in the East to the Iberian Peninsula in the West, and southward into the Indian subcontinent and sub-Saharan Africa. There were also several large zones where milking was not practiced: in the Far East, Equatorial Africa, Oceania and the Americas. Populations which contain a significant minority of absorbers will generally have some history of admixture with a population from the traditional dairying zone.

This correlation between the ethnic and geographical distribution of lactose malabsorption and the traditional geographical distribution of dairying has led Simoons (1970) to formulate the so-called *cultural-historical hypothesis* which, simply stated, suggests that those peoples whose origins lie in the traditionally milk-drinking regions of the world are likely to have become, by genetic selection, lactose absorbers, while peoples whose origins lie elsewhere would never have acquired the enzymatic capacity for lactose digestion in adulthood.

Obviously, it is not possible to devise a direct test of the cultural-historical hypothesis. However, we can identify certain questions whose answers will have a strong bearing on the ultimate acceptance or rejection

% Malabsorbers

	0	20	40	60	80	100

A. GROUPS AMONG WHOM MALABSORPTION PREDOMINATES

I. THOSE WITH ORIGINS IN THE TRADITIONAL ZONE OF NONMILKING (see map) (1038 individuals tested)

1. In Africa	(321)
South Nigeria peoples	(113)
Bantu of Cameroons, Congo, Uganda, Zambia, South Africa	(179)
Surinam bush Negroes	(29)
2. In Eastern Asia	(543)
Thai	(324)
Indonesians	(53)
Chinese	(162)
Koreans	(4)
3. In the Pacific area	(20)
New Guineans	(8)
Fijians	(12)
4. In North and South America	(154)
Eskimo and Indians of Alaska	(36)
Pure-bred Greenland Eskimo	(25)
Indians of Canada's West Coast	(30)
U.S. Indians	(39)
Chami Indians of Colombia	(24)

II. THOSE WITH ORIGINS IN THE TRADITIONAL ZONE OF MILKING (724 individuals tested)

1. Mediterranean and Near East	(533)
Italians in the Naples area	(9)
Greek Cypriots	(17)
Arabs	(121)
Jews	(386)
In Israel	(310)
In Canada and the U.S.	(76)
2. In India	(156)
Indians from areas other than the Northwest	(138)
Overseas Indians	(18)
3. In Africa	(35)
Hausa	(17)
Nilotes and Nilo-Hamites	(18)

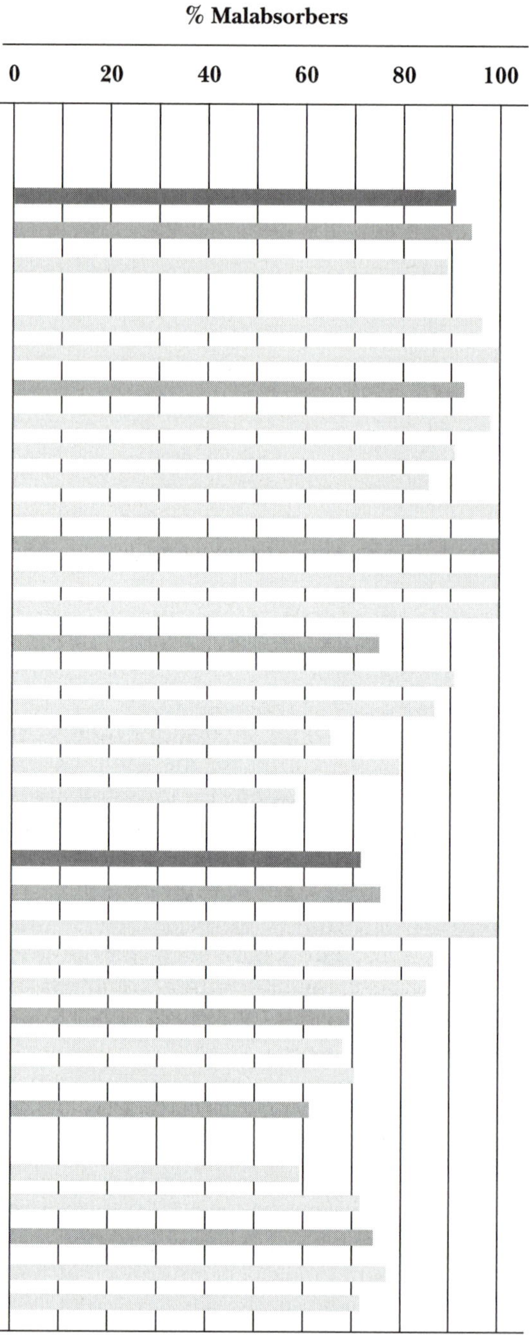

In preparing the above table results of studies were used only if they involved one of the two most reliable, widely used tests of malabsorption: (1) lactose loading test, which measures the rise of blood glucose, and (2) assay of lactase activity following intestinal biopsy. Excluded from consideration were all studies using testing procedures of questionable reliability or studies focusing on symptoms rather than on absorption per se.

Excluded were all studies of children. Also eliminated, insofar as possible, were individuals among whom malabsorption may have been secondary, in cases where the incidence of malabsorption in the study group may have been significantly influenced. Also not taken into our account were those studies in which data presented did not permit the determination of percentage of malabsorption in the group in question.

Figure 2. Differences in lactose malabsorption among the world's peoples (adults) A. Groups among whom malabsorption predominates; B. Groups among whom absorption predominates and whose origins are in the traditional zone of milking; C. Mixed groups: Malabsorbers × absorbers.

% Malabsorbers

0   20   40   60   80   100

B. GROUPS AMONG WHOM ABSORPTION PREDOMINATES
AND WHOSE ORIGINS ARE IN THE TRADITIONAL ZONE
OF MILKING (2102 individuals tested)

  1. In Africa   (52)

    Hima   (11)
    Tussi   (32)
    Nomadic Fulani   (9)

  2. In India   (79)

    Indians born in the Punjab   (9)
    Indians of the New Delhi area   (70)

  3. In Europe   (1971)

    Danes   (670)
    Finns   (293)
    Germans   (55)
    Dutch   (14)
    French   (14)
    Poles   (21)
    Czechs   (17)
    North Italians   (40)
    Greeks in Athens   (226)
    Overseas groups largely of north European origin

      Canadians of northwest European origin   (16)
      White Australians   (133)
      White Americans   (454)
      Others   (18)

C. MIXED GROUPS: MALABSORBERS × ABSORBERS
(Malabsorption incidences intermediate between those
of parental groups) (295 individuals tested)

  1. African malabsorbers × African absorbers   (67)

    Hausa/Fulani   (39)
    Iru   (13)
    Hutu   (15)

  2. African malabsorbers × European absorbers   (138)

    Surinam Creoles   (31)
    American Negroes   (107)

  3. Asian malabsorbers × European absorbers   (6)

    Thai/English   (6)

  4. Native American malabsorbers × European
    absorbers   (84)

    Greenland Eskimos with Danish grandparent   (7)
    Mexican Americans   (11)
    Colombian Mestizos   (16)
    Peruvian Mestizos   (50)

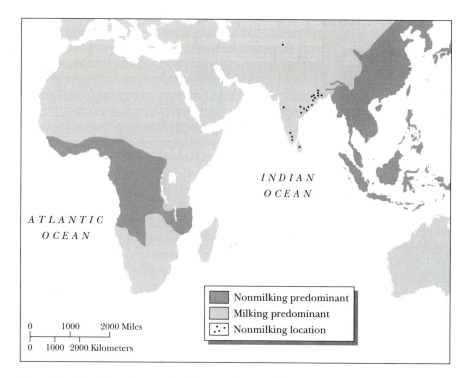

Figure 3. Traditional areas of milking and nonmilking

of the hypothesis. First, what is the pattern of inheritance of lactose malabsorption? Second, which was the original "wild type"—the absorber or the malabsorber? Third, has adequate time elapsed since the advent of dairying to account for the present-day frequency of lactose absorption in the peoples of the so-called "milking zone"?

Investigations aimed at delineating the pattern of inheritance of lactose malabsorption have recently been carried out by Ransome-Kuti et al. (1975) in Nigeria and by Simoons et al. (unpub.) among the Pima and related American Indian tribes of the Phoenix, Arizona, area. In both instances, the investigators have taken advantage of a situation in which the recent admixture of absorbing and nonabsorbing ethnic stocks guarantees a large number of marriages between individuals who differ in their capacity for lactose absorption.

The results of these and other family studies, summarized in Table 1, suggest that the ability to absorb lactose by an adult human is inherited as a dominant trait. Thus, when a heterozygous lactose digestor (Dd) marries either a homozygous lactose nondigestor (dd) or another heterozygous lactose digestor (Dd), statistically the progeny could be expected to be a mixture of both types, i.e., digesters (50–75%) and nondigestors (25–50%). However, in the case of a cross between two lactose nondigestors (dd), none of the progeny should be capable of digesting lactose. There is one report in the literature (Welsh et al. 1968) of a digestor arising

out of a cross between two nondigestors, but this case is exceptional and may indicate nonpaternity.

Continuous intermarriage between a small population of lactose absorbers and a larger population of nonabsorbers should eventually lead to dilution of the gene for adult lactase in the population. This has been the case in Northern Nigeria, where descendants of the nomadic, lactose-absorbing Fulani began to intermarry 200 years ago with the Hausa, a sedentary group of nonabsorbers. The progeny from the Hausa-Fulani crosses have continued to marry into the larger population of Hausa town dwellers, giving rise to a population which is relatively incapable of digesting lactose, but retains many of the cultural traits of the Fulani.

Although the American Negro population is derived primarily from West African peoples who are nondigestors of lactose, it has a surprising frequency of 20–30% adult lactose digesters. This observation could be explained on the basis of unions with Northern European groups composed predominantly (about 90%) of lactose digestors, and fits with information derived from studies of the Gm genotype among American Caucasians and Negroes (Ransome-Kuti et al. 1975).

It is probable that the human ability to digest lactose in adulthood is the result of a mutation in a gene affecting the level of intestinal lactose activity, such that a value of 17 ± 7 units is attained in place of the 2.7 ± 2 units typically present in the nondigestor. Since the usual characteristic of mammals is elevated activity

Table 1.   Summary of families in this study and from the literature

Predicted Genetic Notation	No. of Families	Progeny[1]	
		Digestors (D–)	Nondigestors (dd)
A. Families taken from the literature			
dd × dd	12	1	34
D × dd	15	24	23
D– × D–	3	8	4
B. Nigerian families (Ransome-Kuti et al. 1975)			
dd × dd	9	0	21
D– × dd	10	18	11

[1]The progeny are listed as lactose digestors and nondigestors. The marriages are given a predicted genetic notation.

of the enzyme during infancy and markedly diminished activity in the adult, it seems reasonable to suppose that the nondigestor represents the original "wild type" and the digestor the mutant type. If this is the case, then it seems reasonable to hypothesize that selective pressure may have increased the frequency of lactose digestors in those ethnic groups which practiced milk-drinking.

Cavalli-Sforza (1973) has calculated that a coefficient of selection of 3% operating over a span of 10,000 years would be sufficient to give rise to the high frequency of adult lactose absorption observed among Northern Europeans and certain African tribes today. Direct evidence for the antiquity of dairying can be found in certain rock drawings from the Sahara which depict the milking of cattle, and are dated at ca. 4000 to 3000 B.C. However, the earliest known domestication of a herd animal, that of the sheep, dates to about 9000 B.C. in the Near East. Presumably the initiation of dairying must have occurred sometime between these two events. Further investigations by archaeologists and palaeoanthropologists are needed to determine whether dairying has in fact existed long enough to produce the postulated changes in gene frequency.

If the cultural-historical hypothesis does indeed withstand the test of further investigation, the implications for future nutritional research—and even more significantly, for future nutritional planning—will be enormous. For milk-drinking is only one of dozens of food consumption patterns which have arisen and spread across the world in the last ten thousand years. If differences in milk consumption have in fact led to genetic divergence among human populations, it may well be that other differences have arisen in response to other foodstuffs. There is a definite need for research to determine the true extent of individual and ethnic idiosyncrasies with respect to the most common elements of our diet.

REFERENCES

Cavalli-Sforza, L. L. 1973. Analytic review: Some current problems of human genetics. Am. J. Hum. Gen. *25*, 82–104.

Doell, R. G., and Kretchmer, N. 1962. Studies of small intestine during development. I. Distribution and activity of β-galactosidase. Biochem. Biophys. Acta *62*, 353.

Durand, P. 1958. Idiopathic lactosuria in a patient with chronic acidic diarrhea. Minerva Pediatr. *10*, 706. (Italian)

Holzel, A. 1967. Sugar malabsorption due to deficiencies of disaccharidase activities and of monosaccharide transport. Arch. Dis. Child. *42*, 341.

Johnson, J. D., Kretchmer, N., and Simoons, F. J. 1974. Lactose malabsorption: Its biology and history. Adv. in Pediatr. *21*, 197–238.

Kretchmer, N., and Sunshine, P. 1967. Intestinal disaccharidase deficiency in the sea lion. Gastroenterology *53*, 123.

Ransome-Kuti, O., Kretchmer, N., Johnson, J., and Gribble, J. T. 1975. A genetic study of lactose digestion in Nigerian families. Gastroenterology *68*, 431–436.

Simoons, F. J. 1970. Primary adult lactose intolerance and the milking habit: A problem in biological and cultural interrelations. II. A cultural-historical hypothesis. Am. J. Dig. Dis. *15*, 695.

Simoons, F. J. et al. Lactose malabsorption among the Indians of the American Southwest. (Two unpublished papers)

Sunshine, P., and Kretchmer, N. 1964. Studies of the small intestine during development. III. Infantile diarrhea associated with intolerance to disaccharides. Pediatrics *34*, 38–50.

Welsh, J. D. et al. 1968. Studies of lactose intolerance in families. Arch. Intern. Med. *122*, 315–316.

24

The Tall *and* the Short of It

Barry Bogin

Baffled by your future prospects? As a biological anthropologist, I have just one word of advice for you: plasticity. *Plasticity* refers to the ability of many organisms, including humans, to alter themselves—their behavior or even their biology—in response to changes in the environment. We tend to think that our bodies get locked into their final form by our genes, but in fact we alter our bodies as the conditions surrounding us shift, particularly as we grow during childhood. Plasticity is as much a product of evolution's fine-tuning as any particular gene, and it makes just as much evolutionary good sense. Rather than being able to adapt to a single environment, we can, thanks to plasticity, change our bodies to cope with a wide range of environments. Combined with the genes we inherit from our parents, plasticity accounts for what we are and what we can become.

Anthropologists began to think about human plasticity around the turn of the century, but the concept was first clearly defined in 1969 by Gabriel Lasker, a biological anthropologist at Wayne State University in Detroit. At that time scientists tended to consider only those adaptations that were built into the genetic makeup of a person and passed on automatically to the next generation. A classic example of this is the ability of adults in some human societies to drink milk. As children, we all produce an enzyme called lactase, which we need to break down the sugar lactose in our mother's milk. In many of us, however, the lactase gene slows down dramatically as we approach adolescence—probably as the result of another gene that regulates its activity. When that regulating gene turns down the production of lactase, we can no longer digest milk.

Lactose intolerance—which causes intestinal gas and diarrhea—affects between 70 and 90 percent of African Americans, Native Americans, Asians, and people who come from around the Mediterranean. But others, such as people of central and western European descent and the Fulani of West Africa, typically have no problem drinking milk as adults. That's because they are descended from societies with long histories of raising goats and cattle. Among these people there was a clear benefit to being able to drink milk, so natural selection gradually changed the regulation of their lactase gene, keeping it functioning throughout life.

That kind of adaptation takes many centuries to become established, but Lasker pointed out that there are two other kinds of adaptation in humans that need far less time to kick in. If people have to face a cold winter with little or no heat, for example, their metabolic rates rise over the course of a few weeks and they produce more body heat. When summer returns, the rates sink again.

Lasker's other mode of adaptation concerned the irreversible, lifelong modification of people as they develop—that is, their plasticity. Because we humans take so many years to grow to adulthood, and because we live in so many different environments, from forests to cities and from deserts to the Arctic, we are among the world's most variable species in our physical form and behavior. Indeed, we are one of the most plastic of all species.

One of the most obvious manifestations of human malleability is our great range of height, and it is a subject I've made a special study of for the last 25 years. Consider these statistics: in 1850 Americans were the tallest people in the world, with American men averaging 5' 6". Almost 150 years later, American men now average 5' 8", but we have fallen in the standings and are now only the third tallest people in the world. In first place are the Dutch. Back in 1850 they averaged only 5' 4"—the shortest men in Europe—but today they are a towering 5' 10". (In these two groups, and just about everywhere else, women average about five inches less than men at all times.)

So what happened? Did all the short Dutch sail over to the United States? Did the Dutch back in Europe get an infusion of "tall genes"? Neither. In both America and the Netherlands life got better, but more so for the Dutch, and height increased as a result. We know this is true thanks in part to studies on how height is determined. It's the product of plasticity in our childhood and in our mothers' childhood as well. If a girl is undernourished and suffers poor health, the growth of her body, including her reproductive system, is usually reduced. With a shortage of raw materials, she can't build more cells to construct a bigger body; at the same time, she has to invest what materials she can get into repairing already existing cells and tissues from the damage caused by disease. Her shorter stature as an adult is the result of a compromise her body makes while growing up.

192

Such a woman can pass on her short stature to her child, but genes have nothing to do with it for either of them. If she becomes pregnant, her small reproductive system probably won't be able to supply a normal level of nutrients and oxygen to her fetus. This harsh environment reprograms the fetus to grow more slowly than it would if the woman was healthier, so she is more likely to give birth to a smaller baby. Low-birth-weight babies (weighing less than 5.5 pounds) tend to continue their prenatal program of slow growth through childhood. By the time they are teenagers, they are usually significantly shorter than people of normal birth weight. Some particularly striking evidence of this reprogramming comes from studies on monozygotic twins, which develop from a single fertilized egg cell and are therefore identical genetically. But in certain cases, monozygotic twins end up being nourished by unequal portions of the placenta. The twin with the smaller fraction of the placenta is often born with low birth weight, while the other one is normal. Follow-up studies show that this difference between the twins can last throughout their lives.

As such research suggests, we can use the average height of any group of people as a barometer of the health of their society. After the turn of the century both the United States and the Netherlands began to protect the health of their citizens by purifying drinking water, installing sewer systems, regulating the safety of food, and, most important, providing better health care and diets to children. The children responded to their changed environment by growing taller. But the differences in Dutch and American societies determined their differing heights today. The Dutch decided to provide public health benefits to all the public, including the poor. In the United States, meanwhile, improved health is enjoyed most by those who can afford it. The poor often lack adequate housing, sanitation, and health care. The difference in our two societies can be seen at birth: in 1990 only 4 percent of Dutch babies were born at low birth weight, compared with 7 percent in the United States. For white Americans the rate was 5.7 percent, and for black Americans the rate was a whopping 13.3 percent. The disparity between rich and poor in the United States carries through to adulthood: poor Americans are shorter than the better-off by about one inch. Thus, despite great affluence in the United States, our average height has fallen to third place.

People are often surprised when I tell them the Dutch are the tallest people in the world. Aren't they shrimps compared with the famously tall Tutsi (or "Watusi," as you probably first encountered them) of Central Africa? Actually, the supposed great height of the Tutsi is one of the most durable myths from the age of European exploration. Careful investigation reveals that today's Tutsi men average 5' 7" and that they have maintained that average for more than 100 years. That means that back in the 1800s, when puny European men first met the Tutsi, the Europeans suffered strained necks from looking up all the time. The two-to-three-inch difference in average height back then could easily have turned into fantastic stories of African giants by European adventurers and writers.

The Tutsi could be as tall or taller than the Dutch if equally good health care and diets were available in Rwanda and Burundi, where the Tutsi live. But poverty rules the lives of most African people, punctuated by warfare, which makes the conditions for growth during childhood even worse. And indeed, it turns out that the Tutsi and other Africans who migrate to Western Europe or North America at young ages end up taller than Africans remaining in Africa.

At the other end of the height spectrum, Pygmies tell a similar story. The shortest people in the world today are the Mbuti, the Efe, and other Pygmy peoples of Central Africa. Their average stature is about 4' 9" for adult men and 4' 6" for women. Part of the reason Pygmies are short is indeed genetic: some evidently lack the genes for producing the growth-promoting hormones that course through other people's bodies, while others are genetically incapable of using these hormones to trigger the cascade of reactions that lead to growth. But another important reason for their small size is environmental. Pygmies living as hunter-gatherers in the forests of Central African countries appear to be undernourished, which further limits their growth. Pygmies who live on farms and ranches outside the forest are better fed than their hunter-gatherer relatives and are taller as well. Both genes and nutrition thus account for the size of Pygmies.

Peoples in other parts of the world have also been labeled pygmies, such as some groups in Southeast Asia and the Maya of Guatemala. Well-meaning explorers and scientists have often claimed that they are genetically short, but here we encounter another myth of height. A group of extremely short people in New Guinea, for example, turned out to eat a diet deficient in iodine and other essential nutrients. When they were supplied with cheap mineral and vitamin supplements, their supposedly genetic short stature vanished in their children, who grew to a more normal height.

◆ ◆ ◆

Another way for these so-called pygmies to stop being pygmies is to immigrate to the United States. In my own research, I study the growth of two groups of Mayan children. One group lives in their homeland of Guatemala, and the other is a group of refugees living in the United States. The Maya in Guatemala live in the village of San Pedro, which has no safe source of drinking water. Most of the water is contaminated with fertilizers and pesticides used on nearby agricultural fields. Until recently, when a deep well was dug, the townspeople depended on an unreliable supply of water from rain-swollen streams. Most homes still lack running water and have only pit toilets. The parents of the Mayan children work mostly at clothing factories and are paid only a few dollars a day.

I began working with the schoolchildren in this village in 1979, and my research shows that most of them eat only 80 percent of the food they need. Other research shows that almost 30 percent of the girls and 20 percent of the boys are deficient in iodine, that most of the children suffer from intestinal parasites, and that many have persistent ear and eye infections. As a consequence, their health is poor and their height reflects it: they average about three inches shorter than better-fed Guatemalan children.

The Mayan refugees I work with in the United States live in Los Angeles and in the rural agricultural community of Indiantown in central Florida. Although the adults work mostly in minimum-wage jobs, the children in these communities are generally better off than their counterparts in Guatemala. Most Maya arrived in the 1980s as refugees escaping a civil war as well as a political system that threatened them and their children. In the United States they found security and started new lives, and before long their children began growing faster and bigger. My data show that the average increase in height among the first generation of these immigrants was 2.2 inches, which means that these so-called pygmies have undergone one of the largest single-generation increases in height ever recorded. When people such as my own grandparents migrated from the poverty of rural life in Eastern Europe to the cities of the United States just after World War I, the increase in height of the next generation was only about one inch.

One reason for the rapid increase in stature is that in the United States the Maya have access to treated drinking water and to a reliable supply of food. Especially critical are school breakfast and lunch programs for children from low-income families, as well as public assistance programs such as the federal Women, Infants, and Children (WIC) program and food stamps. That these programs improve health and growth is no secret. What is surprising is how fast they work. Mayan mothers in the United States tell me that even their babies are bigger and healthier than the babies they raised in Guatemala, and hospital statistics bear them out. These women must be enjoying a level of health so improved from that of their lives in Guatemala that their babies are growing faster in the womb. Of course, plasticity means that such changes are dependent on external conditions, and unfortunately the rising height—and health—of the Maya is in danger from

political forces that are attempting to cut funding for food stamps and the WIC program. If that funding is cut, the negative impact on the lives of poor Americans, including the Mayan refugees, will be as dramatic as were the former positive effects.

Height is only the most obvious example of plasticity's power; there are others to be found everywhere you look. The Andes-dwelling Quechua people of Peru are well-adapted to their high-altitude homes. Their large, barrel-shaped chests house big lungs that inspire huge amounts of air with each breath, and they manage to survive on the lower pressure of oxygen they breathe with an unusually high level of red blood cells. Yet these secrets of mountain living are not hereditary. Instead the bodies of young Quechua adapt as they grow in their particular environment, just as those of European children do when they live at high altitudes.

Plasticity may also have a hand in determining our risks for developing a number of diseases. For example, scientists have long been searching for a cause for Parkinson's disease. Because Parkinson's tends to run in families, it is natural to think there is a genetic cause. But while a genetic mutation linked to some types of Parkinson's disease was reported in mid-1997, the gene accounts for only a fraction of people with the disease. Many more people with Parkinson's do not have the gene, and not all people with the mutated gene develop the disease.

Ralph Garruto, a medical researcher and biological anthropologist at the National Institutes of Health, is investigating the role of the environment and human plasticity not only in Parkinson's but in Lou Gehrig's disease as well. Garruto and his team traveled to the islands of Guam and New Guinea, where rates of both diseases are 50 to 100 times higher than in the United States. Among the native Chamorro people of Guam these diseases kill one person out of every five over the age of 25. The scientists found that both diseases are linked to a shortage of calcium in the diet. This shortage sets off a cascade of events that result in the digestive system's absorbing too much of the aluminum present in the diet. The aluminum wreaks havoc on various parts of the body, including the brain, where it destroys neurons and eventually causes paralysis and death.

The most amazing discovery made by Garruto's team is that up to 70 percent of the people they studied in Guam had some brain damage, but only 20 percent progressed all the way to Parkinson's or Lou Gehrig's disease. Genes and plasticity seem to be working hand in hand to produce these lower-than-expected rates of disease. There is a certain amount of genetic variation in the ability that all people have in coping with calcium shortages—some can function better than others. But thanks to plasticity, it's also possible for people's bodies to gradually develop ways to protect themselves against aluminum poisoning. Some people develop biochemical barriers to the aluminum they eat, while others develop ways to prevent the aluminum from reaching the brain.

An appreciation of plasticity may temper some of our fears about these diseases and even offer some hope. For if Parkinson's and Lou Gehrig's diseases can be prevented among the Chamorro by plasticity, then maybe medical researchers can figure out a way to produce the same sort of plastic changes in you and me. Maybe Lou Gehrig's disease and Parkinson's disease—as well as many others, including some cancers—aren't our genetic doom but a product of our development, just like variations in human height. And maybe their danger will in time prove as illusory as the notion that the Tutsi are giants, or the Maya pygmies—or Americans still the tallest of the tall.

Food as Medicine

The distinction between food and medicine may seem clear enough when you inventory your medicine cabinet and your refrigerator. The things in your medicine cabinet are probably tablets of various shapes, colors, and sizes, and bottles of moderately foul-tasting thick liquids, all of which have specific instructions about how often and how much to consume, as well as why you should consume them—that is, a description of the symptoms they promise to alleviate. In the refrigerator, on the other hand, there may be things like bottles of fruit juice, cartons of milk, eggs, carrots, and other things you might consume when hungry. The packaging has lots of printing, but no specific directions as to how often or in what amounts the foods should be consumed, and usually no specific instructions as to why they should be consumed. Consume as desired!

The distinction between medicine and food is less clear when you try to define the two terms. One definition of *medicine* is ". . . a substance that when taken into the living organism may modify one or more of its functions" (Thomas, 1973). That definition would serve for food as well, because the consumption of a food results in some physiological changes, if only the production of digestive enzymes.

The distinction is even murkier when you think about the effects we know some foods have on disease. A classic example is scurvy, an ugly disease characterized by joint pain, muscle weakness, and bleeding gums. We now understand that scurvy is a result of an inadequate intake of vitamin C (ascorbic acid) and would treat the symptoms with vitamin C tablets. In the eighteenth century, when scurvy was devastating the crews of British sailing ships on their voyages of exploration around the globe, no one knew what vitamin C was. However, the British did know that the symptoms could be cured by eating fresh vegetables. Captain James Cook, the famous explorer, reported that outbreaks of scurvy in his crew caused him to make a number of unscheduled stops to get the edible "green stuff" that would cure it (Watt, 1981). The problem on these sailing ships was that the diet was pretty much limited to food that was easily preserved and transported, such as "biscuits," oatmeal, dried peas, butter, cheese, and beer (Lloyd, 1981). The British finally figured out that carrying lemons would prevent scurvy and hence eliminate the need to go ashore for edible green stuff. In essence, British sailors, soon called "limeys" for now obvious reasons, first used particular foods to cure a disease and then learned to use another food to prevent that same disease.

A more familiar example is the use of diet to treat the problem of high serum (blood) cholesterol levels, not a disease per se, but a well-known risk factor for developing cardiovascular disease. In the case of high serum cholesterol, diet therapy is recommended in two ways: (1) to reduce the amount of animal foods in the diet, and hence the amount of cholesterol coming in through the diet (the human body always produces some cholesterol); (2) to increase high-fiber foods, such as oat bran, fruits, and legumes, that act to limit the amount of cholesterol absorbed in the small intestine.

The first article in this part, "Chinese Nutritional Therapy," was written by Eugene Anderson, a cultural anthropologist who has devoted his career to exploring the ways in which traditional societies manage their natural resources. Anderson focuses specifically on the use of food as medicine in traditional Chinese society. He describes a very complex and ancient system of food beliefs relating food to health. In this system, foods are classified into a number of different categories: heating versus cooling, *pu* (strengthening), *tu* (poison-potentiating), *ch'ing* (cleansing), and *hsiao* (dispelling). Anderson argues that the system fits reasonably well, although not perfectly, with actual empirical observations people have made, as well as with Chinese cosmology (beliefs about the form and nature of the universe as a whole). It is a very comprehensive system in that almost any illness can be treated with a change in diet. It is also a system in which the distinction between "food" and "medicine" is blurred. For the Chinese studied by Anderson, food is medicine, and some medicines, such as herbal medicines, are consumed in significant enough quantities to be considered foods.

The second article in this part, "You Are What You Eat: Religious Aspects of the Health Food Movement," brings the discussion of food and medicine closer to home: It is about the health food movement in the United States. The author, Jill Dubisch, is a cultural anthropologist interested in ritual and religion. Her thesis in the article may take you by surprise; it is that the health food movement is not only a way of eating, but a kind of religion. Dubisch describes the health food movement as a belief system centered around the relationship between diet and health that is complete with sacred symbols and sacred texts. The main classification scheme is not hot-cold, but rather "junk foods" versus "natural foods." The purity of foods is a particularly important concern; the purest foods are the most "natural" and least processed. Dubisch's article was published in 1981, and while it was an excellent portrayal of the health food movement then, it may now seem to be describing an unfamiliar culture. Interestingly, what has happened is that the health food movement has moved from the fringes to become a big industry. Many of the practices she describes have become integrated into the mainstream, and many of the food items that could be found only in a health food store in the early 1980s are widely available in supermarkets now.

In summary, the two articles that follow force us to take a closer look at two conceptual categories we probably have taken for granted—food and medicine. There are a number of parallels in the belief systems they describe, but more importantly the examples they present serve to underscore the general observation that all human societies classify foods into a limited set of categories, use these categories to define their diet, and relate diet to health.

SUGGESTIONS FOR THINKING AND DOING NUTRITIONAL ANTHROPOLOGY

1. The articles in this part describe two different food classification systems. What other systems are you familiar with? How do they work? How are they related to health? If you have trouble thinking of one, think of what you were taught as a child at home or in school.

2. Go to a bookstore and look at the titles on diet. How many are directly related to health (not just weight loss)? How many describe ways to address problems, such as psychological problems, through diet?

3. Pretend you are a nutritional anthropologist from Mars. Go to a supermarket and take note of any and all types of information related to diet and health (posters, food displays, leaflets, books, and so on). Do the same exercise at a health food store. What is the difference? Do you agree with Dubisch that health food stores are "temples," where the purity of the health food movement is maintained? Why or why not?

SUGGESTED READINGS AND REFERENCES

Deutsch, R. M. (1977). *The new nuts among the berries*. Palo Alto, CA: Bull Publishing Company. (A delightful history of food fads in the United States.)

Etkin, N. L. (Ed.). (1986). *Plants in indigenous medicine and diet: Biobehavioral approaches*. Bedford Hill, NY: Redgrave Publishing Company.

———. (Ed.). (1994). *Eating on the wild side: The pharmacologic, ecologic, and social implications of using noncultigens*. Tucson: University of Arizona Press.

Lloyd, C. C. (1981). "Victualling of the fleet in the eighteenth and nineteenth centuries." In James Watt, E. J. Freeman, & W. F. Bynum (Eds.), *Starving sailors: The influence of nutrition upon naval and maritime history* (pp. 9–15). Bristol, England: National Maritime Museum.

Thomas, C. L. (1973). *Tabor's cyclopedic medical dictionary*. Philadelphia: F. A. Davis Company.

Watt, J. (1981). "Some consequences of nutritional disorders in eighteenth-century British circumnavigations." In J. Watt, E. J. Freeman, & W. F. Bynum (Eds.), *Starving sailors: The influence of nutrition upon naval and maritime history* (pp. 51–72). Bristol, England: National Maritime Museum.

25

Chinese Nutritional Therapy

Eugene N. Anderson

Chinese nutritional therapy—the use of food as medicine, to treat illness and physical challenge—provides an ideal ground for studies of how people think about their place in the organic world. Unlike many folk systems of medicine, Chinese nutrition has a long written history. Doctors and food experts have devoted much effort to articulating and systematizing a vast amount of information. Much of the data comes from folk observation—the empirical experience of generations of farmers and workers.

In Chinese medicine, humans as total persons confront a world of plants, animals, and minerals that have varied medical functions. The line between food and medicine does not exist; all foods have some medical significance, and many medicinal herbs are eaten in enough quantity to count as foodstuffs.

Theoretically, there is an infinite number of possible ways of thinking about food and health. The Chinese have constructed a system that represents empirical experience well; fits with their cosmology . . . ; and fits with their views on the individual and society. It is a system that classifies and arranges a great number of facts—statements that are true by the standards of Western laboratory science as well as Chinese experience. It incorporates these truths into a plausible and logical structure, and ties the whole thing to the network of emotions, personal values, and deeply held beliefs that sustain Chinese society. To put it a bit crudely, the system wouldn't sell if it didn't work. But, also, it wouldn't sell if it didn't fit with the rest of the Chinese system of thought and feeling.

In this [article], I provide a rather thorough account of the traditional Chinese construction of nutritional knowledge. I then show how and why it is logically compelling, given the assumptions of Chinese logic. Finally, I suggest some ways in which it seems to fit well with the Chinese experience of being a person in society.

Cultural ecology concerns itself with all human relationships with the environment. Food is one of the field's main concerns. Foodways provide good examples of demand-driven systems. Foods are produced because people need to eat and want particular foods. The cultural ecologist studies not only food production, but also food consumption.

Thus, I came to study Chinese food.[1] I adopted the "food system" approach widely used in nutritional anthropology, in which production, distribution, and consumption are studied as one system. I found I needed to employ this model in order to work in fisheries development. People were, after all, producing fish for a market. The nature of the market—pcople's preferences for different types of fish—determined what could be sold.

This led me to investigate Chinese nutritional therapy. Many fish and other food products were produced and sold because they were believed to have medicinal properties. Medical foodways are so important in Chinese culture that they have had important effects on the course of Chinese food production.

Recently, the effects have been disastrous, because many rare species are believed to be medicinally valuable: rhinos are killed for their horn, swiftlets for their edible nests, bears for their gall. Until the last few years, however, Chinese medicinal food use has been a force for ecological good.[2] It has kept the Chinese agricultural system diverse. It has led—and is still leading—to the cultivation of dozens of species, some of which might otherwise have been lost. One hopes that it will continue to serve as an incentive to domestication or preservation. Surely, before the bears run out, someone will take steps to preserve them as a health resource.

Thus, while food consumption may not seem directly related to the ecological mission of this book, it is in fact central. First, food consumption drives food production, and thus affects the whole ecosystem.[3] Second, the logic of Chinese food consumption reveals a great deal about how people think about resources. As such, it is absolutely central to my argument, and necessary for what follows. This [article] may seem long and detailed, but the data simply must be presented with some thoroughness.

Chinese nutritional medicine has its own logic, which is based on a wide and deep empirical knowledge base. Here, as with *feng-shui*, we have a system that has vastly influenced resource management, through a logic that is unique and distinctive.

Chinese medicine is a tradition several thousand years old. It has its general ideological grounding and its separate schools and findings. Put another way, it is an accommodation between an ideology and the experience of millions of Chinese in healing the sick and maintaining strength in the healthy. The Chinese learned many empirical facts—the "natural resources" of information, to be managed like any other resource. This is what psychologists would expect; people relate new information to what they already know, and structure it in terms of their preexisting structures of thought.[4]

China now holds one-fourth of the world's population, yet has only 7 percent of its cropland. Feeding its enormous population has always been an enormous task. Naturally, through millennia of famine and want, the Chinese have learned an inconceivably vast amount about food—how to produce it, how to process it, how to consume it, and how to cope with deficiencies.[5]

Chinese nutritional therapy has relatives worldwide.[6] We shall examine the belief that some foods are heating, others cooling to the body. Most of the world's cultures have beliefs of this kind—often strikingly similar to Chinese beliefs. Thus, the theoretical foundations of Chinese medicine[7] must have some general appeal of plausibility.

As early as the Chou Dynasty (ca. 1100–221 B.C.), the court dietitians were the highest-ranked of the court medical staff. So says the *Chou Li,* the court manual of the Chou. The surviving form of it was heavily reconstructed by the Han Dynasty (206 B.C.–221 A.D.), so we may possibly have a Han courtier's ideal Chou rather than the reality. However, the Han scholars tried hard for accuracy, at least in minor and relatively noncontroversial matters of this sort. The companion work *Li Chi,* in its further accounts of Chou rites, contains much more about food, especially about what dishes are appropriate for what settings: seasonal sacrifices, august banquets, informal entertainments of gentlemen of high or low rank, and so forth. It even specifies appropriate dishes for serving the elderly, and these are easily digestible dishes high in protein, calcium, and iron. The Han Dynasty itself produced a number of medical works, based to some unknown degree on earlier books, that include a considerable amount of sophisticated nutritional knowledge and theory.[8]

There is no question why "China, land of famine"[9] has always put nutrition at the head of the list of medical specializations. Malnutrition was by far the single most important cause of death, killing countless millions directly and weakening countless more so that they died of disease. The Chinese quite properly looked to nutrition in both cases. Moreover, nutrition and its effects were easy to observe in village and family. Herbal medicine probably arose as a handmaiden of nutrition, and has continued to blend into it. The herbals all discuss foods at length. By contrast, the European world focused early on surgery, ranked low by the *Chou Li;* perhaps the Europeans' fondness for war led them to attend more to trauma!

Dominant at this time was a relatively new scientific system, based on the opposition of yang and yin and on the mutual intertransformations of the five elements: water, wood, fire, earth, metal. This system was relatively new at the time, replacing earlier systems that were heavily magical[10] or empirical. The five elements were not like the fixed, perfect elements of ancient Greek thought. In fact, "elements" is a rather arbitrary translation of a word that literally means "goings." (The same word means "street" in some parts of modern China.) Manfred Porkert translated it as "evolutive phases."[11]

We are to understand a dynamic, shifting energy in the universe, whose various manifestations can be conceptualized as woody, metallic, and so on. The same property that makes wood woody makes food sour. Changing according to the laws of cosmic evolution, the energy moves from wood to fire. The same progression is seen when food becomes bitter (scorched-tasting, more or less). Fire produces earth, as wood turns first to flame and then to ash. Similarly, bitter evolves (by some subtle process) into sweet. Earth, smelted, yields metal; sweet yields pungent. Metal collects dew, thus producing water, which is associated with the salt taste (possibly because seawater and salt brines were the Chinese salt sources). The same qualities inform the directions (north is more metallic), the organs of the body, and almost everything else, producing a fivefold classification of the cosmos.

Crosscutting this cycle is the interpenetration of yang and yin, the bright-dry and cool-wet aspects of the universe. Yang and yin do *not* mean, focally, male and female. They are derived from words for the sunny and shady slopes of a hill, as the characters show quite graphically in their early forms. Male sexuality simply involves about twice as much yang as yin energy, female sexuality the reverse.

All these various phases were aspects of *ch'i. Ch'i* means, literally, "breath." It does not really mean "energy," but Westerners (myself included) find convenience in so translating it in medical contexts. (But, still, *ch'i shui* means "aerated water," that is, soda pop—not "energized water.") Like the Greek equivalent *pneuma, ch'i* came to refer to a subtle circulating medium. It pervades the cosmos—including that microcosm, the human body. Herein it circulates by subtle channels, the meridians that acupuncturists tap at certain critical points.

Ch'i can be blocked, necessitating medical intervention, since stagnant *ch'i* is devastating to whatever part of the body it may occupy. *Ch'i* can also be depleted; for the Chinese, as for St. Augustine, evil is the privation of good. The flow and quantity of *ch'i* can also be augmented (*pu*), and it was already known that foods high in easily digestible protein augmented health and strength in just the proper way. Indeed, I suspect that we see in the foods proper to old people the ur-form of *ch'i*-strengthening lore.[12]

During the Han Dynasty, there were many debates about this new all-encompassing system. Tung Chung-shu and other Han Confucianists championed it. An older medicine of witches, ghosts, and demons challenged it,[13] as did a still newer, hardheaded rationalism (exemplified by the teachings of Wang Ch'ung) that put little faith in such grand schemes. But it provided a good scientific paradigm: simpler and clearer than other methods of schematizing the world and accounting better for the facts. The old witch-and-demon theories survived but were greatly weakened by attacks from the newer thinkers. Wang Ch'ung's rationalism succeeded in heavily (but far from totally) discrediting the demons, but had little effect on the new theories of *ch'i*, since he proposed nothing better and seems to have believed in a more cautious version of the same sort of theory.

By the sixth century A.D., when T'ao Hung-ching brought out his epochal new editions of the great medical classics, a new influence had come. In T'ao's works we find, for the first time in China, the theory of heating, cooling, wetting, drying, and neutral qualities in foods and medicines. This theory, sometimes known as the "humoral theory" because of similarities to Western humoral medicine, will be described below. Humoral medicine in China was perhaps a local development, but more likely came from the Western world via Central Asia. It fit so happily with yang-yin theory that it must have been adopted easily and rapidly.

Finally, during the same centuries, some foods came to be seen as cleansing (*ch'ing*) to the system. Others seemed to poison it, and still others potentiated poisons or bad *ch'i*. These were both lumped as *tu*, "poisonous or poison-potentiating," or—better—"dangerously strong in potentially harmful force."

T'ao Hung-ching's synthesis of existing medical and nutritional theory was so masterful that no one since his time could do much more than add to it. Medicine developed in orderly fashion during the subsequent dynasties. Only in Sung (960–1280 A.D.) were genuinely new and exciting theories discussed, and they ultimately failed to replace T'ao's great synthesis, though they were not without effect.[14] Even when Western medical lore entered China in modern times, traditional nutritional lore emerged triumphant until well into the twentieth century. The most important reason, I think, was a very simple one; you stayed healthier if you followed T'ao Hung-ching. As late as the end of the nineteenth century, Western nutritionists either still embraced the heating/cooling theory themselves, or had gone all the way with protein and calories and were advising people not to "waste their

money" on fruits and vegetables. Only the discovery of vitamins would finally give the West a better success rate in dealing with malnutrition cases. Even today, Western nutritional science remains rather less developed than, say, surgery. Most of us who have experienced traditional Chinese nutritional therapy believe it still has much to offer.

But there is, of course, more to Chinese nutritional science than that. It incorporated some major errors—statements that were simply empirically wrong. These persisted. Individuals could see that particular drugs failed to act or particular anatomical claims did not fit with common observation of animals; yet they explained away these experiences or regarded them as mere random fluctuations. I have seen this happen many times. Of course, I have seen Western medicine fail on even more occasions, yet Westerners do not doubt the system. Throughout the world, it takes more than random failures to call the framework of medical knowledge into question.

It is possible to look at Chinese medicine either as a storehouse of useful knowledge to add to the world's pool of healing arts, or as a system (a set of texts, if you will) to study in its own right. If you are primarily interested in curing people, you will gravitate toward the first approach—thereby running the risk of ignoring some important aspects of the system itself. If you are primarily interested in the history of science, you will gravitate to the second, thus tending to ignore China's very real contributions to modern international medical practice.

This contrast of approaches informed a classic recent debate, when Paul Unschuld (historian of science) commented from the second position on the monumental work of Joseph Needham (doctor and medical researcher).[15] In a gentlemanly response, Needham agreed to disagree.[16] I humbly propose a union of approaches. With Unschuld, I try to understand the system as a whole. With Needham, I seek to understand it for ultimately practical ends. I believe the system has value in itself and is part of China's lasting contribution—not for its medical accuracy so much as for its value in showing how people structure information.

My experience with Chinese nutritional therapy was largely in the New Territories of Hong Kong, back when they were still quite isolated, rural, and traditional. In the New Territories, until relatively recently, China's old Imperial laws held force in much of civil life. When I did fieldwork in 1965–66, many peasants and fishermen still lived lives that would have been familiar to their ancestors of two thousand years before. I had to hike five miles to reach some villages. By the time of my last prolonged visit in 1974–75, the old lifeways were almost gone, and the old social and physical framework was completely gone, but all older adults remembered traditional society and moved most familiarly in its cultural universe. I was able to observe the close fit between folk theory and folk practice. The Hong Kong variant of Chinese nutritional therapy had much to offer even to modern urban Americans; but it was much more effective in dealing with the realities of peasant life in old South China.

The system, as known to the peasants and fishermen of the New Territories, was based on maintaining a balance of qualities. They were concerned especially about hot and cold, and to a lesser extent dry and wet, assimilated closely to the wider realm of yang and yin. They had much concern with the flow of ch'i, but cared almost nothing for the five elements. Supplementing, cleaning and poison were still very important to them. Closely similar (but not quite identical) folk systems existed elsewhere among South Chinese[17] and among Chinese in America, Australia, and elsewhere. Aspects of the Hong Kong belief system have been excellently described by medical anthropologists, including Linda Koo and Marjorie Topley.[18]

In the New Territories, a generation ago, the fundamental concept of balance overrode all else. Recently I was asked to give a paper on this topic in a panel on balance in Chinese medicine. I followed Paul Unschuld, who contributed a brilliant and exciting paper critiquing Westerners who have overrated the importance of balance in traditional Chinese medicine. As he pointed out, the great Han texts stress dynamism and eschew balance.[19] I had to follow, lamely, with my words on the very real importance of balance to modern Cantonese.

Westerners did not invent the Chinese concern with balance; they got it from the modern Chinese, who have indeed given it a special place not warranted by the Han texts. This is, in part, a result of Western influence many centuries ago, especially in the form of the humoral system. It is also part of a development within Chinese society. Symptoms are not seen as labels of a particular insult so much as markers of something wrong with the body's equilibrium or dynamic balance. This does not mean that there is no external insult, but rather that the body was not able to cope with it, or that it destabilized the body and the imbalance has to be corrected.

Western medicine was seen by my friends as being directed toward the insult; Chinese medicine was directed toward fixing the body itself.[20] Thus the Cantonese could, and did, combine both for maximal effect, focusing on balance—in the body as a whole or in some particular organ's field of influence within it. (The Chinese terms translated "heart," "kidney," "liver," and so on actually refer to functional subsystems of the bodily system of organs and ch'i flow. They refer focally to networks of functions, centered on the organs named, but extending throughout the body.)

When my friends on the waterfront of Castle Peak Bay, Hong Kong, talked about health and illness, they rarely strayed long from the idea of balance. The simple Chinese word is p'ing, which originally referred to the dynamic, sensitive balance maintained by the beam of a weighing scale. Often, in discussing health, the term was expanded to ho p'ing, "harmony and balance" or "harmonious balance." A healthy person can be described as a p'ing jen. Closely related concepts include the idea of center or median (chung) and the idea of maintaining a harmonious, unobstructed, unrushed flow of ch'i, activity, blood, and life in general. The concept of balance in the western New Territories of Hong Kong, as in classical Chinese tradition, was clearly a dynamic one: the fragile stability of the beam, or even of the spinning top, rather than the solid stability of a rock. Maintaining ho p'ing in life was an ongoing process. Every day brought its disturbances: sudden heat or cold, a stressful event, an attack by wind (literal or medically metaphoric), a snack that was too rich.

Richard Currier, drawing on his research in Mexico and on the theories of George Foster, argued that such attention to balance in medicine serves as a metaphor for attention to balance in society.[21] Groups especially concerned about maintaining social harmony should be similarly concerned about harmony within the human body. For the Chinese this is certainly true. The concepts of balance and harmony are expressly used in discourse about social life and about the relationships of humanity to the cosmos, and they have been so used for several thousand years. For instance, a wedding or other joyous social occasion is a "hot" event,[22] just as ginger and pepper are "hot" foods, and as such can be stressful to the system if not balanced by cool, restful times.

Ping, he, ho p'ing, and p'ing ho are terms that are all commonly used. They tend to merge into each other. My friends would report that they meant more or less the same thing, but not quite. Harmony refers to things working together and working right. Balance refers to the aspects of a thing being in correct proportion, and the thing itself being centered, able to rest without instability. Harmony is thus more active and implies the presence and action of various forces or entities; balance is a property inherent in systems. Each can be seen as a special case of the other (it depends on how broadly one wishes to define one's system), and the two naturally co-occur. P'ing-an, "balance and security," is the Chinese word for "peace." Ho p'ing implies the ideal situation for any system. The resemblance of this and subsequent axioms to systems theory is not coincidental. The folk system is part of the tradition that, formalized as administrative theory in the Chou Dynasty, became one of the ancestors of modern systems theory.[23]

In medicine, balance is most important to maintain between the forces of yin and yang. The dynamic interplay of these forces is basic to human life and to the cosmos. For the people of Castle Peak Bay, the question of balance and harmony came up most frequently in regard to nutrition. Indeed, almost every question of health became first and last a question about food.

In folk nutritional science, balance was most commonly used to refer to the "neutral" point in the humoral system. Foods were coded as heating or cooling, and, less saliently, as wet or dry. Those that were perfectly balanced between heating, cooling, wetting, and drying were referred to as *p'ing* or *ho p'ing*. Our word "neutral" is not a true translation; these foods were not lacking in the forces of heat, coolness, wet, and dry, but had all of them to the ideal degree, so that they balanced each other correctly. The most perfectly balanced food, defining the set point, was ordinary boiled rice, *fan*. Foods of similar whitish color, moderate caloric value, nonirritating quality, and major dietary importance were also balanced: white-fleshed fish, noodles, potatoes, many steamed breads, and the like. Insofar as foods deviated from this, they were classified as increasingly heating or cooling.[24] Sickness almost always resulted from, or involved, some degree of imbalance between these qualities. Balance was restored by appropriate diet therapy. Menus had to be planned to balance the meal; for example, if fat pork (heating) was served, there should be watercress or carrots or cabbage in soup (cooling).

The heating/cooling dimension is far more important in Chinese medicine and nutrition than the wetting/drying one. The latter is almost undocumented. Cantonese of Hong Kong believed that shrimps and similar crustaceans were heating and wetting (and thus made venereal disease worse). Coffee and roasted peanuts were heating and drying, because they irritated the throat. Nothing was cooling and wetting or cooling and drying. The vast majority of foods, then, were evaluated only on the heating/cooling dimension.

Foods that were high in calories and cooked by intense heat were the focal heating foods. These included anything fried; anything baked for any great length of time; anything greasy. Spices that English also labels "hot"—chili, black pepper, ginger—were heating in proportion to their pungency. Alcohol was hot. The higher the calorie levels and the spicier the taste, the more heating was the food. Some other foods were considered heating because of their "hot colors": red beans, for instance. Green beans were cooling, white

beans neutral. Cooling foods were those that were sour, watery, low-calorie, and cool-colored. The focal cooling foods were thus green, leafy vegetables and the green-fleshed large radish (which does not have a "hot" taste). The more sour and watery the vegetable, the more cooling it was. Black tea was heating because it brews to a red color; green tea was cooling. Some foods gave mixed signals: oranges, plums, and tomatoes are a hot color but are watery and sour. About these, people disagreed. There was continual debate and adjustment. Many people, for instance, separated "cold" foods from "cooling" ones; this is a classical distinction that has been debated for centuries.

These codings were based on observed physical responses to food. Feasts—which featured greasy, spicy food, with alcohol—led to indigestion and hangover, pathological conditions easily cured by avoiding the foods in question for a day or so, and eating soothing foods like rice and vegetables. Scurvy is also a "hot" condition, involving sores, dry, flaky skin, rashes, and other burnlike symptoms. Green vegetables cure it. Conversely, a diet of rice and vegetables is apt to lead to thinness, pallor, wasting away, low body temperature, and the like. In Western terms, we would diagnose lack of protein, available iron, and other minerals. Chinese would diagnose too much cold and not enough heat. So heating foods, specifically meat and highly nutritious plant foods like wolfthorn berries, were eaten. They worked. Heating foods of this kind are also eaten for convalescence, recovery from childbirth, and other situations in which rebuilding strength through good protein and mineral nutrition is desirable.

Individual differences that we would explain by "allergies" were explained by differences in basic nature. Some people are basically hotter or cooler than others. They have to eat differently. Some foods that are cooling for most people are heating for a few —these are mostly cases of allergy rash. Conversely, heating foods may cause diarrhea (a cold condition) in a few susceptible people.

I have shown elsewhere that the Chinese did the best they could to make empirical observations comprehensible by a simple scheme.[25] Carol Laderman has confirmed this line of thinking by demonstrating the same for the closely related Malay system of folk nutrition.[26]

Some form of the hot/cold belief system is found in most of the world's cultures, and was obviously invented independently on several occasions. There is much evidence for its existence in the pre-Columbian civilizations of the Americas, for instance. This is obviously due to the fact that sick people usually do show excess heat (fever) or cold (chills). No one can miss the association. Observations of the therapeutic effects of certain foods follow naturally.[27] The heating/cooling belief existed throughout Europe until well into the twentieth century.

In short, we have here a case in which human information processing leads naturally to a particular scheme that is simple, memorable and effective. It is "wrong" by the standards of modern biomedical science, but it is "right" for the pragmatic peasants who use it.

In addition, foods could have value as *pu p'in:* "supplementing" or "patching" foods.[28] The very name implies restoring a balanced condition, though these are seen as strengthening foods more than as restorers of balance. Other foods were used to clean the system, restoring harmony by eliminating bad things that had entered. A standard herbal and nourishing preparation was *ch'ing-pu-liang*, "cleansing, supplementing, and cooling," a mixture of herbs and seeds made into a soup used for those purposes.

In preparing medicines, ingredients such as licorice were introduced to harmonize the other ingredients, producing a balanced system. This led to maximal good effect and minimal side-effects. Cooking served as a model: some ingredients without much flavor were introduced to bind the main ingredients, producing a single dish with a proper balance of flavors rather than a bunch of disparate ingredients lying together in the pot. These last examples showed that *ho p'ing* is not solely a matter of regulating an existing system. It includes actually creating a system from its component parts, or creating a functional system from a nonfunctioning one.

Other medical practices within the traditional Chinese therapeutic universe were also seen as restoring balance, harmony, and proper function to the human system. This extended to the essentially psychological (in Western terms) practices of the spirit mediums (*wu shih* and other categories), of whom there were many in the area. They did much that was far from harmonious—driving away or exorcising ghosts, casting lots, going into ecstatic trances, slashing themselves with swords. Yet, in practice, their treatments consisted of prescribing medicines, performing ceremonies to restore lost components of the souls, calming agitation and stress, and making soothing statements to their clients. One favorite statement was: "Some people have been saying bad things about you, but you are really a good person. Those other people just have some badness in their hearts. Don't pay attention to them and you will be all right." I heard this line many times in spirit medium performances.

The practices of the spirit mediums and other fairly fixed formulas stressed the value of social harmony. In the eyes of both the mediums and the patients, social imbalance and disharmony were specifically pathogenic, causing genuine physical distress.

They had to be treated, if only by telling the victim to rise above them.

Ideally, the disharmony itself would be cured. Indeed, local grassroots leaders were described as restorers of balance and harmony, just as curers were. Leaders healed the body politic in the same general way that curers healed the body physical. Harmony with the gods, spirits, ghosts, and natural world was also necessary. Driving ghosts away from a patient can be seen as restoring harmony between human and ghost realms, rather than as a statement of total war between those realms. Giving deliberate or unintended offense to a supernatural being was a common cause of illness.

Offending the natural landscape could lead to its indwelling spirits visiting one with illness. The similarity of tapping into *feng-shui* channels and acupuncture, for instance, was known to several of my informants. The forces of the cosmos must be properly in balance, in relationship to the individual and the community, at any given time and place. Without that, ill luck and ill health follow. The other principal forms of folk medicine in Castle Peak Bay—herbal therapy, exercise, massage, and physical therapy—also operated from a model of restoring balance. Even the rather dramatic and painful techniques were thought to harmonize the *ch'i*. These included hard massage, coin-rubbing—raising a bruise by rubbing or pinching with a coin—and moxibustion, which involved burning cones of powdered sagebrush on the bare skin to leave a serious blistered welt. By contrast, "Western" medicine (international biomedicine) was seen as usually involved with specifically fixing injuries or exterminating invading pathogens, rather than as restoring a global personal balance to the individual.

The major forms of medicine at Castle Peak Bay were diet therapy (largely a home matter), herbal treatment (largely in the hands of Chinese doctors and pharmacists), and spiritual medicine (practiced by spirit mediums). These overlapped; the gods, speaking through their mediums, routinely prescribed homey herb and food remedies in cases of soul loss, witchcraft, and divine vengeance. The contrast between "naturalistic" and "personalistic" medicine was not very meaningful to Castle Peak Bay people. Indeed, spirit mediums seemed to specialize in naturalizing the personalistic. Exercise, massage, and rest were other harmonizing modalities. Only Western medicine was seen as based on a really different paradigm. (Acupuncture, so dear to the hearts of Western devotees of Chinese medicine, was rarely utilized by Castle Peak Bay individuals.) Medicine was supposed to give not just freedom from disease, but a long and vigorous life. Only a moderate, harmonized life could be prolonged.

However, it is not enough to say that the people of rural Hong Kong were simply following ancient tradition. Cantonese folk culture is extremely different from China's elite culture, let alone the elite culture of Chou. Paul Unschuld has quite correctly pointed out that Chinese medicine has many rhetorics.[29] It includes passages as militaristic as modern American popular writings about the immune system. It includes many strong charges to avoid, prevent, repel, dispel, and evade. It includes many theories of sickness that are quite separate from the concept of balance. Indeed, all these various other theories and modes of discourse are present in Cantonese folk tradition as well.

Yet, they are not only reduced in relative importance (vis-à-vis the classical medical tradition), they are often simply subsumed under the balance-and-harmony rhetoric. They are incorporated into that overarching view, at a lower level. One must explain why this particular net of concepts was so enthusiastically adopted. My friends stressed balance and harmony in health more than the orthodox Chinese medical traditions do, just as in social matters they stressed them even more than orthodox Confucian traditions do. Other concepts of great importance in classical writings were of no interest to the Hong Kong villagers; for instance, they were vaguely aware of the fivefold correspondence doctrine but did not take it very seriously. They had greatly overgeneralized and overextended one part of ancient tradition (that relating to balance and harmony) at the expense of much else (five phases, *ch'i* flow specifics, the apotropaic language cited above, acupuncture, and more).

Following Currier's theory, one would expect to find that this focus on medical harmony implied that social harmony was an extreme, indeed transcendent, value to the villagers. This is, indeed, the case. It is the highest good. When I sought out definitions of the word "good" as applied to individual and social life, discussions invariably turned to the maintenance of social harmony or good relations. Here the related words include *kuan-hsi*, "mutual goodwill" with a sense of "mutual responsibility," and *kan-ch'ing*, which means "sentiment" with a sense of "wanting to help and be helped by someone." A "good person" was one who could create and maintain harmony through these and other means of networking.[30] John Young, in a book about Castle Peak Bay's neighboring market town Yun Long, provides a superb account of these matters.[31] A healthy person was one who maintained a comparable internal state. Once again, the microcosm and the macrocosm function according to the same rules.

Currier's theory implies a corollary: such societies have particular problems with social order. Specifically, Currier finds that balance is stressed in societies that are strongly hierarchic, with a powerful, traditional hierarchy that is strongly represented in the ideology. Here Currier grounds his ideas in George Foster's hypothesis of the "image of limited good" in peasant societies. Foster points out that peasants, living in a frequently static economic order, see human kindness and other virtues as limited in quantity, like land and wealth.[32] They work to make the best of what they have, and to reduce tension or the appearance of tension. Here again China fits the pattern.

In particular, this allows us to differentiate such societies from others with different overarching, fundamental tenets of proper living. The Northwest Coast Indians maximize power, including healing power.[33] Americans, indefatigable competitive individualists, tend to see illnesses as invasions that must be fought off[34] (though Americans, too, have a concept of "balanced diet"; the Cantonese stress on nutrition and the American stress on "germs" clearly have much to do with the relative roles of balance versus defensiveness in the respective rhetorics).

Strongly and stably hierarchic societies could be expected to have such a focus on harmony simply as a result of ideology generated by the elites. One could see the whole belief as simply a way that elites persuade ordinary people to stay calm and amiable. Yet we find that the villagers and fishermen of the South China coast are among the most independent people in China, with a long history of rebelliousness and regionalism, and are quite aware of the importance of ideology in such matters. They do not adopt ideas lightly. They are, in fact, far too aware of the role of ideas to adopt the idea of balance and harmony unless it did in fact promote good health and also produce social benefits to both individuals and communities.

Some biological benefits of the ideology of balance are clear. Dietary excesses, excesses of activity or sloth, exposure to too much sun or too much cold, sexual excesses, and similar mistakes are clearly counterindicated. The individual is charged to find his or her own comfort point or set point, and to deviate from that only with due care. Most South Chinese are in fact careful, and many are continually concerned. They regulate every activity so that it does not take them far from their perceived balance points. This is particularly pronounced in regard to diet, but it affects all aspects of life, notably including physical exercise. These and other benefits seem inadequate to explain the enthusiasm with which the system is accepted.

The need to have some overarching, all-connecting symbol or value is also clearly present. Every system needs something to tie it together at the top—to connect all parts and make them all meaningful in relation to each other. This allows people to store and retrieve information much more easily. Any medical system must have a simple way of organizing its facts, for the convenience of its practitioners. Ordinary laypersons then take over this simple algorithm and simplify it again. Often they then go on to make it more complicated again, but in their own, nonprofessional ways. While international scientific medicine has the idea of rationality and the concept of experimentally verified fact, the Chinese concepts of balance and harmony serve to link medicine to the homologous systems (or subsystems) of thought represented in social management, landscape management, and cosmology.

Yet this leaves the question of why one overarching symbol system is picked over another.

Balance and harmony are picked, in my opinion, because they place the locus of control squarely on the individual, and specifically on the individual in society. If the elite did deliberately sell this belief system to pacify the masses, they captured a Tartar. The overarching message of the valuation of balance, in both social life and personal health, is that the individual exists in relation to the environment and has to take control of how he or she interacts with that environment. Social life is not simply a matter of passive adjustment to a social order; it is a matter of developing wider and deeper personal networks, and working on balancing one's responsibilities. Health, similarly, requires a continual balancing act. One must react to the environment and take control of one's responses to it. This may be related to the concept of "somatization," used by the psychiatrist and anthropologist Arthur Kleinman to describe Chinese medicine's treatment of what Westerners call "psychological" problems.[35] The Chinese use physical therapy, nutrition, and similar methods to deal with what they see as a bodily matter. The idea of a "mind," divorced from the body and subject to its own diseases, is foreign to China.

Life in traditional China is sometimes thought to be constrained. The individual is said to be dominated by gentry, lineage elders, and a rigid code derived from neo-Confucian philosophy. This was true up to a point, but the ordinary people had many ways of maintaining their own integrity and power. Recent studies such as those of Hill Gates, Robert Marks, and Robert Weller have focused on resistance: the ways in which ordinary people managed their lives in spite of elites and rules, and prevailed over these when opportunity afforded.[36] Not only did ordinary people have many means of direct resistance; they had to run their own farms and their own communities. Even the state had to work with them, not against them; the state could not manage every farm, and it depended on the revenue. Therefore, life for the average adult was one of actively negotiating and renegotiating one's place in society and the cosmos.

If one were to write a book on China comparable to Ruth Benedict's *The Chrysanthemum and the Sword,* it would not focus on hierarchic terms but on terms associated with managing cooperation and fine-tuned social relationships. In addition to *he* and *ping*, one would discuss *ho* "cooperation" (as in *lien-ho*—a different word from "harmony"), *kuan-hsi, kan-ch'ing, min* ("face"), and the folk concepts of leadership and friendship.[37] If the Japanese are highly social and Americans highly individualistic, the Chinese may be thought of as combining (balancing!) both: they are individuals-in-society. Certainly the Cantonese word *ian* ("person") conveys this idea. Castle Peak Bay persons put a very high value on individuality, even eccentricity, but an even higher value on being actively participating members of communities and networks. Independence, resistance, and control of one's life grew from such roots. And medical aspects of balance grew as a logical corollary of this view of the world, which in turn developed from the needs of the ordinary person to survive and function in a highly complex social environment. E. P. Thompson has shown how a working class forms as individuals strive to exercise what control they can. Jean Comaroff, among anthropologists, has applied similar concepts to the use of ideology as a means of constructing passive resistance.[38] The Chinese have always used their medical system as a means of asserting individualism. By connecting it directly with the social system, through the concept of balance, they made explicit a concern with internalizing the locus of control over personal life in society and in the environment.

The health consequences of such a belief system are not trivial. Richard Schulz has written a paper describing the human need to feel able to cope with one's life.[39] Psychologists, especially Albert Bandura and Ellen Langer, have stressed the psychological and physical importance of perceived control. Health and even survival under stress depend (in part) on maintaining control.[40]

The traditional Chinese folk system based on humoral medicine, herbal therapy, tonic and strengthening foods and medicines, exercise, and other forms of "nourishment of life"[41] demands that the individual take some control over life, and encourages even more. A person must actively, thoughtfully take over health maintenance for himself or herself, and (to varying degrees) for those for whom he or she is responsible. This is a deeply empowering ideology, and part of the tough, resilient network of grassroots power that allows Chinese to work both alone and together for the common good. It is part of an ideology that grows from practice and, in turn, affects practice. As such, it has been one key part in the survival of the Chinese people over the millennia.

◆ ◆ ◆

Balancing hot and cold is not the only matter of serious importance in Chinese nutritional medicine.

Strengthening, cleansing, and dealing with poisons are also daily concerns. These draw on a very different logic, perhaps more ancient, certainly less social. To understand these systems, we must invoke other theories of how people process knowledge and how they feel about what they know.

Pu p'in ("supplementing things"; *pou pan* in Cantonese) are part of a complex widely known in Asia. My friend Najma Rizvi, who has studied food beliefs and medical practices in the Indian subcontinent, has told me of similar foods used for strengthening, especially for women after childbirth.[42] More research is needed on how far the complex spreads, but there are similar belief systems in Southeast Asia and elsewhere.[43] *Pu p'in* include many medicinal herbs, as well as foods. They supplement energy, tone up the system, and above all strengthen. Some strengthen the whole body; others, a specialized group, strengthen particular organ systems. On the whole, *pu p'in* supplement depleted *ch'i*. They may also repair damaged tissue, or they may act by invigorating *ch'i* and thus empowering the body to repair itself.

The most basic and widespread *pu p'in* is chicken soup, which is as popular with Chinese grandmothers as with proverbial Jewish ones. The Chinese variant should ideally be simmered very slowly for a very long time, with warming and *pu* herbal drugs.

In general, all poultry are *pu*, but wild ones are more so than tame ones. Most meat is *pu*, at least when stewed slowly and delicately in a closed container. As with birds, wild meat is more *pu* (on the whole) than tame. Among herbs, ginseng is the most famous, but there is a vast lore of *pu* herbs. Many fungi are especially important. Especially valuable for preserving the *pu* qualities (while preventing too much heat from getting into the food) is a steaming process known as *tun*. This involves putting the food in a covered dish that is then put in a larger vessel with some water, rather like a bain-marie. A similar cooking process is known by the similar sounding word *dum* or *dam* in India, and there too it serves to retain virtues of the food. I suspect a relationship between the words *tun* and *dam*. After all, the concepts of "strengthening foods" are clearly related.

Almost all *pu p'in* are cooked this way or in a casserole or soup. Almost all *pu p'in* are gently heating; this sort of cooking reduces or tempers their heat still more. The idea is to provide a gentle warming rather than a sudden shock of heat. Prepared this way, *pu p'in* are easy to digest, by both Chinese and Western standards. Such items as chicken are often stewed with enough vinegar to leach calcium and other minerals from the bones.

In explaining *pu* foods, the first and most obvious factor is that they work. The focal situations in which *pu* foods are prescribed are—above all—recovery from childbirth; convalescence from disease or trauma; and the waning of powers that accompanies aging. The *pu p'in* are all either foods that are high in protein and minerals while being low in fat (poultry, game, mushrooms), or else plants with tonic effects that are known (ginseng and its relatives) or likely. The traditional Chinese lived on grain with relatively small amounts of vegetables. Even in the diet of the rich, meat was not heavily represented, vegetables and fruits being choicer than most meats. Protein and mineral nutrition was adequate for ordinary life but marginally adequate for tissue repair. Women got a disproportionately small share of meat and other high-quality protein and mineral sources. As I often observed in the field, pregnancy and childbirth very often pushed them over the edge into out-and-out anemia. At best, they needed all the help they could get. A good diet meant not only their own survival or welfare, but that of their infants. Thus all Chinese women recovered from childbirth by "doing the month":[44] they spent some days, ideally a month, lying still and eating *pu* foods. Many of the foods at this time were explicitly intended to increase milk supply, and these were high in fat or calcium. Others, such as liver, were rich in iron and vitamins. All in all, they worked superbly for their intended purpose. It is impossible to imagine China reaching its current population without the "month."

But the effectiveness does not by any means account for all the facts concerning *pu p'in*. Many highly nutritious items were neglected. More strikingly, many items were considered to have supernaturally spectacular effect, especially on the aged.

One reason to think that a food was a *pu p'in* was a Chinese equivalent of the Doctrine of Signatures. Roots shaped like the human form, for instance, were naturally held to strengthen the actual human body. This is one reason why ginseng was so highly regarded (the other reason is that it actually does contain effective chemicals, apparently tonic to the immune-response system). Also, parts of an animal's body were especially strengthening to corresponding parts of a human's. This was validated by the obvious beneficial effect of animal blood on humans with weak blood; anemia and the effect of pig's and chicken's blood on it were very well known. Red jujube fruits also improve blood, and they too have some iron. By the time we get to port wine, however, we are in the realm of pure magic. Perhaps Westerners, introducing it, convinced the Chinese of its value in order to sell more of it, though many native wines were always believed to have tonic effects, if only because of their alcohol content.

Consuming liver was seen as an ideal way to supplement one's own liver. As in so many other cases, observation had made clear the actual health benefits of liver consumption by anemic patients. This observation was logically extended. Pigs' lungs help the lungs of the eater. Brains improve brain power, and so do walnut meats, which look like brains.

Genitalia, of course, strengthen the genitalia; and it follows, logically (but wrongly), that the best would be from a notoriously randy animal. A male deer can service a whole herd of several dozen does. The same is true of at least some kinds of seal. Their genitalia can be found in all Chinese drug stores, commanding a very high price among men who feel old age creeping upon them. This was even more true in the old days of polygamy. A man was expected to satisfy all his wives. Deer antlers in velvet are also highly valued as a general strengthener with special effect on the male genital system; antlers in velvet do contain hormones and minerals of uncertain effect. *Pu* items such as this are often translated as "aphrodisiacs" by salacious Westerners, but the action is not seen as aphrodisiacal. They improve, strengthen, and repair the system, and —as with ginseng—they act as general tonics. They do not excite the genitals directly, the way Spanish fly does.

Finally, *pu* effects are ascribed to items that appear strange or uncanny. This recalls the work of Lévi-Strauss and of Mary Douglas. The Lele people, whom Douglas studied in Africa, regarded the pangolin as magically powerful, because it seems both mammal and reptile and because it both burrows and runs on the surface or even climbs.[45] The Africans taboo it. The Chinese also see the pangolin as anomalous, but instead of tabooing it, they seek it out as one of the most *pu* of foods. I have seen a recipe from Kweichow for pangolin, which recommends stewing the pangolin for hours with every strong-flavored food item available. Obviously the strong taste of ants and grubs is not one of the animal's selling points; never have I seen the Chinese work so hard to kill a taste.

Other bizarre creatures that are spectacularly *pu* are edible birds' nests, sea cucumbers, sea horses, flying lizards, rhinoceros horns, vultures, and raccoon dogs. It is clear that their bizarreness, their anomalous nature, is the reason they are considered so powerful. Less strange items with comparable nutritional value are less *pu*: white fungus, abalone, and the like. Still less so are wild ducks and pigeons. Finally, ordinary barnyard creatures are *pu*, but only mildly so. My informants were quite realistic about the value of these as food.

In short, the more strange a food, the more power is ascribed to it. Fishermen at Castle Peak Bay ascribed particular potency to a small crustacean parasite of the giant grouper. They held that the *ch'i* of the grouper entered this small creature when the fish died. Thus the strange little crustacean held all the potency of a fish that could run to five hundred pounds of fighting muscle.

This last example gives us a clue to the logic of the system. Weirdness is taken as proof that the animal in question has potent *ch'i*. Strange-looking rock formations such as stalactites (high in calcium!) are also pressed into service. If a creature seems to be two things at once (like the pangolin), or if it simply looks striking, or if it has the appearance of twisted, tortured, knotted energy flow, it is assumed to be a good candidate. In the end it must also exhibit some empirical effect.

A partial opposite of *pu* is *tu*, "poisonous." Often this really means "poison-potentiating." *Tu* foods bring out poisons already present in the system, and thus make disease worse. They are especially dangerous for cancer patients. *Tu* foods include uncastrated male poultry. In a study of cancer epidemiology, M. L. Anderson and I found what our Chinese colleagues already knew: cancer patients rigorously abstained from any poultry that they did not actually see killed and cleaned, and even from chicken broth, for fear that they would get a tiny bit of a male, which would potentiate the cancer. Beef and sheep meats are often considered poisonous, the latter potentiating epilepsy. Several fish are poison-potentiating, especially if they are heating and wetting. Informants and classical herbals differ as to just which foods are *tu* for which conditions. As Carol Laderman points out, allergic reactions such as hives are often at the root of such ascriptions.[46] Rashes are often diagnosed in Chinese folk practice as being due to internal poisons breaking out.

Most *pu* foods are nonpoisonous, but the poison-potentiating foods seem generally *pu* to some degree. Many herbal remedies are poisonous, "using poison to drive out poison," much as the Chinese "used barbarians to control barbarians" in classical political strategy. It seems that such things as uncastrated male poultry combine *pu* and heat in a degree that makes them *pu* to poisons in the human system. They nourish the cancer or the toxin. The tremendous yang energy of a rooster or drake converts it from a gentle nourisher to an uncontrolled, angerous force.

Harder to explain are the many poisonous combinations. Here the belief is not in poison-potentiating; certain foods eaten together react to produce actual, virulent poisons. Gould-Martin gives some examples: "in Taiwan, crab and pumpkin, pork and licorice, mackerel and plums and, in Hong Kong, garlic and honey, crab and persimmon, dog meat and green beans . . ."[47] Very long lists can be compiled by anyone with access to medical books. The lists differ so much from place to place and person to person that they defy all explanation. A delightful article by Libin Cheng recounts his daring experiments. He and his experimental animals survived unhurt, but his gingerly approach to testing the combinations on himself rings clearly through his medical prose! He suspects the whole complex may be due to experiences with allergy, bacterial contamination, adulteration, and the like.[48] Perhaps so; this would explain the lack of system in the whole matter. Yet we find similar beliefs around the world. Growing up in Nebraska, I was solemnly assured by almost everyone around me that eating ice cream at the same meal with fish or shellfish would "kill you for sure." Some combinations appear to be illogical, wrong, uncanny; people suffering indigestion blame it on a union of foods that, to them, seems basically wrong or unacceptable.

We may pass briefly over such minor problems as foods said to be bloating or flatulence-causing; here people merely describe reality. The one other key concept is the one that underlies *ch'ing,* "cleansing," and *hsiao,* "dispelling, clearing away." Foods in these categories are low in calories, mild in flavor, easy to digest, frequently astringent, and almost always herbal or vegetal. They include "honey, brown sugar, sugarcane juice"[49] in Taiwan; honey and sugarcane (juice included) in Hong Kong. They get rid of waste products, poisons, impurities, excess wetness, excess "wind" (i.e., rheumatism and other conditions thought to be related to internal effects of winds on the body), and other pathogenic forces. Their common denominator is that they are bland. They are either astringent or soothing.

It will be immediately evident that they form a contrast set as opposed to strengthening and poison-potentiating foods: bland versus flavorful, soothing versus exciting, cool versus hot, plant versus usually animal, cool-colored versus hot-colored. The set of cleaning foods heavily overlaps the set of bland and cooling foods. However, it is not quite identical; see, for example, brown sugar in Taiwan. More research is needed on these matters. There seems a good likelihood that the Chinese are aware of some quality in many of these herbal remedies that is new or not very familiar to Western medicine and that would repay further investigation. But, so far, all we know is that they are soothing, mild, low-calorie foods that would seem to act by calming an overwrought digestive system or diluting systemic irritants.

◆ ◆ ◆

In all these cases, we have a group of foods that actually have some obvious physical effects, that seem experientially to hang together, and that make good sense as a unit. Yet, in no case did the Chinese see the unity as being produced by an obvious organoleptic or analytic quality. They inferred subtle energies or qualities.

They inferred, on the whole, according to a very simple and straightforward set of rules:

1. Assume the simplest possible linkage. Like goes with like.
2. Assume the widest possible linkage.
3. Assume the linkage that is most consonant with the theories of *ch'i.*
4. Assume that weirdness marks effective power. Anomaly and "mixed signals" are instances of weirdness.

Chinese nutritional therapy, therefore, is a beautiful case of fitting empirical data into a logically derived theory and then making deductions based on that theory. The theory is dubious (but still respectable) by modern scientific standards. The deductions are almost all wrong. So are some of the empirical observations, notably the poisonous nature of certain food combinations. This seems typical of human thought. People are good, but far from perfect, observers. They tread on more dangerous ground when they abstract—inferring theory or generalization. But when they make deductions from inferred and necessarily imperfect theory, they make their really major mistakes.

People classify things by seeing some shared qualities that they think are, somehow, more basic than other qualities. They then overgeneralize and overextend these classifications to produce overarching high-level systems. They then deduce new "truths." Often the deduction is so confidently made that real-world observations are claimed to support it, even when they actually do not. People misperceive the facts, or they count only the hits and explain away the misses. If a cooling food seems heating to a particular person, that person simply has a unique nature. If a *pu* food fails to tone up a patient, that patient was too far gone.

Generalization, chunking of data, and inference are at work. We need not deal with schemas in any strict sense (as my sometime colleague in these researches, the cognitive psychologist Sheng-ping Fan, points out). We are dealing with lists and taxonomies and with simple information processing.

Something very close to a schema does exist in the form of analogic thinking. This is a classic process in Chinese philosophical thought, having triumphed over syllogistic logic in early centuries.[50] Analogic arguments drew on perceived parallels between events. In proving the certainty of mortality, the Chinese were more apt to say that all animals and plants die, so humans must die too; the Greeks, with their syllogistic logic, gave us the classic "All men are mortal; Socrates is a man; therefore Socrates is mortal." The Greeks argue from the general to the particular; the Chinese from one datum to a parallel datum at the same level of generality.

Chinese thinkers recognized that there were analogies and analogies. The idea was to find cases that were more than mere coincidental resemblances—cases where analogy was due to a real, underlying driving dynamic, a cause or process that produced like effects in like situations. There were qualities that were pure labels imposed by humans (such as value judgments). There were qualities that were real and shared but rather superficial and trivial (whiteness). There were still other qualities that are truly basic (ch'i). In the end, analogic incorporated syllogistic logic. One can recast much of the medical system syllogistically: Anomalous appearance is caused by potent ch'i; the pangolin looks anomalous; therefore the pangolin has potent ch'i. The Chinese focused on existential reality seen as process. The whole Western tradition of idealism (focusing on essential reality and on permanent, unchanging ideal forms) was unacceptable to the Chinese, even though it was often introduced, especially by schools of Buddhism.

So far, we have dealt primarily with "cold" cognition: cognition that does not involve the emotions. But the sense of uncanniness one gets from anomalous animals is emotional in nature: this is "hot" cognition in modern psychological terminology. (How readily we fall into using heat and coolness as natural metaphors! Will future psychologists believe in true heat and cold in the mind?)

However, there is more at work. The most salient feature of Chinese traditional medicine, and especially of herbal therapy, is unquestionably its relentless focus on a holistic, somatizing, naturalistic, individually localized view. The locus of control is in the individual, and in that whole individual. Thinking, knowing, and emotional feeling are viewed as clusters of functions of the body, not as a separate "mind" or even a set of functions localized in the brain. Thinking takes place in the brain, but emotion is of the heart and liver. Kleinman, in his discussion of somatization, has not quite shaken the Western notion of a separate "mind" somewhere in there, and wonders why the Chinese do not pay more attention to it.[51] But for the Chinese, mentality is not a thing, but a class of functions, like digesting.

I was raised, like most Westerners, with the belief that bad things are basically external. I would "catch a bug" or get accidentally hit by something. The Cantonese of Hong Kong were more concerned with "nourishment of life."[52] Illness is primarily a destabilization of the body, not an external insult to it. It is caused, usually, by one's own lifestyle, not by accident.

Of course, the distinction is far from total. The humoral system affected my own childhood. I was taught that getting my feet wet would cause me to catch cold—a purely humoral statement. And the Chinese could see that many an accident was just chance. But the difference was real. Their medicine localized control basically within the individual; mine localized it outside the individual.

Moreover, the Chinese of Hong Kong saw most illness as natural. It was not sent by gods, witches, or demons. People I have known elsewhere in China were more afraid of the spirits, but they still saw most illness as naturalistic in causation. This can be contrasted with those many African and Oceanian peoples who ascribe all illness to malevolent or vengeful conscious entities. George Foster and Barbara Anderson make a contrast between "naturalistic" and "personalistic" medicine.[53] They rather overdrive the distinction, but it is nonetheless of interest, especially since Paul Unschuld has shown that Chinese medicine has changed from an ancient personalistic emphasis to its modern naturalistic one.[54] In rural Hong Kong when I did fieldwork there, even the spirits (speaking through spirit mediums) usually diagnosed illness as due to natural causes.

Unschuld points out that the rise of the naturalistic system, with its focus on individual control, tracked the rise of the rational bureaucratic state. Once again, as in the case of the theme of "balance," the connection lies in the desperate need of the Chinese people (both elite and folk) to assert as much control of their lives as they possibly could. Confronted with an impersonal power state and its impersonal, hyperorganized cosmology, they bent that cosmology to their own ends. They deduced a system of medicine that gave them as much control of their lives as possible. This, of course, is what made personalistic medicine succeed so little. When it did succeed, it often succeeded when all other hope had gone, or among marginal populations —in other words, it succeeded among people who had lost even the pretense of maintaining much significant control. Of course, the doctors' view could be very different from the patients', as each side jockeyed to retain or expand their power and control.

Charlotte Furth has given us a brilliant Foucaultian analysis of how this game was played in Ch'ing Dynasty gynecology.[55] Foucault saw that medical discourses are discourses about control—of the body, the mind, and the society—as well as (or, even, instead of) discourses about healing the wounded and the ill. And when an entire people locate control of health firmly in their own individual bodies, we must assume that they are trying to maximize control over their lives. Perhaps they do it to resist the bureaucratic state, using what James Scott calls the "weapons of the weak."[56] Perhaps, in this case, they are not so weak.

Chinese medicine could be bent to the service of doctors, herbalists, and even rulers, but it was superbly used for self-empowerment by the broad people of China. This is what gave it force. They could weave their empirical observations into a pragmatic of power. This is, of course, exactly the same force that is making Chinese medicine popular with some of its Western devotees today. As my student William Bowen has often pointed out to me, the Chinese explicitly attempt to take back control of their health from what they see as an alienated and alienating medical establishment that is trying to take too much control of their lives.

Many ordinary Westerners today concern themselves with "stress" and downplay genes and other aspects of fate, hoping to maximize feelings of control. Recent research shows that cancer and heart disease patients, for instance, focus on the aspects of life they can control, such as diet and stress, and ignore or try to ignore the role of uncontrollable factors such as genetics.[57] Indeed, the modern world could do worse than see the human body-mind system as a dynamic swirl of energy, which must be kept in balance and vigor by proper "nourishment of health."

To some extent, the Chinese had little choice. They had to control their lives and their health, in the old Imperial days, when government officials comprised only 0.1 to 0.2 percent of the population. (About one in ten workers in the United States today is a government employee.) And the Ch'ing didn't even have telephones. Doctors were also few in number. Druggists and herbalists were numerous and widespread, providing much care and also a cultural pipeline between educated elite and ordinary folk. But individuals had to assert control in the teeth of government, community, and kinship organization.

Psychologist Robert Zajonc argued that humans cannot know or think anything without at least some involvement of emotion, if only a vague sense of "good" or "bad."[58] As Zajonc would lead us to expect, the deeper generating dynamic of the special characteristics of the Chinese medical system is "hot," not "cold." As Bandura would lead us to expect, it is a function of the human need to negotiate self-efficacy.[59]

This, and the cosmology of ch'i and its transformations, gives Chinese medicine a very different language from Western therapy. Translation can be dangerous—a fact only now beginning to be realized.[60] Real explanatory dictionaries are needed; Liu and Liu make a good start.[61]

Chinese society required that every science be applied. The Renaissance concept of "pure" science was a revolutionary development in the West, but had strong roots going back to Classical Greece. Plants were to be studied *primarily* in relation to other plants, and only secondarily in regard to their value to humans. Physics was to be studied as *pure* work, or motion, and only secondarily in regard to human work. Mathematics became a wonderful sport. The need to classify newfound plants and model newfound heavenly motions had much to do with this, but it was philosophically congenial. To the Chinese, on the other hand, botany was ever the handmaiden of agriculture and herbal study; mathematics of engineering; anatomy of medical practice. There was a felt need to understand things in themselves, just as there was a pure mathematics. But people were too busy with the practical matters of life to go into either one in very much depth. Chinese applied science went as far as it could without a pure science to back it up, but then it foundered on a maze of reefs: untested inferences, untested mistaken deductions. Even so, it is well to remember that a malnourished person would have been far better advised to trust himself or herself to a Chinese grandmother than to a Western nutritionist, right up into the first part of our own century.

As it confronts the Western world, Chinese medicine is accommodating in methodology and discourse. Medical anthropologist Karin Hilsdale argues that Chinese medicine shows signs of losing its paradigm and becoming a disunited bundle of techniques, as Western concepts of cosmology, biotechnology, and so on are incorporated.[62] Arthur Kleinman's and William Bowen's current research adumbrates on this issue as well.[63] While the demise of the Chinese paradigm is hardly imminent, there is a real chance of losing certain strengths.[64] The irony of adopting an increasingly analytic, if not alienated, approach is evident. *Scientific American* (1985) reports that one recent study concludes that almost a third of deaths in the United States are hastened by abuse of tobacco, alcohol, and other drugs. Add to this the toll of suicide, eating disorders, and other self-destructive behavior, and we probably can say that most deaths in the United States are caused or hastened by processes under the full control (conscious or subconscious, if you will) of the individual.

Chinese medicine has persisted so well because it has a comprehensive, overarching framework that can accommodate everything from spirit mediumship to literally cut-and-dried herbal remedies and because it satisfies its users' need to take control of their lives. I extend Karin Hilsdale's call to preserve the framework in extending Chinese medicine to the West.[65] We not only need to preserve it; we need to transmit it outside the bounds of traditional Chinese practice.

Thus, for confusing and complex reasons relating to human information processing, Chinese nutritional science has moved back and forth from everyday empirical reality to a highly abstract and complex logical scheme that, in turn, influences perception of everyday reality. The net result is better nutrition for billions of people over countless years.

NOTES

1. E. N. Anderson, *The Food of China* (New Haven: Yale University Press, 1988).

2. Ibid.

3. Production affects consumption, too, but in China consumption has often been the clear driving force; see Anderson, *Food of China.*

4. Ulric Neisser, *Cognition and Reality* (San Francisco: Freeman, 1976).

5. Anderson, *Food of China;* Henry Lu, *Chinese System of Food Cures* (New York: Sterling Publishing Co., 1986); and Rance Lee, "Perceptions and Uses of Chinese Medicine among the Chinese of Hong Kong," *Culture, Medicine and Psychiatry* 4 (1980): 345–375.

6. E. N. Anderson, "Why Is Humoral Medicine So Popular?" *Social Science and Medicine* 25 (1987): 331–337; and George Foster, "On the Origin of Humoral Medicine in Latin America," *Medical Anthropology Quarterly* 1 (1987): 355–393.

7. Manfred Pokert, *Theoretical Foundations of Chinese Medicine* (Cambridge, Mass.: M.I.T. Press, 1974).

8. For the history, see Anderson, *Food of China.*

9. Walter H. Mallory, *China, Land of Famine* (New York: American Geographical Society, special publication no. 6, 1926).

10. Paul Unschuld, *Medicine in China: A History of Ideas* (Berkeley: University of California Press, 1985).

11. Pokert, *Theroretical Foundations.*

12. For discussions and definitions of Chinese medical concepts, see Paul Buell, "Theory and Practice of Traditional Chinese Medicine" (paper no. 21 presented at the East Asian Colloquium, Center for East Asian Studies, Bellingham, Wash., 1984); Frank Liu and Yan Mau Liu, *Chinese Medical Terminology* (Hong Kong: Commercial Press, 1980); Pokert, *Theoretical Foundations;* Kristofer Schipper, "The Taoist Body," *History of Religion* 17 (1978): 3–4, 355–386; Unschuld, *Ideas, Medicine in China: A History of Pharmaceutics* (Berkeley: University of California Press, 1986), and *Medicine in China: Nan-Ching: The Classic of Difficult Issues* (Berkeley: University of California Press, 1986).

13. See Unschuld, *Ideas.*

14. Ibid.

15. Ibid.

16. Joseph Needham, review of *Ideas* and *Pharmaceutics,* by Paul Unschuld, *American Ethnologist,* 15 (1 [1988]): 182–183.

17. E.g., Taiwan. See Katherine Gould-Martin, "Hot Cold Clean Poison and Dirt: Chinese Folk Medical Categories," *Social Science and Medicine* 12 (1978): 39–46.

18. Linda Koo, *Nourishment of Life* (Hong Kong: Commercial Press, 1982); and M. Topley, "Chinese Traditional Ideas and the Treatment of Disease: Two Examples from Hong Kong," *Man* 5 (1970): 421–437.

19. Paul Unschuld, Illness and Health in Chinese Medicine (paper presented at the annual conference of the Association for Asian Studies, Boston, MA, 1987).

20. Lee, *Perceptions.*

21. Richard Currier, "The Hot-Cold Syndrome and Symbolic Balance in Mexican and Spanish-American Folk Medicine," *Ethnology* 5 (1966): 251–263. See also George Foster, "Peasant Society and the Image of Limited Good," *American Anthropologist* 67 (1965): 293–315; and George Foster and Barbara Anderson, *Medical Anthropology* (New York: Wiley, 1978).

22. Gould-Martin, *Hot Cold Clean.*

23. H. Creel, *Shen Pu-Hai* (Chicago: University of Chicago Press, 1973); and Anderson, *Food of China.*

24. See Anderson, (1982a), "Ecologies of the Heart," in *Proceedings of the International Chinese Medicine Conference,* ed. Michael Gandy et al. (Oakland, 1984), 205–230, "Heating and Cooling Foods Re-Examined," *Social Science and Medicine* 25 (1984): 331–337, and, especially, "Humoral."

25. E. N. Anderson, "Heating and Cooling Foods in Hong Kong and Taiwan," *Social Science Information* 19 (2 [1980]): 237–268, and "Humoral."

26. Carol Laderman, "Symbolic and Empirical Reality: A New Approach to the Analysis of Food Avoidances," *American Ethnologist* 3 (1981): 468–493.

27. Anderson, "Humoral."

28. E. N. Anderson, "Ecology and Ideology in Chinese Folk Nutritional Therapy" (paper presented at the annual meeting of the American Anthropological Association, Washington, D. C., 1982); and Gould-Martin, *Hot Cold Clean.*

29. Unschuld, *Ideas* and *Illness.*

30. E. N. Anderson, *The Floating World of Castle Peak Bay* (Washington, D.C.: American Anthropological Association, 1970).

31. John Young, *Business and Sentiment in a Chinese Market Town* (Taipei: Orient Cultural Service, 1974).

32. Cf. Foster and Anderson, *Medical Anthropology.*

33. Cf. Diamond Jenness, *The Faith of a Coast Salish Indian* (Victoria, B.C.: British Columbia Provincial Museum, Anthropological Papers no. 3, 1955).

34. Robert Bellah et al., *Habits of the Heart* (Berkeley: University of California Press, 1985).

35. Arthur Kleinman, *Patients and Healers in the Context of Culture* (Berkeley: University of California Press, 1980), and *Social Origins of Distress and Disease* (New Haven: Yale University Press, 1986).

36. Hill Gates, "Dependency and the Part-Time Proletariat in Taiwan," *Modern China* 5 (1979): 381–407; Robert Marks, *Rural Revolution in South China* (Madison: University of Wisconsin Press, 1984); Robert Weller, *Unities and Diversities in Chinese Religion* (Seattle: University of Washington Press, 1987).

37. Anderson, *Floating World.*

38. E. P. Thompson, *The Making of the English Working Class* (1963; reprint, New York: Vintage, 1966); and Jean Comaroff, *Body of Power, Spirit of Resistance* (Chicago: University of Chicago Press, 1985).

39. Richard Schulz, "Some Life and Death Consequences of Perceived Control," *Cognition and Social Behavior,* ed. John S. Carroll and John W. Payne (New York: Academic Press, 1976), 135–153.

40. Albert Bandura, "Self-Efficacy Mechanism in Human Agency," *American Psychologist* 37 (2 [1982]): 122–147; and Ellen Langer, *The Psychology of Control* (Beverly Hills: Sage, 1983).

41. Koo, *Nourishment.*

42. Najma Rizvi, personal communication.

43. See Carol Laderman, "Symbolic and Empirical Reality: A New Approach to the Analysis of Food Avoidances," *American Ethnologist* 3 (1981): 468–493, for Malaysia.

44. Barbara Pillsbury, "Doing the Month" (paper presented at the annual meeting of the American Anthropological Association, 1976).

45. Mary Douglas, *Natural Symbols* (London: Barrie and Rockliff, 1966), and *Implicit Meanings* (London: Routledge, Kegan Paul, 1975). The latter book was published with a cover picture of a pangolin printed upside down, anomalous to the end.

46. Laderman, *Symbolic.*

47. Gould-Martin, *Hot Cold Clean,* 41.

48. Libin Cheng, "Are the So-Called Poisonous Food-Combinations Really Poisonous?" Contributions, Biological Laboratory, Science Society of China, *Zoological Series* 2 (9 [1936]): 307–316.

49. Gould-Martin, *Hot Cold Clean,* 40.

50. See, e.g., A. C. Graham, *Later Mohist Logic* (Hong Kong and London: Chinese University of Hong Kong and University of London School of Oriental and African Studies, 1978); and D. Lau, *Mencius* (Harmondsworth, Sussex: Pelican, 1970).

51. Kleinman, *Patients,* and *Social Origins.*

52. Koo, *Nourishment.*

53. Foster and Anderson, *Medical Anthropology.*

54. Unschuld, *Ideas.*

55. Charlotte Furth, "Concepts of Pregnancy, Childbirth, and Infancy in Ch'ing Dynasty China," *Journal of Asian Studies* 46 (1 [1987]): 7–35.

56. James Scott, *Weapons of the Weak* (New Haven: Yale University Press, 1985).

57. Susan Fiske and Shelley Taylor, *Social Cognition* (Reading, Mass.: Addison-Wesley, 1984); and David Morgan, unpublished research.

58. Robert Zajonc, "Feeling and Thinking: Preferences Need No Inferences," *American Psychologist* 35 (1980): 151–175.

59. Bandura, "Self-Efficacy."

60. See important discussions in Pokert, *Foundations,* and Unschuld, *Ideas.*

61. Liu and Liu, *Terminology.*

62. Karin Hilsdale, "The 'Psychiatry' of Traditional Oriental Medicine: An Exploratory Study in Comparative Diagnosis of Depressed Women" (Ph.D. diss., International College, 1985).

63. See Kleinman, *Social Origins.*

64. Michael Gandy et al. (eds.), *Proceedings of the International Chinese Medicine Conference* (Oakland, 1984).

65. Hilsdale, "'Psychiatry.'"

26

You Are What You Eat:
Religious Aspects of the Health Food Movement

Jill Dubisch

In this article Jill Dubisch shows that the health food movement in this country may be seen as more than a way of eating and more than an alternative healing system. Using Clifford Geertz's definition of religion as a "system of symbols," Dubisch maintains that the health food movement has many of the characteristics of a religion. For example, the anthropological concepts of mana *and* taboo *are used in a discussion of the merits of "health foods" (mana) versus the detrimental nature of "junk foods" (taboo). The health food movement, like religion, offers its adherents salvation of the body, psyche, and even society itself. Followers strive to gain new values and a new world view. Comparing health food devotees to people undergoing a religious revitalization, Dubisch describes how converts learn to criticize prevailing social values and institutions. She notes the process of conversion that individuals entering the movement undergo, their concern for the maintenance of purity, the "temples" (health food stores), the "rabbis" (health food experts), and the sacred writings that establish the movement's principles. Provocative and entertaining,*

Dubisch's analysis of the religious aspects of the health food movement is sound anthropology and is certain to remind each of us of our own, or an acquaintance's, "religious" involvement with health food.

Dr. Robbins was thinking how it might be interesting to make a film from Adelle Davis' perennial best seller, *Let's Eat Right to Keep Fit.* Representing a classic confrontation between good and evil—in this case nutrition versus unhealthy diet—the story had definite box office appeal. The role of the hero, Protein, probably should be filled by Jim Brown, although Burt Reynolds

Reprinted from Susan P. Montague and W. Arens, eds., *The American Dimension: Culture Myths and Social Realities,* 2nd ed. (Palo Alto, Calif., 1981), pp. 115–27, by permission of the author and Mayfield Publishing Company.

undoubtedly would pull strings to get the part. Sunny Doris Day would be a clear choice to play the heroine, Vitamin C, and Orson Welles, oozing saturated fatty acids from the pits of his flesh, could win an Oscar for his interpretation of the villainous Cholesterol. The film might begin on a stormy night in the central nervous system. . . .

—Tom Robbins, *Even Cowgirls Get the Blues*

I intend to examine a certain way of eating; that which is characteristic of the health food movement, and try to determine what people are communicating when they choose to eat in ways which run counter to the dominant patterns of food consumption in our society. This requires looking at health foods as a system of symbols and the adherence to a health food way of life as being, in part, the expression of belief in a particular world view. Analysis of these symbols and the underlying world view reveals that, as a system of beliefs and practices, the health food movement has some of the characteristics of a religion.

Such an interpretation might at first seem strange since we usually think of religion in terms of a belief in a deity or other supernatural beings. These notions, for the most part, are lacking in the health food movement. However, anthropologists do not always consider such beliefs to be a necessary part of a religion. Clifford Geertz, for example, suggests the following broad definition:

> A *religion* is (1) a system of symbols which acts to (2) establish powerful, pervasive, and long-lasting moods and motivations in men by (3) formulating conceptions of a general-order of existence and (4) clothing these conceptions with such an aura of factuality that (5) the moods and motivations seem uniquely realistic. (Geertz 1965: 4)

Let us examine the health food movement in the light of Geertz's definition.

HISTORY OF THE HEALTH FOOD MOVEMENT

The concept of "health foods" can be traced back to the 1830s and the Popular Health movement, which combined a reaction against professional medicine and an emphasis on lay knowledge and health care with broader social concerns such as feminism and the class struggle (see Ehrenreich and English 1979). The Popular Health movement emphasized self-healing and the dissemination of knowledge about the body and health to laymen. One of the early founders of the movement, Sylvester Graham (who gave us the graham cracker), preached that good health was to be found

in temperate living. This included abstinence from alcohol, a vegetarian diet, consumption of whole wheat products, and regular exercise. The writings and preachings of these early "hygienists" (as they called themselves) often had moral overtones, depicting physiological and spiritual reform as going hand in hand (Shryock 1966).

The idea that proper diet can contribute to good health has continued into the twentieth century. The discovery of vitamins provided for many health food people a further "natural" means of healing which could be utilized instead of drugs. Vitamins were promoted as health-giving substances by various writers, including nutritionist Adelle Davis, who has been perhaps the most important "guru" of health foods in this century. Davis preached good diet as well as the use of vitamins to restore and maintain health, and her books have become the best sellers of the movement. (The titles of her books, *Let's Cook It Right, Let's Get Well, Let's Have Healthy Children,* give some sense of her approach.) The health food movement took on its present form, however, during the late 1960s, when it became part of the "counterculture."

Health foods were "in," and their consumption became part of the general protest against the "establishment" and the "straight" life-style. They were associated with other movements centering around social concerns, such as ecology and consumerism (Kandel and Pelto 1980: 328). In contrast to the Popular Health movement, health food advocates of the sixties saw the establishment as not only the medical profession but also the food industry and the society it represented. Food had become highly processed and laden with colorings, preservatives, and other additives so that purity of food became a new issue. Chemicals had also become part of the food-growing process, and in reaction terms such as "organic" and "natural" became watchwords of the movement. Health food consumption received a further impetus from revelations about the high sugar content of many popular breakfast cereals which Americans had been taught since childhood to think of as a nutritious way to start the day. (Kellogg, an early advocate of the Popular Health movement, would have been mortified, since his cereals were originally designed to be part of a hygienic regimen.)

Although some health food users are members of formal groups (such as the Natural Hygiene Society, which claims direct descent from Sylvester Graham), the movement exists primarily as a set of principles and practices rather than as an organization. For those not part of organized groups, these principles and practices are disseminated, and contact is made with other members of the movement, through several means. The most important of these are health food stores, restaurants, and publications. The two most prominent journals in the movement are *Prevention* and *Let's Live,* begun in 1920 and 1932 respectively (Hongladarom 1976).

These journals tell people what foods to eat and how to prepare them. They offer advice about the use of vitamins, the importance of exercise, and the danger of pollutants. They also present testimonials from faithful practitioners. Such testimonials take the form of articles that recount how the author overcame a physical problem through a health food approach, or letters from readers who tell how they have cured their ailments by following methods advocated by the journal or suggested by friends in the movement. In this manner, such magazines not only educate, they also articulate a world view and provide evidence and support for it. They have become the "sacred writings" of the movement. They are a way of "reciting the code"— the cosmology and moral injunctions—which anthropologist Anthony F. C. Wallace describes as one of the important categories of religious behavior (1966: 57).

IDEOLOGICAL CONTENT OF THE HEALTH FOOD MOVEMENT

What exactly is the health food system? First, and most obviously, it centers around certain beliefs regarding the relationship of diet to health. Health foods are seen as an "alternative" healing system, one which people turn to out of their dissatisfaction with conventional medicine (see, for example, Hongladarom 1976). The emphasis is on "wellness" and prevention rather than on illness and curing. Judging from letters and articles found in health food publications, many individuals' initial adherence to the movement is a type of conversion. A specific medical problem, or a general dissatisfaction with the state of their health, leads these converts to an eventual realization of the "truth" as represented by the health food approach, and to a subsequent change in life-style to reflect the principles of that approach. "Why This Psychiatrist 'Switched'," published in *Prevention* (September 1976), carries the following heading: "Dr. H. L. Newbold is a great advocate of better nutrition and a livelier life style. But it took a personal illness to make him see the light." For those who have experienced such conversion, and for others who become convinced by reading about such experiences, health food publications serve an important function by reinforcing the conversion and encouraging a change of life-style. For example, an article entitled "How to Convert Your Kitchen for the New Age of Nutrition" (*Prevention,* February 1975) tells the housewife how to make her kitchen a source of health for her family. The article suggests ways of reorganizing kitchen supplies and reforming cooking

by substituting health foods for substances detrimental to health, and also offers ideas on the preparation of nutritious and delicious meals which will convert the family to this new way of eating without "alienating" them. The pamphlet *The Junk Food Withdrawal Manual* (Kline 1978) details how an individual can, step by step, quit eating junk foods and adopt more healthful eating habits. Publications also urge the readers to convert others by letting them know how much better health foods are than junk foods. Proselytizing may take the form of giving a "natural" birthday party for one's children and their friends, encouraging schools to substitute fruit and nuts for junk food snacks, and even selling one's own baking.

Undergoing the conversion process means learning and accepting the general features of the health food world view. To begin with, there is great concern, as there is in many religions, with purity, in this case, the purity of food, of water, of air. In fact, there are some striking similarities between keeping a "health food kitchen" and the Jewish practice of keeping kosher. Both make distinctions between proper and improper foods, and both involve excluding certain impure foods (whether unhealthful or non-kosher) from the kitchen and table. In addition, a person concerned with maintaining a high degree of purity in food may engage in similar behavior in either case— reading labels carefully to check for impermissible ingredients and even purchasing food from special establishments to guarantee ritual purity.

In the health food movement, the basis of purity is healthfulness and "naturalness." Some foods are considered to be natural and therefore healthier; this concept applies not only to foods but to other aspects of life as well. It is part of the large idea that people should work in harmony with nature and not against it. In this respect, the health food cosmology sets up an opposition of nature (beneficial) versus culture (destructive), or, in particular, the health food movement against our highly technological society. As products of our industrialized way of life, certain foods are unnatural; they produce illness by working against the body. Consistent with this view is the idea that healing, like eating, should proceed in harmony with nature. The assumption is that the body, if allowed to function naturally, will tend to heal itself. Orthodox medicine, on the other hand, with its drugs and surgery and its nonholistic approach to health, works against the body. Physicians are frequently criticized in the literature of the movement for their narrow approach to medical problems, reliance on drugs and surgery, lack of knowledge of nutrition, and unwillingness to accept the validity of the patient's own experience in healing himself. It is believed that doctors may actually cause further health problems rather than effecting a cure. A short item in *Prevention,* "The Delivery Is Normal—But the Baby Isn't," recounts an incident in which drug-induced labor in childbirth resulted in a mentally retarded baby. The conclusion is "nature does a good job—and we should not, without compelling reasons, try to take over" (*Prevention,* May 1979: 38).

The healing process is hastened by natural substances, such as healthful food, and by other "natural" therapeutic measures such as exercise. Vitamins are also very important to many health food people, both for maintaining health and for healing. They are seen as components of food which work with the body and are believed to offer a more natural mode of healing than drugs. Vitamins, often one of the most prominent products offered in many health food stores, provide the greatest source of profit (Hongladarom 1976).

A basic assumption of the movement is that certain foods are good for you while others are not. The practitioner of a health food way of life must learn to distinguish between two kinds of food: those which promote well-being ("health foods") and those which are believed to be detrimental to health ("junk foods"). The former are the only kind of food a person should consume, while the latter are the antithesis of all that food should be and must be avoided. The qualities of these foods may be described by two anthropological concepts, *mana* and *taboo.* Mana is a type of beneficial or valuable power which can pass to individuals from sacred objects through touch (or, in the case of health foods, by ingestion). Taboo, on the other hand, refers to power that is dangerous; objects which are taboo can injure those who touch them (Wallace 1966: 60–61). Not all foods fall clearly into one category or the other. However, those foods which are seen as having health-giving qualities, which contain *mana,* symbolize life, while *taboo* foods symbolize death. ("Junk food is . . . dead. . . . Dead food produces death," proclaims one health food manual [Kline 1978: 2–4].) Much of the space in health food publications is devoted to telling the reader why to consume certain foods and avoid others ("Frozen, Creamed Spinach: Nutritional Disaster," *Prevention,* May 1979; "Let's Sprout Some Seeds," *Better Nutrition,* September 1979).

Those foods in the health food category which are deemed to possess an especially high level of *mana* have come to symbolize the movement as a whole. Foods such as honey, wheat germ, yogurt, and sprouts are seen as representative of the general way of life which health food adherents advocate, and Kandel and Pelto found that certain health food followers attribute mystical powers to the foods they consume. Raw food eaters speak of the "life energy" in uncooked foods. Sprout eaters speak of their food's "growth force" (1980: 336).

Qualities such as color and texture are also important in determining health foods and may acquire symbolic value. "Wholeness" and "whole grain" have come to stand for healthfulness and have entered the jargon of the advertising industry. Raw, coarse, dark, crunchy, and cloudy foods are preferred over those which are cooked, refined, white, soft, and clear. (See Table 1.)

Thus dark bread is preferred over white, raw milk over pasteurized, brown rice over white. The convert must learn to eat foods which at first seem strange and even exotic and to reject many foods which are components of the Standard American diet. A McDonald's hamburger, for example, which is an important symbol of America itself (Kottack 1978), falls into the category of "junk food" and must be rejected.

Just as the magazines and books which articulate the principles of the health food movement and serve as a guide to the convert can be said to comprise the sacred writings of the movement, so the health food store or health food restaurant is the temple where the purity of the movement is guarded and maintained. There individuals find for sale the types of food and other substances advocated by the movement. One does not expect to find items of questionable purity, that is, substances which are not natural or which may be detrimental to health. Within the precincts of the temple adherents can feel safe from the contaminating forces of the larger society, can meet fellow devotees, and can be instructed by the guardians of the sacred area (see, for example, Hongladarom 1976). Health food stores may vary in their degree of purity. Some sell items such as coffee, raw sugar, or "natural" ice cream which are considered questionable by others of the faith. (One health food store I visited had a sign explaining that it did not sell vitamin supplements, which it considered to be "unnatural," i.e., impure.)

People in other places are often viewed as living more "naturally" and healthfully than contemporary Americans. Observation of such peoples may be used to confirm practices of the movement and to acquire ideas about food. Healthy and long-lived people like the Hunza of the Himalayas are studied to determine the secrets of their strength and longevity. Cultures as yet untainted by the food systems of industrialized nations are seen as examples of what better diet can do. In addition, certain foods from other cultures—foods such as humus, falafel, and tofu—have been adopted into the health food repertoire because of their presumed healthful qualities.

Peoples of other times can also serve as models for a more healthful way of life. There is in the health food movement a concept of a "golden age," a past which provides an authority for a better way of living. This past may be scrutinized for clues about how to improve contemporary American society. An archaeologist,

Table 1.   Health food world view

	Health Foods	Junk Foods	
cosmic	LIFE	DEATH	
oppositions	NATURE	CULTURE	
	holistic, organic	fragmented, mechanistic	
basic	harmony with body	working against body	
values	and nature	and nature	undesirable
and	natural and real	manufactured and	attributes
desirable	harmony, self-	artificial disharmony,	
attributes	sufficiency, independence	dependence	
	homemade, small scale	mass-produced	
	layman competence	professional esoteric	
	and understanding	knowledge and jargon	
beneficial	whole	processed	
qualities	coarse	refined	
of food	dark	white	harmful
	crunchy	soft	qualities
	raw	cooked	
	cloudy	clear	
specific	yogurt*	ice cream, candy	
foods with	honey*	sugar*	
mana	carob	chocolate	
	soybeans*	beef	specific
	sprouts*	overcooked vegetables	taboo
	fruit juices	soft drinks*	foods
	herb teas	coffee,* tea	
	foods from other cultures:	"all-American" foods: hot dogs,	
	humus, falafel, kefir, tofu,	McDonald's hamburgers,*	
	stir-fried vegetables,	potato chips,	
	pita bread	Coke	
	return to early American	corruption of this original	
	values, "real" American	and better way of life	
	way of life	and values	

*Denotes foods with especially potent mana or taboo.

writing for *Prevention* magazine, recounts how "I Put Myself on a Caveman Diet—Permanently" (*Prevention*, September 1979). His article explains how he improved his health by utilizing the regular exercise and simpler foods which he had concluded from his research were probably characteristic of our prehistoric ancestors. A general nostalgia about the past seems to exist in the health food movement, along with the feeling that we have departed from a more natural pattern of eating practiced by earlier generations of Americans (see, for example, Hongladarom 1976). (Sylvester Graham, however, presumably did not find the eating habits of his contemporaries to be very admirable.)

The health food movement is concerned with more than the achievement of bodily health. Nutritional problems are often seen as being at the root of emotional, spiritual, and even social problems. An article entitled "Sugar Neurosis" states "Hypoglycemia (low blood sugar) is a medical reality that can trigger wife-beating, divorce, even suicide" (*Prevention*, April 1979: 110). Articles and books claim to show the reader how to overcome depression through vitamins and nutrition and the movement promises happiness and psychological well-being as well as physical health. Social problems, too, may respond to the health food approach. For example, a probation officer recounts how she tried changing offenders' diets in order to change their behavior. Testimonials from two of the individuals helped tell "what it was like to find that good nutrition was their bridge from the wrong side of the law and a frustrated, unhappy life to a vibrant and useful one" (*Prevention,* May 1978: 56). Thus, through more healthful eating and a more natural life-style, the health food movement offers its followers what many religions offer: salvation—in this case salvation for the body, for the psyche, and for society.

Individual effort is the keystone of the health food movement. An individual can take responsibility for his or her own health and does not need to rely on professional medical practitioners. The corollary of this is that it is a person's own behavior which may be the cause of ill health. By sinning, by not listening to our bodies, and by not following a natural way of life, we bring our ailments upon ourselves.

The health food movement also affirms the validity of each individual's experience. No two individuals are alike: needs for different vitamins vary widely; some people are more sensitive to food additives than others; each person has his or her best method of achieving happiness. Therefore, the generalized expertise of professionals and the scientifically verifiable findings of the experts may not be adequate guides for you, the individual, in the search of health. Each person's experience has meaning; if something works for you, then it works. If it works for others also, so much the better, but if it does not, that does not invalidate your own experience. While the movement does not by any means disdain all scientific findings (and indeed they are used extensively when they bolster health food positions), such findings are not seen as the only source of confirmation for the way of life which the health food movement advocates, and the scientific establishment itself tends to be suspect.

In line with its emphasis on individual responsibility for health, the movement seeks to deprofessionalize knowledge and place in every individual's hands the information and means to heal. Drugs used by doctors are usually available only through prescription, but foods and vitamins can be obtained by anyone. Books, magazines, and health food store personnel seek to educate their clientele in ways of healing themselves and maintaining their own health. Articles explain bodily processes, the effects of various substances on health, and the properties of foods and vitamins.

The focus on individual responsibility is frequently tied to a wider concern for self-sufficiency and self-reliance. Growing your own organic garden, grinding your own flour, or even, as one pamphlet suggests, rais-

ing your own cow are not simply ways that one can be assured of obtaining healthful food; they are also expressions of independence and self-reliance. Furthermore, such practices are seen as characteristic of an earlier "golden age" when people lived natural lives. For example, an advertisement for vitamins appearing in a digest distributed in health food stores shows a mother and daughter kneading bread together. The heading reads "America's discovering basics." The copy goes on, "Baking bread at home has been a basic family practice throughout history. The past several decades, however, have seen a shift in the American diet to factory-produced breads. . . . Fortunately, today there are signs that more and more Americans are discovering the advantage of baking bread themselves." Homemade bread, home-canned produce, sprouts growing on the window sill symbolize what are felt to be basic American values, values supposedly predominant in earlier times when people not only lived on self-sufficient farms and produced their own fresh and more natural food, but also stood firmly on their own two feet and took charge of their own lives. A reader writing to *Prevention* praises an article about a man who found "new life at ninety without lawyers or doctors," saying "If that isn't the optimum in the American way of living, I can't imagine what is!" (*Prevention,* May 1978: 16). Thus although it criticizes the contemporary American way of life (and although some vegetarians turn to Eastern religions for guidance—see Kandel and Pelto 1980), the health food movement in general claims to be the true faith, the proponent of basic Americanness, a faith from which the society as a whole has strayed.

SOCIAL SIGNIFICANCE OF THE HEALTH FOOD MOVEMENT FOR AMERICAN ACTORS

Being a "health food person" involves more than simply changing one's diet or utilizing an alternative medical system. Kandel and Pelto suggest that the health food movement derives much of its popularity from the fact that "food may be used simultaneously to cure or prevent illness, as a religious symbol and to forge social bonds. Frequently health food users are trying to improve their health, their lives, and sometimes the world as well" (1980: 332). Use of health foods becomes an affirmation of certain values and a commitment to a certain world view. A person who becomes involved in the health food movement might be said to experience what anthropologist Anthony F. C. Wallace has called "mazeway resynthesis." The "mazeway" is the mental "map" or image of the world which each individual holds. It includes values, the environment and the objects in it, the image of the self and of others, the techniques one uses to manipulate the environment to achieve desired end states (Wallace 1966: 237). Resynthesis of this mazeway—that is, the creation of new "maps," values, and techniques—commonly occurs in times of religious revitalization, when new religious movements are begun and converts to them are made. As individuals, these converts learn to view the world in a new manner and to act accordingly. In the case of the health food movement, those involved learn to see their health problems and other dissatisfactions with their lives as stemming from improper diet and living in disharmony with nature. They are provided with new values, new ways of viewing their environment, and new techniques for achieving their goals. For such individuals, health food use can come to imply "a major redefinition of self-image, role, and one's relationship to others" (Kandel and Pelto 1980: 359). The world comes to "make sense" in the light of this new world view. Achievement of the desired end states of better health and an improved outlook on life through following the precepts of the movement gives further validation.

It is this process which gives the health food movement some of the overtones of a religion. As does any new faith, the movement criticizes the prevailing social values and institutions, in this case the health-threatening features of modern industrial society. While an individual's initial dissatisfaction with prevailing beliefs and practices may stem from experiences with the conventional medical system (for example, failure to find a solution to a health problem through visits to a physician), this dissatisfaction often comes to encompass other facets of the American way of life. This further differentiates the "health food person" from mainstream American society (even when the difference is justified as a return to "real" American values).

In everyday life the consumption of such substances as honey, yogurt, and wheat germ, which have come to symbolize the health food movement, does more than contribute to health. It also serves to represent commitment to the health food world view. Likewise, avoiding those substances, such as sugar and white bread, which are considered "evil" is also a mark of a health food person. Ridding the kitchen of such items—a move often advocated by articles advising readers on how to "convert" successfully to health foods—is an act of ritual as well as practical significance. The symbolic nature of such foods is confirmed by the reactions of outsiders to those who are perceived as being inside the movement. An individual who is perceived as being a health food person is often automatically assumed to use honey instead of sugar,

for example. Conversely, if one is noticed using or not using certain foods (e.g., adding wheat germ to food, not eating white sugar), this can lead to questions from the observer as to whether or not that individual is a health food person (or a health food "nut," depending upon the questioner's own orientation).

The symbolic nature of such foods is especially important for the health food neophyte. The adoption of a certain way of eating and the renunciation of mainstream cultural food habits can constitute "bridge-burning acts of commitment" (Kendel and Pelto 1980: 395), which function to cut the individual off from previous patterns of behavior. However, the symbolic activity which indicates this cutting off need not be as radical as a total change of eating habits. In an interview in *Prevention,* a man who runs a health-oriented television program recounted an incident in which a viewer called up after a show and announced excitedly that he had changed his whole life-style—he had started using honey in his coffee! (*Prevention,* February 1979: 89). While recognizing the absurdity of the action on a practical level, the program's host acknowledged the symbolic importance of this action to the person involved. He also saw it as a step in the right direction since one change can lead to another. Those who sprinkle wheat germ on cereal, toss alfalfa sprouts with a salad, or pass up an ice cream cone for yogurt are not only demonstrating a concern for health but also affirming their commitment to a particular life-style and symbolizing adherence to a set of values and a world view.

CONCLUSION

As this analysis has shown, health foods are more than simply a way of eating and more than an alternative healing system. If we return to Clifford Geertz's definition of religion as a "system of symbols" which produces "powerful, pervasive, and long-lasting moods and motivations" by "formulating conceptions of a general order of existence" and making them appear "uniquely realistic," we see that the health food movement definitely has a religious dimension. There is, first, a system of symbols, in this case based on certain kinds and qualities of food. While the foods are believed to have health-giving properties in themselves, they also symbolize a world view which is concerned with the right way to live one's life and the right way to construct a society. This "right way" is based on an approach to life which stresses harmony with nature and the holistic nature of the body. Consumption of those substances designated as "health foods," as well as participation in other activities associated with the movement which also symbolize its world view (such as exercising or growing an organic garden), can serve to establish the "moods and motivations" of which Geertz speaks. The committed health food follower may come to experience a sense of spiritual as well as physical well-being when he or she adheres to the health food way of life. Followers are thus motivated to persist in this way of life, and they come to see the world view of this movement as correct and "realistic."

In addition to its possession of sacred symbols and its "convincing" world view, the health food movement also has other elements which we usually associate with a religion. Concepts of mana and taboo guide the choice of foods. There is a distinction between the pure and impure and a concern for the maintenance of purity. There are "temples" (health food stores and other such establishments) which are expected to maintain purity within their confines. There are "rabbis," or experts in the "theology" of the movement and its application to everyday life. There are sacred and instructional writings which set out the principles of the movement and teach followers how to utilize them. In addition, like many religious movements, the health food movement harkens back to a "golden age" which it seeks to recreate and assumes that many of the ills of the contemporary world are caused by society's departure from this ideal state.

Individuals entering the movement, like individuals entering any religious movement, may undergo a process of conversion. This can be dramatic, resulting from the cure of an illness or the reversal of a previous state of poor health, or it can be gradual, a step-by-step changing of eating and other habits through exposure to health food doctrine. Individuals who have undergone conversion and mazeway resynthesis, as well as those who have tested and confirmed various aspects of the movement's prescriptions for better health and a better life, may give testimonials to the faith. For those who have adopted, in full or in part, the health food world view, it provides, as do all religions, explanations for existing conditions, answers to specific problems, and a means of gaining control over one's existence. Followers of the movement are also promised "salvation," not in the form of afterlife, but in terms of enhanced physical well-being, greater energy, longer life-span, freedom from illness, and increased peace of mind. However, although the focus is this-worldly, there is a spiritual dimension to the health food movement. And although it does not center its world view around belief in supernatural beings,

it does posit a higher authority—the wisdom of nature —as the source of ultimate legitimacy for its views.

Health food people are often dismissed as "nuts" or "food faddists" by those outside the movement. Such a designation fails to recognize the systematic nature of the health food world view, the symbolic significance of health foods, and the important functions which the movement performs for its followers. Health foods offer an alternative or supplement to conventional medical treatment, and a meaningful and effective way for individuals to bring about changes in lives which are perceived as unsatisfactory because of poor physical and emotional health. It can also provide for its followers a framework of meaning which transcends individual problems. In opposing itself to the predominant American life-style, the health food movement sets up a symbolic system which opposes harmony to disharmony, purity to pollution, nature to culture, and ultimately, as in many religions, life to death. Thus while foods are the beginning point and the most important symbols of the health food movement, food is not the ultimate focus but rather a means to an end: the organization of a meaningful world view and the construction of a satisfying life.

REFERENCES

Ehrenreich, Barbara, and Deidre English. 1979. *For Her Own Good: 150 Years of the Experts' Advice to Women.* Garden City, N.Y.: Anchor Press/Doubleday.

Geertz, Clifford. 1965. "Religion as a Cultural System." In Michael Banton, ed., *Anthropological Approaches to the Study of Religion.* A.S.A. Monograph No. 3. London: Tavistock Publications Ltd.

Hongladarom, Gail Chapman. 1976. "Health Seeking Within the Health Food Movement." Ph.D. Dissertation: University of Washington.

Kandel, Randy F., and Gretel H. Pelto. 1980. "The Health Food Movement: Social Revitalization or Alternative Health Maintenance System." In Norge W. Jerome, Randy F. Kandel, and Gretel H. Pelto, eds., *Nutritional Anthropology.* Pleasantville, N.Y.: Redgrave Publishing Co.

Kline, Monte. 1978. *The Junk Food Withdrawal Manual.* Total Life, Inc.

Kottak, Conrad. 1978. "McDonald's as Myth, Symbol, and Ritual." In *Anthropology: The Study of Human Diversity.* New York: Random House.

Shryock, Richard Harrison. 1966. *Medicine in America: Historical Essays.* Baltimore: Johns Hopkins University Press.

Wallace, Anthony F. C. 1966. *Religion: An Anthropological View.* New York: Random House.

PART IV

Too Little and Too Much: Nutritional Problems in the Contemporary World

Undernutrition: Counting, Classification, and Consequences

The World Health Organization estimates that some 6.6 million children currently die every year from protein-energy malnutrition (PEM) (Table 1). Nearly all of these are infants and children who live in Africa, Asia, and Latin America. On a scale that is easier to relate to, about 396 children—the approximate number of passengers on a jumbo jet—die every half hour of every day of every year. Unlike the publicity that would surround the jet crashes, these children die in relative silence.

Alleviating undernutrition is a great challenge, and many nutritional anthropologists are working on various aspects of this problem. But before the causes of undernutrition can be addressed, it is important, even essential, to understand who is undernourished, how severely and chronically they are undernourished, and which nutrients are involved. Answering these questions is not always easy and without controversy. A theme of this part is the science and politics of quantifying and classifying undernutrition.

What are the consequences of malnutrition? Many individuals die from severe malnutrition, but these are a minority of the malnourished. Protein-energy malnutrition is the most prevalent form of undernutrition, followed by iron deficiency and iodine deficiency (Table 1). Should relief and intervention efforts be directed toward these many mildly malnourished, or to the more severely malnourished who may die? If efforts are to be directed toward individuals with milder forms of malnutrition, then alleviating this level of undernutrition ought to improve lives. A second and important theme of this part's articles concerns the consequences of mild-to-moderate malnutrition (MMM).

In "The Potentiating Effects of Malnutrition on Child Mortality: Epidemiological Evidence and Policy Implications," David Pelletier summarizes data on malnutrition and child mortality. Pelletier's approach is a version of "meta-analysis," an epidemiological technique in which results are compared and summarized for all available studies that meet similar criteria. Pelletier is interested in how often malnutrition leads to child mortality, the strengths and consistency of the effect, and how strong the effect is for different levels of malnutrition. Malnutrition is classified by categories of weight-for-age (WA): WA of >80 percent of the median for children is generally considered normal, a WA of 60–79 percent of the median is considered to reflect mild-to-moderate levels of malnutrition (MMM), and a WA of <60 percent is considered indicative of severe malnutrition.

Among Pelletier's startling findings are that (1) malnutrition predicts increased mortality in almost every study, (2) malnutrition is the most important underlying cause of child mortality in most countries, and (3) even mild-to-moderate malnutrition precedes an increase in mortality. Do these results surprise or shock you? What are some of the policy implications of these data?

Mortality is by far the most dramatic consequence of malnutrition, but does being malnourished have other consequences? To answer this question, Adolfo Chávez and colleagues from the Mexican National Institute of Nutrition conducted a lengthy study of infants and children with mild-to-moderate malnutrition in Mexico. When they began in the 1960s, there were other studies demonstrating the effects of severe malnutrition on experimental animals, as well as on human adults, but very little was known of the effects of MMM on the growing infant and child.

Adolfo Chávez, Celia Martínez, and Beatriz Soberanes summarize the results of their longitudinal study in "The Effect of Malnutrition on Human Development." The study was designed to compare the growth and development of children provided with nutritional supplements with that of nonsupplemented children living in the same highland Mexican town.

As predicted, they found that the supplemented children gained weight more rapidly than the nonsupplemented children (Figure 5, Table 2). More surprising were the effects of supplementation on the percentage of days sick (Figure 6), activity patterns (which were calculated as the number of "foot contacts" per hour) (Figure 8), and behaviors relating to personality and intellectual development (Figures 9–13, Tables 3–4). Questions to consider when reading this article include the following:

♦ Is the study an ethical one? Don't forget what was and was not known about malnutrition at the time of the study.

Table 1.   Estimated numbers of people affected by malnutrition worldwide in the 1990s

Deficiency	Morbidity	Prevalence	Mortality/Year
Protein and energy	stunted growth	230 million children 0–5 years	6.6 million
Iron	anemia	1500 million	—
Vitamin A	blindness	350,000 children 0–5 years	210,000
	clinical deficiency	2.7 million children 0–5 years	—
Iodine	goiter	911 million	—
	brain damage	66 million	—

SOURCE: World Health Organization (http://www.who.int/nut.malnutritionworldwide.htm#pem and http://www.who.int/inf-fs/en/fact119.html and http://www.who.int/gpv-dvacc/diseases/vitamina.htm); Scrimshaw, 1991 (article 29).

✦ How convinced are you that these results may be extrapolated to other communities?

✦ Given these data, what should be done? How? When? By whom?

The focus of Chávez and colleagues' Projecto Puebla was on the general state of nutrition, as was appropriate for the time of the study. Their goal was simply to compare children with and without adequate food. However, in order to intervene, it may be useful to know which nutrients are most important. Is it protein, as was thought in the 1960s? Or energy, as was assumed in the 1980s? Or various micronutrients (vitamins and minerals), which are a focus of research in the 1990s? Or most of the above? Or even all of the above?

In a half century of research and practice, Dr. Nevin Scrimshaw has been instrumental in nearly every major development in international nutrition. He is credited with first explicating the deadly synergy between malnutrition and infection in the 1960s, he helped establish programs to combat undernutrition throughout the world, he trained many of today's leaders in international nutrition, and he continues to contribute to knowledge of the importance of problems such as micronutrient deficiencies. In "Iron Deficiency," Dr. Scrimshaw summarizes what is known of the functional consequences of a mild deficiency of this micronutrient. His article is a review, written for nonspecialists.

Scrimshaw elaborates that iron deficiency is one of the most widespread deficiencies today. The most well-known effect of iron deficiency is anemia, a low concentration of blood hemoglobin. However, there is evidence that iron deficiency has functional consequences even before hemoglobin concentrations are low enough for an individual to be classified as anemic. His findings are as startling as those of Pelletier and Chávez and colleagues. In addition to the synergy between iron deficiency and infection, iron deficiency also has clear functional consequences on work and exercise ability and even on learning and cognition.

One of the important twists in thinking about iron deficiency is that the relationship between iron intake and iron status is more complex than is usually recognized. Iron absorption depends on the form of the iron, what is eaten with the iron, and the state of the body at the time of consumption. For example, consider the following: Heme iron (iron that is part of a hemoglobin molecule) is more readily absorbed than non–heme iron (from vegetable sources), all forms of iron are more readily absorbed when consumed with ascorbic acid (vitamin C), and iron is absorbed more efficiently when an individual is anemic.

The relationship between nutritional status and its consequences on the one hand, and politics and public policy on the other hand, is made clear in the article "Body Size, Adaptation and Function" by Reynaldo Martorell. Trained as a biological anthropologist, Martorell is now best known for work on nutritional problems in Mexico and Central America. This article is a response to what has come to be known as the "small but healthy" hypothesis.

David Seckler, an economist working in India, suggested the "small but healthy" hypothesis in articles published in the early 1980s. Seckler proposed that there was little evidence that individuals who are classified as small by anthropometric comparisons to U.S. standards were compromised in function and were unhealthy. Rather, he hypothesized, these individuals, perhaps a billion or more in Asia alone, were growing appropriately for their environment, and their small bodies were actually an adaptation to a restricted food supply. They were "small but healthy." The important implication of this perspective for public policy is that relief efforts should be focused on the more severely malnourished, rather than the "small but healthy" individuals.

That the "small but healthy" hypothesis may be flawed should be clear from the studies of Pelletier and Chávez and colleagues. Martorell's article provides a focused and direct response to Seckler. Martorell makes four points that link public policy to biology:

1.   Saying that stunting is healthy is akin to condoning the conditions of poverty that cause stunting.

2.   Poor growth is a danger signal.

3. The same factors that lead to stunting affect functions such as cognition.

4. The functional consequences associated with poor growth are lifelong.

How well does Martorell demonstrate that the "small but healthy" hypothesis is invalid and even detrimental?

How do we count and classify the malnourished? The articles in this part make clear that counting and classification are not simple tasks. In cases of severe undernutrition, there are a variety of clinical and biochemical signs, and ambiguities are greatly reduced. However, in the more prevalent forms of MMM, the tool kit is a rather small and crude one. Heights, weights, and sometimes some other anthropometric measurements are recorded and compared to a standard (Figures 1 and 2). Clearly, some individuals are small for genetic reasons; therefore, misclassification of individuals is a fact that needs to be recognized. Nonetheless, stunting (short stature) is an important sign at the individual level, as well as at the level of the group or community.

The most important point of the articles is that subtle levels of nutritional inadequacy and excess may have lasting functional consequences. An ongoing challenge to nutritional scientists and anthropologists is to further isolate and specify the relationship between nutrients and varied consequences. At the same time, many have said we know enough now about counting, classification, and consequences of inadequate nutrition. Articles in subsequent parts will focus on the contexts and causes of undernutrition and possible solutions.

SUGGESTIONS FOR THINKING AND DOING NUTRITIONAL ANTHROPOLOGY

1. Compare the public policy implications of the "small but healthy" hypothesis with the implications of a rejection of this hypothesis.

2. Research the validity of growth in height and weight as a measure of nutritional status. A good starting point is article 28 and Eveleth and Tanner's (1990) data on variation in growth by socioeconomic status.

3. *Anthropometric Measurement of Nutritional Status.* One of the key advantages of anthropometric methods is that they are easily implemented. They do not require expensive equipment, they can be performed almost anywhere, and most methods can be reliably performed by individuals after a short training period. A number of excellent articles and books, such as Gib-

son's *Principles of Nutritional Assessment* (1990), provide detailed information on how to measure and interpret nutritional status data. The following is a brief and simplified guide to measuring heights and weights and converting these measurements to percentiles of height-for-age (HA) and weight-for-age (WA). In order to gain a sense of reliability (the degree of variation in measurement among measurers), students should work in groups of about four. Each student should measure the others in his or her group.

Stature. If anthropometric equipment is not available, attach a measuring tape to the wall (make sure the tape is absolutely vertical) and measure stature (height) against the wall. Subjects should take their shoes off and stand tall, with their heels against the wall, for measurement with eyes looking straight ahead and their head level. Hold a flat object such as a ruler or book vertically on the top of the head and record your measurement to the nearest quarter of an inch.

Weight is best measured on a balance beam type of scale, although a normal household scale may do for our purpose of better understanding reliability. Subjects should be measured without shoes or heavy clothing. Record measurements to the nearest pound.

A. Reliability. Members of each group may now compare their measurements with those of the other students in the group. In a group of four, all four individuals should have been measured three times. Describe the similarity in measurements. Which measurements are more or less similar? Is the measurement of any individual "off" compared with the others? What inferences can you make about the reliability of height and weight measurement?

B. Converting to Percentiles. Converting to growth percentiles allows for the comparison of individuals of different ages and sexes. Figures 1 and 2 are growth charts from the U.S. National Center for Health Statistics (NCHS). A cluster of seven parallel lines represents percentiles of growth in stature (upper set) and weight (lower set) by age for males and females. The lowest line is the 5th percentile, the heavy middle line is the 50th percentile, and the upper line is the 95th percentile. Students should locate individuals they have measured on these charts. Age 18 years can be used for everyone over that age. For the entire class, how many individuals fell between the 25th and 75th percentiles, and how many fell outside of the 10th and 90th percentiles?

C. Now that you have learned some basics of anthropometry, use and extend these tools. Offer to measure children at a local kindergarten. Measure a larger group of students, and plot the relationship between weight and

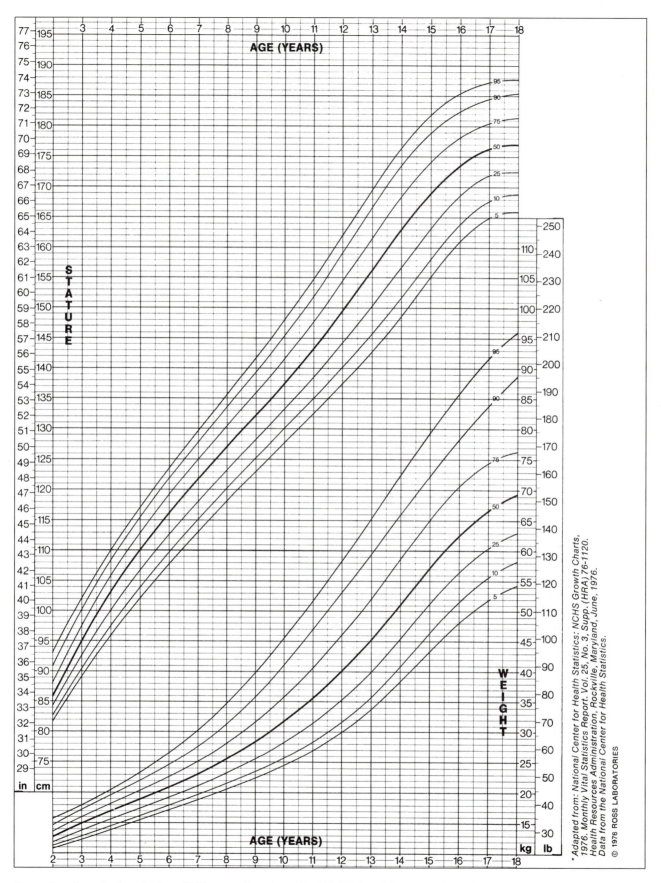

Figure 1.   Growth chart for boys 2–18 years of age from the U.S. National Center for Health Statistics (NCHS).

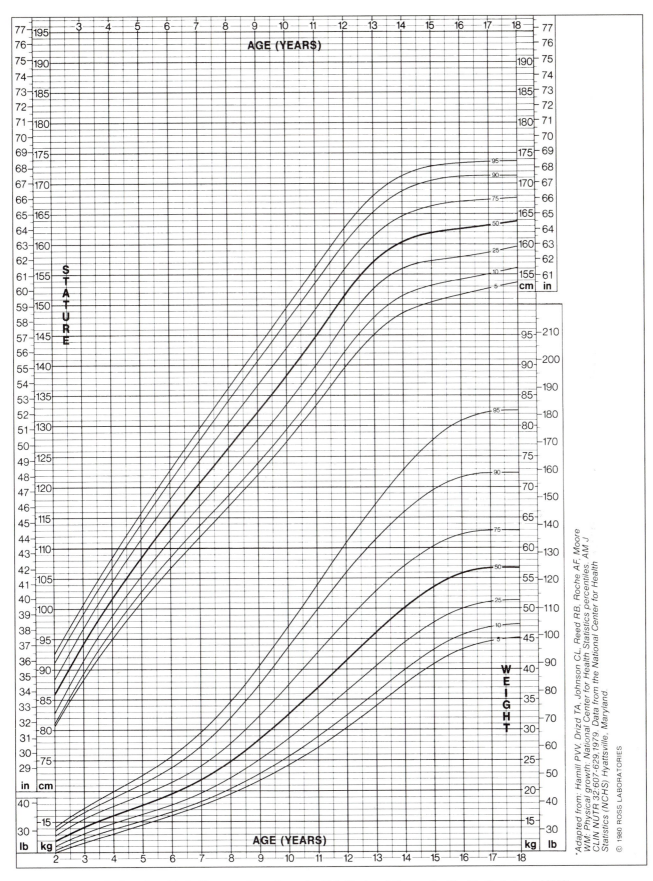

Adapted from: Hamill PVV, Drizd TA, Johnson CL, Reed RB, Roche AF, Moore WM: Physical growth: National Center for Health Statistics percentiles. AM J CLIN NUTR 32:607-629,1979. Data from the National Center for Health Statistics (NCHS) Hyattsville, Maryland.

© 1980 ROSS LABORATORIES

Figure 2.　Growth chart for girls 2–18 years of age from the U.S. National Center for Health Statistics (NCHS).

stature. If equipment is available (measuring tape, skinfold calipers), use one of the references and try measuring upper-arm circumferences and triceps skinfold thickness.

SUGGESTED READINGS

Eveleth, P. B., & Tanner, J. M. (1990). *Worldwide variation in human growth* (2nd ed.). New York: Cambridge University Press. (Excellent source on geographic, economic, and ethnic variation in growth and the environmental and genetic causes of observed differences.)

Gibson, R. (Ed.). (1990). *Principles of nutritional assessment.* Oxford: Oxford University Press. (Comprehensive and clear overview of anthropometric, biochemical, and clinical nutritional assessment methods.)

Himes, J. (Ed.). (1991). *Anthropometric assessment of nutritional status.* New York: John Wiley. (Set of chapters on dietary and nutritional assessment methods. More theoretical and less of a "how to" than Gibson's *Principles of Nutritional Assessment.*)

Seckler, D. (1980). Malnutrition: An intellectual odyssey. *Western Journal of Agricultural Economics, 5*(2), 219–27. (The original source of the "small but healthy" hypothesis.)

Ulijaszek, S. J., Johnson, F. E., & Preece, M. A. (Eds.). (1998). *The Cambridge encyclopedia of human growth and development.* New York: Cambridge University Press. (Excellent compendium of short articles on various aspects of human growth and development.)

27

The Potentiating Effects of Malnutrition on Child Mortality: Epidemiologic Evidence and Policy Implications

David L. Pelletier

The physiologic synergism between malnutrition and infection has been recognized for some time, but its implications have not been addressed in current child survival policies and programs. This [article] summarizes the conclusions from a recent analysis of 28 epidemiologic studies of the malnutrition–mortality relationship. It concludes that the relationship is consistent across diverse world populations, that there is a significant effect of both mild-to-moderate malnutrition and severe malnutrition, and that the effect is not simply due to confounding by socioeconomic factors or intercurrent illness. In addition, evidence is provided supporting the hypothesis that malnutrition and infection have multiplicative effects on child mortality, rather than the additive effects implicitly assumed, and the policy implications of these findings are described.

In 1968, Scrimshaw and colleagues documented the synergistic relationship between malnutrition and infection.[1] This was one of the landmark publications in the recent history of nutrition science. Drawing together extensive evidence from biomedical research, clinical research, and clinical practice, this synthesis formalized the "vicious cycle" concept of malnutrition, which is now widely accepted in both scientific and applied circles. Stated simply, this view holds that malnutrition adversely affects a person's ability to resist and/or respond to infection, and infection adversely affects a person's ability to utilize energy and nutrients obtained from the diet. As illustrated by the case of measles,[2] such physiologic synergism can have devastating consequences.

Despite the broad recognition and acceptance of this phenomenon for more than two decades, the implications of the malnutrition–infection synergism are not yet reflected in policies designed to improve child survival in developing countries. Among some relevant questions are the following: (1) Does the relationship between malnutrition and mortality differ across diverse populations? (2) Is the effect of malnutrition on the risk of death limited to severe malnutrition, or is it also present in mild-to-moderate malnutrition (MMM)? (3) Do malnutrition and infection have multiplicative effects on mortality at the population level, as would be predicted by theory? (4) Is it possible to estimate the percentage of child deaths due to malnutrition in order to decide on the most appropriate mix of intervention strategies on a global, country, and local basis? (5) Does malnutrition have similar effects on many infectious diseases, or is its effect confined to such well-defined examples as measles and diarrhea? Answers to these questions have profound implications for health and development policy and are now forthcoming from a synthesis and reanalysis of epidemiologic studies conducted over the past two decades. Each question is taken up below after a description of the studies used in the meta-analysis.

DESCRIPTION OF STUDIES

A computer-assisted literature search complemented by bibliographic branching generated 28 reports of research that met the basic criteria for meta-analysis. The study criteria included: that studies done in developing countries be community-based rather than hospital-based; that prospective methods be used to relate child mortality to indicators of nutrition status; that anthropometric methods as indicators of nutrition status be used; and that the target population be children under the age of 5. The list of 28 reports is believed to be complete with respect to studies that meet these criteria.

The 28 reports actually refer to 21 separate studies, representing populations in 10 different countries. There is a clear bias favoring Bangladesh (14 reports based on 7 different studies). There are 10 reports from Africa (Guinea-Bissau, Senegal, Zaire, Uganda, Tanzania, and Malawi), 3 reports from Asia outside of Bangladesh (India, Indonesia, and Papua New Guinea), and no reports from Latin America. All reports used one or more of the following anthropometric indicators: weight-for-age (WA), height-for-age, weight-for-height, and mid-upper arm circumference (MUAC). Further details about this sample of studies, methods, and findings are available in the full report.[3]

Consistency Across Populations

The earliest of the prospective studies took place in India,[4] Bangladesh,[5,6] and Papua New Guinea[7] and established the basic finding that the risk of mortality is inversely related to anthropometric indicators of nutrition status. The legitimacy of this conclusion was first called into question by the findings from Kasongo, Zaire.[8] That study found no association between anthropometric indicators and subsequent mortality and led to some discussion about possible population-specific relationships,[8,9] a concept that prevails to this day.[10]

When the Kasongo study is examined in light of the entire set of prospective studies, it appears that the negative results are more likely due to methodologic reasons. This is because more recent studies in Africa have all found the expected inverse relationship between nutrition status and mortality, including studies from Guinea-Bissau,[11] Senegal,[12] Uganda,[13,14] Tanzania,[15] and Malawi.[16,17] This is also confirmed in a recent study from a different region of Zaire.[18] Close inspection of the Kasongo report[8] reveals that mortality was grossly underenumerated (approximately 20% of the expected number of deaths were counted), and the anthropometric measurements were "obtained under conditions that are similar to operational conditions of screening in clinics."[8] Thus, the overwhelming body of evidence continues to support the notion that the fundamental inverse relationship between nutrition status and mortality is consistent across populations. In fact, a surprising degree of consistency is observed even in the details of the relationship, as revealed by a subset of studies described below.

Mild-to-Moderate Malnutrition

The perception that MMM may have no consequences for child mortality was created in large part by the early findings from Chen et al.[6] They empirically observed elevated mortality among children with severe weight deficits (WA below 65% of the international reference) but noted no consistent relationship above that threshold. Commenting on this, Trowbridge and Sommer[19] presented results based on MUAC from an earlier Bangladesh study. Those results showed a sharp increase in mortality among the severely malnourished (MUAC < 12.0 cm), with a more modest elevation among those children with moderate deficits (MUAC 12–12.9 cm). Since then, many studies have confirmed the characteristic exponential relationship between mortality and anthropometric indicators,[3] which seemingly supports the concept that anthropometric deficits are a serious concern only at the extremes of the distribution. This has reinforced the theories of adaptation to malnutrition[20] and small but healthy,[21] and seems to reinforce the widespread practice of screening for severe malnutrition in many supplementary feeding programs.

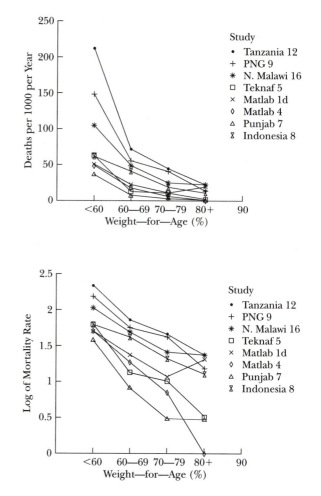

Figure 1. Relationship between child mortality and weight-for-age as a percentage of international median. The Chen et al. study is labelled "Matlab 1d" in this figure and is based on a reanalysis by Cogill.[22] Reprinted with permission from Pelletier DL. The relationship between child anthropometry and mortality in developing countries: implications for policy, programs, and future research. (*Source: J Nutr 1994:124:2047S–81S*)

With this historic perspective, it is of great interest to note that the results of Chen et al.[6] have not been replicated by prospective studies since that time, including studies in the same geographic region of Bangladesh, other areas of Bangladesh, other Asian countries, and several African countries. Figure 1 shows the results of seven other studies that employed similar methodologies. These studies can be compared in detail with those from Chen et al.[6] The top panel depicts mortality in natural units, and the bottom panel depicts the log (base 10) of mortality. The dominant impression from the top panel is a marked elevation in mortality below 60% WA, especially in Tanzania, Papua New Guinea, and Malawi, all of which have high mortality rates at any given WA. However, the figure also reveals a clear elevation in mortality even at moderate (60–69% WA) and mild (70–79% WA) anthropometric deficits. The bottom panel depicts mortality using the log scale, and merely accentuates this observation. It is interesting that the MUAC results of Trowbridge and Sommer[19] fit this pattern exactly, although at the time they were interpreted as confirmation of a threshold effect as seen by Chen et al.[6]

The data from Figure 1 suggest that the study by Chen et al.[6] produced unusual results for inexplicable reasons. They also reveal a clear elevation in mortality among children with MMM that is remarkably consistent across populations, albeit not as marked as that seen in severe malnutrition. It is important to note that the modest elevation in mortality associated with MMM results in a lower screening efficiency for this group, and one that is probably unacceptably low in practical settings. However, it still has relevance for a broader policy formulation in light of the much higher prevalence of MMM as compared to severe malnutrition. This is highlighted by the quantitative estimates of malnutrition provided below.

Although the accumulated results of malnutrition–mortality relationships are striking for their consistency, the hypothesis can be made that the association is simply or largely due to statistical confounding. According to this hypothesis, malnutrition and mortality may co-occur in the same households simply because both are associated with poverty or low socioeconomic status. For instance, it may be that the malnutrition noted in these households is caused by poor nutrient intake and an increased exposure to disease, whereas mortality may be caused by low immunization rates or inappropriate treatment of illness. Another possibility is that low WA is a by-product of increased exposure to disease and appears to be associated with mortality for this reason but actually plays no causal role in mortality. Several studies have examined the possibility of confounding[3] and all of them have found that a significant association between malnutrition and mortality persists even after controlling for confounding through various statistical techniques.

THE MULTIPLICATIVE EFFECTS OF MALNUTRITION AND MORBIDITY

The above discussions suggest that the effects of malnutrition on mortality are consistent across populations, are found in MMM as well as severe malnutrition, and are not simply due to confounding by socioeconomic factors or intercurrent illness. The eight studies represented in Figure 1 are important for another reason, as well. They provide confirmation that the physiologic synergism described by Scrimshaw et al.[1] does have multiplicative effects on mortality at the population level. As shown earlier,[23] a simple specification of the synergism between malnutrition and morbidity is that exposure to disease is constant within any given population, but the fatality rate per exposure varies with the degree of malnutrition. If this is so, then the risk of death for an individual child is related to the product (not the sum) of the probability of exposure to disease and the probability of being malnourished (a multiplicative rather than an additive model). At the population level, it follows that the mortality rate should be related to the product of the burden of disease (exposure) and the prevalence of malnutrition. Note that one indicator of the burden of disease in a given population is simply the mortality rate among the well-nourished, because some proportion of well-nourished children will die of infectious diseases at some "baseline" rate determined by the types of diseases present and the health care available to treat them.

The data shown in Figure 1 (especially the lower panel) conform precisely to this theoretical model of synergism. It reveals that populations with high "baseline mortality" (mortality among the relatively well-nourished, reflecting the population's burden of disease) have a systematically higher response to malnutrition. For instance, the population in Punjab, India, initially had the lowest level of baseline mortality (2.8/1000/year) but experienced an increase of 34/1000/year when the WA went from >80% to <60%. By contrast, Iringa, Tanzania, had the highest baseline mortality (23/1000/year) and experienced an increase of 189/1000/year in going from >80% WA to <60% WA. With an additive model, Tanzania would have experienced roughly the same number of excess deaths as India (34/1000/year) in progressing from the well-nourished to the severely malnourished category. The parallelism in the eight lines reveals that there is a consistent tendency across the eight studies in which the mortality response* to malnutrition is proportional to the baseline mortality level. This has been formally tested and confirmed by Pelletier et al.[23,24]

The above results and the inferences drawn from them are important because the sample sizes in the only controlled intervention were not adequate for testing the multiplicative effects of malnutrition and morbidity.[4] Thus, the present results provide the only evidence currently available for testing this hypothesis.

---

*In this paragraph, "mortality response" and "increase in mortality" are used as a shorthand for attributable risk, which is the difference in mortality rates between the malnourished and the well-nourished.

These observations have important implications for conceptualizing the relationships between malnutrition, morbidity and mortality, classifying causes of death, and planning actions to improve health and survival in developing countries. Specifically, malnutrition should not be viewed as a cause of death on its own. Instead, malnutrition acts as a potentiator of existing infectious diseases, with the degree of potentiation proportional to the severity of malnutrition. Consequently, it is both meaningless and misleading to ascribe a certain number of deaths to either malnutrition or infectious disease alone, the latter being a common practice. In developing countries with high rates of malnutrition, the excessive number of deaths attributed to diarrhea, acute respiratory infection (ARI), measles, and other common infections places primacy on the proximate and clinically obvious cause, while ignoring the potentiating effects that severe and (less obvious) MMM have on those diseases. For example, the 1993 World Development Report attributes only 2.4% of Disability Adjusted Life Years (DALYs) lost to protein–energy malnutrition, as compared to 63% for common infectious diseases. At the policy level, one consequence of ignoring this potentiation may be a neglect of improvement in nutrition status as a broad strategy to reduce mortality due to infectious diseases.

MALNUTRITION AND MORTALITY: QUANTIFYING THE EFFECTS

Bearing in mind the "potentiation paradigm" of the effect of malnutrition on mortality, the results shown in the lower panel of Figure 1 indicate that the absolute value of child mortality can be accurately modeled simply as a function of (1) baseline mortality among those with WA >80% and (2) the percentage of children falling in each of the grades of malnutrition below 80% of median. However, this observation has limited practical utility when stated in those terms because most countries do not know the mortality level among those with WA >80% of median. Thus, it would not be possible to estimate the contribution of malnutrition to child mortality in most populations.

An alternative formulation relies upon the fact that the relative risk (RR) of mortality at various grades of WA can be calculated from the data in Figure 1. The RRs are 8.4 for severe (WA < 60%), 4.6 for moderate (WA = 60–69%), and 2.4 for mild (WA = 70–79%) malnutrition. The contribution of malnutrition to child mortality because of its potentiating effect on infectious disease can then be calculated using the standard epidemiologic statistic of population attributable risk (PAR). The PAR simply combines the RR estimates with estimates of the prevalence of low WA in a given population. The methodology has been fully described and tested elsewhere[24] but is discussed here to present the results that have emerged from this approach when applied to 53 countries for which suitable anthropometric data have been published.[25]

Figure 2 shows the percentage of child deaths due to the potentiating effects of malnutrition on disease in each of 53 countries. The total PAR is divided into the portion due to severe malnutrition (WA < 60%) and that due to MMM (WA = 60–79%). Based on the average for all 53 countries, the results indicate that 56% of all child deaths are due to the potentiating effects of malnutrition on disease, of which 83% is due to MMM. The values for any given country vary in proportion to its prevalence of low WA. Among the countries shown here, the range for total PAR is from 15% in Paraguay to approximately 85% in India. The percentage due to MMM varies from zero among several countries where severe malnutrition is extremely rare to a high of 68% in India.[26]

These estimates are remarkably close to those arising from the Inter-American Investigation of Childhood Mortality more than two decades ago.[27] That study was based on Latin American and selected North American samples and used clinical and verbal autopsy methods to ascertain cause of death. As in the present study, it reported that in the Latin American countries, 54% of deaths in children ages 2–4 had malnutrition as an underlying or associated cause, of which about 15% was severe malnutrition. Among infants 0–11 months, malnutrition was an underlying or associated cause of death in one quarter to one third of all deaths. The estimates for infants are lower than for children because a large proportion of neonatal deaths are due to congenital and obstetric complications. Thus, although the Inter-American Investigation employed a different methodology than the prospective studies depicted in Figure 1, it confirms the quantitative estimates of malnutrition on child mortality and demonstrates that the Latin American results are similar to those from Africa and Asia. In addition, both studies confirm that conventional methods for classifying cause of death[25] underestimate the importance of malnutrition by a factor of 8–10-fold.

EFFECTS OF MALNUTRITION ON DIFFERENT CAUSES OF DEATH

The consistency in the slope of mortality on WA shown earlier in Figure 1 is striking in light of the differences

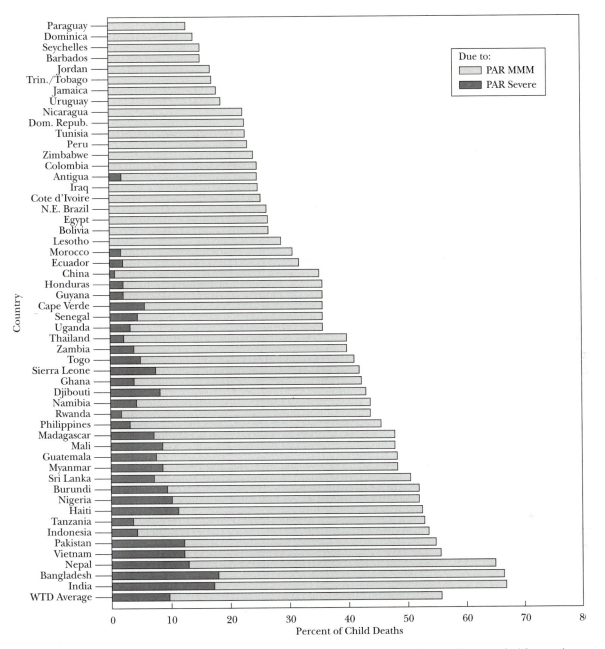

Figure 2.   Deaths due to the potentiating effects of malnutrition on infectious diseases. Reprinted with permission from Pelletier DL, Frongillo EA, Schroeder DG, Habicht J-P. The effects of malnutrition on child mortality in developing countries. *(Source: Bulletin of the World Health Organization 73(4), 1994)*

in ecologic circumstances and associated disease exposure, as well as cultural differences across studies. For example, the Papua New Guinea study took place in the highlands where ARI was noted as a major cause of death and malaria was presumably absent. Yet, it has a slope similar to Bangladesh, Tanzania, and Malawi, where diarrhea and malaria are combined with ARI as major diseases. This empiric observation of relative uniformity in slope across populations suggests that malnutrition may potentiate the effects of many or all of the common infectious diseases.

Somewhat more direct confirmation of this is provided by three of the prospective studies as well as the Inter-American Investigation. Two studies in Bangladesh and one in Uganda collected verbal reports of symptoms at the time of death and thus were able to estimate the RR of death due to malnutrition for each symptomatic cause of death separately.[3] All three studies show elevated RRs for diarrhea and measles, the only diseases reported separately in all three studies. In addition, the Uganda study shows elevated RRs for fever and ARI. In clinical practice, fever is usually assumed to be due to malaria in African settings with endemic malaria. The Ugandan study did not collect detailed clinical data to confirm this, however. The two Bangladesh studies grouped fever and ARI with other infections and found elevated RRs for that combined category. Thus, these three studies are consistent with the evidence presented in Figure 1, confirming that malnutrition may have a potentiating effect on many or all infectious diseases.

The Inter-American Investigation was based on 13 Latin American studies and found that malnutrition was an associated cause in 47% of all deaths of children under 5 years of age (excluding neonatal deaths). It was an associated cause in roughly 60% of deaths due to diarrhea, measles, and other infective and parasitic diseases, compared to about 32% of deaths due to respiratory disease or other causes. The latter figure was no higher than that seen in the "other" category, which represents a pseudo-control category.

A recent study from Zaire has challenged the notion that subclinical MMM is associated with child mortality, perhaps due to the uniformity with which malaria kills children regardless of nutrition status.[18] It is difficult to interpret this study for two reasons. First, the authors note that it was carried out in an area that has been the target of an integrated health and development program for the past 20 years. As such, immunization levels are higher and the incidence of diarrhea is lower than in most parts of Africa, and access to curative care is presumably greater. The authors suggest that this may help to explain the absence of an overall effect of MMM on mortality in their study. If so, it may have limited relevance to areas that do not share in those characteristics.

A second difficulty relates to the analytic strategy. In contrast to other prospective studies, these authors removed from the MMM sample any children who showed clinical signs of malnutrition, including muscle wasting (by inspection or palpation), with or without loss of subcutaneous fat, visible skeletal structures, or hanging skin. Pitting edema was also considered a clinical sign. The difficulty in interpretation arises from the fact that children with any of these signs were all considered severely malnourished but did not come exclusively from the category with WA < 60%. Results published separately[28] indicate that roughly 20% of all children below 80% WA showed these signs and were excluded from the analysis. This makes it extremely difficult to compare this study with other prospective studies. It appears that the possibility of disease-specific effects of malnutrition is a question that deserves further study, and it may be most amenable to study through case-control analysis of clinical data.

SUMMARY AND POLICY IMPLICATIONS

Analysis of 28 reports from 10 developing countries leads to a number of clear conclusions regarding malnutrition and child mortality:

♦   The inverse association between nutrition status and mortality is a consistent finding across diverse world populations, thereby contradicting the earlier suggestion that the results may be region or population specific.

♦   Mortality is elevated even among children with MMM, contrary to the widely held view that the effects are confined to the severely malnourished.

♦   The association between malnutrition and child mortality does not appear to be due simply to the confounding effects of socioeconomic factors and intercurrent illness.

♦   The long-recognized physiologic synergism between malnutrition and infection leads to the prediction that these two factors should have multiplicative effects on mortality at the population level. This prediction is fully consistent with the results from eight epidemiologic studies of malnutrition and mortality. Malnutrition is observed to multiply the number of deaths caused by infectious disease, rather than acting in a simple additive fashion. The effects are strong and consistent across populations.

♦   When applying the results of these eight studies to a larger set of 53 countries for which suitable anthropometric data exist, it is found that malnutrition contributes to 56% of all child deaths due to its potentiating effects on infectious diseases. This is roughly 8–10 times higher than conventional estimates that ignore the potentiating effects of malnutrition on disease and the effects of MMM. Of the malnutrition-related deaths, 83% are due to MMM as opposed to severe malnutrition, which is more significant than commonly recognized.

♦   The quantitative relationship between malnutrition and mortality is remarkably consistent across eight populations representing diverse ecologic, disease, and cultural environments. Based on a smaller number of more detailed studies, malnutrition is observed to potentiate deaths due to several infectious diseases. However, some studies raise doubts as to its effect on malaria and respiratory infection, leading to the need for further study.

These results have a number of implications for health policy and, more generally, for equity-oriented development policy. The PAR estimates suggest that programs directed at screening and treating only the severely malnourished could potentially only prevent about 17% of malnutrition-related deaths, representing approximately only 10% of all child deaths. The actual preventable fraction in current health facilities and child survival projects is likely to be even smaller than this, because existing interventions are not 100% effective. Greater impact could be achieved by pursuing policies and programs that attempt to shift the entire distribution of nutrition status, thereby improving MMM (which accounts for most of the malnutrition-related deaths). In addition, because of the multiplicative effects arising from the synergism between malnutrition and morbidity, the largest impacts could be expected in populations with the greatest exposure to disease and/or the highest prevalence of malnutrition. The results suggest that improving the nutrition status of populations would be expected to reduce mortality due to several diseases simultaneously (even if not all of them), regardless of whether exposure to those diseases remained unchanged. This is as opposed to a disease-focused approach that employs separate interventions to prevent or treat each disease. It is clearly desirable to improve nutrition status as well as to reduce disease exposure, but the suggestive cross-disease impacts of nutrition improvement should be taken into account when attempting to design the most cross-effective interventions in the face of resource constraints.

Finally, the focus on the malnutrition–morbidity synergism has led to a neglect of the other important variable in child survival policies, namely curative health care. Analysis of gender differentials in the effects of malnutrition on mortality in these prospective studies has confirmed that the mortality consequences of this powerful synergism can be ameliorated by access to health care (as seen among males in Bangladesh).[29,30] However, this analysis also reveals that the failure to address the synergism, either by reducing exposure to disease or improving nutrition status, places children in a high-risk situation for mortality when access to health care is limited (as seen among females in Bangladesh). This suggests that the relative risk of mortality (and percentage of deaths) due to the potentiating effects of malnutrition may be higher when access to health care is limited and lower when access to health care is improved. This has implications for the cost-effectiveness and sustainability of alternative approaches to reducing child mortality. Specifically, it suggests that cost-effectiveness calculations could be performed for various intervention strategies that combine health care, nutritional improvement, and reductions in disease exposure in order to determine the most cost-effective strategies in the medium term. However, the sustainability of strategies weighted heavily toward curative health care is likely to be lower than those strategies that give more attention to reducing malnutrition and disease exposure and would do little to improve social equity.

Acknowledgments. The author acknowledges the support of the Rockefeller Foundation, Thrasher Research Fund, and UNICEF, as well as the contributions of Drs. EA Frongillo, Jr., D Schroeder, and JP Habicht.

1. Scrimshaw NS, Taylor CE, Gordon JE. Interaction of nutrition and infection. Geneva: World Health Organization, Monograph Series 57

2. Morley D. *Pediatric Priorities in the Developing World.* London, England: Butterworth and Company, 1973

3. Pelletier DL. The relationship between child anthropometry and mortality in developing countries: implications for policy, programs, and future research. J Nutr 1994;124:2047S–81S

4. Keilmann AA, McCord C. Weight-for-age as an index of risk for death in children. Lancet 1978;1:1247–50

5. Sommer A, Loewenstein MS. Nutritional status and mortality: a prospective validation of the QUAC stick. Am J Clin Nutr 1975;28:287–92

6. Chen LC, Chowdhury A, Huffman SL. Anthropometric assessment of energy-protein malnutrition and subsequent risk of mortality among preschool aged children. Am J Clin Nutr 1980;38:1836–45

7. Heywood P. The functional significance of malnutrition: growth and prospective risk of death in the highlands of Papua, New Guinea. J Food Nutr 1982;39:13–9

8. Kasongo Project Team. Anthropometric assessment of young children's nutritional status as an indicator of subsequent risk of dying. J Trop Pediatr 1983;29:69–75

9. Bairagi R. Why mortality-discriminating power of anthropometric indicators differs among populations. J Trop Pediatr 1985;31:63–4

10. Ewbank DC, Gribble JN. Effects of health programs on child mortality in sub-Saharan Africa. Commission on Behavioral and Social Sciences Education. National Research Council. Washington, DC: Academic Press, 1993

11. Smedman L, Sterky G, Mellander L, Wall S. Anthropometry and subsequent mortality in groups of children aged 6–59 months in Guinea-Bissau. Am J Clin Nutr 1987;46:369–73

12. Briend A, Bari A. Critical assessment of the use of growth monitoring for identifying high risk children in primary health care programmes. Br Med J 1989;298:1607–11

13. Vella V, Tomikins A, Borghesi A, Migliori GB, Nidku J, Adriko BC. Anthropometry and childhood mortality in northwest and southwest Uganda. Am J Publ Health 1993;83:1616–8

14. Vella V, Tomkins A, Ndiku J, Marshal T, Cortinovis I. Anthropometry as a predictor for mortality among Ugandan children. Eur J Clin Nutr 1994;48:189

15. Yambi O. Nutritional status and the risk of death: a prospective study of children six to thirty months old in

Iringa region, Tanzania. Ph.D. Thesis, Cornell University, Ithaca, NY

16. Lindskog U, Lindskog P, Carstensen J, Larsson Y, Gebre-Medhin M. Childhood mortality in relation to nutritional status and water supply: a prospective study from rural Malawi. Acta Paediatr Scand 1988;77:260–8

17. Pelletier DL, Low JW, Johnson FC, Msukwa LAH. Child anthropometry and mortality in Malawi. Testing for effect modification by age and length of followup and confounding by socioeconomic factors. J Nutr 1994;124:2082S–105S

18. Van Den Broeck J, Eeckels R, Uylsteke J. Influence of nutritional status on child mortality in rural Zaire. Lancet 1993;341:1491–5

19. Trowbridge FL, Sommer A. Nutritional anthropometry and mortality risk. Am J Clin Nutr 1981;34:2591–2

20. Lipton M. Poverty, undernutrition and hunger. Staff Working Paper No. 597. Washington, DC: World Bank

21. Seckler D. Small but healthy: a basic hypothesis in the theory, measurement, and policy of malnutrition. In: Sukhatme PV, ed. *Newer Concepts in Nutrition and the Implications for Policy.* Pune, India: Maharashtra Association for the Cultivation of Science Research Institute, 1982

22. Cogill B. Ranking anthropometric indicators using mortality in rural Bangladesh children. M.Sc. Thesis, Cornell University, Ithaca, NY, 1982

23. Pelletier DL, Frongillo EA, Habicht J-P. Epidemiologic evidence for a potentiating effect of malnutrition on child mortality. Am J Publ Health 1993;83:1130–3

24. Pelletier DL, Frongillo EA, Schroeder DG, Habicht J-P. A methodology for estimating the contribution of malnutrition to child mortality in developing countries. J Nutr 1994;124:2106S–22S

25. World Bank. *World Development Report: Investing in Health.* Oxford, England: Oxford University Press, 1993

26. UNICEF. Child malnutrition: progress toward the World Summit for Children Goal. Statistics and Monitoring Section, 1993

27. Puffer RC, Serrano CV. Patterns of mortality in childhood. Scientific Publication No. 262. Washington, DC: PAHO, 1973

28. Van Den Broeck J. Assessment of child health and nutritional status in a rural tropical area. Ph.D. thesis, Katholieke Universiteit, Leuven, Belgium, 1994

29. Pelletier DL. The relationship between malnutrition, morbidity, and child mortality in developing countries. Cornell Food and Nutrition Policy Program, Ithaca, NY, 1994

30. Pelletier DL, Frongillo EA Jr, Schroeder DG, Habicht J-P. The effects of malnutrition on child mortality in developing countries. Bulletin of the World Health Organization, 73(4), 1995

28

The Effect of Malnutrition on Human Development: A 24-Year Study of Well-Nourished and Malnourished Children Living in a Poor Mexican Village

Adolfo Chávez, Celia Martínez, and Beatriz Soberanes[1]

INTRODUCTION: CHRONIC MALNUTRITION

It was recognized in the 1950s that the severe forms of protein-energy malnutrition, kwashiorkor and marasmus, were associated with marked cognitive effects (Scrimshaw et al., 1968) although the lasting effects on survivors were unknown. The predominant type of malnutrition in Latin America has changed dramatically during the second half of this century. On the one hand, the prevalence of acute and severe forms of malnutrition that bring death to children has steadily declined. On the other hand, chronic malnutrition, which causes physical and intellectual impairments in the affected populations, has increased substantially.

Marginal or chronic malnutrition is a consequence of early malnutrition that is more noticeable between 8 and 20 months of age. Many individuals who experience childhood malnutrition survive and reach adult age. However, these individuals are "vulnerable survivors" with very specific developmental deficiencies that are the result of chronic malnutrition experienced during early childhood.

This study reports on an 18-year follow-up that gives us the opportunity to describe the natural history of two exceedingly important problems in developing countries: poverty and malnutrition. These data contribute to our understanding of the consequences of early childhood poverty and malnutrition for the individual's performance at birth, during the school-age period, and during adolescence and young adulthood.

The worldwide problem of malnutrition is related to the consumption of deficient and monotonous diets that are based on roots and cereals. Cross-sectional studies conducted in developing countries have shown that few children have the symptoms and clinical signs of severe protein-energy or micronutrient malnutrition. Furthermore, the majority of these children seemed to tolerate well their chronic exposure to suboptimal diets. However, pioneering studies in Mexico (Ramos-Galván, 1949; Cravioto et al., 1966; Cravioto and DeLicardie, 1968) showed that subclinical malnutrition, manifested only by impaired growth, significantly impaired intersensory perception. Concurrently Mönckeberg (1967) showed a significant relationship between growth retardation and reduced cognitive performance in low socioeconomic groups in Chile.

In this period, Federico Gómez, the Director of the Hospital Infantil de Mexico, proposed a classification of malnutrition based on weight-for-age that has been widely adopted. First degree malnutrition was identified as 10 to 25% below normal weight-for-age, second degree as 25 to 40% below and third degree as greater than 40% below standards for well-nourished children for whom the normal range was plus or minus 10%. First and second degree malnutrition correspond to what is now called *marginal nutrition* (Gómez, 1946; Canosa et al., 1968).

The longitudinal study described in this [article] was carried out to understand the consequences of moderate malnutrition. Emphasis was on determining the relationship between chronic malnutrition and the physical, mental, and behavioral development of the individuals. To understand this relationship, the research design must control for nonnutritional factors that also affect human developmental needs by including longitudinal observations of both malnourished and well-nourished children living under the same social and ecological conditions.

By 1967, the year in which this study was planned, it was recognized that subclinical malnutrition associated with growth retardation was associated with deficits in learning and behavior. However, there was no agreement as to the extent with which these associations were due to malnutrition or to concurrent genetic, cultural or other environmental factors. As a result of this debate, this study was designed as an intervention in which it was possible to control for nonnutritional factors.

We decided to follow a small number of subjects prospectively in great detail, for two reasons. The data collection, which included measurements of milk volumes, interviews, and direct observations of child behavior, required field workers to live with the families for at least three consecutive days every two months. The ethics of observing a control group of subjects without nutritional supplementation during the study has been questioned. The researchers considered the study to be ethical because its results would help to motivate decision-makers to invest in and support efforts to improve the nutritional status of the poor in Mexico and throughout the world, an expectation amply realized. Moreover, the control group benefited from the same enhanced medical care and stimulation as the supplemented group. Without a control group no children would have received a supplement.

Several of the social goals of the project were achieved. In 1973, a few months after the first report of the project was presented, the Mexican government launched a major program called Orientación Familiar, which taught women how to improve their infant feeding practices. The program promoted partial breast-feeding at three months of age, which meant the inclusion of clean foods available at home in addition to breast milk (Muñoz de Chávez and Chávez, 1986). This program was delivered to more than two million households by a large number of rural women who were trained in the use of educational materials. This was the largest public health effort that resulted from the study in Tezonteopan, which together with other smaller studies, was instrumental in decreasing the severity of malnutrition in Mexico.

Most of the original observations in Tezonteopan were made by the resident researcher Celia Martínez between 1968 and 1973. She still lives in the village 24 years after the initiation of the study and has also conducted, at times with few resources and little support, follow-up studies during adolescence and young adulthood. It is to her that we owe the accumulation of knowledge from this extraordinarily detailed study that illustrates how the functioning of poor Mexican infants is damaged by malnutrition and how it can be improved with better primary health care and nutrition.

A POOR VILLAGE: ITS REALITY AND PROBLEMS

Tezonteopan had 1,495 inhabitants when the study was initiated in 1968. The village was very isolated, even though it was only 9 km from a paved road to Mexico City, only 2.5 hours away.

Tezonteopan covers 200 ha of agricultural land and was founded in 1884 by 18 families that ran away from a neighboring hacienda. In 1938 the government provided the village with an additional 552 ha of agricultural land. Agriculture is the main source of income

Table 1. Demographic data on the community (mean of 5 years around the annual rate)

Demographic Data	1966	1972	1978	1984	1990
Total population	1355	1779	2195	2577	2918
Birth rate	58.8	50.4	45.1	40.0	33.2
General mortality rate	18.5	12.5	9.6	9.7	6.9
Demographic growth rate	38.3	40.3	35.5	30.3	26.3
Preschooler mortality rate	16.9	7.5	11.9	6.3	2.6
Infant mortality rate	126	108	77	78	62

for the villagers, who grow corn, beans, and squash for subsistence and peanuts as a cash crop.

The vast majority of the families are poor and have access to only 2 or 3 ha of land. Income received from crops is just enough to pay for the loans that are provided in kind or as cash by the local shop owners. These loans are usually used to acquire consumption and production goods and to cover expenses related to social events and health care.

In 1968 most of the dwellings were built of reeds or adobe and had only one room. The quality of life, including the level of hygiene, was very poor and the village lacked basic infrastructure such as electricity and potable water. At the beginning of the study, the average family income was 1 US$ per day.

In the two years prior to the initiation of the study, overall mortality was 18.5/1,000, infant mortality was 126/1,000 births, and the preschool mortality was 16.9/1,000 inhabitants. The annual birth rate was 58.8/1,000, which in part can be explained by the predominantly young population living in the village. Despite the high mortality, the birth rate was still high and the population increased. The secular trends (1966–1990) of fertility and mortality are presented in Table 1.

The period of fertility was short because the onset of menarche usually was late, at about 15.5 years of age, and the women reached menopause at the relatively young age of 40.5 years (A Chávez and Martínez, 1973). The period of postpartum amenorrhea was very long and lasted for 13.5 months. Therefore the birth intervals were long, with a mean duration of 27 months. The fecundity rates were high because the women had nine children in their short reproductive lives, only five of whom survived until adolescence or early adulthood.

The diet in the village was deficient in nutrients because meat products were hardly ever consumed. Corn provided two-thirds of the daily energy intake, and the remaining calories were provided by beans, sugar (in coffee and tea), and sometimes pasta, bread, and wild vegetables. The infant feeding patterns were

very consistent in the village. Infants were given only breast milk up to 8 to 10 months of age. At this age other foods—*atole* (corn gruel), soups, and tortillas—were gradually introduced into the diet.

Since the project was designed around a nutritional intervention, it was decided to minimize the inclusion of other types of interventions such as health care and community development. For this reason, only basic health care was provided, and community events were supported only when this was specifically requested by the villagers.

Important changes took place in the community during the study. This was undoubtedly the result of the presence of the research team and the interest of the Mexican government in the community development of rural areas. At the beginning, these changes were slow; electricity and potable water were not requested by the villagers until the third and fifth year of the study, respectively. After this period the villagers wanted to experience a faster rate of community development, and by 1980 several projects were planned. These included the introduction of irrigation pumps, more profitable crops such as tomatoes, machines for removing peanut husks, and trucks for transporting agricultural products. The research center fully supported and communicated all these requests to the authorities in charge of making these decisions.

The process of change in the village was interrupted in 1982 as a result of a national economic crisis. The sharp increment in outmigration by young villagers that took place around this time probably reflected the fear and anguish caused by this crisis. In 1982, the first peasants went to work in a neighboring community, and now, 10 years after the first migrations, there are 150 villagers working in the United States and Canada.

In spite of the several changes that have taken place since 1975 as a result of social and economic openness, many aspects of basic life in the village have not changed. For example, in the 1990s almost all families have television and video sets. However, the villagers still sleep on a mat on the floor, and the houses still have the same appearance and size, even though they now use more brick and concrete. Most of the houses still lack windows and are as contaminated as before. The food habits and environmental conditions of the people are still the same, even though they now have higher incomes and water taps inside the households.

Infant feeding habits have changed: infants are now given more foods in addition to breast milk and are introduced to these foods at earlier ages. The families are now more likely to give cows' milk as a complement to breast milk. These changes in infant feeding practices are due to the fact that the families have seen the superior development of the children who were supplemented in the study.

There have been important improvements in health in the village. It is paradoxical that small changes could bring about such large effects. The community is still trying to produce more agricultural products, in spite of the national economic crisis of the last 10 years. However, the villagers are also obtaining resources by more diversified strategies that include migration. These recent migration patterns have brought about the most important changes that have benefited the village. In spite of the scarcity of credit and the decline in the prices of agricultural products, the community is now less isolated and more likely to seek external resources. Chronic or moderate malnutrition still persists today at about the same level as before, but there has been a decline in the number of cases of severe malnutrition. Regretfully, these changes have not been enough to promote the healthy development of the survivors.

THE LONGITUDINAL INTERVENTION STUDY: DESIGN AND IMPLEMENTATION

The study was planned as an intervention in which one group of mother-infant dyads received food supplementation while a second group remained untreated. Whereas the treated group would tell us if an adequate nutritional status could be attained even under adverse socioeconomic conditions, the untreated group would provide important information about the natural course and consequences of chronic malnutrition (Madrigal and Avila, 1990).

This project was conceived as a study of cases and not as an epidemiological survey. At that time there were data suggesting that the problem of marginal malnutrition was related to breast-feeding (Martínez and Chávez, 1967). For this reason it was decided to devote a substantial amount of effort to measuring the quantity of breast milk produced and ingested. A great deal of effort also went into making behavioral observations of the children. This component was included because the research team believed that suboptimal child behavior was one of the main consequences of malnutrition. Because behavioral studies can only be done by direct observation in the households, the sample size could not be large. Based on a statistical procedure for taking into account the possibility of dropouts from the study, it was estimated that 20 dyads would be enough to test the behavioral hypotheses.

The supplemented and unsupplemented groups did not enter the study at the same time, because the people in the villages could have questioned the provision of food to some but not to other children. For this reason, during the first year of the study, only the non-supplemented women and their newborns were recruited into the study. During the second and third year of the study, all the women who became pregnant received food supplementation. At the time of birth of the children, dyads with similar physical and socioeconomic characteristics to the unsupplemented group were recruited for continued supplementation.

The United States National Institutes of Health (NIH) initially funded the study for four years and later extended this period to seven years. The Mexican Council for Science and Technology (CONACYT) funded the project for another seven years. The project has continued to be funded by smaller grants, one of which was provided by the United Nations University (UNU).

The study was initiated in February 1968, and the first three months were devoted to a general study of the community and to establishing a close relationship with the families. Following this period, all the pregnant women in the village were studied. By the end of the first year, in June 1969, a group of 41 mother-infant dyads had been recruited. Twenty of these 41 women were selected for the measurements of milk production and intake and behavioral observations. The selection was based on socioeconomic status and maternal health, age, and anthropometry. The growth of the children of the remaining 21 dyads was followed longitudinally into the adolescent period.

The women and their children born in 1968 and 1969 were not given supplemental food and did not receive any type of intervention except in emergency situations. These children grew up with the support of their families under the usual conditions of the village. They were breast-fed for a prolonged period of time, and weaning foods were usually introduced with hesitation and at a very late age in an insanitary environment that constantly led to constant infections.

These children were born with low birth weight. They grew well in the first three months but then their growth velocity declined and therefore they began to suffer malnutrition. Of the 20 children who were selected for the full study, two were treated and dropped from the study because they developed severe malnutrition, one with edema and the other with marasmus. One of them was replaced by another child. Another child died of an infection under very difficult circumstances and one child emigrated. Therefore this group had a final sample size for the full study of 17 children. The total number of newborns of that year was later further reduced from 41 to 36 due to two additional migrations. This group has been analyzed and included in several reports dealing with preschoolers and teenagers.

The following year a second group of pregnant women was recruited and supplemented twice per day with a nutritious drink immediately following the first report of amenorrhea. The drink was made by mixing milk with fruits and was designed to provide 400 kcal per day and appropriate amounts of iron, niacin, riboflavin, and vitamins A and C. The intake of the food supplement was monitored, and it was shown that it provided 325 kcal per day. Supplemented women had similar socioeconomic and physical characteristics as the women in the nonsupplemented group that was recruited the previous year.

Supplemented subjects were matched at birth with their counterparts in the unsupplemented group, according to the physical and social characteristics of the mother-infant dyad. In addition to the 20 supplemented women who were included in the full study, another 20 women were also given food supplements and studied in some aspects of their development. The fact that the experimental and the control groups entered the study at different times was necessary, not only for interactions with the community but for logistic reasons.

The children in the experimental group began to receive supplementary food as soon as they showed the first signs of growth faltering, at about 12 weeks of age. First, the children were offered a bottle with milk during the night. When the children started to request to be breast-fed more often, even though they were being offered the bottle with milk, they were also given fruits and vegetables. Afterwards the infants were fed ad libitum with milk and a variety of strained foods. The research team always advised the women to continue breast-feeding during this time.

When the children were four years old, they were supplemented twice per day with a sandwich and a glass of milk. When the children began attending school, they sometimes missed one of the daily episodes of supplementation because they preferred to remain playing at school during recess instead of going out to receive their supplement. However, the children always received the supplementation after school hours. The supplementation intervention ended when the children were 10 years of age.

Throughout the study, special care was taken to ensure that the only between-group difference was the nutritional supplementation. Measures were taken to balance the amount of contact with research workers and any other procedure that could have been considered a nonnutritional intervention.

Throughout the 24 years of existence of the Centro Rural de Tezonteopan, a variety of nutrition and child development parameters have been studied. The unsupplemented children are, as this report is being written, 22 years old and therefore have become young adults. The children in the supplemented group are now between 17 and 20 years of age. The range of ages in the latter group is explained by the fact that the

large amount of effort needed for planning and implementing the project caused a slowdown in the rate of recruitment of subjects during the last years of the intervention phase.

The different types of studies are presented in the Results. The special methodologies that were employed are presented and discussed below.

a. All the women were included in longitudinal follow-ups of anthropometry and in a special study on fertility and reproduction.

b. The studies on food intake during early infancy included measurements of milk volume using a 72-hour test-weighing procedure at 2, 8, 16, 24, 36, 56, and 78 weeks of age.

c. The behavioral follow-up looking at mother-child interactions was the most significant component of the study. These observations were made between breast-feeding episodes while the observer was seated in a corner of the house pretending to read a book. Every 40 seconds the investigator looked over the book to make a "visual photograph" of the mother-child interaction (e.g., holding, feeding, kissing, verbalizing, degree of physical activity, etc.). Seventeen parameters were captured and written down every time a "visual photograph" was created. This procedure was carried out for 1.5 hours during the morning after the child woke up and for another 1.5 hours in the afternoon. This methodology is derived from that used for ethological observations of primates and is the one that captured the most important differences between the supplemented and unsupplemented children.

d. A similar methodology was used during the school period. The researchers made a hole in the wall of the classroom so that they could make behavioral observations of the children (e.g., standing, sleeping, attention span) while attending class. Each observation period lasted 1.5 hours and yielded information that discriminated between supplemented and unsupplemented children. Several national and international knowledge and problem-solving tests were also administered during the school period.

e. The physical activity of the infants was evaluated by observing the number of contacts that the heel made with the bed. Afterwards physical activity was measured as the number of steps taken in a specified period of time (10 minutes per hour for 10 consecutive hours).

f. The longitudinal assessments involving neurological, psychological, and cognitive measurements were done following traditional methods (A Chávez and Martínez, 1982).

g. Morbidity was recorded daily and the study also included a microbiological assessment of fecal contamination of household objects and members.

The experimental design was selected to test the hypothesis that nutrition during early childhood is an environmental factor that has a strong negative impact on long-term human development and function. The design of the study also contributed to a better understanding of the development of children in a deprived environment. It was also possible to study the life cycle in the families, since it included the follow-up of subjects from the time that they were in their mother's womb until they became pregnant.

The final objective of the project was to identify the critical point at which interventions that will achieve an optimal development in socioeconomically disadvantaged populations are most cost-effective.

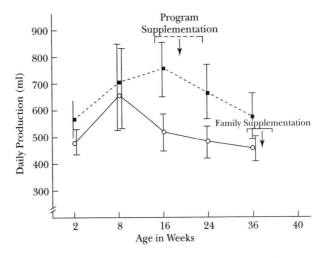

Figure 1. Milk consumption by the infants of supplemented (- - -) and unsupplemented (—) mothers.

THE FIRST EIGHT MONTHS OF LIFE

The first impact of the supplementation interventions was on the mothers themselves. By the eighth month of pregnancy, the supplemented women consumed 20% more food (2,410 cal and 70.7 g protein vs 2,055 cal and 53.3 g protein) and had a higher pregnancy weight gain (+3.4 kg) than unsupplemented women. Among supplemented women, menstruation returned by 7.5+2.6 months postpartum, 6.2 months earlier than among unsupplemented women. An important consequence of this delayed return of menstruation was that the birth interval decreased from an average of 27 months to 19 months (A Chávez and Martínez, 1973). This effect cannot be attributed to decreased rates of breast-feeding, because *all* the supplemented women were breast-feeding an average of 7.3 times per day by the time that menses returned.

In this community, infants can be considered as extrauterine fetuses who depend on their mothers for survival during their first months of life. Then infants are fed almost exclusively on breast milk. Solid foods usually begin to make a critical nutritional contribution when the infant is beyond six to eight months of age.

The placenta is a very efficient organ for the transfer of nutrients from the mother to the fetus even when she is poorly nourished. However, this study demonstrates that maternal supplementation under these circumstances can improve birth weight. The newborns of supplemented mothers weighed 2,970 g at birth and were 180 g heavier than their counterparts in the unsupplemented group (A Chávez and Martínez, 1979c). This 6.5% increase in birth weight, as

trivial as it might seem, is important for several reasons. First, this was the beginning of the anthropometric differences that persisted throughout life. Second, 39% (14/39) of the newborns in the unsupplemented group, but only 7.5% (3/40) of those in the supplemented group, were low birth weight (<2.5 kg) infants. Third, food supplementation was also associated with increased total length, leg length, thorax circumference, ratio of head to thorax circumference, and ratio of leg to total length (A Chávez, 1978).

An important question is whether the decline in breast milk production even in the supplemented mothers is due to maternal malnutrition or is a natural phenomenon in the human species. The latter is a possibility, because all mammals follow a parabolic pattern of milk production, with a short incremental period and a long and progressive decremental stage. There is no reason for the human species to follow a different pattern of lactation. To respond to this question, the women who were supplemented during pregnancy continued to be supplemented during lactation. The total milk volumes plotted in Figure 1 show remarkable between-group differences. As with other mammals, breast milk production among supplemented women followed a parabolic pattern, peaking at four months, followed by a gentle decline.

The literature indicates that in developing countries, children begin to slow their growth at about three months of age. Therefore, it is important to consider the role of breast-feeding in the future of the child. A key finding from this study is that intake or production of breast milk in the unsupplemented group increased during the first eight weeks of lactation and fell thereafter (Martínez and Chávez, 1971). In the supplemented group it increased at least to 16 weeks. Unfortunately, milk volume measurements

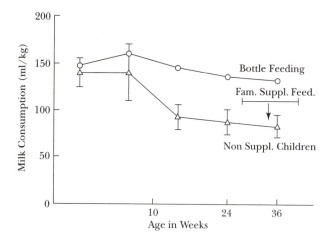

Figure 2. Milk consumption per kg of weight by age during the first nine months by infants receiving breast milk alone without complementary cow's milk feeding, cow's milk by bottle to complement breast milk, and children given complementary cow's milk and whose family was given additional food from 27 to 41 weeks that was partially shared with the infant.

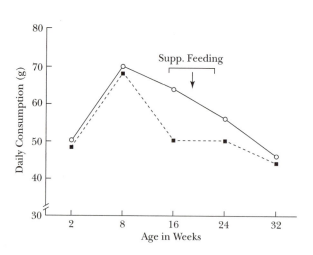

Figure 3. Milk solids consumed by the infants of supplemented (—) and unsupplemented (- - -) mothers.

were not taken within the 8- to 16-week interval. However, by 16 weeks the milk volume had already decreased.

At eight weeks, the infants of unsupplemented mothers were consuming 32 ml per nursing episode, and by 16 weeks this figure decreased to 41 ml per episode. In Figure 2 a comparison of the breast milk intake per kilogram of body weight between the village children and Japanese children fed breast milk ad libitum with bottles indicates that the decrease in milk volume observed in the village after eight weeks is abnormal. This decline in breast milk production occurred despite the fact that children were breast-feeding about 13 times every 24 hours. Therefore, it is important to underscore that the decline in breast milk production is due to maternal supply and not infant demand. This decrease in breast milk production has important nutritional and developmental consequences for the child.

Chemical analysis of the milk samples indicated that the breast milk of unsupplemented women was not diluted according to the progressive pattern typical of other mammals. Unsupplemented women continued producing concentrated milk after their infants were eight weeks of age. By contrast, the milk of supplemented women was diluted beyond the expected range. Figure 3 includes the consumption of breast milk solids and shows that both groups of women secreted the nutrients following a pyramid-type pattern, although the peak is sharper among supplemented women. The peak for supplemented women was followed by a more gradual decline in the concentration of nutrients in breast milk after the infants were 3 months of age.

The between-group difference in the nutrient content of breast milk was 16% less in the supplemented group during the first eight months of life of the child. Although this difference does not seem large, it is important to underscore that it was greatest between 8 and 24 weeks. During this short period of time, the unsupplemented children ceased to be able to obtain all the breast milk that they demanded. To a certain extent, this also happened with the supplemented children, although in this case this phenomenon was observed at an older age and with a more gradual onset.

The decline in breast milk consumption by the children of poorly nourished mothers that begins at two to three months of age is the first insult that leads to malnutrition during early childhood. This situation could be easily corrected by introducing complementary foods available in the household by three months of age as required to maintain weight gain.

Figure 4 shows the between-group differences in energy intake. The deficiency in energy intake in the unsupplemented group begins at 12 weeks and is not corrected later. By eight months of age, the between-group differences in nutritional status are not readily apparent to the observer, i.e., the unsupplemented children were not obviously malnourished. However, more detailed analysis of their nutritional status shows some impairments. Photographs confirmed that supplemented and unsupplemented mother-child pairs had different attitudes and different characteristics of the skin, adipose and muscular tissues (Chávez and Martínez, 1982).

By eight months, the unsupplemented children had already been exposed to two nutritional insults. The first occurred in utero due to a deficient transfer of nutrients across the placenta. The second occurred

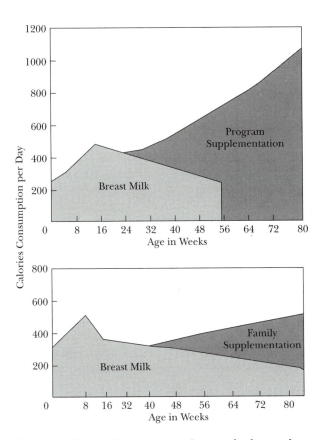

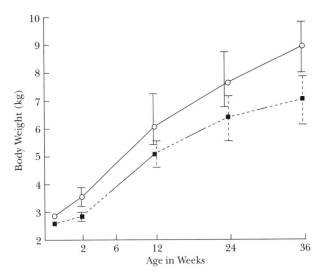

Figure 5.   Weight increase in the first 36 weeks of children in the maternal supplementation and complementary feeding group (—) compared with children breast-fed by unsupplemented mothers who received no complementary food from the program (- - -).

Figure 4.   Mean caloric consumption per day by age during the first two years after birth by infants whose mothers received food supplementation during pregnancy and who were given complementary feeding when growth began to falter (upper diagram) compared with the caloric intake of infants whose mothers were unsupplemented and who received only the complementary food spontaneously provided by the family (lower diagram).

at about three months of age due to a decrease in maternal breast milk production. In view of these insults, why were there so few clinical manifestations? First, breast-feeding allows infants to recover partially from the in utero insult. During the first three months of life, the infant has access to an abundant supply of milk and grows at a very fast rate. Second, biological mechanisms protect the child against nutritional insults. This is illustrated by the fact that the child can maintain lean tissue at the expense of his fat reserves. Another coping mechanism is a reduction in physical activity. This hidden malnutrition is likely to have negative long-term consequences for the future development of the child, even though dramatic effects are not evident by eight months of age.

As shown in Figure 5, the between-group difference in weight is small at eight months. Furthermore, it is still not possible to detect significant differences in the infants' utilization of nutrients, physical activity, or behavior. However, some indicators show consistent differences. Perhaps the most pronounced differences

can be seen in neurological development both at birth and during early infancy (Rodríguez et al., 1979). By eight months, the unsupplemented child had less reflex control and poorer psychomotor development (A Chávez et al., 1975). There were also some behavioral differences. Unsupplemented children cried more, played less, and had less than optimal family interaction (A Chávez and Martínez, 1975).

The fact that there were no obvious clinical manifestations of malnutrition up to eight months of age has led some people to recommend exclusive breast-feeding for a minimum of six months. However, this study does not support this argument, since the breast milk supply begins to decline by three months, and small developmental, biological, and behavioral deficits begin to appear. These deficits become larger as the child grows older in a socioeconomically deprived environment.

In short, on the one hand, children who reach eight months of age with acceptable growth, such as weighing more than 8 kg, will be more likely to crawl, to demand attention, and to have better immunological defenses. On the other hand, a child who reaches eight months under adverse conditions, grows less well, has a poor appetite and low levels of physical activity and social interaction and is likely to become more malnourished.

THE "VALLEY OF DEATH" BETWEEN 8 AND 20 MONTHS

Even though breast-fed, socioeconomically disadvantaged children living in developing countries go through a period of particularly high health risks between 8 and 20 months of age. The most vulnerable children die during this period that can be characterized as the "valley of death." The vast majority of those individuals who survive this period are the "vulnerable survivors."

The child needs to have adequate reserves to survive the passage through this period. The valley of death represents both a biological and a cultural reality. It is a biological phenomenon because it is linked with nutrition and infections. It is also related to culture because it is in part determined by child-rearing practices. Both adverse cultural and biological factors are present simultaneously during weaning and illness. In the valley of death, there are three situations in which feeding practices and health interact with each other.

The *first* is related to the finding that by eight months, the mothers, both supplemented and unsupplemented, cannot produce enough milk to meet the nutritional demand of their infants. At around this age, the volume of milk produced plateaus at about 450 ml per day. It is likely that this is a common situation among poor people, since similar findings were obtained in an urban area (Pérez-Hidalgo, 1970). This amount of breast milk is valuable for the nutrition of the infant. Therefore, prolonged breast-feeding is recommended for those women who do not have enough resources to obtain and safely handle cow's milk or a combination of foods. Although breast milk should be a major component of the infant's diet during the valley of death, it is also important to feed clean digestible foods as soon as possible.

The *second* feeding problem that occurs during this period is the tendency of children of this age to develop anorexia when the organism is exposed to an insult, particularly an infection. The anorexia during the passage through the valley of death contrasts with the good appetite of children younger than eight months who demand to be breast-fed even during episodes of severe diarrhea. This is desirable, because the infant replenishes nutrients that are being lost because of diarrhea. Some of this anorexia could be due to malnutrition, or perhaps it is normal at this age since the same phenomenon is observed among well-nourished children.

The *third* issue that needs to be considered is that during this period many children are weaned from the breast. Earlier it was believed that this was the cause of malnutrition, because the children were abruptly weaned without being offered foods of adequate protein quality and content. There is no doubt that weaning from the breast is an important event; however, it is often done at an age when the child is already malnourished. In fact, it is possible that women decide to

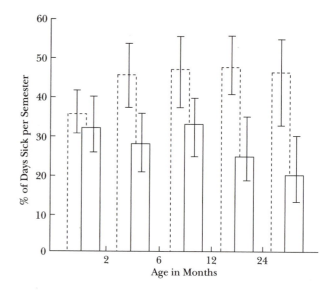

Figure 6. Percentage of days sick per semester in the first 30 weeks of children in the maternal supplementation and complementary feeding group (—) compared with children, breast-fed by unsupplemented mothers, who received no complementary food from the program (- - -).

stop breast-feeding because they notice an insufficient milk supply long before weaning. In the case of Tezonteopan, weaning from the breast during this period was not an issue, since only three of the unsupplemented women stopped breast-feeding before 20 months, and this did not pose a health risk to their children at this time.

A second period of decline in breast milk production was observed when the children were about 13 months of age. This is often associated with a new pregnancy. According to common wisdom, when a mother becomes pregnant during the period encompassing the valley of death, the child becomes jealous and changes his personality. What happens in reality is that the malnourished child becomes sad and irritated, and cries frequently. These signs could be interpreted as indicators of an increase in the severity of malnutrition related to the low milk supply produced by the mother.

The other biological phenomenon characteristic of the valley of death is related to infections, since this is the period when the child loses the passive immunity received from his mother and has acquired only limited active immunity. It is also the time when the child moves around in unsanitary areas and foods contaminated with pathogens are introduced. While not all immunity is lost by eight months, the epidemiological observations, however, show clearly that the supplemented and unsupplemented children had different patterns of frequency, duration, and severity of infectious diseases (Figure 6).

The role played by culture is similar to what has been reported for other socioeconomically disadvantaged groups. For this reason, it is possible to talk about a culture of poverty during the valley of death. In Tezonteopan weaning foods are introduced very late and in small quantities at about eight months of age. These foods are often withdrawn from the infant's diet with illness, particularly fevers and diarrhea, without taking into account the nutritional needs of the child. Another example is the practice of giving the child a corn tortilla to lick. Every time the tortilla falls down, the caretaker picks it up and gives it back to the child, even though it has dirt on it. The child is not able to ingest the tortilla and for this reason it obtains a minimum nutritional benefit from it. The same could be said of other foods that were given to the unsupplemented group, such as *atoles* and soups. Very frequently these foods contain fewer nutrients and are contaminated.

The differences in energy consumption after eight months between the supplemented and unsupplemented groups can be seen in Figure 4. In the supplemented group, the energy intake increases gradually, following the children's requirements. In the unsupplemented group, on the other hand, energy intake declines and reaches a nadir at about 10 to 11 months of age, unfortunately. At this point, the intake of non-breast-milk foods is still very small. Given the low nutrient intakes observed among the unsupplemented group in the valley of death, it is surprising that children survive and even show a small advance in their development. At two months of age, when the child weighs about 4 kg, he obtains almost 500 kcal from breast milk. Afterwards the energy intake declines from breast milk.

The growth curve shown in Figure 7 corresponds to the increments in body surface (Wetzel plot) and shows that by the third month, the growth of the unsupplemented child begins to falter in relation to that of the supplemented child. This difference becomes more pronounced between four and eight months of age. The figure represents the averages of 17 cases that were followed closely. However, if individual cases were plotted, a zigzag pattern with arrested, accelerated, or decelerated periods of growth would appear. This is due to episodes of illness that have negative growth effects through direct biological mechanisms (i.e., altered metabolism, anorexia, reduced absorption) and exogenous cultural mechanisms (i.e., withdrawal of solid food).

The growth patterns of supplemented and unsupplemented children differ not so much in the number and severity of infections as in the speed of recuperation from infections. Supplemented children had frequent episodes of infections during this period, and

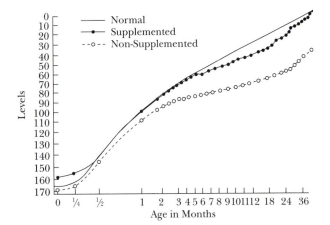

Figure 7. Levels of growth in the first 36 weeks of children in the maternal supplementation and complementary feeding group (—•—) compared with children breast-fed by unsupplemented mothers and who received no complementary food from the program (--o--). Children in the supplemented group of children match levels of growth for well-nourished children (—) during the first four months of infancy.

their growth and appetite were also affected. However, they recovered sooner from illness and ate very well while recovering from infections. Their anthropometry was better than that of the unsupplemented children. Between 6 and 18 months, the supplemented children grew less than normal, but they returned rapidly to their expected growth pattern between 18 and 24 months. The unsupplemented children recover very slowly, and before they can catch up fully, another episode of infection commonly occurs.

With the findings from this study, it is possible to clarify the relative importance of malnutrition and infection as determinants of child health in developing countries. Several researchers insist that infectious diseases are the main determinants, but this study shows that supplemented children are able to recover from infections sooner. This observation allows us to ascertain that nutrition is a more important determinant of child health than disease, because a well-nourished child is able to recuperate and return to his normal growth pattern in spite of suffering frequent episodes of infectious diseases.

It is not clear how the unsupplemented children can survive the valley of death while consuming less than 500 kcal/day and facing so many illnesses. However, the two principal factors are their reduced body size and less physical activity (A Chávez et al., 1972). Figure 8 shows clear between-group differences in physical activity.

There was no apparent between-group difference in physical activity at eight months of age. It is possible that the method of measurement of physical activity

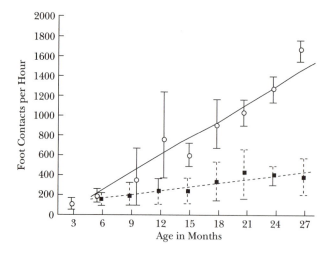

Figure 8.   Number of foot contacts per hour in the first 27 weeks of children in the maternal supplementation and complementary feeding group (—) compared with children breast-fed by unsupplemented mothers and who received no complementary food from the program (- - -).

(i.e., the number of times that the feet touched the side of the crib) was not sensitive enough to pick up differences, because it is common to wrap the infants with blankets in the study village. After 10 months of age, however, the differences were remarkable, showing that as they grew older, the supplemented children increased their physical activity whereas the unsupplemented children did not.

As in other underdeveloped communities, almost all the children developed clinical signs of malnutrition at some point during the study. However, their symptoms were transient and improved even without medical care. Cross-sectional studies conducted in underdeveloped villages have reported similar nutritional findings to those encountered in Tezonteopan. Only 26.3% of the children under five years of age can be classified as having type II or type III malnutrition (i.e., moderate to severe malnutrition). This would suggest that the nutritional status of the population is heterogeneous. This is misleading, however, because the studies have examined children of different ages and at different stages of nutritional stress.

A frequency distribution of the nutritional status of the 41 unsupplemented children indicated that 14.6% were severely malnourished (i.e., type III malnutrition) when they were experiencing their worst nutritional status, 78.1% had type II malnutrition at worst, and only 7.3% had no worse than type I malnutrition at some point during the study. This is the real distribution of malnutrition in the community and is different from the prevalence estimates. With a cross-sectional study, it would have not been possible to

detect these high levels of severe malnutrition, because all the children do not become malnourished at the same point in time and several of them could have already been dead when the study was conducted. Therefore severely malnourished children in the sample did not die in the Tezonteopan study, because they received medical care as soon as they began to become severely malnourished if they were not recovering spontaneously.

The previous data show that underdeveloped regions can have only a moderate prevalence but a high incidence of moderate to severe malnutrition. Therefore malnutrition can be the underlying cause of mortality during the critical period of human development studied in Tezonteopan. Furthermore, prenatal malnutrition associated with low birth weight, immaturity at birth, and low breast milk output after two to three months increases the relevance of nutrition for public health.

There is no doubt that malnutrition between 8 and 20 months adversely affects neurological function and other phenomena that have social repercussions. The low energy intake in the unsupplemented children and their reduced levels of physical activity are directly related to behavioral outcomes such as longer sleep periods and desire to remain in the crib for longer periods of time. It is also possible that malnourished children are carried for longer periods of time on their mothers' backs because they do not move and remain quiet. It is also possible that the low levels of physical activity have an indirect relationship with the suboptimal level of stimulation and interaction between the fathers and siblings and the malnourished child (A Chávez et al., 1975; A Chávez and Martínez, 1975).

In sharp contrast with the unsupplemented group, the supplemented children were more active, slept less, and did not want to remain in the crib or to be carried by their mothers for a long period of time. Fathers were often involved with the care of the supplemented children and smiled at and played with their offspring. The siblings also had to participate sooner and more intensely in the care of the child. All these events brought relatively more stimulation and interaction to the supplemented children.

Although the differences in physical activity explain part of the differences in behavior, stimulation, and degree of interaction, there might be other factors that also contribute to explaining these outcomes.

It is possible that malnutrition by itself is related directly to several personality traits. The unsupplemented children were withdrawn and insecure, and they cried frequently. The crying can be attributed to hunger and to the request to be breast-fed. However, the facts that even after eight months of age these chil-

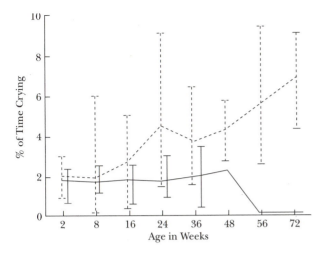

Figure 9.   Percentage of time crying in the first 27 weeks by children in the maternal supplementation and complementary feeding group (—) compared with children breast-fed by unsupplemented mothers and who received no complementary food from the program (- - -).

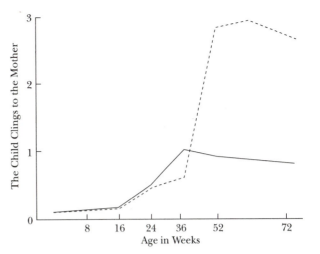

Figure 10.   Children observed clinging to the mother in the first 72 weeks in the maternal supplementation and complementary feeding group (—) compared with children breast-fed by unsupplemented mothers, who received no complementary food from the program (- - -).

dren still cried frequently and with anguish during periods of anorexia and had low levels of physical activity (Figure 9) indicate different personality traits of supplemented and unsupplemented children.

Between 8 and 20 months, the unsupplemented children did not smile at their fathers, played less by themselves or with other individuals, and felt secure only if they were close to their mothers. The need to be in direct physical contact was so strong that several of them held to their mothers with great force for prolonged periods of time (Figure 10). Several of the unsupplemented children were afraid of their fathers and siblings and did not like to be cleaned. They hardly ever vocalized and only communicated by crying (Figure 11).

In general, the results show that the malnourished child is very insecure, and this leads to a passive and dependent personality. These characteristics of infant behavior become even worse as a result of several cultural practices that are frequently found in underdeveloped communities. In general, the mothers do not take the initiative to stimulate their offspring. As a result, there is a poor maternal-child interaction, which is limited to breast-feeding when the child cries or simply swinging the child in the crib or carrying him on her back.

In the case of the supplemented group, it is clear that the children stimulated responses from other people, demonstrating that supplementary feeding can break the passivity and apathy in the family. The children initiated interactions not only with their mothers but also with their fathers, siblings, neighbors, and ani-

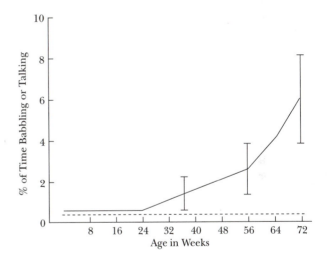

Figure 11.   Babbling in the first 72 weeks by children in the maternal supplementation and complementary feeding group (—) compared with children breast-fed by unsupplemented mothers, who received no complementary food from the program (- - -).

mals. The behavior of the supplemented children changed traditional cultural patterns, since the fathers became involved with the care of young children. This was possible because the supplemented children were too active and difficult to be taken care of by their mothers alone, and also had happy personalities that attracted the fathers.

The different behavioral characteristics of supplemented and unsupplemented children influenced

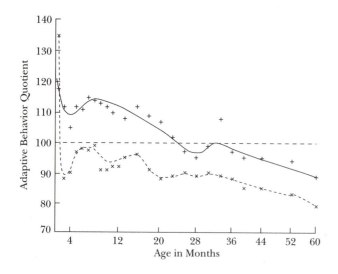

Figure 12. Changes in adaptive behavior of children in the maternal supplementation group (—) compared with children of unsupplemented mothers (- - -).

their mental development scores. It is curious, however, that between-group differences in intellectual performance were present as early as two months of age.

The psychomotor development of the unsupplemented group was higher from birth up to four to six weeks of age, when the lines crossed. The results for adaptive behavior are shown in Figure 12. The results for the first two months of life are not shown, because the scores of both groups, and in particular of the unsupplemented group, were very high. The finding that children born in underdeveloped communities are "smarter" at birth has also been reported in Africa and Guatemala. However, it is an artifact, because the scores are reported as percentage of days ahead in development with respect to the birth date. Therefore, for example, a three-day-old child who has a psychomotor age of 15 days has an advantage of 520%. This child seems to have very precocious development, when in fact he is only 12 days ahead, which might be trivial for his future development.

It is also possible that being far ahead in psychomotor development might be a sign of delayed and not of improved development. It is possible that it represents a delay in cortical function which allows for the presence of hypothalamic reflexes, as has been observed in other mammals that stand, walk, and even run during the first hours of life. When the cortex matures, these reflexes disappear and the movements become voluntary.

A remarkable finding is that, beginning at three to four months of life, the developmental lines of the two groups cross, and the supplemented children score 10 to 20 points above their unsupplemented counterparts. As will be shown, in spite of the fact that the differences in mental development vary as a function of

age and the specific test that is applied, these differences are present even at adult age.

There is concern about the meaning of results from Western-type mental development tests applied to rural children in developing countries. However, the between-group comparison in this study is a valid one, because both groups were equally rural and similar in their socioeconomic conditions.

The only potential confounder of the mental development results is the between-group personality differences. However, the fact that there were developmental differences very early in life, when there were still no differences in personality, demonstrates that the tests captured differences not only in personality but also in mental capacity. In domains such as language and social development, the between-group differential patterns presented oscillations. However, in tests of adaptive behavior and motor development, the unsupplemented children were constantly below their supplemented counterparts and at points almost reached the lower limits of normality.

The time trends in the figures suggest that the between-group developmental differences could have originated in utero. This is likely if the "early advantage" of the unsupplemented children in reality represents a developmental delay, because it would mean that the two groups were different from birth until adulthood. This could be the result of delayed neurological maturation in utero caused by poor maternal nutrition during a time when the brain is highly vulnerable.

However, another potential explanation for the poor development of the unsupplemented children is the lack of stimulation received from their environment, which is caused by their own withdrawn personality and low levels of physical activity.

Of the three factors that have been postulated, the authors think, based on their intensive contact with the maternal-infant dyads, that the low energy intake and physical activity of the children are the leading causes of poor mental and behavioral performance. If the brain is considered as a computer that cannot program itself but that is structured according to the needs of the user, it is possible to argue that the lack of stimulation received by the vulnerable survivor is what causes the important limitations on the development of the intellect.

The onset of low energy consumption, low physical activity, poor stimulation, and poor brain development takes place when the production of breast milk falls at around three months of age. The delay in the development of the brain increases until the age of 20 months and then stabilizes.

The interpretation of the results by the authors is reinforced by the fact that malnutrition after eight months of age has a clear negative impact on the development of language, which is essential for an adequate performance in the tests of mental development.

The developmental delays of the unsupplemented children stabilize at the end of the valley of death at 20 months of age. Afterwards their developmental curves run parallel to and always below those of the supplemented and reference children. As a result, the unsupplemented child leaves the valley of death as a vulnerable survivor.

THE PRESCHOOL SURVIVOR AND THE NUTRITIONAL CRISIS AT SCHOOL ENTRANCE

The nutritional status of the children who grow up in Tezonteopan stabilizes at about 20 months of age, and their rate of weight growth becomes similar to that observed in well-nourished populations. The increments in linear growth are of a smaller magnitude than those in weight, and as a result, the children from the village experience a progressive increment in weight relative to height. Ramos Galván (1969) refers to this phenomenon as homeorrhexis.

All the study children were still being breast-fed at 20 months, and their breast milk intake was about 400 ml/day (i.e., 35 ml/kg of body weight). The consumption of non-breast-milk foods, such as tortillas, corn *atole*, and beans, was low, and these foods were of poor quality. The total daily energy and protein consumption were 526 kcal and 11.2 g, respectively (A Chávez and Martínez, 1982).

How is it possible that the 20-month-old children from Tezonteopan can stabilize their nutritional status if they are surviving on such a low food intake? It almost seems impossible that the unsupplemented children could gain weight as fast as the supplemented or well-nourished children who consumed at least twice the amount of food. At this age the physiological needs of the child decrease and there is also a large adaptive reduction in physical activity; however, the child may still be unhealthy. The findings that by 20 months the unsupplemented child has a stable food consumption and energy expenditure, and that his activity level decreases in relation to the supplemented child, support this hypothesis.

The pattern of changes in body proportions is interesting. The malnourished children are born with shorter legs, and during the first eight months the size of the legs substantially catches up with that of the rest of the body. Between 8 and 20 months, the legs and the trunk of malnourished and well-nourished children grow at the same rate. However, after 20 months the growth rate of the legs of malnourished children again declines in relation to the well-nourished children.

The rate of increase in head circumference is analogous to the growth rate of the legs. This rate is the same in supplemented and unsupplemented children until 20 months of age, after which the rate declines among the unsupplemented children. Given this finding, why do the unsupplemented children who experience homeorrhexis seem to have large heads? The reason is that the small circumference of the thorax, coupled with a relatively large waist circumference, gives the child the appearance of being younger with a normal head size.

It is possible that the ratio between head and thorax circumference, rather than weight-for-age or weight-for-height, is the best indicator of nutritional status between 20 months and six years. This ratio is always <1 for malnourished and >1 for well-nourished children. Other indicators that might be sensitive to the nutritional status at this age are the ratios of upper to lower body length and of thorax to head circumference.

The severity and frequency of infections decrease beginning at 20 months. The duration per episode of diseases such as respiratory infections and diarrhea declines among the well-nourished relative to the malnourished.

At this age there is also some degree of stabilization in neurological function and mental performance. Beginning at 20 months of age, the unsupplemented children increase their performance at the same rate as the supplemented children, although the latter maintain a constant 10% to 15% advantage. By three years of age, the unsupplemented children almost reach the level of the supplemented children in language development and social behavior. However, after a short time their curves separate again, and later the unsupplemented show similar improvement rates as the supplemented children.

The differences in physical activity that can be attributed to the food supplementation are remarkable, and between 20 and 36 months there is a seven-fold difference in favor of the supplemented children.

Between 20 and 40 months, the household time-sampling methodology that was previously used to assess behavior was switched to a method based on placing the child in an open-field square area that had toys on one side and the mother on the other. This method allowed behavior to be studied at a predetermined time and place. The differences in behavior between supplemented and unsupplemented children remained constant. The unsupplemented children did not move around the square area, did not play with the toys, and did not move from their mothers' sides, where they remained crying and requesting to be held in their arms. By contrast, the supplemented children played with the toys, showed them to their mothers, and moved around the square area without fear or insecurity.

These results show that the malnourished children do not experience complete compensatory adaptations beginning at 20 months of age. These children

Table 2. Differences in average weight and height between supplemented and unsupplemented children

Age (yrs)	Weight (kgs)	Height (cms)
5.0	3,989	9.5
5.5	4,109	9.0
6.0	4,387	8.2
6.5	4,629	7.4
7.0	5,030	7.0
7.5	4,845	5.4
8.0	4,869	5.6

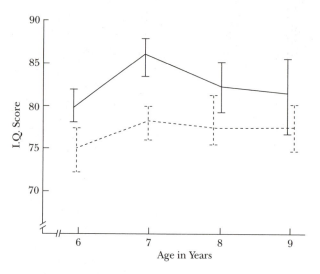

Figure 13. Intelligence quotients (I.Q.) of children in the maternal supplementation and complementary feeding group (—) compared with children breast-fed by unsupplemented mothers, who received no complementary food from the program (---).

are shorter, more ill, and heavily dependent on their mothers because they have a withdrawn personality. It is difficult to understand the basis for the insecurity experienced by malnourished children. It could be caused by a general feeling of weakness or lack of control of the environment, and/or by their immature personalities. These characteristics of insecurity and fear are responsible for the crisis faced by the malnourished child when he enters school for the first time.

At around six or seven years of age, the homeorrhetic mechanism observed among malnourished children (i.e., to spare weight at the expense of height) is reversed. At this age the children increase their linear growth rate at the expense of weight, and several symptoms of malnutrition begin to appear. Table 2 shows the difference in weight and height between the well-nourished and the malnourished children at the end of the preschool and at the beginning of the school period.

Beginning at five years, the unsupplemented children begin to catch up in linear growth, and by eight years they have reduced their deficit with respect to the supplemented children by about 4 cm. By contrast, the deficit in weight of the unsupplemented children increases during this period of time.

When applying the Jenss reference growth model to the children of Tezonteopan, it was found that the unsupplemented children experience their maximum deviation in growth rates at five to seven years of age (A Chávez and Martínez, 1982).

The morbidity data indicated that at six and seven years of age the malnourished children experience a small and statistically nonsignificant increase in the number of episodes and duration per episode of illness when compared with the supplemented group. This finding might be explained by the exposure to new microbes in school.

Results from the Terman Merrill development test, which was periodically applied after the children were four years of age, show statistically significant between-group differences at both six and seven years of age (Figure 13). Whereas the supplemented children improved their IQ scores substantially, the unsupplemented children showed negligible improvements. This indicates that the village environment limited the mental performance of the unsupplemented children but not that of the supplemented children.

In the school, the children were observed every 45 seconds for 1.5 hours at arrival and before leaving the school for the day. Twelve behavioral items were recorded, and the children were unaware that they were being observed (Schlaefper, 1986). There were large between-group differences in school behavior and performance. Table 3 summarizes 3,240 behavioral observations per year per child. Statistics are not presented, due to the large sample size and the large between-group differences. The first column shows the results of the second daily observations and the second column shows the results that include both daily observations. These two columns are presented because the unsupplemented children performed even worse at the end of the day, perhaps because of fatigue. This is likely to have occurred because by the end of the day these children reduced their level of activity and increased the time spent sleeping. Unsupplemented children participated less in class, were more distracted, slept more, played less, and cried more on arrival at school than their supplemented counterparts.

There were also substantial between-group differences, which are difficult to interpret, at six and seven

Table 3. Classroom activities of children (percentage of time in activity in 3,240 observations during 3 hours in the first school year)

Behavior	End of Day Observations		Total Observations	
	Not Supplemented	Supplemented	Not Supplemented	Supplemented
Active participation[a]	1.9%	11.7%	4.3%	13.9%
Passive participation[b]	11.3%	19.3%	10.1%	18.1%
Classroom movement	4.8%	23.1%	7.7%	24.5%
Distracted	52.6%	31.6%	54.4%	30.2%
Sleepy	8.5%	0.0%	4.5%	0.7%
Crying	3.0%	1.4%	4.7%	0.6%
Fighting	0.8%	1.3%	0.4%	1.0%
Out of classroom/ other behavior	17.1%	11.6%	13.9%	11.0%

[a]Obey instructions, participate or interact with the teacher.

[b]Look at the teacher, read or look at the book or answer in chorus.

Table 4. Results of tests in the first school year

Test	Not Supplemented	Supplemented
Beginning of year Detroit-Engel	6.5 ± 1.9	8.1 ± 0.5
Middle of year L. Filho	8.8 ± 1.4	13.3 ± 0.9
End of year Detroit-Engel	19.4 ± 2.5	36.1 ± 3.1
End of year International	6.2 ± 1.0	7.9 ± 0.7
End of year National	6.3 ± 1.2	8.6 ± 0.9

years of age in a series of written tests. The unsupplemented children had an average grade of 6.5 ± 1.9 out of 10, and 38.3% failed to pass the school year. By contrast, none of the supplemented children had to repeat the school year, and their average grade was 8.1 ± 0.5.

Several teachers, who were unaware of which group the children belonged to, were trained to apply several tests of knowledge to the study children. Table 4 shows the results of these tests. It indicates that there were between-group differences in favor of the supplemented children, even at the beginning of the school period (see Detroit-Engel test). This result is interesting, because none of the children received preschool education. By the end of the school year, the between-group differences in the knowledge tests were even larger, perhaps as a result of the school learning experience.

The knowledge of the children was also measured during the second year. However, the between-group comparisons are invalid, because the large proportion of unsupplemented children who repeated the school year had been previously exposed to these tests. In

addition, two unsupplemented children were taken out of school by their parents.

COMMENTS: NUTRITION IN THE LIFE CYCLE AND SOCIAL DEVELOPMENT

The results of this study show that malnutrition is tightly linked to health, well-being, and educational opportunities in the community. Malnutrition is both the cause and the effect of the limited opportunities for socioeconomic development of the study population.

Malnutrition begins at birth, as illustrated by the finding that newborns of unsupplemented mothers were 180 g lighter. Almost 40% of these children were born with low birth weight (<2.5 kg). During the first two to three months of life, the unsupplemented children experienced only a partial recovery from in utero malnutrition. This is because they had access to adequate nutrition after birth, since their mothers had an initially adequate milk supply until this age. However, the maternal milk supply was soon no longer sufficient, and the children's nutritional status deteriorated. However, because this deterioration took place slowly it was not obvious to the parents or even the physicians. This is unfortunate, because this is the period when the functional deficits associated with malnutrition begin to appear (Chávez and Martínez, 1979a). It can be detected by periodic weighing.

From three to eight months the children were hungry, as evidenced by their demand to be breast-fed 20 or more times per day, and they began to change their morphology and general appearance, as illustrated by changes in skin texture and adipose tissue. During this period the children began to be insecure and unhappy. However, the mothers and the physicians were unable to interpret these signs correctly, as illustrated by the practice of prolonged exclusive breast-feeding.

The period between 8 and 20 months of age is the valley of death, when malnutrition becomes apparent. During this period, when the transfer of maternal immunity decreases, there is a synergism between malnutrition and infection, resulting from the unsanitary environment in which the child lives, and lower resistance due to malnutrition. The valley of death is also characterized by many behavioral deficiencies, some of which may be triggered by lower levels of physical activity and a more timid and apprehensive personality, both traits that lead to reduced interaction between the child and his mother, family, and environment (Allen et al., 1992).

The interaction between malnutrition and poverty is apparent throughout the life cycle. Maternal malnutrition, as reflected by low weight gain during pregnancy, and poor health are related to low birth weight (Allen et al., 1992). Afterwards, the mother influences the nutritional status of her child through her breast-feeding practices. The consequences of an inadequate maternal milk supply in this population, for satisfactory development after the infant reaches about three months of age, are far more serious than is currently accepted.

Breast milk is the first "push" for the development of the child, but among malnourished women this push is short-lived and not as strong as it should be. The maternal production of breast milk in Tezonteopan is enough to meet the nutritional requirements of the infant only for the first two to three months of life. During this period, the mother increases her milk supply, but it suddenly drops to a level of 500 to 600 ml and remains at this lower level. It is likely that this is a common phenomenon throughout the disadvantaged areas of the world. The decreased milk supply is not enough to continue "pushing" the child in his development and is responsible for a deterioration of his nutritional status. By eight months of age, the milk deficit,

together with inadequate complementary feeding and the increased nutritional needs for physical activity and recovery from infection, worsens the situation of the child. The survivors in communities like Tezonteopan grow less, spend less energy, and interact less with their environment than well-nourished children (A Chávez and Martínez, 1979b).

The sudden stabilization in nutritional status and reactivation of growth and development that takes place at 20 months of age is surprising. However, this reactivation takes place at a pace adequate for the chronological, but not for the biological or functional, age of the child. Therefore, there is no catch-up in the developmental processes in this period. Between 20 months and six to seven years of age, the unsupplemented child's appearance and behavior are those of a younger individual. Character and personality are withdrawn, but nutrition problems are not apparent. At the beginning of the school period, the linear growth of the supplemented children is similar to that of the unsupplemented children, but the latter exhibit deficits in weight and in mental and behavioral development. Moreover, the unsupplemented children did not do well in school. More than one-third failed to pass the first year of school, and the remaining perhaps should have also failed because their grades were very low. The poor school performance of these children can be attributed to malnutrition, since the supplemented children passed their first year of school without problems.

Adolescence is usually considered a period of nutritional crisis. In this study, however, the between-group differences tended to narrow during this period. This is related to adaptation mechanisms of the unsupplemented children, including delayed onset and longer duration of puberty, which allowed them to partially recover from their deficits. In addition, cultural factors that limit the opportunities for progress slowed down the development of supplemented children during adolescence. However, it is important to note that unsupplemented subjects did not reach the levels of performance of the supplemented children during adolescence. Their physical, mental, and behavioral performance was also worse.

From these results it seems likely that certain behavioral and cultural characteristics that have been considered as typical of poor agricultural societies are due to malnutrition. Among them are passivity, lack of motivation for change, and limited decision-making abilities, which together explain the tendencies for the limited progress and development in these communities. It is possible to break the vicious cycle of malnutrition and social development in several ways. The approach adopted has almost always been to promote investment in increased production and create the conditions for savings and reinvestment. This has not worked in the poor rural environment, where it is difficult to save and reinvest. Nutrition is an area that deserves special attention because, as this study shows, it improves the quality of human resources, an essential factor for development. A society with more capable individuals not only can produce more but can improve its technological competence. Improved nutrition is both an instrument for development and an end in itself. Better nutrition improves health and physical and mental capabilities, the instruments and outcomes of development.

This study shows that it is not difficult to improve the nutritional status of individuals. While more material and human resources were expended in this study due to the research nature of the project, than would be required, it shows that much can be achieved with relatively little investment. Applied nutrition programs are needed because they can maximize the benefits per unit of investment. The data from this study show that the target age for nutritional interventions should be three to eight months to prepare the child for a healthy entrance into the valley of death. Children should weigh 8 kg by eight months of age. The second priority of these programs should be the valley of death, because this is the period when the nutritional problem becomes worse. At this age, programs are curative rather than preventive, since the children are already malnourished (VA Chávez et al., 1988).

An important programmatic priority is the care of the pregnant woman. Gestation is an extremely important period because, as this study shows, the deficits in physical development observed in the unsupplemented group at the end of the study are proportional to those present at birth. The issue of how best to improve the nutritional status of pregnant women has not been resolved. Suboptimal nutrition during pregnancy is related to social conditions, the treatment of women in society, employment, age at marriage, birth interval, and many other factors that currently cannot be addressed with cost-effective programs.

Programmatic actions need to address the malnutrition-infection complex with simple measures. These should be driven by a primary health approach involving food and hygiene, sometimes called the "bread and soap" approach. With political commitment, this is a feasible strategy. The implementation of primary health care measures in the communities involving essential nutrition and health interventions at the household level is within the reach of most Latin American countries. These measures should include immunization, provision of essential micronutrients, elimination of parasites, and educational messages regarding the need for complementary feeding beginning at three months of age. Measures that will improve nutrition during pregnancy are also needed.

These and other studies have documented the nature of the malnutrition problem and its conse-quences. Furthermore, the technology to combat the problem of malnutrition is available. It is hoped that the findings of this study will help to mobilize the sociopolitical will to solve the problem that is still lacking in many developing countries.

REFERENCES

Allen LH, Backstrand JR, Chávez, A, Pelto GH. 1992. *Functional implications of malnutrition. People cannot live by tortillas alone: the results of Mexico CRSP. Final Report of Mexico Project.* Human Nutrition Collaborative Research Program, USAID, Washington, DC, June 1992.

Canosa C, Salomón, JB, Klein R. 1968. "Nutrition growth and mental development." In: *Proceedings of the International Congress of Pediatrics,* Mexico.

Chávez A. 1978. "Effects of mother's nutrition on infant body morphology." In: *Birth-Weight Distribution as an Indicator of Social Development.* SAREL/WHO Report R:2, Sweden.

Chávez A, Martínez C. 1973. "Nutrition and development of infants from poor rural areas III. Maternal nutrition and its consequences on fertility." *Nutr Rep Intern* 7:1.

Chávez A, Martínez C. 1975. "Nutrition and development of children from poor rural areas. V. Nutrition and behavioral development." *Nutr Rep Intern* 11:466.

Chávez A, Martínez C. 1979a. "Effects of maternal undernutrition and dietary supplementation on milk production." In: Aebi H, Whitehead, RG, eds. *Maternal Nutrition During Pregnancy and Lactation.* Bern: Hans Huber Publ.

Chávez A, Martínez C. 1979b. *Nutrición y Desarrollo Infantil.* Nueva Editorial Interamericana, México.

Chávez A, Martínez C. 1979c. "The effect of maternal supplementation on infant development." In: Effects of maternal nutrition on infant health. Arch Latinoamer Nutr Supplement 1, Dec 1979.

Chávez A, Martínez C. 1982. *Growing Up in a Developing Community.* INCAP-UNU Publ.

Chávez A, Martínez C, Bourges H. 1972. "Nutrition and development of infants from poor rural areas. II. Nutritional level and physical activity." *Nutr Rep Intern* 5:139.

Chávez A, Martínez C, Soberanes B. 1991. "Effects of early malnutrition on the physical, mental and social condition of rural adolescents." Symposium of the IX Meeting of the L.S. Nutrition Society, San Juan, PR.

Chávez A, Martínez C, Yashine T. 1975. "Nutrition, behavioral development and mother-child interaction in young rural children." *Fed Proc* 34:1574.

Chávez VA, González-Richmond A, Cifuentes E, Batrouni L, Madrigal H, Martínez C, Mata A. 1988. "Alcances del sistema de paquetes selectivos en los programas de atención primaria." *Rev Sal Pub Méx* 30:446.

Cravioto J, DeLicardie ER. 1968. "Intersensory development of school aged children." In: Scrimshaw NS, Gordon JE, eds. *Malnutrition, Learning and Behavior.* Cambridge, MIT Press: 252–69.

Cravioto J, DeLicardie ER, Birch HG. 1966. "Nutrition, growth and neurointegrative development: an experimental and ecologic study." *Pediatrics* 38(suppl. 2, Pt. 2):319–72.

Gómez F. 1946. "Desnutrición." *Bol Med Hosp Inf Méx* 3:543.

Jelliffe DB. 1966. *The Assessment of Nutritional Status of the Community (with Special Reference to Field Surveys in Developing Regions of the World).* Geneva: WHO.

Madrigal H, Avila CA. 1990. *Encuesta Nacional de Alimentación del Medio Rural.* Publ División de Nutrición L-89, Tlalpan, D.F., México.

Martínez C, Chávez A. 1967. "La lactancia y los hábitos de alimentación infantil en una comunidad indígena." *Rev Méx Sociol* 29:223.

Martínez C, Chávez A. 1971. "Nutrition and development of children from poor rural areas. I. Consumption of mothers' milk by infants." *Nutr Rep Intern* 4:139.

Mönckeberg F. 1978. "Effect of early marasmic malnutrition on subsequent physical and psychological development." In: Scrimshaw NS, Gordon JE, eds. *Malnutrition, learning and behavior.* Cambridge, MA: MIT Press: 269–77.

Muñoz de Chávez M, Chávez A. 1986. "Evaluación de un programa de educación masiva para mejorar la alimentación infantil rural." *Rev Inv Clín Méx* 38(Suppl: La Nutrición en México 1980–1985):153.

Pérez-Hidalgo C. 1970. "Valor nutritivo de la leche materna procedente de madres Méxicanas urbanas." *Salud Publ Méx* 12:236.

Ramos-Galván R. 1949. "La desnutrición infantil en México: sus aspectos estadísticos, clínicos, dietéticos y sociales." *Bol Med Hosp Inf Méx* 5:84.

Ramos-Galván R. 1969. "El significado de las edades pediátricas." *Acta Pediatr Latinoamer* 1:65.

Rodríguez R, Rubio F, Martínez C, Chávez A. 1979. "Nutrition and development of children from poor rural areas. VIII. The effect of mild malnutrition on children's neurological development." *Nutr Rep Intern* 19:315.

Schlaepfer LVA. 1986. "A longitudinal study in a rural Mexican community: analysis of the growth, health and nutrition aspects (0–10 years of age)." Doctoral thesis, University of Maryland, College Park, MD.

Scrimshaw NS, Taylor CE, Gordon J. 1968. *Interactions of Nutrition and Infection.* Geneva: WHO.

Seckler D. 1982. "Small but healthy. A basic hypothesis in the theory, measurement and policy of malnutrition." In: Sukhatme PV, ed. *New Concepts in Nutrition and Their Implications for Policy.* Pune, India: Maharasthra Assoc Sc Res Institute.

NOTES

1. The authors are affiliated with the Division of Community Nutrition in the Instituto Nacional de la Nutrición "Salvador Zubirán," in Mexico, D.F., Mexico.

29

Iron Deficiency

Nevin S. Scrimshaw

Iron deficiency is the most prevalent nutritional problem in the world today. Two thirds of children and women of childbearing age in most developing nations are estimated to suffer from iron deficiency; one third of them have the more severe form of the disorder, anemia. Furthermore, unlike classical nutritional diseases—such as vitamin A deficiency, which can lead to blindness, and iodine deficiency, which can cause retardation and deafness—iron deficiency is found in all societies, developing and industrial alike. In the U.S., Japan and Europe, for instance, between 10 and 20 percent of women of childbearing age are anemic.

Iron deficiency commonly remains unrecognized. Because of subtle symptoms such as pallor, listlessness and fatigue, the disorder is not regarded as life-threatening. Yet iron deficiency can have a multitude of effects—and can even result in death.

In the past several years researchers have found that iron deficiency is associated with the often irreversible impairment of a child's learning ability and other behavioral abnormalities. Although the neurochemical roles of iron are not fully understood, it is clear that low levels of the nutrient can have a significant adverse impact on brain function. In addition, diminished levels of iron in adults can affect work capacity and productivity and, by impairing the immune system, increase the chances of acquiring and dying from infection.

Despite the possibilities for low-cost intervention, many countries lack an effective system for diagnosing, treating and preventing iron deficiency. Consequently, progress in combating iron deficiency has been slight. Whereas the administration of effective treatments for deficiency in vitamin A and in iodine can be made uniform in nearly all countries, therapies for iron deficiency must be tailored to suit individual cultures and countries.

The situation could soon improve. This year a United Nations subcommittee on nutrition established a working group to promote the control of iron deficiency. The group is collaborating with the World Health Organization (WHO) in developing a 10-year plan to eliminate this public health scourge. Understanding the multiple functional consequences of iron deficiency is crucial to that effort.

Iron has diverse biological functions, and it is this diversity that accounts for the wide-ranging impact of its deficiency. The metal is best known for its role in the transport of oxygen in blood. As a component of hemoglobin, iron helps the molecule pick up oxygen in the lungs and shuttle and release it throughout the body. Approximately 73 percent of the body's iron is found in hemoglobin, where it is constantly recycled as more red blood cells are created.

◆ ◆ ◆

Of the balance of the body's iron, 12 to 17 percent is stored in two molecules—ferritin and hemosiderin—both of which can bind large numbers of iron atoms. (Each molecule of ferritin alone binds 4,500 iron atoms.) Myoglobin accounts for another 15 percent of the iron, acting as a reservoir of oxygen for muscle cells. A small but extremely important amount (0.2 percent) of body iron is bound to transferrin, a compound that shuttles iron from sites of release to sites of need. Lactoferrin—a compound found in breast milk, mucosal tissues and white blood cells, or leukocytes—also binds a percentage of the body's iron so that it is not available for bacterial growth, thereby stemming infection.

The minute amount of iron not accounted for by these compounds is found in myriad enzymes crucial to metabolism. These enzymes include oxidases, catalases, reductases, peroxidases and dehydrogenases. Each enzyme plays an important role as a reversible donor or acceptor of electrons during cellular metabolism.

All the iron needed to execute these diverse tasks comes from diet. Although vegetables, particularly spinach, are regarded as impressive sources of iron, plant (nonheme) iron is relatively poorly absorbed. For instance, only 1.4 percent of the iron from spinach can be taken in by the body; other vegetables yield slightly more: 1.6 percent from black beans, 4.4 percent from lettuce and 7 percent from soybeans.

In contrast, 20 percent of iron from red meat, in the form of heme iron, can be absorbed. Iron from poultry, fish and breast milk is equally well assimilated, but the concentrations are lower. The composition of a meal can influence the amount of iron that is retained. For example, if a meal contains both heme and nonheme iron, the former will improve the absorption of the latter. Vitamin C enhances the utilization of nonheme iron, but substances like tannin from tea as well as fiber and phytates from plants inhibit it. Absorption also changes in accordance with the amount of iron in the body: it decreases if individuals are iron replete and increases if they are iron deficient.

Poor absorption from the predominantly vegetarian diets of most people in developing countries is a primary cause of iron deficiency. For the poor, meat is expensive and consumed in small quantities or not at all. Iron deficiency and anemia affect the majority of individuals in such populations.

Iron deficiency is not caused by dietary imbalances alone—it can occur even when the diet has adequate iron. Other culprits are chronic blood loss caused by hookworm and schistosomiasis and the excessive storage of iron as hemosiderin, a result of malaria. Abnormal uterine bleeding is another cause.

◆ ◆ ◆

Hookworm eggs from human feces hatch on moist soil to produce tiny larvae that painlessly enter the skin of the feet. The bloodstream and lymph vessels then carry these larvae to the lungs. From there they find their way into the trachea, or windpipe, to the pharynx and, ultimately, to the small intestine after they are swallowed. They bind to the intestinal lining and secrete an anticoagulant that causes bleeding proportional to the number of worms. As many as three million worms may be recovered after severe cases are treated.

Hookworm rarely kills its victims, but it can leave them weak and listless. Children with hookworm disease are not only pale and anemic but slow and dull. Indeed, the parasite was largely responsible for the image of laziness of poor Southern whites in the U.S. Because poor whites formed the bulk of the Confederate Army during the Civil War, some scholars have suggested that hookworm disease was a significant factor in the army's defeat by the North.

Although hookworm has been largely eradicated in the U.S. and other industrialized nations, it continues to plague over 900 million people—more than one fifth of the world's population. Schistosomiasis afflicts more than 200 million people, and malaria causes 200 to 300 million deaths every year.

Shortages of iron, whether caused by disease or diet, or both, are described in three overlapping stages, beginning as deficiency and culminating as anemia. (There are many additional causes for anemia, including genetic defects and other nutritional disorders.) Although anemia is the more severe condition, the impairment of many bodily functions, such as harmful changes in biochemistry and in the effectiveness of important iron-containing enzymes, occurs long before anemia sets in.

In the first stage, stored iron is depleted, a process reflected in declining levels of ferritin. Next, levels of serum iron plummet, and as a result the iron transport protein, transferrin, is no longer fully saturated. At this second stage, cellular compounds requiring iron begin to be affected. As the deficiency persists, the synthesis of hemoglobin is inhibited, and anemia develops. This

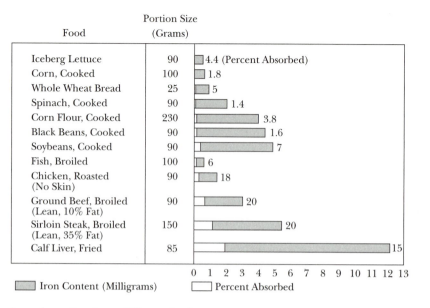

Iron absorption from different foods

last stage is characterized by reduced numbers of now small, pale blood cells.

One of the more devastating consequences of iron deficiency and anemia has been elucidated over the past 15 years, although it is far from clearly understood. Anemic children and adults have often been described as backward or apathetic, but these behavioral aspects were historically attributed to the lack of oxygen transported in the blood. Recently remarkable advances in probing the relation between iron status and cognition have illuminated these symptoms.

Although there were a number of early studies in animals, it was not until 1973 that Frank A. Oski of Johns Hopkins University School of Medicine and his colleagues at Syracuse University reported that anemic infants improved their performance on certain behavioral tests after a single large injection of iron. The tests, called the Bayley Scales of Infant Development, measure a broad range of activities, including motor skills, affective responses and attention span, as well as general cognitive function. Five years later Oski and Alice S. Honig, also at Syracuse, found similar improvements after such treatment in anemic infants when compared with normal infants who received the same treatment.

In 1982 Ernesto Pollitt of the University of California at Davis provided the first demonstration of the adverse effects of subclinical iron deficiency as opposed to anemia. Pollitt, then at the Massachusetts Institute of Technology, found that three- to six-year-olds, in Cambridge, Mass., who were mildly iron deficient had poorer scores on a battery of behavioral tests than did preschoolers whose iron status was normal. He then showed that the scores significantly improved after 11 to 12 weeks of iron therapy.

Pollitt repeated these studies with both iron-deficient and anemic preschool children in Egypt, Guatemala and Indonesia. This time he found only limited improvement in the Guatemalan and Egyptian children, even when their blood levels of iron returned to normal. Only the Indonesian children, who were from a town near Bandung, did significantly better on the test after iron supplementation, presumably because their deficiency was less severe. Other researchers have found the same irreversibility during double-blind studies in Costa Rica, Chile and various parts of Guatemala.

The adverse effects of iron deficiency on cognitive performance also proved irreversible in a study of 2,000 children in Thailand. There, Pollitt and his collaborators found a significant correlation between iron levels, IQ and a Thai language achievement test: the higher the iron levels, the better the scores. Studies in other parts of the world, including India, Papua New Guinea and Semerang in Indonesia, have consistently found a similar association.

Apparently iron deficiency is educationally deleterious regardless of ethnicity or physical or social environment. The lack of recovery in many children after iron supplementation underscores the importance of preventing iron deficiency.

◆ ◆ ◆

A possible neurochemical basis for these problems has recently been suggested. Moussa B. H. Youdim of the Technion Medical School in Haifa and Shlomo Yehuda at Bar-Ilan University in Ramat-Gan, Israel, found that rats with low levels of iron had fewer D_2 receptors—one of several families of dopamine receptors—in certain regions of the brain. These findings suggest that iron is important to the normal develop-

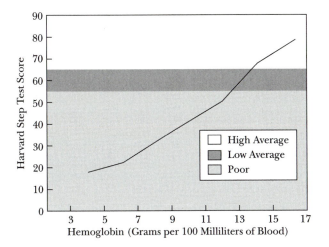

Work performance has been linked to the level of iron in the blood. Anemic Guatemalan laborers performed poorly on a physical test (the Harvard Step Test), whereas those with higher hemoglobin levels performed well.

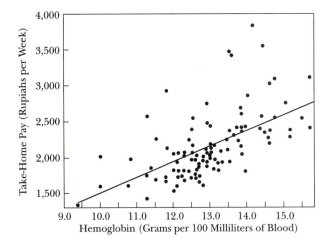

Productivity of Indonesian rubber tappers varies with hemoglobin levels. The diagonal line marks the association between income and hemoglobin.

ment and functioning of dopaminergic neurons and that early changes could lead to permanent damage.

The precise role of iron in the brain, however, has not been determined. The nutrient is distributed quite unevenly but appears to reflect the location of certain neurons that release the neurotransmitter gamma-aminobutyric acid, or GABA. The release of GABA inhibits neuronal transmission. It is also noteworthy that iron is found in monoamine oxidase, an enzyme vital to the production of a host of neurotransmitters, including serotonin, norepinephrine and epinephrine as well as dopamine. Thus, there are tantalizing indications of how iron deficiency might affect the central nervous system.

Behavioral changes caused by iron deficiency are not found solely in infants and young children. Physicians visiting developing countries have repeatedly demonstrated a connection between iron levels and work capacity and productivity in adults. In 1970 I found that certain laborers on Guatemalan sugar and coffee plantations performed poorly on the Harvard Step Test (HST), which requires that they step up on and then down off a bench every two seconds for a maximum of five minutes, if possible. All these workers, considered lethargic and stupid by the plantation owner, proved to be anemic.

My observation was confirmed by Fernando E. Viteri of the University of California at Berkeley. Earlier studies in animals had shown an association between poor performance on a treadmill and low hemoglobin levels. Viteri, then at the Institute of Nutrition of Central America and Panama, saw the same correlation in Guatemalan laborers. After treatment with iron, the subjects' HST results improved

remarkably. Coincidentally, Samir S. Basta, who was then my graduate student at M.I.T., made similar discoveries among road construction workers and rubber tappers in Indonesia.

A question remained: Did these differences in physical capacity have any effect on the laborers' productivity? Basta, who is now director of UNICEF in Europe, established a strong correlation between hemoglobin levels, HST results and the amount of rubber the Indonesian tappers collected. He determined that anemic tappers who were given iron supplements for 60 days augmented their take-home pay by 30 percent. Iron supplementation also increased the productivity of tea pickers in Indonesia and Sri Lanka and of laborers in Kenya and Colombia.

One of Basta's observations suggested the mechanism by which iron depletion hindered performance. He discovered that both the road construction workers and the tappers were better able to work after only 30 days of iron supplementation—before there was any significant increase in hemoglobin. It became clear that iron depletion did not solely affect oxygen transport in the blood but also interfered with oxygen exchange in muscles. Indeed, blood transfusions that restored hemoglobin levels to normal in anemic tea pickers in Sri Lanka failed to improve their treadmill performance: further evidence that the oxygen-carrying capacity of blood is not the single culprit.

Studies in animals further clarified some of the biochemical mechanisms at work in muscles. For example, iron-deficient rats were found to have lower levels of such important proteins as myoglobin, cytochromes and mitochondrial and other oxidative enzymes. Human studies are still lacking, in part because it is inconvenient to take biopsies of muscles.

In addition to reducing the ability of premenopausal women to perform work, iron deficiency curtails their ability to successfully produce and raise healthy children. In many underprivileged populations the limited availability of iron in the diet and the pathological losses associated with parasites increase the likelihood that a woman will experience iron deficiency. Already struggling with poverty and the demands of procuring and preparing food, maintaining a home and caring for a family, many such women are jeopardizing their own health and that of their fetuses.

✦ ✦ ✦

Although the shortage of iron affects both sexes, women are particularly at risk. Normally men lose only one milligram of iron every day through urine, skin and feces, an amount easily replenished. Such losses are proportionally less in women because of their smaller body size: only about 0.7 to 0.8 milligram a day.

Over the course of a month, however, women lose far greater amounts than men. Menstrual bleeding causes an additional average daily loss of 0.4 to 0.5 milligram, and 10 percent of women lose three times that amount. Intrauterine devices can lead to even more bleeding. Although menstruation ceases during pregnancy, women lose iron to the placenta and to the fetus—roughly five milligrams a day during the second and third trimesters, or a total of 370 milligrams by delivery. This loss is compounded by blood lost during and after delivery.

Iron deficiency during pregnancy can prove dangerous. Maternal mortality, prenatal and perinatal infant death and prematurity are significantly increased. If the mother is iron deficient while she is pregnant, the child is born with poor iron reserves and is at greater risk of morbidity, mortality and learning disorders. Low-birth-weight babies exhaust their iron stores at an earlier age than do normal infants, and they soon require more iron than breast milk can supply.

Treatment works—if it reaches the child in time. In studies in Indonesia, children receiving iron grew more than did those receiving placebo. (Studies of this kind receive ethical approval if they are designed to determine the need for iron supplementation and if, after it is determined that such therapy is effective, the placebo group is also given iron until hemoglobin levels become normal.) The results suggest that iron either has a direct metabolic effect on the child or exerts an indirect effect by increasing appetite, a known boon of iron therapy in people of all ages.

Iron supplementation may also help children by reducing the severity or incidence of infection. Malnutrition in any form is likely to decrease resistance to infection, and nutritional deficiencies are ubiquitous among underprivileged populations. Still, iron deficiency remains the most common, and it is clearly associated with increased illness resulting from infection.

As early as 1928, British physicians reported that bronchitis and gastroenteritis were more likely to develop in poorly nourished infants than in well babies. When malnourished infants received iron supplementation, the incidence of these diseases decreased.

Almost 40 years later the first controlled study of iron and morbidity was published. Morten B. Andelman and Bernard R. Sered of the Chicago Board of Health studied more than 1,000 infants from poor Illinois families. One group received a formula containing vitamins but no iron; the other group received formula with vitamins and iron. The results were striking: the second group had half as many respiratory infections as the first.

Similar findings were reported in Alaska by the wife-and-husband team of Carolyn and Robert Brown of the U.S. Public Health Service. They found a direct correlation between low hemoglobin levels and the prevalence of diarrheal and respiratory diseases in native Alaskan children. Another researcher, Robert Fortuine, also with the U.S. Public Health Service in Alaska, found that meningitis in anemic children often proved deadly, whereas the disease did not prove fatal in any of the nonanemic children he studied.

Although knowledge of the mechanisms by which iron deficiency results in increased morbidity is far from complete, both animal and human studies offer clues. Raymond B. Baggs, a graduate student at M.I.T., fed rats progressively less iron and simultaneously infected the animals with salmonella, a bacterium that causes diarrhea. He found that as the amount of iron in the animals' diet declined, the incidence of morbidity and mortality from the infection rose.

To kill bacteria, white blood cells sharply increase oxygen consumption, a process called respiratory burst. Respiratory burst, in turn, produces an oxygen radical, peroxide. Baggs searched for the cause of the findings and discovered that although white blood cells in the gastrointestinal tract of iron-deficient animals could engulf bacteria, the cells had low levels of the iron-dependent enzyme myeloperoxidase. Without this enzyme, a cell cannot create the free oxygen radicals needed to kill the ingested bacteria.

In studies in Indian children, Ranjit K. Chandra, now at the Memorial University of Newfoundland, showed that respiratory burst diminishes as levels of transferrin fall. At the same time, there is an increase in the number of surviving bacteria in lymphocytes infected in vitro and a fall in the production of new lymphocytes, also in vitro.

Other researchers in India have shown that as the amount of serum transferrin falls, the capacity of tuberculosis patients to respond to a skin test gradually disappears. This failure could result either from the protein deficiency responsible for the decrease in transferrin or from the associated decline in serum iron. This type of response, referred to as delayed cutaneous hypersensitivity, is an important indicator of the health of the cell-mediated immune system.

◆ ◆ ◆

Another little-known consequence of iron deficiency was discovered by chance during a study of behavioral changes in iron-deficient children. Oski noticed that the blood levels and the urinary excretion of epinephrine were much higher in his subjects than in normal children. In 1975 he speculated that his finding was related to the behavioral changes he had observed. It is common for animal studies to point to the need for confirmatory investigations in human subjects, but in this case the opposite occurred.

Three years later Erick Dillman of the Institute of Nutrition in the Hospital for Nutritional Diseases in Mexico City and a group of collaborators at the University of Washington decided to explore Oski's findings, this time using rats. They discovered that iron-deficient rats were unable to maintain a normal body temperature when exposed to cold. In these rats, oxygen consumption was also reduced, indicating a lower metabolic rate and therefore less heat production. In addition to epinephrine, the hormone thyroxine, which is secreted by the thyroid gland and which regulates metabolic rates, was abnormally high in the rats' urine.

Miguel Layrisse of the Institute of Scientific Investigations in Caracas, Venezuela, learned of these results and decided to investigate further. He placed anemic and nonanemic men in a water tank under conditions in which blood pressure, body temperature and oxygen consumption could be monitored and periodic blood samples obtained. The water in the tank was held at body temperature (37 degrees Celsius) for one hour and then lowered to 28 degrees C.

Layrisse's findings paralleled Dillman's. Five subjects with severe iron deficiency proved unable to maintain their body temperature. Moreover, oxygen consumption decreased and epinephrine levels in urine increased in individuals with mild as well as severe iron deficiency. When they were given 60 milligrams of iron three times a day for seven days, oxygen consumption returned to normal, even though there was not time enough for the hemoglobin levels to change significantly. The observation that iron deficiency lowers resistance to cold exposure and that this phenomenon is reversible may be particularly significant for those anemic elderly who are already more susceptible to cold because of less subcutaneous fat or poor circulation.

Despite the clear advantage of iron supplementation in restoring temperature regulation or counteracting reduced work capacity, treating iron deficiency is not as straightforward as treating some other nutritional disorders. For example, in iodine deficiency, iodine is easily supplied by iodized salt and, unlike iron, is not harmful in large amounts. The same is true for vitamin A deficiency: a dosage of 300,000 international units every four to six months is safe and effective.

Iron supplementation at a level not exceeding 100 milligrams of ferrous sulfate daily is beneficial for normal individuals who are deficient because of poor absorption of dietary iron and the effects of parasites and other infections. Most populations can also benefit from a staple food fortified with somewhat less iron—for example, cereals, bread, sugar, salt and even monosodium glutamate. Yet the fortification of multiple dietary sources for a population should be avoided.

◆ ◆ ◆

The old adage that too much of a good thing is no longer good is particularly relevant to iron supplementation. One of the first insights into the dangers of iron excess was provided by South African Bantu men, who have a high incidence of a serious liver disease called hemochromatosis. In this disease the liver is characterized by the excessive accumulation of iron, the development of fibrous tissue and often the occurrence of fatal cancer.

Investigation revealed that the individuals affected were, and still are, accustomed to consuming large quantities of beer fermented locally in iron pots. Because the acid of fermentation leaches iron into the beer and because the quantities consumed daily are very large, toxic iron overloads develop. Obviously these circumstances are unusual, but they have also been reported in a number of other African countries. (Hemochromatosis can also develop in individuals who have a relatively rare genetic defect that destroys the person's ability to modulate the absorption of iron in response to need.)

In 1970 Hylton McFarlane of Manchester University in England reported from South Africa that intramuscular injections of iron given to severely malnourished children to correct their anemia were associated with fatal infections. Reports from Nigeria, New Guinea and Somalia have also indicated that iron injections exacerbate malaria.

The reason for such a result is that iron is valuable not only to the individual but also to the organism infecting that individual. Usually the body has several mechanisms for withholding iron as part of its resistance to such infections. When white blood cells disintegrate after ingesting and killing bacteria and viruses, they release interleukin-1, whose many functions include stimulating the synthesis of ferritin, the efficient iron storage protein. Ferritin production ensures that the iron released from decaying red blood cells will not be available to invading organisms. Disintegrating leukocytes will also discharge lactoferrin at sites of inflammation. Lactoferrin binds iron more strongly than can infecting organisms.

There is little doubt that the body's methods of withholding the iron needed by microorganisms for their multiplication constitute an important way of reducing the virulence of bacterial and protozoan infections. (These mechanisms have been extensively reviewed by Eugene D. Weinberg of Indiana University.) In the presence of too much iron, however, these protective mechanisms are overwhelmed and ineffective.

This complication does not mean that iron deficiency is ever a desirable state. It does mean, however, that giving malnourished individuals large doses of iron is potentially dangerous. Particular care must be taken so that individuals whose cell-mediated immunity has been compromised by iron deficiency do not become overwhelmed by infection before recovery of immunity can occur. Modest daily amounts of iron contribute to a healthy immune system without weakening the protective mechanisms that withhold iron from microorganisms.

The serious consequences of iron deficiency for human health, behavior and performance and the wide prevalence of this disorder are urgent reasons for the strong national and international efforts to curb this illness. Both UNICEF and WHO will need to coordinate strategies for fortifying appropriate foods with iron and providing iron supplements to vulnerable groups. At the same time, infections must be prevented, particularly those causing blood loss, such as hookworm, schistosomiasis and malaria. With concerted international effort, iron deficiency, and the unacceptable suffering it causes so many people around the world, could become another of the major public health problems eliminated in this century.

FURTHER READING

Iron Deficiency: Brain Biochemistry and Behavior. Edited by Ernesto Pollitt and Rudolf L. Leibel. Raven Press, 1982.

Iron Deficiency and Work Performance. Edited by Leif Hallberg and Nevin S. Scrimshaw. INACG, 1983. Available from the Nutrition Foundation, Washington, D.C.

International Conference on Iron Deficiency and Behavioral Development. Edited by Ernesto Pollitt, Jere Haas and David A. Levitsky. Supplement to American Journal of Clinical Nutrition, Vol. 50, No. 3; September 1989.

Functional Significance of Iron Deficiency. Edited by Cyril O. Enwonwu. Nashville. Tenn., Meharry Medical College, 1990.

30

Body Size, Adaptation and Function

Reynaldo Martorell

This is a brief discussion of the "small but healthy" hypothesis proposed by David Seckler in the early 1980s. Four basic points are made. First, adults in developing countries have small body sizes largely as a result of poor diets and infection during childhood. Therefore, to acclaim small body size as a desirable attribute for populations is also to affirm that its causes are desirable. Second, monitoring the growth of children is widely recognized as an excellent tool for detecting health problems. Growth retardation, rather than an innocuous response to environmental stimuli, is a warning signal of increased risk of morbidity and mortality. Third, the conditions which give rise to stunted children also affect other aspects such as cognitive development. Finally, stunted girls who survive to be short women are at greater risk of delivering growth retarded infants with a greater probability of dying in infancy. For all these reasons, small is not healthy.

Key words: nutrition, child growth, health, adaptation, function

An economist by the name of David Seckler proposed the "small but healthy" hypothesis a few years ago (Seckler 1980, 1982). This hypothesis has generated a lively literature (Messer 1986), including heated debates and thoughtful but sometimes emotionally charged rebuttals from nutritionists such as Gopalan

(1983) and Latham (1984). Seckler's views have sparked a great deal of interest because they result in policy and programmatic implications which differ markedly from the conventional. The "small but healthy" hypothesis implies a world in which the problem of malnutrition is no longer of massive proportions since most of the world is "small but healthy." In Seckler's world, the only individuals who are "truly" malnourished are those showing clinical signs of malnutrition. The latter, Seckler tells us, should be the first priority of nutrition policy, and nutritional resources should not be squandered on the "small but healthy population." My presentation is not a comprehensive critique of Seckler's ideas nor of the resulting policy implications, but rather it is a selective discussion of issues that seem to have been ignored by Seckler. First allow me to briefly describe some of the principal elements of the "small but healthy" hypothesis.

SECKLER'S "SMALL BUT HEALTHY" HYPOTHESIS

Seckler's "small but healthy" child is the child who is short but not thin. In the Waterlow classification, this refers to children whose heights are two standard deviations below the median of the reference population but whose weight for heights are above this criterion (see Table 1). In the jargon of the day, these children are said to be "stunted but not wasted." This group of children makes up a significant proportion of the population in many Third World countries and is the majority in India, Bangladesh, and some African nations (Martorell 1985). Children who are wasted, on the other hand, are far less common, and rarely exceed 10% of the population, even in areas where nutritional problems are a serious concern (Martorell 1985). Wasting is synonymous with marasmus and Seckler has no objection to classifying these children

as unhealthy. To repeat, it is the stunted but not wasted child who Seckler calls "small but healthy."

According to Seckler (1980, 1982), most nutritional scientists believe in what he calls the "Deprivation Theory." This view holds that an individual is healthy and well nourished if he grows along his genetically determined growth curve. On the other hand, growth significantly below this curve indicates that the individual is malnourished and in poor health. Seckler believes that this view is incorrect and instead proposes the "Homeostatic Theory of Growth." In this theory, the single potential growth curve is replaced by the concept of a broad array of potential growth curves. Within the bounds of this potential growth space, the child may move through various paths of size and shape without suffering any functional implications. Seckler tells us that while the *deprivation* theory of nutritionists postulates a continuous functional relationship between small size and impairments, his *homeostatic* theory postulates a threshold relationship. Seckler (1982:129) goes on to tell us that "smallness may not be associated with functional impairments over a rather large range of variation; but the system explodes into a high incidence of functional impairments at the lower bound of size." The stunted but not wasted child is within this safe zone, or to use his words, "small but healthy."

I am certain that the vast majority of researchers do not agree with the "deprivation theory" as formulated by Seckler. Growth retardation is widely recognized as a response to a limited nutrient supply at the cellular level. The maintenance of basic metabolic functions takes precedence and resources are diverted away from growth and physical activity. The concurrence of growth retardation and functional impairments is the rationale for the use of anthropometric indicators as risk indicators of poor health and as predictors of mortality. It is incorrect to claim that nutritional scientists uniformly hold that growth retardation and functional impairments are linearly related. In fact, much of the research shows curvilinear relationships (see Martorell and Ho 1984 for a review of the literature). Minor and brief interruptions in growth are not likely to be a cause of concern, whereas chronic patterns of growth retardation leading to stunting invariably are.

My remarks are limited to a discussion of four issues. The first issue is that the causes of stunting are unhealthy. Second, I will emphasize that linear growth retardation is a danger signal and not an innocuous adjustment to environmental stimuli. Third, I will discuss the fact that the factors that affect linear growth also affect other functional domains. Finally, I will refer to the fact that stunted adults suffer certain disadvantages.

Table 1. Waterlow's classification

		Height	
		<2 SD	**≥2 SD**
Weight for height	<2 SD	Stunted and wasted	Not stunted but wasted
	≥2 SD	Stunted but not wasted	Normal

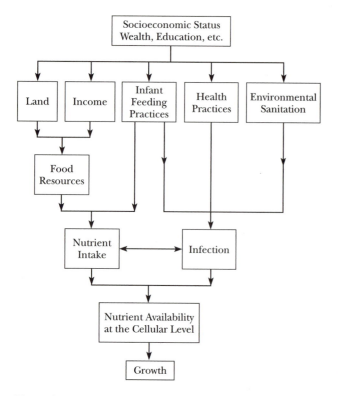

Figure 1. Examples of mechanisms through which poverty influences growth in children

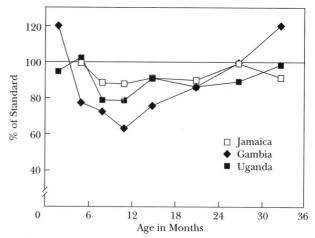

Figure 2. Relative velocity curves for length for young children from three countries *(from Waterlow and Rutishauser 1974)*

THE PROCESS OF STUNTING IS UNHEALTHY

First, I would like to underscore that the *process* of stunting is unhealthy. Seckler implies that the child is healthy while he is becoming stunted so long as he avoids wasting, and that stunting has no functional implications once it has occurred. Throughout his writings we are presented with the image of the child who "indifferently" adjusts his growth trajectory in response to environmental stimuli while enjoying perfect health. Moreover, he seems to ascribe only a small role to nutrition and infection factors in causing smallness. Seckler proposes that there are two kinds of smallness. The first, he says, is "smallness due to poverty, and to poor physical and socio-economic environments" (Seckler 1982:134). The second is "smallness due to malnutrition, a pathological state of deficiency entailing functional impairment of individuals" (Seckler 1982:134).

There are no known mechanisms through which poverty can affect growth which do not involve nutrition and infection. Examples of mechanisms through which socio-economic factors influence growth in children are shown in Figure 1. The relative importance of the components of poverty will vary from place to place, but these will always lead to low dietary intakes

and/or infection which result in decreased nutrient availability at the cellular level and which then gives rise to growth retardation (Chen 1983). The diets of poor children are generally deficient in both quantity and quality and these characteristics are the result of several factors: limited food availability *per se,* inappropriate infant feeding practices and the influence of infections on appetite. Infections will also have direct effects on nutrient metabolism and thus lead to poor nutrient utilization. In short, there are not two kinds of smallness. Rather, the basic cause of stunting is poverty and the effects on size are mediated through poor diets and infection.

We know a great deal about the timing of stunting (see Martorell and Habicht 1986 for a detailed discussion of this subject). One of the best available illustrations of the development of stunting is a figure published in Waterlow and Rutishauser (1974; see Figure 2). By expressing mean growth rates in length in populations of preschool children from developing countries as a percentage of the average velocity in the reference population, one will obtain curves which are similar to the ones shown in Figure 2 for Jamaica, Gambia, and Uganda. The choice of reference population, as noted below, matters little if at all. Growth in length in the first few months of life is generally as fast in Third World children as in reference populations. Growth retardation begins anywhere from the second to the sixth month and continues till about three years of age. Growth rates generally equal those in reference populations after about three years of age.

The period from three months to as long as three years is the period of weaning in traditional societies, which I define as the transition from total dependence

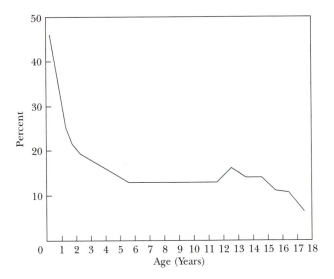

Figure 3. Proportion of protein requirement due to growth needs at various ages in boys *(from data in FAO/WHO/ UNU 1985)*

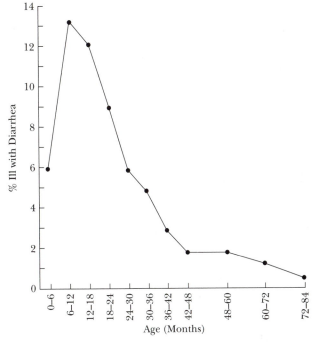

Figure 4. Mean percentage of time ill with diarrhea from birth to seven years of age in Guatemalan children *(from Martorell and Habicht 1986)*

on mother's milk to complete reliance on the local diet. Stunting is a phenomenon intimately associated with the perils of this period. Numerous factors play a role in determining nutrient intake and infectious disease patterns, including infant feeding practices, the nature of the local diet and the foods offered to children, environmental sanitation, and the degree of contamination of foods and liquids.

Weaning brings together powerful factors which lead to stunting. The first two years of life is a time when growth is very rapid and therefore a time when adverse factors are going to have a significant and lasting effect. Also, infancy and the second year of life are when nutritional requirements, expressed as energy or as nutrients per kg per day, are greater than at any other subsequent time of life. As shown in Figure 3, a greater proportion of the requirement for protein is due to growth during this critical phase of human development than is the case later. Thus, growth rates are not only fastest during the weaning period, but also account for a greater share of the total nutrient demand than is the case later on in life.

Another feature is that infections, particularly diarrheal diseases, occur most frequently during the first two to three years of life. This is illustrated in Figure 4 which shows the percent of time Guatemalan children are ill with diarrhea from birth to seven years of age. The first two years or so of life is a time when children's immunological systems are maturing rapidly and when they are first coming into contact with disease pathogens. If children survive to four or five years of age, they will be healthier than they were earlier in life.

There is now considerable evidence from a variety of settings showing that almost all of the growth retardation observed in Third World populations has its origin in this stormy period of weaning (Billewicz and McGregor 1982; Hauspie et al. 1980; Dahlmann and Petersen 1977; Satyanarayana et al. 1980, 1981). By the time children in developing countries are three to four years of age, many are already destined to be stunted adults.

Ethnicity or race plays a minor role in determining population differences in length during the weaning period. In fact, it has been rather difficult to show that there are ethnic differences in growth potential in prepubescent children. Differences associated with poverty, on the other hand, are easy to demonstrate (Victora et al. 1986) and far overshadow those which might be ascribed to race or ethnicity (see Martorell 1985 for a review of the literature).

GROWTH RETARDATION IS A RISK INDICATOR

The second issue I want to address is that linear growth is our best indicator of child health. *Good growth means*

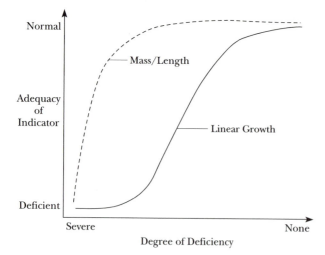

Figure 5.   Response of anthropometric indicators to varying degrees of deficiency

good health. Seckler, you will recall, claims that linear growth retardation has no functional implications. Only wasting implies an impaired state and therefore only wasting represents a nutritional and public health problem. This is a very narrow and out-dated clinical view of the problem of malnutrition.

Seckler's views ignore that there is a continuum of responses as children face nutritional deficits. As indicated in Figure 5, at severe levels of deficiency, linear growth ceases altogether and it becomes necessary to use tissue reserves as an energy and nutrient source to maintain vital functions. However, at less severe stages, normal mass to length dimensions will be maintained as it may be possible to cope with dietary deficits simply by slowing down in growth and by decreasing physical activity. This seems to be the situation in Latin America where moderate linear growth retardation occurs but where wasting is rare. However, in parts of Africa and the Indian subcontinent, the burden is much greater and marked growth retardation prevails and severe wasting is more common (Martorell 1985).

A fundamental principle of pediatrics and of modern public health nutrition is the notion that a child who is growing normally is more likely to be healthy than one who is growing poorly. This is the philosophy behind growth monitoring programs which seek to identify children who are failing to grow adequately in order to intervene with appropriate measures before the situation progresses to wasting and malnutrition (Morley 1976; Rohde et al. 1975).

The rationale for growth monitoring is evidence that children who grow poorly are more likely to be severely ill when infected and more likely to die than

children who grow well. Wasting appears to be a stronger predictor of risk than stunting, as one would expect, but indicators of stunting are definitely important, even after controlling for socioeconomic status (Martorell and Ho 1984).

OTHER FUNCTIONAL EFFECTS

A third and related point I would like to make is that the factors which cause growth to be retarded also affect other functional domains as well. One reason growth retardation is predictive of morbidity and mortality is that immunocompetence is impaired, thus rendering the child more vulnerable to infections (Kielmann et al. 1976; McMurray et al. 1981). Physical activity is probably affected even at early stages of energy deficiency but the evidence on this is lacking. This is unfortunate because activity may be an important factor in child development since it is one determinant of the ability of the child to explore the environment and to learn from it.

There are a number of studies showing strong relationships between stunting and poor psychological test performance (Pollitt and Thomson 1977). The relationship is complex and probably due to third factors, such as those related to poverty, which cause both physical and developmental retardation. The point we should remember is that stunting is a marker for poor psychological performance.

FUNCTIONAL IMPLICATIONS OF STUNTING IN ADULTS

So far I have focused on the functional implications of stunting in children. However, is the child who survives to become a stunted adult healthy? In other words, does stunting in adults have any functional implications? This is the fourth and last point of my presentation.

To answer this question, I would like to focus on two aspects: work capacity and productivity in males, and reproductive performance in females.

In discussing the relationship between body size and work, we should distinguish between capacity and productivity. Work capacity is largely a measure of the biological potential to do work and is determined in the laboratory, whereas productivity is an economic term measured in terms of goods produced per unit time. There is overwhelming evidence showing that stunted men have reduced muscle masses and significantly diminished work capacities (Spurr 1983). How-

Table 2. Maternal stature, infant mortality, parity, and number of surviving children in Mayan women
(data from Martorell et al. 1981)

	Terciles of Height[a]			Analysis of Variance Main Effects	
	Lower (N = 127)	Middle (N = 124)	Upper (N = 129)	F	p
Infant mortality[b]	205	150	101	7.9	<.001
Parity[b]	4.75	4.10	4.22	2.1	.12
Surviving children[b]	2.83	3.02	3.15	1.7	.18

[a] Means and ranges for height (cm) for each of the three groups were as follows: Lower (mean 137.7, range 126.3–140.2), middle (mean 142.0, range 140.3–144.7) and upper (mean 148.2, range 144.8–158.6).

[b] Values standardized for age by analyses of covariance. Adjusted to the mean age of 28.4 years.

ever, many jobs in agriculture, manufacturing and industry are not that physically demanding. Also, many factors other than work capacity determine productivity, and among these we can include motivation and training. Hence, one would not necessarily expect small body sizes to be a limiting factor for light to moderate activities. As it turns out, current nutritional status—as measured by weight for height, iron status, and energy intakes—seems to be a better predictor of productivity than height for many types of activities (see Martorell and Arroyave 1988 for a review of the literature). There are, of course, physically demanding tasks such as sugarcane cutting where physical size has been found to be related to productivity. This is to be expected since at a strenuous work load, those with a lower work capacity would be closer to a maximal effort and would function at faster heart rates. Such overtaxed individuals may not be able to maintain the work pace for very long and may produce less (Spurr 1983).

Greater height in women in areas where malnutrition is endemic is associated with an enhanced capacity to conceive, and to deliver a baby more likely to survive and to have better growth and development. The results of a study of maternal stature and infant mortality in several hundred Mayan women illustrate this point (Table 2). Variations in socioeconomic status were minimal because all families lived [on] and were employed by owners of coffee plantations, and because all received the same low salaries and small amounts of corn in payment for their labor. Mothers were very short; in fact, the population studied appears to be among the shortest in the world. The mean height was 142.4 cm and the tallest woman was only 158.6 cm or 5 ft 2 in. As shown in Table 2, maternal height was significantly associated with infant mortality which was 205 per 1,000 live births for the shortest group, 150 for the middle group, and 101 for the tallest group. This is not a new finding. Low maternal height is widely recognized as a risk indicator of low birth weight and infant mortality.

CONCLUDING REMARKS

It is clear I do not believe small is healthy. This is largely because the process by which children become small is associated with major functional impairment and because its causes are undesirable. I also do not embrace policies which are targeted only at the severely malnourished. Rather, I favor broad public health and nutrition measures which aim to prevent severe malnutrition. Promoting actions which prevent growth failure in young children will reduce the risk of progression to severe malnutrition and death. Throughout my presentation I have emphasized four key points.

First, it is a travesty to call the process of stunting healthy since its causes are deficient diets and infections. To acclaim the end result of the process, small body size, as a desirable attribute of populations is also to affirm that its causes are desirable.

Second, *good growth means good health*. I am not promoting maximal size, but rather insisting that growth retardation is an early warning signal. Linear growth retardation is one of our best indicators that something is going wrong and it should be a call for action.

Third, the stunted child has other unfortunate characteristics such as poor cognitive development. This simply reflects the fact that the harsh conditions which give rise to markedly reduced stature have other undesirable repercussions as well.

And finally, small body size does have functional implications in adults. Productivity may be limited in small individuals engaged in very strenuous activities, and very short stature in mothers is a powerful predictor of low birth weight and infant mortality.

For all these reasons, small is not healthy. Quite the contrary, poor growth in a child is an indicator of major functional impairment. A society in which a major proportion of its children are stunted is one with serious public health problems.

REFERENCES CITED

Billewicz, W. Z., and I. A. McGregor
  1982 A Birth-to-Maturity Longitudinal Study of Heights and Weights in Two West African (Gambian) Villages, 1951–1975. Annals of Human Biology 9(4): 309–320.
Chen, L. C.
  1983 Interactions of Diarrhea and Malnutrition: Mechanisms and Interventions. *In* Diarrhea and Malnutrition: Interactions, Mechanisms, and Interventions. L. C. Chen and N. Scrimshaw, eds. Pp. 3–19. New York: Plenum Press.
Dahlman, N., and K. Petersen
  1977 Influences of Environmental Conditions During Infancy on Final Body Stature. Pediatric Research 11:695–700.
FAO/WHO/UNU Joint Expert Consultation
  1985 Energy and Protein Requirements. Technical Report Series 724. Geneva, Switzerland: World Health Organization.
Gopalan, C.
  1983 Small Is Healthy? For the Poor, Not for the Rich. Nutrition Foundation of India Bulletin, October.
Hauspie, R. C., S. R. Das, M. A. Preece, and J. M. Tanner
  1980 A Longitudinal Study of the Growth in Height of Boys and Girls of West Bengal (India) Aged Six Months to 20 Years. Annals of Human Biology 7:429–441.
Kielmann, A. A., I. S. Uberoi, R. K. Chandra, and V. L. Mehra
  1976 The Effect of Nutritional Status on Immune Capacity and Immune Responses in Preschool Children in a Rural Community in India. Bulletin of the World Health Organization 54:477–483.
Latham, M. C.
  1984 Smallness—a Symptom of Deprivation. Nutrition Foundation of India Bulletin 5(6), July.
Martorell, R.
  1985 Child Growth Retardation: A Discussion of Its Causes and Its Relationship to Health. *In* Nutritional Adaptation in Man. Sir Kenneth Blaxter and J. C. Waterlow, eds. Pp. 13–30. London: John Libbey.
Martorell, R., and G. Arroyave
  1988 Malnutrition, Work Output and Energy Needs. *In* Capacity for Work in the Tropics. K. J. Collins and

D. F. Roberts, eds. Pp. 57–75. Cambridge: Cambridge University Press.
Martorell, R., H. L. Delgado, V. Valverde, and R. E. Klein
  1981 Maternal Stature, Fertility, and Infant Mortality. Human Biology 53(3):303–312.
Martorell, R., and J-P. Habicht
  1986 Growth in Early Childhood in Developing Countries. *In* Human Growth: A Comprehensive Treatise, 2nd ed. Vol. 3: Methodology: Ecological, Genetic, and Nutritional Effects on Growth. F. Falkner and J. M. Tanner, eds. Pp. 241–262. New York: Plenum Press.
Martorell, R., and T. J. Ho
  1984 Malnutrition, Morbidity, and Mortality. *In* Child Survival: Strategies for Research. H. Mosley and L. Chen, eds. Pp. 49–68. Supplement to Volume 10 of the Population and Development Review.
McMurray, D. N., S. A. Loomis, L. J. Casazza, H. Rey, and R. Miranda
  1981 Development of Impaired Cell-Mediated Immunity in Mild and Moderate Malnutrition. American Journal of Clinical Nutrition 34:68–77.
Messer, E.
  1986 The "Small but Healthy" Hypothesis: Historical, Political, and Ecological Influences on Nutritional Standards. Human Ecology 14(1):57–75.
Morley, D.
  1976 Nutritional Surveillance of Young Children in Developing Countries. International Journal of Epidemiology 5(1):51–55.
Pollitt, E., and C. Thomson
  1977 Protein-Calorie Malnutrition and Behavior: A Review from Psychology. *In* Nutrition and the Brain, Vol. 2. R. J. Wurtman and J. J. Wurtman, eds. Pp. 261–307. New York: Raven Press.
Rohde, J. E., D. Ismail, and R. Sutrisno
  1975 Mothers as Weight Watchers: The Road to Child Health in the Village. Environmental Child Health 21:295–297.
Satyanarayana, K., A. Nadamuni Naidu, M. C. Swaminatham, and B. S. Narasinga Rao
  1980 Adolescent Growth Spurt Among Rural Indian Boys in Relation to Their Nutritional Status in Early Childhood. Annals of Human Biology 7:359–366.
  1981 Effect of Nutritional Deprivation in Early Childhood on Later Growth—a Community Study Without Intervention. American Journal of Clinical Nutrition 34(8):1636–1637.
Seckler, D.
  1980 Malnutrition: An Intellectual Odyssey. Western Journal of Agricultural Economics 5(2):219–227.
  1982 "Small but Healthy": A Basic Hypothesis in the Theory, Measurement, and Policy of Malnutrition. *In* Newer Concepts in Nutrition and Their Implications for Policy. P. V. Sukhatme, ed. Pp. 127–137. Maharashtra Association for the Cultivation of Science Research Institute. Law College Road, Pune, India.
Spurr, G. B.
  1983 Nutritional Status and Physical Work Capacity. Yearbook of Physical Anthropology 26:1–35.

Victora, C. G., J. P. Vaughan, B. R. Kirkwood, J. C. Martines, and L. B. Barcelos
1986 Risk Factors for Malnutrition in Brazilian Children: The Role of Social and Environmental Variables. Bulletin of the World Health Organization 64(2): 299–309.

Waterlow, J. C., and I. H. E. Rutishauser
1974 Malnutrition in Man. *In* Early Malnutrition and Mental Development. Symposia of the Swedish Nutrition Foundation XII. J. Cravioto, L. Harnbreaus, and B. Vahlquiest, eds. Pp. 13–26. Uppsala, Sweden: Almquist and Wiksell.

Dietary "Delocalization" and Development

Coca-Cola™ is one of the United States' biggest exports. Like their thirsty cousins in the United States, the average Mexican and Icelander drink almost 8 ounces of Coca-Cola per day. Coca-Cola is not merely a major economic commodity, but a major contributor to diets. The drinking of two to three soft drinks in a day by a 10-year-old Mayan boy accounts for about a third of his energy intake.

In the 1980s, a popular movie, *The Gods Must Be Crazy,* centered on an empty bottle of Coca-Cola found by a !Kung San. The soft drink bottle was a well-chosen metaphor for the intrusion of Western culture. It appears that the unique diets noted in previous articles, including the hunting and gathering lifestyle of the San, are becoming increasingly cosmopolitan and, at the same time, increasingly similar. The global village is dominated by American fast foods and perhaps genetically engineered foods. How did this come to be? What are the consequences for culture, environment, and human biology?

Half a millennium ago, the local populace of each region had independent responsibility for producing their food. Food systems developed in response to ecological limits and cultural patterns. Local independence began to change with long-distance exploration and trade. First, explorers such as Marco Polo came back with easily transported spices, teas, and condiments. These exotic items were made available to sponsors, and the tastes of the wealthy and the nobility began to change. Full-blown globalization of diets began at about the time of the colonization and conquest of the Americas. Increased transcontinental transport provided a means for supplying goods to the middle classes. Staples began to be traded, and seeds of fruits, vegetables, tubers, and grains were transported and replanted in faraway places. Some of these "ecological exchanges" likely failed miserably and became of little historical consequence. Others proved to be great successes, at least initially, as, for example, the migration of the potato from Peru to Ireland.

The articles in this part focus on various aspects of the key historical trends of dietary delocalization and commoditization. Pelto and Pelto (article 31) define *delocalization* as "processes in which food varieties, production methods, and consumption patterns are dis-

seminated throughout the world in an ever-increasing and intensifying network of socioeconomic and political interdependency." Commoditization of food systems, a process embedded in dietary delocalization, is defined by Dewey (1989:415) as "the use of agricultural goods for sale rather than home consumption." The articles that follow illustrate general aspects of these processes with specific examples.

In "Diet and Delocalization: Dietary Changes Since 1750," anthropologists Gretel and Pertti Pelto outline the idea of delocalization, how it might vary from place to place, and its potential impact on nutritional status. As stated in their definition of *delocalization,* they view this process as "ever-increasing and intensifying." It is clear that more and more groups are being drawn into national and international markets and systems of trade. Trade agreements such as NAFTA and those of the WTO support this trend.

Delocalization is in reality a number of interrelated processes involving the movement of foods, ideas, and peoples. Key processes include new foods being introduced through trade, locally produced foods now purchased in stores, new foods grown locally, and new knowledge and food preferences brought about by migration of individuals and ideologies. Because the mix of subprocesses varies, the consequences of delocalization for diet and nutrition are complex. The end result, however, is typically an increase in energy needs due in part to transportation. Local autonomy is frequently lost because external "market forces" control prices.

Pelto and Pelto suggest that one means to evaluate delocalization is via its consequence on dietary diversity. *Dietary diversity* is important because more diverse diets are more likely to provide a healthy mix of nutrients. They hypothesize that delocalization has had a positive effect on dietary diversity for wealthy individuals. However, for individuals who cannot afford to purchase exotic foods, delocalization may lead to decreased diversity.

In "Time, Sugar, and Sweetness," anthropologist Sidney Mintz demonstrates the key role of one food item—sugar—in the development of England and Europe and the "underdevelopment" of the Caribbean. In Mintz's analysis, the developed taste for sugar among the working class of Europe provided the impetus for an extractive industry that changed the Caribbean forever and helped to fuel the Atlantic slave trade.

Following sugar around the globe, as Mintz does, provides an excellent illustration of the importance of delocalization and commoditization. The production of sugar from sugarcane began in South Asia and was imported to the Caribbean along with enslaved Africans. Sugar production was an industry on new soil (the Caribbean) run by nonlocal, wealthy Europeans and maintained by the labor of enslaved Africans. The dietary consequences are also systemic and delocalized. At the beginning of the seventeenth century, sugar in Britain was a luxury and a medicine. But with mass production and transatlantic trade, by the end of the century it had become a necessity. Everyone wanted sugar, and consumption rates dramatically rose. Paradoxically, the craving for sugar is expanding still. Sugar has returned to Central America and the Caribbean in a soft drink bottle.

It is easy to envision why subsistence farmers would become increasingly drawn into markets. Selling their crops provides cash that offers the flexibility to buy commodities of choice. In the best of situations, they can increase the intake of nutrient-dense foods. For example, fruits and vegetables that do not grow well in local soils and climates might be purchased. Fish may be brought to inland areas. Additionally, nonfood items can be purchased with money from growing export foods. More often, delocalization involves the loss of control over pricing, and the amount of funds available for purchasing foods is limited. What is bought may be more a function of the power of advertisement than of family nutritional needs.

In "When the Turtle Collapses, the World Ends," Bernard Nietschmann tells the story of the Miskito Indians of the Atlantic coast of Nicaragua and their change from subsistence agriculture and fishing to exporting turtle to distant world markets. Along with cassava, a high-energy source, green turtle meat had been a dietary staple of the Miskito. Turtle meat is highly esteemed, but until recently there was no need to catch more turtles than could be locally consumed. In the late 1960s, two export companies began processing turtles for their meat and other products to market in Europe and North America. For the first time, the Miskito Indians had the option of selling turtles—in fact, selling as many as they could catch. Unfortunately, the ecological reality is not "turtles all the way down" (a quote from the opening of Nietschmann's article). Turtles are a finite resource. When turtle production declines or competition increases, financial yield decreases and nutrition suffers. What is the lesson to be learned from this article? How generalizable

is it? What could and should be done to prevent this type of exploitation from occurring in the future?

Debbie Mack's "Food for All" presents some of the current and hotly contested issues around a new type of delocalization: genetic engineering of foods. The public relations program of Monsanto, a company that is heavily involved in genetic engineering, optimistically declares that they will be able to feed the world with their new insect-resistant and high-yield varieties of seeds. They claim that their genetic engineering will even provide more nutritious varieties of maize and other foods. But at least two problems persist. First, many are skeptical that the promise of genetic engineering can be achieved. There may be upper limits to manipulating crop nutrient composition and crop yields without sacrificing resistance or creating other unforeseen problems. The track record, from the worst of the Green Revolution to Monsanto's marketing of Roundup-resistant soya beans, does not engender great confidence. Second, these technological fixes are controlled by multinationals. Using them requires that local farmers become less independent. Is the Faustian bargain of poor farmers: "buy seed, or die"?

Delocalization has prevented starvation and allowed more individuals to be fed. Delocalization has led to wonderfully tasteful mixes of food. If diversity is the spice of life, then delocalization is the spice factory. But delocalization can go too far. Will the pressures to make wages to pay for other goods pull many peasants worldwide even further away from tending their small gardens and agricultural plots? If local autonomy is lost, then delocalization can have horrific economic, social, and nutritional consequences. Cokes and chips and genetically engineered seeds will replace tortillas and fruits.

SUGGESTIONS FOR THINKING AND DOING NUTRITIONAL ANTHROPOLOGY

1. *The Turtle People* is a film about the plight of the Miskito Indians. It follows very well the article by Nietschmann. Another view of commoditization is found in the film *Jungle Burger*. View one or both films and consider the consequences of commoditization of systems of exchange.

2. Select a favorite dish that you associate with an ethnic group. Identify each ingredient. Where did each ingredient originate, and how did it become incorporated into this cuisine?

3. Select a processed food item and trace its origins. Where did the various components originate? Try to identify where they are now grown or produced.

4. Calculate your dietary diversity. As a class, first construct food categories. Your categories should not be too broad (all carbohydrate-based foods) or too narrow (chicken). For three days, place each of your foods into these categories and score the total number of categories you eat from for each day. Compare your diversity to that of fellow students.

5. One of the most serious debates of the coming years will be over the introduction of genetically engineered foods. Assuming that these foods will be developed, what might be some of the ways to make sure the benefits are shared by those who are most in need?

FURTHER READINGS

Bindon, J. R. (1982). Breadfruit, banana, beef and beer: Modernization of the Samoan diet. *Ecology of Food and Nutrition, 12,* 49–60. (An excellent study of changes in food systems with "modernization.")

Daly, D. C. (1996, January). The leaf that launched a thousand ships. *Natural History,* pp. 24–30. (Along with other articles in this issue, Daly's is a good starting point on the history of the potato and the "Great Famine" in Ireland.)

Dewey, K. G. (1989). Nutrition and the commoditization of food systems in Latin America and the Carribbean. *Social Science and Medicine, 28,* 415–424.

Kloppenburg, J. (1990). *First the seed: The political economy of plant biotechnology 1492–2000.* New York: Cambridge University Press. (Kloppenburg was one of the first and most outspoken critics of the role of multinationals in controlling seed distribution.)

Mintz, Sidney. (1985). *Sweetness and power.* New York: Viking Press. (A classic on the role of sugar in world history. Essentially, an expansion of the article that is included here.)

Ross, E. (1980). History and ascendancy of beef in the United States diet. In *Beyond the myth of culture: Essays in cultural materialism* (pp. 181–225). New York: Academic Press. (A fine essay on the interrelationship of technology, ideology, and economics in changing national diets.)

Sokolov, R. (1991). *Why we eat what we eat.* New York: Simon and Schuster. (A lively series of short articles by a food writer on the spread of foods and condiments around the world and the process of increasing hybridity of food traditions.)

Viola, H. J., & Margolis, C. (Eds.). (1991). *Seeds of change.* Washington, D.C.: Smithsonian Institution Press. (Chapters trace the routes of Old World crops into the Americas and vice versa.)

31

Diet and Delocalization: Dietary Changes Since 1750

Gretel H. Pelto and Pertti J. Pelto

During the past two centuries virtually all of the populations in the world have experienced dramatic changes in their dietary patterns. In the industrialized countries changes in food patterns have been associated with improved levels of nutrition and public health, although some nutrition-related diseases are increasing. Similar processes of change in the less industrialized nations, however, have often had serious negative effects. We examine here some of the primary processes of change in food resources and distribution over the past 250 years, focusing on three main transformations that have had profound effects on global eating patterns. Our primary thesis is:

First, the general direction of transformations in food use throughout the world in the past two or three centuries has involved an increasingly rapid "delocalization" of food production and distribution. By "delocalization" (discussed more fully below) we refer to processes in which food varieties, production methods, and consumption patterns are disseminated throughout the world in an ever-increasing and intensifying network of socioeconomic and political interdependency. From the point of view of individuals and families at any one place on the globe, delocalization means that an increasing portion of the daily diet comes from distant places, usually through commercial channels.

Second, in the industrialized nations, delocalization has been associated with an increase in the diversity of available foods and the quantity of food imports, and, therefore, with improved diets. In earlier periods this improvement of diet, especially through diversification, primarily benefited the upper social classes, but during the twentieth century the effects have diffused to a wide spectrum of people in the "developed" world.

Third, in the less industrialized countries of the world, the same processes of delocalization have tended to produce opposite effects on dietary quality, except for the elite. Until recent times many peoples in the Third World have been primarily dependent on locally produced food supplies, which remained largely outside the networks of commerce. As these populations have been drawn more and more into full commercial participation, economic and political forces have encouraged concentration on one or two main cash crops, with an accompanying deterioration of food diversity, as well as a loss of local control over the distribution system. Thus, world-wide food distribution and food-use transformations have occurred at the expense of economically marginal populations.

These general ideas about changes in food availability and dietary patterns have been discussed for a number of years. Here we present them in a manner that is intended to encourage historical research on these associations. To date there has been relatively little careful empirical investigation of the relationships among social change, dietary change, and nutritional status and health. Research questions need to be framed in a manner that permits hypothesis-testing and a refinement of the general model.[1]

THREE MAJOR PROCESSES OF DIETARY CHANGE

The dramatic transformations in dietary patterns that have taken place in the past two and a half centuries are one key aspect of the much larger picture of massive social and economic change that has affected all parts of the world. The specific dimensions have varied widely in relation to particular historical, political, and ecological conditions, but the basic food-use changes of interest to us have largely come about as a result of three fundamental developments:

1. A world-wide dissemination of domesticated plant and animal varieties.

2. The rise of increasingly complex, international food distribution networks, and the growth of food-processing industries.

3. The migration of people from rural to urban centers, and from one continent to another, on a hitherto unprecedented scale, with a resulting exchange of culinary and dietary techniques and preferences.

Each of these processes has been powerfully influenced by national and international politico-economic forces, cultural and religious movements, and other factors. One fundamental sector of great importance has been the development of new technologies; in particular, transportation and communications technologies have played major roles.

Our rationale for focusing on the three processes listed above rests on a view of the basic elements of delocalization as they affect the behavior of particular local communities. That is, if we picture the dietary possibilities of people in a French rural commune, a small valley in Mexico, or an island in Polynesia, their food selections will change if:

a.   New plant and animal varieties are introduced to the community for local production, or locally produced foods are removed from the community for sale elsewhere.

b.   New foods are made available through commercial or governmental channels.

c.   The people themselves move to a new area, or they receive immigrants from elsewhere, resulting in cultural exchange of culinary/dietary preferences.

Changes may also occur because of purely local developments of new food production or preparation techniques, but such occurrences are generally much less frequent.

Throughout our discussion of dietary change we confront the philosophical question of basic causes. Attempting to isolate clear, necessary and sufficient causes may have some utility in relatively simple systems. However, human behavior is more understandable if we conceptualize a system of complex, interconnected forces (including biological, psychological, economic, political, technological, and other factors), so that a focus on one component as a prime mover rests more on philosophical or stylistic preference rather than on demonstrable, empirical evidence. Understanding the developments in human food use patterns of the past 250 years depends, first of all, on sorting out the primary (descriptive) trends and processes, leaving for the future the search for the more or less clear prime movers.

THE CONCEPT
OF DELOCALIZATION

The concept of delocalization, which is central to our analysis of changes in human dietary patterns, is one major aspect of all the historical changes to which people give various labels such as modernization, development, progress, acculturation, and so on. In using the term delocalization we are focusing attention on one fundamental, apparently undirectional tendency in human history, particularly of more recent centuries.

Delocalization has many different facets, but there are two that are most important for our discussion here.

First, there is the delocalization that results in the reduction of local autonomy of energy resources, due to dependence on gasoline-driven equipment for transportation, local industry, and other essential processes. In recent times this loss of local energy autonomy has been quite striking in the remoter areas of the globe where motor-driven boats, snowmobiles, and other equipment have been widely adopted.

Second, in more complex urban centers, delocalization is evidenced in the increased sensitivity (of prices, costs, etc.) to political fluctuations in any sector of the world energy and food network, as can be seen, for example, in the world-wide impact of Soviet grain purchasing policies, OPEC price manipulations, coffee and sugar production levels, and the beef consumption demands of the international fast-food industry.

DELOCALIZATION
AND FOOD SYSTEMS

One way to gain an understanding of delocalization in matters of human food use is to consider the opposite —local autonomy. In small-scale hunting and gathering societies, such as those of the Inuit (Eskimo) and the San peoples of the Kalahari, or among our ancestors of preagricultural times, the great bulk of food supplies and other energy resources had to be obtained from the immediate local environment. For that reason hunting-gathering societies have always been rather small—usually no more than 300 to 400 persons in the local group (often much less), with population densities that seldom exceeded ten persons per 100 square miles.

Among a great many small-scale cultivator peoples of central Africa, the Amazon rainforest areas, and the South Pacific, local groups have been largely dependent on their own food and energy resources, although some trading of food and other goods has been common between coastal and inland peoples, and between animal-keeping pastoralists and their more sedentary neighbors; occasionally, trade has been widespread among the various islands of the South Pacific.

Despite the presence of small-scale regional trading, human societies of earlier times were, to a considerable extent, unaffected by the state of food supplies in other areas. If crops failed or herds were decimated by disease in any particular area, famine was the usual result; there was no way to send for disaster relief.

In contrast to small-scale, semi-autonomous communities, peasant populations in Europe, Asia, and Latin America, in past centuries, have been a good deal more dependent on at least some commercial exchanges with other regions and nations. A common feature of peasant societies, however, has been the dependence on a wider marketing system for the purchase of non-food supplies and equipment, in exchange for which local peasant peoples were able to transfer their surplus food production, thus feeding not only themselves but the non-food producing people of the cities. A large proportion of the peasant family's food needs were met from their own farm, even though they were dependent on the commercial system for iron equipment, some clothing, a few luxury items, and (in recent decades) special foods such as sugar, salt, tea or coffee, and spices.

Before the fifteenth century there was a slow and gradual dissemination of certain major crops and food animals into ever-wider parts of the world. For example, the wheat, barley, and dairy food complex spread into all parts of Europe, south into Africa, and eastwards into Asia, from the presumed origins in the Far East. A similar process of diffusion occurred with the rice-growing complex in East and South Asia. These slow processes of diffusion certainly had significant effects on food systems in the world but the impact of changes precipitated by the age of discovery were dramatic and rapid.

WORLD-WIDE DISSEMINATION OF DOMESTICATED PLANTS AND ANIMALS

Beginning with Columbus' voyages to the New World, and other fifteenth-century expeditions into hitherto unknown parts, Europeans acquired knowledge about food crops and production systems that was formerly unavailable to them. At the same time, European settlers, missionaries, and adventurers spread the knowledge (and requisite seeds and other materials) of both Old World and New World animal domesticates to other parts of the world. By the beginning of the seventeenth century the boundaries of the various plant and animal species were transformed, as the major crops and animals were introduced into different ecological zones. By 1700 maize, rice, wheat, barley, oats, and potatoes, as well as cattle and other livestock had spread throughout most of the world, whereas earlier each of these food sources had been grown by only a segment of the world's population.

The consequences of the world-wide dissemination of domesticated plants and animals were dramatic. In Europe the slow but steady adoption of maize, potatoes, and other American cultigens began to have powerful effects by the eighteenth century. The addition of potatoes to the basic subsistence economy has been seen by some researchers as a cause of major changes in demographic patterns. For example, Vanderbroek has claimed that potatoes sustained rapid population expansion in the southern Netherlands in the middle of the eighteenth century. His data indicate that potato cultivation grew rapidly in the 1740s and 1750s, returning a five times greater yield per acre than wheat, which had previously been the main crop. Rapid population increases in that part of the Netherlands contrasts, in his view, with slower population growth in areas where potatoes were not adopted at that time.[2]

In approximately the same period the potato spread to northern Europe, where in Sweden, Finland, and Russia its cultivation was seen as an important hedge against famine. Governmental and private groups propagandized on behalf of potato cultivation, and free seed potatoes were made widely available. In Finland at the end of the eighteenth century the Finnish Economics Society distributed free seed potatoes and gave monetary prizes and medals to potato growers. "A famine and epidemic in 1765 persuaded Catherine the Great of the potential importance of the tuber to Russia, and her government launched a campaign to encourage its cultivation. However, the potato did not become a major crop in central Russia until after the crop failures of 1838 and 1839."[3]

Some writers may have exaggerated the importance of the potato in the economics of Europe, but considerable weight may be given to the remarks of Morineau, who noted that ". . . the potato, thanks in part to its very real advantages, became the only short-term solution (to increased food needs) everywhere in Western Europe. This it remained, despite some periods of blight, as long as new granaries had not opened in other parts of the world and until, in due course, agricultural science was able to produce much higher grain yields than the traditional agriculture."[4]

Negative consequences of the role of potatoes have been noted, particularly in the great potato famines in Ireland in the nineteenth century.

Ho and other scholars consider American cultigens to have been central to the growth of ecological carrying capacity in China. Ho suggests that by the end of the eighteenth century rice cultivation areas (the wetlands) and the dry region lands of millet and wheat had neared their limits of production, so that any further expansion of Chinese population would have been at the cost of increased nutritional deficiencies and periodic famine. However, the adoption of maize and sweet potatoes significantly increased the food supply.[5]

In presenting these observations concerning the world-wide diffusion of major cultigens, we do not need to subscribe to the theory that new foods caused population expansions in various regions of the world. In fact, it would appear that the causal arrows have often been in the opposite direction, in that population pressures have triggered the intensification of food production techniques. It is plausible that both types of situations have occurred repeatedly in different human populations: at times the fortuitous importation of new food crops or production methods has occurred before population expansion; in other circumstances the reverse has happened.[6]

Europe and Asia were not the only continents that experienced large-scale changes in food production as a result of contacts with new cultigens. Africa was an early recipient of new production ideas, in part because slave traders introduced maize and other crops to West Africa in order to provision their ships. Maize was introduced so early in some parts of Africa that some researchers have argued for its aboriginal development there.[7]

In the Americas the powerful influences of wheat, barley, and other Old World crops have been overshadowed by the effects of the massive infusion of meat animals. Before the coming of the Europeans, the natives of North and South America had only turkeys, dogs, llamas, chickens, and guinea pigs as sources of meat. The meat of pigs, cattle, sheep, and other food animals were quickly included in the diet of both the European settlers and the native inhabitants.

THE RISE OF COMMERCIAL FOOD DISTRIBUTION NETWORKS

A second major process in the delocalization of food occurs with the proliferation of commercial food distribution systems, which now affect virtually all societies. Food patterns in formerly remote communities are powerfully affected by the presence of commercially distributed food.

The growth of commercial food distribution networks has been intricately related to the development of food processing technologies. Food processing involves a wide spectrum of manipulation, from relatively simple preservation, such as canning and freezing, to the preparation of cooked, ready-to-eat meals and a variety of snack foods. The great expansion in commercial food processing has taken place in the twentieth century, although important developments occurred throughout the nineteenth century. French, British, and American inventors all contributed to the development of hermetically sealed canning processes in the 1830s and 1840s, followed by the processing of condensed milk and the mechanization of biscuit making.[8]

Prior to the nineteenth century the scope and scale of commercial operations in foodstuffs were limited. The larger and more important commercial houses dealt mainly in a few specialized items—coffee, sugar, spices, tea, salt, and alcoholic beverages. Some researchers have claimed that liquor and beer were practically the only foodstuffs for which production was responsive to demand before the latter half of the nineteenth century. However exaggerated such a statement, it does serve to highlight the importance of the commercial enterprises, and the more complex food marketing, that came into existence in the middle of the last century.[9]

SUGAR: THE COMMERCIAL FOOD PAR EXCELLENCE

Sugar is one processed food item that has played a major role in dietary transformations since the eighteenth century. The history of sugar documents the growing significance of commercial food marketing over the past 200 years. Like many other food products, cane sugar was known and used for centuries in some parts of the world before it rose to prominence in European trade. Gourmets of ancient India knew sugar, and there was some cultivation of sugar cane in Arab Spain and southern France in the eighth century. However, it was a rare and costly luxury until cane production was initiated in the New World.

The special conditions of the Americas, which combined favorable growing conditions, large acreages, and the importation of relatively low-cost (slave) labor, brought about rapid increases in production. During the eighteenth century it was still a costly commodity, but as production increased there was a fairly steady drop in price, and public demand for sugar rose rapidly. The use of by-products of the sugar cane process in the manufacture of rum contributed to the profitability of the sugar business. By the early years of the nineteenth century the average per capita consumption of sugar in the United States had risen to twelve or thirteen pounds per year. From that point the rise was relatively steady to 1929, when a peak of

109 pounds per capita per year was reached. During the Great Depression sugar intake decreased but rose again with better economic times. Patterns of consumption in England were similar, with a peak in 1960 of 112 pounds per capita per year.[10]

MIGRATION: RURAL TO URBAN AND CROSS-NATIONAL POPULATION MOVEMENTS

The processes of change discussed thus far all refer to the transfer of ideas and materials—the food products themselves—from one area to another, accompanied by mechanisms of interdependency. The third mechanism is, superficially at least, different because the basic feature is the movement of persons. Migration to urban areas from rural regions, and movements from one nation or continent to another, introduce an additional dimension—food preferences and food knowledge are transferred by the migrants themselves. The migrants may exert their influence simply as individuals (or groups of individuals) with specific food preferences, but they also introduce change by actions, such as the establishment of food stores, restaurants, or other special enterprises.

Ethnic foods were introduced by migrants in earlier centuries and especially in America in the nineteenth century. There is a dual feature to the impact of migrant peoples on dietary practices: on the one hand, emigrés from distant places often preserved their traditional food patterns, so that, for example, Italian immigrants in major United States cities were soon able to maintain their consumption of pasta, sausages, olive oil, and other products in neighborhood cafes and restaurants, as well as in their homes; on the other hand these ethnic foods became available to non-Italians as well, and the growingly sophisticated urban-dwellers could select from a variety of different cuisines.

In most cases the old ethnic diets were not maintained in their traditional forms. Working hours—in factories, shops, and offices—soon made the old schedules (e.g. the large midday meal that is common in many European countries) difficult to continue. Even strongly held religious food patterns (e.g. among orthodox Jews) had to be modified to meet the new conditions.

One of the first ecumenical movements in ethnic food adoption was the spread of French cooking as a high prestige practice among upper-class and middle-class people around the world. Equally significant in influencing multi-cultural sophistication in food has

been the spread of Chinese restaurants, which can be found in most major cities of the world today. Many of the international exchanges manifested in ethnic restaurants and grocery stores testify to the final phases of the colonial era, during which increasing numbers of families from "the colonies" established ethnic enclaves and food patterns in Europe: Indonesians in Holland, Indian restaurants and shops in England, and Moroccan and other North African coffee houses in France.

The latest phases of world-wide ecumenical sharing of cuisine (as opposed to dissemination of the raw materials) has taken the form of an accelerated development of international cooking at home. Also, visible today throughout the world is the rapid spread of multi-national, fast-food chains.

MECHANISMS OF CHANGE AND CONSUMPTION TRENDS

The three main processes outlined above have been vehicles by which long-standing dietary patterns have been more and more radically altered in practically all parts of the world. The results of these changes are reflected in consumption statistics and nutrient profiles, which show, for example, continuing increases in the percentages of sugar consumed as diets become "modernized." In the United States the consumption of flour and cereal products dropped from 680 pounds per capita per year in 1910 to 450 pounds in 1970. During the same period vegetable fat consumption increased from 20 grams per capita per day to nearly 50 grams. Viewed in terms of nutrient consumption (rather than types of foods) in the period from 1910 to 1970 iron has declined from 15.2 mg. per capita per day to 8.0 mg., while riboflavin increased from 1.86 mg. to 2.46 mg.; another eight vitamins showed similar increases during that sixty-year span.[11]

It is difficult to find adequate statistical information on dietary changes in small-scale, non-modern societies because of the paucity of careful, quantitative studies. However, some of the main dimensions of change can be inferred from recent ethnographic studies. For example, in the Alaskan Eskimo community of Napaskiak, Oswalt noted that "everyone regards certain [store foods] as absolute necessities. These include sugar, salt, flour, milk, coffee, tea, tobacco, and cooking fats. Other foods frequently purchased include various canned meats and fish, crackers, candy, carbonated beverages, canned fruits, potatoes, onions, and rice." Similarly, among the Miskito Indians of Nicaragua, store-bought foods already accounted for over 30 percent of the diet in 1969, when Nietschmann made a detailed analysis of their food system. The store-purchased foods, including sugar, flour, beans, rice, and coffee, had captured two thirds of the Miskito food economy by 1973, mainly because of the depletion of the green sea turtles, which are now sold to international food companies rather than consumed locally. Since the purchased foods are quite different in nutrient content from the wild foods that they replace and are especially high in carbohydrates, the Miskito, like virtually all small-scale societies, are undergoing rapid dietary change.[12]

The Eskimo and Miskito examples are particularly illustrative because they clearly reflect two different aspects of the world-wide commercial food system: in the Miskito situation commercial food distributors have taken away a primary food resource—the sea turtles—thus forcing the local people to change their food patterns. In the North Alaskan situation the emphasis is on the increased availability of modern foods in the local stores. Even in cases where local traditional food resources are not depleted, the availability of sugar, flour, canned goods, and other store food has a powerful effect on diets.

DELOCALIZATION AND THE FINNISH FOOD SYSTEM

Changes in food use brought about by delocalization are clearly revealed in Finland, which was transformed from an underdeveloped nation into an urban, industrialized society from the 1930s to 1970. Until 1940 the great majority of Finnish families were rural; the major cities, other than Helsinki, were little more than overgrown market centers. In 1950 the infant mortality rate was still 43 per 1,000; before the war it had been considerably higher. In other health and welfare statistics, as well as in its income and occupational profile, Finland contrasted sharply with the more industrialized nations of Europe and America.

The traditional Finnish dietary pattern was heavily dependent on dairy products. Finland still ranks as the leading nation in the world in per capita milk consumption, in addition to which Finns consume large amounts of butter, cheese, buttermilk, and viili, a fermented milk product, which is somewhat akin to yogurt.

Grain products made up another major portion of the diet. Rye, oats, and barley had been the most important cereals in earlier centuries, with increasing amounts of wheat in the nineteenth and twentieth centuries. Potatoes were eaten practically every day in considerable quantity, a pattern that continues today for

Table 1. Consumption trends in Finland, 1950–1973 (annual per capita consumption)

Item	Year					
	1950	1955	1960	1965	1970	1973
Wheat(ks)	81.5	86	75	70	65	60
Meat	60	60	60	60	60	60
Sugar(ks)	28.3	38	40	40	45	45
Rye	48	42	39	32	25	24
Butter/margarine	22	22	22	22	22	22
Fruit/vegetables	33	48	53	52	65	81

SOURCE: *Elinolosuhteet 1950–1975* [Living Conditions 1950–1975], Central Statistical Office of Finland, 86.

most of the population. Meat, and to a lesser extent fish, although consumed in modest quantities, have been important sources of protein.[13]

In the pre-World War II Finnish diet a major source of vitamin C was the wild lingonberry (and other berries), gathered in large quantities and stored for use throughout the winter. Also characteristic was a lack of green vegetables and fresh fruit, other than berries. Throughout the 1950s the supplies of imported fresh fruit in Finnish grocery stores was irregular.

During the 1960s the commercial food system changed drastically, as large supermarkets were established by several cooperative associations and by private entrepreneurs. Frozen foods, food freezers in stores and in homes, and many other technological features were introduced. A rapid expansion of the network of paved roads also contributed to these developments. At the same time, Finnish nutritionists and government policy-makers mounted extensive informational campaigns to increase the consumption of vegetables and fruit and decrease the intake of saturated fats and sugar. The nutrition information programs were fueled, in part, by the realization that Finland had, until very recently, the highest rates of cardiovascular disease in the world.[14]

Food consumption trends from 1950 to 1973 show the interesting changes that have occurred during the recent decades of delocalization (see Table 1). These changes reflect delocalization both within the Finnish economy, and in relation to world-wide markets. Much of the increase in fruit and vegetables represents greatly expanded imports from Eastern Europe and the Mediterranean countries, made possible by the expansion of the modern European trucking network equipped with refrigeration, air conditioning, and other technological features. Meanwhile producers in Finland have begun to use artificially heated greenhouses (relying on new developments in plastic sheeting) to grow cucumbers and tomatoes, which are now in great demand since the introduction of salads into the Finnish diet.

From 1940 to 1970 Finnish farm families gave up most aspects of their earlier self-sufficiency in basic foods. In short, they changed from being peasants to being commercial farmers. The highly developed system of producers' cooperatives played a major part in these changes, augmented by the growth of private food-producing companies. Meat animals, milk, and cereal grains are now delivered directly to the cooperatives or to private buyers. In turn, the farmers buy back selected meat products at a members' discount. Certain parts of slaughtered animals (including the blood), that were routinely used in the family food economy, are now unavailable or must be purchased in processed form from the cooperatives. Blood pancakes and bloodbread, for example, are now generally made from packaged mixes. Even butter and cheese are usually purchased from the cooperatives to which the farmers sell their raw milk, unlike the pre-war days, when families prepared a large share of their own basic foods, from barn and field to the dinner table.

The changes in utilization of home-produced food in Finnish farming households represents delocalization at the local, or micro-level. Thus delocalization refers not only to the increased availability of foods from distant lands; it also means the giving up of local community control to the regional and national food-processing systems.

Although the impact of delocalization in terms of making new foods available was more dramatic in Finland than in some other Western European countries, the general process has been much the same throughout the industrialized world. The example of Finland is instructive because the major changes have occurred largely in the past fifty years, nearly a century later than in most parts of Western Europe. There have been major differences in some aspects of delocalization, as the pattern of land tenure, differences in international trading networks, and political processes have all strongly affected the course of developments in food distribution and dietary patterns.

DELOCALIZATION IN THE THIRD WORLD

A major feature of food delocalization in the nineteenth and twentieth centuries has been the transformation of food systems in non-industrialized areas as they have become involved in supplying some of the food needs of Euro-American communities. Sugar plantations were among the first manifestations of a rapidly developing commerce in food products. A large-scale banana trade developed later, mainly in the twentieth century. Shipments of bananas, like many other fruits and vegetables, could not become major world trade commodities until the development of effective storage technologies, in addition to faster shipping times.

In countries such as Jamaica the economic livelihood of many small farmers became tied to the fluctuations in world prices of bananas (or other cash crops), as well as to government policies of encouragement or discouragement of farm production. Jamaica is highly delocalized in terms of food resources, as most of the daily diet depends on imports from North America and other sources. The significance of delocalization for the Jamaican (as an example of the effects of modernization in Third World countries) is illustrated by events in the 1970s. As analyzed in a study by Marchione in the mid-1970s, the cost of food in Jamaica (not adjusted to take account of inflation) soared as a result of the oil crisis and other factors in international markets. In the period from 1973 to 1975 the retail price of wheat flour increased 142 percent, corn meal 100 percent, salt cod 75 percent, rice 65 percent, and sugar 60 percent. Banana prices, however, paid to local, mostly small-scale producers, did not rise.[15]

Marchione studied the impact of a nutrition program in the St. James area of Jamaica during this period and found that world market forces resulted in a return to subsistence crop-growing by many farmers. The expected negative effects of highly inflationary food prices appear to have been offset by increases in home-grown foods. Instead of declining, the nutritional status of small children in the St. James area improved during this period. The research design of the evaluation study made it possible to determine that it was mainly the farmers' food production responses to market conditions, rather than the local nutrition education program, that brought about improved nutritional status in the children.

It is also important, Marchione suggests, to note that during this period the climate of commerce in food was affected by the Jamaican government's policy of striving for greater national self-sufficiency. "Jamaican government policies to ban food exports, levy taxes on foreign-owned bauxite companies, create public service jobs and redistribute or force idle land into production represent concerted efforts to gain local control of energy forms and flows; i.e. power."[16]

Another striking example of the negative consequences of delocalization is the widespread adoption of beef cattle production in many parts of Latin America in response to the growth of hamburger and other fast-food merchandizing in the United States. In

Guatemala, beef production nearly doubled from 1960 to 1972, yet domestic per capita consumption of beef fell by approximately 20 percent during the same period. In Costa Rica during the same period total production of beef rose from 53.3 to 108 million pounds, yet the amount available for domestic consumption remained constant (34.8 million pounds), resulting in a reduction of nearly one third in beef consumption while exports climbed from 17.5 to 73.7 millions of pounds.[17]

Analyzing the impact of this large-scale shift to beef production, DeWalt found that large areas of forest in Honduras were being cut down to make room for cattle. From 1952 to 1974 the forested area in southern Honduras was reduced from approximately 74,000 to only 41,000 hectares. During the same period the land area in permanent crops actually declined. DeWalt comments that the "implications of the conversion of southern Honduras into a vast pasture for export-oriented cattle production . . . are the following: first in the long run fewer individuals will have access to land on which to produce their own subsistence crops. Employment opportunities in the local region will decline because livestock raising is less labor intensive than grain crop production. The permanent and temporary migration that these processes produce can only exacerbate the already explosive social, economic, and political situation that exists in Central America."[18]

These cases are intended to illustrate how worldwide delocalization of food production and distribution has created a complex web of interrelations, changes which place local food-producing populations in serious jeopardy, particularly if they are dependent for their livelihood on one or two principal cash crops. In the developing world, delocalization results in a loss of food resources and flexibility as productive agricultural land is put to use for cash crops in competition with land use for local food production, and national food systems become increasingly dependent on the developed nations for shipments of grain and other basic foods.

DIETARY DIVERSITY, NUTRITIONAL STATUS, AND DELOCALIZATION

Good nutrition depends on adequate consumption of calories, protein, fats, vitamins and minerals. Whereas a sufficient intake of calories (and, to some extent, protein and fat) depends on quantity of food consumed, adequate consumption of other nutrients depends on the utilization of foods that are high in these substances. Because vitamins and minerals are differentially distributed in food, it is generally felt that more varied and diverse diets are more likely to be adequate from a nutritional perspective. A "mixed portfolio" also seems advisable on ecological grounds and may provide some protection from overexposure to mildly toxic components of foods.

When delocalization results in an expanded food supply and greater diversity of available foods, one would hypothesize that there should be an improvement in nutritional status, whereas a reduction in diversity, as well as in the quantity of available foods should be associated with a decline in nutritional status. In the industrialized world, it appears that there have generally been significant improvements in nutrition in the past century. There are several lines of evidence to support this statement. The major vitamin-deficiency diseases have now virtually disappeared in developed countries and, although mineral-deficiency diseases are still prevalent, they tend to be much less severely manifested than in developing countries. Except for anorexia nervosa, obesity rather than emaciation is the primary problem of caloric consumption.

Another indicator of improved nutrition is the secular growth trend that makes modern Europeans and North Americans seem like giants compared to the average size of people in the seventeenth and eighteenth centuries. In 1876 Charles Roberts, a doctor employed in a British factory, noted that "a factory child of the present day at the age of nine years weighs as much as one of ten years did in 1833 . . . each age has gained one year in forty." This comparison was possible because a large-scale program of measurements of children was carried out in 1833 to provide evidence for Parliament to consider the effects of child labor. "At that time, working boys aged ten years averaged 121 cm. in height compared with 140 cm. today; those aged eighteen years averaged 160 cm. compared with 175 cm. today." The recent trends in Japan from 1950 to 1970 show a nearly 3 cm. increase per decade among seven year olds, and a 5 cm. per decade increase in twelve year olds. Other factors, including improved sanitary conditions, have also played a part in these trends, but the role of nutrition seems clear.[19]

Although the secular trends in industrialized countries point to a general improvement in nutrition, it is important to note the complexities that are involved in the interpretation of data on height. The issues are ably discussed by Fogel and his colleagues, who point out the significance of "cycles of height" in the past two centuries in British and American populations. Fogel argues that these fluctuations reflect different levels of nutrition and this supports Tanner's and others' interpretation of the meaning of secular trends in height.[20]

Age at menarche is another measure frequently cited in connection with the overall improved nutrition levels of Europeans, North Americans, and other industrialized populations. Tanner has demonstrated that the average age at menarche for girls in Finland, Norway, and Sweden was between sixteen and seventeen years in the middle of the nineteenth century, from which there has been a progressive decline to the present day. Now, the averages hover around thirteen years.

Increased caloric and protein intakes throughout the nineteenth and twentieth centuries have had major impacts, but the increased diversity of available foods has also played a role. In Britain from 1950 to 1973 total fruit as a component of household consumption increased from 18 ounces to 25 ounces per week per person, while in the same period bread dropped from 56 ounces to 34 ounces. Diversification of protein resources was evident in the rise in poultry consumption.[21]

DELOCALIZATION AND FAMINE

One of the more obvious, yet infrequently noted, results of the delocalization of food products in the industrialized world is the elimination, except during wartime, of disastrous famines. Food catastrophes, such as the Irish potato famine, or the less well-known famine between 1865 and 1867 in northeastern Europe, are no longer a threat in developed nations. Recent Soviet grain purchases and shipments of food to Poland show how modern commercial channels can redistribute food in times of serious regional shortages.

In most of the world the channels of food distribution can be expanded in response to regional shortages, although serious distribution problems still remain. Recent crises in Bangladesh, India, and parts of Africa demonstrate that in extreme situations appropriate foods cannot be transported and distributed effectively enough to the populations in need.[22]

McAlpin notes that population growth rates fluctuated widely in India well into the twentieth century because of the interrelated effects of periodic famine and disease. She points out that the development of an effective railroad network helped reduce the sharp impact of regional food shortages.[23]

Famines still occur in isolated parts of India, as they do in some other parts of Asia, but McAlpin's data indicate that "mortality from famines was not an important force in slowing India's population growth after 1921." Thus, the forces of delocalization—the spread of transportation systems and food distribution networks, plus governmental communications and food relief systems—have effectively eliminated most (but not all) of the impacts of regional crop failures and other disasters that in the past led to severe periodic famine conditions.

DEVELOPING NATIONS: SHORTAGES AND DISTORTIONS

Many of the changes that we have described for the industrialized nations have also affected parts of the Third World. The spread of diverse food resources by means of the New World-Old World exchange of cultigens and livestock has had a powerful impact on most of the world. Thus, potentially, the populations of Latin America, much of Asia, and many parts of Africa could have a greatly expanded diversity of foods. Despite that potential, the lack of economic purchasing power for all but a minority in the most affluent sectors means that the diets of the majority are restricted in quantity and quality.

Inequality of wealth is not the only factor that has contributed to the declines in quality and quantity of food in rural sectors of developing nations. Modern farming practices, including the widespread use of chemicals—pesticides and herbicides—may have unexpected, often unnoticed, side-effects on food use. For example, the widespread use of herbicides in the maize fields of Mexico has resulted in the elimination of a number of "weeds" that had been regular, vitamin-rich additions to the peasant diets.[24]

Global delocalization of food resources involves a number of major cost increases. A large part of the price of food items pays for the processing, packaging, advertising, and shipment of foods, as well as the profits of various entrepreneurs in the food chain. Poor people cannot afford to pay these added costs, and hence they are reduced to a narrower selection of the cheaper foods.

Although there continues to be some argument about "how to define" malnutrition, there is little disagreement that for sheer numbers, there are more millions of malnourished people in the world than ever before. The most telling and shocking statistic is the effect of malnutrition on child mortality. Berg estimates that in 1978 "malnutrition was a factor in the deaths of at least 10 million children."[25]

A discussion of all the complex factors involved in contemporary problems of malnutrition is beyond the scope of this article, but we suggest that the poorer populations in developing countries, especially in rural areas, have experienced declines in total caloric consumption (per capita) and in dietary diversity as traditional subsistence systems have been severely disrupted by the forces of modernization, especially delocalization.

✦ ✦ ✦

Delocalization captures some of the main dimensions of change in food production and diet over the past 250 years. Historically, the process appears to be unidirectional, as most regions of the world give up local autonomy to increased linkages with global food distribution networks. The example of Jamaica, however, is only one of many national policy attempts to counter delocalization through political encouragement of self-sufficiency. Although the process of delocalization is so complex as to appear to be outside the range of local political decision-making, it may not be an inevitable aspect of development.

In examining the relationship between delocalization and changes in nutrition and health status, we are not claiming that the process has been wholly positive in the industrialized countries and completely negative in the Third World. Increased obesity, problems of food sensitivities, and other, more subtle nutrition-related problems may well be related to delocalization of food patterns in the industrialized countries. At the same time, traditional food systems in developing countries are often far from ideal from a nutritional standpoint, and, in many circumstances, environmental factors severely constrain local food production.

There have been massive changes in local food systems over the past 250 years as the world community has become knit into a tightly inter-connected network of economic, social, and political relations. The effects on nutrition and dietary patterns have been powerful. World-wide food production capabilities have increased greatly. However, serious problems of maldistribution of food resources remain, and some problems are becoming worse, not better. Although a considerable proportion of the global community derives clear benefit from food delocalization, many rural and urban low-income communities are experiencing serious malnutrition.

Further analysis of delocalization of food may help to explicate historical conditions. At the same time, improved understanding of the relationship between delocalization and nutritional status may help to make nutrition planning and policy development more effective in the future.

NOTES

1. Cf. Alan Berg, *The Nutrition Factor* (Washington, D.C., 1973); Frances Moore Lappé and Joseph Collins, *Food First* (Boston, 1977).

2. Christian Vanderbroek, "Aardappelteelt en Aardappelverbruik in de 17e en 18e Eeuw," *Tijdschrift voor Geschiedenis*, LXXXII (1969), 49–68.

3. Alfred W. Crosby, Jr., *The Columbian Exchange* (Westport, Conn., 1972), 184.

4. Michel Morineau, "The Potato in the Eighteenth Century," in Robert Forster and Orest Ranum (eds.), *Food and Drink in History* (Baltimore, 1979), 17–36.

5. Ping-ti Ho, *Studies on the Population of China, 1368–1953* (Cambridge, Mass., 1959). Crosby, *Columbian Exchange*, 199–200.

6. Ester Boserup, *The Conditions of Agricultural Growth* (Chicago, 1965). William T. Sanders, "Population, Agricultural History, and Societal Evolution in Mesoamerica," in Brian Spooner (ed.), *Population Growth: Anthropological Implications* (Cambridge, Mass., 1972), 101–153.

7. Carl O. Sauer, *Seeds, Spades, Hearths, and Herbs* (Cambridge, Mass., 1952). Cf. Michael D. Gwynne, "The Origin and Spread of Some Domestic Food Plants of Eastern Africa," in H. Neville Chittick and Robert I. Rotberg (eds.), *East Africa and the Orient: Cultural Synthesis in Pre-Colonial Times* (New York, 1975), 248–271.

8. Waverly Root and Richard de Rochemont, *Eating in America* (New York, 1976), 158; James P. Johnston, *A Hundred Years of Eating: Food, Drink, and Family Diet in Britain Since the Late Nineteenth Century* (Montreal, 1977), 33.

9. Maurice Aymard, "Toward the History of Nutrition," in Forster and Ranum. *Food and Drink*, 1–16.

10. Root and Rochemont, *Eating in America*, 418; Richard O. Cummings, *The American and His Food* (Chicago, 1940); Chris Wardle, *Changing Food Habits in the U.K.* (London, 1977).

11. United States Dept. of Agriculture, Report No. 138 (Washington, D.C., 1974); Willis A. Gortner, "Nutrition in the United States—1900 to 1974," *Cancer Research*, XXXV (1975), 3246–3253.

12. Wendell Oswalt, *Napaskiak: An Alaskan Eskimo Community* (Tucson, 1963), 102; Bernard Nietschmann, *Between Land and Water* (New York, 1973).

13. I. Talve, *Suommen Kansanomaisesta Ruokataloudesta* (Turku, 1973).

14. Ancel Keys, *Seven Countries: A Multivariate Analysis of Death and Coronary Heart Disease Rates* (Cambridge, Mass., 1980).

15. Thomas J. Marchione, "Food and Nutrition in Self-Reliant National Development," *Medical Anthropology*, I (1977), 57–79.

16. *Ibid.*, 73.

17. Billie R. DeWalt, "The Cattle Are Eating the Forest," unpub. ms. (1981).

18. *Ibid.*, 24–25.

19. J. M. Tanner, *Foetus into Man* (Cambridge, Mass., 1978), 150–151.

20. Robert W. Fogel et al., "Secular Changes in American and British Stature and Nutrition."

21. Wardle, *Changing Food Habits*, 72.

22. For a discussion of entitlements, see Louise A. Tilly, "Food Entitlement, Famine, and Conflict."

23. Michelle B. McAlpin, "Famines, Epidemics, and Population Growth: The Case of India."

24. Ellen Messer, "The Ecology of Vegetarian Diet in a Modernizing Mexican Community," in Thomas K. Fitzgerald (ed.), *Nutrition and Anthropology in Action* (Amsterdam, 1977), 117–124.

25. Berg, *Malnourished People: A Policy View* (Washington, D.C., 1981), 2.

32

Time, Sugar, and Sweetness

Sidney W. Mintz

Food and eating as subjects of serious inquiry have engaged anthropology from its very beginnings. Varieties of foods and modes of preparation have always evoked the attention, sometimes horrified, of observant travelers, particularly when the processing techniques (e.g., chewing and spitting to encourage fermentation) and the substances (e.g., live larvae, insects, the contents of animal intestines, rotten eggs) have been foreign to their experience and eating habits. At the same time, repeated demonstrations of the intimate relationship between ingestion and sociality among living peoples of all sorts, as well as the importance attributed to it in classic literary accounts, including the Bible, have led to active reflection about the nature of the links that connect them. Long before students of Native America had invented "culture areas," or students of the Old World had formulated evolutionary stages for pastoralism or semiagriculture, W. Robertson Smith had set forth elegantly the concept of commensality and had sought to explain the food prohibitions of the ancient Semites.[1] But food and eating were studies for the most part in their more unusual aspects—food prohibitions and taboos, cannibalism, the consumption of unfamiliar and distasteful items—rather than as everyday and essential features of the life of all humankind.

Food and eating are now becoming actively of interest to anthropologists once more, and in certain new ways. An awakened concern with resources, including variant forms of energy and the relative costs of their trade-offs—the perception of real finitudes that may not always respond to higher prices with increased production—seems to have made some anthropological relativism stylish, and has led to the rediscovery of a treasure-trove of old ideas, mostly bad, about natural, healthful, and energy-saving foods. Interest in the everyday life of everyday people and in categories of the oppressed—women, slaves, serfs, Untouchables, "racial" minorities, as well as those who simply work with their hands—has led, among other things, to interest in women's work, slave food, and discriminations and exclusions. (It is surely no accident that the best early anthropological studies of food should have come from the pens of women, Audrey Richards[2] and Rosemary Firth.[3]) What is more, the upsurge of interest in meaning among anthropologists has also reenlivened the study of any subject matter that can be treated by seeing the patterned relationships between substances and human groups as forms of communication.

While these and other anthropological trends are resulting in the appearance of much provocative and imaginative scholarship, the anthropology of food and eating remains poorly demarcated, so that there ought still to be room for speculative inquiry. Here, I shall suggest some topics for a study of which the skills of anthropology and history might be usefully combined; and I shall raise questions about the relationship between production and consumption, with respect to some specific ingestible, for some specific time period, in order to see if light may be thrown on what foods mean to those who consume them.

During and after the so-called Age of Discovery and the beginning of the incorporation of Asia, Africa, and the New World within the sphere of European power, Europe experienced a deluge of new substances, including foods, some of them similar to items they then supplemented or supplanted, others not readily comparable to prior dietary components. Among the new items were many imports from the New World, including maize, potatoes, tomatoes, the so-called "hot" peppers (*Capsicum annuum, Capsicum frutescens*, etc.), fruits like the papaya, and the food and beverage base called chocolate or cacao.

Two of what came to rank among the most important post-Columbian introductions, however, did not originate in the New World, but in the non-European Old World: tea and coffee. And one item that originated in the Old World and was already known to Europeans, the sugar cane, was diffused to the New World, where it became, especially after the seventeenth century, an important crop and the source of sugar, molasses, and rum for Europe itself. Sugar, the ingestible of special interest here, cannot easily be discussed without reference to other foods, for it partly supplemented, partly supplanted, alternatives. Moreover, the character of its uses, its association with other items, and, it can be argued, the ways it was perceived, changed greatly over time. Since its uses, interlaced with those of many other substances, expressed or embodied certain continuing changes in the consuming society itself, it would be neither feasible nor convincing to study sugar in isolation. Sweetness is a "taste," sugar a product of seemingly infinite uses and functions; but the foods that satisfy a taste for sweetness vary immensely. Thus, a host of problems arise.

Until the seventeenth century, ordinary folk in Northern Europe secured sweetness in food mostly from honey and from fruit. Lévi-Strauss is quite right to emphasize the "natural" character of honey,[4] for he has in mind the manner of its production. Sugar, molasses, and rum made from the sugar cane require advanced technical processes. Sugar can be extracted from many sources, such as the sugar palm, the sugar beet, and all fruits, but the white granulated product familiar today, which represents the highest technical achievement in sugar processing, is made from sugar cane and sugar beet. The sugar-beet extraction process was developed late, but sugar-cane processing is ancient. When the Europeans came to know the product we call sugar, it was cane sugar. And though we know sugar cane was grown in South Asia at least as early as the fourth century B.C., definite evidence of processing—of boiling, clarification and crystallization—dates from almost a millennium later.

Even so, sugar crudely similar to the modern product was being produced on the southern littoral of the Mediterranean Sea by the eighth century A.D., and thereafter on Mediterranean islands and in Spain as well. During those centuries it remained costly, prized, and less a food than a medicine. It appears to have been regarded much as were spices, and its special place in contemporary European tastes—counterpoised, so to speak, against bitter, sour, and salt, as the opposite of them all—would not be achieved until much later. Those who dealt in imported spices dealt in sugar as well. By the thirteenth century English monarchs had grown fond of sugar, most of it probably from the Eastern Mediterranean. In 1226 Henry III appealed to the Mayor of Winchester to obtain for him three pounds of Alexandrine sugar, if possible; the famous fair near Winchester made it an entrepôt of exotic imports. By 1243, when ordering the purchase of spices at Sandwich for the royal household, Henry III included 300 pounds of *zucre de Roche* (presumably, white sugar). By the end of that century the court was consuming several tons of sugar a year, and early in the fourteenth century a full cargo of sugar reached Britain from Venice. The inventory of a fifteenth-century chapman in York—by which time sugar was beginning to reach England from the Atlantic plantation islands of Spain and Portugal—included not only cinnamon, saffron, ginger, and galingale, but also sugar and "casson sugar." By that time, it appears, sugar had entered into the tastes and recipe books of the rich; and the two fifteenth-century cookbooks edited by Thomas Austin[5] contain many sugar recipes, employing several different kinds of sugar.

Although there is no generally reliable source upon which we can base confident estimates of sugar consumption in Great Britain before the eighteenth century—or even for long after—there is no doubt that it rose spectacularly, in spite of occasional dips and troughs. One authority estimates that English sugar consumption increased about fourfold in the last four decades of the seventeenth century. Consumption trebled again during the first four decades of the eighteenth century; then more than doubled again from 1741–1745 to 1771–1775. If only one-half of the imports were retained in 1663, then English and Welsh consumption increased about twenty times, in the period 1663–1775. Since population increased only from four and one-half million to seven and one-half million, the per capita increase in sugar consumption appears dramatic.[6] By the end of the eighteenth century average annual per capita consumption stood at thirteen pounds. Interesting, then, that the nineteenth century showed equally impressive increases—the more so, when substantial consumption at the start of the nineteenth century is taken into account—and the twentieth century showed no remission until the last decade or so. Present consumption levels in Britain, and in certain other North European countries, are high enough to be nearly unbelievable, much as they are in the United States.

Sugar consumption in Great Britain rose together with the consumption of other tropical ingestibles, though at differing rates for different regions, groups, and classes. France never became the sugar or tea consumer that Britain became, though coffee was more successful in France than in Britain. Yet, the general spread of these substances through the Western world since the seventeenth century has been one of the truly important economic and cultural phenomena of the modern age. These were, it seems, the first edible luxuries to become proletarian commonplaces; they were surely the first luxuries to become regarded as necessities by vast masses of people who had not produced them; and they were probably the first substances to become the basis of advertising campaigns to increase consumption. In all of these ways, they, particularly sugar, have remained unmistakably modern.

Not long ago, economists and geographers, not to mention occasional anthropologists, were in the habit of referring to sugar, tea, coffee, cocoa, and like products as "dessert crops." A more misleading misnomer is hard to imagine, for these were among the most important commodities of the eighteenth- and nineteenth-century world, and my own name for them is somewhat nastier:

> Almost insignificant in Europe's diet before the thirteenth century, sugar gradually changed from a medicine for royalty into a preservative and confectionery ingredient and, finally, into a basic commodity. By the seventeenth century, sugar was becoming a staple in

European cities; soon, even the poor knew sugar and prized it. As a relatively cheap source of quick energy, sugar was valuable more as a substitute for food than as a food itself; in western Europe it probably supplanted other food in proletarian diets. In urban centres, it became the perfect accompaniment to tea, and West Indian sugar production kept perfect pace with Indian tea production. Together with other plantation products such as coffee, rum and tobacco, sugar formed part of a complex of "proletarian hunger-killers," and played a crucial role in the linked contribution that Caribbean slaves, Indian peasants, and European urban proletarians were able to make to the growth of western civilization.[7]

If allowance is made for hyperbole, it remains true that these substances, not even known for the most part by ordinary people in Europe before about 1650, had become by 1800 common items of ingestion for members of privileged classes in much of Western Europe—though decidedly not in all—and, well before 1900, were viewed as daily necessities by all classes.

Though research by chemists and physiologists on these substances continues apace, some general statements about them are probably safe. Coffee and tea are stimulants without calories or other food value. Rum and tobacco are both probably best described as drugs, one very high in caloric yield, and the other without any food value at all, though apparently having the effect at times of reducing hunger. Sugar, consisting of about 99.9 percent pure sucrose, is, together with salt, the purest chemical substance human beings ingest and is often labeled "empty calories" by physicians and nutritionists. From a nutritional perspective, all are, in short, rather unusual substances. With the exception of tea, these hunger-killers or "drug foods" destined for European markets were mostly produced in the tropical Americas from the sixteenth century onward until the nineteenth century; and most of them continue to be produced there in substantial amounts. What, one may ask, was the three-hundred-year relationship between the systems of production of these commodities, their political and economic geography, and the steady increase in demand for them?

Though remote from his principal concerns, Marx considered the plantations of the New World among "the chief momenta of primitive accumulation":[8]

> Freedom and slavery constitute an antagonism. . . . We are not dealing with the indirect slavery, the slavery of the proletariat, but with direct slavery, the slavery of the black races in Surinam, in Brazil, in the Southern States of North America. Direct slavery is as much the pivot of our industrialism today as machinery, credit, etc. Without slavery, no cotton; without cotton, no modern

industry. Slavery has given their value to the colonies; the colonies have created world trade; world trade is the necessary condition of large-scale machine industry. Before the traffic in Negroes began, the colonies only supplied the Old World with very few products and made no visible change in the face of the earth. Thus slavery is an economic category of the highest importance.[9]

These and similar assertions have been taken up by many scholars, most notably, Eric Williams, who develops the theme in his famous study, *Capitalism and Slavery* (1944). In recent years a lively controversy has developed over the precise contribution of the West India plantations to capitalist growth in the metropolises, particularly Britain. The potential contribution of the plantations has been viewed in two principal ways: fairly direct capital transfers of plantation profits to European banks for reinvestment; and the demand created by the needs of the plantations for such metropolitan products as machinery, cloth, torture instruments, and other industrial commodities. Disputes continue about both of these potential sources of gain to metropolitan capital, at least about their aggregate effect. But there is a third potential contribution, which at the moment amounts only to a hunch: Possibly, European enterprise accumulated considerable savings by the provision of low-cost foods and food substitutes to European working classes. Even if not, an attractive argument may be made that Europeans consumed more and more of these products simply because they were so good to consume. But it hardly seems fair to stop the questions precisely where they might fruitfully begin. Of the items enumerated, it seems likely that sweet things will prove most persuasively "natural" for human consumption—if the word dare be used at all. Hence, a few comments on sweetness may be in order.

Claude Lévi-Strauss in his remarkable *From Honey to Ashes* (1973) writes of the stingless bees of the Tropical Forest and of the astoundingly sweet honeys they produce, which, he says,

> have a richness and subtlety difficult to describe to those who have never tasted them, and indeed can seem almost unbearably exquisite in flavour. A delight more piercing than any normally afforded by taste or smell breaks down the boundaries of sensibility, and blurs its registers, so much so that the eater of honey wonders whether he is savouring a delicacy or burning with the fire of love.[10]

I shall resist an inclination here to rhapsodize about music, sausage, flowers, love and revenge, and the way languages everywhere seem to employ the idiom of sweetness to describe them—and so much else—but only in order to suggest a more important point. The general position on sweetness appears to be that our hominid capacity to identify it had some positive evolutionary significance—that it enabled omnivores to locate and use suitable plant nutrients in the environment. There is no doubt at all that this capacity, which presumably works if the eating experience is coupled with what nutritionists call "a hedonic tone," is everywhere heavily overladen with culturally specific preferences. Indeed, we know well that ingestibles with all four of the principal "tastes"—salt, sweet, sour, and bitter—figure importantly in many if not most cuisines, even if a good argument can be made for the evolutionary value of a capacity to taste sweetness.

Overlaid preferences can run against what appears to be "natural," as well as with it. Sugar-cane cultivation and sugar production flourished in Syria from the seventh century to the sixteenth, and it was there, after the First Crusade, that north Europeans got their first sustained taste of sugar. But the Syrian industry disappeared during the sixteenth century, apparently suppressed by the Turks, who, according to Iban Battuta, "regard as shameful the use of sugar houses." Since no innate predisposition, by itself, explains much about human behavior, and since innate predispositions rarely get studied before social learning occurs—though there is at least some evidence that fetal behavior is intensified by the presence of sucrose, while human newborns apparently show a clear preference for sweetened liquids—how much to weigh the possible significance of a "natural" preference remains moot. For the moment, let it suffice that, whether there exists a natural craving for sweetness, few are the world's peoples who respond negatively to sugar, whatever their prior experience, and countless those who have reacted to it with intensified craving and enthusiasm.

Before Britons had sugar, they had honey. Honey was a common ingredient in prescriptions; in time, sugar supplanted it in many or most of them. (The term "treacle," which came to mean molasses in English usage, originally meant a medical antidote composed of many ingredients, including honey. That it should have come to mean molasses and naught else suggests, in a minor way, how sugar and its byproducts overcame and supplanted honey in most regards.) Honey had also been used as a preservative of sorts; sugar turned out to be much better and, eventually, cheaper. At the time of the marriage of Henry IV and Joan of Navarre (1403), their wedding banquet included among its many courses "Perys in syrippe." "Almost the only way of preserving fruit," write Drummond and Wilbraham, "was to boil it in syrup and flavour it heavily with spices."[11] Such syrup can be made by supersaturating water with sugar by boiling; spices can be added during the preparation. Microorganisms that spoil fruit in the absence of sugar can be controlled by 70 percent sugar solutions, which draw off water from their cells and kill them by dehydration. Sugar is a superior preservative medium—by far.

Honey also provided the basis of such alcohol drinks as mead, metheglin, and hypomel. Sugar used with wine and fruit to make hypocras became an important alternative to these drinks; ciders and other fermented fruit drinks made with English fruit and West Indian sugars represented another; and rum manufactured from molasses represented an important third. Here again, sugar soon bested honey.

The uses of spices raise different issues. Until nearly the end of the seventeenth century, a yearly shortage of cattle fodder in Western Europe resulted in heavy fall butchering and the preservation of large quantities of meat by salting, pickling, and other methods. Though some writers consider the emphasis on spices and the spice trade in explanation of European exploration excessive, this much of the received wisdom, at least, seems well founded. Such spices were often used to flavor meat, not simply to conceal its taste; nearly all were of tropical or subtropical origin (e.g., nutmeg, mace, ginger, pepper, coriander, cardamom, turmeric—saffron is an important exception among others). Like these rare flavorings, sugar was a condiment, a preservative, and a medicine; like them, it was sold by Grocers (*Grossarii*) who garbled (mixed) their precious wares, and was dispensed by apothecaries, who used them in medicines. Sugar was employed, as were spices, with cooked meats, sometimes combined with fruits. Such foods still provide a festive element in modern Western cuisine: ham, goose, the use of crab apples and pineapple slices, coating with brown sugar, spiking with cloves. These uses are evidence of the obvious: that holidays preserve better what ordinary days may lose—just as familial crises reveal the nature of the family in ways that ordinary days do not. Much as the spices of holiday cookies—ginger, mace, cinnamon—suggest the past, so too do the brown sugar, molasses, and cloves of the holiday ham. More than just a hearkening to the past, however, such practices may speak to some of the more common ways that fruit was preserved and meat flavored at an earlier time.

Thus, the uses and functions of sugar are many and interesting. Sugar was a medicine, but it also disguised the bitter taste of other medicines by sweetening. It was a sweetener, which, by 1700, was sweetening tea, chocolate, and coffee, all of them bitter and all of them stimulants. It was a food, rich in calories if little else, though less refined sugars and molasses, far commoner in past centuries, possessed some slight additional food value. It was a preservative, which, when eaten with what it preserved, both made it sweeter and increased its caloric content. Its byproduct molasses (treacle) yielded rum, beyond serving as a food itself. For long, the poorest people ate more treacle than sugar; treacle even turns up in the budget of the English almshouses. Nor is this list by any means complete, for sugar turns out to be a flavor-enhancer, often in rather unexpected ways. Rather than a series of successive replacements, these new and varied uses intersect, overlap, are added on rather than lost or supplanted. Other substances may be eliminated or supplanted; sugar is not. And while there are medical concerns voiced in the historical record, it appears that no one considered sugar sinful, whatever they may have thought of the systems of labor that produced it or its effects on dentition. It may well be that, among all of the "dessert crops," it alone was never perceived as an instrument of the Devil.[12]

By the end of the seventeenth century sugar had become an English food, even if still costly and a delicacy. When Edmund Verney went up to Trinity College, Oxford in 1685, his father packed in his trunk for him eighteen oranges, six lemons, three pounds of brown sugar, one pound of powdered white sugar in quarter-pound bags, one pound of brown sugar candy, one-quarter pound of white sugar candy, one pound of "pickt Raisons, good for a cough," and four nutmegs.[13] If the seventeenth century was the century in which sugar changed in Britain from luxury and medicine to necessity and food, an additional statistic may help to underline this transformation. Elizabeth Boody Schumpeter has divided her overseas trade statistics for England into nine groups, of which "groceries," including tea, coffee, sugar, rice, pepper, and other tropical products, is most important. Richard Sheridan points out that in 1700 this group comprised 16.9 percent of all imports by official value; in 1800 it comprised 34.9 percent. The most prominent grocery items were brown sugar and molasses, making up by official value two-thirds of the group in 1700 and two-fifths in 1800. During the same century tea ranked next: The amount imported rose, during that hundred years, from 167,000 pounds to 23 *million* pounds.[14]

The economic and political forces that underlay and supported the remarkable concentration of interest in the West India and East India trade between the seventeenth and nineteenth centuries cannot be discussed here. But it may be enough to note Eric Hobsbawm's admirably succinct summary of the shift of the centers of expansion to the north of Europe, from the seventeenth century onward:

> The shift was not merely geographical, but structural. The new kind of relationship between the "advanced" areas and the rest of the world, unlike the old, tended constantly to intensify and widen the flows of commerce. The powerful, growing and accelerating current of overseas trade which swept the infant industries of Europe with it—which, in fact, sometimes actually *created* them—was hardly conceivable without this change. It rested on three things: in Europe, the rise of a market for overseas products for everyday use, whose market could be expanded as they became available in larger quantities and more cheaply; and overseas the creation of economic systems for producing such goods (such as, for instance, slave-operated plantations) and the conquest of colonies designed to serve the economic advantage of their European owners.[15]

So remarkably does this statement illuminate the history of sugar—and other "dessert crops"—between 1650 and 1900 that it is almost as if it had been written with sugar in mind. But the argument must be developed to lay bare the relationships between demand and supply, between production and consumption, between urban proletarians in the metropolis and African slaves in the colonies. Precisely how demand "arises"; precisely how supply "stimulates" demand even while filling it—and yielding a profit besides; precisely how "demand" is transformed into the ritual of daily necessity and even into images of daily decency: These are questions, not answers. That mothers' milk is sweet can give rise to many imaginative constructions, but it should be clear by now that the so-called English sweet tooth probably needs—and deserves—more than either Freud or evolutionary predispositions in order to be convincingly explained.

One of Bess Lomax's better-known songs in this country is "Drill, ye Tarriers, Drill."[16] Its chorus goes:

> And drill, ye tarriers, drill,
>   Drill, ye tarriers, drill,
> It's work all day for the sugar in your tay,
>   Down behind the railway . . .

As such, perhaps it has no particular significance. But the last two verses, separated and followed by that chorus, are more pointed:

> Now our new foreman was Gene McCann,
>   By God, he was a blamey man.
> Last week a premature blast went off
>   And a mile in the air went Big Jim Goff.
> Next time pay day comes around,
>   Jim Goff a dollar short was found.
> When asked what for, came this reply,
>   You're docked for the time you was up in the sky.

The period during which so many new ingestibles became encysted within European diet was also the period when the factory system took root, flourished, and spread. The precise relationships between the emergence of the industrial workday and the substances under consideration remain unclear. But a few guesses may be permissible. Massive increases in consumption of the drug-food complex occurred during the eighteenth and nineteenth centuries. There also appears to have been some sequence of uses in the case of sugar; and there seems no doubt that there were changes in the use, by class, of sugar and these other products over time, much as the substances in association with which sugar was used also changed. Although these are the fundamentals upon which further research might be based, except for the first (the overall increases in consumption) none may be considered demonstrated or proved. Yet, they are so general and obvious that it would be surprising if any turned out to be wrong. Plainly, the more important questions lie concealed behind such assertions. An example may help.

To some degree it could be argued that sugar, which seems to have begun as a medicine in England and then soon became a preservative, much later changed from being a direct-use product into an indirect-use product, reverting in some curious way to an earlier function but on a wholly different scale. In 1403, pears in syrup were served at the feast following the marriage of Henry IV to Joan of Navarre. Nearly two centuries later, we learn from the household book of Lord Middleton, at Woollaton Hall, Nottinghamshire, of the purchase of two pounds and one ounce of "marmalade" at the astronomical price of 5s. 3d., which, say Drummond and Wilbraham, "shows what a luxury such imported preserved fruits were."[17]

Only the privileged few could enjoy these luxuries even in the sixteenth century in England. In subsequent centuries, however, the combination of sugars and fruit became more common, and the cost of jams, jellies, marmalades, and preserved fruits declined. These changes accompanied many other dietary changes, such as the development of ready-made (store-bought) bread, the gradual replacement of milk-drinking by tea-drinking, a sharp decline in the preparation of oatmeal—especially important in Scotland—and a decrease in the use of butter. Just how such changes took place and the nature of their interrelationship require considerable detailed study. But factory production of jams and the increasing use of store-bought (and factory-made) bread plainly go along with the decline in butter use; it seems likely that the replacement of milk with tea and sugar are also connected. All such changes mark the decline of home-prepared food. These observations do not add up to a lament over the passage of some bucolic perfection, and people have certainly been eating what is now fashionably called "junk food" for a very long time. Yet, it is true that the changes mentioned fit well with a reduction in the time which must be spent in the kitchen or in obtaining foodstuffs, and that they have eased the transition to the taking of more and more meals outside the home. "Only in the worst cases," writes Angeliki Torode of the mid-nineteenth-century English working class, "would a mother hesitate to open her jam jar, because her children ate more bread if there was jam on it."[18] The replacement of oatmeal by bread hurt working-class nutrition; so, presumably, did the other changes, including the replacement of butter by jam. Sugar continues to be used in tea—and in coffee, which never became a lower-class staple in England—but its use in tea is direct, its use in jam indirect. Jam, when produced on a factory basis and consumed with bread, provides an efficient, calorie-high and relatively cheap means of feeding people quickly, wherever they are. It fits well with changes in the rhythm of effort, the organisation of the family, and, perhaps, with new ideas about the relationship between ingestion and time.

"What is wanted," wrote Lindsay, a nutritionist of the early twentieth century, about Glasgow, "is a partial return to the national dish of porridge and milk, in place of tea, bread and jam, which have so universally replaced it in the towns, and which are replacing it even in the rural districts."[19] But why, asks R. H. Campbell, the author of the article in which Lindsay is cited, did people fail to retain the more satisfactory yet cheap diet of the rural areas?[20] Investigators in Glasgow found a ready answer: "When it becomes a question of using the ready cooked bread or the uncooked oatmeal, laziness decides which, and the family suffers." In the city of Dundee, home of famous jams and marmalades, other investigators made an additional observation: The composition of the family diet appears to change sharply when the housewife goes to work. There, it was noted that such time-consuming practices as broth-making and oatmeal-cooking dropped out of domestic cuisine. Bread consumption increases; Campbell cites a statistic for the nineteenth century indicating that one family of seven ate an average of fifty-six pounds of bread per week.[21] Jam goes with bread. The place of laziness in these changes in diet remains to be established; the place of a higher value on women's labor—labor, say, in jam factories (though women worked mainly in jute factories in Dundee)—may matter more.

The rise of industrial production and the introduction of enormous quantities of new ingestibles occurred during the same centuries in Britain. The relationship between these phenomena is, on one level, fairly straightforward: As people produced less and less of their own food, they ate more and more food produced by others, elsewhere. As they spent more and more time away from farm and home, the kinds of foods they ate changed. Those changes reflected changing availabilities of a kind. But the availabilities themselves were functions of economic and political forces remote from the consumers and not at all understood as "forces." People were certainly not compelled to eat the specific foods they ate. But the range of foods they came to eat, and the way they came to see foods and eating, inevitably conformed well with other, vaster changes in the character of daily life—changes over which they plainly had no direct control.

E. P. Thompson has provided an illuminating overview of how industry changed for working people the meaning—nay, the very perception—of the day, of time itself, and of self within time: "If men are to meet both the demands of a highly-synchronized automated industry, and of greatly enlarged areas of 'free time,' they must somehow combine in a new synthesis elements of the old, and the new, finding an imagery based neither upon the seasons nor upon the market but upon human occasions."[22] It is the special character of the substances described here that, like sugar, they provide calories without nutrition; or, like coffee and tea, neither nutrition nor calories, but stimulus to greater effort, or, like tobacco and alcohol, respite from reality. Their study might enable one to see better how an "imagery based . . . upon human occasions" can take shape partly by employing such substances, but not always with much success. Perhaps high tea can one day become a cozy cuppa; perhaps the afternoon sherry can find its equivalent in the grog shop. But a great amount of manufactured sweetness may eventually lubricate only poorly, or even partly take the place of, human relations on all occasions.

The coffee break, which almost always features coffee or tea, frequently sugar, and commonly tobacco, must have had its equivalent before the industrial system arose, just as it has its equivalent outside that system today. I have been accused of seeing an inextricable connection between capitalism and coffee-drinking or sugar use; but coffee and sugar are too seductive, and capitalism too flexible, for the connection to be more than one out of many. It is not that the drug-food habits of the English working classes are the consequence of long-term conspiracies to wreck their nutrition or to make them addicted. But if the changing consumption patterns are the result of class domination, its particular nature and the forms that it has taken require both documentation and specification. What were the ways in which, over time, the changing

occupational and class structure of English society was accompanied by, and reflected in, changes in the uses of particular ingestibles? How did those ingestibles come to occupy the paramount place they do in English consumption? Within these processes were, first, innovations and imitations; later, there were ritualizations as well, expressing that imagery based upon human occasions to which Thompson refers. But an understanding of those processes, of those meanings, cannot go forward, I believe, without first understanding how the production of the substances was so brilliantly separated by the workings of the world economy from so-called meanings of the substances themselves.

I have suggested that political and economic "forces" underlay the availabilities of such items as sugar; that these substances gradually percolated downward through the class structure; and that this percolation, in turn, probably fit together social occasion and substance in accord with new conceptions of work and time. And probably, the less privileged and the poorer imitated those above them in the class system. Yet, if one accepts this idea uncritically, it might appear to obviate the research itself. But such "imitation" is, surely, immeasurably more complicated than a bald assertion makes it seem. My research to date is uncovering the ways in which a modern notion of advertising and early conceptions of a large clientele— a mass market, or "target audience" for a mass market —arose, perhaps particularly in connection with sweet things and what I have labeled here "drug-foods." How direct appeals, combined with some tendency on the part of working people to mimic the consumption norms of those more privileged than they, can combine to influence "demand" may turn out to be a significant part of what is meant by meaning, in the history of such foods as sugar.

As anthropologists turn back to the study of food and eating and pursue their interest in meaning, they display a stronger tendency to look at food in its message-bearing, symbolic form. This has resulted in an enlivening of the discipline, as well as in attracting the admiration and attention of scholars in kindred fields. Such development is surely all to the good. But for one interested in history, there is reason to wonder why so few anthropological studies have dealt with long-term changes in such things as food preferences and consumption patterns, to which historians and economic historians have paid much more attention. In part, the relative lack of anthropological interest may be owing to the romanticism of an anthropology once resolutely reluctant to study anything not "primitive." But it appears also to stem from a readiness to look upon symbolic structures as timeless representations of meaning.

Hence, we confront difficult questions about what we take "meaning" to mean and within what limits of space and time we choose to define what things mean. No answers will be ventured here. But if time is defined as outside the sphere of meaning in which we are interested, then certain categories of meaning will remain and may then be considered adequate and complete. In practice, and for the immediate subject-matter, the structure of meaning would in effect be made coterminous with the political economy. For the substances of concern here—plantation products, tropical products, slave products, imported from afar, detached from their producers—the search for meaning can then be confined within convenient boundaries: the boundaries of consumption.

But if one is interested in the world economy created by capitalism from the sixteenth century onward, and in the relationships between the core of that economy and its subsidiary but interdependent outer sectors, then the structure of meaning will not be coterminous with the metropolitan heartland. If one thinks of modern societies as composed of different groups, vertebrated by institutional arrangements for the distribution and maintenance of power, and divided by class interests as well as by perceptions, values, and attitudes, then there cannot be a single system of meaning for a class-divided society. And if one thinks that meanings arise, then the separation of how goods are produced from how they are consumed, the separation of colony from metropolis, and the separation of proletarian from slave (the splitting in two of the world economy that spawned them both in their modern form) are unjustified and spurious.

Such substances as sugar are, from the point of view of the metropolis, raw materials, until systems of symbolic extrusion and transformation can operate upon them. But those systems do not bring them forth or make them available; such availabilities are differently determined. To find out what these substances come to mean is to reunite their availabilities with their uses—in space and in time.

For some time now anthropology has been struggling uncomfortably with the recognition that so-called primitive society is not what it used to be—if, indeed, it ever was. Betrayed by its own romanticism, it has sought to discover new subject-matters by imputations of a certain sort—as if pimps constituted the best equivalent of "the primitive" available for study. Without meaning to impugn in the least the scientific value of such research, I suggest that there is a much more mundane modernity equally in need of study, some of it reposing on supermarket shelves. Anthropological interest in things—material objects—is old and highly respectable. When Alfred Kroeber referred to "the fundamental thing about culture . . . the way in which

men relate themselves to one another by relating themselves to their cultural material . . . ,"[23] he meant objects as well as ideas. Studies of the everyday in modern life, of the changing character of such humble matters as food, viewed from the perspective of production and consumption, use and function, and concerned with the emergence and variation of meaning, might be one way to try to renovate a discipline now dangerously close to losing its purpose.

NOTES

Versions of this [article] were presented during the past few years at the University of Minnesota, Bryn Mawr College, Rice University, Wellesley College, Cornell University, the University of Pennsylvania, and at Johns Hopkins University's Seminar in Atlantic History and Culture. In radically modified form, these materials also formed part of my 1979 Christian Gauss Lectures at Princeton University. I benefited from comments by participants at all of these presentations, and from criticisms from other friends, including Carol Breckinridge, Carol Heim, and Professors Fred Damon, Nancy Dorian, Eugene Genovese, Jane Goodale, Richard Macksey, Kenneth Sharpe, and William Sturtevant.

1. W. Robertson Smith, *Lectures on the Religion of the Semites* (New York, 1889).

2. Audrey I. Richards, *Hunger and Work in a Savage Tribe: A Functional Study of Nutrition Among the Southern Bantu* (London, 1932); *Land, Labour and Diet in Northern Rhodesia: An Economic Study of the Bemba Tribe* (London, 1939).

3. Rosemary Firth, *Housekeeping Among Malay Peasants* (London, 1943).

4. Claude Lévi-Strauss, *From Honey to Ashes* (New York, 1973).

5. Thomas Austin, *Two Fifteenth-Century Cookbooks* (London, 1888).

6. Richard Sheridan, *Sugar and Slavery* (Baltimore, 1974).

7. Sidney W. Mintz, "The Caribbean as a Socio-cultural Area," *Cahiers d'Histoire Mondiale* IX (1966), 916–941.

8. Karl Marx, *Capital* (New York, 1939), I, 738.

9. Karl Marx to P. V. Annenkov, Dec. 28, 1846, *Karl Marx to Friedrich Engels: Selected Works* (New York, 1968).

10. Lévi-Strauss, *From Honey to Ashes*, 52.

11. J. C. Drummond and Anne Wilbraham, *The Englishman's Food* (London, 1958), 58.

12. I am indebted to Professor Jane Goodale of Bryn Mawr College, who first suggested to me that I investigate this possibility.

13. Drummond and Wilbraham, *Englishmen's Food*, 111.

14. Sheridan, *Sugar and Slavery*, 19–20. Statistics on tea are somewhat troublesome. Smuggling was common, and figures on exports are not always reliable. That the increases in consumption were staggering during the eighteenth century, however, is not open to argument. See Elizabeth Schumpeter, *English Overseas Trade Statistics, 1697–1808* (Oxford, 1960).

15. Eric Hobsbawm, *Industry and Empire* (London, 1968), 52.

16. See A. Lomax, *The Folk Songs of North America* (Garden City, N.Y., 1975).

17. Drummond and Wilbraham, *Englishmen's Food,* 54.

18. Angeliki Torode, "Trends in Fruit Consumption," in T. C. Barker, J. C. McKenzie, and John Yudkin, eds., *Our Changing Fare* (London, 1966), 122.

19. R. H. Campbell, "Diet in Scotland: An Example of Regional Variation," in ibid., 57.

20. Ibid.

21. Ibid., 58.

22. E. P. Thompson, "Time, Work Discipline and Industrial Capitalism," *Past and Present*, no. 38 (1967), 96.

23. Alfred Kroeber, *Anthropology* (New York, 1948), 68.

33

When the Turtle Collapses, the World Ends

Bernard Nietschmann

After delivering a lecture on the solar system, philosopher-psychologist William James was approached by an elderly lady who claimed she had a theory superior to the one described by him.

"We don't live on a ball rotating around the sun," she said. "We live on a crust of earth on the back of a giant turtle."

Not wishing to demolish this absurd argument with the massive scientific evidence at his command, James decided to dissuade his opponent gently.

"If your theory is correct, madam, what does this turtle stand on?"

"You're a very clever man, Mr. James, and that's a good question, but I can answer that. The first turtle stands on the back of a second, far larger, turtle."

"But what does this second turtle stand on?" James asked patiently.

The old lady crowed triumphantly, "It's no use, Mr. James—it's turtles all the way down."

In the half-light of dawn, a sailing canoe approaches a shoal where nets have been set the day before. A Miskito turtleman stands in the bow and points to a distant splash that breaks the gray sheen of the Caribbean waters. Even from a hundred yards, he can tell that a green turtle has been caught in one of the nets. His two companions quickly bring the craft alongside the turtle, and as they pull it from the sea, its glistening shell reflects the first rays of the rising sun. As two men work to remove the heavy reptile from the net, the third keeps the canoe headed into the swells and beside the anchored net. After its fins have been pierced and lashed with bark fiber cord, the 250-pound turtle is placed on its back in the bottom of the canoe. The turtlemen are happy. Perhaps their luck will be good today and their other nets will also yield many turtles.

These green turtles, caught by Miskito Indian turtlemen off the eastern coast of Nicaragua, are destined for distant markets. Their butchered bodies will pass through many hands, local and foreign, eventually ending up in tins, bottles, and freezers far away. Their meat, leather, shell, oil, and calipee, a gelatinous substance that is the base for turtle soup, will be used to produce goods consumed in more affluent parts of the world.

The coastal Miskito Indians are very dependent on green turtles. Their culture has long been adapted to utilizing the once vast populations that inhabited the largest sea turtle feeding grounds in the Western Hemisphere. As the most important link between livelihood, social interaction, and environment, green turtles were the pivotal resource around which traditional Miskito Indian society revolved. These large reptiles also provided the major source of protein for Miskito subsistence. Now this priceless and limited resource has become a prized commodity that is being exploited almost entirely for economic reasons.

In the past, turtles fulfilled the nutritional needs as well as the social responsibilities of Miskito society. Today, however, the Miskito depend mainly on the sale of turtles to provide them with the money they need to purchase household goods and other necessities. But turtles are a declining resource; overdependence on them is leading the Miskito into an ecological blind alley. The cultural control mechanisms that once adapted the Miskito to their environment and faunal resources are now circumvented or inoperative, and they are caught up in a system of continued intensification of turtle fishing, which threatens to provide neither cash nor subsistence.

I have been studying this situation for several years, unraveling its historical context and piecing together its past and future effect on Miskito society, economy, and diet, and on the turtle population.

The coastal Miskito Indians are among the world's most adept small-craft seamen and turtlemen. Their traditional subsistence system provided dependable yields from the judicious scheduling of resource procurement activities. Agriculture, hunting, fishing, and gathering were organized in accordance with seasonal fluctuations in weather and resource availability and provided adequate amounts of food and materials—without overexploiting any one species or site. Women cultivated the crops while men hunted and fished. Turtle fishing was the backbone of subsistence, providing meat throughout the year.

Miskito society and economy were interdependent. There was no economic activity without a social context and every social act had a reciprocal economic aspect. To the Miskito, meat, especially turtle meat, was the most esteemed and valuable resource, for it was not only a mainstay of subsistence, it was the item most commonly distributed to relatives and friends. Meat shared in this way satisfied mutual obligations and responsibilities and smoothed out daily and seasonal differences in the acquisition of animal protein. In this way, those too young, old, sick, or otherwise unable to secure meat received their share, and a certain balance in the village was achieved: minimal food requirements were met, meat surplus was disposed of to others, and social responsibilities were satisfied.

Today, the older Miskito recall that when meat was scarce in the village, a few turtlemen would put out to sea in their dugout canoes for a day's harpooning on the turtle feeding grounds. In the afternoon, the men would return, sailing before the northeast trade wind, bringing meat for all. Gathered on the beach, the villagers helped drag the canoes into thatched storage sheds. After the turtles were butchered and the meat distributed, everyone returned home to the cooking fires.

Historical circumstances and a series of boom–bust economic cycles disrupted the Miskito's society and environment. In the seventeenth and eighteenth centuries, intermittent trade with English and French buccaneers—based on the exchange of forest and marine resources for metal tools and utensils, rum, and firearms—prompted the Miskito to extend hunting, fishing, and gathering beyond subsistence needs to exploitative enterprises.

During the nineteenth and early twentieth centuries, foreign-owned companies operating in eastern Nicaragua exported rubber, lumber, and gold, and initiated commercial banana production. As alien economic and ecological influences were intensified, contract wage labor replaced seasonal, short-term economic relationships; company commissaries replaced limited trade goods; and large-scale exploitation of natural resources replaced sporadic, selective extraction. During economic boom periods the relationship between resources, subsistence, and environment was drastically altered for the Miskito. Resources became a commodity with a price tag, market exploitation a livelihood, and foreign wages and goods a necessity.

For more than 200 years, relations between the coastal Miskito and the English were based on sea turtles. It was from the Miskito that the English learned the art of turtling, which they then organized into intensive commercial exploitation of Caribbean turtle grounds and nesting beaches. Sea turtles were among the first resources involved in trade relations and foreign commerce in the Caribbean. Zoologist Archie Carr, an authority on sea turtles, has remarked that "more than any other dietary factor, the green turtle supported the opening up of the Caribbean." The once abundant turtle populations provided sustenance to ships' crews and to the new settlers and plantation laborers.

The Cayman Islands, settled by the English, became in the seventeenth and eighteenth centuries the center of commercial turtle fishing in the Caribbean. By the early nineteenth century, pressure on the Cayman turtle grounds and nesting beaches to supply meat to Caribbean and European markets became so great that the turtle population was decimated. The Cayman Islanders were forced to shift to other turtle areas off Cuba, the Gulf of Honduras, and the coast of eastern Nicaragua. They made annual expeditions, lasting four to seven weeks, to the Miskito turtle grounds to net green turtles, occasionally purchasing live ones, dried calipee, and the shells of hawksbill turtles (*Eretmochelys imbricata*) from the Miskito Indians. Reported catches of green turtles by the Cayman turtlers generally ranged between 2,000 and 3,000 a year up to the early 1960s, when the Nicaraguan government failed to renew the islanders' fishing privileges.

Intensive resource extraction by foreign companies led to seriously depleted and altered environments. By the 1940s, many of the economic booms had turned to busts. As the resources ran out and operating costs mounted, companies shut down production and moved to other areas in Central America. Thus, the economic mainstays that had helped provide the Miskito with jobs, currency, markets, and foreign goods were gone. The company supply ships and commissaries disappeared, money became scarce, and store-bought items expensive.

In the backwater of the passing golden boom period, the Miskito were left with an ethic of poverty,

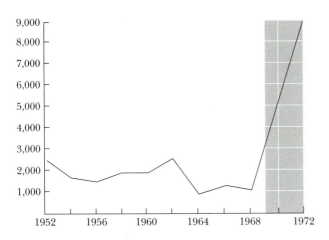

Number of green turtles exported annually from eastern Nicaragua

but they still had the subsistence skills that had maintained their culture for hundreds of years. Their land and water environment was still capable of providing reliable resources for local consumption. As it had been in the past, turtle fishing became a way of life, a provider of life itself. But traditional subsistence culture could no longer integrate Miskito society and environment in a state of equilibrium. Resources were now viewed as having a value and labor a price tag. All that was needed was a market.

Recently, two foreign turtle companies began operations along the east coast of Nicaragua. One was built in Puerto Cabezas in late 1968, and another was completed in Bluefields in 1969. Both companies were capable of processing and shipping large amounts of green turtle meat and by-products to markets in North America and Europe. Turtles were acquired by purchase from the Miskito. Each week company boats visited coastal Miskito communities and offshore island turtle camps to buy green turtles. The "company" was back, money was again available, and the Miskito were expert in securing the desired commodity. Another economic boom period was at hand. But the significant difference between this boom and previous ones was that the Miskito were now selling a subsistence resource.

As a result, the last large surviving green turtle population in the Caribbean was opened to intensive, almost year-round exploitation. Paradoxically, it would be the Miskito Indians, who once caught only what they needed for food, who would conduct the assault on the remaining turtle population.

Another contradictory element in the Miskito—turtle story is that only some 200 miles to the south at Tortuguero, Costa Rica, Archie Carr had devoted fifteen years to the study of sea turtles and to the conservation and protection of the Caribbean's last major sea turtle nesting beach. Carr estimates that more than half the green turtles that nest at Tortuguero are from Nicaraguan waters. The sad and exasperating paradox is that a conservation program insured the survival of an endangered species for commercial exploitation in nearby waters.

Green turtles, *Chelonia mydas,* are large, airbreathing, herbivorous marine reptiles. They congregate in large populations and graze on underwater beds of vegetation in relatively clear, shallow, tropical waters. A mature turtle can weigh 250 pounds or more and when caught, can live indefinitely in a saltwater enclosure or for a couple of weeks if kept in shade on land. Green turtles have at least six behavioral characteristics that are important in their exploitation: they occur in large numbers in localized areas; they are air breathing, so they have to surface; they are mass social nesters; they have an acute location-finding ability; when mature, they migrate seasonally on an overlapping two- or three-year cycle for mating and nesting; and they exhibit predictable local distributional patterns.

The extensive shallow shelf off eastern Nicaragua is dotted with numerous small coral islands, thousands of reefs, and vast underwater pastures of marine vegetation called "turtle banks." During the day, a large group of turtles may be found feeding at one of the many turtle banks, while adjacent marine pastures may have only a few turtles. They graze on the vegetation, rising periodically to the surface for air and to float for awhile before diving again. In the late afternoon, groups of turtles will leave the feeding areas and swim to shoals, some up to four or five miles away, to spend the night. By five the next morning, they gather to depart again for the banks. The turtles' precise, commuterlike behavior between sleeping and feeding areas is well known to the Miskito and helps insure good turtling.

Each coastal turtling village exploits an immense sea area, containing many turtle banks and shoals. For example, the Miskito of Tasbapauni utilize a marine area of approximately 600 square miles, with twenty major turtle banks and almost forty important shoals.

Having rather predictable patterns of movement and habitat preference, green turtles are commonly caught by the Miskito in three ways: on the turtle banks with harpoons; along the shoal-to-feeding area route with harpoons; and on the shoals using nets, which entangle the turtles when they surface for air.

The Miskito's traditional means of taking turtles was by harpoon—an eight- to ten-foot shaft fitted with a detachable short point tied to a strong line. The simple technology pitted two turtlemen in a small, seagoing canoe against the elusive turtles. Successful turtling with harpoons requires an extensive knowledge of turtle behavior and habits and tremendous skill and experience in handling a small canoe in what can be very rough seas. Turtlemen work in partnerships: a "strikerman" in the bow; the "captain" in the stern. Together, they make a single unit engaged in the delicate and almost silent pursuit of a wary prey, their movements coordinated by experience and rewarded by proficiency. Turtlemen have mental maps of all the banks and shoals in their area, each one named and located through a complex system of celestial navigation, distance reckoning, wind and current direction, and the individual surface-swell motion over each site. Traditionally, not all Miskito were sufficiently expert in seamanship and turtle lore to become respected "strikermen," capable of securing turtles even during hazardous sea conditions. Theirs was a very specialized calling. Harpooning restrained possible overexploitation since turtles were taken one at a time by two men directly involved in the chase, and there were only a limited number of really proficient "strikermen" in each village.

Those who still use harpoons must leave early to take advantage of the land breeze and to have enough time to reach the distant offshore turtle grounds by first light. Turtlemen who are going for the day, or for several days, will meet on the beach by 2:00 A.M. They drag the canoes on bamboo rollers from beachfront sheds to the water's edge. There, in the swash of spent breakers, food, water, paddles, lines, harpoons, and sails are loaded and secured. Using a long pole, the standing bowman propels the canoe through the foaming surf while the captain in the stern keeps the craft running straight with a six-foot mahogany paddle. Once past the inside break, the men count the dark rolling seas building outside until there is a momentary pause in the sets; then with paddles digging deep, they drive the narrow, twenty-foot canoe over the cresting swells, rising precipitously on each wave face and then plunging down the far side as the sea and sky seesaw into view. Once past the breakers, they rig the sail and, running with the land breeze, point the canoe toward a star in the eastern sky.

A course is set by star fix and by backsight on a prominent coconut palm on the mainland horizon. Course alterations are made to correct for the direction and intensity of winds and currents. After two or three hours of sailing the men reach a distant spot located between a turtle sleeping shoal and feeding bank. There they intercept and follow the turtles as they leave for specific banks.

On the banks the turtlemen paddle quietly, listening for the sound of a "blowing" turtle. When a turtle surfaces for air it emits a hissing sound audible for fifty yards or more on a calm day. Since a turtle will stay near the surface for only a minute or two before diving to feed, the men must approach quickly and silently,

maneuvering the canoe directly in front of or behind the turtle. These are its blind spots. Once harpooned, a turtle explodes into a frenzy of action, pulling the canoe along at high speeds in its hopeless, underwater dash for escape until it tires and can be pulled alongside the canoe.

But turtle harpooning is a dying art. The dominant method of turtling today is the use of nets. Since their introduction, the widespread use of turtle nets has drastically altered turtling strategy and productivity. Originally brought to the Miskito by the Cayman Islanders, nets are now extensively distributed on credit by the turtle companies. This simple technological change, along with a market demand for turtles, has resulted in intensified pressure on green turtle populations.

Buoyed by wooden floats and anchored to the bottom by a single line, the fifty-foot-long by fourteen-foot-wide nets hang from the surface like underwater flags, shifting direction with the current. Nets are set in place during midday when the turtlemen can see the dark shoal areas. Two Miskito will set five to thirty nets from one canoe, often completely saturating a small shoal. In the late afternoon, green turtles return to their shoals to spend the night. There they will sleep beside or beneath a coral outcrop, periodically surfacing for air where a canopy of nets awaits them.

Catching turtles with nets requires little skill; anyone with a canoe can now be a turtleman. The Miskito set thousands of nets daily, providing continuous coverage in densely populated nocturnal habitats. Younger Miskito can become turtlemen almost overnight simply by following more experienced men to the shoal areas, thus circumventing the need for years of accumulated skill and knowledge that once were the domain of the "strikermen." All one has to do is learn where to set the nets, retire for the night, remove the entangled turtles the next morning, and reset the nets. The outcome is predictable: more turtlemen, using more effective methods, catch more turtles.

With an assured market for turtles, the Miskito devote more time to catching turtles, traveling farther and staying at sea longer. Increased dependence on turtles as a source of income and greater time inputs have meant disruption of subsistence agriculture and hunting and fishing. The Miskito no longer produce foodstuffs for themselves; they buy imported foods with money gained from the sale of turtles. Caught between contradictory priorities—their traditional subsistence system and the market economy—the Miskito are opting for cash.

The Miskito are now enveloped in a positive feedback system where change spawns change. Coastal villages rely on turtles for a livelihood. Decline of subsistence provisioning has led to the need to secure food from local shopkeepers on credit to feed the families in the villages and the men during their turtling expeditions. Initial high catches of turtles encouraged more Miskito to participate, and by 1972 the per person and per day catch began to decline noticeably.

In late 1972, several months after I had returned to Michigan, I received a letter from an old turtleman, who wrote: "Turtle is getting scarce, Mr. Barney. You said it would happen in five or ten years but it is happening now."

Burdened by an overdependence on an endangered species and with accumulating debts for food and nets, the Miskito are finding it increasingly difficult to break even, much less secure a profit. With few other economic alternatives, the inevitable step is to use more nets and stay out at sea longer.

The turtle companies encourage the Miskito to expand turtling activities by providing them with building materials so that they can construct houses on offshore cays, thereby eliminating the need to return to the mainland during rough weather. On their weekly runs up and down the coast, company boats bring food, turtle gear, and cash for turtles to fishing camps from the Miskito Cays to the Set Net Cays. Frequent visits keep the Miskito from becoming discouraged and returning to their villages with the turtles. On Saturdays, villagers look to sea, watching for returning canoes. A few men will bring turtle for their families; the majority will bring only money. Many return with neither.

Most Miskito prefer to be home on Sunday to visit with friends and for religious reasons. (There are Moravian, Anglican, and Catholic mission churches in many of the villages.) But more and more, turtlemen are staying out for two to four weeks. The church may promise salvation, but only the turtle companies can provide money.

Returning to their villages, turtlemen are confronted with a complex dilemma: how to satisfy both social and economic demands with a limited resource. Traditional Miskito social rules stipulate that turtle meat should be shared among kin, but the new economic system requires that turtles be sold for personal economic gain. Kin expect gifts of meat, and friends expect to be sold meat. Turtlemen are besieged with requests forcing them to decide between who will or will not receive meat. This is contrary to the traditional Miskito ethic, which is based on generosity and mutual concern for the well-being of others. The older Miskito ask why the turtlemen should have to allocate a food that was once abundant and available to all. Turtlemen sell and give to other turtlemen, thereby insuring reciprocal treatment for themselves, but there simply are not enough turtles to accommodate other economic and social requirements. In order to have enough tur-

Distribution of turtle meat by gift and purchase

Percent of Villagers*	Pounds Received per Person
18	10–14+
28	6–9
32	2–5
22	0–1.9

During the one-month period from April 15 to May 15, 1971, 125 green turtles were caught by the turtlemen of Tasbapauni, Nicaragua. Of these, 91 were sold to turtle companies; the remaining 34 were butchered and the meat sold or given to villagers. In all, 3,900 pounds of turtle meat were distributed, but 54 percent of the villagers received 5 pounds or less, an insufficient amount for adult dietary protein requirements.
* Population of 998 converted to 711 adult male equivalents.

tles to sell, fewer are butchered in the villages. This means that less meat is being consumed than before the turtle companies began operations. The Miskito presently sell 70 to 90 percent of the turtles they catch; in the near future they will sell even more and eat less.

Social tension and friction are growing in the villages. Kinship relationships are being strained by what some villagers interpret as preferential and stingy meat distribution. Rather than endure the trauma caused by having to ration a limited item to fellow villagers, many turtlemen prefer to sell all their turtles to the company and return with money, which does not have to be shared. However, if a Miskito sells out to the company, he will probably be unable to acquire meat for himself in the village, regardless of kinship or purchasing power. I overheard an elderly turtleman muttering to himself as he butchered a turtle: "I no going to sell, neither give dem meat. Let dem eat de money."

The situation is bad and getting worse. Individuals too old or sick to provide for themselves often receive little meat or money from relatives. Families without turtlemen are families without money or access to meat. The trend is toward the individualization of nuclear families, operating for their own economic ends. Miskito villages are becoming neighborhoods rather than communities.

The Miskito diet has suffered in quality and quantity. Less protein and fewer diverse vegetables and fruits are consumed. Present dietary staples—rice, white flour, beans, sugar, and coffee—come from the store. In one Miskito village, 65 percent of all food eaten in a year was purchased.

Besides the nutritional significance of what is becoming a largely carbohydrate diet, dependence on purchased foods has also had major economic reverberations. Generated by national and international scarcities, inflationary fallout has hit the Miskito. Most of their purchased foods are imported, much coming from the United States. In the last five years prices for staples have increased 100 to 150 percent. This has had an overwhelming impact on the Miskito, who spend 50 to 75 percent of their income for food. Consequently, their entry into the market by selling a subsistence resource, diverting labor from agriculture, and intensifying exploitation of a vanishing species has resulted in their living off poorer-quality, higher-priced foods.

The Miskito now depend on outside systems to supply them with money and materials that are subject to world market fluctuations. They have lost their autonomy and their adaptive relationship with their environment. Life is no longer socially rewarding nor is their diet satisfying. The coastal Miskito have become a specialized and highly vulnerable sector of the global market economy.

Loss of the turtle market would be a serious economic blow to the Miskito, who have almost no other means of securing cash for what have now become necessities. Nevertheless, continued exploitation will surely reduce the turtle population to a critical level.

National and international legislation is urgently needed. At the very least, commercial turtle fishing must be curtailed for several years until the *Chelonia* population can rebound and exploitation quotas can be set. While turtle fishing for subsistence should be permitted, exportation of sea turtle products used in the gourmet, cosmetic, or jewelry trade should be banned.

Restrictive environmental legislation, however, is not a popular subject in Nicaragua, a country that has recently been torn by earthquakes, volcanic eruption, and hurricanes. A program for sea turtle conservation submitted to the Nicaraguan government for consideration ended up in a pile of rubble during the earthquake that devastated Managua in December, 1972, adding a sad footnote to the Miskito–sea turtle situation. With other problems to face, the government has not yet reviewed what is happening on the distant east coast, separated from the capital by more than 200 miles of rain forest—and years of neglect.

As it is now, the turtles are going down and along with them, the Miskito—seemingly, a small problem in terms of the scale of ongoing ecological and cultural change in the world. But each localized situation involves species and societies with long histories and, perhaps, short futures. They are weathervanes in the conflicting winds of economic and environmental priorities. As Bob Dylan sang: "You don't need a weatherman to tell which way the wind blows."

34

Food for All

Debbie Mack

Five million Brazilians faced starvation this year. This time it was a drought related to El Niño that halved grain crops in the northeast of the country, but next year it will be something else. Famine is perennial in Brazil.

In September Monsanto, the world's largest supplier of genetically modified seeds, announced it would invest $550 million in Brazil to build a factory producing its herbicide Roundup. Shortly afterwards the Brazilian government made Monsanto's Roundup-resistant soya beans the country's first legally approved, genetically engineered crop. The soya beans will boost profits for the big landowners who grow them to feed beef cattle for export. But most rural Brazilians are subsistence farmers who do not grow soya. No help will trickle down from Monsanto's beans to the starving millions.

The story exemplifies the limited contribution genetically modified crops have made so far to eradicating world hunger. It is not that biotech companies are uninterested in the developing world. Far from it: Brazil and other newly industrialising countries are in fact prime targets, with their growing demand for agricultural products, little opposition to biotechnology, and farmers who have risen above hard graft subsistence, but have not yet become customers of the world's seed and agrochemicals conglomerates.

But who will benefit from genetically modified crops in these countries? The companies speak of feeding the starving millions, while conserving the environment. They say that the new technology will have greater benefits in the Third World than anywhere else. "Biotechnology is a key factor in the fight against famine," claims the literature from EuropaBio, the association of European biotechnology companies. "Biotechnology will help increase the yield on limited land." Critics maintain that there is little evidence of this. Instead, they say most of the engineered crops developed or in the pipeline will benefit rich farmers, not the needy. Worse still, they fear the biotech industry's increasing domination of crop research will hurt, not help, the poor.

Agriculture does need a new technological saviour. Most of the world's food calories come from grain. A simple redistribution of what we grow now, even if it were possible, will not feed the 10 billion humans expected by 2030. Traditional methods of improving crops seem to have gone about as far as they can. "The fact that we start from the results of more than 5000 years of selective breeding makes further staggering yield increases unlikely," says Lloyd Evans of the CSIRO Division of Plant Industry in Canberra, Australia. "The biggest opportunity for increasing grain yields is to produce varieties more precisely adapted to local conditions."

Yet few of these crops have emerged so far. Those that are on or near the market aim to increase farmers' profits by cutting expensive "inputs," such as pesticides. This is little help to farmers who can afford no inputs to begin with, not even the reduced levels needed for these crops, and no help if they cannot afford the patented seed. Steven Briggs, head of the Novartis Agricultural Discovery Institute in San Diego, which sequences plant genomes, points to several innovations in the pipeline which might help: fodder crops that contain more calories, so more meat can be produced per hectare of corn or soya; crops that destroy toxins produced by moulds, such as fumonisin, which cause massive crop losses after harvest; and disease-resistant crops, such as sweet potatoes and cassava, staples of the poor, which fend off viruses.

Crops that thrive despite drought and salty soils could also let farmers expand production into marginal lands. And the nutritional content of staples could be improved. If maize, for example, can be made to produce more of the amino acids it naturally lacks, the 80 million people who live almost exclusively on maize would get more protein. Ganesh Kishore, head of nutrition at Monsanto, says: "We can make it into a complete balanced meal."

Briggs agrees that there are contradictions inherent in bringing high-tech remedies to low-tech farmers. Breeding crops for subsistence, he says, is "emergency aid, not a path to economic growth." Pol Bamelis, from the German giant Bayer and chair of the German and European biotechnology associations, says that the industry "cannot help the fact that there are rich and poor in the world."

BUY OUT

Biotech companies think genetic engineering will be in the best position to help once farmers everywhere switch from small-scale subsistence to large-scale mechanisation. But many activists fear just that process. The high price of the technology could allow the few farmers who can afford it to out-compete their poorer neighbours and eventually buy them out, driving people from the land, says Hope Shand, of the Rural Advancement Fund International in Canada.

Monsanto also argues that helping poor farmers would reap another kind of benefit: richer peasants who no longer need to destroy forests to get more land. But this could be simplistic. Steve Vosti, of the International Food Policy Research Institute in Washington DC, has studied poor farmers and deforestation in Amazonia. He says any technology that increases a farmer's profits, or reduces the labour needed per hectare, will cause the farmer to cut down trees to get more land. It is not clear whether the kind of farmer who needs to fell forests to get land, or who eats little but maize meal, will ever be able to afford genetically modified crops. But even if only rich farmers benefit, says Vosti, their expansion would tend to push poorer farmers into forest margins.

And there are other disadvantages for the poorest farmers. "New biotechnologies threaten to aggravate problems of genetic uniformity, and increase the dependence of farmers on transnational corporations," says Shand. Even in the industrialised world, people are worried about genetic uniformity arising from the widespread introduction of genetically modified crops. In Missouri this summer, half the soya plants on some farms died of *Fusarium* mould, after three-quarters of the land was planted with Roundup-resistant varieties which turned out not to resist mould.

The handful of modified varieties offered by biotech companies will inevitably be more genetically uniform, hence more susceptible to unforeseen stress, than the plethora of classically bred varieties grown now. That problem could be worse in the tropics, where there is more existing crop diversity together with stresses that seed breeders based in the North may not have anticipated. Tropical countries will also have less money to pay multinationals for the rights to incorporate proprietary genes into several local varieties.

The last problem stems from the big companies' growing control of both markets and plant genes. Crop scientists must continually breed new crop varieties to meet the ever-evolving threats of pests and disease. In the Third World, this is mainly done by government-funded institutions, and the Consultative Group for International Agricultural Research. But public sector breeders are losing funding, while companies such as Monsanto are rapidly becoming the only source for improved varieties. It already, for example, sells half the maize seed in Argentina.

LOSING ACCESS

The public breeders are also losing access to plant genes. Last May the CGIAR completed a detailed study of the problems posed by the fact that the genes it needs to do its work are increasingly available only at a price, because companies hold the patents. India recently declined to pay Monsanto $8 million for the use, by its state-owned crop laboratories, of Monsanto's *Bt* insecticide gene. Those labs will not be able to provide Indian farmers with cheap, locally bred insect-resistant crops. Farmers who can afford to will have to buy whatever Monsanto has to offer.

Even if Third World breeders get access to patented genes, they may be forced to protect them in ways that put them out of reach of the poor. *Terminator*, a gene owned by Monsanto, keeps a plant from producing viable seed. So farmers cannot save seed from patented, genetically modified varieties for the next harvest. It also keeps farmers from crossing patented strains with other crops to create new varieties. "Public sector breeders could be under great pressure to use *Terminator* to protect patented genes in the breeds they produce, in exchange for access to those genes," says Shand.

The overall effect could be that breeders will not be able to create new varieties to meet evolving threats unless they pay for the genes, and couple them with technologies to prevent the saving of seed. That means fewer, more expensive varieties, plus increased costs for the 1.4 billion poorest farmers who grow 80 per cent of subsistence crops from saved seed. As big northern companies expand their control of crop genes, their choice may be to buy seed, or die.

Cultural Ecology of Infant Feeding

THE VALUE OF HUMAN MILK FOR HUMAN BABIES

Together with the rest of the mammalian world, human females have the capacity to produce milk, a complete food, to meet the needs of their newborn offspring. As would be expected for a substance that is so central to survival, the composition of milk is finely adapted to the specific nutrient requirements of offspring. Human milk is no exception. In addition to containing the appropriate balance of essential nutrients, human milk also contains antibodies and other substances that help to protect infants from potentially life-threatening infection. Although the milk of other animals is not ideal for human infants, it is possible for babies to consume and derive nutrients from it. This feature of human adaptability has led to the use of other animal milks to supplement or replace breastmilk. Bottle-feeding is not a new invention, and the use of feeding bottles and animal milks was known in classic Greek and Roman times. However, artificial feeding did not become a common practice across the populations of the world until this century, in particular after the Second World War.

The significance of the massive culture change in infant feeding practices began to be carefully studied in the 1960s and 1970s. The more that biological, medical, and social scientists discovered about breastfeeding, the more serious were the concerns about the consequences of the major behavioral change from breastfeeeding to bottle-feeding. The more breastmilk an infant receives, the better the health outcome.

WHY DO MOTHERS CHOOSE TO BREASTFEED OR BOTTLE-FEED?

As the importance of breastfeeding for child health became more and more widely known, the reasons for the worldwide change in infant feeding also began to be discussed and studied. Scientists, politicians, social observers, and other types of people who were concerned with social change offered a number of different theories about why bottle-feeding had become so popular. In the beginning of her article "Perspectives on Infant Feeding: Decision-Making and Ecology," nutritional anthropologist Gretel Pelto provides an overview of the different approaches that were taken to explain the phenomenon of bottle-feeding. She then goes on to argue that the different philosophical approaches to understanding the problem fall short because they do not consider the cultural-ecological context. She suggests that infant feeding, like other aspects of child care, needs to be understood in the larger context of economic, social, and cultural roles within families and societies. She suggests that it is useful to think about infant feeding practices as the result of deliberate decisions rather than as simply customary behaviors. One can then ask, What are the factors that influence or determine those decisions? Her article describes the various determinants and gives examples from different cultural settings to show how these influences can operate.

The article by biological anthropologist Katherine Dettwyler, "More Than Nutrition: Breastfeeding in Urban Mali," is a case study from West Africa that richly illustrates the ways in which several of the factors identified by Pelto affect infant feeding. In this example, economic factors, government policy, and cultural beliefs all operated to positively influence mothers to breastfeed. For more than a year, Dettwyler carried out research as a participant-observer in Farimabougou, a town near Bamako, the capital of Mali. (The story of her second field trip to Mali, which she recounts in her book *Dancing Skeletons: Life and Death in West Africa* [1994], is not only a moving account of the process of conducting scientific research on malnutrition but also an insightful examination of the meaning of malnutrition and disease in the lives of poor families.) Dettwyler describes family structure in the peri-urban community of Farimabougou and discusses the economic constraints within which family decisions about cash expenditures are made. She also provides a description of the ways infants are fed—the pattern of breastfeeding behavior—and outlines the specific cultural beliefs that support and reinforce the value of breastmilk. She sets these beliefs within the context of social structure and discusses the relationship of this structure to the social and economic functioning of the family unit. Of particular importance is the conception of breastfeeding as "a special process that creates bonds of kinship between women and children and among children." These beliefs also dovetail well with government pro-breastfeeding educational programs and policies that discourage the use of infant formulas. In this example, we see clearly the effects on infants' food intake of the interaction between two components of the ecological model—"culture" (ideology) and "social organization" (that is, economy, family structure, government)—which we outline in article 1.

FROM BREASTFEEDING TO COMPLEMENTARY FEEDING

Breastmilk alone is generally adequate to support optimal infant growth for four to six months. After that, additional foods are needed. The degree to which mothers complement breastmilk with other foods as the child makes the transition to the family diet is influenced by many factors. In many industrialized societies, the recommendations of health care providers are often an important influence on caregivers' decisions to begin adding other foods to infants' diets, and beliefs about how to introduce children to "food" can be found in virtually every society. In some societies, the introduction of the first food is recognized with a formal ritual, much like naming ceremonies, infant circumcision, baptism, or the first birthday are ritual occasions in the life of children.

Apart from ritual or beliefs related to people's ideas about child health, the introduction of complementary foods is often influenced by women's work roles. The ecological model outlined by Pelto applies as well to decisions about giving babies complementary foods. A number of years ago, Nerlove (1974) examined information about the age of introduction of complementary foods. This information was available for a sample of 83 traditional cultures, ranging from hunting-gathering groups to peasant agriculturalists. She found that in societies where there was a high level of women's participation in food production, foods were often introduced before one month of age. A corollary of this finding is that the frequency of breastfeeding is also affected by women's work roles, and in some traditional societies women leave their infants in the care of others while they engage in agricultural work.

The importance of women's work in affecting the frequency of breastfeeding and the use of other foods is very clearly illustrated in the case study by cultural anthropologist Nancy Levine's fieldwork in Nepal. Levine worked in a region that presents people with serious challenges for meeting their food needs.

Humla is in the mountains of northwest Nepal, in an area where people depend heavily on human labor to raise crops, and where women have a major role in producing family foods. Because of the difficult conditions under which agricultural work is carried out, most women leave their infants at home, to be cared for by others. They are away from home for long hours at a time, and their babies must be fed during their absence. In this poverty-stricken region of the world, the trade-offs that these women must make between family food security and infant feeding leave their infants at risk of malnutrition. Levine's article helps to make it clear why it is essential to examine nutrition problems, such as the too-early introduction of complementary foods, within the wider context of social and economic organization. For example, nutrition education messages that exhort mothers to not introduce complementary foods until their infant is four to six months old would not help them to deal with the underlying reasons for this behavior.

MOTHERS' HEALTH, HIV, AND BREASTFEEDING: EMERGING CONCERNS

Breastfeeding is not only beneficial for infants; it is also good for mothers. In the immediate postdelivery period, the action of infant suckling helps the uterus to contract, which stems postpartum bleeding. Most important from the perspective of women's health is the contraceptive effect of exclusive or intensive breastfeeding. Although the protection is not absolute, on average, women who breastfeed intensively and who are not taking other contraceptive measures are protected from a new pregnancy for nearly a year. This biological protection is particularly important in our species, in which the danger of too short a spacing between births is high because there are no cycles of sexual receptivity and because the adult male-female couple is the fundamental unit of social organization.

Now, perhaps for the first time in human history, the physical and psychological health of the mother-infant dyad is seriously threatened by a disease that has reached epidemic proportions, at least in parts of Africa. Already the AIDS epidemic was viewed as a serious threat, particularly as the death rates among men and women of childbearing age began rising. But with the recent discovery that the HIV virus can be transmitted from mother to child via breastmilk, the picture becomes even more grim. Across the world, countries are being encouraged to adopt, as health policy, the position that women who are HIV positive should be counseled to bottle-feed rather than breastfeed.

While the "HIV+/ no breastfeeding" policy appears to be scientifically sound from the standpoint of preventing infants of infected mothers from acquiring the virus, it raises a series of other difficult problems. Among the most serious questions are the following: How can families ensure safe bottle-feeding in environments where lack of refrigeration, contaminated water supplies, and inadequate financial resources make it very difficult for this to be achieved? Will the decrease in child deaths from AIDS be more than offset by an increase in deaths from diarrhea? How can women avoid the stigma and potentially profound social consequences of being identified as HIV positive when they bottle-feed in a social environment that respects and expects breastfeeding? How can poor women who typically have little contact with health care be adequately advised, supported, and counseled about the decision? How can the spread of pro-bottle-feeding, anti-breast-feeding attitudes be avoided if messages and policies to encourage bottle-feeding are introduced, albeit for only a segment of the population? These and related questions about the social and public health significance of this policy raise serious doubts about its wisdom. While the answers to these questions are being hotly debated, other alternatives to prevent mother-to-infant infection are being explored, and the much-hoped-for outcome is that these questions will then become irrelevant.

SUGGESTIONS FOR THINKING AND DOING NUTRITIONAL ANTHROPOLOGY

1.   From art history books, museum catalogs, and books on important archaeological sites, put together a collection of pictures that illustrate cultural values about breastfeeding.

2.   Using magazine and newspaper stories and advertising, identify the types of messages concerning infant feeding that Americans receive through these mass media sources. What kind of practices are being promoted? What practices are being discouraged?

3.   Conduct a survey among students and in an older sample to find out whether there are any age-related differences in beliefs about how to feed infants and young children.

SUGGESTIONS FOR FURTHER READINGS

Dettwyler, K. A. (1994). *Dancing skeletons: Life and death in West Africa.* Prospect Heights, Ill.: Waveland Press. (A personal account of Dettwyler's research in Mali on infant nutrition.)

Nerlove, S. (1974). Women's workload and infant feeding practices: A relationship with demographic implications. *Ethnology, 13,* 207–214. (Excellent overview of the interrelationship between work and infant feeding.)

Stuart-Macadam, P., & Dettwyler, K. (Eds.). (1995). *Breastfeeding: Biocultural perspectives.* Chicago: Aldine. (A wide-ranging set of articles on the evolution of infant feeding and current health, nutrition, and social issues.)

Van Estrick, P. (1989). *Beyond the breast and bottle controversy.* New Brunswick, N.J.: Rutgers University Press. (An anthropological perspective on issues underlying the promotion of bottle-feeding in the developing world.)

35

Perspectives on Infant Feeding: Decision-Making and Ecology

Gretel H. Pelto

INTRODUCTION

Near the end of the eighteenth century the conical glass infant feeding bottle was developed, fitted with a "tubular mouthpiece enclosed in an overlapping finger of linen, parchment or wash-leather" (1). This new low-cost device replaced earlier feeding devices such as perforated cow horns and various forms of pap spoons. Thus, concurrent with the beginning of the Industrial Revolution, technological developments for the first time made possible a widespread shift away from breast-feeding of human infants. Before the advent of this technological breakthrough, those women who wished to avoid some of the responsibilities of breast-feeding had resorted to the use of wet nurses—a practice that is of considerable antiquity in the western world.

Bottle-feeding did not, however, spread rapidly in the early nineteenth century, in part because both medical and lay opinion was against the practice. As the London obstetrician Underwood wrote in his *Treatise on the Diseases of Children,* "Every child should be suckled, and always by its own mother, where her health can safely admit of it." To this opinion, an editorial footnote was added:

> I am convinced that the attempt to bring up children by hand proves fatal, *in London,* to at least seven out of eight. . . . *In the country,* the mortality among dry nursed children is not so great as in London, but it is abundantly greater than is generally imagined. [Quoted in ref. 1, p. 1141.]

These medical observations at the dawning of the "bottle-feeding era" set forth some of the outlines of the controversy that has become one of the most celebrated issues in contemporary nutrition. Despite the attention and debate—involving scientists as well as political, social, and commercial interests—our knowledge about the dynamic forces shaping current practices lacks coherence, and many critical questions remain unanswered.

An examination of the sizeable body of empirical studies on the social correlates of infant-feeding practices reveals that many investigations have proceeded without a systematic theoretical framework to guide the research.

Variables often appear to be selected on an ad hoc basis, without regard to the underlying dimensions they represent. Many potentially important factors have not been studied. For those that have, methodological problems in conceptualizing and operationalizing variables reduces the usefulness of the research.

The clouded state of data on infant-feeding practices has been discussed by Butz in a paper in which he offers a "conceptual model of breast-feeding behavior," based on economic concepts of supply and demand. After setting out a series of hypotheses (to be discussed below) he notes:

> It is a remarkable fact that not one of the above predictions has received testing adequate for making even a preliminary judgement as to support or refutation. Most of the predictions have not been tested at all. We are unfortunately in the position of looking around for empirical generalizations that *seem* consistent or inconsistent with particular predictions. [2, p. 247]

In a similar fashion, Dugdale and Doessel have commented that "this inability to quantitate factors because of lack of data has allowed the current controversy on infant feeding to develop by emphasizing one or another factor while ignoring the remainder and has prevented a rational solution" (3, p. 1). Furthermore, a significant component of the literature consists of programmatic statements, opinions, and pronouncements that lack empirical documentation.

At present, a number of comprehensive research programmes on infant feeding are in various stages of planning and execution. The purpose of this [article] is to contribute to the effort to understand infant-feeding behaviour by setting what is currently known about patterns of infant feeding in a framework of bio-cultural and socio-cultural theory.

INFANT-FEEDING PRACTICES IN TRADITIONAL, NON-WESTERN SOCIETIES

As members of the class Mammalia, infants of *Homo sapiens* have been sustained on their mother's milk throughout the history of our species. Prior to the recent development of artificial feeding, almost all traditional societies encouraged long-term breast-feeding, as is documented by Whiting and Child in a cross-cultural study of 75 societies undertaken nearly 30 years ago. The researchers reported:

> There are 52 societies for which we have our judges' estimates of the age at which serious efforts at weaning are typically begun. For the median case, weaning is reported to begin at the age of two and a half years. Approximately this age is indeed typical of primitive societies in general, for the estimate for 33 out of the 52 societies falls between the ages of two years and three years.
>
> At the upper extreme there are only two societies for which the usual age at weaning appears to be greater than three and a half years. . . . At the lower extreme there are only two primitive societies in our sample who attempt to wean their children before they are a year old. [4, pp. 70, 71]

Of interest here is not only the information about long breast-feeding but also the fact of *variability* from one society to another. Whiting and Child report differences in the intensity of breast-feeding—the degree of "oral indulgence" of the infant—and in maternal attitudes toward breast-feeding, as well as in duration of breast-feeding. According to their research, differences in infant-feeding practices are systematically related to other features of child training, as well as to differences in religious ideology and belief systems. In later research Whiting and colleagues demonstrated that cultural differences in infant and child feeding were also related to other social and cultural characteristics of those societies (5).

The duration of breast-feeding represents one aspect of infant feeding that varies from one non-western society to another. The timing of the introduction of supplemental foods and the degree of reliance on foods other than human milk also vary in systematic ways, as demonstrated by Nerlove. In a cross-cultural study that reviewed ethnographic reports on 83 societies, Nerlove found strong support for her hypothesis that societies in which women are involved to a greater degree in subsistence activities are statistically more likely to have patterns of early supplemental feeding (before one month of age) than societies where women play less important roles in food production. She reports that, while "the primary responsibility for child care is nowhere in the world left to men," there are "societies in which women do make a substantial contribution to subsistence food production activities" (6, p. 207). In such societies infant-feeding practices are apparently adjusted to fit with other demands on the lactating woman through early introduction of supplemental foods.

Anthropologists commonly classify societies on the basis of subsistence (economic/ecological) systems. These broad classifications distinguish between:

a. hunting/gathering systems, in which crops are not grown and domestic animals are not used for food;

b. intermediate cultivators, gardening societies such as those in Central Africa, the Amazon rainforest, and other tropical areas;

c. pastoralist herders, including East African cattle herders and Lapland reindeer herders;

d. complex agriculturalists, e.g., the rice cultivators of South and South-East Asia, the great civilizations of the New World and preindustrial Europe.

There is evidence that child-training practices tend to be different in different types of subsistence systems (7), and, by extension, we can expect that infant-feeding practices are also patterned in relation to subsistence type, although this has been less systematically documented. Beyond the broad outlines of social organization associated with different types of subsistence systems, cross-cultural studies—such as those by Whiting and Child and Nerlove (4, 6)—as well as ethnographic studies of child-rearing practices (5, 8, 9) provide ample evidence that in non-western, traditional societies, where human milk is the primary source of nutrients for infants, there are distinct variations in infant-feeding practices that are relatable to social and environmental conditions. One non-western culture, that of the Marquesans, sounds surprisingly like some industrial societies, for the Marquesans

> believe that nursing makes a child hard to raise and not properly submissive. There was probably a certain amount of nursing, dependent upon the will of the mother, but in any event the nursing period was very short. Women took great pride in the firmness and beautiful shape of their breasts, which were important in sexual play. They believed that prolonged nursing spoiled the breasts. [4, pp. 59–70]

At the other extreme in infant feeding are the ethnographic reports on the Chenchu people of India, who supposedly nurse children until five or six years of age (ibid., p. 71).

INFANT FEEDING IN THE WESTERN WORLD

Western societies in earlier centuries depended on mother's milk to feed infants, just as all other cultures have. However, both the employment of wet nurses and the use of bottles have a long history in western culture and appear to have been well-developed practices in ancient Greece and Rome not limited to situations of maternal lactation failure (1, 10–13). In some respects, the controversies about artificial feeding are centuries old.

The eleventh-century physician Avicenna presented in his *Canon of Medicine* a medical opinion concerning the advantages of women nursing their own babies:

> Whenever possible, the mother's milk should be given and by suckling. For that is the aliment of all others most like in substance to the nutrient material which the infant received while in the womb. [Quoted in ref. 1, p. 1141.]

It is implied in this statement that alternatives to mother's milk and suckling were options for some segments of the population. Avicenna goes on to outline the desirable characteristics of a wet nurse. He recommends that the woman be of medium build, between 25 and 35 years of age, "strong-necked and broad-chested, the breasts firm, the nipples well-formed but not too large. Her character and personal habits must be good, her nature equable and slowly aroused by the bad passions of the mind" (ibid.). Moreover, the wet nurse should not engage in sexual intercourse because it would have a bad effect on the milk, he felt.

Michelangelo was wet-nursed by a stone-cutter's wife—a circumstance he regarded as having affected his career: "With my mother's milk I sucked in the hammer and chisels I use for my statues" (12, p. 284).

There is a tragic and sympathetic document recording a mother's plaintive directive to future generations, after she herself had relied (unsuccessfully) on wet nurses:

> Be not so unnatural as to thrust away your own children; be not so hardy as to venture accessory to that disorder of causing a poorer woman to banish her own infant for the entertaining of a richer woman's child, as it were, bidding her to unlove her own to love yours. [Quoted in ref. 12, from the original pamphlet of Elizabeth Clinton, Dowager Countess of Lincoln, 1662.]

In the seventeenth and eighteenth centuries, employment of a wet nurse was a standard practice in the upper classes of Europe and England (10), a feature of child training that was taken up in North American society as well. As late as the middle of the nineteenth century, well-to-do American women employed wet nurses. In a social history of a nineteenth-century Pennsylvania mill town, Wallace reports that some of the educated, élite women "employed wet-nurses for

their infants at birth, or shortly after, thus freeing themselves to move about, to work and to travel. This practice entailed the occasional inconvenience of losing some of the intimacies of motherhood; but the mothers took a practical view of the matter" (14, p. 24). Styles of infant care carried through to management of older children:

> Nor were children . . . allowed to disrupt their mothers' lives at older ages. . . . Boarding school at ten or eleven ended the child's residential connection for several years during the teens, except for summer vacations. . . . It was a no-nonsense system, which functioned (and no doubt was designed) to protect the mother's role as hostess and household administrator and increasingly, her continued intellectual development and participation in evangelical and reform activities in the community. [Ibid.]

INFANT FEEDING IN THE TWENTIETH CENTURY

All cultures include provision for the feeding of babies who are orphaned or whose mothers experience lactation failure. In many cultures, especially those of the western tradition, there has been a minority of élite women who have delegated child-care responsibilities (including infant feeding) to others. Until the twentieth century, however, mother's milk was the major source of nutrition for the great majority of human infants. By the middle of the twentieth century this was no longer true. Large segments of the world's population of infants now receive their food in a bottle containing something other than human milk.

The trend toward bottle-feeding began in the industrialized, western world. Sweetened, condensed milk was commercially produced in the United States in the late 1850s, followed 30 years later by canned, evaporated milk; infant formulas became available in 1916 (15). Utilization of these new products developed rapidly. By the end of the Second World War only one mother in four in the northeastern United States left the hospital breast-feeding (16). Nationally, about 60 per cent of babies were bottle-fed at the time of discharge from the hospital. The percentage of women who chose bottle-feeding continued to increase rapidly throughout the 1950s, levelling off at more than 80 per cent. Trends in the industrialized countries of Europe were similar to those in the United States, although the percentage of breast-feeding remained somewhat higher (17).

Recently, there has been some reversal of the trends toward bottle-feeding (17). By 1975, 30 per cent of US infants were breast-fed to some extent, and "by

1974 about one-half of babies born to women with some college education were breast fed" (18, p. 3). Other industrialized countries, especially in northern Europe, appear to be experiencing a similar tendency toward increased breast-feeding. As in the United States, the selection of breast-feeding in Europe is generally associated with higher socio-economic status and higher education (19).

In developing countries it has been more difficult to obtain statistics on infant-feeding practices. There have been a number of studies of specific subgroups in various countries, but data on a national level have not generally been available. Studies reveal great variability of practices, both within and between countries. For example, in Ghana 88 per cent of infants in the northern part of the country were fully breast-fed at six months of age, but in the south the corresponding figure was only 54 per cent (20). Considerable use of bottles is reported in some urban communities (for example, in Costa Rica and Chile), especially among upper income groups (ibid). The multinational collaborative study undertaken by WHO confirms the impression conveyed by earlier reports:

> Marked urban/rural differences in patterns of breast-feeding . . . emerge in the majority of countries studied; mothers in urban areas seem less likely to breastfeed than rural mothers, or to breastfeed for as long as rural mothers. . . . In the Philippines, where the lowest prevalence of breastfeeding was documented, 33% of urban well-to-do mothers who were interviewed had not breastfed the youngest child; similarly 15% of all urban poor mothers interviewed had not breastfed the youngest child. In Guatemala, the corresponding percentages were 23% among the urban well-to-do and 9% among urban poor mothers. [Ibid., p. 21]

Interpretation of the statistics on modes of infant feeding is complicated by several methodological problems (17). First, there are the typical problems that characterize public health statistics, especially in countries that do not have adequate resources for statistical data gathering. Secondly, there are problems in the definitions of modes of infant feeding. Many studies report results simply as "breast-fed" and "bottle-fed." A further refinement includes the category "mixed feeding." The reality behind these labels, however, is a behavioural complex which exhibits great intra-group variability (21). The meaning of "mixed feeding" or even an affirmative response to the question, "Are you breast-feeding this infant?" is very broad, covering a wide range of behaviour.

The lack of specificity in the labels presents a problem for the investigator who wants to accurately describe the distribution of infant-feeding modes. It also creates a problem for interpreting the social dynamics that lie behind the statistics. In broad outline it is clear that large numbers of babies in the western world are bottle-fed and that a significant number of babies in developing countries are also bottle-fed, at least to some degree. Our concern here is not with the consequences of a particular mode of infant feeding but with understanding why and how selections of modes of feeding occur.

EXPLANATIONS FOR CHANGING INFANT-FEEDING PRACTICES

As the controversy over bottle-feeding has expanded, the changing patterns have become a social and political issue as well as a scientific concern. In reviewing suggested explanations of the phenomena, it may be useful to distinguish between positions that are essentially "social philosophies" and those that contain a more-or-less articulated theory of social and/or biological processes. In the first category, we can identify at least three orientations: the "women's rights/feminist" position, the "anti-commercial" position, and the "biological determinist" position.

Women's Rights/Feminist Orientation

Interestingly, the contemporary social philosophy associated with the women's rights movement has been used to argue both for and against bottle-feeding. On the one hand, artificial feeding can be regarded as a boon to women, giving them the opportunity to engage freely in other activities without being tied to a schedule of infant feeding. The trend toward bottle-feeding can, therefore, be interpreted as a reflection of women's increasing expression of their right to control their own time and activities.

On the other hand, members of the women's movement have argued strongly for a woman's rights to fulfil her biological function as a nurturer of her infant without penalty (e.g., loss of job, pay) and without interference or coercion. From this perspective, the increase in bottle-feeding can be regarded in a negative light—a reflection of increased male dominance over women, caused, in part, by the increasing dominance of male physicians over female reproductive activities.

Anti-Commercial Orientation

The significance of promotional activities by the corporations that manufacture infant formulas has been approached in several ways. On the one hand, questions about the role of advertising and promotion are being framed as testable hypotheses for which research data can be collected. Also, documentation of the nature and extent of these activities is being undertaken as a descriptive research task (Marchione, personal communication). On the other hand, the adoption of bottle-feeding by women in the third world is being incorporated into anti-capitalist philosophy as an example of contemporary world-wide economic processes. Often this philosophical position has been presented with little concern for establishing clear causal links between the commercial advertising and the supposed dependent variable—bottle-feeding behaviour. Discussion of the contradiction between feminist positions (which generally include an assumption that women are intelligent and make rational choices) and the anti-commercial rhetoric (which portrays women as gullible victims of multinational promotion efforts) is surprisingly absent from the literature (22).

Biological Determinist Position

In much of the popular writing concerning women's roles there has continued to be an underlying biological determinism, focused on concepts of women's "natural" biological qualities in relation to child care. From that perspective any deviations from long-established patterns of infant feeding are generally thought of as "deviance" or "warping" of women's personalities and essential nature. As a writer in the sixteenth century put the matter, "Wherefore it is agreeing to nature so it is also necessary and comely for the own mother to nurse the own child . . . it shall be commendable and wholesome" (23).

In a recent expression of the "biological determinist" position, anthropologists Lionel Tiger and Robin Fox discuss breast-feeding in the context of "bonding," a concept that is central to their construction of human behaviour. They first suggest that "the reason behind the invariability of the mother-child bond in mammals—as compared with the extreme variability of the male-female bond—is very simple: suckling" (24, p. 61). They go on to state:

> The human mother is a splendid mammal—the epitome of her order. Her physiology is more highly developed for suckling behavior—with permanent breasts, for example—than any of her cousins, except domesticated ungulates bred specially for milk-giving. But more than this, she is, like any other mammal, emotionally programmed to be responsive to the growing child. [Ibid., p. 65]

However, Tiger and Fox urge their readers to understand that the dependence of the infant "does not hinge wholly on food, but on emotional security, of which food is but a part."

The biological determinist orientation is subtly at work in the new advertising gambit of the formula manufacturers, reflected in such phrases as, "When mother's milk fails . . . ," or "The best substitute when mothers can't nurse." The implication is that women's biological capacity is weak, requiring the benign assistance of industrial progress. The explanation, then, for the recent trends toward bottle-feeding is founded on a biological determinist orientation, in this case couched as "biological failure."

These three social orientations have appeared in both the popular and the scientific literature, sometimes presented with great eloquence, sometimes in strident, polemical fashion. They contain ideas about causes of infant-feeding trends, some of which can be transformed into scientifically testable hypotheses. They are also important for study as social phenomena in their own right. As Gerlach has suggested (25, 26), it is important to understand the impact of these social philosophies on selection of infant-feeding modes and on the institutions (commercial, governmental, educational, and medical) to which they are addressed.

In contrast to the preceding orientations, which can be characterized as social philosophies, there are a number of approaches to an explanation of infant-feeding trends which are either directly theoretical (i.e., presentation of a causal model) or *imply* a theory in the selection of variables for empirical study. These approaches can be characterized as follows: modernization models, economic models, and bio-cultural models.

Modernization Models

This is probably the most widely evoked of all theories, some formulation of "modernization" being frequently used to explain trends in infant feeding. In the context of discussing "the dramatic decline in breast feeding" in the developing world, Berg expresses this position in the following words:

> Encroaching urbanization and modernization and new social values are significant influences. Breast feeding is often viewed as an old-fashioned or backward custom and, by some, as a vulgar peasant practice. Indeed, anthropologists, struck by the relationship of artificial feeding to societal change, have used the duration of nursing as an inverse measure of acculturation for some countries. In most developing countries, the greater the sophistication, the worse the lactation: the bottle has become a status symbol. [27, p. 99]

The influence of mass media, improvements in transportation and communication, and exposure to new ideas from health care personnel can be regarded as additional aspects of "modernization." The language is sometimes different but the underlying theme is the same in discussions about the spread of bottle-feeding in industrialized countries. For example, the following statements by sociologists C. Hirschman and J. Sweet in their analysis of the 1965 National Fertility Survey reflect a "modernization" model:

> We know of no adequate theoretical perspective that can guide empirical research in this area. At most, the ideas from popular culture suggest that breast-feeding has declined as society moved from a traditional, rural-based, family-centered structure to the modern urban social milieu where traditional culture regarding child-birth and child-care was discarded. [28, p. 42]

The authors hypothesize that the resurgence of interest in traditional values may be associated with a renewed interest in breast-feeding:

> Similarly, we might expect that resurgence of popular interest in natural foods, natural childbirth, bicycling to work, etc., represent attempts to recapture less modern or mechanized ways of dealing with the basic tasks of life. Thus, there might be some basis to believe that breastfeeding may have been making a comeback in recent years. Although we will not be able to test these speculations directly, our data will allow us to examine trends in breastfeeding behavior until 1965. [Ibid.]

In this study, as in a number of others carried out in both western and developing countries, the researchers look for associations with such variables as education, income, place of residence, region of origin, and other "social background" characteristics. In a sense, these may all be regarded as aspects of modernization, for they capture those features of modern life that depart from the types of social systems in which breast-feeding was the only mode of infant feeding. In these studies, investigators generally find significant correlations between feeding mode and a variety of social background characteristics (29–32). Generally, these associations can be regarded as support for "modernization hypotheses." However, since they are basically descriptive, merely documenting associations of infant-feeding modes with characteristics of contemporary life, they provide little insight into the causal factors. As Hirschman and Sweet say at the end of their article:

> Although we think that this analysis has provided some conclusion on this subject where only speculation existed before, it has raised more questions than it answered. Why has the rate of breastfeeding been declining so rapidly over the past few decades? What is it about certain ethnic, religious and regional groups that causes differentials in breastfeeding behavior? Do the effects of educational attainment upon the rate of breastfeeding represent a true education "effect" or is it an indicator of some other socioeconomic factor that is correlated with education? Analysis of these and other questions will require further research.

Berg's comments quoted above (27, p. 99) and the preceding statement about "a true educational 'effect'" suggest that one of the major components of modernization is adherence to a set of beliefs or values which provide guidelines for behaviour. That is, one may logically conclude that a belief that breast-feeding is vulgar would lead a woman to select bottle-feeding and, similarly, that the belief that breast milk is best for babies should be associated with a decision to breast-feed.

These statements reflect a long-standing theoretical position in anthropology and other social sciences. The premise on which this position is based is that behaviour results from an individual's attitudes and values. The prime source of these attitudes is generally "the culture." Women's ideas about proper infant feeding are transmitted from one generation to the next through the process of enculturation. Thus rural, peasant women breast-feed their infants for a year or more because it is the custom. When new ideas are introduced, either through outside cultural influences or through migration to new cultural settings, behaviour changes as well.

As a theoretical perspective, the "ideational" or "cultural norms" frame of reference has come under increasing criticism (32–34). When analysis is presented in the form of descriptive associations, we are left unenlightened about the causal relationship. To date, researchers have made little effort to design studies that would untangle the difficult questions about the role of beliefs and attitudes in affecting behavioural choices.

There is a paucity of studies directly addressed to questions of the relationships between *attitudes* on infant feeding and actual behaviour. The available information is ambiguous. Several studies have documented a disparity between belief and practice and have shown that many women who believe that breast milk is better for babies nonetheless choose to bottle-feed (35–37). On the other hand, there are also strong statistical associations between positive attitudes about breast-feeding and the selection of this mode of infant feeding. The same holds for associations between the expression of negative attitudes about breast-feeding and the selection of bottle-feeding (35, 36). In order to increase our understanding about the role of beliefs and attitudes in the selection of infant-feeding modes, we will need further studies in which beliefs and attitudes are carefully measured prospectively and are followed by a recording of actual behaviour with respect to infant feeding.

Economic Models of Infant-Feeding Practices

To date, serious analytic efforts to understand the factors that influence infant feeding have been limited mainly to economic variables. As noted above, Butz has developed a sophisticated theoretical model to explain the demand for breast-feeding:

> In trying to explain and predict how a particular scarce resource is allocated among competing uses, economists generally find it helpful to investigate determinants of the supply of that resource and of the demand for it that arises out of each competing use . . . In this case the scarce resources . . . are a woman's time and her stock of nutrients. [2, p. 233]

After pointing out the variety of competing uses of a woman's time, Butz notes that "some values, like wages for market work, are relatively easily measured. Others, like the value of sleep or social activity are conceptually and empirically very difficult to evaluate."

After defining the main dimensions of the model, constructed to show the effects of alterations in the supply and demand curves, Butz describes a series of implications (hypotheses) derived from it. Several of the implications deal with the effect of changes in the market:

1. An increase in the market demand for female labor tends to reduce breast-feeding if the jobs are less than fully compatible with maternal child care.

2. An increase in the supply of female labor to the market . . . tends to reduce breast-feeding if many labor market jobs are less than fully compatible with breast-feeding.

3. An increase in the price of food staples consumed by adults tends to reduce breast-feeding in populations suffering mild to moderate or worse malnutrition.

4. An increase in the marginal value product schedule of a woman's time in home agriculture or cottage industry tends to reduce breast-feeding if these activities are less compatible with child care than alternative activities engaged in.

5. Factors that reduce the supply curve of a woman's breast-feeding . . . tend to reduce her actual breast-feeding more if alternative foods are available. . . . [Ibid.]

Butz goes on to consider a series of other factors that could have effects on his primary factors. These further items include the availability of modern contraceptives, infant-weaning foods, substitutes for the economic and non-economic benefits bestowed by children, and so on. His model therefore suggests a number of significant areas for further research.

Women's Employment and the Feeding of Infants

At the outset it is important to note that "employment" is often far from being a simple variable in its effect on women's lives and roles. We tend to think of people in our society as either employed or "unemployed" in relation to "jobs" that earn wages or salaries. In much of the world (including major sectors of North American society) the gradations of "jobs" and "employment" (in and outside the home) can be complex indeed.

One of the few studies that directly addressed the interrelations of women's employment and infant feeding is the work of Popkin and Solon (38). Their study is focused on the Philippines, where they note first of all that

> women are more actively involved in trade, service, professional, industrial and other work which draws her [sic] outside the home for employment. . . . Nevertheless market related activities which take place in the home such as embroidery, basket weaving and sari-sari store management play a major role in her economic activities. [38, p. 197]

In their sample of women on the island of Cebu, they found that "26% of the urban and 31% of the rural women were engaged in some form of market employment." They note that some studies in the Philippines report infants nursed 7 to 8 times per day, with each feeding lasting 15 minutes to half an hour. This schedule of nursing could require from 3 to 4 hours, in addition to which one should allow for "travel time" if the mother is working somewhere and returns to her infant for breast-feeding. In any case, the scheduling of breast-feeding requires a very considerable time investment from the mother.

Dugdale (39) examined data on breast-feeding patterns for 2,009 infants in Kuala Lumpur, Malaysia, for the years 1960, 1962, and 1965. The information included family income (divided into high and low), number of children in the family (presumably of that particular mother), and ethnicity (Chinese, Malay, Indian). The data are interesting because they are

Table 1. Percentage of mothers breast-feeding at 28 weeks in Kuala Lumpur (1965) according to income and ethnicity

Income	Ethnicity					
	Malay		**Chinese**		**Indian**	
High	(28)*	18%	(109)	28%	(19)	33%
Low	(41)	65%	(96)	39%	(42)	44%

*n in parentheses.

SOURCE: Dugdale (39).

roughly comparable to situations in many other developing nations, especially in Asia. Focusing on the data for families of two to four children (the modal category) in 1965, according to the different ethnicities, we find that the income variable is important in each of the ethnic groups, with the higher income (higher socio-economic status) women breast-feeding less often (and for shorter duration) than the lower status mothers (table 1). Dugdale feels that there are two possible reasons for the differentials based on income:

> The first is that the social and advertising pressures are all away from breastfeeding. The mother who has a higher income is probably more educated and is more able to afford artificial feeding. The second reason is that many families have a higher income *because both parents work* outside the home. Under these circumstances, breast-feeding is not possible. [39, p. 233]

Also, as the author comments, "the extended family and the availability of domestic help both make possible the care of infants while the mother works." Further, among the Malays the mothers with children go out to work much less than do the Chinese, hence an overall higher incidence of breast-feeding among the Malay mothers (in the three years surveyed).

A comparison of the data for 1960 with the 1965 data shows a consistent decrease in breast-feeding in the Chinese sample (n is 1020), and an increase in breast-feeding among the Malay women. The author does not comment on this difference in the trends but notes that the increase in breast-feeding is mainly among low income mothers with one child.

Marchione (40) has developed an economic model to explain infant-feeding patterns in the Caribbean. He emphasizes the relationship of women's work activities with the type of economy in which those activities take place as a significant factor in infant-feeding patterns. In a plantation economy—first under slavery, then as low-pay resident workers—women in the Caribbean have for centuries been under pressure to devote long hours to work and short hours to breast-feeding. Marchione's study suggests that, wherever we find the combination of a past or present plantation agricultural system and the presence of a variety of breast milk substitutes such as bush teas, starchy gruels, or paps, we can hypothesize on the existence of direct pressures on women to limit breast-feeding.

Another type of economic model also concentrates on structures outside the household, specifically on the economic motivations of the commercial interests that stand to gain from a large-scale shift to bottle-feeding—the infant food manufacturers, the advertising media, and, to a limited extent, health-care professionals. The research strategy that has been pursued to develop this model has focused primarily on describing the economic structures of the formula-manufacturing companies and the promotional strategies of corporation and advertising agencies (41, 42). There has been little linking of these structures and activities to maternal selection of feeding mode, perhaps largely because it presents serious methodological and ethical problems for investigators.

Bio-Cultural Models of Infant Feeding

Another approach to explaining infant-feeding patterns examines issues from a biological perspective, seeking to understand the extent to which problems with lactation, as a socially mediated biological process, may be involved in current trends. It is important to note that this approach is more limited in that it applies only to one segment of the women who make up the statistics—those who *attempt* breast-feeding but shift rapidly to bottle-feeding. In any examination of infant-feeding practices it is necessary to separate exclusive bottle-feeders from those women who begin breast-feeding, even if they only breast-feed for a few days. The decision to bottle-feed an infant—if the decision is made before the infant is born—is conceptually a different kind of decision from the decision to try breast-feeding. Bio-cultural explanations which seek to understand "lactation failure" or "premature weaning" apply, of course, only to those women who attempt breast-feeding.

While a biological failure of the capacity to initiate lactation is rare, post partum problems in lactation are not (43). It has been hypothesized that separation of infants from their mothers at birth, which has been a common practice in western medicine, affects lactation success. Klaus and Kennell (44) have studied the relationship of early separation to problems in mother-infant bonding, which, in turn, appears to be implicated in lactation problems. Newton and Newton (45) and others have suggested that separation, which delays the onset and frequency of breast-feeding in the immediate post partum period, may be related to breast over-engorgement and sucking problems for the infant that lead to a "vicious cycle," resulting in early termination of breast-feeding.

Raphael has also proposed a bio-cultural explanation of lactation failure, an explanation based on the "let down reflex" in the absence of supportive social networks for the newly delivered mother (46). The breakdown of social networks and social support is postulated as an urban phenomenon which, together with other stresses of urbanization and modernization, leads to psychophysiological stress inhibiting milk production (47, 48).

Recently Gussler and Briesemeister (43) have presented a bio-cultural explanation for what they refer to as the "insufficient milk syndrome." Their discussion begins with a review of a significant finding in many studies, namely, that the most common reason mothers give for premature weaning or early termination of breast-feeding is "insufficient milk." From many different cultural and social settings in both industrialized and developing countries, mothers report that their milk was insufficient or inadequate to satisfy their infant's needs:

> Anecdotal and research data suggest that, quite naturally, mothers become concerned about presumably unhappy or uncomfortable infants, and respond to their behavioral cues with an explanation of breast milk insufficiency, even though the explanation is not confirmed by poor weight gain.
>
> These mothers are both right and wrong. They are probably correct in interpreting the behavior of their fussy infants as caused by hunger. They are incorrect that this necessarily indicates that something is inherently "wrong" with their milk or ability to lactate. [43, p. 6]

From this base the authors develop their theory. The primary source of the problem is what they call "non-biologic breast-feeding," the pattern of "scheduled, widely spaced feedings of breast milk." Scheduled, infrequent feeding leads, in turn, to a crying baby, to sucking difficulties, to maternal anxiety, to insufficient sucking and emptying of the breast, and hence through several neural and cognitive pathways to the interpretation of "insufficient milk." In many cases the interpretation becomes a biological self-fulfilling prophecy. The authors conclude their paper with a call for research on this important aspect of contemporary breast-feeding experiences.

Each of these approaches—socio-cultural (modernization), economic, and psycho-physiological—has much to offer to our understanding of contemporary infant-feeding practices. Of course, the significance of

particular factors will vary in different contexts. To date, none of the theoretical approaches have been fully explored through systematic research, nor have efforts been made to integrate them. While the bio-cultural approach of Gussler and Briesemeister does present a theory that integrates social behaviour (frequency of feeding) with biological variables, it does not provide a full framework since it is focused specifically on milk insufficiency. The development of a full framework is probably best achieved through successive approximations based on feedback from empirical research. The remainder of this [article] is devoted to outlining some of the features of a "first approximation," noting several key components of what can be regarded as a "cultural-ecology" approach.

THE CULTURAL-ECOLOGY FRAME OF REFERENCE

An ecological perspective directs attention to the specific features of the physical and social environments within which behaviour takes place. The question of how individuals and groups meet essential needs (for food, shelter, and so on) remains a central concern. Although people are seen as acting within a system of environmental constraints and opportunities (and having available resources and technologies), they are considered to be making conscious choices about behaviour. The ecological approach thus emphasizes people's rational decision-making behaviour and calls attention to intra-community, intra-population variations in the specific choices, as related to situational (environmental) differences (34).

Anthropologist John Bennett has described the theoretical perspective of cultural ecology clearly:

> A second meaning of the term ecology emphasizes adaptation or *adaptive behavior*. Here we refer to coping mechanisms or ways of dealing with people and resources in order to attain goals and solve problems. Our emphasis here is not on relationships between institutions, groups or aggregates of data, but on patterns of behavior: problem-solving, decision-making, consuming or not consuming, inventing, innovating, migrating, staying. [49, p. 11]

In the nutrition and public health field, the issue of infant feeding is often approached from a narrow viewpoint in which the infant is seen as a passive receiver of food and the mother as the giver of food. Problems arise when the mother fails to fulfil adequately her role as food-giver. However, the woman's behaviour with respect to feeding her infant is rarely examined in the total context of her life. While a new infant may seem to be a major focus of a mother's energy and attention, the fact is that a new mother can be said to have acquired an additional role—that of mother of her new-born—but she does not necessarily lose her other roles. In most circumstances she may continue to have the responsibilities of being a wife, a daughter-in-law, a mother to her other children, a farmer, a housekeeper, a lawyer, and so on.

While the extension of biologically oriented theory places primary emphasis on women's roles as child-bearers and child-rearers, an ecological approach would tend to focus on women's responsibilities in the economic subsistence system, as well as in maternal tasks. The contrast between the two approaches is evidenced in this statement from the study by Nerlove:

> In her discussion of the division of labor by sex, Brown (1970) stated that the degree to which women participate in subsistence activities depends upon the compatibility of the latter with simultaneous child care responsibilities. The present study qualified this statement by showing that child care responsibilities may be adjusted to accommodate the mother's subsistence activities. [6, p. 212]

The ecological framework is not one of economic determinism, but a search for all the relevant factors (economic and others) affecting women's roles. Aside from direct food production practices and ways of making a living, many other factors must be taken into account in an ecological perspective, including such features as shelter, modes of travel, and environmental characteristics. Political organization and religious beliefs and other ideological components are also examined. Perhaps the major feature of the cultural-ecology approach is the attention to a multiplicity of factors affecting every aspect of human behaviour.

ECOLOGICAL THEORY AND WOMEN'S ROLES

The growing body of literature on women's situations in various cultures and diverse environmental contexts is beginning to provide a base for generalizations about women's roles. These studies point to some of the major variables and parameters that are necessary for a well-developed model of women's roles in the care and feeding of offspring. It would appear that throughout history women have played a very significant and primary role in child care, not least because of the nature of their biological relationship with their offspring. It is also clear that in many societies women have major responsibilities for food production and

that, in these societies, their child-care roles are adjusted to these responsibilities.

The introduction of new crops into traditional societies can have various and diverse effects on women's roles. The economic position of Afikpo Ibo women of Nigeria is an interesting illustration. According to LeVine, when the new crop cassava was introduced in the region, it was considered to be of very low prestige and value. Women were allowed (by the men) to grow the cassava as a marginal activity:

> This despised crop eliminated the annual famine before the yam harvest and attained a high and stable market value. The Afikpo women became capable of supporting themselves and their children without aid from their husbands. . . . Afikpo husbands have found it increasingly difficult to keep their wives at home in their formerly subordinate position. [50, p. 178]

A different sort of example is provided by the Azande people in East Africa. Until recent times the Azande engaged in frequent warfare, and women were the main source of labour and symbols of wealth. Traditionally, women were "treated much like slaves and . . . barred from the main source of power." Increasing contacts with Europeans and the introduction of cash crops brought large-scale changes. "Women became emancipated, crops acquired cash value, war disappeared, hunting was reduced, and men were compelled to invest most of their efforts in agriculture" (51, p. 201). In contrast to the Afikpo situation, the Azande men placed high value on the major cash crops and controlled the access of women to this new sphere of activity. Although the women gained a new measure of freedom, they did not become anything like as economically powerful as the Afikpo women.

The growing number of studies of women's roles in different types of societies have underscored two major themes:

a. Women's overall status and prestige and the degree they contribute to the basic economic system exhibit a very wide range of variations in non-modern societies.

b. Degrees of participation in food production and other economic activities have strong effects on the patterning of child-care activities.

Some of the other variables that have important effects on women's roles include the patterning and degree of warfare (52), kinship structure and household composition (53), and religious system (54). This is hardly an exhaustive list of the variables that may be important in affecting women's roles and infant-feeding practices, but it provides a starting point for an examination of individual cases and contexts.

THE SHAPING OF WOMEN'S ROLES

From an ecological perspective, women's roles in a social system can be seen as composed of a number of crucial dimensions that can take on a range of values. Following role theory we can conceptualize that an individual has a *cluster* of roles. Many of the roles an individual assumes are of long standing and taken to be stable over the generations. For example, the central roles of wife and mother are thought of as relatively unchanging in basic content from one generation to the next. Also, in a stable society the supposed rules of behaviour are sufficiently well established and pragmatic that regular expectations about conduct in the role of "wife" do not seriously conflict with the requirements of the role set to "mother." On the other hand, everyone is familiar with examples in which different aspects of role expectations come into sharp conflict. In such situations individuals have had to make agonizing choices: "Shall I give up my family ties to marry this man?" "Shall I protect my husband from this unwarranted demand by our son?"

The factors that shape the multiple-role behaviour of any given women in any particular society are variable and specific to the situation. At the same time, it can be argued that these factors have regular, patterned effects, so that generalizations can be made about the nature of role behaviour:

1.   Although people do not always act in their own best interests, in general individuals weigh alternatives and make choices based on their perceptions of the relative merits and shortcomings of particular actions. All persons seek to be optimizers in their daily behaviour.

2.   "Micro-differences" in characteristics such as household composition, distance from resources, material wealth, etc., create differential behaviour within even the smallest and most traditional populations.

3.   Therefore women within practically all communities will exhibit a range of variation in their tendencies toward particular types of role behaviour, including breast-feeding. Intra-community variation is a pervasive fact of life.

4.   Individual choice behaviour is, of course, always constrained by knowledge of what other persons—kin and non-kin—expect as appropriate, right conduct.

5.   For most categories of behaviour and activities there are alternatives that people can choose. Life is not a rigid prescription.

6.   Recent decades have brought new dimensions of choice in practically all parts of the world. People have many more options to consider, even though poverty and lack of technical skills may in practice limit their selections from the theoretically available alternatives.

7.   Although new options and alternatives have spread rapidly in recent decades, change and development occurred in most societies and communities in past centuries as well. Most people are used to the prospect of change.

INFANT FEEDING AND DECISION-MAKING

The statistics on trends in both breast-feeding and bottle-feeding can be regarded as a reflection of multiple decisions by numerous women and their families. The concept of decision implies, of course, a choice among alternatives. With the advent of large-scale availability of bottles, it is apparent that many women *perceive* themselves as having an alternative. Seen against the whole of human history the decision to use a bottle *appears* to represent the exercise of choice, comparable to the choice involved in using contraceptives to regulate fertility.

However, just as with the use or non-use of contraceptives, we must be careful not to assume that choices are made in a vacuum, without constraints. It is apparent from the available literature that many factors influence and constrain a woman's decision to breast-feed or bottle-feed her infant. Among the factors that influence this decision are the views of significant other persons, particularly spouses, as the following illustrations make clear.

In an Egyptian village, anthropologist Soheir El Sukkary interviewed women concerning their views and decisions about infant feeding. One woman, the mother of seven, told her,

> In our village all women have to breast-feed. I told my husband that I was tired of breast-feeding after seven children and I want to use cow's milk. You know what he said? He told me even if I break my neck I still have to breast-feed. We are no city girls. [El Sukkary, personal communication]

Contrast the constraints on this woman with those on a young Puerto Rican woman interviewed in Miami by anthropologist Carol Bryant:

The doctor said to breast-feed them, especially the boy. But I can't explain it, maybe it has a lot to do with my husband. He's sort of shy about that, too . . . You know, I think he's jealous. When I told him I wanted to breast-feed, he said, "You're going to breast-feed? Well, I don't know about that." And stuff like that. But if I had to do it again, I'd try it. [37]

In another cultural context, it is the in-laws who effectively control the decision-making concerning infant feeding. Johnston (55) has reported about the situation in West Indian households in Trinidad, where the low-status young wife is subordinate to her mother-in-law in an extended family household. According to Johnston, the young mother is expected to "entrust the daytime care and feeding of the infant to her in-laws and devote her attention to chores for the benefit of the whole family." The grandparents therefore give bottles, filled with a variety of substances from skim milk powder to sugar water and tea, while the mother works at other types of activities for the household. This Trinidad study is perhaps the clearest example yet reported of bottle-feeding motivated by the work demands of a woman's extended household. The bottle-feeding regimen does not, however, eliminate breast-feeding. Moreover, Johnston reports that the ratio of breast-feeders to bottle-feeders has not changed substantially during the past decade.

In this Trinidad example, the significance of in-laws in the infant-feeding process lies in the fact that they are in the *same economically integrated household*. Clearly the variable of household size and structure may in this case be more significant than simply the "cultural attitudes" of in-laws per se. There are a few other cases, however, in which the in-laws appear to have some influence. In a small-scale study in New England, for example, the opinions of the subjects' in-laws appeared to be the only major anti-breastfeeding influence.

MEDICAL ADVICE

The doctor Avicenna's advice against any substitutions for natural (mother's) breast-feeding (1) reminds us that health professionals may be among the most important sources of influence on women's infant-feeding practices. Jelliffe and Jelliffe (48, 56), Cole (57), and others have noted the significance of health professionals in affecting infant feeding. Halpern et al., for example, reported that among 1,700 infants in Dallas, Texas, there was a strong correlation between breast-feeding and the paediatrician's attitudes (58). In developing countries, the role of western medical care may significantly influence women to adopt

bottle-feeding (42), and lack of encouragement and assistance from medical and nursing staff has been identified as a factor in lactation failure among Asians recently migrated to Great Britain (59).

MULTIPLE SOURCES OF ADVICE

Many of the studies of infant feeding in both industrialized and developing societies have provided information on the effects of social ties, significant others, opinions of relatives, and other influences on women's decision-making. While these are undoubtedly important factors, they appear to assume significance mainly in relation to other variables.

In practically all situations where the opinions of significant others—kin and non-kin—appear to be important, there is likely to be a considerable mixture of sources of information and opinion. Karkal reports that in a survey conducted in Bombay the following were identified as sources of advice regarding supplemental foods: tradition, 11 per cent; elders, 19.2 per cent; self, 17.1 per cent; doctor or nurse, 13 per cent; radio or reading, 4.7 per cent; and "cannot say," 34 per cent (60). An effective explanatory model must make sense of this mixture.

BIOLOGICAL INFLUENCES

In the earlier discussion on bio-cultural approaches, the role of birth practices, feeding schedule, and the absence of a supporting social network were mentioned as factors that affect infant-feeding practices. Additional features of maternal health and pregnancy experience, fatigue, maternal intake of fluids and calories, and other dietary variables must also be carefully considered. In pursuing a cultural-ecology approach, the problem will be to identify the ways in which biological variables enter into the complex calculus of decision-making of individuals.

CONCLUSION

The main features of a cultural-ecology framework as a guide to research and application of research for programme planning and development in infant feeding include the following:

1.   The aggregate pattern of infant-feeding modes for any particular population or identifiable social groups is a composite result of a series of individual decisions.

2.   To understand these decisions, attention must be focused both on the individual decision-makers (mothers and their households) and on the characteristics of the environment in which the decisions are made.

3.   In choosing among alternative strategies for feeding their infants, mothers may be influenced by a series of factors: economic conditions; health characteristics and concerns (their own and their baby's); requirements and desires related to allocation of their own time; the presence of alternative caretakers; beliefs and values related to the social acceptability of the choices; and advice from other people and media sources.

4.   Selection from theoretically available alternatives is strongly conditioned by external (environmental) and internal (individual) constraints. Thus, such features as the availability of work, characteristics of the economic system, characteristics of the health care system, family and community structure, and organization may all exert powerful constraining influences on an individual mother's decisions about how to feed her infant.

5.   Decisions on infant feeding, as with most other activities, are not made simply at a single point in time but should more properly be regarded as a process, in which the key actors (mothers, infants, families, and other significant participants) monitor and adjust their behaviour over time.

These points suggest that the reasons for particular patterns of feeding will differ from one social setting to another over time. It is fallacious to conclude that a common pattern is necessarily the result of common causes. The utilization of a cultural-ecology approach does not imply a simple eclecticism in which "all variables are equal." As conditions change, the "power" or significance of particular factors in the decision-making process may change.

Following a cultural-ecology framework, the next steps to improving our understanding of contemporary infant-feeding patterns is to develop research that is holistic and multidisciplinary. Attention must be directed to include mother-infant pairs, the households in which they reside, the communities and environments in which the households exist, and the larger socio-political, cultural, and economic systems from which the new choices (e.g., bottles and formulas) and new constraints (e.g., wage employment) are ultimately derived.

There is no evidence, at present, that justifies eliminating any of the major domains of causal influence from investigation. The extent to which economic fac-tors, household characteristics, the individual's beliefs, goals, desires, and values, and psycho-biological characteristics affect decisions about infant feeding is amenable to empirical investigation. Since the relative importance of these characteristics is likely to be different in different environments, future research must be cross-cultural and must be carried out in different regions and cultural conditions. This does not mean that research on infant feeding has to be undertaken in every community on the face of the earth before we can have a better understanding of the contemporary situation. But it does mean that we must be careful not to assume that the picture is the same in all urban centers of the industrialized world or that we can easily extrapolate findings from a rural Asian community to a plantation in Guatemala.

Direct interventions by policy-makers can bring about dramatic changes in the environment, changes which presumably will have powerful effects on individuals' decisions. It would seem logical to conclude, for example, that banning bottles from the market-place would create an environmental constraint of overwhelming proportions. However, alternative routes to utilization of artificial feeding may develop readily if the other factors that are influencing mothers to select bottle-feeding remain unchanged. We return to the basic premise: decision-making about infant care (including infant feeding) is a rational process in which the outcome reflects the "best choice" or the "best compromise" among competing demands, conditions, and values. When the "best choice" conflicts with "best" psycho-physiological and health outcomes (as judged from a bio-medical perspective), health care professionals and other people are appropriately distressed. The problems, however, cannot begin to be resolved unless infant-feeding patterns are examined in the complex context in which they occur. Thus, research that is sensitive to differences in micro-ecological variations (for example, in the WHO research and action projects) is essential for progress in our understanding of these issues (61). A cultural-ecology approach contains the guidelines for beginning that process.

REFERENCES

1. B. M. Duncum, "Some Notes on the History of Lactation," *Brit. Med. Bull.,* 5:1141 (1947).

2. W. Butz, "Economic Aspects of Breast Feeding," in W. H. Mosley, ed., *Nutrition and Human Reproduction* (Plenum, New York, 1977).

3. A. E. Dugdale and D. P. Doessel, "Family Well-being and Infant Feeding (unpublished paper, Department of Child Health, University of Queensland, Brisbane, Australia, n.d.).

4. J. W. M. Whiting and I. L. Child, *Child Training and Personality: A Cross Cultural Study*, (Yale University Press, New Haven and London, 1953).

5. L. McInturn and W. W. Lambert, *Mothers of Six Cultures: Antecedents of Child Rearing* (John Wiley and Sons, New York, 1964).

6. S. B. Nerlove, "Women's Workload and Infant Feeding Practices: A Relationship with Demographic Implications," *Ethnology*, 13:125–214 (1974).

7. H. Barry, I. L. Child, and M. K. Bacon, "Relation of Child Training to Subsistence Economy," *American Anthropology*, 61:51–63 (1959).

8. R. LeVine and B. B. LeVine, *Nyansongo: A Gusii Community in Kenya* (John Wiley and Sons, New York, 1966).

9. B. B. Whiting, ed., *Six Cultures: Studies of Child Rearing* (John Wiley and Co., New York, 1963).

10. I. G. Wickes, "A History of Infant Feeding," *Arch. Dis. Childhood*, 28:151–158, 232–240, 495–502 (1953).

11. P. Aries, *Centuries of Childhood: A Social History of Family Life* (Random House, Vintage Books, New York, 1962).

12. J. Prince, "Infant Feeding through the Ages," *Midwives Chronicle and Nursing Notes*, Dec. 1976, pp. 283–285.

13. A. L. Wood, "The History of Artificial Feeding of Infants," *Journal Amer. Dietet. Assoc.*, 31:474–482 (1955).

14. A. F. C. Wallace, *Rockdale: The Growth of an American Village in the Early Industrial Revolution* (Alfred A. Knopf, New York, 1972).

15. D. A. Sehring, "Infant Feeding Trends in an Industrialized Culture," *Mod. Prob. Paediat.*, 15 (1975): 231–237.

16. H. Meyer, "Breastfeeding in the United States," *Clin. Pediat.*, 7:708–715 (1968).

17. B. A. Underwood, H. Van Arsdell, E. Blumenstiel, and N. S. Scrimshaw, "Implications of Available Information on Breast-feeding Worldwide" (paper presented at the International Symposium on Infant and Child Feeding, Michigan State University, East Lansing, Mich., USA, 1978).

18. G. E. Hendershot, "Trends in Breastfeeding," *Advanced Data*, Vital and Health Statistics of the National Center for Health Statistics, PHS No. 59 (Washington, D.C., 1980).

19. E. Helsing, "Feeding Practices in Europe—Beliefs and Motivations and Possibilities for Change" (paper presented at the International Symposium on Infant and Child Feeding, Michigan State University, East Lansing, Mich., USA, 1978).

20. WHO/UNICEF, part one of the working paper of the Meeting on Infant and Young Child Feeding (organized by WHO and UNICEF, Geneva, 1979).

21. A. Ferris, Ph.D. dissertation (Department of Food Science and Nutrition, University of Massachusetts, Amherst, Mass., USA, 1979).

22. N. W. Jerome, "Do Families and Women of the Third World Have the Right to Establish Their Own Priorities?" (paper presented at the Conference on Infant Formula in the Third World: Does It Serve a Useful Role?, New York, 1979).

23. T. Phayer, *Boke for Children* (1510–1560).

24. L. Tiger and R. Fox, *The Imperial Animal* (Holt, Rinehart and Winston, New York, 1971).

25. L. P. Gerlach, "Milk, Movements and Multinationals: Complex Interactions and Social Responsibilities," in *Responsibilities of Multinational Corporations to Society*, vol. III, proceedings of the Fifth Panel Discussion, Council of Better Business Bureaus, Washington, D.C.

26. L. P. Gerlach, "The Flea and the Elephant: Protest, Response and Consequences in the Infant Formula Controversy," *Transaction/Society*, special issue on food, agriculture, and development (1979).

27. A. Berg, *The Nutrition Factor: Its Role in National Development* (The Brookings Institution, Washington, D.C, 1973).

28. C. Hirschmann and J. A. Sweet, "Social Background and Breastfeeding among American Mothers," *Social Biology*, 21:39–57.

29. W. O. Robertson, "Breastfeeding Practices: Some Implications of Regional Variations," *Amer. J. Publ. Health*, 51: 1035–1042 (1961).

30. E. J. Salber and M. Feinleib, "Breastfeeding in Boston," *Pediatrics*, 37:299–303 (1966).

31. A. Yankauer, A. Boek, E. D. Lawson, and F. A. J. Ianni, "Social Stratification and Health Practices in Childbearing and Child Rearing," *Amer. J. Publ. Health*, 48: 732–741 (1958).

32. M. Harris, *The Rise of Anthropological Theory* (Crowell, New York, 1968).

33. C. M. Woods and T. D. Graves, *The Process of Medical Change in a Highland Guatemalan Town*, Latin American Studies, 21 (University of California Press, Los Angeles, 1973).

34. P. J. Pelto and G. H. Pelto, "Intracultural Diversity: Some Theoretical Issues," *Amer. Ethnologist*, 2:1–18 (1975).

35. J. Mohrer, "Breast and Bottle Feeding in an Inner-City Community: An Assessment of Perceptions and Practices," *Med. Anthro.*, 3:125–145 (1979).

36. R. A. K. Jones and E. M. Belsey, "Breastfeeding in an Inner London Borough—A Study of Cultural Factors," *Soc. Sci. Med.*, 11:175–179 (1977).

37. C. Bryant, "The Impact of Kin, Friend and Neighbor Networks on Infantile Obesity" (Ph.D. dissertation, University of Kentucky, Lexington, Ky., USA, 1978).

38. B. Popkin and F. Solon, "Income, Time, the Working Mother and Child Nutriture," *J. Trop. Pediat.*, 22:156–165 (1976).

39. A. E. Dugdale, "Breastfeeding in a South East Asian City," *Far East Med. J.*, 6:230–234 (1970).

40. T. Marchione, "A History of Breast-feeding Practices in the English-Speaking Caribbean of the Twentieth Century," *Food and Nutr. Bull.*, 2 (2): 9–18 (1980).

41. T. Greiner, *The Promotion of Bottle Feeding by Multinational Corporations*, Cornell International Nutrition Monograph Series, No. 2 (Cornell University, Ithaca, N.Y., 1975).

42. T. Greiner, *Regulation and Education: Strategies for Solving the Bottle Feeding Problem*, Cornell International Nutrition Monograph Series, No. 4 (Cornell University, Ithaca, N.Y., 1977).

43. J. D. Gussler and Briesemeister, "The Insufficient Milk Syndrome: a Biocultural Explanation," *Med. Anthro.*, 4:1–24 (1980).

44. M. Klaus and J. Kennell, *Maternal-Infant Bonding: The Impact of Early Separation or Loss on Family Development* (C. V. Mosby, St. Louis, Mo., USA, 1976).

45. M. Newton and N. Newton, "The Normal Course and Management of Lactation," *Child and Family*, vol. 9 (1) (1970).

46. D. Raphael, *The Tender Gift: Breast Feeding* (Schocken Books, New York, 1976).

47. N. R. Newton and M. Newton, "Psychological Aspects of Lactation," *New Engl. J. Med.*, 277:1179–1188 (1967).

48. D. B. Jelliffe and E. F. P. Jelliffe, *Human Milk in the Modern World* (Oxford University Press, London, 1978).

49. J. W. Bennett, *Northern Plainsmen: Adaptive Strategy and Agrarian Life* (Aldine/Atherton, Chicago, 1969).

50. R. LeVine, "Sex Roles and Economic Change in Africa," in J. Middleton, ed., *Black Africa* (Macmillan Co., New York, 1970), pp. 174–180.

51. P. R. Sanday, "Female Status in the Public Domain," in M. Z. Rosaldo and L. Lamphere, eds., *Women, Culture and Society* (Stanford University Press, Stanford, Calif., USA, 1974), pp. 189–206.

52. M. Ember and C. R. Ember, "The Conditions Favoring Matrilocal Versus Patrilocal Residence," *American Anthropologist*, 73:571–594 (1971).

53. A. Schlegel, *Male Dominance and Female Autonomy* (HRAF Press, New Haven, 1972).

54. M. Z. Rosaldo, "Women, Culture and Society: A Theoretical Overview," in M. Z. Rosaldo and L. Lamphere, eds., *Woman, Culture and Society* (Stanford University Press, Stanford, Calif., USA, 1974), pp. 17–42.

55. J. Johnston, "The Household Context of Infant Feeding Practices in South Trinidad" (paper presented at the annual meeting of the American Anthropological Association, Houston, Texas, 1977).

56. D. B. Jelliffe and E. F. P. Jelliffe, "The Uniqueness of Human Milk," *Am. J. Clin. Nutr.*, 24:968–1024 (1971).

57. J. Cole, "Breastfeeding in the Boston Suburbs in Relation to Personal-Social Factors," *Clin. Pediat.*, 16:352–356 (1977).

58. S. R. Halpern, W. A. Sellars, R. B. Johnson, D. W. Anderson, S. Saperstein, and S. Shannon, Jr., "Factors Influencing Breastfeeding: Notes on Observations in Dallas, Texas," *South. Med. J.*, 65:100–102 (1972).

59. N. Evans, I. R. Walpole, M. U. Qureshi, M. H. Memon, and H. W. E. Jones, "Lack of Breastfeeding and Early Weaning in Infants of Asian Immigrants to Wolverhampton," *Arch. of Dis. in Childhood*, 51:608–612 (1976).

60. M. Karkal, "Sociocultural and Economic Aspects of Infant Feeding," *Indian Pediatrics*, 12:13–19 (1975).

61. M. Carvallo, "World Health Organization Programs in Breastfeeding," in D. Rafael, ed., *Breastfeeding and Food Policy in a Hungry World* (Academic Press, New York, 1979), pp. 245–252.

36

More Than Nutrition: Breastfeeding in Urban Mali

Katherine A. Dettwyler

Ethnographic research on infant feeding among women in Mali reveals that breast milk substitutes are not widely used, with only 15 out of 136 children (11%) ever having received a breast milk substitute. This is an exception to the general trend toward substantial use of breast milk substitutes in urban Third World contexts. Economic constraints, pro-breastfeeding government policies, and beliefs about the value of breast milk all function to support the maintenance of breastfeeding. In addition, traditional kinship beliefs strongly affect maternal perceptions of the opportunity costs of alternative infant feeding choices, since only breastfeeding creates maternal kinship.

In all societies, maternal choices among alternative infant feeding strategies are based on a number of complex factors, including environmental constraints, economic and political conditions, women's workloads, and cultural beliefs about the nature of children and the nature of food. They are seldom, if ever, made simply on the basis of which alternative is cheaper or more convenient. Indeed, even the relative cost of breast milk substitutes in terms of time, money, and convenience are culturally defined. However, the role that cultural beliefs play in defining and constraining women's infant feeding choices has often been ignored in favor of simple economic or "convenience" models.

During the past decade, a number of cross-cultural surveys of infant feeding practices have been published. Much of this literature has focused on the "infant formula controversy"—the trend in the urban centers of many Third World countries away from breastfeeding and toward the use of infant-feeding bottles and/or commercial formula, with detrimental effects on the health of children (Jelliffe and Jelliffe 1978; Raphael and King 1977; Stupiansky 1982; World Health Organization 1981). Often the blame for this shift has been laid at the feet of multinational corporations, such as Nestlé, whose aggressive advertising campaigns have suggested that formula/bottle[1] feeding is the "Western" or "modern" way to feed infants. Lacking money, education, and sanitary water sources, so the argument goes, poor urban mothers prepare infant formula improperly, diluting it to make it go further and mixing it with contaminated water. The result is a dramatic increase in infant morbidity and mortality in these communities. More recently, Raphael and Davis (1985) have suggested that multinational corporations are not to blame. They suggest that other factors account for the rise in infant morbidity and mortality, that mothers choose the infant feeding option that is best suited for their particular situation, and that formula/bottle feeding may be the best option in certain circumstances.

It is not my intent here either to refute Raphael and Davis or to repeat the arguments that have surrounded this controversy. Instead, I will present data from Farimabougou, Mali, an urban Third World community in which breastfeeding is still overwhelmingly the infant feeding choice, and try to answer the question, "Why has breastfeeding persisted in this community?" Or, conversely, "What particular economic or political factors and/or cultural beliefs prohibit women from considering formula as a viable option for infant feeding?" In this discussion I will show that Van Esterik's distinction between breastfeeding as a *process* and breast milk as a *product* (Van Esterik 1985) is a particularly useful concept for understanding women's behavior in this community.

RESEARCH METHODS

Research on infant feeding and growth was conducted in Farimabougou, Mali, during 1982 and 1983. The community is one of approximately ten peri-urban squatter settlements located across the Niger River from the capital city of Bamako. Information concerning breastfeeding and weaning beliefs and practices comes from two sources. The first source is a sample, selected for the collection of mixed-longitudinal data on growth and development.[2] The sample consists of approximately 5% of the compounds in the community, and was selected primarily on the basis of the infant's age and the mother's willingness to cooperate over the extended research period of 20 months. A detailed description of the sample selection procedure is available elsewhere (Dettwyler 1986). The sample includes 136 infants from 117 compounds, and includes 20 sibling pairs. These 117 compounds were visited once every four to eight weeks. A number of anthropometric measurements were taken, and information was collected about feeding patterns and health. These visits also provided observational data

about actual infant feeding practices. All interviews were conducted in Bambara, which is the native language of most of the informants and is spoken as a second language by the rest.

At each visit, if the mother had time after we collected these standard items of information, we discussed other topics, such as breastfeeding and weaning practices, beliefs about child rearing in general, and attitudes toward pregnancy. Fathers, relatives, and visiting friends sometimes contributed information on these topics, but since mothers have virtually total responsibility for infant feeding, the majority of my information comes from them. These discussions, which were open-ended and often provided extremely detailed information, constitute the second source of data concerning the breastfeeding and weaning beliefs and practices that are presented in this article.

ETHNOGRAPHIC BACKGROUND

According to estimates made by the World Bank in 1979, the population of Farimabougou in 1983 was approximately 22,000 people, contained within 2,336 compounds (World Bank 1979). In terms of ethnic identity, the parents of children involved in the study identify themselves primarily as either Bambara or Mandinka (67%), with smaller numbers of Fulani, Senoufo, Songhai, Bobo, and Dogon.[3]

Houses in Farimabougou are mostly of mud brick construction with corrugated iron roofs, and are located inside mud-walled compounds which are closely packed along narrow dirt streets. Compounds have neither running water nor electricity. Light is provided by kerosene lanterns, and water either comes from a deep well inside each compound or is purchased from water trucks filled at the river. Each compound has a pit latrine. The daily open marketplace is centrally located and serves as the source of most food and the focus of public activities.

Traditionally, the Malian economy has been based on subsistence agriculture. Bamako and squatter settlements like Farimabougou, however, operate primarily on a cash economy. The most common occupations of fathers are merchant, cash crop farmer, chauffeur (taxi driver, bus driver), and carpenter, with a variety of other skilled and unskilled occupations represented.

In addition to the fathers, three of the mothers of children in the sample are employed: one as a schoolteacher, one as a nurse, and one as a cook. Some of the mothers occasionally sell food or herbs in the daily market, and one regularly sells fried potatoes door-to-door. Some families grow a few vegetables in their compounds or have a small garden plot near the river, but essentially all food is purchased in the daily market with cash obtained from wage labor.

The Malian diet is based on the consumption of two cereal staples, rice and millet. The noon and evening meals consist of a large quantity of rice (*kini*) or millet (*to*), served with a sauce. The most common sauces are made from okra, peanut butter, tomatoes and onions, green leaves, or *soumbala* (fermented locust bean). Animal protein in the diet usually comes from beef or fish and is pounded before being added to the sauce. According to several food consumption surveys, adult Malians have an adequate diet in terms of both protein and calories (Clairin, cited in May 1968; Diakite 1968; Mondot-Bernard and Labonne 1982).

Traditional Bambara social organization entailed patrilineal descent, patrilocal residence, and polygynous marriages. Compounds thus contained large extended families formed by a core of patrilineally related men, plus their wives and children (N'Diaye 1970). This type of social organization is seldom realized in Farimabougou. Usually only one adult male in a family migrates to the city, and he usually has only one wife because of economic constraints. In view of these factors, the majority of children in the study (72%) belong to parents in monogamous marriages; most (65%) live in compounds containing only nuclear family members.

Except for a few Christian families, the people of Farimabougou are Moslem. For the most part, however, women do not follow strict Moslem teachings: they are not secluded, seldom go to the mosque or pray at home, rarely fast during Ramadan, and are not familiar with Koranic guidelines concerning infant feeding. (The Koran recommends breastfeeding for two years but states that children may be weaned earlier by mutual consent of the mother and father.) For both men and women, Islamic beliefs coexist with traditional religious beliefs and practices. Sickness and death, however, are usually attributed to Allah rather than to either organic causes or witchcraft and sorcery.

The majority of women who participated in the study were born in rural villages and have lived in the urban environment for less than 20 years. Data on length of residence reveal a tendency to report this information in five-year intervals, with approximately equal numbers of women reporting urban residence of five, ten, fifteen, and twenty years. The women have had little or no formal education, speak Bambara but not French, and can neither read nor write. More detailed descriptions of the study community can be found in Dettwyler (1985, 1986).

RESULTS

To understand Farimabougou mothers' selection of breastfeeding over bottle or formula use, one must first comprehend the local culture of breastfeeding.

The Cultural Context of Breastfeeding and Women's Work

Traditionally, breastfeeding was the only infant feeding option available to Malian women. Even today, so few women use breast milk substitutes that young women seldom can be said to "choose" whether or not to breastfeed. They grow up surrounded by older women nursing babies and expect to be successful at nursing their own children. Infants are nursed on demand, day and night. It is considered a primary right of children to be nursed whenever they want, for as long as they want, as often as they want. In addition to providing nourishment, babies are also nursed for comfort if they are hurt, sick, tired, or frightened. This aspect of nursing is considered as important as nursing for nourishment. If for some reason the mother is not available and the baby is crying, another woman, such as the maternal grandmother or a co-wife, will allow the baby to suckle. Solid foods are added to the diet at the median age of 7 months, with a range of 3 to 24+ months, and a mode of 6 months; the median age of complete weaning from the breast is 21 months, with a range of 6 to 32 months, and a mode of 24 months (see Dettwyler 1987 for more complete descriptions of breastfeeding and weaning practices).

Generally speaking, nursing bouts (separate nursing episodes) are very frequent—on the order of several to many times per hour—and usually last less than 15 minutes. This pattern continues until complete weaning. Despite the fact that most children nurse very often both day and night, women do not view this as a burden or an inconvenience. Breastfeeding is not culturally defined as an activity that significantly constrains a woman's activities.

When very young, an infant's head is supported during breastfeeding, but by the age of four months the infant, lying across the mother's lap, is expected to find the breast by herself, and the mother gives the baby little physical support or attention during feedings. This leaves both of the mother's arms free for other tasks, which means that nursing her baby need not interrupt her work. Breasts are not considered sexual objects, and nursing is not considered to be a private activity. When a woman needs to work or travel somewhere, her infant is tied on her back with a cloth wrap. It is not considered dangerous for infants or new mothers to go outside their compounds, and young infants are often taken on walking trips involving miles, or they may travel with their mothers on mopeds or in "bush taxis." When the baby needs to nurse, he is simply pulled around onto the mother's hip where he can reach her breast while still supported by the sling.

Women take babies and young children everywhere—to the market, to the fields, on visits to friends, to rural villages, even to work. Market women almost always have a baby on their laps or seated at their feet. The infants nurse, sleep, and play while their mothers sell food or other market items. Even in the formal sector, returning to wage employment does not necessarily mean giving up breastfeeding, as some employers allow women to bring their infants to the job. In view of the few women involved in formal-sector employment, this variable was not a major factor in my study. However, other women employed in the formal sector were observed at work with their nursing babies at an engineering consulting firm, a government hospital, various government offices, the Meteorological Society, and the English language school run by the Agency for International Development. In such cases babies were observed to spend the day tied on their mothers' backs or playing or sleeping on the floor by the desk. Sometimes the baby of an employed mother is cared for outside by an older sibling or hired nursemaid, who brings the baby in for feeding when it cries. This lenient attitude on the part of employers reflects the importance of breastfeeding in this culture and the general tolerance of infants by adult men.

With regard to the effects of women's work on infant feeding strategies in other societies, the evidence is mixed. Brown (1970) concludes that women are limited to certain types of productive activities by breastfeeding, because it requires the mother's constant presence and frequent interruptions of her work. Nerlove's (1974) comparative data suggest that women supplement earlier (with solids or breast milk substitutes) when their productive activities are not compatible with breastfeeding. However, Van Esterik and Greiner (1981), in summarizing the arguments about the relationship between increasing formal sector employment among women and declining breastfeeding frequencies and durations in the developing world, point out that many women successfully combine breastfeeding and employment, and that the often-cited "evidence" does not, in fact, support the claim that breastfeeding and women's work are incompatible. At the same time, evidence from Melanesia (Akin 1985; Barlow 1985) and Nepal (Levine 1986) suggests that in some societies even domestic or subsistence labor in rural settings may be incompatible with breastfeeding both because of cultural beliefs about dangers to infants and children outside the home and because of the perceived inconvenience to the mother of having the infant with her.

In Mali, because women and their infants are allowed to travel everywhere together, the mother does not have to stay at home to nurse her infant. The infant is simply taken along wherever the mother cares to go and is welcome in almost any situation. Even in the formal sector, there are few contexts requiring the presence of the mother that forbid the presence of the infant. Thus, cultural definitions of when and where it is appropriate for infants to go and for mothers to nurse have at least as much impact on infant feeding choices as the conditions of women's work.

Bottle/Formula Use

Breast milk substances available in Farimabougou include powdered commercial infant formula, powdered whole milk, Cerelac (a cereal-milk combination), pasteurized cow's milk, and raw cow's milk. Powdered commercial infant formula is sold only in pharmacies, the nearest of which is approximately two kilometers away. In 1982 the cost of a can of formula ranged from 1,400 to 1,800 Malian francs (700 FM = $1.00). Equivalent cans of powdered whole milk cost only 1,000 FM and were sold at the local shops in every neighborhood. Thus, powdered milk is cheaper and more widely available than infant formula. In addition, families often keep powdered milk on hand for use in the breakfast porridge and coffee.

Cerelac comes in several varieties (wheat, rice, oat). When prepared it has the consistency of thin Cream of Wheat and must be diluted further to be given in a bottle with a nipple. Cerelac is only rarely used as a substitute for breast milk; occasionally it serves as an infant's first "solid" food.

Pasteurized cow's milk must be refrigerated, and is generally sold only in larger stores outside the community. It is sometimes available in the local market in the late afternoon, however. Raw cow's milk from Fulani herds is sold door-to-door in the late afternoons during the rainy season (June–August). While usually cheaper than other forms of milk, it must be used immediately and is often already soured by the time it is offered for sale, which prevents it from flowing smoothly through the nipple. It is also said to upset children's stomachs. For these reasons, its use as a breast milk substitute is limited.

Like commercial infant formula, bottles and nipples are offered for sale only in pharmacies. Although some women use baby bottles with nipples, most women who use breast milk substitutes offer them in cups or empty formula or powdered milk cans. This means that infants must learn to swallow from the cup at an early age if given a breast milk substitute.

Only 15 of the 136 children in the sample (11%) had ever received any kind of breast milk substitute. In 14 of the 15 cases, the bottle/formula was used to supplement breast milk, rather than replace it, and in 11 cases it was added to the diet because the mother had experienced problems with breastfeeding. These included "insufficient milk" (nine cases) and sore breasts or nipples (two cases). One woman had used formula with an older set of twins, who were quite healthy, and decided to continue it with her next child. Two women could not provide any specific reason for their decision to use bottles/formula to supplement breastfeeding. The one case where infant formula was used to replace breast milk involved the child of a maternity nurse. The infant was exclusively breastfed for six months and then weaned onto formula when the mother returned to work full-time. Although the mother could have taken her baby to work with her, she preferred leaving him in the care of his father, who worked at home building furniture.[4]

Economic Constraints

The World Bank has defined the "urban poverty threshold" for Bamako as 30,000 FM (approximately $60.00) per household per month (1979). According to the World Bank, almost half of the households in Farimabougou have an income below the urban poverty threshold, and the average income is 40% lower than that of Bamako (World Bank 1979). Given the low average income, the cost of using formula and/or other breast milk substitutes on a regular basis would be prohibitive for almost all community residents. For example, if a child were given only properly prepared formula, and one can costing 1,600 FM lasted approximately five days, the cost per month to feed an infant would be 9,600 FM. This represents almost one-third of the total income for families at the urban poverty threshold, and an even greater proportion for families below the threshold.

Even for families with greater discretionary income, other items are usually given higher priority than the purchase of breast milk substitutes. These include school fees, medical care, remittances to rural relatives, gasoline for mobylettes, bus fare, and clothing, to name only a few. For these reasons, it is impossible to specify whether a family can or cannot "afford" infant formula. Most do not choose to spend any of their income, regardless of its adequacy, on breast milk

substitutes—or, for that matter, on more or better food for other family members (Dettwyler 1986). The few women who use formula or powdered milk to supplement their own breast milk buy it when their other needs have already been met at some minimal level—for example, if no one has been sick that week. When they are short of funds, the child receives only breast milk until money is available again.

Government Policy

The Malian government has developed a number of programs to promote breastfeeding and discourage the use of formula. Radio programs, restrictions against the advertising of formula in printed media, regulations against the promotion of formula in maternity clinics (where 85% of children are born), and recommendations by clinic personnel not to use formula all operate to reinforce traditional feeding practices.

Breast Milk as a Product

In her summary to Marshall's *Infant Care and Feeding in the South Pacific* (1985), Van Esterik draws a distinction between viewing breastfeeding as a *process* and breast milk as a *product:*

> It is likely that the more traditional interpretations are primarily process models in societies where women breastfeed successfully. The biomedical model built on accumulated scientific evidence about breastmilk composition and the functions of specific nutrients in breastmilk is a product oriented model. . . . It is this emphasis on breastmilk as a product which has been particularly advantageous to the expansion of the market for breastmilk substitutes. Infant formula is an item to be sold, and as such, can be compared with another product, breastmilk. . . . It would be difficult to imagine a process oriented campaign for breastmilk substitutes. [1985:339–340]

The conceptual distinction between product and process is useful for understanding how women in any community feel about nursing their children. Women in Farimabougou do perceive of breast milk as a product and will discuss its attributes. In general, people say that breast milk is the best food for infants and makes them strong and healthy. A baby's own mother's milk is considered better for it than another woman's milk or formula. People also claim that babies were stronger in the "old days," when they were nursed until three or four years of age and before bottle-feeding was introduced. Bottle-fed infants are perceived as being weaker and more sickly than breastfed infants, because the product is inferior. Several women stated specifically that breast milk acts to protect babies from illness. In addition, women report that a sick baby will often refuse to eat but will always nurse, so that breast milk may provide the only nourishment during an illness. If a child becomes thin after weaning, its mother will say that it is not as "heavy" as before, because breast milk makes a child "heavy." Some people also say that formula can make a child tall, but only breast milk can make a child "heavy," healthy, and strong.

The women of Farimabougou also believe that breast milk can vary in both quality and quantity from woman to woman. It is a widespread belief in the community that a fat baby results from a mother with "good" milk. Women say that it is the quality rather than the quantity of milk that is the important factor. Likewise, a thin baby may be the result of the mother having "bad" milk.

The women of Farimabougou believe that during lactation breast milk is produced "from the blood" and that each woman has a finite amount of blood in her body during her lifetime. Therefore it is impossible to increase or compensate for any lost blood or to affect the quantity of breast milk available through diet or medicine. If a woman loses a lot of blood in an accident, for example, she will probably not have enough breast milk for her children and will have to supplement with breast milk substitutes or solid foods. Older women who have already nursed many children will likewise have a poor milk supply and will be tired all the time because they have "used up" all of their blood (Dettwyler 1987). Thus, women do perceive breast milk as a product, transformed from blood, which can vary in quality but is generally superior to infant formula.

Breastfeeding as a Process

Perhaps the most widespread belief about breast milk in this community, cutting across all ethnic, age, and socioeconomic categories, is that because it is made from a woman's blood, the process of breastfeeding creates a special relationship between a child and the woman from whom it nurses, whether or not she is the baby's biological mother. In addition, breastfeeding creates a bond among all children who nurse from the same woman, whether or not they are biological siblings.[5]

In this strongly patrilineal society, children of the same father are bound by ties of common "blood." Children inherit their father's "blood" via his semen, which, through intercourse, is the cause of pregnancy. The children of one man, even if they have different

mothers, cannot marry or have sexual relations because they "share the same blood." Some people extend this relationship another generation to include all the grandchildren of one man (thus ruling out marriage between cousins), while others limit the marriage taboo to one generation and even encourage marriage between cousins. Of particular importance to this discussion is the fact that the marriage taboo is predicated on the concept of "shared blood."

Analogous to the belief that children of one father share the same blood by virtue of inheritance, children who nurse from the same woman are said to share the same blood through her breast milk. In fact, children of the same woman are related to each other on the maternal side not because they were all born from her body, but because they all nursed from her breast. Thus, breast milk is thought of as a "product" with some very special attributes, and these attributes are incorporated by the infant during the "process" of breastfeeding itself. Two children who nurse from the same woman are related through the process itself and cannot marry, whether they are "genetically" related or not. *Shin-kelen* (literally, "one breast"—i.e., nursing from the same woman) creates an even stronger taboo against incest or marriage (in terms of punishment for transgressions) than having the same father. For the same reason, bonds of kinship between full siblings (same mother and father) are considered stronger than bonds between half-siblings (same father, different mothers). This belief is also reflected in the kinship terminology: a man may refer to his full brother as *shin-ji* (literally, "breast milk").

Every woman hopes that her children will grow up and marry her friends' children, and a son's wife is often chosen from among the daughters of his mother's friends. Therefore, women do not nurse their friends' babies, as this would eliminate the possibility of their children marrying as adults. Only in an extreme situation would a woman nurse a friend's child—for example, if the friend died in childbirth and no one else was available to nurse the infant.

Women routinely nurse children other than their own, if doing so will not jeopardize future marriage prospects. That is, women can and do nurse children who are already of "the same blood" and therefore not marriageable. Depending on which of the two aforementioned marriage prohibitions one adopts, this may include co-wives' children, grandchildren through daughters, brothers' children, and husband's brothers' children. In the latter case, only co-wives' children could be nursed.

The most commonly occurring instance of a woman nursing a child other than her own in Farimabougou is that of a woman and her daughter's baby. According to the rules of kinship and exogamy, a woman could technically also nurse her sons' children, but this does not happen. A woman's daughters may marry as young as 13 years of age and have children while their mother is also still bearing and nursing children of her own. In addition, women say that "a woman and her daughters are the same," especially with regard to nursing. Conversely, a woman's sons usually do not marry and have children until relatively late (25 years or older). Thus, women say they will be too old to nurse their sons' children. Even if a woman still has milk at the time her son has a child, the traditional antagonism between a woman and her daughter-in-law makes it unlikely that a woman will nurse her son's children.

During the study, a number of women were observed nursing children other than their own biological offspring. Most often this involved a woman nursing her oldest daughter's first baby, but instances involving co-wives or other relationships were also observed.

The belief that women become related to their children primarily through the process of breastfeeding is not unique to the Bambara and related peoples of Mali. Similar beliefs have been reported by Davis (1985) for Haiti, Counts and Counts (1983) for the Kaliai of Papua New Guinea, Farb and Armelagos (1980) for an area reaching from the Balkans east to Burma, and Dickson (1949) for the Badawin of Kuwait and Saudi Arabia.

DISCUSSION AND CONCLUSIONS

In this article I have discussed infant feeding beliefs and practices in a peri-urban squatter community in Mali where breastfeeding is still the overwhelming infant feeding choice. Economic constraints and explicit pro-breastfeeding government policies contribute to the maintenance of breastfeeding. Most important, traditional beliefs about the qualities of human milk and the process of breastfeeding itself function very strongly to inhibit the use of breast milk substitutes.

In this community, breastfeeding is seen as a special process that creates bonds of kinship between women and children and among children. Breastfeeding is *more* than nutrition. The decision to substitute infant formula in a bottle for the complex process of breastfeeding is more than just a decision about the relative cost or nutritional value of the two products or the practical convenience of the two processes. A woman in Farimabougou who decides not to breastfeed is, in effect, deciding not to be related to her chil-

dren. On numerous occasions, when discussing the use of breast milk substitutes, women expressed uneasiness at the implications for maternal kinship of giving up breastfeeding. Economic constraints were clearly viewed as secondary considerations. Even if breast milk substitutes were relatively inexpensive, in this strongly patrilineal society where a woman's rights to her children are tenuous at best, few women at the present time will willingly choose to give up their primary tie to their children. Thus, where breast milk has more than nutritional importance, and where breastfeeding is viewed not as a constraint on women's activities but as a process that provides contact and comfort and that creates kinship, bottle feeding has been resisted.

NOTES

Acknowledgments. This research was supported in part by grants from Sigma Xi and the Graduate School of Indiana University. The ideas were developed further during participation in a National Endowment for the Humanities Summer Seminar for College Teachers, "Anthropology of Food and Foodways," in 1987. The author also wishes to thank Rita Gallin, Alan Harwood, Sheila Cosminsky, and the anonymous reviewers for helpful comments on earlier drafts.

Correspondence may be addressed to the author at the Department of Anthropology, Texas A & M University, College Station, TX 77843.

1. It is important to recognize that infant bottles may contain a variety of products used as breast milk substitutes, including commercial infant formula, powdered milk, diluted commercial infant cereals, and diluted gruels made from the local carbohydrate staple. Additionally, any of these breast milk substitutes may be given in a cup or with a bowl and spoon, rather than in a bottle. The phrase "formula/bottle" is used in this article to indicate the use of a breast milk substitute, which may or may not be commercial infant formula, and may or may not be given in a bottle.

2. A mixed-longitudinal study is one in which children enter and leave at different ages, thus providing varying degrees of longitudinality. As such, it represents a combination of a cross-sectional study, in which individual children are measured only once, and a pure longitudinal study, in which all children enter at the same time and are retained until the end of the study. Children left the sample through death, migration, or parental decisions not to continue cooperation. Children were added to the sample through birth (younger siblings of children already in the sample), parental requests to be included, or recruitment because they represented some aspect of the population not present in the original sample (twins, older mothers, etc.).

3. Two-thirds of the sample consists of people who identify themselves as either Bambara or Mandinka. These are closely related ethnic groups, speaking mutually intelligible

languages, and sharing many features of culture and social organization. Although there are a variety of other ethnic groups identified in the sample, "ethnic identity" is a problematic issue in this region, where people assume the ethnic identity of their fathers. Many of the children in the study have parents of differing ethnic backgrounds, and many of the parents themselves are of mixed ethnic origin. So, for example, a woman who identifies herself as "Bambara" based on her father's lineage, may have a mother who is ethnically Dogon. If she is married to a Fulani, her children will be ethnically Fulani. In addition, many generations of migration and contact have resulted in situations where, for example, people retain Fulani surnames and ethnic identity, but speak Bambara and live as sedentary agriculturalists. Analyses of the data reveal no consistent differences in beliefs relating to infant feeding according to ethnic affiliation. Geographic differences, on the other hand, were often cited by the women themselves as explanations for why other Bambara women held different beliefs about infant feeding. The beliefs about breastfeeding reported in this article are ascribed to by the majority of the women in the sample.

4. More detailed information about children supplemented with formula can be found in Dettwyler (1987).

5. According to my informants, the creation of kinship ties via breastfeeding does not operate in a linear, additive fashion. That is, a woman who nurses her child for two years is not somehow *more* related to that child than to the child she nurses for only one year. The women did not specify an exact minimum duration of breastfeeding necessary to establish definite bonds of kinship, but felt that women who nursed their children for only a few months were definitely taking a risk in that regard.

REFERENCES CITED

Akin, K. Gillogly
1985 Women's Work and Infant Feeding: Traditional and Transitional Practices on Malaita, Solomon Islands. *In* Infant Care and Feeding in the South Pacific. Leslie B. Marshall, ed. Pp. 207–233. New York: Gordon and Breach.

Barlow, Kathleen
1985 The Social Context of Infant Feeding in the Murik Lakes of Papua New Guinea. *In* Infant Care and Feeding in the South Pacific. Leslie B. Marshall, ed. Pp. 137–154. New York: Gordon and Breach.

Brown, Judith K.
1970 A Note on the Division of Labor by Sex. American Anthropologist 72:1073–1078.

Counts, Dorothy Ayers, and David R. Counts
1983 Father's Water Equals Mother's Milk: The Conception of Parentage in Kaliai, West New Britain. *In* Ideologies of Conception in Papua New Guinea. D. Jorgensen, ed. Mankind 14(1):46–56.

Davis, Wade
1995 The Serpent and the Rainbow. New York: Simon and Schuster.

Dettwyler, Katherine A.
1985 Breastfeeding, Weaning, and Other Infant Feeding Practices in Mali and Their Effects on Growth and Development. Ph.D. dissertation, Department of Anthropology, Indiana University. Ann Arbor: University Microfilms.
1986 Infant Feeding in Mali: Variations in Belief and Practice. Social Science and Medicine 23(7):651–664.
1987 Breastfeeding and Weaning in Mali: Cultural Context and Hard Data. Social Science and Medicine 24(8):633–644.

Diakite, Seydou
1968 Nutrition in Mali. Proceedings of the West African Conference on Nutrition and Child Feeding, Dakar, Senegal, March 25–29, 1969. Pp. 87–97. Washington: U.S. Department of Health, Education, and Welfare, Public Health Service.

Dickson, H. P. R.
1949 The Arab of the Desert: A Glimpse into Badawin Life in Kuwait and Sau'di Arabia. London: George Allen & Unwin, Ltd.

Farb, Peter, and George Armelagos
1980 Consuming Passions: The Anthropology of Eating. Boston: Houghton Mifflin.

Jelliffe, Derrick B., and E. F. Patrice Jelliffe
1978 Human Milk in the Modern World. St. Louis: C. V. Mosby.

Levine, Nancy E.
1986 Patterns of Fertility, Child Care, and Mortality in Rural Nepal. Paper read at the 85th annual meeting of the American Anthropological Association, Philadelphia, PA, December 3–7, 1986.

Marshall, Leslie B., ed.
1985 Infant Care and Feeding in the South Pacific. New York: Gordon and Breach.

May, Jacques M.
1968 The Ecology of Malnutrition in the French Speaking Countries of West Africa and Madagascar. New York: Hafner Publishing Company.

Mondot-Bernard, J., and M. Labonne
1982 Satisfaction of Food Requirements in Mali to 2000 A.D. Paris: Development Centre of the Organization for Economic Co-operation and Development.

N'Diaye, Bokar
1970 Groupes ethniques au Mali. Bamako: Edition Populaires.

Nerlove, Sara B.
1974 Women's Workload and Infant Feeding Practices: A Relationship with Demographic Implications. Ethnology 13:207–214.

Raphael, Dana, and Flora Davis
1985 Only Mothers Know: Patterns of Infant Feeding in Traditional Cultures. Westport, CT: Greenwood Press.

Raphael, Dana, and Joyce King
1977 Mothers in Poverty: Breastfeeding and the Maternal Struggle for Infant Survival. Lactation Review 2(3) (special issue).

Stupiansky, Sandra Waite
1982 The Infant Formula Marketing Controversy: A Sociopolitical Case History. Ph.D. dissertation, Interdis-

ciplinary Doctoral Program on Young Children, Indiana University, Bloomington.

Van Esterik, Penny
  1985 Commentary: An Anthropological Perspective on Infant Feeding in Oceania. *In* Infant Care and Feeding in the South Pacific. Leslie B. Marshall, ed. Pp. 331–343. New York: Gordon and Breach.

Van Esterik, Penny, and Ted Greiner
  1981 Breastfeeding and Women's Work: Constraints and Opportunities. Studies in Family Planning 12(4): 184–197.

World Bank
  1979 Report and Recommendations of the President of the International Development Association to the Executive Directors on a Proposed Credit to the Republic of Mali for an Urban Development Project. Report No. WP-2595-MLI, June 12, 1979.

World Health Organization
  1981 Contemporary Patterns of Breast-Feeding: Report on the WHO Collaborative Study on Breast-Feeding. Geneva: World Health Organization.

37

Women's Work and Infant Feeding: A Case from Rural Nepal[1]

Nancy E. Levine

It is commonly presumed that women's work in traditional societies is organized in ways compatible with childbearing and childrearing (Brown 1970; Hammond and Jablow 1976:54; Nardi 1984; and Quinn 1977:192), in contrast to observed realities in modern industrial societies.[2] This view is pervasive; it is implicit in demographic transition theory and informs the dichotomy drawn between domestic and public domains. Yet such presumptions call for closer scrutiny, as an examination of the cross-cultural literature reveals, and the present case of Himalayan agriculturists makes particularly clear. Mountain agriculture involves special, intensive systems of cultivation, and in the Himalayas this entails heavy reliance upon the work of women. At the same time, practices of male seasonal labor migration add to women's work responsibilities. One of the consequences is decreased time for child care and, as this study shows, diminished opportunities for infant feeding. The demands of work can be so compelling as to constrict the effects of cultural differences, so that communities with comparable labor requirements follow similar patterns in feeding infants regardless of their cultural or ethnic affiliation. Although women in many societies are burdened with heavy work and child care responsibilities, our understanding of how the two are accommodated and how systems of labor management vary cross-culturally with systems of infant and child care remains fragmented. Such information, moreover, could offer a fuller perspective on the widespread transition to bottle feeding in modern urban societies in recent decades.

The data to be discussed here derive from field research conducted in Humla, a mountainous district of northwest Nepal and one of the poorest regions in that country. Development programs have bypassed the region, agricultural techniques remain primitive, failed harvests and famines are frequent, and even in good years, poor families suffer hunger in pre-harvest months. In consequence, men leave their homes for months at a time to participate in seasonal labor migration or trade. This increases the burdens on women, the poorer of whom also must supplement work on their own lands with ill-paid labor for others. At the same time, women bear seven-and-a-half children on average by the end of their reproductive careers, and hold the major responsibility for child care. Thus women have to balance major involvements in productive labor with those in childbearing and childrearing.

These problems are intensified by the special demands of mountain agriculture, which is intrinsically arduous and imposes added difficulties of transport and travel. In Humla these problems and the necessity for long periods of uninterrupted work discourage women from taking infants and small children to their work sites. Most leave the children behind with substitute caretakers. This, however, creates its own problem: how to feed the infants left behind. The solution for many mothers is early supplementation of breast milk, beginning the first few weeks after birth, so that they can go out to work.

Patterns of breast feeding in traditional societies have been incompletely examined. As Nerlove (1974) notes, the studies that exist have tended to focus on the late weaning characteristic of such societies, while neglecting practices of very early supplementation. The fact is that early supplementation is quite prevalent and, moreover, positively correlated with women's work contributions.[3] The potential harm in very early supplementation similarly has drawn little comment, while far greater attention has been paid to the negative effects of bottle feeding in less developed countries. Yet the two may be responses to the same problem: the difficulties of combining work away from home with child care.[4]

MOUNTAIN AGRICULTURE AND WOMEN'S WORK

Mountain agriculture in Nepal, as elsewhere, requires tremendous labor inputs for much lower levels of productivity than realized in plains regions (Guillet 1983:563). First, simply traversing the land is difficult. Heavy loads of compost must be carried up or down steep, sometimes dangerous trails at high altitudes, and the harvested grain carried in the opposite direction. Second, farmers commonly own small, dispersed plots. This has its advantages: it allows each household to cultivate under the full range of available ecological conditions and altitudes, divides up land in more favored areas, gives each household the opportunity to grow diverse crops, spreads the risk of localized fluctuations, and staggers the workload across a longer season (Rhoades and Thompson 1975; Netting 1981: 17–18). But it also adds to the work by creating plots that are small and inefficient to plow and cultivate, and by increasing travel time. Many of the plots in Humla are smaller than a twelfth of an acre and located thousands of feet (vertically) and several miles (horizontally) apart. Finally, the mountain location limits possibilities for improving existing technologies, increasing yields, or lowering labor inputs. Even if modern farm machinery were affordable and easily transportable, it would prove impractical in such areas. Small, narrow terraces resist mechanized farming and are difficult to plow even with cattle. Expanding irrigation channels is expensive, too, and in the western Himalayas made more difficult by limited water sources. Bringing water from major rivers several thousand feet down the hillside is, of course, not feasible.

These constraints make large holdings difficult to manage, which hinders large accumulations of land.[5] Since land is the predominant resource, the result is limited economic differentiation. This is why a recent survey of Nepalese groups found the greatest economic inequality in villages on the Tibetan border, where people rely more on trade, and in the Terai, the portion of Nepal adjoining and ecologically similar to the North Indian plains (Acharya and Bennett 1981:33).[6] Himalayan groups also have milder systems of social stratification: Hindus have fewer castes, with the majority assigned to the middle ranks, and easier mobility exists between them (Höfer 1981). Forms of inequality seem to be moderated among the ethnic Tibetans in Nepal as well, increasing opportunities for social mobility.

In consequence, most mountain dwellers are workers on their own land, and no one is wealthy enough to absent himself or herself from productive labor. Households with more than average landholdings, however, may have to employ hired workers at peak periods. The wealthiest households may employ workers year-round, and they may do so to help overburdened household women. This can free wealthier women for work at home, while it takes poorer women away from home—often far from home—facts that have significance for child care.

There are other aspects of mountain agriculture bearing upon women's work and their time to care for their children. Among them are the ecological micro-variations and seasonality in production found at high altitude. These problems are felt even more strongly in Humla, where communities have access to land within a narrow altitudinal and territorial range. Altitude and chance factors of location (e.g., exposure to sunshine, availability of water, soil quality) all contribute to the mix of crops grown. Differing access to pastureland also affects involvements in herding. The combination of crops and other productive strategies in turn affect seasonal cycles of labor. Since women work more on some crops and activities than others, this affects their relative work burdens, as the case studies below show.[7]

WOMEN'S WORK AND CHILD CARE: THE NEPALESE CONTEXT

Juxtaposing conditions of women's work in the Himalayas with that of the neighboring North Indian plains is quite instructive. In North India, the ideal is to keep women at home (which is associated with purdah and norms of female seclusion) and involved only in work that can be done at home. Such restrictions on women and their separation from economic life are common in the so-called male farming systems of extensive plow agriculture (Boserup 1970:35, 50; Goody 1976:31–37). While hill-dwelling Hindus in Nepal share North Indian ideals, their agriculture is

Table 1.   Time spent by Nepalese women on work and child care

	Average Hours per Day at:			
	Conventional Economic Activity	Subsistence Domestic Tasks	Other Domestic Work	Child Care
Highland and Middle Hills Communities				
Baragaonle[a]	3.64	1.38	3.22	0.56
Lohorung Rai	4.99	3.20	4.05	0.14
Kham Magar	4.93	1.73	1.59	0.78
Tamang	5.80	1.17	1.46	0.03
Kathmandu Valley Communities				
Parbatiya	5.51	1.71	4.37	0.91
Newar	2.42	2.50	3.14	1.27
Terai or Plains Communities				
Tharu[a]	3.39	2.51	2.83	1.88
Maithili	2.36	2.02	4.35	1.25

These data derive from Acharya and Bennett 1981:426.

[a]The data summarize observations of all members of twenty-four households per community over a minimum six month period. The Baragaonle were observed for two and the Tharu for one hour less than households in the other villages, and the figures for these communities may underrepresent work involvements proportionately.

intensive (Boserup 1970:35), and households cannot afford to dispense with women's labor.[8] Although Tibetan women may be free of comparable restrictions, ethnic Tibetan women in Humla who raised the issue invariably said they would prefer to stay home, engaged in domestic chores and child care, and avoid the exhausting round of agriculture.

Patterns of women's time usage in work and child care were documented in a recent study of eight Nepalese communities. These communities constitute three groups: highland and middle hill dwellers, peoples living in the Kathmandu valley, and those in the Terai or plains. The data on time allocation are aggregated into four categories (see Table 1). The first includes conventional economic activities such as agriculture, animal husbandry, manufacturing, and paid labor outside the home; the second includes food processing, water, and fuel collection; the third includes domestic work, such as cooking, washing dishes and clothing, and house cleaning; and the fourth includes child care (defined as feeding, carrying, and direct attendance upon, but not playing with, a child (Bennett 1981:146).[9]

As these data show, ethnic and religious affiliations have little effect on women's work responsibilities. Parbatiya and Maithili are the groups that most strongly voice Hindu ideals, yet Parbatiya women are among the most heavily engaged in agricultural and other productive work. Location seems to count more, which is why we find women in the Terai spending less time on conventional economic activities than the women of all but one Kathmandu valley group. Notably, we find women in the mountains and middle hills spending the least, women in the Terai the most, and women in the Kathmandu valley an intermediate amount of time on child care.

The time documented as spent on child care also seems surprisingly low, especially in view of the fact that the average married woman had 2.76 children alive at the time of the survey (Acharya and Bennett 1981:103). This partly is a consequence of practices of collective responsibility for children. All adult women in the household, responsible girls, and, to lesser degree, adult men and boys help care for household children. While the study shows considerable interhousehold variation, it also makes clear that mothers' efforts tend to be diverted to other tasks.[10]

The implication is that women place great emphasis on productive labor and arrange child care around it, and this seems even truer for poorer women who work more and spend less time on child care than those better-off (Acharya 1981:157; Bennett 1981: 137). Whether this means that women's productive contributions are considered more important than the welfare of children is a moot point. What my discussions with Humla women suggest is that productive efforts are treated as more inflexible and agricultural work more demanding, while child care is regarded as simpler and manageable even by children. Sharma (1980:128–129) sums up similar attitudes held in the North Indian hills and plains and the contrast with our own:

> In British middle-class culture there is an emphasis on spending time with one's child, the idea that the moral training and cultivation of the child's potential is achieved by the parents (and particularly the mother). . . . But few Punjabi or Himachali women saw child care as something that 'takes up time' except in so far as the physical needs of children have to be satisfied. The proper training of children was seen . . . not as some kind of specific task for which time had to be allocated. . . .

COMMUNITIES IN HUMLA: ETHNIC AND AGRICULTURAL VARIATIONS

Humla is a mountainous district in far northwest Nepal with one of the lowest population densities in the country. Most of the land is too high in altitude or too steep to be cultivated, and villages cluster along major river valleys where agriculture is practicable. The population includes three ethnic groups: Hindu Parbatiyas, the great majority of them high caste; ethnic Tibetans (who are Buddhist); and Bura, who cite ancestry from Tibetans, local Hindus, and the Byansis of Darchula, although they are heavily Nepalicized and Hindu today (Levine 1987a). The Parbatiya tend to farm the land at the valley bottoms, the ethnic Tibetans occupy the higher valleys and those closer to Tibet, while Bura cultivate land at a middle range of altitudes, where unreclaimed forest lands still provide opportunities for agricultural expansion.

Despite fundamental cultural differences (most markedly between Parbatiya and ethnic Tibetans) all groups have a similar sexual division of labor. Plowing and planting everywhere are the responsibility of men, while women may help prepare the soil, smooth it after plowing, or, less commonly, help plant seed. Women do most or all the weeding, mostly take charge of the preparation and application of compost, and do most of the wood and grass collection.[11] Women also take responsibility for almost all phases of millet cultivation, including its intensive weeding, and typically harvest millets alone, while both sexes share in the harvesting of buckwheat and wheat. Humla people explain women's role in the millet harvest by their gentler touch, which makes them less apt to shake grains from the stalk. Whatever the factors responsible, a similar division of labor is found throughout the country. Par-

batiya women in the Kathmandu valley also weed, prepare and apply compost, and work more on maize (which is not grown to any great extent in Humla) and millet (Bennett 1981:161, 165). In Humla and Nepal generally, women seem to do the great majority of food processing, as well as domestic work and child care.

Because the sexual division of labor tends to be relatively fixed, the types of crops a community grows and circumstances such as the proximity of water and wood or the need for grass (which depends upon the number of domestic animals kept) determine demands upon women's time. Thus a community with more wheat and buckwheat, less millet, fewer domestic animals, and water and wood nearby will call less on the extra-domestic labor of its women than one with the opposite conditions. There are other factors that have an effect on the work of women and men alike, such as the length of the growing season and the general productivity of the soil. Communities with poorer land or other unfavorable conditions are likelier to have men and women seeking additional work with wealthier neighbors. Men in ethnic Tibetan communities tend to sponsor their own trading enterprises (centered around exchanges of Tibetan salt for grain grown in the south), while those from other ethnic groups are likelier to work as their hired shepherds. Thus cultural factors have this effect and combine with environmental ones to produce a distinctive pattern of work for each community. Within the community, such factors as the extent of landholdings and the location of fields can lead to interhousehold variation in crops sown and thus in household members' workloads.[12]

While there are substantial differences between communities in the phasing of labor, all experience peak labor requirements at some point in the middle of summer and in autumn. It is in summer that millets are weeded, barley and wheat harvested, and the late buckwheat crop sown. Autumn marks the final harvest of the year. Following this are several months of relative ease, when women's work involves domestic chores, the processing of grains, and weaving of woolen clothing. This work takes place at home and can be co-ordinated with infant and child care. Agricultural work resumes in March, the precise time depending upon altitude and other environmental conditions.

INFANT FEEDING IN HUMLA

The following discussion derives from a segment of a formal questionnaire administered to the women of six communities, drawn from Humla's three ethnic groups. In the two largest communities households were randomly sampled; elsewhere all village households were surveyed. One woman in each of these households was asked to provide a retrospective fertility history.[13] The final set of questions concerned infant feeding. Women were asked how old their last and next-to-last (from the last closed birth interval) children were when they began regularly giving them supplementary foods. Approximately 19 per cent of the women provided no answer for their last and 23 per cent of the women provided no answer for their next-to-last children. Some of the women reported this event by the month of the year, and a few gave the child's stage of development, but most specified the child's precise age, either in days, weeks, or months. The question was phrased not to determine when children first tasted solid foods, as in ceremonies of first rice feeding, nor when a caretaker left briefly with an infant gave it some food to keep it from crying, but rather when supplements were added to the infant's regular diet.

There was space on the questionnaire to write down additional remarks that women made. Many women from ethnic Tibetan communities described early provision of supplements as a Nepali custom and said that they had learned this from their Parbatiya and Bura neighbors. This, however, simply may reflect observations of ceremonial practices. Parbatiya and Bura are Hindus and regard childbirth as extremely polluting: the mother gives birth in a separate room and stays there about three weeks. When she returns, the infant is given its first taste of rice in a mash mixed with water. Most of the mothers then resume full breastfeeding. Other than this, there is no relationship between ethnic identity and timing of supplementation.

Another comment many women made was that they had given cereal supplements earlier than they would have liked, because of their heavy workloads. Women in Humla, as I have mentioned, prefer not to take their children to the fields because of difficulties of transport and of working while caring for a child. This preference is reinforced by the notion that it is mystically dangerous to take vulnerable infants on public roads through lonely places, which are the supposed haunts of demons and ghosts.[14] The choices are to stay home with a nursing infant and neglect work, take the infant to the fields, and not only do a poorer job but also expose it to mystical dangers, or leave it at home. Women usually leave their children with household members, although they also may make arrangements with sisters and good friends in other households and occasionally leave infants alone, securely wedged in baskets. What a woman does depends on whether her household can afford the loss of her labor, whether there are other workers to replace her in the fields, whether there are responsible adults or

children to leave the infant with who are not themselves needed in agricultural work, and also depends on seasonal labor demands.

There is no published study on Nepal that addresses these issues in a systematic way, so it is impossible to determine the generality of child care patterns or even to say when supplementary foods are most commonly introduced. Graves reports that supplements, principally rice, are introduced before six months of age in the Kathmandu valley (Graves 1978:542), but does not specify in which month or months this generally takes place.[15] Other studies describe women of diverse ethnic affiliations taking their nursing infants with them to the fields and working with them tied to their backs or putting them on blankets at the fields' edge (Molnar 1981:55; Panter-Brick 1986:141–2; Schuler 1981:22). It is unclear, however, how common this is and whether it varies with the distance or difficulty in reaching a given place.[16]

In Humla, patterns of supplementing breast milk vary markedly both within and across the different ethnic groups. Three communities of ethnic Tibetans were studied: Ladog, with a population of approximately 1,400 people; Rongphug, with approximately 350 people; and Gyaling, with approximately 650 people.[17] Also studied was one Parbatiya community, Jajarkot. It is predominantly Chetri in caste, with a few untouchable artisan households, and included approximately 1,100 people at the time of the survey. The two Bura communities are Daiba and Sankhagaon, which included approximately 500 and 600 people respectively. All of these communities also vary greatly in wealth, as their average landholdings show (Tables 2 and 3).

It becomes immediately apparent that Tibetan versus Parbatiya versus Bura ethnic identity bears no relationship to the timing of supplementing breast milk. Thus ethnic Tibetans can be found at both ends of the spectrum: those in Ladog tend to give supplements latest, while those in Gyaling do so earliest. Within communities there is considerable variation as well. Informant interviews suggest that this reflects factors of individual choice, for women hold differing opinions about when it is best to start supplements. Factors beyond a woman's control also figure in this, such as illness and demand for her labor. Predictably there is the least internal variation in communities that provide supplements earliest, where the decision is made before other factors can intervene.

There does, however, appear to be an association between a community's general economic standing, as measured by average landholdings, and the timing of supplementation. In Humla (and it probably is not atypical for Nepal) average incomes and standards of living vary widely between different communities. Certain villages are better situated for agriculture, with

Table 2. Providing supplementary feedings, Tibetan communities

Child's Age When Introduced	Community Name		
	Ladog	Rongphug	Gyaling
	Percent of Children		
Less Than One Month	3.5	25.0	75.5
One to Two Months	18.3	25.0	14.9
Three to Four Months	12.7	14.6	2.1
Five to Six Months	10.6	12.5	4.3
Seven Months to One Year	24.6	12.5	1.1
More Than One Year[a]	30.3	10.4	2.1
Landholdings (In Plow Days)[b]	10.9	4.5	9.7
N. of Cases	142	48	94

[a] Including the responses: after he/she was walking, took the food him/herself.

[b] This is based on the number of days it takes to plow family holdings with an ox-yak crossbreed. Each day is equivalent to about thirty percent of an acre.

richer soils and more irrigation sources or with room for expansion, while others may be better situated for herding or trade. Certain villages are more recently settled or have experienced less population growth, thus face less pressure on land. The Parbatiya village Jajarkot suffers on all accounts. Its soils are overworked, there is no pasture for herding (and thus no animals for compost to improve the soils), and most fields are on a steep slope, now deforested and increasingly eroded. Jajarkot also is located at the bottom of a narrow river valley, hemmed in by its neighbors, with nowhere to expand. Its population is large, and each household has very little land (see Table 3).

Wealth can affect infant feeding and child care in several ways. People who are wealthier can hire substitute labor and relieve their women from some of their tasks. Wealthier households tend to be larger too, and have more people available to share the labor. Thus a wealthy woman may be able to stay home with her infant more, instead of relying mostly on caretakers. In addition, members of wealthier households tend to have a better diet: more meat, milk, and greater variety in grains, pulses, and vegetables. Local women feel that diet is a significant factor in their ability to produce adequate breast milk, an issue to be raised again. And people's own ideas—the fact that they regard prolonged full breast-feeding as a sign of affluence—surely are significant as well.[18]

Landholdings, however, fail to explain all the variation between communities. Ladog, which has the most land and the greatest income from trade, does have the latest dates of introducing supplements, and land-short Jajarkot and Rongphug do provide supplements early. Yet Gyaling, a relatively well-off community, provides supplements earliest of all, and Daiba women tend to provide supplements much later than their Bura counterparts in Sankhagaon, despite roughly equivalent landholdings. Thus other factors are involved, among them local needs for and demands on women's time.

This becomes particularly clear in Gyaling, where women repeatedly complain that they had to give supplements early because of their work responsibilities. These women are known locally for their extremely heavy workloads, and it seemed to me that they worked harder than women in the other communities I studied, although I lack data on actual time allocations. There are two reasons for this situation. 1) The extensive cultivation of millets is particularly demanding of a woman's time. The average Gyaling household planted 3.3 plow days of millet in 1982, versus 1.8 in Ladog (where supplementation is quite late). The other communities planted comparable amounts: 2.2 plow days of millet in Rongphug and Sankhagaon, and 2.6 in Jajarkot and Daiba. 2) Gyaling women also manage large cattle herds pastured at great distances from the village. In spring the pasture site is 3,600 feet above the village. Women prefer to keep infants there (they believe it is a healthier place) and so they must descend a steep path to village fields every morning and ascend that same path every evening. It is no wonder then that they provide supplements for the infants left behind. In autumn, they engage in day-long searches for hay, that they forage from distant hillsides and sometimes pilfer from the land of adjacent communities.

Daiba women are the only ones in the study who customarily take their young infants to the field. The Daiba study was completed after I left Humla, and I was unable to find out why it differs in this regard. It may be because the village is in a less rugged area, where transport poses fewer problems. It also may be due to the system of double village residence. Villagers keep two homes, one near their upper and the other near lower altitude fields. This may result in mothers working close to home, or the division of the family across two homes may reduce the number of substitute caretakers available. Another relevant fact is that Daiba lands are relatively more productive and food shortages less widespread.[19] Thus people are better off than landholding data would suggest, and this may have an impact on infant care. Daiba women, nonetheless, also said that they start infants on supplements in order to

Table 3.   Providing supplementary feedings, Nepali speakers

	Community Name		
	Parbatiya	Bura	
Child's Age When Introduced	Jajarkot	Daiba	Sankhagaon
	Percent of Children		
Less Than One Month	15.3	2.9	7.6
One to Two Months	38.2	14.3	60.2
Three to Four Months	27.4	31.4	25.4
Five to Six Months	8.3	45.7	6.8
Seven Months to One Year	8.3	5.7	0.0
More Than One Year[a]	2.6	0.0	0.0
Landholdings (In Plow Days)[b]	4.7	8.0	7.9
N. of Cases	157	105	118

[a]Including the responses: after he/she was walking, took the food him/herself.

[b]This is based on the number of days it takes to plow family holdings with an ox-yak crossbreed. Each day is equivalent to about thirty percent of an acre.

go off on their own to work; they simply delay doing so longer than most.

SEASONAL CYCLES OF WORK AND INFANT FEEDING IN HUMLA

The seasonal cycle of women's work has an impact upon infant feeding, as studies of other societies have shown. Infants in parts of Gambia, for example, are likelier to be weaned at the height of the agricultural season (Ware 1981:64). In African countries and in Bangladesh, a decline in suckling frequency has been reported for peak agricultural seasons (Huffman and Lamphere 1984:97; Chen, Chowdhury and Huffman 1979:180). Ethnic Tibetan women in Humla also are likelier to introduce supplementary food during busy agricultural months (Table 4). Proportionately more of these women report introducing supplementary foods between late February and early April, which is when the agricultural cycle begins, and these higher rates persist through late summer or autumn. There is considerable month-to-month variation, which may be attributable to the small sample size but also may be due to variations in the intensity of work. Notably, the seasonal pattern holds even in Gyaling, where most women give supplements within the first month. This is because they tend to delay supplementation for children born in winter, when they are at home and more

easily can feed and attend to an infant's needs. Finally, the data suggest that women introduce supplements somewhat in advance of the time of greatest demand on their labor and delay supplementation toward its end. This is consistent with the reported practice of getting infants used to cereals. Women say they do this intentionally, so that when supplements become necessary the infant will accept them without difficulty. If Rongphug differs slightly, it may be the lower altitude and the prolonged agricultural season, although the pronounced fluctuations also may be attributable to the small sample size.[20]

These patterns are not repeated among Parbatiya and Bura, with Sankhagaon a possible exception (Table 5). There are two possible reasons for this. These women may have been less careful in reporting when they began to give supplements. Approximately two-thirds gave the same ages for last and next-to-last children. That is, two-thirds of the women who said that they first regularly gave supplements when their last child was two months old said the same about the next-to-last child. By contrast, one-quarter or fewer of the ethnic Tibetans gave the same answer for last and next-to-last children. Thus Parbatiya and Bura women may have given conventional answers that reflected general experience (theirs, or kin and friends) despite being asked about their particular infants. It also is possible that seasonal agricultural cycles have less effect upon decisions to provide supplements in these communities, and that women judge this by the child's

Table 4. Seasonality of supplementary feeding, Tibetan speakers

Month of Introducing Cereal Foods	Community Name			
	Ladog	Rongphug	Gyaling	All Tibetans
	Percent of Children			
12 /16–1/15[a]	5.0	7.1	3.3	4.7
1/16–2/15	4.0	2.4	5.4	4.3
2/16–3/15	7.1	14.3	7.6	8.6
3/16–4/15	13.1	4.8	14.1	12.0
4/16–5/15	9.1	7.1	10.9	9.4
5/16–6/15	12.1	16.7	11.9	12.9
6/16–7/15	11.1	9.5	8.7	9.9
7/16–8/15	10.1	11.9	11.9	11.2
8/16–9/15	8.1	2.4	7.6	6.9
9/16–10/15	11.1	2.4	7.6	8.1
10/16–11/15	4.0	14.3	4.4	6.0
11/16–12/15	5.0	7.1	6.5	6.0
N. of Cases	99	42	92	233

[a]These months conform to the Nepali lunar calendar.

Table 5. Seasonality of supplementary feeding, Parbatiya and Bura

Date of Introducing Cereal Foods	Community Name			
	Jajarkot	Daiba	Sankhagaon	Chetri-Bura
	Percent of Children			
12 /16–1/15[a]	10.3	13.3	5.9	9.8
1/16–2/15	8.9	3.8	4.3	5.9
2/16–3/15	7.6	4.8	14.5	8.9
3/16–4/15	8.3	8.6	9.4	8.7
4/16–5/15	8.3	3.8	9.4	7.4
5/16–6/15	9.7	14.3	13.7	12.3
6/16–7/15	9.7	6.7	8.6	8.4
7/16–8/15	7.6	6.7	11.1	8.4
8/16–9/15	8.3	14.3	5.9	9.3
9/16–10/15	6.2	5.7	8.6	6.8
10/16–11/15	11.7	12.4	5.1	9.8
11/16–12/15	3.4	5.7	3.4	4.1
N. of Cases	145	105	117	367

[a]These months conform to the Nepali lunar calendar.

age, not work demands. This certainly could be the case in Daiba where women take their infants to the fields for a time.

EARLY SUPPLEMENTARY FEEDING

Humla women of all communities say that when they lack sufficient food, their breast milk suffers and their infants remain hungry. Thus inadequate maternal diet was one of the commonest reasons volunteered for early supplementation, second only to excessive workload. Humla, as I have said, is one of the poorest districts in Nepal and has experienced several famines in recent decades. Food shortages are particularly acute in the poorest communities, Rongphug and Jajarkot—reaching their peak in spring and early summer—while wealthy communities like Ladog suffer slightly even in the worst of years.

Studies on breast milk composition suggest that Humla women have reason to be concerned, for the quantity and quality of breast milk appears to be affected by nutritional status. There is evidence of lower fat content in the milk of undernourished women and some indication of lower levels of protein and lactose (Rowland, Paul and Whitehead 1981; Wray 1978:199–200). Dietary deficiencies also have been implicated in diminished production of breast milk and in shortened duration of lactation, both quantity and duration declining as these deficiencies increase (Wray 1978:203). Some studies suggest that breast milk quantity declines when women's nutrition falls below a threshold level (World Health Organization 1985:38, 44).

Rural peasant women cannot make precise assessments about the quality of their milk. What they notice, and what they say, is that their milk is inadequate and that it does not satisfy their infants; some also say that it dries up sooner than they would like. The notion common to all these communities is that women with better diets have adequate breast milk. Also shared are notions about the constituents of a good diet: meat, milk products, honey, and rice and barley, the preferred grains.

Women's concerns about the adequacy of breast milk were revealed in a segment of the questionnaire on problems experienced breast feeding. The questions prompted discursive answers about inadequate nutrition and difficulties of work and reveal the prevalence of women's concerns about their abilities to meet their infants' needs (Table 6). These data cannot be taken as an accurate index to problems, but rather of perceptions of (and willingness to discuss) problems. This may explain why ethnic Tibetan women

voiced these concerns more often about male than female infants (Levine 1987b).

Women's opinions are divided on the effects of early supplementation. Some argue that it makes children strong and helps them to grow, and eases the lot of mothers, while others speak against it. Most, however, agree on the ill effects of leaving infants all day with caretakers. The concern is not about the supplements, but about the effects upon breast milk, which women say spoils over the long day while they work in the hot sun (cf. Raphael and Davis 1985:83–4).[21] Yet there certainly are problems with the supplements. Women make them by masticating some of the grain foods prepared for family members and mixing this mash with untreated water or butter. The food is then left indoors near the fire or outdoors in the sun, where it soon is covered by houseflies.[22] Caretakers then scoop bits out with their fingers to feed infants during the day.

We only can speculate about the effects these contaminated supplements have on young infants. While studies have examined the impact of inappropriately prepared formula foods on morbidity and mortality in less developed countries, there have been no tests of the effects of traditional foods prepared under similar conditions. We know that infants from developed countries in the early to mid-twentieth century who were given mixed feedings had levels of mortality intermediate between wholly breast fed and wholly artificially fed infants (Knodel 1977:1112; Winikoff 1982:124; Wray 1978:209–213). In rural Chile, however, children receiving mixed feedings early on (at four weeks and three months) had mortality rates close to children wholly artificially fed and more than twice the mortality rate of children wholly breast fed (Wray 1978:216–7).[23] It seems likely too that the timing of introducing supplements is significant (see Huffman and Lamphere 1984:96).

The contamination of traditional foods probably rises in summer, because of heat and increased populations of houseflies, and this is precisely when Humla women are likeliest to initiate supplementary feeding. Not surprisingly, infant and child deaths also rise in summer and early fall, which may be associated with increased diarrheal disease. Nonetheless, local people blame summer diarrhea on the spoilage of a working mother's milk in the hot sun. In several communities, chronic summer diarrhea is seen as a hereditary disease transferred through the mother's milk. No one linked such illnesses with contaminated supplements, and women with whom I shared my concerns rejected this notion. Early supplementation has other negative consequences too, including a shortened period of protection from conception for the mother, an effect whose extent is unclear.[24] Women in these societies say they prefer births spaced three or four years apart, and

Table 6.   Reported breast feeding problems

	No Problems Reported	Inadequate Milk or Other Problems[a]	N. of Cases
Ladog			
Male	57.9%	42.1%	88
Female	71.6	28.4	74
Rongphug			
Male	72.2	27.8	36
Female	69.2	30.8	26
Gyaling			
Male	39.0	60.9	41
Female	50.9	49.1	57
Parbatiya-Bura[b]			
Male	74.7	25.3	261
Female	79.8	20.2	238

[a]The other problems included: milk "drying up," baby not feeding well, and separation because of mother's work (which is believed to result in lowered milk output).

[b]This also includes a fourth community for which adequate data on supplementation and weaning are lacking. These women may have offered fewer complaints because the interviewers were men.

they believe that prolonging lactation helps in this, but do not appear to recognize that this might be compromised by early supplementation.

The opposite problem, that of late supplementation, exists as well. As Table 2 shows, more than half of Ladog women reported starting supplementary foods when their children were six months or more, and almost a third delayed this for longer than a year, which I have linked to these women's greater wealth and lesser workload. The problem is that supplements should be added between four and nine months to ensure an infant's continued growth and well-being.[25] Thus delaying supplementation has its own risks, which increase with the delay (Wyon and Gordon 1971).

DURATION OF BREAST FEEDING

Despite early supplementation and practices of leaving children all day with caretakers, total weaning is quite late here, as in many traditional societies. Women continue to feed their children whenever they are home, regularly and on demand. Women sleep with infants and small children, who thus can suckle freely at night. They feed them before leaving for work in the morning, return home if possible to feed them at midday, and feed them immediately upon return in the evening. Women reported breast feeding their next-to-last children for over two years and their most recent child up to four years (Table 7). In many cases that meant a woman's last child and last children are

breast-fed for very long periods, sometimes extending for five or six and even seven or eight years.[26] These practices show effects of ethnicity, for the Parbatiya and Bura women wean their children latest. The Nepal Fertility Survey found a similar pattern, with Hindu women breast feeding their children longer than Buddhist women (World Fertility Survey 1979:174–75).

Most women feed a child until their milk dries up with subsequent pregnancies.[27] If their milk continues, weaning may be delayed almost until childbirth, and if the new infant dies, the mother may start breast feeding the previous child again. This is because breast feeding is seen as beneficial, physically and emotionally, and as an unquestioned obligation. Moreover, it is seen as having no costs. Thus prolonged breast feeding occurs with all children and seems not to differ for boys and girls.

Once children reach age three or four, however, they may be weaned intentionally, either because women feel that breast feeding is no longer necessary or because they find it somewhat unseemly, in addition to interfering with their work. They first try to discourage the child verbally, and, if that fails, put bitter substances on their breasts. Women in Rongphug sometimes wean an insistent child by sending it to its grandmother's house. Only Gyaling women customarily wean their children abruptly. They do so when they decide to stay in the village and send a child to the distant midsummer pastures with its grandmother. This is why Gyaling tends to wean earliest and why weaning is twice as common from mid-June through mid-July. Otherwise Gyaling women, like those in the other communities, breast feed as long as they can.

Table 7. Average duration of breast feeding in months

	Community Name					
	Tibetan-Speakers			Parbatiya-Bura		
	Ladog	Rongphug	Gyaling	Jajarkot	Daiba	Sankhagaon
	All Sexes[a]					
Last Child[b]	42.9	32.6	31.0	41.9	45.8	42.9
N. of Cases	(33)	(14)	(11)	(25)	(16)	(27)
Previous Child[c]	32.5	26.2	25.7	27.0	31.8	34.4
N. of Cases	(57)	(12)	(35)	(54)	(39)	(37)
Landholdings[d]	10.9	4.5	9.7	4.7	8.0	7.9

[a]This only includes children who survived to weaning.

[b]These cases are fewer, because many "last children" were still being breast-fed. Since a certain proportion of these last children were not followed by later siblings, the average duration of breast feeding tends to be longer in this category.

[c]That is, the next to last child (in the last closed birth interval).

[d]As above, this figure is given in plow days.

CONCLUSION

The patterns I have described for Humla, where supplementary cereal foods commonly are introduced within the first few months, where breast feeding is prolonged for at least two years and often more, where there is a mix of frequent and indulgent nursing when the mother is present and supplementary foods when she must work, still may be found among other traditional groups and may have been more common in the past (Zeitlen et al. 1982:31). The existence of such long-standing, traditional patterns of early supplementation to facilitate mothers' work may lend a certain perspective on the use of bottle feeding by urban working women in less developed countries today. The difference is that bottle feeding seems likelier to replace, than to supplement, breast milk, and thus carries greater risks.

What is striking in this case are the similarities in the ways women of different ethnic groups accommodate the demands of work and of feeding and caring for their infants and young children. The cultural and social systems of these communities hardly could be more diverse. Ethnic Tibetans, high caste Hindu Parbatiyas, and Buras have different religions and different systems of social stratification, marriage, and household organization. Yet such factors seem to have little impact on patterns of infant feeding. Instead existing variations appear to have their source in systems of labor management, the exigencies of local resource use, and relative prosperity, which influences how long a new mother can be spared from full pro-

ductive work. Since the heavy agricultural labor women perform is not compatible with full attention to child care, these women tend to compartmentalize the two. Other household members are called into service for child care, and there is relatively little concern about their ability to substitute for the mother. This is because child care is seen as comparatively nondemanding and as not requiring special skills. The major problem is that caretakers only can provide supplementary foods in the mother's absence, and for reasons other than the ones members of these societies identify, this can have negative consequences for children. Although unaware of the sources of the problem, people recognize that infants do best when mothers stay home and can breast feed on demand. However, this is impossible for most women.

NOTES

1. Research in northwest Nepal was carried out between September 1982 and April 1984, supported by the National Science Foundation and the Population Council. Surveys in Tibetan-speaking villages were completed by myself and in the Nepali-speaking Parbatiya and Bura villages by Netra B. Tumbahangfe and Tshewang B. Lama. I thank Tahir Ali, Carole Browner, Allen Johnson, Augusta Molnar, and B. J. Williams for their helpful comments and suggestions on an earlier draft.

2. Comparative data provide a more complex picture of compatibility varying with productive technologies and

accommodations varying with social arrangements (see the essays in Marshall 1985 and Ware 1984:205).

3. Nerlove (1974:208–210) found that women who gave supplements before one month contributed an average of 38 per cent to subsistence activities, while those who did so after one month contributed an average of 27 per cent. This excluded gathering work, which generally is viewed as compatible with child care; but on gathering see Katz (1985:276) and Lee (1980:332, 343).

4. There is no empirical support for the common viewpoint that urban employment is responsible for declines in breastfeeding (Van Esterik and Greiner 1981).

5. Thus when land reform was instituted in Nepal in 1964, no highland holding exceeded the legal maximum.

6. Apart from these two communities, the wealthiest households in each village had assets worth less than three times those of the poorest (Acharya and Bennett 1981:33).

7. The variations in patterns of labor in different Nepalese communities are vividly illustrated by Acharya and Bennett (1981:402–424).

8. Only better-off farmers in the plains can meet this ideal, and conformance to it seems to be rising nowadays, supported by rising agricultural income. The concern apparently not only is purdah, but also securing women's relief from physical labor (see Sharma 1980:29, 43, 116–7 and also Boserup 1970:24–27).

9. Data on time use were collected through random spot checks of a representative sample of households on alternate days over a period of at least six months (Acharya and Bennett 1981:16–23).

10. On the extent of household variations, see Bennett (1981:151). Nag, White, and Peet (1978:295–6) report higher rates of sibling caretaking in a Thami (Nepalese) group than Acharya and Bennett (1981:426–48). but their methods of data collection differed. (On the phenomenon of sibling caretaking generally see Weisner and Gallimore [1977].)

11. Minor variations in this depend on local conditions and traditions. For one example, a community in an intensively cultivated valley collects most of its grass in the space of a few days from individually owned grass fields. During this brief period, both men and women work on grass collection. Another community has fields so far from the village that horses are used to carry compost to them. Since men generally manage horses, they help in transporting compost.

12. Crop selection and rotational schedules involve collective village decisions. The result is that a particular sector of land may be sown with millet one year and double cropped with winter barley and buckwheat the next. Women in households holding disproportionate amounts of land in that sector may find themselves more burdened with work the first year than the next.

13. Many households included extended families with two or more generations of women. The procedure followed here involved interviewing a junior woman in one extended family household, a senior woman in the next, and so on.

14. Similar notions have been reported for Yemen (Ware 1984:203).

15. Rajaure (1981:75–6) reports that Tharu of the Terai, or plains, do not introduce supplements until the child is six to eight months old. Sharma (1980:129) reports that North Indian mothers may take their infants and children to the fields, or leave them at home, depending upon the structure of the household, but does not elaborate on this or note any differences between hill and plains practices.

16. Molnar (personal communication) adds that Kham Magar women bring sibling caretakers along to their work sites and suggests that mothers may be more likely to take their infants to distant fields because of the impossibility of returning home at midday for breast feeding.

17. The community names used here are pseudonyms.

18. Wealth differences within a community, however, do not have a significant effect on the timing of introducing supplements.

19. Reports on grain production involved approximations and may be biased by underestimates due to Humla people's justifiable fear of tax increases. Thus the 25 per cent higher yields that Daiba households report must be treated as suggestive only.

20. Rongphug lies in a low valley just below 8,000 feet, while Ladog villages range between 10,000 and 11,000 feet. Gyaling, though only 9,000 feet, lies in a cool northern valley, which curtails the growing season. Jajarkot is located at 8,300 feet; Sankhagaon at 8,900 feet; the lower village of Daiba must be below 7,500 feet and the upper village above 9,000 feet.

21. No one thinks an infant can survive on cereal foods alone, and people make great efforts to find someone, ideally a close relative, to feed an infant whose mother has died (cf. Gordon et al. 1963; Wray 1978:210, 214).

22. Mastication and the action of the enzyme ptyalin, enhanced by the warmth of the sun, may accelerate the conversion of these cooked starches into glucose and make these foods more digestible by infants.

23. Winikoff (1982:124) suggests that disparities in reports on the effects of mixed feeding (that is, with modern formulas) may be due to problems of study design, such as differences in defining mixed feeding and failures to control for parental socio-economic status, conditions of sanitation, and the birth weights and ages of the babies concerned.

24. Studies suggesting that partial breast feeding shortens the duration of amenorrhea do not specify what level of supplementation prompts the return of ovulation and what other factors might be involved in this (Gray 1981:101; Ridley 1978:176).

25. This depends upon the mother's nutrition (Scrimshaw, Taylor and Gordon 1968; Rowland, Paul and Whitehead 1981; Winikoff 1982:125).

26. Women were asked how old the child was when they ceased breast feeding, and their answers show marked heaping at six month intervals. As Ware (1984:202) points out, weaning "is not an event . . . that anyone is likely to recall by exact date." Instead it is a process prolonged over several months, which makes the request for a precise date inappropriate and answers heaped at six month intervals quite justifiable. By contrast, questions about first supplementation did not yield answers heaped on any particular months.

27. Women say that milk tends to dry up when they are four to seven months pregnant. A study in India showed a sharp decline in the output of milk occurring twelve weeks after the onset of pregnancy (reported in Gray 1981:103).

BIBLIOGRAPHY

Acharya, M. 1981. The Maithili Women of Sirsia. Manila.

Acharya, M., and L. Bennett. 1981. The Rural Women of Nepal. An Aggregate Analysis and Summary of 8 Village Studies. Manila.

Bennett, L. 1981. The Parbatiya Women of Bakundol. Manila.

Boserup, E. 1970. Women's Role in Economic Development. New York.

Brown, J. K. 1970. A Note on the Division of Labor by Sex. American Anthropologist 72:1073–1078.

Chen, L. C., A. K. M. Alauddin Chowdhury, and S. L. Huffman. 1979. Seasonal Dimensions of Energy Protein Malnutrition in Rural Bangladesh: The Role of Agriculture, Dietary Practices, and Infection. Ecology of Food and Nutrition 8:175–87.

Goody, J. 1976. Production and Reproduction. Cambridge.

Gordon, J. E., I. D. Chitkara, and J. B. Wyon. 1963. Weanling Diarrhea. American Journal of Medical Science 245:345–377.

Graves, P. L. 1978. Nutrition and Infant Behavior: A Replication Study in the Kathmandu Valley, Nepal. American Journal of Clinical Nutrition 31:541–551.

Gray, R. H. 1981. Birth Intervals, Postpartum Sexual Abstinence and Child Health. Child Spacing in Tropical Africa, eds. H. J. Page and R. Lesthaeghe. London.

Guillet, D. 1983. Toward a Cultural Ecology of Mountains: The Central Andes and the Himalayas Compared. Current Anthropology 24:561–574.

Hammond, D., and A. Jablow. 1976. Women in Cultures of the World. Menlo Park, California.

Höfer, A. 1979. The Caste Hierarchy and the State in Nepal. A Study of the Muluki Ain of 1854. Innsbruck.

Huffman, S. L., and B. B. Lamphere. 1984. Breastfeeding Performance and Child Survival. Child Survival Strategies for Research, eds. W. Henry Mosley and Lincoln C. Chen. Population and Development Review. Supplement to Volume 10.

Katz, M. M. 1985. Infant Care in a Group of Outer Fiji Islands. Infant Care and Feeding in the South Pacific, ed. Leslie B. Marshall. New York.

Knodel, J. 1977. Breast Feeding and Population Growth. Science 98:1111–1115.

Lee, R. B. 1980. Lactation, Ovulation, Infanticide, and Women's Work: A Study of Hunter-Gatherer Population Regulation. Biosocial Mechanisms of Population Regulation, eds. R. Malpass and H. Klein. New Haven.

Levine, N. E. 1987a. Caste, State and Ethnic Boundaries in Nepal. Journal of Asian Studies 46:71–88.

———. 1987b. Differential Child Care in Three Tibetan Communities: Beyond Son Preference. Population and Development Review 13:281–304.

Marshall, L. B., ed. 1985. Infant Care and Feeding in the South Pacific. New York.

Molnar, A. 1981. The Kham Magar Women of Thabang. Manila.

Nag, M., B. N. F. White, and R. C. Peet. 1978. An Anthropological Approach to the Economic Value of Children in Java and Nepal. Current Anthropology 19:293–306.

Nardi, B. A. 1984. Infant Feeding and Women's Work in Western Samoa: A Hypothesis, Some Evidence and Suggestions for Future Research. Ecology of Food and Nutrition 14:277–286.

Nerlove, S. B. 1974. Women's Workload and Infant Feeding Practices: A Relationship with Demographic Implications. Ethnology 13:207–214.

Netting, R. McC. 1981. Balancing on an Alp. Cambridge.

Panter-Brick, C. 1986. Women's Work and Child-bearing Experience. Two Ethnic Groups of Salme Nepal. Contributions to Nepalese Studies 13:137–147.

Popkin, B. M. 1980. Time Allocation of the Mother and Child Nutrition. Ecology of Food and Nutrition 9:1–14.

Quinn, N. 1977. Anthropological Studies on Women's Status. Annual Review of Anthropology 6:181–225.

Rajaure, D. 1981. The Tharu Women of Sukhrwar. Manila.

Raphael, D., and F. Davis. 1985. Only Mothers Know. Westport, CT.

Rhoades, R. E., and S. I. Thompson. 1975. Adaptive Strategies in Alpine Environments: Beyond Ecological Particularism. American Ethnologist 2:535–551.

Ridley, J. C. Nutrition and Breast Feeding. Introductory Statement. Nutrition and Human Reproduction, ed. W. Henry Mosley. New York.

Rowland, M. G. M., Alison A. Paul, and R. G. Whitehead. Lactation and Infant Nutrition. British Medical Bulletin 37:77–82.

Schuler, S. 1981. The Women of Baragaon. Manila.

Scrimshaw, N. S., C. E. Taylor, and J. E. Gordon. 1968. Interactions of Nutrition and Infection. Monograph No. 57. W.H.O. Geneva.

Sharma, U. 1980. Women, Work and Property in North-west India. London.

Van Esterik, P., and T. Greiner. 1981. Breastfeeding and Women's Work: Constraints and Opportunities. Studies in Family Planning 12:184–197.

Ware, H. 1981. Women, Demography and Development. Canberra.

———. 1984. Effects of Maternal Education. Women's Roles and Child Care in Child Mortality. Child Survival. Strategies for Research, eds. W. H. Mosley and L. C. Chen. Population and Development Review. Supplement to Volume 10.

Weisner, T. S., and R. Gallimore. 1977. My Brother's Keeper: Child and Sibling Caretaking. Current Anthropology 18:169–90.

Winikoff, B. 1982. Weaning: Nutrition, Morbidity, and Mortality Consequences. Biological and Social Aspects of Mortality and the Length of Life, ed. S. H. Preston. Liege.

World Fertility Survey. 1979. Nepal Fertility Survey. First Report. Voorburg, Netherlands.

World Health Organization. 1985. The Quantity and Quality of Breast Milk. Report on the WHO Collaborative Study on Breastfeeding. Geneva.

Wray, J. D. 1978. Maternal Nutrition. Breast-feeding and Infant Survival. Nutrition and Human Reproduction, ed. W. Henry Mosley. New York.

Wyon, J. B., and J. E. Gordon. 1971. The Khanna Study. Cambridge, MA.

Zeitlin, M. F. et al. 1982. Nutrition and Population Growth. The Delicate Balance. West Germany.

Undernutrition, Overnutrition, and Hunger in Lands of Plenty

The nutritional problems of individuals in the United States and other "lands of plenty" are seemingly paradoxical. While not as obvious and severe as the problems faced by individuals living in extreme poverty, in various ways these problems diminish lives and demand better understanding. The articles in this part explore this complex of problems.

There are two apparent and interrelated paradoxes: (1) the paradox of hunger and undernutrition in a land of great wealth and (2) the simultaneous occurrence of overnutrition and undernutrition. Despite great overall wealth, many families have difficulty providing nutritious foods for their children. With regard to energy and protein, it is rare to find examples of anything more than mild levels of deficiency in the United States. Deficient quality, rather than deficient quantity, is the problem. Diets that are all too commonly dominated by processed foods and snack foods are low in nutrient density (the ratio of micronutrients to calories). This eating pattern promotes deficiencies in iron, calcium, and other micronutrients and consequent problems in learning, resistance to disease, and other functional domains.

Culture and ideology play roles in determining who may be at risk for micronutrient deficiency. It is important to know the forces shaping food purchase and consumption decisions. Without doubt these decisions are shaped by food availability in local markets and the multiple ways that foods are advertised. Age and sex are key, too. For many nutrients, younger individuals have greater needs relative to energy intakes (that is, they require a more nutrient-dense diet). But they may be the most susceptible to quick satisfaction. Economic status may be the most common cause of nutrient deficiencies. Poor school districts may obtain needed funds by allowing companies such as Coca-Cola to place vending machines in their halls and to advertise at sporting events.

Hunger is the perception of inadequate food. To many, because hunger is "only a perception" that may or may not be associated with undernutrition, it is not a public health problem. But in fact, the threat and perception of hunger determine behaviors. Hunger is quickly alleviated by inexpensive snacks, such as a soft drink.

Despite the billions of dollars spent on diet programs and on purchases of exercise equipment, overnutrition is increasing in the United States and around the world. The simple equation for the etiology of obesity is that more energy is consumed than is expended. But why does this seem to happen so easily? How do we explain obesity at a deeper and more meaningful level? Why is weight so easy to gain, and why are these gains so hard to reverse?

Overnutrition, or obesity, is a sign of health and beauty in some cultures and among some ethnic groups. There, the trend to desire obesity, especially in women, may conflict with health workers' efforts to reduce obesity (obesity is clearly associated with chronic disease and disability). Conversely, the mainstream media in the United States portray thinness as healthy, sexy, and a sign of control. A popular saying is that you can neither be too rich nor too thin! Thinness is so desired that the stigma of obesity may exacerbate and even override health concerns. We must, therefore, come to grips with the conflicting cultural meanings of the body.

The complicating paradox is the co-occurrence of hunger, micronutrient undernutrition, and obesity. Often the same individuals who are consuming excess energy also suffer from micronutrient malnutrition and bouts of hunger. In a sense, this complex is the "worst of both worlds." It is the worst of the world of poverty and the worst of the world of plenty. Article 38 focuses on the nexus of hunger and malnutrition, and the last two articles focus on the nexus of obesity (articles 39 and 40).

In "Hunger, Malnutrition, and Poverty in the Contemporary United States: Some Observations on Their Social and Cultural Context," Janet Fitchen provides a powerful argument for the significance of hunger and malnutrition in the United States. She presents a statistical and historical background to hunger and malnutrition, including efforts to combat these problems. However, her greatest contribution is in her analysis of the sociocultural milieu of poverty that fosters and perpetuates these problems. Fitchen shows how eating patterns are shaped by, among other things, lack of funds, unavailability of produce in impoverished areas, food "handouts" from government programs, and cultural valuation of prestige foods.

In "An Anthropological Perspective on Obesity," Peter Brown and Melvin Konner provide a broad anthropological overview of obesity. Their basic thesis is that obesity is an intractable problem in part because genes and culture coevolved to maximize weight gain in past societies. Excess weight increased chances of survival and increased fertility in preagricultural groups that maintained only the most minimal or no food surplus. From an evolutionary perspective, obesity appears to be an example of culture and biology being out of sync. Physiologies are designed to add weight out of fear of famine, but such fears are no longer warranted. Instead, we live well past our reproductive primes, and in later years the excess body weight can lead to chronic diseases.

There is a clear trend toward thinness as beautiful in advertisements. The public has responded with skyrocketing purchases of exercise equipment and enrollment in weight-loss plans. Yet, obesity increases. Between a survey in 1976–80 and one in 1988–94, male obesity increased 38 percent and female obesity increased 33 percent. The result is a double problem: increased risk of chronic disease and the stigma of obesity in a culture that values thinness. Obesity is related to new "hungers." Many individuals who consider themselves to be obese develop eating disorders, and many still will intermittently "go hungry" in an effort to reduce weight. Obesity, therefore, is much more than a biomedical problem.

In the last article in this part, "The Pima Paradox," Malcolm Gladwell reports on studies of obesity in the Pima of Arizona and northern Mexico, and what these studies may say about obesity in the rest of us. Gladwell travels around the Gila River reservation of the Pima, into the world of diet books and weight-loss drugs, and finally over the Mexican border to the world of the Mexican Pima. Along the way, he evaluates the superficial explanations (weight = excess calories) and, at a deeper level, a conflicting set of explanations for why certain people gain weight so readily and what can be done about it. It is no wonder that most of us are confused about weight.

The main lesson is from the Mexican Pima, the southern cousins of the Gila River Pima. The Mexican Pima appear to be genetically indistinguishable from their U.S. cousins. But unlike the Gila River Pima, who live on a reservation and have very low activity levels, the Mexican Pima still subsist by maintaining small farms. They are active and thin. What is the lesson to be learned from the Pima? What does this say for the health care system's approach to obesity?

SUGGESTIONS FOR THINKING AND DOING NUTRITIONAL ANTHROPOLOGY

1. Compare the protein density of some foods you commonly consume. First, look for food labels that contain the protein content of a serving in grams and the energy content in calories. Second, simply divide the protein by the calories to get a protein content per calorie of energy. How variable are the protein densities of your foods?

2. Today the most frequently used definition of obesity is based on body mass index (BMI), which is weight (in kilograms) divided by height squared (in meters).

$$BMI = weight\ (kg)/ht^2\ (meters)$$

What is your BMI? If you have previously been measured for height and weight, then use these measures.

3. What is a healthy body? Cut out pictures from magazines and have the class evaluate the healthiness of each body on a scale from 1 (very unhealthy) to 5 (very healthy). Then rank the same bodies from 1 (very obese) to 5 (very thin). What is the relationship between obesity and ideas of healthiness?

4. Travel around a neighborhood. What is easier to purchase: beer, soft drinks, cigarettes, or a fresh orange?

FURTHER READINGS

Bray, G. A., Bouchard, C., & James, W. P. T. (Eds.). (1997). *Handbook of obesity*. New York: Marcel Dekker. (A well-rounded compendium of articles, mostly on the etiology and treatment of obesity.)

Brown, L. (1987, February). Hunger in America. *Scientific American*, pp. 36–41. (Essentially, a short version of the Physician Task Force on Hunger in America [see below] on the epidemiology of hunger in the 1980s.)

deGarine, I., & Pollock, N. J. (Eds.). (1995). *Social aspects of obesity*. New York: Gordon and Breach. (A good source of readings on the social milieu of obesity worldwide.)

Maurer, D., & Sobal, J., (Eds.). (1995). *Eating agendas: Food and nutrition as social problems*. New York: Aldine de Gruyter. (A wide-ranging set of chapters on social aspects of food, especially pertaining to obesity, hunger, and body image.)

Physician Task Force on Hunger in America. (1985). *Hunger in America: The growing epidemic*. Boston: Harvard University School of Public Health. (A report on hunger and malnutrition in the United States that helped to alert many individuals to the growing problem.)

38

Hunger, Malnutrition, and Poverty in the Contemporary United States: Some Observations on Their Social and Cultural Context

Janet M. Fitchen

That malnutrition and hunger exist in the contemporary United States seems unbelievable to people in other nations who assume that Americans can have whatever they want in life. Even within the United States, most people are not aware of domestic hunger or else believe that government programs and volunteer efforts must surely be taking care of any hunger that does exist here. And, to some extent, the focus of American public attention on "Third World hunger" and the enthusiasm for mass media events to raise money for famine relief divert attention from hunger and malnutrition at home. After all, the television pictures of distended bellies, matchstick legs, and gaunt faces are from Ethiopia, not the United States.

In the United States, hunger can go unnoticed because there is little overt begging for food and little obvious starvation. In fact, people who are poor enough to qualify for government-issued food stamps may be seen in grocery stores purchasing not only basic, inexpensive staples but also such widely popular items as frozen pizza, potato chips, soda pop, prepared desserts, and sometimes a beef steak. With such purchases, low-income people may be seeking to satisfy subjective as well us metabolic aspects of eating, perhaps attempting to convert their perceived hunger into a sense of well-being or to affirm that they can live like other Americans. But in so doing, they may inadvertently be transforming their hunger into malnutrition and also hiding their hunger from public awareness. The public, observing such "luxury" items among the grocery purchases of the poor, concludes that if poor people can eat steak, then they must be neither very poor nor very hungry. And so the problem of hunger receives little serious public attention.

But the diet of Americans who are poor should be compared to the nutritional status and eating patterns of the rest of the American population rather than to the condition of starving refugees in Africa. Although hunger anywhere is fundamentally a metabolic phenomenon with absolute dimensions, it also has important cognitive and relativistic attributes. Hunger in America, like the poverty that spawns it, must be understood in relation to the standards of living and

eating in the surrounding society. In this article I argue that hunger is a significant problem in the United States today, in both its physical and its cognitive forms; and also that malnutrition, which is a more purely physical condition involving insufficient nutrients for growth and health, is a serious problem. I emphasize the need to understand the cultural aspects of hunger.

Hunger in the United States is not the result of insufficient foodstuffs for the total population: in fact, national food production is at unprecedentedly high levels, and farm surpluses continue to be a problem for the economy. It is, instead, a matter of some people regularly having inadequate access to sufficient food. And the recent increase in hunger outlined below is not solely a result of the policies and priorities of the present federal administration. True, the problem has been exacerbated as government programs providing food assistance to needy people have been cut back, altered, or eliminated. But simply to blame the current administration is to fail to understand the complexity of the situation.

To provide increased understanding of what hunger means in the American context and why this society has tolerated the continued existence of hunger and malnutrition in the midst of affluence, I look more deeply at the cultural dimensions of hunger, of eating, and of food assistance programs. I look not only at the people who go chronically underfed but also at the cultural context in which their hunger is embedded. The first part of the article presents the case that hunger and malnutrition do indeed exist in the United States, that they are closely associated with poverty, and that currently they are growing more prevalent. The main part of the article presents ethnographic data on the food and eating patterns of low-income people, suggesting that these patterns result both from the economic constraints of poverty and from the fact that the poor, despite their limited economic resources, follow many dominant American cultural ideas and practices. I indicate how these two sets of factors together shape eating patterns that may actually exacerbate malnourishment. In the following section I summarize prevailing American cultural assumptions about poverty and the poor, showing that these assumptions generate societal ideas about how the poor should eat. I then demonstrate that the same assumptions shape governmental policy and programs for food assistance. I conclude with the suggestion that in America there is a strong cultural belief, enshrined in government food assistance programs, that the poor should eat differently from other Americans because they are different: the poor should not buy steak.

RECENT HISTORY OF HUNGER AND MALNUTRITION IN AMERICA

Hunger Is Closely Associated with Poverty

A brief review of recent trends of hunger and poverty at the national level underscores the correlation between the two phenomena. In the 1950s it was widely assumed that the poverty and hunger of the Depression era had been totally eradicated by a combination of federal New Deal programs, the economic stimulus of World War II, and post-war economic growth. But in the early 1960s serious poverty was "discovered" in the midst of America's affluence: it was estimated that between 22 percent and 25 percent of the U.S. population was living in poverty.[1] The John F. Kennedy campaign and presidency gave public recognition to the extent and severity of poverty and to the hunger and malnutrition associated with it. In 1967, when a group of U.S. senators and teams of physicians toured some of the newly discovered pockets of poverty, they found staggering evidence of hunger and malnutrition. These forays into the underclass led to books and television documentaries that stirred public opinion and to congressional testimony that galvanized the government into action.[2] From the mid-1960s through the mid-1970s, a massive effort was undertaken to combat poverty through community action programs, job training, various compensatory educational programs (such as Head Start), regional development schemes, and so forth.

While the "war on poverty" was attacking some of the underlying causes of poverty that contributed to hunger and malnutrition, new food assistance programs were also developed to attack hunger directly. The commodity distribution program, which provided handouts of such commodities as lard, milk powder, cheese, and dried beans from federal stockpiles to those of the poor who could get to the pick-up stations,

was expanded to reach more people with more food items. Later the program was replaced by nationwide food stamps as a more effective form of assistance.[3] In 1969 President Richard Nixon, responding to the growing tide of public and congressional concern, declared to the nation that he would work "to put an end to hunger in America for all time." In a spirit of real commitment that surmounted entrenched opposition (see Kotz, 1969), Congress made adjustments in the new food stamp program to extend its benefits to a greater percentage of the needy. The federal program to provide free school lunches was expanded, advertised, and more adequately funded; and free breakfasts became available in many schools. A home-based nutrition education program was set up at the national level and implemented in all states, tailoring nutrition lessons to the exigencies of low-income living.[4] Extra food assistance was made available to poor people with particular needs, such as pregnant or lactating mothers, infants, and small children.[5]

As a result of the combined effort to combat hunger directly and to attack the underlying problem of poverty, and with a generally strong economy, both poverty and hunger decreased significantly. The poverty rate fell dramatically from its 1959 level of approximately 25 percent, nearly 40 million people, to a 1979 low of just under 12 percent (using a constant definition of poverty with dollar levels adjusted for inflation).[6] In 1977, when two Senate committees and a team of physicians restudied the same poverty pockets they had visited a decade earlier, they found real improvement in nutrition levels. Nationwide surveys conducted by the United States Department of Agriculture also found that although deficiencies of calories, calcium, iron, and vitamin C were still more common in low-income populations than in the general population, there was substantial improvement from 1966 to 1977 (Physician Task Force on Hunger in America, 1985:68–69).

Recently, however, the figures on poverty, hunger, and malnutrition have deteriorated again. Nationwide, poverty rose to 13 percent in 1980 and to 15.2 percent in 1984—the highest level in two decades. Although by late 1985 the poverty rate had fallen back down to 14 percent, 33.1 million Americans were officially classified as poor. And there is little to suggest that the poverty rate will once again decline to the 12 percent level of 1979. The position of the poor relative to the rest of the society has also deteriorated recently, as is evidenced by the fact that the official poverty level for a family of four in 1985, $10,989, was almost the same as the median national income in that same year, $11,013 (Pear, 1986). Figures on the percentage of people below the officially defined poverty line, moreover, give no indication of how far below that income level people actually are; most observers report that many people are further below the line now than they were a decade ago. The poor are getting poorer.

If the poor are more numerous and poorer now than when this decade began, they are hungrier and less well nourished also, as two recent studies show. One was coordinated by the Harvard School of Public Health and compiled under the title *Hunger in America: The Growing Epidemic* (Physician Task Force on Hunger in America, 1985); the other, compiled by Public Voice for Food and Health Policy, is entitled *Rising Poverty, Declining Health: The Nutritional Status of the Rural Poor* (Shotland, 1986). The poor are less well fed now not only because of reduced purchasing power (due to increased food costs relative to wages and welfare benefit levels) but also because fewer of them are currently receiving government food assistance and those who do get assistance are receiving less of it. As a result of more stringent eligibility guidelines for the food stamp program, which is the major form of federal food assistance, the number of households receiving food stamps decreased by 6.1 percent from 1983 to 1984 (from 21,073,000 to 19,778,000 people)—while the poverty rate dropped a mere 0.8 percent (Physician Task Force on Hunger in America, 1985:99). (Even among those who are potentially eligible, only about 60 percent actually participate in the program.) For those who do receive food stamps, the monthly allotments have been reduced. The stamp allotment has never been intended to cover all household food needs, but generally it has been thought to fill the gap between food a household can afford to purchase on its own and food it should have to approach minimum daily requirements for all of its members. At present, the food stamp allotments fill a smaller part of that gap: the average bonus level for a four-person household in 1984 was only $147 (ibid.:91). Within the poverty population, specific groups who are at high risk for malnutrition now get less assistance than previously. For example, the number of children receiving free and reduced-price school lunches has decreased by 12 percent since 1980, according to United States Department of Agriculture figures (ibid.:98). Since most poor people lack food reserves, either in their bodies or in their cupboards, their being dropped from a government food assistance program or having benefit levels reduced is likely to have serious consequences for nutritional well-being.

Ample evidence of the recent increase in hunger and malnutrition appears throughout the Harvard study, including disturbing reports from pediatricians around the country. For example, doctors in Chicago report cases of marasmus (protein-calorie deficiency) and kwashiorkor (protein deficiency) reminiscent of the findings in the 1960s (ibid.:49–50). Children from low-income families continue to have high rates of anemia: in Minneapolis, 13 percent of the infants and 21 percent of the children among families applying for supplementary food assistance were determined by the Health Department to be anemic (ibid.:78).

Evidence of another kind comes from across the nation where in the last few years churches, volunteer groups, and local governments have found it necessary to set up soup kitchens, food banks, and other emergency food give-aways to supplement federal food assistance programs. Despite the rapid growth of such facilities, the number of people coming to each of them rose remarkably. In 1983 a random sample survey of 181 emergency food programs in the United States found that one-third of them had experienced at least a 100 percent increase in one year in the number of people coming for food (ibid.:9). In the Boston area food pantries served about 13,000 people monthly in 1982, nearly 30,000 in 1984 (ibid.:14). In Alabama, the Birmingham Community Kitchens that had served only 1,200 meals in 1980 served over 130,000 in 1984 (ibid.:25). A recently completed survey in New York State indicated dramatic rises in the number of people regularly turning to such food sources, with 63 percent of the programs reporting an increase in people served from 1984 to 1985 alone and only 5.5 percent reporting a decrease (Cornell University and New York State Department of Health, 1985). It can safely be assumed that most of the people who are turning increasingly to these food sources do so because they cannot afford to eat sufficiently well on their own—because they are hungry.

Corroborating evidence of the worsening problem of hunger comes from human-service workers in various states and programs. Nutrition educators conducting lessons in low-income homes increasingly observe empty cupboards and refrigerators and see more families lacking food or resources for the next day's meals. Teachers in Head Start have told me that children are eating voraciously at school on Monday mornings. And volunteers who operate soup kitchens have felt it necessary to give their Friday diners an extra bag of food for the weekend.

Hunger Is Unevenly Distributed in the Population

Within the national figures, those population groups, geographic regions, and age ranges most likely to fall below the poverty line (such as blacks, Hispanics, Indians, members of households headed by women, and children) are also most at risk for being hungry and malnourished. Children, for example, are disproportionately hungry or malnourished due to poverty. With the poverty rate at about 15 percent in 1983, more than 20 percent of all children under eighteen were living in households below the poverty line (O'Hare, 1985:17). Probably at least 15 percent of all children in the United States routinely experience sufficient hunger and malnutrition to cause such problems as anemia and lowered resistance to infection. If malnutrition occurs early enough, is severe enough, or persists for long periods, many of these children may also suffer long-term consequences such as impaired brain development and stunted body growth.

The South as a region is vulnerable to poverty-related hunger; and blacks as a group are particularly vulnerable. Predictably, therefore, in Mississippi there is again, or still, a serious problem of hunger in the black population (Physician Task Force on Hunger in America, 1985:18–28). In many of that state's counties, 50 percent to 75 percent of the black population falls below the poverty line (Mississippi Research and Development Center, 1981). However, only slightly over half of the state's households potentially eligible for food stamps are receiving them. Low levels of welfare benefit and a 6 percent sales tax on food exacerbate the hunger problem among black Mississippians.

Closely associated with both poverty and hunger is a high infant mortality rate (number of children per thousand who die before reaching age one). Among some populations, especially low-income blacks, infant mortality has risen recently despite technological advances in neonatal care. For American blacks as a whole, the infant mortality rate is roughly equal to the national rate in Costa Rica; and the disparity between infant mortality rates for blacks and whites in the United States, currently at a ratio of 2 to 1, continues to grow. In Pittsburgh, Pennsylvania, a city recently dubbed in a national survey one of the best places in America to live, the infant mortality rate among blacks is higher than in any other city in the United States, and nearly three times the rate for whites in the city (Physician Task Force on Hunger in America, 1985:72). The major causes of infant mortality in the United States are premature birth and low birth weight, which are closely associated with malnutrition of mothers, especially young mothers. Studies have shown that making supplemental foods available to pregnant women decreases the infant mortality rate by as much as 22 percent.[7] Even for those infants of low birth weight who do survive, as for all other infants, inadequate nutrition may lead to or exacerbate mental, developmental, and physical limitations that cannot be erased later. Born of an undernourished mother and undernourished during its first years of life, a child is likely to grow up to repeat the cycle: hungry because poor, and poor because hungry.

EATING PATTERNS OF THE POOR

In any human population, hunger is embedded in the larger context of eating, and so to understand hunger we need to understand eating. Eating is not simply a matter of ingesting calories, proteins, vitamins, and minerals. And just as eating is a culturally shaped act, so too is hunger culturally defined and invested with meanings that may outweigh its metabolic or nutritional aspects.

The cultural dimensions of hunger among poor Americans can be elucidated by the use of ethnographic research methods, which are particularly well suited for examining such food-related patterns as food preferences, frequency, quantity, and regularity of eating, distribution of food within the household, attitudes about foods, and social interactions associated with food. Several years of participant-observation research among rural poor people living in pockets of poverty in upstate New York have given me ample opportunity to witness food-related activities, including shopping and cooking as well as eating, within the context of everyday life (Fitchen, 1981). My research focused on over forty families living in several rural depressed neighborhoods, with twenty families studied quite intensively. During frequent, unscheduled, drop-in visits in homes, I listened to many food-related conversations and observed innumerable interactions involving food.

I have since supplemented this ethnographic research about hunger and foodways in one poverty setting with both first-hand and indirect observation in other regions of the nation. Particular insight has come from conducting training workshops for EFNEP, the Expanded Food and Nutrition Education Program that is operated nationwide by Co-operative Extension to bring nutrition information to low-income homemakers. From discussions with hundreds of EFNEP staff who conduct lessons in the homes of low-income families, I have learned about nutritional conditions and food patterns among the poor of various regions and ethnic and racial backgrounds, for example, southwestern Hispanics, urban blacks in the Northeast and deep South, rural whites in the Northwest, Indians in the upper Midwest, and Samoans in Hawaii. The opportunity to accompany EFNEP outreach educators in several states as they conducted lessons in the homes of their low-income clients has enabled me to observe mothers and children interacting over food and to listen to women talk about their food buying and preparation. These observations, though brief, have added breadth to the case study research and have confirmed that the eating patterns observed in the smaller sample can indeed be generalized. Additional insight has come from years of interaction with various food assistance and antipoverty programs at the federal, state, and local levels.

Low-income people probably vary as much as any other population segment in the United States in terms of individual and family food behaviors. But there are also some important similarities, so we can generalize about eating patterns of the poor without doing violence to variations among individuals and between groups.

Eating Patterns Are Shaped by the Constraints of Poverty

Poverty obviously affects the total amount of money a household can spend on food. Although the amount spent by a poor household on food may be considerably smaller than what a similar-size household with more available money spends, the poorer household is likely to spend a greater percentage of its income on food. Some low-income people are able to supplement their food supply from noncash sources, such as fishing and hunting, vegetable gardening and gathering wild fruits, raising chickens or other animals, and of course food stamps, free school lunches, and other forms of food assistance. Most poor people also obtain additional food by using their social resources, for example, by trading services and goods with relatives and neighbors to obtain food or food stamps. But for most poor Americans, as in the population as a whole, the majority of food is purchased (cf. Whitehead in Douglas, 1984:112).

Poverty also affects the amount of food that poor people can obtain for their money or their food stamps. Because of the constraints of poverty, the foods purchased by America's poor often cost more than the same foods purchased by more affluent people. Most poor people generally lack the surplus cash needed to take advantage of sale prices or to buy in quantity. Furthermore, inadequate storage space and refrigeration at home necessitate frequent trips to the store and smaller-scale purchases, usually at higher unit prices. Limited cash for public transportation (where it is available) and the lack of private cars restrict some people to shopping in small neighborhood stores rather than in more distant supermarkets with lower prices. From the inner cities of the eastern seaboard to the small towns on southwestern Indian reservations, food may cost more for those who are poor.

The economic exigencies of poverty also determine the types of foods that people eat most frequently. Interesting (and tasty) variations certainly exist in the foods preferred by different poverty populations; but in their menu combinations, in cuts of meat used (ibid.:118), and in modes of preparation (Goode et al. in Douglas, 1984:148) the inescapable constraints of poverty tend to override ethnic and regional differences. Indeed, I have been struck by overall similarities in the diets of America's poor, from Maine to Hawaii, from Mississippi to Alaska. By and large, poverty diets nationwide appear to be excessive in starches, fats, and sugars while being deficient in any or all of: meats and other proteins, vegetables and fruits, and milk products. Particular dietary excesses and deficiencies vary considerably, as do particular preferences within any single food group. For example, the main starch may be rice, potatoes, tortillas, or Indian fry bread, according to ethnic preference, but whatever the case the preferred starch constitutes the bulk of a diet that may achieve satiety but also produces malnutrition. As a consequence of these dietary similarities, diet-related health problems are also similar across different poverty populations. For example, obesity and adult-onset diabetes, both common in many low-income populations, have been reported as epidemic among the Zuñi Indians, whose diet consists of an abundance of fats, sugar, and fast foods (Peterson, 1986). In Hawaii and American Samoa, low-income people are purchasing such high-fat, imported, and expensive starches as potato chips, a trend that EFNEP nutrition educators hope to reverse by stimulating new interest in the native, traditional taro, which is both cheaper and nutritionally better.

A common eating pattern in poverty populations across the nation is a marked periodicity in food consumption levels. Both purchase and consumption peak immediately after the paycheck, welfare check, or food stamps arrive. (Grocery stores may be especially crowded with customers using food stamps just after the first of each month.) Quantity and variety of food consumed subsequently taper down and level off, then take a nosedive in the last few days before the next check or stamp allotment. One mother I observed in Boston fried potatoes—with no accompaniment—for dinner for her four children on three successive nights at the end of one month. Even preschool children in the rural households I studied were fully aware of the check-to-check cycle of food availability: while examining bare cupboards, they eagerly listed treats they would ask for on payday. These periodic reductions in availability of food can create problems of both hunger and malnutrition, and EFNEP nutrition educators, who see this pattern frequently among their low-income clients, are attempting to help families stretch money, food stamps, and food to avoid the end-of-month hunger periods. There is some evidence that families receiving welfare, food stamps, and food assistance maintain relatively constant, if inadequate, nutrient intake throughout the month (Emmons, 1986).

The amount of food consumed also drops from time to time, when decreased income or unexpected expenses place additional strains on household finances. The unreliability of household income is only one source of fluctuations in food expenditures. Food is a nonfixed cost, and money set aside for food may go to the bill collector instead: one woman called this "eating light to pay for the lights." Human service workers, from nutrition educators to budget counselors, report that money allocated for food is often diverted to other uses when expenses increase unexpectedly, when debts become more pressing, or when income drops. Even personal family pleasure may sometimes come ahead of eating well, as long as the children are not complaining much.

The amount and quality of food that people eat is also frequently reduced by the necessity to stretch the household's food supply to feed extra people temporarily eating in or staying at the home. This sharing of food has been reported with increasing frequency in the last few years by nutrition educators in EFNEP in all states, and especially among black, Indian, and Hispanic populations. Although food sharing may temporarily diminish the food intake of the host household, it is an important coping strategy found in many poverty populations: it enables people to get through tight times by maintaining a system of reciprocity, an informal security network (Stack, 1974; Fitchen, 1981:106). Young children in families I observed were explicitly encouraged to share food and praised for food generosity; it was common to see an elementary school child bring home to share with a younger sibling a pocket full of cookies or candies from a party at school.

Another eating pattern found in diverse populations of low-income people is that food consumption is unevenly distributed within households. Although I collected no quantified food intake data in my case study to prove the point, observations during mealtimes and conversations with women indicated this tendency. When the cost of feeding a family must be eked out of a small income, always competing with other urgent needs, some individuals may go seriously underfed. Although the man of the household may receive ample quantities of food, for example, an older relative living in the household, perhaps an otherwise homeless person, may receive an insufficient amount of food. Some individual children routinely have insufficient access to food, through differential size or order of serving, outright denial of certain foods, or

parental failure to accommodate a child's particular food needs. The vulnerable children are often those who occupy problematic positions within the household, for example children of a previous marriage or handicapped children. Some children may eat very little because of chronic untreated health problems, such as bad teeth, gastroenteritis, or anemia; but even if the health problem is addressed, the portions served may not be sufficiently increased as the child's health improves.

Even more common than the vulnerable child pattern is the phenomenon of the wife-mother who short-changes her own food needs. In many poor households the woman eats only starches without any of the meats or vegetables she serves to the rest of the family. For herself, she may scrape the pot or lick the spoon and take whatever her children leave uneaten on their plates, but basically she eats just plain macaroni—or potatoes, or fry bread, or tortillas and beans. This pattern, which I observed during my field research, is recognized by EFNEP workers as one of the most common causes of nutritional problems among low-income women throughout the nation. It shows up clearly in the 24-hour food recalls, in which women enrolled in EFNEP are asked to record their own food intake. Many of these women proudly report that they have fixed a certain nutritious recipe for their children but admit that they did not eat any themselves. Although American women of other socioeconomic levels may also place the food needs and wants of family ahead of their own (see Whitehead in Douglas, 1984:126), "sacrificing for the sake of the children" has more deleterious nutritional consequences for poor women. It undoubtedly contributes to the observably high incidence of obesity, poor dental health, and generally low nutritional status of low-income women as compared to their nonpoor counterparts and even to other members of their families.[8]

The perpetual condition of limited financial resources also affects when, where, and with whom people eat. Shortage of chairs, plates, or forks may mean that in many households meals are not taken with all members of the household assembled in one place or at one time. Some young children I observed were given or helped themselves to food off and on throughout the day: a nursing bottle filled with milk, juice, or soda pop or other artificially flavored sweet drink; a bowl of dry cereal; a peanut butter and jelly sandwich; soup eaten directly out of a can; doughnuts or a bag of potato chips. When a greater proportion of food is taken as snacks rather than meals, the result is apt to be a less well balanced diet, perhaps seriously so. In some homes, however, women went to considerable effort to cook meals, especially the evening dinner, and some were excellent cooks and ingenious at devising substitutes for ingredients or equipment they lacked. (One woman made her own bread, baking it in coffee cans in an oven that had been retrieved from the local garbage dump, propping the oven door shut with a stick.) But when financial or other problems overwhelmed these women, mealtime eating ceased to be planned, organized, or nutritionally balanced. During fieldwork, I was often able to gain a quick estimate of the current state of family life by observing or hearing about eating. For example, one woman in my sample was very conscious of nutritional needs and normally made a real effort to feed her family as well as possible. But during periods of parental depression or alcoholism, or marital violence, often brought on by money problems, each child helped herself from whatever happened to be in the cupboards.

Poverty also shapes the eating patterns of the poor by generating anxieties that center on food. Many adults, in recounting their childhood, cited periods when "there was no food in the house and no way to get any" and when "all we had for supper in those years was boiled potatoes and the water they were cooked in —we called it potato soup." The sense of deprivation engendered by such food shortages in early childhood seems to leave a lifelong sensitivity to the problem of having sufficient and desirable food. It may cause some adults to eat beyond the point of satiety or metabolic need, to overeat regularly and become obese. Food anxiety often carries over to the next generation too. Many of the mothers in my study consciously linked recollections of food deprivation in childhood and a present desire to give their children whatever foods they request, including soda pop and potato chips, so that the children might never feel denied or deprived. Thus for people living a whole lifetime in poverty, as for many of America's poor, the memory of childhood hunger in one generation may be a factor leading to malnutrition in the next.

For all poor people, the constraints of having to feed a family on an inadequate budget are exacerbated by the fact that hunger is cognitive as well as metabolic. The necessity of keeping children reasonably satisfied despite the shortage of money may take its toll on nutritious eating. In one common management strategy a mother responds to her children's complaints about being hungry by giving them a food item that is not only filling but also desired and liked. A package of frosting-covered cupcakes (high in desirability, sugar, and cost, but low in needed nutrients) may quickly pacify a child, thereby addressing the perceived and expressed hunger of the moment and allowing the mother to turn to other demands on her time and attention. Repeated reliance on this strategy, however, may lead to long-term nutritional deficit for the child. But the child's fussing now is more pressing and imme-

diate and cannot be ignored; malnourishment, on the other hand, is delayed, is not so readily apparent, and has a less clear cause. Consciously as well as unconsciously, mothers may be dealing with the problem of inadequate access to food by trading off between hunger in the present and malnutrition in the future. In responding to cognitive hunger, they are inadvertently contributing to physical malnutrition.

Food may also occupy people's attention more when obtaining enough of it is problematic. Some young children I observed during my studies of rural poverty-stricken families seemed preoccupied with food: when not actually eating or begging a parent for something to eat, they would stand for whole minutes at a time just looking at whatever foods were still in the cupboard or refrigerator. One such child seemed simply to be reassuring himself that there was something left to eat. Perhaps this visual reassurance is part of the reason, along with limited kitchen storage space, why many food items always remain out on the kitchen table: bottles of ketchup, jars of instant coffee, bread, jam, peanut butter. (Perhaps it is also a literal manifestation of a saying one hears frequently among low-income people: "We may be poor, but at least we have managed to keep a roof over our heads and food on the table.") Some babies cling to the learned security of a nursing bottle until they are three or four; some carry the bottle around the house, hide it, and return to it periodically throughout the day.

Food is the source or the center of considerable interpersonal friction in many low-income homes. Many of the young children's temper tantrums I observed were connected with a demand for food. Minor disputes between mothers and children often revolved around the child's demands for something to eat and the mother's refusal—followed frequently by her capitulation. In many homes, arguments between spouses or lovers began over expenditures for food or the selection and preparation of foods. The most frequent form of this argument that I observed or heard about was a man castigating a woman for wasting "his" money on the purchase of some "unnecessary" food such as fruit juice, fruit, or vegetables. Food was sometimes used as a weapon (both literally and figuratively) in marital quarreling: a man who throws a plate full of food at his wife, a woman who punishes her man by preparing a dinner that she knows he dislikes. Where such food disagreements were common in the home some children developed strong negative associations with all food and eating and ate very little even when food was available; other children, even in the same family, reacted in the opposite way, with an insatiable, voracious appetite.

Just as eating takes up a large portion of the budget and thoughts of low-income people, so also it occupies a large part of their actions. During the vast majority of my home visits in various poverty-stricken communities around the nation, at least one person in the household was eating. But it is not sheer physical hunger or metabolic need alone that fastens people's attention so much on food. Food and eating are enmeshed in feelings about self, interpersonal relationships, and dreams for the future, and these in turn are shaped by the surrounding culture.

Eating Patterns Are Shaped by General American Culture

As Mary Douglas (1984:3) has said, "unlike livestock, humans make some choices that are not governed by physiological processes. They choose what to eat, when and how often to eat, in what order, and with whom." As in any society, so in America, the definitions of acceptable and preferred foods are largely cultural. Contemporary food preferences that lean towards finger foods, fun foods, snack foods, and fast and convenient foods express basic American cultural values (Jerome, 1969). Low-income people express their membership in the society and their adherence to its dominant values through many of the same food choices that characterize the rest of the population. And so they, too, desire and purchase foods with these characteristics. Like most other Americans, poor people want to exercise "freedom of choice" in their food selection. (This is one reason why food stamps or vouchers for purchasing food at the grocery store are generally preferred to commodities.) In exercising this freedom, poor people select not only for price but also for desirability and therefore often purchase heavily advertised, status-invested foods "seen on television." Hence among the poor, as for the nation as a whole, diets may be high in processed foods, in sugars and fats, and in the category loosely termed "junk food."

The effect of junk foods on the nutritional status of the poor is probably worse than it is on the affluent. The well-to-do can afford both junk food and nutritious food; the poor can seldom afford both. The low-income parent who frequently succumbs to children's constant pleading for potato chips, soda pop, cheese-flavored puffs, and creme-filled cupcakes has no money left over for milk or carrots or apples. From the corner convenience store in inner-city Boston to the street vans parked by public housing projects in Honolulu, low-income parents have difficulty denying their children these advertised, desired products that are high in cost but low in nutritional value. One important factor contributing to the purchase of these products for children is the low self-image and sense of failure of the parent, a problem that seems pervasive in the American poverty population. Mothers with low

self-esteem report that they have difficulty saying no to their children's demands for junk foods, even when they know that these foods are economically costly and nutritionally detrimental. (The association between poverty and low self-image is attested to by the responses of EFNEP outreach educators to a questionnaire about problems affecting the homemakers they teach. With over a thousand responses received from different regions of the country, I have found that the vast majority ranked "low self-esteem" as number one, two, or three in prevalence.) Single low-income mothers have told me that they are particularly vulnerable to buying treats for their children as an attempt to make up for the fact that the child has only one parent.

Foods and drink are as important to social interaction among the poor as they are in other segments of the American population—or any population. Some items, such as coffee, are more social than dietary. During field research, I was offered—and accepted—a cup of coffee almost every time I entered a home. The cost to the financially strapped family was outweighed in their minds by the importance of making this gesture of hospitality, this culturally prescribed presentation of themselves. In many homes, coffee was also consumed in great quantities whenever a family was going through some calamity and relatives and neighbors were dropping in to discuss events.

Poor people also reflect general American cultural patterns in their use of foods for celebrating. In rural poor households, I found, people were fully aware of the food choices and food consumption patterns appropriate for holidays and rites of passage. One woman started in September to use food stamps to purchase one Thanksgiving item each week: a can of cranberry sauce, a can of pumpkin, and so on. A mother on a very limited budget made a child's birthday more special by purchasing a "real" birthday cake, with icing and lettering on it, rather than buying the ingredients and making it herself at lower cost. Women regarded the scrimping before and after these celebrations as preferable to the sense of deprivation felt when such socially prescribed foods of celebration are missing.

If people ate entirely on the basis of rational appraisal of nutritive value relative to dollars spent, then poor people could be convinced to ignore the preferences of their society. But poor people cling to and may even exaggerate dominant American food preferences because, despite their poverty, they are American—by culture if not by riches. And so, to the detriment of their own nutritional well-being, they may spend their food stamps and their scarce money on foods that are both expensive and nutritionally inferior. Despite what they may learn about nutritional needs and smart shopping, low-income people will continue to purchase convenience foods, snack foods, holiday foods, and status foods because they continue to classify themselves first of all as Americans and only second as poor Americans. If they could only accomplish it, most poor people would eat their way into the middle class.

CULTURAL ASPECTS OF THE RESPONSE TO HUNGER IN THE UNITED STATES

Dominant Cultural Values Shape Societal Attitudes About the Poor and What They Should Eat

Dominant American culture not only influences the foods poor people eat; it also influences the way the nonpoor think about eating, about poverty, and about what the poor should eat. To a considerable extent Americans are unaware of the impact of culture on what they eat. When asked, most claim that their food selections are purely a matter of individual preference, a claim that fits well with the cultural emphasis on individualism and individual choice. Most are equally unaware of the multiple functions served by their own food behaviors. Because of this general oversight, the public seriously underestimates the cultural and psychosocial factors shaping food patterns of people who are poor; and so there is ample room for societal attitudes about poverty to shape ideas about what poor people should eat.

The American cultural system rests on a belief that in this land of opportunity, the individual can and should shape his or her own destiny. One corollary is a pervasive conviction that the poor are casualties not of society but of their own shortcomings. Poverty is a condition of individuals not of society: people are poor, the assumption is, because they are lazy and won't work and because they spend their money foolishly, purchasing only for immediate gratification, with no care for the future. It is an article of faith that the opportunity to escape poverty exists; the responsibility of poor people is to seize that opportunity and pull themselves up.

These beliefs about poverty and poor people shape dominant societal beliefs about what and how poor people should eat. Because the poor have little money, they should eat rationally on a cost/benefit basis, where costs are measured only in dollars and benefits solely in terms of nutrition. If poor people would eat this way, then surely there would not be malnutrition and hunger in America. By this reasoning,

just as poverty is the fault of the poor, so hunger and malnutrition are the fault of the hungry and malnourished. The proposed solution, then, is that poor people should change their eating habits:

a.   People who are poor should eat only the basics, consume only the foods needed by the body to maintain growth and health. (In fact, the official federal definition of poverty, and the determination of the poverty level, is based on a calculation involving the cost of a minimally adequate diet, actually 80 percent of it, assuming no expenditure for any foods other than minimal daily requirements.)

b.   Poor people should not waste their money buying convenience foods. (Since the poor are too lazy to work, it is thought, they have plenty of time on their hands. They should economize by spending their unused time making meals from scratch rather than purchasing the convenience foods that busy working people eat.)

c.   People who are poor should forego the favored, advertised, status foods, purchasing only cheap substitutes. (If people remain poor because they seek instant gratification, then to escape poverty they should learn to postpone pleasures for the future.)

These common public attitudes about poverty and what the poor should eat reveal a complete lack of awareness of the cultural aspects of eating. And they have important consequences, for they blend with our attitudes about food to shape the governmental response to hunger and malnutrition.

Cultural Attitudes about Poverty Shape Food Assistance Programs

The inadequacy of government food assistance programs goes deeper than the political conservatism of the present administration and the current constraints of budget deficits. The inadequacy exists—and is tolerated by the public—because of the ascendant myth that any individual who really wants to can overcome poverty and the accompanying assumption that if the poor are hungry and malnourished it must be of their own doing; they eat wrongly. Another deep and long-standing reason for the failure to guarantee decent, reliable food assistance to anyone who needs it may be a culturally generated fear that guaranteed food assistance (like guaranteed income) would create recipients dependent on government help. In a society that strongly favors independence and individual effort, aversion to creating dependence carries sufficient political appeal to outweigh concern that government food assistance is insufficient to prevent many children from growing up badly nourished, unhealthy, and poorly developed. When concern does rise, the more culturally appropriate solution involves voluntary efforts rather than governmental assistance.

Government assistance programs for the needy also reflect the fact that food is used instrumentally in our society. Early in life we learn that food is given or withheld at the discretion of the donor; food is a means by which we are controlled and can control others; food is used to reward and punish. So it is culturally appropriate that government food assistance is politically more palatable than the provision of a guaranteed minimum income, since the former contains an element of control over recipients. Food programs give assistance on their own terms: the donor determines what is given, when and where it is given, to whom, and under what conditions.

Government food assistance is neither shaped by nor solely conducted for the benefit of the people in need of food. In general, the interests and political power of the food industry and the agricultural sector of the economy exert a strong influence on food assistance programs. The food stamp program, the major form of food assistance, is entirely under the supervision of the United States Department of Agriculture (USDA) and subject to congressional and lobbying interests mostly representing agricultural producers, processors, and distributors—not the poor.[9] The USDA controls other food assistance programs as well, including the free and reduced-price school lunches and nutrition education for the poor. However, the poor are not the USDA's major constituency, and their needs do not claim top priority. Among the major food assistance programs, only the Women, Infants, and Children program is under a federal department primarily charged with people's well-being, the Department of Health and Human Services.

Some government food assistance programs also contain an element of "feeding the poor our leftovers." Consider, for example, the commodity distributions to the poor, also administered by the USDA. Such a program was used in the 1950s and early 1960s but was phased out in the late 1960s when it was decided that food stamps would better assist the poor in obtaining food. In the early 1980s, however, the commodity distribution program was reinstated as a supplement to food stamps, ostensibly in response to concern about reports of increasing hunger in America. The new version of the food give-away program started with cheese —more accurately, with blocks of pasteurized processed cheese food—and was subsequently expanded to include other commodities with seasonal and regional variations, depending on availability and deliv-

eries. For example, in 1985 in an upstate New York county, families who proved or declared their poverty could receive every other month, on a first-come-first-served basis, the following goods: two five-pound blocks of processed cheese, two one-pound blocks of butter, and a choice of any two of the following items: 10 lbs. cornmeal, 4 lbs. powdered milk, 3 lbs. honey, 5 lbs. flour, or 2 lbs. rice. Many low-income people have responded positively to the give-aways, standing in lines at Salvation Army centers, churches, community halls, fire stations, and hospitals all across the nation to receive their generically packaged handouts.[10] (There are also nongovernmental food give-aways, many organized by church groups, in which excess or unsold foods donated by manufacturers and distributors are given to poor people.)

The foodstuffs given out by the government are not exactly scraps front the tables of the affluent, but they are clearly the leftovers from the food production industry. They represent the overproduction that threatens to bring down the price received by the producer/processor, the "surplus" purchased by the federal government to keep it off the market. The real objectives of the commodity distribution program, it appears, are to reduce the supply reaching the market, to dispose of government-owned surplus commodities in a way that obviates long-term storage costs, and to reduce embarrassment over surplus in the face of reportedly growing hunger. Although the public may believe that food distribution is designed, funded, and carried out solely for the altruistic purpose of reducing hunger, one could easily argue that the beneficiaries include not only the hungry but also the well-fed.

CONCLUSION: THE RICH BUY STEAK AND THE POOR GET CHEESE

Hunger, eating, and helping hungry people to eat— each is a cultural as well as a metabolic phenomenon. Food is culturally embedded for both the affluent and the poor. Through food patterns, all Americans enact cultural values and conduct interpersonal relationships. Cultural preferences, group identity, social interactions, and psychological needs all shape food-related behavior, no matter what the income level. Poor people are also subject to the same general, systemwide economic and social factors that tend to prevent most Americans from getting maximum nourishment per dollar. Because Americans are captive consumers in a total food production system that emphasizes profits rather than national nutritional well-being (Silverstein, 1984), and because all Americans buy foods to satisfy a variety of needs beside caloric and nutritional ones (Counihan, 1985), few Americans are as well nourished as they could afford to be.

The problem is significantly worse for low-income people, however, because for them there is no cushion of good health to tide them over periods of inadequate eating. The chronically poor have little opportunity to eat both the nutritious foods and also the heavily advertised, status-invested, and culturally preferred foods available to the upper classes. If they opt only for nutritionally "sensible" and cheaper foods, and forego the foods "that everyone else eats," their perceived sense of deprivation will be as genuine and gnawing as are the pangs of an empty stomach. But if they give in to the pressures of advertising, to the desire to eat like other people, and to the pleading of their children, then they will remain nutritionally and financially shortchanged—and also criticized by societal opinion for their "wasteful spending." It is a difficult set of choices, choices that have to be made every day but provide no clear way to win.

Because poverty-stricken Americans are influenced by dominant cultural values as well as by financial exigencies and metabolic requirements, a low-income person may occasionally purchase a beef steak. When other shoppers and grocery store employees observe such a purchase, behavioral conventions may restrict immediate reaction to a stare, but subsequent comments are uniformly negative. That the grocery cart is filled mostly with macaroni, potatoes, and bread may go unnoticed. The image of a poor person purchasing a steak sticks in the public mind as undeniable proof that in America the poor are living in luxury. If the poor are hungry in this land, it is thought to be their own fault, a result of their unwise spending.

The purchase of a steak by a poor person represents more than just an "unwise" use of money, however, and it carries significance far beyond the act itself. It is also culturally "inappropriate" behavior, for it violates an implicit cultural statement about the way things are or ought to be: the rich buy steak and the poor get cheese. This cultural statement actually encompasses three significant oppositions. The rich are the opposite of the poor. Buying food is the opposite of getting or being given food. And steak and cheese are familiar opposites: a thick piece of red meat is an ultimate desired food for Americans, while ordinary processed cheese, such as the government gives to the poor, is a well-known cheap substitute for meat. Rich—poor; buy—get; steak—cheese. Each of these three pairs is a culturally recognized opposition, and the first term of each pair should be combined with only the first term of the other pairs. Rich is appropri-

ately associated with buy and with steak. Poor is appropriately associated with getting and with cheese.

Thus it is culturally fitting that the government gives handouts of cheese to the poor: by defining what they shall eat and how they shall obtain it, the "cheese give-away" also defines who the poor are. When a poor person buys a steak, she or he is committing a symbolic inversion, performing an action associated with the rich and acquiring a food appropriate only to the rich. If the poor person gets the steak with food stamps rather than with cash, the purchase further violates what is thought to be appropriate because it violates the notion of how certain categories of food should be obtained: luxury foods should not be obtained with food stamps. But whether the steak is obtained with money or stamps, steak for the poor is a notable transgression because it violates the idea that the poor are different from the rest of us. It mocks our sense of societal order that demands separation of rich and poor.

NOTES

Adapted from a paper presented at the annual meeting of the Northeastern Anthropological Association, Buffalo, N.Y., March 1986, as part of a symposium, "Feast or Famine," organized by Carole Counihan.

1. Michael Harrington stirred public and governmental concern with his *The Other America* (1962), which documented the high incidence of poverty. He stressed both the uneven distribution of poverty in the population and its invisibility. Journalist Nick Kotz examined the politics of hunger and food programs (1969). The widely read works of anthropologist Oscar Lewis called attention to the intergenerational persistence of poverty. The untiring efforts of philanthropist-activist Robert Choate, of psychiatrist-writer Robert Coles (1969), and of political leaders such as senators George McGovern and Robert Kennedy contributed greatly to public awareness and demand for government action. Private foundations, such as the Field Foundation, were also instrumental in funding research and publicizing findings.

2. Investigations into the problem of hunger and malnutrition around the nation were sponsored or directly carried out by the Senate Select Committee on Nutrition and Human Needs, the Senate Subcommittee on Employment, Manpower, and Poverty, and the Citizens' Board of Inquiry (the last funded by the Field Foundation). In 1968 the powerful CBS television documentary *Hunger in America*, which was based on these investigations, brought action from Washington—despite sharp criticism from some in government.

3. The Food Stamp Program provides coupons that can be used like money in purchasing any foods (but no pet foods and no nonedible household supplies). The value of the coupons allotted is determined by household income and size. Booklets of coupons are issued monthly to eligible families. Originally participating households paid a set

amount each month, calculated according to their income, and received an amount of stamps equal to payment plus the bonus level (based on income and the household size). Subsequently the cash payment has been eliminated, so households receive stamps equivalent to the bonus level alone.

4. EFNEP, the Expanded Food and Nutrition Education Program, has been active in all states for 15 years as part of Co-operative Extension (which transmits information about agricultural and household topics from the state land-grant colleges to the public). EFNEP uses the extension mode of education to carry information about food and nutrition directly to a low-income audience. Through EFNEP low-income people (usually women) receive training in food and nutrition and then conduct individualized lessons in the homes of program participants. Lessons include not only nutrition needs and nutrient values but also food selection, preparation, and handling. Funded by a combination of federal, state, and local money, the program has recently been jeopardized by a threat of complete withdrawal of federal money.

5. This nationwide program, available in most counties of most states, is the Special Supplementary Food Program for Women, Infants, Children, commonly known as WIC. Participating women are issued vouchers that are redeemable only on specified foods, such as milk, cheese, infant formula, infant cereals, and fruit juices.

6. The official definition of poverty used by the federal government to count the poor, and by most federal, state, and local programs to determine eligibility and benefit levels for assistance, is a straight income definition adjusted to the number of people in the household. It is based on the cost of obtaining food that would provide only about 80 percent of minimum daily dietary requirements and assumes that people need three times this much income to meet minimally adequate nutritional levels and other basic needs as well. The poverty level thus calculated is adjusted periodically to reflect the cost of living. In 1970 the poverty level for a family of 4, for example, was about $4,000; during 15 years of inflation it has been adjusted upward, reaching $10,989 for the same size household in 1985. All 4-person households with less than that level of income are officially defined as poor.

7. The Women, Infants, and Children program, WIC, has perpetually been underfunded and threatened with reductions in funds, which will mean longer waiting periods to obtain WIC benefits. For a single mother with little money to spend on food, a wait of just a few months before receiving WIC coupons for supplemental foods can have serious effects on her infant's well-being. For the pregnant woman, delay in obtaining WIC may affect the outcome of the pregnancy (premature birth, low birth weight). In many states the WIC program has lacked sufficient federal funding and staff to certify all those who apply. In New York State, as of March 1985, 16,300 low-income women who were pregnant and/or had young children were on the waiting list to obtain WIC benefits. Some states have recently had to reduce costs by dropping the eligibility age limit for children from six to three or below. In New Mexico only 28 percent of eligible infants and children could be served by WIC. Figures from Physician Task Force on Hunger in America, 1985.

8. Roe, 1973, in a study conducted on rural and urban women in the same region, reports a high number of medical complaints and chronic ailments, as well as obesity, among the low-income women to whom her team administered questionnaires, physical examinations, and laboratory tests.

9. See Kotz, 1969. When the Food Stamp program began, participants could not use their stamps to purchase any imported items. When it was seen that this regulation meant no coffee, tea, or bananas for the poor, the ruling was changed to allow imports if no domestic product were available. Thus tinned corned beef from Argentina could not be purchased with food stamps even when cheaper than its domestic counterpart. Even this restriction was subsequently dropped, but agricultural interests still prevail in shaping this program. Hence food stamps cannot be used to purchase essential kitchen cleaning supplies that might contribute to better health of the nation's poor: only food items are allowed.

10. Some products given out in the current distribution are not necessarily nutritionally advisable for all recipients. "Pasteurized process cheese food" is not an allowable purchase on WIC vouchers because this product is felt to be inadvisable for pregnant/lactating mothers and small children. The elderly have been cautioned about their free cheese because of its sodium content. Nutritionists warn recipients that honey should not be given to babies; but with the ending of federal honey subsidies, this commodity will no longer be distributed.

REFERENCES

Coles, Robert. 1969. *Still Hungry in America*. New York: New American Library.

Cornell University and New York State Department of Health. 1985. *Joint Report on Emergency Food Relief in New York State*. Ithaca, N.Y.: Cornell University, Division of Nutritional Sciences.

Counihan, Carole M. 1985. "What Does It Mean to Be Fat, Thin, and Female in the United States? A Review Essay." *Food and Foodways* 1:77–94.

Douglas, Mary. 1984. *Food in the Social Order: Studies of Food and Festivities in Three American Communities*. New York: Russell Sage Foundation.

Emmons, Lillian. 1986. "Food Procurement and the Nutritional Adequacy of Diets in Low-income Families." *Journal of the American Dietetic Association* 86:1684–93.

Fitchen, Janet M. 1981. *Poverty in Rural America: A Case Study*. Boulder: Westview.

Harrington, Michael. 1962. *The Other America: Poverty in the United States*. New York: Macmillan.

Jerome, Norge W. 1969. "American Culture and Food Habits: Communicating through Food in the U.S.A." In Jacqueline Dupont, ed., *Dimensions of Nutrition*, pp. 223–34. Fort Collins: Colorado Dietetic Association.

Kotz, Nick. 1969. *Let Them Eat Promises: The Politics of Hunger in America*. Englewood Cliffs, N.J.: Prentice-Hall.

Lewis, Oscar. 1961. *The Children of Sanchez*. New York: Random House.

———. 1966. "The Culture of Poverty." *Scientific American* 215:19–25.

Mississippi Research and Development Center. 1981. *Handbook of Selected Data for Mississippi*. Jackson: State of Mississippi.

O'Hare, William P. 1985. "Poverty in America: Trends and New Patterns." *Population Bulletin* 40, 3.

Pear, Robert. 1986. "Poverty Rate Shows Slight Drop for '85, Census Bureau Says." *New York*, 27 August.

Peterson, Iver. 1986. "Surge in Indians' Diabetes Linked to Their History." *New York Times*, 18 February.

Physician Task Force on Hunger in America. 1985. *Hunger in America: The Growing Epidemic*. Boston: Harvard University School of Public Health.

Roe, Daphne A., and Kathleen R. Eickwort. 1973. "Health and Nutritional Status of Working and Non-Working Mothers in Poverty Groups." Report prepared for the U.S. Department of Labor, Manpower Administration. Ithaca, N.Y.: Cornell University, School of Nutrition.

Shotland, Jeffrey. 1986. *Rising Poverty, Declining Health: The Nutritional Status of the Rural Poor*. Washington, D.C.: Public Voice for Food and Health Policy.

Silverstein, Brett. 1984. *Fed Up: The Food Forces That Make You Fat, Sick and Poor*. Boston: South End.

Stack, Carol B. 1974. *All Our Kin: Strategies for Survival in a Black Community*. New York: Harper & Row.

39

An Anthropological Perspective on Obesity

Peter J. Brown and Melvin Konner

An anthropological approach to human obesity involves both an evolutionary and a cross-cultural dimension. That is, it attempts to understand how the human predisposition to obesity so evident in modern affluent societies may have been determined during our species' long evolutionary history as hunters and gatherers, as well as the variation in obesity prevalence in different societies, social classes, or ethnic groups.

The evolutionary success of *Homo sapiens* is best understood by reference to the operation of natural selection on our dual system of inheritance; that is, on genes and culture, but also, and perhaps especially, on their interaction. Human biology and culture are the product of adaptation to environmental constraints; traits that enhance an individual's ability to survive and reproduce should become common in human societies. In this view, the health and illness of a population can be conceived as measures of biocultural adaptation to a particular ecological setting. Changing patterns of morbidity and mortality, such as the epidemiological transition from infectious to chronic diseases, are the result of historical changes in lifestyle (*i.e.* culture) that affect health.

It is valuable to view obesity from this evolutionary perspective because of its great historical scope. The first appearance of the genus *Homo* occurred over two million years ago, and the first anatomically modern humans (*Homo sapiens sapiens*) became predominant about 40,000 years ago.[1] From either prehistoric point of departure, during most of human history, the exclusive cultural pattern was one of hunting and gathering. This original human lifestyle is rare, but a few such groups have been the subject of detailed anthropological study.[2]

Culture, in an anthropological sense, entails learned patterns of behavior and belief characteristic of a particular society. This second dimension of the anthropological perspective includes variables demonstrably related to the prevalence of obesity in a particular group—material aspects of lifestyle, like diet and productive economy—as well as more idealistic variables, the relationship of which to obesity is more speculative—such as aesthetic standards of ideal body type or the symbolic meaning of fatness.

Cross-cultural comparison thus serves two purposes, one relating to each of the two dimensions. First, technologically simple or primitive societies provide ethnographic analogies to amplify our understanding of prehistoric periods, or to test hypotheses about biocultural evolution. Such societies provide useful analogies to prehistoric societies, particularly in terms of economic production and diet. Second, cross-cultural comparison allows us to see our own society's health problems and cultural beliefs about health in a new way. In a heterogeneous society like the United States, where particular social groups have markedly high prevalences of obesity, attention to cultural variation in beliefs and behaviors has practical value for medicine. Going beyond the U.S. to the numerous cultural varieties in the anthropological record gives us a fascinating range of further variation for systematic analysis. Such analysis is likely to reveal relationships that may not appear in other approaches, and attention to this wider range of cultures becomes even more relevant as obesity becomes a factor in international health.

In this [article] we argue that throughout most of human history, obesity was never a common health problem, nor was it a realistic possibility for most people. This was because, despite the qualitative adequacy of their diet, most primitive societies have been regularly subjected to food shortages. Scarcity has been a powerful agent of natural selection in human biocultural evolution. Both genes and cultural traits that may have been adaptive in the context of past food scarcities today play a role in the etiology of maladaptive adult obesity in affluent societies. Following this evolutionary argument about the origins of obesity, we turn our attention to the cross-cultural range of beliefs about ideal body characteristics and the social meanings of obesity. A prerequisite for both discussions is a review of some basic facts concerning the social epidemiology of obesity.

HUMAN OBESITY: THREE SOCIAL EPIDEMIOLOGICAL FACTS

Humans are among the fattest of all mammals;[3] the proportion of fat to total body mass ranges from approximately 10 percent in the very lean to over 35 percent in the obese.[4] In other mammals, the primary function of fat deposits is insulation from cold, but in humans, it is now widely accepted that much (but not all) fat serves as an energy reserve. The social distribution of adiposity within and between human populations is not random, and that distribution provides a key to understanding obesity. Three widely recognized social epidemiological facts about obesity are particularly salient for this discussion: (1) higher levels of fatness and risk of obesity in females represents a fundamental aspect of sexual dimorphism in *Homo sapiens;* (2) obesity is rare in unacculturated primitive populations, but the prevalence often increases rapidly during modernization; and (3) the prevalence of obesity is related to social class, usually positively; but among females in affluent societies, that relationship is inverted.

Obesity and Gender

Differences in fat deposition are an important aspect of sexual dimorphism in *Homo sapiens*.[5] Sexual dimorphism is found in many primate species, and it is more pronounced in terrestrial, polygynous species. Humans are only mildly dimorphic in morphological variables like stature; a survey of human populations

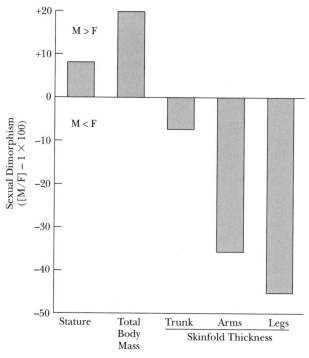

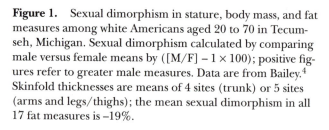

Figure 1.   Sexual dimorphism in stature, body mass, and fat measures among white Americans aged 20 to 70 in Tecumseh, Michigan. Sexual dimorphism calculated by comparing male versus female means by ([M/F] – 1 × 100); positive figures refer to greater male measures. Data are from Bailey.[4] Skinfold thicknesses are means of 4 sites (trunk) or 5 sites (arms and legs/thighs); the mean sexual dimorphism in all 17 fat measures is –19%.

around the world reveals a range of dimorphism in stature from 4.7 to 9.0 percent.[6] The most significant aspects of sexual dimorphism reside predominantly in soft tissue. On average for young adults in an affluent society, adipose tissue constitutes approximately 15 percent of body weight in males and about 27 percent in females.[4]

Fatness, particularly peripheral or limb body fat, is the most dimorphic of the morphological variables, as shown in Figure 1. Adult men are larger than women in stature (+8%) and total body mass (+20%), whereas women have more subcutaneous fat as measured in skinfold thicknesses. Bailey's analysis of sex differences in body composition using data from white Americans in Tecumseh, Michigan shows greater female skinfolds in 16 of 17 measurement sites (the exception is the suprailiac). In general, adult limb fatness was much more dimorphic than trunk fatness: trunk: –7.5% (mean of 5 measures); arms: –35.4% (mean of 4 measures); and legs/thighs: –46.7% (mean of 5 measures).[4]

It is noteworthy that peripheral body fat does not have the same close association with chronic diseases

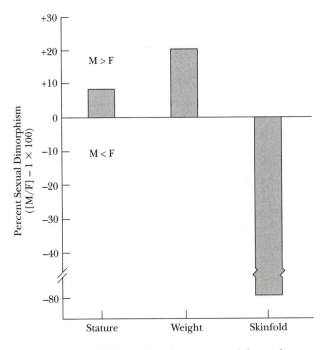

Figure 2. Sexual dimorphism in stature, weight, and mid-triceps skinfolds among !Kung San hunter-gatherers of Botswana. Sample includes 527 men and women, aged 10–80, all living in a traditional lifestyle. Sexual dimorphism calculated by comparing male versus female means by ([M/F] – 1 × 100); positive figures refer to greater male measures. Note the larger male/female difference in fat than among white Americans shown in Figure 1.

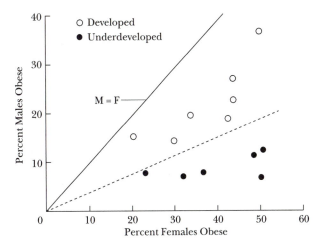

Figure 3. Gender differences in prevalence of obesity in 14 populations by general economic development. Only complete society prevalences were used, and underdeveloped populations were limited to groups with a significant degree of obesity. Operational definitions of obesity differ between studies. Populations include: Pukapuka, Rarotonga and New Zealand urban Maori,[13] Capetown Bantu, Guyana, Lagos (Nigeria), Puerto Rico, Germany, London,[12] U.S. Blacks, and U.S. Whites.[16] The unbroken line demarcates equal male/female obesity rates. The broken line indicates an apparent division between the proportion of gender difference in obesity between developed and underdeveloped countries.

(*i.e.* Type II diabetes mellitus or hypertension) as centripetal or trunk fatness. Thus the sexual dimorphism in fat deposition may be unrelated to the dimension of obesity that most affects health. The developmental course of this dimorphism is also of interest. It is present in childhood, but increases markedly during adolescence, due to greatly increased divergence in the rate of fat gain.[7] Thus this divergence occurs at the time of reproductive maturation.

Although there is some population-specific variation in fat distribution, human sexual dimorphism in overall fat and peripheral fat appears to be universal. Although very small in stature and extremely lean by worldwide standards, the !Kung San, a hunting and gathering society of the Kalahari desert, show a similar pattern of sexual dimorphism, with a pronounced difference in measures of subcutaneous fat for women (see Figure 2). The sexual dimorphism of the !Kung San is about +6.7% for stature, +20% in weight, and –80% in midtriceps skinfolds.[8]

Sex differences are also seen in the prevalence of obesity. Despite methodological differences in the operational definition of obesity and in sampling frameworks, data from the 14 populations shown in Figure 3 show that in all of the surveys, females have a higher prevalence of obesity than males. Variations in the male/female ratio of proportions of obesity seen in this figure reveal a new regularity that remains to be explained—namely, that more affluent western populations have more equivalent male/female ratios of obesity prevalence than poor populations in the underdeveloped world.

Obesity and Modernization

The second social epidemiological fact regards culture change and the origins of obesity. It is significant that anthropometric studies of traditional hunting and gathering populations report no obesity. By contrast, numerous studies of traditional societies undergoing the process of modernization (or Westernization) report rapid increases in the prevalence of obesity.[9–12] A classic natural experiment study by Prior and colleagues compared the diet and health of Polynesian islanders at different stages of acculturation: the prevalence of obesity in the most traditional island (Pukapuka) was 15.4%; for a rapidly modernizing population (Rarotonga), it was 29.3%; and for urban Maoris it was 35.4 percent.[13] Trowell and Burkitt, whose recent volume contains 15 case studies of societies experiencing increased obesity and associated Western diseases during modernization, conclude that obesity is the first of these diseases of civilization to appear.[14]

Change in diet appears to be a primary cause for the link between modernization and obesity. More precisely, westernization of traditional diets involves decreased intake of fiber and increased intake of fats and sugar. The seeming inevitability of this change toward a less healthy diet is impressive but not well understood. We suspect that more is involved in this dietary change than the simple imitation of prestigious western foodways: the quick shift from primitive to high fat, high sugar diets with the advent of affluence may have evolutionary roots.

Obesity and Social Class

The third and possibly most important fact concerning the social epidemiology of obesity is its association with social class and ethnicity. Research primarily by Stunkard and colleagues has shown that social class and obesity are inversely related, at least in heterogeneous and affluent societies like the United States.[15,16] The inverse correlation of social class and obesity is very strong, particularly for females. A few studies, however, have found a weak association of class and obesity for groups including men, children, and certain ethnic groups.[17] But there is no doubt that social factors play a role in the epidemiology of obesity, and that the high prevalence of obesity for lower class women reflects that, "obesity may always be unhealthy, but it is not always abnormal."[15]

The association between socioeconomic class and obesity among adult women, therefore, merits special attention. This association is not constant through the life cycle. Garn and Clark describe a pattern of growth called "the socioeconomic reversal of fatness in females": in childhood, middle and upper class girls (and boys) are consistently fatter than poorer girls; at around the time of puberty, the relative level of fatness in the two groups switches; and in adulthood, lower class women are consistently fatter than middle and upper class women.[18]

In the traditional societies typically studied by anthropologists, the social epidemiology of adult obesity is not well documented. The data indirectly suggest, however, that the relationship of obesity and social class is often a positive one. Surveys from developing countries show a positive association between social class and obesity prevalence and, as expected, an inverse correlation between class and protein-calorie malnutrition.[19]

EVOLUTION AND OBESITY: DIET, FOOD SCARCITIES, AND ADAPTATION

Both genes and lifestyle are involved in the etiology of obesity, although the relative importance of either factor, and the ways in which they interact, are not thoroughly understood.[20] We suggest that both genetic and cultural predispositions to obesity may be products of the same evolutionary pressures, involving two related processes: first, traits that cause fatness were selected because they improved chances of survival in the face of food scarcities, particularly for pregnant and nursing women; second, fatness may have been directly selected because it is a cultural symbol of social prestige and an index of general health.

Cultural Evolution from Food Foraging to Food Production

For 95 to 99 percent of our history, humans lived exclusively as hunters and gatherers. Studies of contemporary food foragers reveal some cultural and biological commonalities despite variation in their ecological context. Food foragers live in small, socially flexible, seminomadic bands; experience slow population growth due to prolonged nursing and high childhood mortality; enjoy high quality diets and spend proportionately little time directly involved in food collection; and are generally healthier and better nourished than many contemporary third world populations relying on agriculture.

The reality of food foraging life is to be found somewhere between the Hobbesian "nasty, brutish, and short" and the "original affluent society," a phrase popularized by some anthropologists during the 1960s.[21] It is important to dispel romantic notions of food foragers, like the !Kung San of Botswana, as innocents leading a carefree existence; they suffer from a 50 percent child mortality rate, a low life expectancy at birth, and even a homicide rate that rivals that of many metropolitan areas. Yet, given the length of time that it has survived, food foraging must be considered a successful strategy of adaptation.

Approximately 12,000 years ago, some human groups shifted from a food foraging economy to one of food production. This shift required the domestication of plants and animals, an evolutionary process in which humans acted as agents of selection for domestic phenotypes. This economic transformation, known as the neolithic revolution, may be considered the most important event in human history because it allowed population growth and the evolution of complex societies and civilization. The current consensus among archeologists is that the new economy based on

Table 1. Late Paleolithic, contemporary American, and currently recommended dietary composition[26]

	Late Paleolithic Diet	Contemporary American Diet	Current Recommendations
Total dietary energy (percent)			
Protein	34	12	12
Carbohydrate	45	46	58
Fat	21	42	30
P:S ratio[a]	1.41	0.44	1.00
Cholesterol (mg)	591	600	300
Fiber (gm)	45.7	19.7	30–60
Sodium (mg)	690	2300–6900	1100–3300
Calcium (mg)	1580	740	800–1200
Ascorbic Acid (mg)	392.3	87.7	45

[a]Polyunsaturated:saturated fat ratio.

agriculture was something that people were effectively forced to adopt because of ecological pressures from population growth and food scarcities.[22] Nearly everywhere it has been studied, the switch from food foraging to agriculture is associated with osteological evidence of nutritional stress, poor health, and diminished stature.[23]

It is important to note that the beginning of agriculture is linked to the emergence of social stratification. Civilization was made possible by the political, economic, and military power of urban elites over agricultural surpluses collected in the form of tribute. For members of the ruling class, social stratification has numerous advantages, the most important of which is guaranteed access to food during periods of relative food scarcity. In state level societies, nutritional stress is never evenly distributed across the social spectrum. Functionally, the poor insulate the rich from the threat of starvation.

Obesity is thus not simply a disease of civilization. It is common only in certain kinds of civilized societies —ones with an absolute level of affluence so that even the poor have access to enough food to become obese. Trowell has suggested that obesity became common in Europe, first in elites and then the rest of society, only about 200 years ago.[24]

The Adequacy of Preindustrial Diets

The adequacy of the diet of food foragers, and by close analogy that of our prehistoric ancestors, has been the subject of considerable interest. New analytical techniques now being applied to skeletal populations by archeologists are expanding our knowledge of prehistoric diet.[25] A recent analysis of the nutritional components of the Paleolithic diet,[26] shown in Table 1,

suggests that the diet of prehistoric food foragers was high in protein, fiber, and vegetable carbohydrates and low in sugar and saturated fats. There are striking similarities of this reconstructed stone age diet and the daily nutritional requirements recommended by the U.S. Senate Select Committee, in all areas except cholesterol intake. With this exception, the Paleolithic diet could be considered a model preventive diet, more stringent and thus probably more healthy even than the currently recommended one. But this fact reflects limitations in the availability and choice of foods rather than some primitive wisdom about a nutritionally optimal diet. Studies of culture change have repeatedly shown that when traditional populations with healthy diets have the opportunity, they readily switch to the less healthy (except in terms of abundance) Western diets.

Another method of estimation of the adequacy of the preindustrial diet is through cross-cultural comparison. Marjorie Whiting used ethnographic data from the Human Relations Area Files (HRAF) and nutritional studies to survey some major components of diet in a representative sample of 118 nonindustrial societies with economies based on food-foraging, pastoralism, simple horticulture, and agriculture.[27] (The HRAF is a compilation of ethnographic information on over 300 of the most thoroughly studied societies in the anthropological and historical record, cross-indexed for hundreds of variables. Subsamples of societies are chosen for representativeness of world areas and economic types.) In general, the quality of nonindustrial diets is high, the mean percent of calories derived from fat and carbohydrates falling within the recommended U.S. standards, and the percentage of protein nearly twice the recommended amount.[26] For the 84% of societies where food supply is adequate or plentiful, therefore, the diet seems superior to that of the United States. The major inadequacy of preindustrial diets and productive economies, however, is their susceptibility to food shortages.

The Ubiquity of Food Shortages

Food shortages have been so common in human prehistory and history that they could be considered a virtually inevitable fact of life in the past. Whiting's cross-cultural survey found some form of food shortages for all of the societies in the sample. . . . In 28.7 percent of the societies, food shortages are rare, occurring every 10 to 15 years, whereas in 24.3 percent they happen every 2 to 3 years. Shortages occur annually or even more frequently in 47 percent of the societies. Half of these are annual shortfalls, which Whiting described as happening "a few weeks preceding harvest, anticipated and expected, recognized as temporary," and in the other 23.5 percent of the societies, shortages are more frequent than once a year. This distribution has great evolutionary significance.

. . . For the 113 societies with adequate data, 29.3 percent had severe shortages that were characterized by the exhaustion of emergency foods, many people desperate for food, and starvation deaths—in short, a famine. Moderate shortages, in which food stores were used up, where emergency foods were used, and where people lost considerable weight, were found in 34.4 percent of the societies. Finally, 36.3 percent had mild food shortages, with fewer meals than usual, some weight loss, but no great hardships.[27] Two examples, one archeological and one ethnographic, will serve to illustrate these patterns and their relationship to the relative reliance on food foraging or food production.

The southwestern United States, where we today find Native American groups like the Pima, with endemic obesity and a high prevalence of Type II diabetes,[28] was in the prehistoric past the frequent site of food shortages. Tree-ring analysis has been used to calculate the frequency of ecological stresses and resulting food shortages affecting these people, the builders of the impressive kivas and cliff dwellings. The data from southern New Mexico suggest that, between 600 and 1249 A.D., every other year had inadequate rainfall for dry farming, and that there was severe stress (more than two successive years of total crop failures) at least once every 25 years.[29] The complex agricultural societies of the prehistoric southwest expanded quickly during a period of uncharacteristically good weather. Despite a variety of social adaptations to food shortages, when lower rainfall pattern resumed, the complex chiefdomships could not be maintained: the population declined, and the culture devolved back to food foraging.

Medical studies of the !Kung San hunter-gatherers have found that adults were in generally good health, but exhibited periodic mild caloric undernutrition.[30] Seasonal variation in the availability of food resulted in an annual cycle of weight loss and weight gain in both food-foraging and food-producing societies. Agriculturalists, however, experience greater seasonal swings of weight loss and gain. Seasonal weight loss among the !Kung, although it varied by ecological region and year, averaged between 1 and 2 percent of adult body weight.[8,31] Seasonal weight losses among African agriculturalists are more severe, averaging 4 to 6.5 percent of total body weight in typical years.[32]

Biological and Cultural Adaptations to Scarcity

Food shortages suggest a hypothesis of the evolution of obesity. Because shortages were ubiquitous for humans under natural conditions, selection favored individuals who could effectively store calories in times of surplus. For three-fourths of the societies, such stores would be depleted, or at least called on, every two to three years, and sometimes more frequently.

Medical data on famine victims show that, in addition to outright starvation, malnutrition from food shortages has a synergistic effect on infectious disease mortality, as well as decreasing birth weights and rates of child growth.[33] Females with greater energy reserves in fat have a selective advantage over their lean counterparts in withstanding the stress of food shortage, not only for themselves, but for their fetuses or nursing children. Humans have evolved to "save up" food energy for the inevitability of food shortages through the synthesis and storage of fat. Moreover, females, whose reproductive fitness depends upon their ability to withstand the nutritional demands of pregnancy and lactation, appear to have been selected for more slow-releasing peripheral body fat than males.

In this evolutionary context the usual range of human metabolic variation must have produced many individuals with a predisposition to become obese; yet they would, in all likelihood, never have the opportunity to do so. Furthermore, in this context there could be little or no natural selection against such a tendency. Selection could not provide for the eventuality of continuous surplus because it had simply never existed.

There is little evidence that obesity, at least moderate obesity, reduces Darwinian reproductive fitness. A follow-up study of participants to the Third Harvard Growth Study found a positive correlation between fatness and fertility when holding both social class and ethnicity constant.[34] The influence of social class is important and complex: in developed countries, fatness, lower social class, and fertility are all positively associated, whereas in underdeveloped countries, fatness and fertility are associated only in upper socioeconomic classes.[35] A minimal level of female fatness may increase lifetime reproductive success because of its association with regular cycling as well as earlier menarche. In preindustrial societies, social status is related, both symbolically and statistically, to fertility and fatness.

It is likely that under some conditions fatness is an adaptation to successful completion of pregnancy. Recommended weight gain during pregnancy is between 20 and 30 pounds, and failure to gain weight (which may be caused by inadequate caloric intake) is considered a clinically ominous sign.[36,37] Especially for women with lower gains and lower pregravid weight, weight gain is positively correlated with birth weight and negatively correlated with perinatal mortality. The energy cost of pregnancy is estimated to be 80,000 kcal (300 kcal/d), assuming no change in energy output[38] —a reasonable assumption for nonindustrial societies. Intrauterine growth retardation associated with working during pregnancy is greatest against the background of low pregravid weight and low pregnancy weight gain.[39] Failure to supplement usual intake adequately will result in a depletion of pregravid tissue reserves.

The ongoing energy cost of lactation, if milk is the sole primary infant food, is higher than that of pregnancy, and lactation in traditional societies may last up to four years and be superimposed on early pregnancy. Estimated needed supplements, converted to energy in milk with high efficiency (around 90%), range from 500 kcal/d in the early postpartum period to 1000 kcal/d by the end of the first year.[36,40] Well-fed women with high pregnancy weight gains can supplement less and safely attain a deliberately negative energy balance during lactation by drawing on prepartum fatty tissue reserves.[41] At the other extreme, experimental interventions in Gambia[42] and Guatemala[43] provided caloric supplementation to pregnant and lactating women. In the Gambian case, women readily took supplements larger than the above-mentioned estimates, and supplemented women who completed pregnancy in the lean season experienced a six-fold reduction of the proportion of low-birth-weight infants, ending up with an incidence typical of developed countries (4.7%). In both populations, supplements during lactation also increased the duration of postpartum infertility.

Using the figure 80,000 kcal for pregnancy, and a conversion rate of 9.1 kcal/g, pregnancy with no supplementation could be maintained by pregravid tissue reserves amounting to 8.8 kg of fat. Viewed from the perspective of the costs of shortage rather than the costs of pregnancy *per se*, an annual or less frequent shortage of the length and type experienced by the Gambian women, whether occurring during pregnancy or lactation, would be cushioned against by excess fat amounting to 15 to 20% of body weight. In as much as women in traditional societies spend the great majority of their reproductive lives either pregnant or nursing, an ideal of plumpness would be adaptive throughout that period. A custom such as the fattening hut for brides-to-be (see below) might provide a critical head-start on this lifelong reproductive energy drain.

Humans have also evolved other cultural mechanisms to minimize the effects of food shortages, including economic diversification, storage of foods, knowledge of possible famine foods, conversion of surplus food into durable valuables to be exchanged for food in emergencies, and cultivation of strong social relations with individuals in other regions.[44] These mechanisms act as buffers between environmental fluctuation and biological adaptation.

THE SOCIAL MEANING OF OBESITY: CROSS-CULTURAL COMPARISONS

Fatness is symbolically linked to psychological dimensions such as self-worth and sexuality in many societies of the world, including our own, but the nature of that symbolic association is not constant. In mainstream U.S. culture, obesity is socially stigmatized[45] even to the point of abhorrence. Weight loss is a major industry in the U.S., with annual expenditures of over five billion dollars. Most cultures of the world, by contrast, view fatness as a welcome sign of health and prosperity.

In an obesity-prevention campaign in a Zulu community outside of Durban,[46] one of the health education posters depicted an obese woman and an overloaded truck with a flat tire, with a caption "Both carry too much weight." Another poster showed a slender woman easily sweeping under a table next to an obese woman who is using the table for support; it has the caption "Who do you prefer to look like?" The intended message of these posters was misinterpreted by the community because of a cultural connection between obesity and social status. The woman in the first poster was perceived to be rich and happy, since she was not only fat, but had a truck overflowing with her possessions. The second poster was perceived as a scene of an affluent mistress directing her underfed servant.

Given the rarity of obesity in unacculturated pre-industrial societies, it is not surprising that many groups have no ethnomedical definition of or concern with obesity. Given the frequency of food shortages, it is equally predictable that thinness, rather than fatness, will be deemed a serious medical symptom. The Tupinamba of Brazil have no descriptive term for fat people, but are reported to fear the symptom of thinness (*angaiuare*).[47] In the preindustrial context, thin people are to be pitied; this is the case for food foragers like the !Kung San, where culturally defined thinness (*zham*) is viewed as a symptom of starvation.

It may be large body size rather than obesity *per se* that in agricultural societies becomes an admired symbol of health, prestige, prosperity, or maternity. The agricultural Tiv of Nigeria, for example, distinguish between a very positive category, too big (*kehe*), and an unpleasant condition, to grow fat (*ahon*).[48] The first is a compliment—sign of prosperity that also refers to the seasonal weight gain of the early dry season when food is plentiful. The second term refers to a rare and undesirable condition.

Even in the industrialized U.S., there is ethnic variation in definitions of obesity. Some Mexican-Americans have coined a new term, *gordura mala* (bad fatness) because the original term *gordura* continues to have positive cultural connotations.[49] There has also been historical variation in clinical standardized definitions of obesity in American medicine. Between 1943 and 1980, definitions of ideal weights declined for women but not for men; more recently, upward revision of those standards has been proposed, due to an apparent disjunction in some data sets between cosmetically ideal weights and the weights at which mortality is minimized. This, however, remains controversial.[50,51] In any case, the definition of obesity is ultimately linked to cultural conceptions of normality, beauty, and health.

Cross-Cultural Variation in Ideal Body Type

In addition to the basic association between plumpness and health, culturally defined standards of beauty may have been a factor in the sexual selection for phenotypes predisposed to obesity. In a classic example, Malcom described the custom of fattening huts for the seclusion of elite Efik pubescent girls in traditional Nigeria.[52] A girl spent up to two years in seclusion before marriage, and at the end of this rite of passage she possessed symbols of womanhood and marriageability: a three-tiered hairstyle, clitoridectomy, and fatness. This fatness was a primary criterion of beauty as it was defined by the elites, who had the economic resources to participate in this custom. Similar fattening huts were found in other parts of West Africa.

Table 2. Cross-cultural standards of female beauty

	Number of Societies	Percent of Category
Overall Body		
Extreme obesity	0	0
Plumpness/moderate fat	31	81
Thin/abhorrence of fat	7	19
Breasts		
Large or long	9	50
Small/abhorrence of large	9	50
Hips and Legs		
Large or Fat	9	90
Slender	1	10
Stature		
Tall	3	30
Moderate	6	60
Small	1	10

Among the Havasupai of the American Southwest, if a girl at puberty is thin, a fat woman stands (places her foot) on the girl's back so that she will become attractively plump. In this society, fat legs, and to a lesser extent arms, are considered essential to beauty.[53] The Tarahumara of Northern Mexico, whose men are famous as long-distance runners, reportedly consider large, fat thighs as the first requisite of beauty; a good-looking woman is called a "beautiful thigh."[54] Among the Amhara of the Horn of Africa, thin hips are called "dog hips" in a typical insult.[55] A South African Bemba courting song has the following verse: "Hullo Mama, the beautiful one, let us go to town/You will be very fat, you girl, if you stay with me."[56]

But how common is such a cultural connection between beauty and fat? There has been no systematic cross-cultural survey of definitions of feminine beauty or ideal body type among the societies of the world. The lack of a survey reflects, in part, the failure of ethnographers and historians to report adequately on this cultural element. Of the 325 cultures coded by the Human Relation Area Files, only 58 have adequate data to estimate some characteristic of ideal female body type.

The data summarized in Table 2 must be considered cautiously for a number of reasons: Because of the paucity of ethnographic data, a representative sample is impossible. Although limited to sources rated good or better, there is potential ethnographer bias toward the exotic. Observations cover a wide historical time span, often characterized by substantial cultural changes. There is the problem of relative standards; given the endemic obesity in modern society, what we consider normal may be fat to members of a society where obesity is uncommon. There is no consideration of intracultural diversity. Because the unit of analysis is a culture, the HRAF data base is skewed toward demographically small and technologically simple societies; the HRAF data base does not include the U.S. or modern European societies.

Granting the weaknesses of the data base, some guarded generalizations still seem possible. Cultural standards of beauty seem to be based on the normal characteristics of the dominant group of a society; they do not refer to physical extremes. No society on record has an ideal of extreme obesity. On the other hand, the desirability of plumpness or being filled out is found in 81 percent of societies for which there is data. This standard, which probably includes the clinical categories of overweight and mild obesity, apparently refers to the desirability of subcutaneous fat deposits. For societies where data on ideal standards on hips and legs is available, it appears that plumpness in peripheral body fat is commonly preferred. Societies that favor plumpness as a standard of beauty are found in all of the major world culture areas, with the exception of Asia. There appears to be no trend in preference for breast-size or stature. Ethnographic discussion of beauty in other societies often emphasizes cultural enhancements to the body, such as scarification, clothes, body paint, jewelry, and other adornments, rather than attributes of the body itself.[57] Standards of sexual beauty are based upon images of nubile, postpubertal, young-adult years in virtually all societies.

Fatness may also be a symbol of maternity and nurturance. In traditional societies where a woman attains her proper status only through motherhood, this symbolic association increases the cultural acceptability of obesity. A fat woman, symbolically, is well taken care of, and she in turn takes good care of her children. Fellahin Arabs in Egypt describe the proper woman as an "envelope for conception," and therefore a fat woman is a desirable ideal because she has more room to bear the child, lactate abundantly, and give warmth to her children.[58]

Although there is cross-cultural variation in standards of beauty, this variation falls within a certain range. American ideals of thinness occur in a setting where it is easy to become fat, and preference for plumpness occurs in settings where it is easy to remain lean. In context, both standards require the investment of individual effort and economic resources; furthermore, each in its context involves a display of wealth. In poor societies the rich impress the poor by becoming fat, which the poor cannot do. In rich societies even the poor can become fat, and avidly do; therefore, the rich must impress by staying thin, as if to say, "We have so little doubt about where our next meal is coming from, that we don't need a single gram of fat store." Cultural relativism in feminine beauty standards, therefore, may be limited by evolutionarily determined human universals on the one hand and by lawful cross-cultural variation on the other.

The ethnographic record concerning body preferences in males is very weak. The HRAF data base includes only 12 societies with adequate information to gauge ideal male body type. In all of these societies, the expressed preference was for a muscular physique and for tall or moderately tall stature. Other characteristics mentioned include broad shoulders and being well filled out. One extreme in this admiration of large body size would be Japanese Sumo wrestlers whose program to build large bodies is really purposeful obesity; [a] similar pattern of fattening young male wrestlers is found in Polynesia.[59] With few exceptions (e.g. the !Kung San)[8] human societies admire large body size, but not necessarily fatness, as an attribute of attractiveness in men. All of these physical characteristics can be considered as indicators of general health and nutritional status. Large body size and even obesity, however, are desirable because they symbolize economic success, political power, and social status in some societies.

Big Men, political leaders in tribal New Guinea, are described by their constituents in terms of their size and physical well-being (as well as other attributes). A Big Man may be described as a tall forest beech tree or as a man "whose skin swells with 'grease' [or fat] underneath."[60] Large body size may, in fact, be an index of differential access to food resources. This is seen in chiefdomships, as in ancient Polynesia, where hereditary political leaders sit at the hub of a redistribution system in which chiefly families are assured a portion of each family's harvest. The spiritual power (mana) and noble breeding of a Polynesian chief is expected to be seen in his physical appearance. One ethnographer in Polynesia was asked, "Can't you see he is a chief? See how big he is?"[61] The Bemba of South Africa believe that fatness in a man demonstrates not only his economic success but also his spiritual power in fending off the sorcery attacks.[62] A similar symbolic association can be assigned to deities. The corpulence of the seated Buddha, for example, symbolizes his divinity and otherworldliness.

Cultural variation in the meaning of fatness is also found among ethnic groups in the United States. Massara's ethnographic study of the cultural meanings of weight in a Puerto Rican community in Philadelphia[63] documents the positive associations and lack of social stigma of obesity. In addition, quantitative evidence[64] suggests that there are significant differences in ideal body preferences between this ethnic community and mainstream American culture. Positive evaluations of fatness may also occur in lower class Black Americans[65] and Mexican Americans.[17] There is also heterogeneity within these ethnic groups; upwardly mobile ethnics more closely resemble mainstream American culture in attitudes about obesity and ideal body shape.

In contrast to these ethnic minorities, and most of the cultures of the world, the ideal of female body shape in dominant middle/upper class America is thin. Studies suggest that females hold this cultural value more strongly than males,[66] who tend to be more satisfied with their own current body shape. Over the past three decades cosmetic ideals of female body shape have gotten thinner,[67] even thinner than medical ideals. Cultural beliefs about attractive body shape, therefore, place pressure on females to lose weight, and appear to be involved in the etiology of anorexia and bulimia. Neither the socioeconomic reversal of fatness in females nor the social history of symbolism of thinness has been adequately examined. Thinness, like tanning, is a contemporary symbol of economic status and leisure time for women. Both may be unhealthy, and both represent reversals of previous ideals.

Finally, although we have focused on the role of food shortages in human history, they are unfortunately not limited to the past. The drought and famine in the Horn of Africa and the Sahel have justifiably received world attention. Even in the United States, arguably the richest nation in human history, an estimated 20 million people are hungry.[68] This continuing worldwide epidemic of hunger presents a powerful and tragic counterbalance to our contemplation of the new epidemic of obesity and a reminder of the sometimes harsh realities of our history.

SUMMARY

An anthropological perspective on obesity considers both its evolutionary background and cross-cultural variation. It must explain three basic facts about obesity: gender dimorphism (women > men), an increase with modernization, and a positive association with socioeconomic status. Preindustrial diets varied in quality but shared a tendency to periodic shortages. Such shortages, particularly disadvantageous to women in their reproductive years, favored individuals who for biological and cultural reasons stored fat. Not surprisingly, the majority of the world's cultures had or have ideals of feminine beauty that include plumpness. This is consistent with the hypothesis that fat stores functioned as a cushion against food shortages during pregnancy and lactation. As obesity has increased, the traditional gap between males and females in its prevalence has narrowed. Under Western conditions of abundance, our biological tendency to regulate body weight at levels above our ideal cannot be easily controlled even with a complete reversal of the widespread cultural ideal of plumpness.

REFERENCES

1. Pilbeam, D. 1984. The descent of hominoids and hominids. Sci. Am. 250: 84–96.
2. Lee, R. B. & I. DeVore, Eds. 1968. Man the Hunter. Aldine. Chicago, IL.
3. Pitts, G. C. & T. R. Bullard. 1968. Some interspecific aspects of body composition in mammals. *In* Body Composition in Animals and Man. National Academy of Science, Washington, D.C. Pub. No. 1598:45–70.
4. Bailey, S. M. 1982. Absolute and relative sex differences in body composition. *In* Sexual Dimorphism in *Homo sapiens*. R. L. Hall, Ed. Praeger Scientific. New York.
5. Pond, C. M. 1978. Morphological aspects and the ecological and mechanical consequences of fat deposition in wild vertebrates. Ann. Rev. Ecol. Syste. 9: 519–570.
6. Stini, W. A. 1978. Malnutrition, body size and proportion. Ecol. Food Nutr. 1: 125–132.
7. Tanner, J. M. 1962. Growth at Adolescence. Blackwell Scientific. Oxford.
8. Lee, R. B. 1979. The !Kung San: Men, Women, and Work in a Foraging Society. Harvard University Press. Cambridge, MA.
9. Page, L. B., A. Damon & R. C. Moellering. 1974. Antecedents of cardiovascular disease in six Solomon Islands societies. Circulation 49: 1132–1146.
10. Zimmet, P. 1979. Epidemiology of diabetes and its macrovascular manifestations in Pacific populations: the medical effects of social progress. Diabetes Care 2: 144–153.
11. West, K. 1978. Diabetes in American Indians. *In* Advances in Metabolic Disorders. Academic Press. New York.
12. Christakis, G. 1973. The prevalence of adult obesity. *In* Obesity in Perspective. G. Bray, Ed. 2: 209–213. Fogarty International Center Series on Preventive Medicine.
13. Prior, I. A. 1971. The price of civilization. Nutr. Today 6(4): 2–11.
14. Trowell, H. C. & D. P. Burkitt. 1981. Western Diseases: Their Emergence and Prevention. Harvard University Press. Cambridge, MA.
15. Goldblatt, P. B., M. E. Moore & A. J. Stunkard. 1965. Social factors in obesity. J. Am. Med. Assoc. 192: 1039–1044.
16. Burnight, R. G. & P. G. Marden. 1967. Social correlates of weight in an aging population. Milbank Mem. Fund. 45: 75–92.
17. Ross, C. E. & J. Mirowsky. 1983. Social epidemiology of overweight: a substantive and methodological investigation. J. Health Soc. Behav. 24: 288–298.

18. Garn, S. M. & D. C. Clark. 1976. Trends in fatness and the origins of obesity. Pediatrics 57: 443–456.
19. Arteaga, P., J. E. Dos Santos & J. E. Dutra De Oliveira. 1982. Obesity among school-children of different socioeconomic levels in a developing country. Int. J. Obesity 6: 291–297.
20. Stunkard, A. J., T. I. A. Sorenson, C. Hanis, T. W. Teasdale, R. Chakaborty, W. J. Schull & F. Schulsinger. 1986. An adoption study of obesity. N. Engl. J. Med. 314: 193–198.
21. Sahlins, M. 1972. Stone Age Economics. Aldine. Chicago, IL.
22. Wenke, R. J. 1980. Patterns in Prehistory. Oxford. New York.
23. Cohen, M. N. & G. J. Armelagos, Eds. 1984. Paleopathology at the Origins of Agriculture. Academic Press. New York.
24. Trowell, H. 1975. Obesity in the western world. Plant Foods for Man 1: 157–165.
25. Gilbert, R. I. & J. H. Mielke, Eds. 1985. The Analysis of Prehistoric Diets. Academic Press. New York.
26. Eaton, S. B. & M. Konner. 1985. Paleolithic nutrition: a consideration of its nature and current implications. N. Eng. J. Med. 312: 283–289.
27. Whiting, M. G. 1958. A cross-cultural nutrition survey. Doctoral Thesis. Harvard School of Public Health. Cambridge, MA.
28. Knowler, W. C., D. J. Pettitt, P. J. Savage & P. H. Bennett. 1981. Diabetes incidence in Pima Indians: contribution of obesity and parental diabetes. Am. J. Epidemiol. 113: 144–156.
29. Minnis, P. E. 1985. Social Adaptation to Food Stress: A Prehistoric Southwestern Example. University of Chicago Press. Chicago, IL.
30. Truswell, A. S. & J. D. L. Hansen. 1977. Diet and nutrition of hunter-gatherers. In Health and Disease in Tribal Societies. Ciba Foundation, Eds. 213–226. Elsevier. Amsterdam.
31. Wilmsen, E. 1978. Seasonal effects of dietary intake in the Kalahari San. Fed. Proc. Fed. Am. Soc. Exp. Bio. 37: 65–71.
32. Hunter, J. M. 1967. Seasonal hunger in a part of the west African savanna: a survey of body weights in Nangodi, north-east Ghana. Trans. Inst. Br. Geog. 41: 167–185.
33. Stein, Z. & M. Susser. 1975. The Dutch famine, 1944–1945, and the reproductive process. Pediatr. Res. 9: 70–76.
34. Scott, E. C. & C. J. Bajema. 1982. Height, weight and fertility among participants of the third Harvard growth study. Hum. Biol. 54: 501–516.
35. Garn, S. M., S. M. Bailey & I. T. T. Higgens. 1980. Effects of socioeconomic status, family life, and living together on fatness and obesity. In Childhood Prevention of Atherosclerosis and Hypertension. R. Lauer & R. Skekelle, Eds. Raven Press. New York.
36. Eastman, N. J. & E. Jackson. 1968. Weight relationships in pregnancy. Obstet. Gynecol. Surv. 23: 1003–1025.
37. Naeye, R. L. 1979. Weight gain and outcome of pregnancy. Am. J. Obstet. Gynecol. 135: 3–9.
38. Blackburn, M. W. & D. H. Calloway. 1976. Energy expenditure and consumption of mature, pregnant and lactating women. J. Am. Diet. Assoc. 69: 29–37.
39. Naeye, R. L. & E. C. Peters. 1982. Working during pregnancy: effects on the fetus. Pediatrics 69: 725–727.
40. Thomson, A. M., F. E. Hytten & W. Z. Billewicz. 1970. The energy cost of human lactation. Br. J. Nutr. 24: 565–572.
41. Butte, N. F., C. Garza, J. E. Stuff, E. O. Smith & B. L. Nichols. 1984. Effect of maternal diet and body composition on lactational performance. Am. J. Clin. Nutr. 39: 296–306.
42. Prentice, A. M., R. G. Whitehead, M. Watkinson, W. H. Lamb & T. J. Cole. 1983. Prenatal dietary supplementation of African women and birth-weight. Lancet 1: 489–492.
43. Delgado, H., A. Lechug, C. Yarbrough, R. Martorell, R. E. Klein & M. Irwin. 1977. Maternal nutrition—its effect on infant growth and development and birth spacing. In Nutritional Impacts on Women. K. S. Moghissi & T. N. Evans, Eds. Harper & Row. Hagerstown, MD.
44. Colson, E. 1979. In good years and bad: food strategies of self-reliant societies. J. Anthropol. Res. 35: 18–29.
45. Cahnman, W. J. 1968. The stigma of obesity. Sociol. Q. 9: 294–297.
46. Gampel, B. 1962. The "Hilltops" community. In Practice of Social Medicine. S. L. Kark & G. E. Steuart, Eds. E. & S. Livingstone. London.
47. Evreux, Y. 1864. Voyage dans le Nord du Bresil Fait durant les Annees 1613 et 1614. F. Denis, Ed. A. Franch. Paris and Leipzig.
48. Bohannan, P. & L. Bohannan. 1969. A source notebook on Tiv religion (5 vol.). Human Relations Area Files. New Haven, CT.
49. Ritenbaugh, C. 1982. Obesity as a culture-bound syndrome. Cult. Med. Psychiatry 6: 347–361.
50. Metropolitan Life Foundation. 1983. Height and Weight Tables. Metropolitan Life Insurance Company.
51. Burton, B. T., W. R. Foster, J. Hirsch & T. B. Van Itallie. 1985. Health implications of obesity: an NIH consensus development conference. Intl. J. Obesity 9: 155–169.
52. Malcom, L. W. G. 1925. Note on the seclusion of girls among the Efik at Old Calabar. Man 25: 113–114.
53. Smithson, C. L. 1959. The Havasupai Woman. U. Utah Press. Salt Lake City, UT.
54. Bennett, W. C. & R. M. Zingg. 1935. The Tarahumara: an Indian Tribe of Northern Mexico. U. Chicago Press. Chicago, IL.
55. Messing, S. D. 1957. The Highland Plateau Amhara of Ethiopia. Doctoral Dissertation (Anthropology). U Pennsylvania. Philadelphia, PA.
56. Powdermaker, H. 1960. An anthropological approach to the problem of obesity. Bull. N.Y. Acad. Sci. 36: 286–295.
57. Brain, R. 1979. The Decorated Body. Harper & Row. New York.
58. Amnar, H. 1954. Growing Up in an Egyptian Village. Routledge & Kegan Paul. London.

59. Beaglehole, E. & P. Beaglehole. 1938. Ethnology of Pukapuka. Bernice P. Bishop Museum. Honolulu, HI.

60. Strahern, A. 1971. The Rope of Moka. Cambridge University Press. New York.

61. Gifford, E. W. 1929. Tongan Society. Bernice P. Bishop Mus. Bull. 61. Honolulu, HI.

62. Richards, A. I. 1939. Land, Labour and Diet in Northern Rhodesia: an Economic Study of the Bemba Tribe. Oxford University Press. London.

63. Massara, E. B. 1979. Que gordita! a study of weight among women in a Puerto Rican community. Ph.D. dissertation. Bryn Mawr College. Philadelphia, PA.

64. Massara, E. B. 1980. Obesity and cultural weight evaluations. Appetite 1: 291–298.

65. Styles, M. H. 1980. Soul, black women and food. In A Woman's Conflict: The Special Relationship between Women and Food. J. R. Kaplan, Ed. Prentice Hall. Englewood Cliffs, N.J.

66. Garner, D. M., P. E. Garfinkel, D. Schwartz & M. Thompson. 1980. Cultural expectations of thinness in women. Psychol. Rep. 47: 483–491.

67. Fallon, A. E. & P. Rozin. 1985. Sex differences in perceptions of desirable body shape. J. Abnorm. Psychol. 94: 102–105.

68. Physician Task Force on Hunger in America. 1985. Hunger in America: the Growing Epidemic. Harvard University School of Public Health. Boston, MA.

40

The Pima Paradox

Malcolm Gladwell

Sacaton lies in the center of Arizona, just off Interstate 10, on the Gila River reservation of the Pima Indian tribe. It is a small town, dusty and unremarkable, which looks as if it had been blown there by a gust of desert wind. Shacks and plywood bungalows are scattered along a dirt-and-asphalt grid. Dogs crisscross the streets. Back yards are filled with rusted trucks and junk. The desert in these parts is scruffy and barren, drained of water by the rapid growth of Phoenix, just half an hour's drive to the north. The nearby Gila River is dry, and the fields of wheat and cushaw squash and tepary beans which the Pima used to cultivate are long gone. The only prepossessing building in Sacaton is a gleaming low-slung modern structure on the outskirts of town—the Hu Hu Kam Memorial Hospital. There is nothing bigger or more impressive for miles, and that is appropriate, since medicine is what has brought Sacaton any wisp of renown it has.

Thirty-five years ago, a team of National Institutes of Health researchers arrived in Sacaton to study rheumatoid arthritis. They wanted to see whether the Pima had higher or lower rates of the disease than the Blackfoot of Montana. A third of the way through their survey, however, they realized that they had stumbled on something altogether strange—a population in the grip of a plague. Two years later, the N.I.H. returned to the Gila River Indian Reservation in force. An exhaustive epidemiological expedition was launched, in which thousands of Pima were examined every two years by government scientists, their weight and height

and blood pressure checked, their blood sugar monitored, and their eyes and kidneys scrutinized. In Phoenix, a modern medical center devoted to Native Americans was built; on its top floor, the N.I.H. installed a state-of-the-art research lab, including the first metabolic chamber in North America—a sealed room in which to measure the precise energy intake and expenditure of Pima research subjects. Genetic samples were taken; family histories were mapped; patterns of illness and death were traced from relative to relative and generation to generation. Today, the original study group has grown from four thousand people to seven thousand five hundred, and so many new studies have been added to the old that the total number of research papers arising from the Gila River reservation takes up almost forty feet of shelf space in the N.I.H. library in Phoenix.

The Pima are famous now—famous for being fatter than any other group in the world, with the exception only of the Nauru Islanders of the West Pacific. Among those over thirty-five on the reservation, the rate of diabetes, the disease most closely associated with obesity, is fifty per cent, eight times the national average and a figure unmatched in medical history. It is not unheard of in Sacaton for adults to weigh five hundred pounds, for teen-agers to be suffering from diabetes, or for relatively young men and women to be already disabled by the disease—to be blind, to have lost a limb, to be confined to a wheelchair, or to be dependent on kidney dialysis. When I visited the town, on a monotonously bright desert day not long ago, I watched a group of children on a playing field behind the middle school moving at what seemed to be half speed, their generous shirts and baggy jeans barely concealing their bulk. At the hospital, one of the tribe's public-health workers told me that when she began an education program on nutrition several years ago she wanted to start with second graders, to catch the children before it was too late. "We were under the delusion that kids didn't gain weight until the second grade," she said, shaking her head. "But then we realized we'd have to go younger. Those kids couldn't run around the block."

From the beginning, the N.I.H. researchers have hoped that if they can understand why the Pima are so obese they can better understand obesity in the rest of us; the assumption is that obesity in the Pima is different only in degree, not in kind. One hypothesis for the Pima's plight, favored by Eric Ravussin, of the N.I.H.'s Phoenix team, is that after generations of living in the desert the only Pima who survived famine and drought were those highly adept at storing fat in times of plenty. Under normal circumstances, this disposition was kept in check by the Pima's traditional diet: cholla-cactus buds, honey mesquite, poverty-weed, and prickly pears from the desert floor; mule deer, white-winged dove, and black-tailed jackrabbit; squawfish from the Gila River; and wheat, squash, and beans grown in irrigated desert fields. By the end of the Second World War, however, the Pima had almost entirely left the land, and they began to eat like other Americans. Their traditional diet had been fifteen to twenty per cent fat. Their new diet was closer to forty per cent fat. Famine, which had long been a recurrent condition, gave way to permanent plenty, and so the Pima's "thrifty" genes, once an advantage, were now a liability. N.I.H. researchers are trying to find these genes, on the theory that they may be the same genes that contribute to obesity in the rest of us. Their studies at Sacaton have also uncovered valuable clues to how diabetes works, how obesity in pregnant women affects their children, and how human metabolism is altered by weight gain. All told, the collaboration between the N.I.H. and the Pima is one of the most fruitful relationships in modern medical science—with one fateful exception. After thirty-five years, no one has had any success helping the Pima lose weight. For all the prodding and poking, the hundreds of research papers describing their bodily processes, and the determined efforts of health workers, year after year the tribe grows fatter.

"I used to be a nurse. I used to work in the clinic. I used to be all gung ho about going out and teaching people about diabetics and obesity," Teresa Wall, who heads the tribe's public-health department, told me. "I thought that was all people needed—information. But they weren't interested. They had other issues." Wall is a Pima, short and stocky, who has long, straight black hair, worn halfway down her back. She spoke softly. "There's something missing. It's one thing to say to people, 'This is what you should do.' It's another to actually get them to take it in."

The Pima have built a new wellness center in downtown Sacaton, with a weight room and a gymnasium. They now have an education program on nutrition aimed at preschoolers and first graders, and at all tribal functions signs identify healthful food choices—a tray of vegetables or of fruit, say. They are doing, in other words, what public-health professionals are supposed to be doing. But results are hard to see.

"We've had kids who were diabetic, whose mothers had diabetes and were on dialysis and had died of kidney failure," one of the tribe's nutritionists told me. "You'd think that that would make a difference—that it would motivate them to keep their diet under control. It doesn't." She got up from her desk, walked to a bookshelf, and pulled out two bottles of Coca-Cola. One was an old glass bottle. The other was a modern plastic bottle, which towered over it. "The original Coke bottle, in the nineteen-thirties, was six and a half ounces." She held up the plastic bottle. "Now they are marketing one litre as a single serving. That's five times the original serving size. The McDonald's regular hamburger is two hundred and sixty calories, but now you've got the double cheeseburger, which is four hundred and forty-five calories. Portion sizes are getting way out of whack. Eating is not about hunger anymore. The fact that people are hungry is way down on the list of why they eat." I told her that I had come to Sacaton, the front lines of the weight battle, in order to find out what really works in fighting obesity. She looked at me and shrugged. "We're the last people who could tell you that," she said.

In the early nineteen-sixties, at about the time the N.I.H. team stumbled on the Pima, seventeen per cent of middle-aged Americans met the clinical definition of obesity. Today, that figure is 32.3 per cent. Between the early nineteen-seventies and the early nineteen-nineties, the percentage of preschool girls who were overweight went from 5.8 per cent to ten per cent. The number of Americans who fall into what epidemiologists call Class Three Obesity—that is, people too grossly overweight, say, to fit into an airline seat—has risen three hundred and fifty per cent in the past thirty years. "We've looked at trends by educational level, race, and ethnic group, we've compared smokers and non-smokers, and it's very hard to say that there is any group that is not experiencing this kind of weight gain," Katherine Flegal, a senior research epidemiologist at the National Center for Health Statistics, says. "It's all over the world. In China, the prevalence of obesity is vanishingly low, yet they are showing an increase. In Western Samoa, it is very high, and they are showing an increase." In the same period, science has unlocked many of obesity's secrets, the American public has been given a thorough education in the principles of good nutrition, health clubs have sprung up from one end of the country to another, dieting has become a religion, and health food a marketing phenomenon. None of it has mattered. It is the Pima paradox: in the fight against obesity all the things that worked in curbing behaviors like drunk driving and smoking and in encouraging things like safe sex and the use of seat belts—education, awareness, motivation—don't seem to work. For one reason or another, we cannot stop eating. "Since many people cannot lose much weight no matter how hard they try, and promptly regain whatever they do lose," the editors of *The New England Journal of Medicine* wearily concluded last month, "the vast amount of money spent on diet clubs, special foods and over-the-counter remedies, estimated to be on the order of $30 billion to $50 billion yearly, is wasted." Who could argue? If the Pima—who are surrounded by the immediate and tangible consequences of obesity, who have every conceivable motivation—can't stop themselves from eating their way to illness, what hope is there for the rest of us?

In the scientific literature, there is something called Gourmand Syndrome—a neurological condition caused by anterior brain lesions and characterized by an unusual passion for eating. The syndrome was described in a recent issue of the journal *Neurology*, and the irrational, seemingly uncontrollable obsession with food evinced by its victims seems a perfect metaphor for the irrational, apparently uncontrollable obsession with food which seems to have overtaken American society as a whole. Here is a diary entry from a Gourmand Syndrome patient, a fifty-five-year-old stroke victim who had previously displayed no more than a perfunctory interest in food:

> After I could stand on my feet again, I dreamt to go downtown and sit down in this well-known restaurant. There I would get a beer, sausage, and potatoes. Slowly my diet improved again and thus did quality of life. The day after discharge, my first trip brought me to this restaurant, and here I order potato salad, sausage, and a beer. I feel wonderful. My spouse anxiously registers everything I eat and nibble. It irritates me. A few steps down the street, we enter a coffee-house. My hand is reaching for a pastry, my wife's hand reaches between. Through the window I see my bank. If I choose, I could

buy all the pastry I wanted, including the whole store. The creamy pastry slips from the foil like a mermaid. I take a bite.

✦ ✦ ✦

Is there an easy way out of this problem? Every year, millions of Americans buy books outlining new approaches to nutrition and diet, nearly all of which are based on the idea that overcoming our obsession with food is really just a matter of technique: that the right foods eaten in the right combination can succeed where more traditional approaches to nutrition have failed. A cynic would say, of course, that the seemingly endless supply of these books proves their lack of efficacy, since if one of these diets actually worked there would be no need for another. But that's not quite fair. After all, the medical establishment, too, has been giving Americans nutritional advice without visible effect. We have been told that we must not take in more calories than we burn, that we cannot lose weight if we don't exercise consistently, that an excess of eggs, red meat, cheese, and fried food clogs arteries, that fresh vegetables and fruits help to ward off cancer, that fibre is good and sugar is bad and whole-wheat bread is better than white bread. That few of us are able to actually follow this advice is either our fault or the fault of the advice. Medical orthodoxy, naturally, tends toward the former position. Diet books tend toward the latter. Given how often the medical orthodoxy has been wrong in the past, that position is not, on its face, irrational. It's worth finding out whether it is true.

Arguably the most popular diet of the moment, for example, is one invented by the biotechnology entrepreneur Barry Sears. Sears's first book, "The Zone," written with Bill Lawren, sold a million and a half copies and has been translated into fourteen languages. His second book, "Mastering the Zone," was on the best-seller lists for eleven weeks. Madonna is rumored to be on the Zone diet, and so are Howard Stern and President Clinton, and if you walk into almost any major bookstore in the country right now Sears's two best-sellers—plus a new book, "Zone Perfect Meals in Minutes"—will quite likely be featured on a display table near the front. They are ambitious books, filled with technical discussions of food chemistry, metabolism, evolutionary theory, and obscure scientific studies, all apparently serving as proof of the idea that through careful management of "the most powerful and ubiquitous drug we have: food" we can enter a kind of high-efficiency, optimal metabolic state —the Zone.

The key to entering the Zone, according to Sears, is limiting your carbohydrates. When you eat carbohydrates, he writes, you stimulate the production of insulin, and insulin is a hormone that evolved to put aside excess carbohydrate calories in the form of fat in case of future famine. So the insulin that's stimulated by excess carbohydrates aggressively promotes the accumulation of body fat. In other words, when we eat too much carbohydrate, we're essentially sending a hormonal message, via insulin, to the body (actually to the adipose cells). The message: "Store fat."

His solution is a diet in which carbohydrates make up no more than forty per cent of all calories consumed (as opposed to the fifty per cent or more consumed by most Americans), with fat and protein coming to thirty per cent each. Maintaining that precise four-to-three ratio between carbohydrates and protein is, in Sears's opinion, critical for keeping insulin in check. "The Zone" includes all kinds of complicated instructions to help readers figure out how to do things like calculate their precise protein requirements in restaurants. ("Start with the protein, using the palm of your hand as a guide. The amount of protein that can fit into your palm is usually four protein blocks. That's about one chicken breast or 4 ounces sliced turkey.")

It should be said that the kind of diet Sears suggests is perfectly nutritious. Following the Zone diet, you'll eat lots of fibre, fresh fruit, fresh vegetables, and fish, and very little red meat. Good nutrition, though, isn't really the point. Sears's argument is that being in the Zone can induce permanent weight loss—that by controlling carbohydrates and the production of insulin you can break your obsession with food and fundamentally alter the way your body works. "Weight loss . . . can be an ongoing and usually frustrating struggle for most people," he writes. "In the Zone it is painless, almost automatic."

Does the Zone exist? Yes and no. Certainly, if people start eating a more healthful diet they'll feel better about themselves. But the idea that there is something magical about keeping insulin within a specific range is a little strange. Insulin is simply a hormone that regulates the storage of energy. Precisely how much insulin you need to store carbohydrates is dependent on all kinds of things, including how fit you are and whether, like many diabetics, you have a genetic predisposition toward insulin resistance. Generally speaking, the heavier and more out of shape you are, the more insulin your body needs to do its job. The Pima have a problem with obesity and that makes their problem with diabetes worse—not the other way around. High levels of insulin are the result of obesity. They aren't the cause of obesity. When I read the insulin section of "The Zone" to Gerald Reaven, an emeritus professor of medicine at Stanford University, who is acknowledged to be the country's leading insulin

expert, I could hear him grinding his teeth. "I had the experience of being on a panel discussion with Sears, and I couldn't believe the stuff that comes out of this guy's mouth," he said. "I think he's full of it."

What Sears would have us believe is that when it comes to weight loss your body treats some kinds of calories differently from others—that the combination of the food we eat is more critical than the amount. To this end, he cites what he calls an "amazing" and "landmark" study published in 1956 in the British medical journal *Lancet*. (It should be a tipoff that the best corroborating research he can come up with here is more than forty years old.) In the study, a couple of researchers compared the effects of two different thousand-calorie diets—the first high in fat and protein and low in carbohydrates, and the second low in fat and protein and high in carbohydrates—on two groups of obese men. After eight to ten days, the men on the low-carbohydrate diet had lost more weight than the men on the high-carbohydrate diet. Sears concludes from the study that if you want to lose weight you should eat protein and shun carbohydrates. Actually, it shows nothing of the sort. Carbohydrates promote water retention; protein acts like a diuretic. Over a week or so, someone on a high-protein diet will always look better than someone on a high-carbohydrate diet, simply because of dehydration. When a similar study was conducted several years later, researchers found that after about three weeks—when the effects of dehydration had evened out—the weight loss on the two diets was virtually identical. The key isn't how you eat, in other words; it's how much you eat. Calories, not carbohydrates, are still what matters. The dirty little secret of the Zone system is that, despite Sears's expostulations about insulin, all he has done is come up with another low-calorie diet. He doesn't do the math for his readers, but some nutritionists have calculated that if you follow Sears's prescriptions religiously you'll take in at most seventeen hundred calories a day, and at seventeen hundred calories a day virtually anyone can lose weight. The problem with low-calorie diets, of course, is that no one can stay on them for very long. Just ask Sears. "Diets based on choice restriction and calorie limits usually fail," he writes in the second chapter of "The Zone," just as he is about to present his own choice-restricted and calorie-limited diet. "People on restrictive diets get tired of feeling hungry and deprived. They go off their diets, put the weight back on (primarily, as increased body fat) and then feel bad about themselves for not having enough will power, discipline, or motivation."

These are not, however, the kinds of contradiction that seem to bother Sears. His first book's dust jacket claims that in the Zone you can "reset your genetic code" and "burn more fat watching TV than by exercising." By the time he's finished, Sears has held up his diet as the answer to virtually every medical ill facing Western society, from heart disease to cancer and on to alcoholism and PMS. He writes, "Dr. Paul Kahl, the same physician with whom I did the AIDS pilot study" —yes, Sears's diet is just the thing for AIDS, too—"told me the story of one of his patients, a fifty-year-old woman with MS."

> Paul put her on a Zone-favorable diet, and after a few months on the program she came in for a checkup. Paul asked the basic question: "How are you feeling?" Her answer was "Great!" Noticing that she was still using a cane for stability, Paul asked her, "If you're feeling so great, why are you still using the cane?" Her only response was that since developing MS she always had. Paul took the cane away and told her to walk to the end of the hallway and back. After a few tentative steps, she made the round trip quickly. When Paul asked her if she wanted her cane back, she just smiled and told him to keep it for someone who really needed it.

Put down your carbohydrates and walk!

It is hard, while reading this kind of thing, to escape the conclusion that what is said in a diet book somehow matters less than how it's said. Sears, after all, isn't the only diet specialist who seems to be making things up. They all seem to be making things up. But if you read a large number of popular diet books in succession, what is striking is that they all seem to be making things up in precisely the same way. It is as if the diet-book genre had an unspoken set of narrative rules and conventions, and all that matters is how skillfully those rules and conventions are adhered to. Sears, for example, begins fearful and despondent, his father dead of a heart attack at fifty-three, a "sword of Damocles" over his head. Judy Moscovitz, author of "The Rice Diet Report" (three months on the *Times* bestseller list), tells us, "I was always the fattest kid in the class, and I knew all the pain that only a fat kid can know. . . . I was always the last one reluctantly chosen for the teams." Martin Katahn, in his best-seller "The Rotation Diet," writes, "I was one of those fat kids who had no memory of ever being thin. Instead, I have memories such as not being able to run fast enough to keep up with my playmates, being chosen last for all games that required physical movement."

Out of that darkness comes light: the Eureka Moment, when the author explains how he stumbled on the radical truth that inspired his diet. Sears found himself in the library of the Boston University School of Medicine, reading everything he could on the subject: "I had no preconceptions, no base of knowledge to work from, so I read everything. I eventually came

across an obscure report . . ." Rachael Heller, who was a co-author of the best-selling "The Carbohydrate Addict's Diet" (and, incidentally, so fat growing up that she was "always the last one picked for the team"), was at home in bed when her doctor called, postponing her appointment and thereby setting in motion an extraordinary chain of events that involved veal parmigiana, a Greek salad, and two French crullers: "I will always be grateful for that particular arrangement of circumstances. . . . Sometimes we are fortunate enough to recognize and take advantage of them, sometimes not. This time I did. I believe it saved my life." Harvey Diamond, the co-author of the three-million-copy-selling "Fit for Life," was at a music festival two thousand miles from home, when he happened to overhear two people in front of him discussing the theories of a friend in Santa Barbara: "'Excuse me,' I interrupted, 'who is this fellow you are discussing?' In less than twenty-four hours I was on my way to Santa Barbara. Little did I know that I was on the brink of one of the most remarkable discoveries of my life."

The Eureka Moment is followed, typically within a few pages, by the Patent Claim—the point at which the author shows why his Eureka Moment, which explains how weight can be lost without sacrifice, is different from the Eureka Moment of all those other diet books explaining how weight can be lost without sacrifice. This is harder than it appears. Dieters are actually attracted to the idea of discipline, because they attribute their condition to a failure of discipline. It's just that they know themselves well enough to realize that if a diet requires discipline they won't be able to follow it. At the same time, of course, even as the dieter realizes that what he is looking for—discipline without the discipline—has never been possible, he still clings to the hope that someday it might be. The Patent Claim must negotiate both paradoxes. Here is Sears, in his deft six-paragraph Patent Claim: "These are not unique claims. The proponents of every new diet that comes along say essentially the same thing. But if you're reading this book, you probably know that these diets don't really work." Why don't they work? Because they "violate the basic biochemical laws required to enter the Zone." Other diets don't have discipline. The Zone does. Yet, he adds, "The beauty of the dietary system presented in this book is that . . . it doesn't call for a great deal of the kind of unrealistic self-sacrifice that causes many people to fall off the diet wagon. . . . In fact, I can even show you how to stay within these dietary guidelines while eating at fast-food restaurants." It is the very discipline of the Zone system that allows its adherent to lose weight without discipline.

Or consider this from Adele Puhn's recent runaway best-seller, "The 5-Day Miracle Diet." America's

No. 1 diet myth, she writes, is that "you have to deprive yourself to lose weight":

> Even though countless diet programs have said you can have your cake and eat it, too, in your heart of hearts, you have that "nibbling" doubt: For a diet to really work, you have to sacrifice. I know. I bought into this myth for a long time myself. And the fact is that on every other diet, deprivation is involved. Motivation can only take you so far. Eventually you're going to grab for that extra piece of cake, that box of cookies, that cheeseburger and fries. But not the 5-Day Miracle Diet.

Let us pause and savor the five-hundred-and-forty-degree rhetorical triple gainer taken in those few sentences: (1) the idea that diet involves sacrifice is a myth; (2) all diets, to be sure, say that on their diets dieting without sacrifice is not a myth; (3) but you believe that dieting without sacrifice is a myth; (4) and I, too, believed that dieting without sacrifice is a myth; (5) because in fact on all diets dieting without sacrifice is a myth; (6) except on my diet, where dieting without sacrifice is not a myth.

The expository sequence that these books follow —last one picked, moment of enlightenment, assertion of the one true way—finally amounts to nothing less than a conversion narrative. In conception and execution, diet books are self-consciously theological. (Whom did Harvey Diamond meet after his impulsive, desperate mission to Santa Barbara? A man he will only identify, pseudonymously and mysteriously, as Mr. Jensen, an ethereal figure with "clear eyes, radiant skin, serene demeanor and well-proportioned body.") It is the appropriation of this religious narrative that permits the suspension of disbelief.

There is a more general explanation for all this in the psychological literature—a phenomenon that might be called the Photocopier Effect, after the experiments of the Harvard social scientist Ellen Langer. Langer examined the apparently common-sense idea that if you are trying to persuade someone to do something for you, you are always better off if you provide a reason. She went up to a group of people waiting in line to use a library copying machine and said, "Excuse me, I have five pages. May I use the Xerox machine?" Sixty per cent said yes. Then she repeated the experiment on another group, except that she changed her request to "Excuse me, I have five pages. May I use the Xerox machine, because I'm in a rush?" Ninety-four per cent said yes. This much sounds like common sense: if you say, "Because I'm in a rush"—if you explain your need—people are willing to step aside. But here's where the study gets interesting. Langer then did the experiment a third time, in this case replacing the specific reason with a statement of the obvious: "Excuse me, I have five pages. May I use the Xerox machine, because I have to make some copies?" The percentage who let her do so this time was almost exactly the same as the one in the previous round—ninety-three per cent. The key to getting people to say yes, in other words, wasn't the explanation "because I'm in a rush" but merely the use of the word "because." What mattered wasn't the substance of the explanation but merely the rhetorical form—the conjunctional footprint—of an explanation.

Isn't this how diet books work? Consider the following paragraph, taken at random from "The Zone":

> In paracrine hormonal responses, the hormone travels only a very short distance from a secreting cell to a target cell. Because of the short distance between the secreting cell and the target cell, paracrine responses don't need the long-distance capabilities of the bloodstream. Instead, they use the body's version of a regional system: the paracrine system. Finally, there are the autocrine hormone systems, analogous to the cord that links the handset of the phone to the phone itself. Here the secreting cells release a hormone that comes immediately back to affect the secreting cell itself.

Don't worry if you can't follow what Sears is talking about here—following isn't really the point. It is enough that he is using the word "because."

✦ ✦ ✦

If there is any book that defines the diet genre, however, it is "Dr. Atkins' New Diet Revolution." Here is the conversion narrative at its finest. Dr. Atkins, a humble corporate physician, is fat. ("I had three chins.") He begins searching for answers. ("One evening I read about the work that Dr. Garfield Duncan had done in nutrition at the University of Pennsylvania. Fasting patients, he reported, lose all sense of hunger after forty-eight hours without food. That *stunned* me. . . . That defied logic.") He tests his unorthodox views on himself. As if by magic, he loses weight. He tests his unorthodox views on a group of executives at A.T. & T. As if by magic, they lose weight. Incredibly, he has come up with a diet that "produces steady weight loss" while setting "no limit on the amount of food you can eat." In 1972, inspired by his vision, he puts pen to paper. The result is "Dr. Atkins' Diet Revolution," one of the fifty best-selling books of all time. In the early nineties, he publishes "Dr. Atkins' New Diet Revolution," which sells more than three million copies and is on the *Times* best-seller list for almost all of 1997. More than two decades of scientific research into health and nutrition have elapsed in the interim, but Atkins' message has remained the same. Carbohydrates are bad. Everything else is good. Eat the hamburger, hold the bun. Eat the steak, hold the French fries. Here is the list of ingredients for one of his breakfast "weight loss" recommendations: scrambled eggs for six. Keep in mind that Atkins is probably the most influential diet doctor in the world.

12 link sausages (be sure they contain no sugar)

1 3-ounce package cream cheese

1 tablespoon butter

3/4 cup cream

1/4 cup water

1 teaspoon seasoned salt

2 teaspoons parsley

8 eggs, beaten

Atkins' Patent Claim centers on the magical weight-loss properties of something called "ketosis." When you eat carbohydrates, your body converts them into glycogen and stores them for ready use. If you are deprived of carbohydrates, however, your body has to turn to its own stores of fat and muscle for energy. Among the intermediate metabolic products of this fat breakdown are ketones, and when you produce lots of ketones, you're in ketosis. Since an accumulation of these chemicals swiftly becomes toxic, your body works very hard to get rid of them, either through the kidneys, as urine, or through the lungs, by exhaling, so people in ketosis commonly spend a lot of time in the bathroom and have breath that smells like rotten apples. Ketosis can also raise the risk of bone fracture and cardiac arrhythmia and can result in light-headedness, nausea, and the loss of nutrients like potassium and sodium. There is no doubt that you can lose weight while you're in ketosis. Between all that protein and those trips to the bathroom, you'll quickly become dehydrated and drop several pounds just through water loss. The nausea will probably curb your appetite. And if you do what Atkins says, and suddenly cut out virtually all carbohydrates, it will take a little while for your body to compensate for all those lost calories by demanding extra protein and fat. The weight loss isn't permanent, though. After a few weeks your body adjusts, and the weight—and your appetite —comes back.

For Atkins, however, ketosis is as "delightful as sex and sunshine," which is why he wants dieters to cut out carbohydrates almost entirely. (To avoid bad breath he recommends carrying chlorophyll tablets and purse-size aerosol breath fresheners at all times; to avoid other complications, he recommends regular blood tests.) Somehow, he has convinced himself that his kind of ketosis is different from the bad kind of ketosis, and that his ketosis can actually lead to permanent weight loss. Why he thinks this, however, is a little

unclear. In "Dr. Atkins' Diet Revolution" he thought that the key was in the many trips to the bathroom: "Hundreds of calories are sneaked out of your body every day in the form of ketones and a host of other incompletely broken down molecules of fat. You are disposing of these calories *not* by work or violent exercise—but just by breathing and allowing your kidneys to function. All this is achieved merely by cutting out your carbohydrates." Unfortunately, the year after that original edition of Atkins' book came out, the American Medical Association published a devastating critique of this theory, pointing out, among other things, that ketone losses in the urine and the breath rarely exceed a hundred calories a day—a quantity, the A.M.A. pointed out, "that could not possibly account for the dramatic results claimed for such diets." In "Dr. Atkins' New Diet Revolution," not surprisingly, he's become rather vague on the subject, mysteriously invoking something he calls Fat Mobilizing Substance. Last year, when I interviewed him, he offered a new hypothesis: that ketosis takes more energy than conventional food metabolism does, and that it is "a much less efficient pathway to burn up your calories via stored fat than it is via glucose." But he didn't want to be pinned down. "Nobody has really been able to work out that mechanism as well as I would have liked," he conceded.

Atkins is a big, white-haired man in his late sixties, well over six feet, with a barrel chest and a gruff, hard-edged voice. On the day we met, he was wearing a high-lapelled, four-button black suit. Given a holster and a six-shooter, he could have passed for the sheriff in a spaghetti Western. He is an intimidating figure, his manner brusque and impatient. He gives the impression that he doesn't like having to explain his theories, that he finds the details tedious and unnecessary. Given the Photocopier Effect, of course, he is quite right. The appearance of an explanation is more important than the explanation itself. But Atkins seems to take this principle farther than anyone else.

For example, in an attempt to convince his readers that eating pork chops, steaks, duck, and rack of lamb in abundance is good for them, Atkins points out that primitive Eskimo cultures had virtually no heart disease, despite a high-fat diet of fish and seal meat. But one obvious explanation for the Eskimo paradox is that cold-water fish and seal meat are rich in n-3 fatty acids —the "good" kind of fat. Red meat, on the other hand, is rich in saturated fat—the "bad" kind of fat. That dietary fats come in different forms, some of which are particularly bad for you and some of which are not, is the kind of basic fact that seventh graders are taught in Introduction to Nutrition. Atkins has a whole chapter on dietary fat in "New Diet Revolution" and doesn't make the distinction once. All diet-book authors profit from the Photocopier Effect. Atkins *lives* it.

I watched Atkins recently as he conducted his daily one-hour radio show on New York's WEVD. We were in a Manhattan town house in the East Fifties, where he has his headquarters, in a sleek, modernist office filled with leather furniture and soapstone sculpture. He sat behind his desk—John Wayne in headphones—as his producer perched in front of him. It was a bravura performance. He spoke quickly and easily, glancing at his notes only briefly, and then deftly gave counsel to listeners around the region.

The first call came from George, on his car phone. George told Atkins his ratio of triglycerides to cholesterol. It wasn't good. George was a very unhealthy man. "You're in big trouble," Atkins said. "You have to change your diet. What do you generally eat? What's your breakfast?"

"I've stopped taking junk foods," George says. "I don't eat eggs. I don't eat bacon."

"Then that's—See there." Atkins' voice rose in exasperation. "What do you have for breakfast?"

"I have skim milk, cereal, with banana."

"That's three carbs!" Atkins couldn't believe that in this day and age people were still consuming fruit and skim milk. "That's how you are getting into trouble! . . . What you need to do, George, seriously, is get ahold of 'New Diet Revolution' and just read what it says."

Atkins took another call. This time, it was from Robert, forty-one years old, three hundred pounds, and possessed of a formidable Brooklyn accent. He was desperate to lose weight—up on a ledge and wanting Atkins to talk him down. "I really don't know anything about dieting," he said. "I'm getting a little discouraged."

"It's really very easy," Atkins told him, switching artfully to the Socratic method. "Do you like meat?"

"Yes."

"Could you eat a steak?"

"Yes."

"All by itself, without any French fries?"

"Yes."

"And let's say we threw in a salad, but you couldn't have any bread or anything else."

"Yeah, I could do that."

"Well, if you could go through life like that. . . . Do you like eggs in the morning? Or a cheese omelette?"

"Yes," Robert said, his voice almost giddy with relief. He called expecting a life sentence of rice cakes. Now he was being sent forth to eat cheeseburgers. "Yes, I do!"

"If you just eat that way," Atkins told him, "you'll have eighty pounds off in six months."

When I first arrived at Atkins' headquarters, two members of his staff took me on a quick tour of the facility, a vast medical center, where Atkins administers concoctions of his own creation to people suffering from a variety of disorders. Starting from the fifth floor, we went down to the third, and then from the third to the second, taking the elevator each time. It's a small point, but it did strike me as odd that I should be in the headquarters of the world's most popular weight-loss expert and be taking the elevator one floor at a time. After watching Atkins' show, I was escorted out by his public-relations assistant. We were on the second floor. He pressed the elevator button, down. "Why don't we take the stairs?" I asked. It was just a suggestion. He looked at me and then at the series of closed doors along the corridor. Tentatively, he opened the second. "I think this is it," he said, and we headed down, first one flight and then another. At the base of the steps was a door. The P.R. man, a slender fellow in a beautiful Italian suit, peered through it: for the moment, he was utterly lost. We were in the basement. It seemed as if nobody had gone down those stairs in a long time.

✦ ✦ ✦

Why are the Pima so fat? The answer that diet books would give is that the Pima don't eat as well as they used to. But that's what is ultimately wrong with diet books. They talk as if food were the only cause of obesity and its only solution, and we know, from just looking at the Pima, that things are not that simple. The diet of the Pima is bad, but no worse than anyone else's diet.

Exercise is also clearly part of the explanation for why obesity has become epidemic in recent years. Half as many Americans walk to work today as did twenty years ago. Over the same period, the number of calories burned by the average American every day has dropped by about two hundred and fifty. But this doesn't explain why obesity has hit the Pima so hard, either, since they don't seem to be any less active than the rest of us.

The answer, of course, is that there is something beyond diet and exercise that influences obesity—that can make the consequences of a bad diet or of a lack of exercise much worse than they otherwise would be—and this is genetic inheritance. Claude Bouchard, a professor of social and preventive medicine at Laval University, in Quebec City, and one of the world's leading obesity specialists, estimates that we human beings probably carry several dozen genes that are directly related to our weight. "Some affect appetite, some affect satiety. Some affect metabolic rate, some affect the partitioning of excess energy in fat or lean tissue," he told me. "There are also reasons to believe that there are genes affecting physical-activity level." Bouchard did a study not long ago in which he took a group of men of similar height, weight, and life style and overfed them by a thousand calories a day, six days a week, for a hundred days. The average weight gain in the group was eighteen pounds. But the range was from nine to twenty-six pounds. Clearly, the men who gained just nine pounds were the ones whose genes had given them the fastest possible metabolism—the ones who burn the most calories in daily living and are the least efficient at storing fat. These are people who have the easiest time staying thin. The men at the other end of the scale are closer to the Pima in physiology. Their obesity genes thriftily stored away as much of the thousand extra calories a day as possible.

One of the key roles for genes appears to be in determining what obesity researchers refer to as setpoints. In the classic experiment in the field, researchers took a group of rats and made a series of lesions in the base of each rat's brain. As a result, the rats began overeating and ended up much more obese than normal rats. The first conclusion is plain: there is a kind of thermostat in the brain that governs appetite and weight, and if you change the setting on that thermostat appetite and weight will change accordingly. With that finding in mind, the researchers took a second step. They took those same brain-damaged rats and put them on a diet, severely limiting the amount of food they could eat. What happened? The rats didn't lose weight. In fact, after some initial fluctuations, they ended up at exactly the same weight as before. Only, this time, being unable to attain their new thermostat setting by eating, they reached it by becoming less active—by burning less energy.

Two years ago, a group at Rockefeller University in New York published a landmark study essentially duplicating in human beings what had been done years ago in rats. They found that if you lose weight your body responds by starting to conserve energy: your metabolism slows down; your muscles seem to work more efficiently, burning fewer calories to do the same work. "Let's say you have two people, side by side, and these people have exactly the same body composition," Jules Hirsch, a member of the Rockefeller team, says. "They both weigh a hundred and thirty pounds. But there is one difference—the first person maintains his weight effortlessly, while the second person, who used to weigh two hundred pounds, is trying to maintain a lower weight. The second will need fifteen per cent fewer calories per day to do his work. He needs less oxygen and will burn less energy." The body of the second person is backpedalling furiously in response to all that lost weight. It is doing everything it can to gain it back. In response to weight gain, by contrast, the Rockefeller team found that the body speeds up metabolism and burns more calories during exercise. It tries to lose that extra weight. Human beings, like

rats, seem to have a predetermined setpoint, a weight that their body will go to great lengths to maintain.

One key player in this regulatory system may be a chemical called leptin—or, as it is sometimes known, Ob protein—whose discovery four years ago, by Jeff Friedman, of the Howard Hughes Medical Institute at Rockefeller University, prompted a flurry of headlines. In lab animals, leptin tells the brain to cut back on appetite, to speed up metabolism, and to burn stored fat. The theory is that the same mechanism may work in human beings. If you start to overeat, your fat cells will produce more leptin, so your body will do everything it can to get back to the setpoint. That's why after gaining a few pounds over the holiday season most of us soon return to our normal weight. But if you eat too little or exercise too much, the theory goes, the opposite happens: leptin levels fall. "This is probably the reason that virtually every weight-loss program known to man fails," José F. Caro, vice-president of endocrine research and clinical investigation at Eli Lilly & Company, told me. "You go to Weight Watchers. You start losing weight. You feel good. But then your fat cells stop producing leptin. Remember, leptin is the hormone that decreases appetite and increases energy expenditure, so just as you are trying to lose weight you lose the hormone that helps you lose weight."

Obviously, our body's fat thermostat doesn't keep us at one weight all our adult lives. "There isn't a single setpoint for a human being or an animal," Thomas Wadden, the director of the Weight and Eating Disorders Clinic at the University of Pennsylvania, told me. "The body will regulate a stable weight but at very different levels, depending on food intake—quality of the diet, high fat versus low fat, high sweet versus low sweet—and depending on the amount of physical activity." It also seems to be a great deal easier to move the setpoint up than to move it down—which, if you think about the Pima, makes perfect sense. In their long history in the desert, those Pima who survived were the ones who were very good at gaining weight during times of plenty—very good, in other words, at overriding the leptin system at the high end. But there would have been no advantage for the ones who were good at losing weight in hard times. The same is probably true for the rest of us, albeit in a less dramatic form. In our evolutionary history, there was advantage in being able to store away whatever calorific windfalls came our way. To understand this interplay between genes and environment, imagine two women, both five feet five. The first might have a setpoint range of a hundred and ten to a hundred and fifty pounds; the second a range of a hundred and twenty-five to a hundred and eighty. The difference in the ranges of the two women is determined by their genes. Where they are in that range is determined by their life styles.

Not long after leptin was discovered, researchers began testing obese people for the hormone, to see whether a fat person was fat because his body didn't produce enough leptin. They found the opposite: fat people had lots of leptin. Some of the researchers thought this meant that the leptin theory was wrong—that leptin didn't do what it was supposed to do. But some other scientists now think that as people get fatter and fatter, their bodies simply get less and less sensitive to leptin. The body still pumps out messages to the brain calling for the metabolism to speed up and the appetite to shrink, but the brain just doesn't respond to those messages with as much sensitivity as it did. This is probably why it is so much easier to gain weight than it is to lose it. The fatter you get, the less effective your own natural weight-control system becomes.

This doesn't mean that diets can't work. In those instances in which dieters have the discipline and the will power to restrict their calories permanently, to get regular and vigorous exercise, and to fight the attempt by their own bodies to maintain their current weight, pounds can be lost. (There is also some evidence that if you can keep weight off for an extensive period—three years, say—a lower setpoint can be established.) Most people, though, don't have that kind of discipline, and even if they do have it the amount of weight that most dieters can expect to lose on a permanent basis may be limited by their setpoint range. The N.I.H. has a national six-year diabetes-prevention study going on right now, in which it is using a program of intensive, one-on-one counselling, dietary modification, and two and a half hours of exercise weekly to see if it can get overweight volunteers to lose seven per cent of their body weight. If that sounds like a modest goal, it should. "A lot of studies look at ten-per-cent weight loss," said Mary Hoskin, who is coördinating the section of the N.I.H. study involving the Pima. "But if you look at long-term weight loss nobody can maintain ten per cent. That's why we did seven."

On the other hand, now that we're coming to understand the biology of weight gain, it is possible to conceive of diet drugs that would actually work. If your body sabotages your diet by lowering leptin levels as you lose weight, why not give extra leptin to people on diets? That's what a number of drug companies, including Amgen and Eli Lilly, are working on now. They are trying to develop a leptin or leptin-analogue pill that dieters could take to fool their bodies into thinking they're getting fatter when they're actually getting thinner. "It is very easy to lose weight," José Caro told me. "The difficult thing is to maintain your weight loss. The thinking is that people fail because their leptin goes down. Here is where replacement therapy with leptin or an Ob-protein analogue might prevent the relapse.

It is a subtle and important concept. What it tells you is that leptin is not going to be a magic bullet that allows you to eat whatever you want. You have to initiate the weight loss. Then leptin comes in."

Another idea, which the Hoffmann-La Roche company is exploring, is to focus on the problems obese people have with leptin. Just as Type II diabetics can become resistant to insulin, many overweight people may become resistant to leptin. So why not try to resensitize them? The idea is to find the leptin receptor in the brain and tinker with it to make it work as well in a fat person as it does in a thin person. (Drug companies have actually been pursuing the same strategy with the insulin receptors of diabetics.) Arthur Campfield, who heads the leptin project for Roche, likens the process by which leptin passes the signal about fat to the brain to a firemen's bucket brigade, where water is passed from hand to hand. "If you have all tall people, you can pass the bucket and it's very efficient," he said. "But if two of the people in the chain are small children, then you're going to spill a lot of water and slow everything down. We want to take a tablet or a capsule that goes into your brain and puts a muscular person in the chain and overcomes that weakness. The elegant solution is to find the place in the chain where we are losing water."

The steps that take place in the brain when it receives the leptin message are known as the Ob pathway, and any number of these steps may lend themselves to pharmaceutical intervention. Using the Ob pathway to fight obesity represents a quantum leap beyond the kinds of diet drugs that have been available so far. Fen-phen, the popular medication removed from the market last year because of serious side effects, was, by comparison, a relatively crude product, which worked indirectly to suppress appetite. Hoffmann-La Roche is working now on a drug called Xenical, a compound that blocks the absorption of dietary fat by the intestine. You can eat fat; you just don't keep as much of it in your system. The drug is safe and has shown real, if modest, success in helping chronically obese patients lose weight. It will probably be the next big diet drug. But no one is pretending that it has anywhere near the potential of, say, a drug that would resensitize your leptin receptors.

Campfield talks about the next wave of drug therapy as the third leg of a three-legged stool—as the additional element that could finally make diet and exercise an easy and reliable way to lose weight. Wadden speaks of the new drugs as restoring sanity: "What I think will happen is that people on these medications will report that they are less responsive to their environment. They'll say that they are not as turned on by Wendy's or McDonald's. Food in America has become a recreational activity. It is divorced from nutritional need and hunger. We eat to kill time, to stimulate ourselves, to alter our mood. What these drugs may mean is that we're going to become less susceptible to these messages." In the past thirty years, the natural relationship between our bodies and our environment—a relation that was developed over thousands of years—has fallen out of balance. For people who cannot restore that natural balance themselves—who lack the discipline, the wherewithal, or, like the Pima, the genes—drugs could be a way of restoring it for them.

◆ ◆ ◆

Seven years ago, Peter Bennett, the epidemiologist who first stumbled on the Gila River Pima twenty-eight years earlier, led an N.I.H. expedition to Mexico's Sierra Madre Mountains. Their destination was a tiny Indian community on the border of Sonora and Chihuahua, seven thousand feet above the desert. "I had known about their existence for at least fifteen years before that," Bennett says. "The problem was that I could never find anyone who knew much about them. In 1991, it just happened that we linked up with an investigator down in Mexico." The journey was a difficult one, but the Mexican government had just built a road linking Sonora and Chihuahua, so the team didn't have to make the final fifty- or sixty-mile trek on horseback. "They were clearly a group who have got along together for a very long time," Bennett recalls. "My reaction as a stranger going in was: Gee, I think these people are really very friendly, very coöperative. They seem to be interested in what we want to do, and they are willing to stick their arms out and let us take blood samples." He laughed. "Which is always a good sign."

The little town in the Sierra Madre is home to the Mexican Pima, the southern remnants of a tribe that once stretched from present-day Arizona down to central Mexico. Like the Pima of the Gila River reservation, they are farmers, living in small clusters of wood-and-adobe *rancherías* among the pine trees, cultivating beans, corn, and potatoes in the valleys. On that first trip, the N.I.H. team examined no more than a few dozen Pima. Since then, the team has been back five or six times, staying for as many as ten days at a time. Two hundred and fifty of the mountain Pima have now been studied. They have been measured and weighed, their blood sugar has been checked, and their kidneys and eyes have been examined for signs of damage. Genetic samples have been taken and their metabolism has been monitored. The Mexican Pima, it turns out, eat a diet consisting almost entirely of beans, potatoes, and corn tortillas, with chicken perhaps once a month. They take in twenty-two hundred calories a day, which is slightly more than the Pima of Arizona do. But on the average each of them puts in twenty-three hours a week of moderate to hard physical labor, whereas the average Arizona Pima puts in two hours. The Mexican Pima's rates of diabetes are normal. They are slightly shorter than their American counterparts. In weight, there is no comparison: "I would say they are thin," Bennett says. "*Thin.* Certainly by American standards."

There are, of course, a hundred reasons not to draw any great lessons from this. Subsistence farming is no way to make a living in America today, nor are twenty-three hours of hard physical labor feasible in a society where most people sit at a desk from nine to five. And even if the Arizona Pima wanted to return to the land, they couldn't. It has been more than a hundred years since the Gila River, which used to provide the tribe with fresh fish and with water for growing beans and squash, was diverted upstream for commercial farming. Yet there is value in the example of the Mexican Pima. People who work with the Pima of Arizona say that the biggest problem they have in trying to fight diabetes and obesity is fatalism—a sense among the tribe that nothing can be done, that the way things are is the way things have to be. It is possible to see in the attitudes of Americans toward weight loss the same creeping resignation. As the world grows fatter, and as one best-selling diet scheme after another inevitably fails, the idea that being slender is an attainable—or even an advisable—condition is slowly receding. Last month, when *The New England Journal of Medicine* published a study suggesting that the mortality costs of obesity had been overstated, the news was greeted with resounding relief, as if we were all somehow off the hook, as if the issue with obesity were only mortality and not the thousand ways in which being fat undermines our quality of life: the heightened risk of heart disease, hypertension, diabetes, cancer, arthritis, gallbladder disease, trauma, gout, blindness, birth defects, and other aches, pains, and physical indignities too numerous to mention. What we are in danger of losing in the epidemic of obesity is not merely our health but our memory of health. Those Indian towns high in the Sierra Madre should remind the people of Sacaton—and all the rest of us as well—that it is still possible, even for a Pima, to be fit.

Recommended Dietary Allowances

Age (years)	Weight (kg)	Weight (lb)	Height (cm)	Height (inches)	Protein (g)	Vitamin A (RE)	Vitamin D (µg)	Vitamin E (mg)	Vitamin K (µg)	Vitamin C (mg)	Thiamin (mg)	Riboflavin (mg)	Niacin (mg equiv.)	Vitamin B$_6$ (mg)	Folate (µg)	Vitamin B$_{12}$ (µg)	Calcium (mg)	Phosphorus (mg)	Magnesium (mg)	Iron (mg)	Zinc (mg)	Iodine (µg)	Selenium (µg)
Infants																							
00.–0.5	6	13	60	24	13	375	7.5	3	5	30	0.3	0.4	5	0.3	25	0.3	400	300	40	6	5	40	10
0.5–1.0	9	20	71	28	14	375	10	4	10	35	0.4	0.5	6	0.6	35	0.5	600	500	60	10	5	50	15
Children																							
1–3	13	29	90	35	16	400	10	6	15	40	0.7	0.8	9	1.0	50	0.7	800	800	80	10	10	70	20
4–6	20	44	112	44	24	500	10	7	20	45	0.9	1.1	12	1.1	75	1.0	800	800	120	10	10	90	20
7–10	28	62	132	52	28	700	10	7	30	45	1.0	1.2	13	1.4	100	1.4	800	800	170	10	10	120	30
Males																							
11–14	45	99	157	62	45	1000	10	10	45	50	1.3	1.5	17	1.7	150	2.0	1200	1200	270	12	15	150	40
15–18	66	145	176	69	59	1000	10	10	65	60	1.5	1.8	20	2.0	200	2.0	1200	1200	400	12	15	150	50
19–24	72	160	177	70	58	1000	10	10	70	60	1.5	1.7	19	2.0	200	2.0	1200	1200	350	10	15	150	70
25–50	79	174	176	70	63	1000	5	10	80	60	1.5	1.7	19	2.0	200	2.0	800	800	350	10	15	150	70
51+	77	170	173	68	63	1000	5	10	80	60	1.2	1.4	15	2.0	200	2.0	800	800	350	10	15	150	70
Females																							
11–14	46	101	157	62	46	800	10	8	45	50	1.1	1.3	15	1.4	150	2.0	1200	1200	280	15	12	150	45
15–18	55	120	163	64	44	800	10	8	55	60	1.1	1.3	15	1.5	180	2.0	1200	1200	300	15	12	150	50
19–24	58	128	164	65	46	800	10	8	60	60	1.1	1.3	15	1.6	180	2.0	1200	1200	280	15	12	150	55
25–50	63	138	163	64	50	800	5	8	65	60	1.1	1.3	15	1.6	180	2.0	800	800	280	15	12	150	55
51+	65	143	160	63	50	800	5	8	65	60	1.0	1.2	13	1.6	180	2.0	800	800	280	10	12	150	55
Pregnant					60	800	10	10	65	70	1.5	1.6	17	2.2	400	2.2	1200	1200	320	30	15	175	65
Lactating																							
1st 6 mo					65	1300	10	12	65	95	1.6	1.8	20	2.1	280	2.6	1200	1200	355	15	19	200	75
2nd 6 mo					62	1200	10	11	65	90	1.6	1.7	20	2.1	260	2.6	1200	1200	340	15	16	200	75

The allowances are intended to provide for individual variations among most normal, healthy people in the United States under usual environmental stresses. Diets should be based on a variety of common foods in order to provide nutrients for which human requirements have been less well defined.

SOURCE: *Recommended Dietary Allowance.* © 1989 by the National Academy of Sciences, National Academy Press, Washington, D.C.

Some Principles:
Nutrition ABCs, Measurement, and Classification

There are two questions affecting health about any food.

1. Is it safe, or will it harm me (*a*) immediately or (*b*) later if I eat it repeatedly?
2. Is it good for me?

Is It "Food"?

For a food one has not eaten before question 1*a* predominates. If it has not been contaminated or infected the answer depends ultimately on folklore. In every culture there are parts of plants and animals that the group recognises as food which other cultures do not. Only a minority of plants can be expected to be freely edible. For most plants it would be an evolutionary advantage to possess a toxin that discourages animals from eating it. Our folklore about which plants are edible comes down from unknown ancestors who took the risk of eating an unfamiliar plant, sometimes with unfortunate results.

Is This Food Good for Me?

Simple trial and error by people with primitive technology cannot answer questions 1*b* or 2. One of the difficulties for professionals who give advice about healthy diets is that there is no immediate symptom of well being corresponding to the surge of amino acids or vitamins that blood samples can show. The feelings of satiety and of inner warmth after a meal are much the same after a good nutritious one as after a meal that contains only "empty calories." One rare exception is the gratifying faecal result that occurs within hours of eating wheat bran in people inclined to constipation. This is probably why the fibre hypothesis was accepted by lay people years before it was well supported by human experiments. The only reliable way to answer questions 1*b* and 2 is by the methods of nutritional science.

ORIGINS OF OUR SCIENTIFIC KNOWLEDGE ABOUT HUMAN NUTRITION

✦ *Comparative and evolutionary*—Homo sapiens and his predecessors have been on the earth one million years or more. Ninety-nine per cent of this time our ancestors lived as hunter-gatherers. Agriculture started only 10,000 years ago. There has not been enough time for our species to evolve any new mechanisms required by the recent food supply but presumably our bodies have evolved well adapted for doing what hunter-gatherers did and eating what they ate. We have information from archaeological records and from studies of the few fast disappearing groups of contemporary hunter-gatherers.

✦ *Experiments of nature and travellers' tales*—From peoples who eat different foods from us, under stable conditions or during a disaster, we can form hypotheses about the physiological effects of different food patterns that we could not easily persuade our fellow countrymen to adopt. We have, for example, learnt about the physiological role of very long chain polyunsaturated fatty acids from the Eskimos, and about deficiency diseases from nutritional experiences of prisoners of war.

✦ *Epidemiological studies* range in the power of their design. Associations and correlations of disease characteristics and dietary variables do not prove cause and effect, but prospective studies, especially if repeated in different groups, give valuable information on the relation between usual diets and chronic diseases.

✦ *Animal experiments* were the principal technique for working out the vitamins. The right animal model has to be used. Understanding of scurvy was static and controversial until Norwegian workers found (in 1910) that guinea pigs are susceptible like man because, unlike most animals, they cannot synthesise ascorbic acid from glucose.

✦ *Clinical records* have been informative about the role of diet in disease, including inborn errors of metabolism. Information about requirements for

Some Examples of Human Experiments and Trials

❦

♦ Intervention trial of low saturated fat diet in half of 850 middle aged male veterans in Los Angeles over five years

♦ Trials of vitamin C against placebo for preventing colds during winter

♦ Experimental depletion of a single nutrient in human volunteers

♦ Long term testing of the value of novel protein foods

♦ Experiments measuring energy expenditure

♦ Metabolic balance studies—for example, to assess the effect of diet on plasma cholesterol

♦ Absorption and uptake studies—for example, glycaemic index after different foods containing carbohydrates

---

trace elements has come recently from experiences with total parenteral nutrition.

♦ *Food analysis*—The independent variables in nutritional epidemiology and in dietetic treatment of disease are food constituents. Food analysis is work that is never finished; foods keep changing and demand develops for constituents not measured before, such as different types of dietary fibre and fatty acids C20:5 and C22:6. To facilitate international sharing of what food composition data there is INFOODS (the International Network of Food Data Systems) was set up in 1983.

♦ *Human experiments and trials* last from hours to years and many different variables can be measured.

THE THREE GROUPS OF SUBSTANCES IN FOODS

(1) Energy and Nutrients

Man needs oxygen and enough food energy (calories), water, 8 to 10 essential amino acids in proteins, essential fatty acids—for example, linoleic acid—a small amount of carbohydrate, 13 vitamins, and 18 elements scattered across the upper half of the periodic table (in addition to hydrogen, carbon, nitrogen, and oxygen).

Together they add up to over 40 nutrients, and many are normally taken for granted: the minor nutrients are present in sufficient amounts in a mixed diet of foods. But for long term total parenteral nutrition all the minor vitamins and trace elements must be included in the required postabsorptive amounts.

For some of the nutrients *you can have too much of a good thing*. Generous intakes of saturated fat raise the plasma cholesterol concentration and contribute to

Size of adult requirements for different nutrients

Adult Daily Requirement in Foods	Essential Nutrients for Man
2–10 μg	Vitamin D, vitamin B-12, Cr, vitamin K
c 100 μg	Biotin, I, Se
200 μg	Folate, Mo
1–2 mg	Vitamin A, thiamine, riboflavin, vitamin B-6, F, Cu
5–10 mg	Mn, pantothenate
c 15 mg	Niacin, vitamin E, Zn, Fe
c 50 mg	Vitamin C
300 mg	Mg
c 1 g	Ca, P
1–5 g	Na, Cl, K, essential fatty acids
c 50 g	Protein (8–10 essential amino acids)
50–100 g	Available carbohydrate
1 kg (1)	Water

Figures are approximate and in places rounded. The range of requirements for different nutrients is about 10^9.

coronary heart disease. People with high salt intakes have more hypertension. Too much food energy leads to obesity.

(2) Water and Packing

All foods contain water. In many it is more than half the weight. The percentage of water is higher in some fruits and vegetables than in milk. The more water a food contains the fewer calories. But this water has to

Periodic table of the elements. Those essential for man are blocked in. Vanadium is provisional. In addition, Ni, Si, and traces of As have been shown to be essential in some animals.

be counted in the diet of patients with anuria. The "packing" of plant foods—that is, dietary fibre—is not all inert. Some fractions have physiological effects: arabinoxylans (hemicelluloses) of wheat increase faecal bulk and speed colonic transit; pectins slow absorption of lipids and carbohydrate.

(3) All the Rest and Toxins

All the many other substances in foods are nonnutritive. They produce most of the flavour, colour, and other sensory qualities. In most natural foods there are inherent substances that are potentially toxic but usually present in small amounts—for example, solanine in potatoes, nitrates and oxalates in spinach, thyroid antagonists in brassica vegetables, cyanogenetic glycosides in cassava and apricot stones, etc. Then there are substances that only some people are sensitive to—for example, in some people wheat causes gluten enteropathy, broad beans favism, and cheese a tyramine effect in patients taking monoamine oxidase inhibitors.

Other toxins get into foods when their environment is unusual—for example, toxic shellfish after a "red tide"—or if polluted with industrial contaminants, such as methyl mercury, PCB, etc. Microbiological infection can produce very potent toxins, such as botulism and aflatoxin. Deliberate food additives are not known to be toxic—if they were they would not be permitted by international or national food administrations. A few can cause sensitivity reactions in a minority of people.

PATTERNS OF NUTRIENTS IN DIFFERENT FOODS

If animals are fed only one food sooner or later they will become ill and die. No single food contains all the essential nutrients. Wheat (wholemeal flour) lacks vitamins A, B-12, C, and D and is very low in calcium (if unfortified); beef contains little or no calcium, vitamins A, C, or D, or dietary fibre. On the other hand, wheat is a good source of dietary fibre and beef of iron and vitamin B-12. The two together provide more nutrients than either alone but between them have no vitamin C or D or hardly any calcium. Addition of citrus fruit or salad brings vitamin C into the mixture, and milk or cheese adds the missing calcium and a little vitamin D.

This is the theory behind the "basic four" food groups for educating the public about nutrition. Each group has some deficiencies which the other three

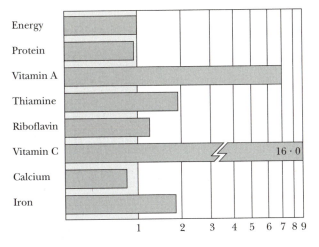

Average nutrient density of fruit and vegetables. Nutrient density is the ratio of a nutrient (expressed as % recommended daily intake) to energy (expressed as % of recommended intake). In the total diet of mixed foods the density for each nutrient should exceed 1 · 0. (From Hansen RG, *Nutrition Reviews* 1973; 31:1–7.)

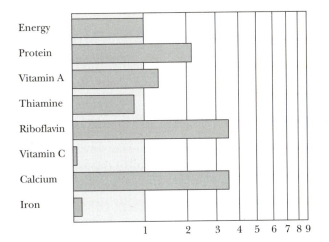

Average nutrient density of milk and milk products

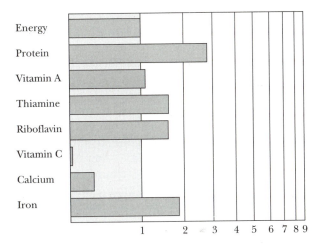

Average nutrient density of meat group

make up between them. You should aim to eat more than one serving each day from each of: the bread and cereals group; the meat, poultry, and fish group; the vegetable and fruit group; and the milk group.

Variety

It is not enough to have daily servings of the same food from each group. One should choose a variety within food groups for two reasons. Firstly, the characteristic nutrients in each group vary greatly for individual foods. Among fruits the vitamin C ranges from negligible (for dried fruits, raw pears, and figs) up to 140 to 150 mg/100 g for stewed blackcurrants and canned guavas (this is in the British food tables; the international range goes up to about 3000 mg/100 g [Brand JC, Cherikoff V, Lee A, Truswell AS. *Lancet* 1982; ii:873]).

Secondly, natural toxins do not follow any of our arbitrary groupings of foods. The wider the variety of individual foods that people eat, the less their chance of acquiring harmful amounts of the toxins that are inevitable in foods but usually in small and subclinical amounts.

Blending Dietary Guidelines with Food Groups

The four groups are intended to minimise deficiency of traditional nutrients—protein, calcium, vitamin C, etc. In affluent countries, however, more disease is probably caused by too much fat, salt, and alcohol and not enough carbohydrate or fibre. So we have to mod-

ify the older message. In Holland each of their four food groups is now subdivided into first preference and second preference subgroups, based on the amounts of fat, sugar, and fibre in individual foods.

Junk Foods and Nutritious Foods

Whether a food is nutritionally bad or good depends on the rest of the diet. As Hippocrates taught, "All things in nutriment are good or bad relatively." An extra portion of saturated fat is bad in Britain but would be good for starving children in north east Africa. An orange does nothing for someone who takes vitamin C tablets but is important for an elderly person who eats no vegetables. Value judgments about foods are being made all the time; they are nearly always subjective and usually wrong.

A good objective method is to work out for a typical serving of the food its provision of important nutrients as a percentage of their recommended dietary

---

Possible Modifications of Four Food Groups
to Incorporate Dietary Guidelines

◆ *Bread*—Yes but wholegrain and with lower salt. Prefer lower fat, low salt *cakes* and *biscuits*.

◆ *Meat*—Lean cuts with the fat removed and not fried. Alternate with *fish* (grilled) and *legumes*.

◆ *Vegetables* slightly cooked, not with salt.

◆ *Fruit* fresh, not canned in syrup or dried.

◆ *Milk* with half or all the cream removed.

---

intakes compared with its content of energy (calories), also as a percentage of the recommended dietary intake. For each nutrient

$$\text{the index of nutritional quality} = \frac{\text{nutrient as \% standard}}{\text{energy as \% standard}}.$$

The profile of indices for major nutrients can be put in an array. The other components, like cholesterol saturated fatty acids, and dietary fibre can be treated in a similar way by using a dietary goal as the standard.

The example, modified from an American book, shows that egg contains a smaller proportion of fat per energy than butter; it is less saturated and egg is also a good source of protein and some other nutrients. Egg and butter both contain some vitamin A but this is the only essential nutrient (other than a tiny amount of linoleic acid) in butter. However, an egg contains much more cholesterol than ½ oz butter.

Calculations of this type should be made before authorities advise whole communities to eat more or less of a food. Applying them to the recent DHSS recommendations about diet to prevent cardiovascular disease means that the amount of butter eaten should be reduced more than the amount of egg, because reduced saturated fat is recommended but current cholesterol intake is not considered excessive. In the USA, however, a dietary guideline advises against high levels of dietary cholesterol and so recommends the general public to moderate its consumption of egg yolks.

Calories Do Count

The law of conservation of energy applies to human nutrition as in the rest of nature. Atwater established this around 1900. A little more heat may be produced after some foods or in some people but the more calories (or kilojoules) you eat the more you can expect to store as adipose tissue.

Foods differ in their calorie content from 7 kcal/100 g (29kJ/100 g) for boiled French beans, cab-

bage, celery, and vegetable marrow up to 899 kcal/100 g (3 · 8 MJ/100 g) for vegetable oils—a 128-fold range. This great range depends on the different energy values of fat, alcohol, protein, and carbohydrate and how much these are diluted by water. It is useful for doctors to know the energy values of average servings of common foods.

No Perfect Diet

There are several diets that appear (in our present state of knowledge) to be good. We can advise on a better diet for Mr Smith or, as in a US report, make recommendations "Towards healthful diets," but there is no best diet. The reason is that man is an omnivore with enzyme systems that can adapt to ranges of intakes of many food components. There is, for example, an inducible enzyme sucrase in the small intestinal epithelium; if people eat sucrose this enzyme appears and digests it. There are several enzymes in the liver which oxidise proteins; their activity increases when protein intake is high and falls in people on low protein diets.

When the intake of one nutrient is varied and the rest of the diet is held constant there is a middle range, over which health does not improve or deteriorate as the intake is changed. For most nutrients this is quite a long range. There is therefore no single optimal intake figure. The recommended daily amount is intended to be at the top of the left hand slope in the diagram.

Replacement

For every food you remove from the diet another has to take its place. This principle is prominent in the design and interpretation of metabolic ward experiments. Does consumption of milk raise or lower the plasma cholesterol concentration? To test this an adequate but physiological amount of milk is to be given in a middle two week period and the plasma cholesterol value measured at the end of this period and at

Indices of nutritional quality (INQ) for butter and egg

	Butter (½ oz; 14 g)			Egg (50 g), Hard Boiled		
	Amount	% of Standard	INQ	Amount	% of Standard	INQ
Energy (kcal)	100	5	1 · 0	80	4	1 · 0
Vitamin A (mg)	0 · 129	11	2 · 2	0 · 078	7	1 · 6
Thiamine (mg)	0	0	0	0 · 04	4	1 · 0
Riboflavin (mg)	0	0	0	0 · 14	12	2 · 9
Niacin (mg)	0	0	0	0 · 03	0	0
Vitamin C (mg)	0	0	0	0	0	0
Iron (mg)	0	0	0	1 · 0	6	1 · 5
Calcium (mg)	3	0	0 · 07	28 · 0	3	0 · 8
Potassium (mg)	4	0	0 · 02	65	1	0 · 3
Protein (g)	0	0	0	6	12	3 · 0
Carbohydrate (g)	0	0	0	1	0	0 · 1
Fat (g)	12	15	3 · 1	6	8	1 · 9
Oleic acid (g)	2 · 9	12	2 · 4	2	8	2 · 0
Linoleic acid (g)	0 · 3	2	0 · 3	0 · 6	3	0 · 8
Saturated fatty acids (g)*	7 · 2	25	5 · 1	1 · 7	6	1 · 5
Cholesterol (mg)*	32	11	2 · 2	225	75	19

Based on Hansen RG, Wyse BW, Sorenson AW. *Nutritional Quality Index of Foods*. Westport, Connecticut: Avi Press, 1979. [The standards they used are energy 2000 kcal (8 · 4 MJ), vitamin A 1 · 2 mg, thiamin 1 mg, vitamin C 60 mg, riboflavin 1 · 2 mg, niacin 14 mg, iron 16 mg, calcium 900 mg, potassium 5000 mg, protein 50 g, carbohydrate 275 g, fat 78 g, oleic acid 24 · 5 g, linoleic acid 20 g, saturated fatty acids 28 · 5 g.] I have taken 300 mg as standard for cholesterol.

*Not essential nutrients.

Energy values as metabolised in the body of the main energy-yielding groups of food components (Atwater factors)

	kcal/g	kJ/g
Fat	9	37
Alcohol	7	29
Protein	4	17
Carbohydrate	3 · 75	16

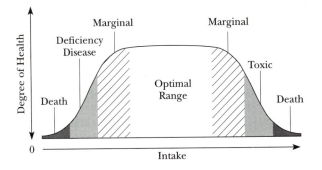

the end of equal length control periods before and after. What should be given to replace the calories of the milk in the control periods? If nothing is given the periods will not be isocaloric. To some extent the effect of milk on plasma cholesterol could be manipulated by the choice of the control food. We do not want to influence the experiment so might ask, "If people here stop drinking milk what would they drink (or eat) in its place: beer, water, fruit juice, fizzy drink, etc?" A similar situation applies in outpatients when the doctor or dietitian instructs a patient to cut out one food from his diet. Unless he is to lose weight he will sooner or later choose other food(s) as replacement, which may affect the outcome.

SOME CONCLUDING PROVERBS

People have been thinking about the safety and goodness of food as well as its social roles and tastiness ever since the Garden of Eden or its evolutionary counterpart. So it is perhaps not surprising that a number of

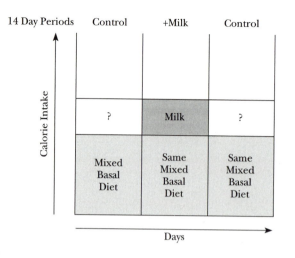

proverbs about food and eating are being confirmed by nutritional science.

Moderation in all things—The recommendation of many expert committees on nutrition. Don't eat too much or too little of anything and don't follow one of the extreme unorthodox regimens.

Variety is the spice of life—You should eat a mixed and varied choice of foods.

Enough is as good as a feast—More leads to obesity. People's energy requirements differ. "Enough" is an individual amount.

You can have too much of a good thing—For example, saturated fat, salt, dietary cholesterol, vitamins A, D, and B-6.

One man's meat is another man's poison—For each of us there are foods we dislike and may well be foods that can make us ill.

There's no accounting for taste—Taste has to be considered in planning therapeutic diets.

A little of what you fancy does you good—Dietary prescriptions are sometimes more rigid than they need be. This proverb also speaks of the placebo effect: if someone believes a food is doing him good he may feel better for a time after eating it.

Old habits die hard—Food habits must be respected. Prescribed dietary changes are likely to be followed better if they are fitted into the least strongly held of an individual's food habits.

There's many a slip twixt cup and lip—People don't necessarily eat what they intend or say they eat. That patient you just put on a diabetic diet may not have understood you.

Glossary

Acculturated   Adopting the cultural or social traits of another group, especially a dominant one

Adipose   Body fat tissue

Adiposity   The state of being fat; obesity

Aflatoxin   A potent toxin produced by a mold (*Aspergillus flavus*) that may grow on grains and peanuts

Albumins   A class of water-soluble proteins found in many foods as well as in human blood (serum albumin)

Aleurone   Finely granulated protein found in the outer layer of cereal seeds

Ameloblast   Enamel forming cells in teeth

Anthropogenic   Caused or produced by humans

Antiatherosclerotic   Preventing the formation of plaque deposits on the lining of artery walls

Apanados   Breaded fried foods typical of Ecuador

Araceae   Family of plants with large leaves, includes *Philodendrum* (a common house plant), taro (an important food crop in tropical Asia and the main ingredient in the Hawaiian dish poi), and mafafa (a food crop in tropical South America)

Arboreal   Adapted to life in the trees

Brassica   Genus of plants, one species of which, *Brassica oleracea*, includes cabbage, kale, brussels sprouts, cauliflower, broccoli, and kohlrabi

Cannaceae   Family of plants with edible roots

Catechists   Individuals who teach the basic principles of a religion in a question-and-answer form

Ceviche   A typical South American dish consisting of small pieces of raw fish or shellfish marinated in lime juice and often flavored with onions and peppers

Chirimoya   A tropical fruit also known as anon; species *Anona cherimolia*

Churrascos   Spanish for "grilled beef steaks"

Cissus   Family of plants with edible roots

Concomitant   Occurring with something else; accompanying

Corm   Underground stem of a plant

Cyanogenic   Cyanide-producing

Cyanogenic glucoside   Cyanide-containing compounds found in plants, especially cassava

Cysteine   One of the two amino acids with sulfur groups

Degenerative pathologies   Diseases like arthritis that are age related and worsen over time

Desiccator   A device to remove the moisture from foods

Detritus   Disintegrated material; debris

Diacritica   Things distinguishing one group from another

Disulfide linkage   A chemical bond formed by two sulfur atoms

Dyad   A pair; a couple

Ectomorphic   Referring to a person with a thin, linear body build (contrasts with mesomorphic, referring to a muscular, stocky body build; and endomorphic, referring to a heavy body build)

Edaphic   Pertaining to the chemical and physical characteristics of the soil

Endogamous   Marriage that occurs within a particular social, ethic, or religious group

Endogenous   Resulting from internal conditions; occurring or produced within

Endosperm   The starchy inner portion of seeds such as maize and rice

Etiologic   Refers to the cause or origin of a disease

Ferritin   A protein that stores iron in the body

Finados   A celebration for the dead observed by traditional people throughout the Andes of South America

Forbs   Herbaceous (not woody-stemmed) plants, except for grasses

Ganbaru   Japanese term meaning "persevere" or "hang in there"

Genus   The main subdivision of a family in biological classification; includes one or more species; the genus name is capitalized and precedes the species name, which is not capitalized (example: *Homo sapiens*)

Geophagy   Practice of eating earth, particularly clay

Geral   A South American language

Globulins   A class of proteins soluble in salty solutions and found in both plant and animal tissues

Glutelin   A single protein found in grain seeds

Gluten   The component of wheat and other grains that gives dough a sticky texture; composed mainly of proteins gliadin and glutenin

Gluten enteropathy   A condition resulting in malabsorption of food from the gastrointestinal tract; usually controlled by eliminating gluten from the diet; same as celiac disease in adults

Gourmand syndrome   A neurological condition characterized by an unusual passion for eating

Grenadilla   Spanish for "pomegranate"

Hegemonic   Dominating

Hemoglobinopathies   Disorders such as sickle-cell anemia caused by abnormal forms of hemoglobin, the iron-containing protein in red blood cells

Hemosiderin   A protein that stores iron in the body and releases it more slowly than ferritin

Heuristic   A device encouraging a person to discover and learn on his or her own

Homeorrhetic   Pertains to the growth pattern seen in malnourished children, in which children have a normal weight for height but are unusually short in stature

Homeostatic system   A system, such as a physiological system, that is capable of maintaining internal stability or equilibrium

Humoral   Pertaining to body fluids or substances in them

Hydrolysis   A chemical reaction in which a compound is split into other compounds or elements by reacting with water

Hypoplasia   An abnormal deficiency of cells or structural elements (example: dental hypoplasia is a deficiency in enamel)

Immunocompetence   Having the ability to develop an immunological response

Interfluvial   Between rivers

Isocaloric   Similar food energy intake

Isoleucine   One of the essential amino acids

Kii   Class of high-cyanide-containing varieties of cassava used by Tukanoan Indians in the Amazon

Kwashiorkor   A form of severe undernutrition in infancy or early childhood that results from inadequate protein intake

Lactase   Enzyme responsible for the hydrolysis (breakdown) of lactose (milk sugar) in digestion

Leptin   A protein that acts as a hormone and is involved in the regulation of appetite and energy expenditure

Leucine   One of the essential amino acids

Linamarase   Enzyme in cassava responsible for the release of cyanide from the cyanogenic glucoside linamarin

Lulo   A cherry tomato–like fruit

Mafafa   A tropical crop with an edible underground portion, or corm; New World counterpart of taro; also known as yautia

Maize   *Corn* in American English

Makasera   Class of low-cyanide-containing cassava varieties used by Tukanoan Indians in the Amazon

Marantacea   Family of plants with edible roots, one of which is arrowroot, a root with finely textured, highly digestible starch

Marasmus   A severe form of undernutrition in children mainly due to energy deficiency; same as starvation in adults

Mesic   Pertaining to a very dry environment

Metate   A flat stone used to grind maize or other grains with a second stone (mano) held in the hands

Monoamine oxidase inhibitors   A class of drugs

Natal comuna   Ecuadorian Spanish for "village of birth"

Organoleptic   Perceived by a sense organ such as the nose

Oxalate   A salt of oxalic acid that occurs naturally in plants

Pangolin   Group of mammals found in Asia and Africa that subsists on ants and termites

Pathogen   Disease-causing agent such as a virus, bacterium, or other microorganism

Peccary   A piglike mammal found in the New World family Tayassuidae

Pedagogical   Typical of teaching

Pellagra   Disease caused by a deficiency of the B vitamin niacin in the diet and characterized by diarrhea, dementia, and dermatitis (skin disorder) in areas of the body exposed to sunlight

Pericarp   The outermost layer of a seed

Periosteal   Referring to the periosteum, the layer of dense fibrous connective tissue covering bone and the outer bone

Phenology   The scientific study of the influence of climate on annual phenomena such as bird migration, plant flowering, and so on

Pinnipeds   A group of sea mammals

Pollo dorado   Spanish for "fried chicken"

Porotic hyperostosis   A porous, sievelike appearance of bone possibly resulting from iron-deficiency anemia

Pregravid   Before pregnancy

Prolamine   A class of proteins found especially in the seeds of cereal crops such as maize

Proletarianization   Conversion into proletarians (that is, workers, especially in Marxist theory) who do not possess capital or property and must sell their labor in order to survive

Prosimians   Animals in the suborder of Primates, Prosimii, traditionally including lemurs, lorises, and tarsiers

Scutellum   A shield-shaped plant part

Seco   Spanish for "dry"; a traditional Ecuadorian dish containing a portion of meat, white rice, potatoes, or other vegetables, and a relish of finely chopped onions and tomatoes

Seco de chivo   A *seco* containing goat meat

Simulacrum   A representation or image

Solanine   A toxic alkaloid found in potatoes that have been exposed to light and turned green

Somatization   Transformation of so-called psychological problems into physical symptoms such as aches and pains

Sopa   Spanish for "soup"

Strontium   A chemical element similar to calcium, but not essential in the diet

Supernatant   Something that floats on the surface

Syntagmatic   Refers to elements (usually linguistic) that occur sequentially, as in "the dog" and "is barking"

Tertiary   Third

Tryptophan   An essential amino acid and the dietary precursor to niacin, a B vitamin

Ungulates   Mammals with hoofs

Volatilize   Leave as a vapor

Zein   Group of yellow-colored proteins found in maize (corn)

Zingiberaceae   Family of plants with edible underground stems (rhizomes); includes ginger (*Zingiber officinale*) and turmeric (*Curcuma lonja*), the spice that gives curry powder its yellowish color

Credits

Page 12 Richard Borshay Lee, "Eating Christmas in the Kalahari," *Natural History*, December 1969. Copyright © 1969 American Museum of Natural History. With permission from the publisher.

Page 16 John Grossmann, "How Many Calories Are There in a 230-Calorie Dinner?" *Hippocrates*, September/October 1987: 47–51. With permission from Time, Inc.

Page 20 Lavinia Edmonds, "The Magic Bullet?" *Johns Hopkins Magazine*, August 1989: 13–20. Copyright © 1989 *Johns Hopkins Magazine*. Reprinted with permission from the publisher.

Page 32 Pat Shipman, "Scavenger Hunt," *Natural History*, April 1984. Copyright © 1984 American Museum of Natural History. With permission from the publisher.

Page 35 Richard B. Lee and Irven Devore, *Man the Hunter*, Aldine de Gruyter, 1968. Copyright © 1968 by the Wenner-Gren Foundation for Anthropological Research. Reprinted with permission from the publisher.

Page 46 Katharine Milton, "Diet and Primate Evolution," *Scientific American*, August 1993: 86–93. Reprinted with permission from the author.

Page 58 Alan H. Goodman and George J. Armelagos, "Disease and Death at Dr. Dickson's Mounds," *Natural History*, September 1985. Copyright © 1985 American Museum of Natural History. With permission from the publisher.

Page 62 S. Boyd Eaton and Melvin Konner, "Paleolithic Nutrition: A Consideration of Its Nature and Current Implications," *The New England Journal of Medicine*, January 31, 1985: 312(5):283–289. Reprinted with permission from the publisher.

Page 71 Robert Sapolsky, "Junk Food Monkeys," *Discover*, September 1989: 48–51. With permission from the publisher.

Page 77 Darna L. Dufour, "Use of Tropical Rainforests by Native Amazonians," *BioScience*, 1990, 40:9:652–659. Reprinted with permission from the publisher.

Page 86 Kathy A. Galvin, D. L. Coppock, and P. W. Leslie, "Diet, Nutrition, and the Pastoral Strategy," from *African Pastoralist Systems: An Integrated Approach*, edited by Elliot Fratkin, Kathleen A. Galvin, and Eric Abella Roth. Copyright © 1994 by Lynne Rienner Publishers, Inc. Reprinted with permission of the publisher.

Page 96 Gretel H. Pelto, "Social Class and Diet in Contemporary Mexico," from *Food and Evolution: Toward a Theory of Human Food Habits*, edited by Marvin Harris and Eric B. Ross. Copyright © 1987 by Temple University. All rights reserved. Reprinted by permission of Temple University Press.

Page 111 Marvin Harris, "India's Sacred Cow," *Human Nature*, February 1978: 28–36. Reprinted with permission from the author.

Page 116 Michael Harner, "The Enigma of Aztec Sacrifice," *Natural History*, April 1977. Copyright © 1977 Michael Harner. Reprinted with permission from the author.

Page 120 Timothy Johns, "A Well-Grounded Diet," *The Sciences*, September/October 1991. Reprinted with permission from the publisher. Individual subscriptions are $28 per year. Write to: The Sciences, 2 East 63rd Street, New York, NY 10021.

Page 128 C. Paige Gutierrez, "The Social and Symbolic Uses of Ethnic/Regional Foodways: Cajuns and Crawfish in South Louisiana," from *Ethnic and Regional Foodways in the United States: The Performance of Group Identity*, edited by Linda Keller Brown and Kay Mussell. Copyright © 1984 by The University of Tennessee Press.

Page 134 Mary J. Weismantel, "The Children Cry for Bread: Hegemony and the Transformation of Consumption," in *The Social Economy of Consumption*, edited by B. Orlove and J. J. Ruiz, University Press of America, 1989. Reprinted with permission from the publisher.

Page 143 Anne Alison, "Japanese Mothers and *Obentōs*: The Lunch-Box as Ideological State Apparatus," *Anthropological Quarterly*, 1991, 64(4):195–208. Reprinted with permission from the publisher.

Page 155 Conrad Kottak, "Rituals at McDonald's," *Natural History*, January 1978. Copyright © 1978 American Museum of Natural History. With permission from the publisher.

Page 164 Darna L. Dufour, "A Closer Look at the Nutritional Implications of Bitter Cassava Use, " from *Indigenous Peoples and the Future of Amazonia: An Ecological Anthropology of an Endangered World*, edited by Leslie Sponsel. Copyright © 1995 The Arizona Board of Regents. Reprinted by permission of the University of Arizona Press.

Page 172 Solomon H. Katz, M. L. Hediger, and L. A. Valleroy, "Traditional Maize Processing Techniques in the New World," *Science*, May 17, 1975, Vol. 184. Copyright © 1975 by the American Association for the Advancement of Science. Reprinted with permission from the publisher.

Page 186 Norman Kretchmer, "Genetic Variability and Lactose Tolerance," *Progress in Human Nutrition*, 1978, 197–205. Reprinted with permission from the publisher.

Page 192 Barry Bogin, "The Tall *and* the Short of It," *Discover* 1998. Copyright © 1998 Barry Bogin. Reprinted with permission of *Discover* magazine.

Page 198 Eugene N. Anderson, *Ecologies of the Heart: Emotion, Belief, and the Environment*, Oxford University Press, 1996. Copyright © 1996 by Oxford University Press, Inc. Used by permission of the publisher.

Page 212 Jill Dubisch, "You Are What You Eat: Religious Aspects of the Health Food Movement," from *The American*

Dimension, Susan P. Montague and William Arens, editors, Mayfield Publishing Company, 1981: 115–127. Copyright © 1981 Susan P. Montague and William Arens. Reprinted with permission from the authors.

Page 227 David Pelletier, "The Potential Effects of Malnutrition on Child Mortality: Epidemiologic Evidence and Policy Implications," *Nutrition Reviews,* 1994, 52:12, 409–415. Copyright © 1994 by the International Life Sciences Institute, Washington, D.C. Reprinted with permission. All rights reserved.

Page 234 Adolfo Chávez, Celia Martinez, and Beatriz Soberanes, "The Effect of Malnutrition on Human Development: A 24-Year Study of Well-Nourished and Malnourished Children Living in a Mexican Village," from *Community-Based Longitudinal Nutrition and Health Studies: Classic Examples from Guatemala, Haiti and Mexico,* N. S. Scrimshaw, editor, 1995. Reprinted with permission from the International Nutrition Foundation, Boston, MA.

Page 252 Nevin S. Scrimshaw, "Iron Deficiency," *Scientific American,* October 1991. Reprinted with permission from the publisher.

Page 258 Reynaldo Martorell, "Body Size, Adaptation and Function," *Human Organization,* 1989:48(1):15–20. Reprinted with permission from the publisher.

Page 269 Gretel H. Pelto and Pertti J. Pelto, "Diet and Delocalization: Dietary Changes Since 1750," *Journal of Interdisciplinary History,* XIX, 1983, 507–528. Copyright © 1983 by The Massachusetts Institute of Technology and the editors of *The Journal of Interdisciplinary History.* Reprinted with permission from the editors and the publisher.

Page 279 Sidney Mintz, "Time, Sugar, and Sweetness," *Marxist Perspectives,* 1981. Reprinted with permission of the author.

Page 287 Bernard Nietschmann, "When the Turtle Collapses, the World Ends," *Natural History,* June/July 1974.

Copyright © 1974 American Museum of Natural History. With permission from the publisher.

Page 292 Debbie Mack, "Food for All," *New Scientists,* October 31, 1998, No. 2158, 50–52. Reprinted with permission from the publisher.

Page 298 Gretel H. Pelto, "Perspectives on Infant Feeding, Decision-Making and Ecology," *Food and Nutrition Bulletin,* 1981, 3:16–29.

Page 312 Katherine A. Dettwyler, "More than Nutrition: Breastfeeding in Urban Mali," *Medical Anthropology Quarterly* 2:2, June 1988. Reproduced by permission of the American Anthropological Association. Not for further reproduction.

Page 320 Nancy E. Levine, "Women's Work and Infant Feeding: A Case from Rural Nepal," *Ethnology,* 27(3):231–251. Reprinted with permission from the publisher.

Page 335 Janet M. Fitchen, "Hunger, Malnutrition, and Poverty in the Contemporary United States: Some Observations on Their Social and Cultural Context," *Food and Foodways,* 1988, 2:309–333. Reprinted with permission from the publisher.

Page 347 Peter J. Brown and Melvin Konner, "An Anthropological Perspective on Obesity," *Annals of New York Academy of Sciences,* 1987, 499:29–46. Reprinted with permission.

Page 358 Malcolm Gladwell, "The Pima Paradox," *The New Yorker,* February 2, 1998, 44–57. Reprinted with permission from the author.

Page 369 Reprinted with permission from *Recommended Dietary Allowances, 10th Edition,* National Academy Press, 1989. Copyright © 1989 by the National Academy of Sciences. Courtesy of the National Academy Press, Washington, D.C.

Page 370 From A. Steward Truswell, "ABCs of Nutrition," *British Medical Journal,* vol. 291, 1985, 1486–1490. Reprinted with permission.

Index

Pages with illustrations are set in italic type.